Private Eyes:
One Hundred And One Knights

Private Eyes:

One Hundred And One Knights

A Survey of American Detective Fiction 1922-1984

Robert A. Baker & Michael T. Nietzel

Bowling Green State University Popular Press
Bowling Green, Ohio 43403

Contents

Introduction

Bill Pronzini

THE PRIVATE EYE STORY, that acclaimed (and sometimes unfairly vilified) sub-genre of crime fiction, is important for the contributions of its best writers and for its influences on other aspects of popular culture (films, radio and television drama). The P.I.'s antecedents may be traced all the way back to Sherlock Holmes, himself a "private inquiry agent," although it was in the pages of the pioneering pulp magazine *Black Mask* in the early 1920s that the modern realistic school of private detective fiction was established by Carroll John Daly and, far more importantly, by Dashiell Hammett. During the past sixty years there have been thousands of novels and stories featuring the tough, often cynical and hard-drinking loner who, in Raymond Chandler's now-famous phrase, walks "the mean streets" of such urban centers as New York, Los Angeles, and San Francisco. ("...But down these mean streets a man must go who is not himself mean—who is neither tarnished nor afraid...") Many of these novels and stories have been very good; many more have been very bad or (cardinal sin!) indifferent. Yet there has been no waning of the private eye's popularity, as evidenced by the number of writers successfully producing this type of detective story today, and the enthusiasm with which their work is received.

Such widespread interest has naturally led in recent years to a growing body of book-length critical works—some good, some bad, and some (same cardinal sin) indifferent. Yet without exception, *all* these books fall into one of two categories:

Biographies of, collections of letters by and about, and literary and sociological dissections of the fiction of Dashiell Hammett, Raymond Chandler, Ross Macdonald, and, to a much lesser degree, Mickey Spillane.

Studies devoted to the influences of these four men on the contemporary writers who most obviously carry on their traditions and visions; i.e., their most successful imitators.

There is no question that Hammett, Chandler, Macdonald, and Spillane *are* the most influential practitioners of private eye fiction over the past six decades; Hammett virtually invented the modern "hardboiled" school, Chandler and Macdonald each refined it in different ways, and Spillane bent it in a perverse new direction. But these four writers are not the *only* important ones in P.I. literature, as the spate of critical works devoted to them presupposes. Not by any means. Others have played important roles in the development of the sub-genre; indeed, certain writers are still playing them. They, too, have added dimension and scope to the form; they, too, in their quiet way, have shaped it in the past and are reshaping it for the future.

None of these writers is a strict and slavish imitator of the "Big Four." Each has his own style, his own quirks and embellishments and innovations. Robert Leslie Bellem, for instance, delighted a generation of pulp magazine readers with his wonderfully slangy, campy Dan Turner stories; these spawned a number of his own imitators, attracted the attention of humorist S.J. Perelman, whose *New Yorker* essay on Bellem and Turner, "Somewhere a Roscoe...," is a minor classic, and in modern reprint form have begun to delight a whole new generation of crime-fiction addicts. Richard S. Prather injected a strong element of sexy, farcical humor into his Shell Scott series, a combination that sold millions of paperbacks in the 1950s and 1960s and also begat a host of imitators. During the same period, Thomas B. Dewey imbued his Chicago investigator, "Mac," with human instead of super-human qualities and thereby paved the way for a new type of private eye novel, one which emphasizes the detective's private life and the short- and long-range effects his walks down the mean streets have on *him*, as well as on those whose paths he crosses. Also in the 50s, the husband and wife team of Skip and Gloria (G.G.) Fickling sired the first significant female private eye, Honey West, a creation whose popularity led to a TV series starring Anne Francis. On the contemporary scene, Marcia Muller, Sue Grafton, Sara Paretsky, Liza Cody, and P.D. James have entered what was previously the all-but-exclusive domain of men by establishing significant female private eyes of their own—not merely reflections of their male counterparts, but realistic and fully realized women who happen to be private investigators and whose attitudes and methods have added yet another new dimension to P.I. literature.

A complete and proper critical assessment of "private eyedom" would be impossible without the inclusion of these, and many other, writers. Robert A. Baker and Michael T. Nietzel, astute fellows both, realized this fact long before they undertook their project. And that is why *Private Eyes: One Hundred and One Knights* unequivocally *is* a complete and proper critical assessment of private eyedom—the definitive work by far on this sub-genre.

It is an important book for this reason, and for the valuable insights it offers, and for its personal glimpses of the men and women behind the untarnished and unafraid heroes. Meticulously researched, skillfully and affectionately written, it is a book for the savant, a book for the aficionado, a book for the casual reader of detective stories. In short, a most effective piece of popular-culture scholarship.

Dr. Baker and Dr. Nietzel are to be congratulated, especially and most warmly by those of us who write private eye fiction and who have labored in obscurity, misunderstanding, apathy, and dismissal for any number of years. Lord, how nice it is at long, long last to have our work taken *seriously*!

Bill Pronzini
San Francisco, California

Chapter I
The Realm of the Private Eye

THE TOUGH DETECTIVE SCHOOL of contemporary mystery fiction is a mixture of cynicism, violence, native American pragmatism and social psychology. This amalgam featuring a private investigator hero or heroine who manages to be both sentimental and hard-boiled emerged in the 1920s from the untrimmed pages of the early pulp magazines. History has shown the private eye novel to be one of the most popular fiction genres ever developed. Sam Spade, Philip Marlowe and Lew Archer are as familiar to the average American library patron and movie goer as Mickey Mouse and Sherlock Holmes. Today every new Travis McGee novel soars to the top of the bestseller lists a week or so after publication. The novels of Dashiell Hammett, Raymond Chandler and the two MacDonalds—John and Ross—are never out of print. Moreover their work is taken seriously enough to furnish the subject matter of courses and graduate seminars in colleges and universities across the nation.

The PI novel is equally popular abroad. The works of Hammett, Chandler, et al have been translated into a dozen or more languages and their books are collected and treasured by admirers in France, both Germanys, Italy, Denmark, Norway and Sweden, Spain, Japan and the USSR.

Besides the appeal of the PI novel to the general public there is something about it that is equally attractive to professional writers. A number of so-called serious writers have yielded to the temptation to try their hand at this literary form. Among the literary lights who have written at least one PI novel are Thomas Berger (*Who is Teddy Villanova?*), Richard Brautigan (*Dreaming of Babylon*), William Hjortsberg (*Fallen Angel*), Nicholas Meyer (*Target Practice*) and Stanley Ellin (*The Eighth Circle*). As for the last named, Julian Symons has called it "the perfect mystery novel, perhaps the greatest mystery novel of all time." And, in many ways, Faulkner's Gavin Stevens—the hero of *Intruder in the Dust* and *Knight's Gambit*—also qualifies as a member of the genre.

What is the appeal of the Private Eye as hero and why are PI novels so popular? This is the question we will answer in the following pages, and we hope that you will find these fictional private investigators as fascinating and as entertaining as we do. We believe that the PI novel is the superior form of the mystery novel and that it is by far the most exciting

1

and intriguing. We believe that it not only deserves to be read and remembered but that over the past sixty years too many excellent American writers of the hard-boiled PI novel have been overlooked. Their books remain unread and their living and breathing heroes unappreciated and unknown. Some of the work of these novelists, even though it was published in the 1920s and 1930s, is as fresh and entertaining today as anything written in the 1980s. These unsung artists and their knights without armor deserve to be read and enjoyed by new generations of readers.

In every decade since the PI novel was born a large number of writers of mystery fiction have created a central PI character and led him or her through several cases to the acclaim of only a few appreciative readers. There are hundreds of superb novels with excellent plots, well-drawn characters and exciting climaxes that are no longer in print and that have been removed from the library shelves to make room for less deserving contemporary material. Even today, because of the voluminous mass of printed material, too many excellent novels within the realm of PI fiction remain unread and unknown. The purpose of this book, therefore, is to call the interested reader's attention to some of the strongest of these books—both present and past.

As dedicated students of the PI genre know, the tough Private Eye was born in the untrimmed pages of *Black Mask* magazine in the early 1920s. Among his creators were Carroll John Daly, Dashiell Hammett, Frederick Nebel, Frank Gruber, Raoul Whitfield, George Harman Coxe and Erle Stanley Gardner. Historically, the first Private Eye was a hard-boiled character, created by Daly, named Race Williams. Race made his initial appearance in a June 1, 1923 *Black Mask* story entitled "Knights of the Open Palm." He narrated his own adventures and described himself as, "half-way between the cops and the crooks .... I do a little honest shooting once in a while—just in the way of business—but I never bumped off a guy that didn't deserve it." Williams was tough, wise and often sentimental like the PIs of today. His human characteristics—his weaknesses and strengths—and his peculiar habit of holding a loaded gun in his hand while he slept, as well as his tough, somewhat ghoulish sense of humor—made him consistently interesting and exciting. As in many of the PI novels to follow, Race Williams told his stories in his own unique way: "I shot him five times. Five times in the stomach before he could even squeeze the trigger. Surprised? He was amazed. At least he should have been. Anyway, he was dead—deader than hell before he folded up and sat down on the floor." In point of fact, Race grew out of an even earlier prototype, Daly's 3-gun Mack who was also known for his quick trigger finger and his tough talk. Mack and Race were the early prototypes of Spillane's Mike Hammer. Race appeared not only in the pages of *Black Mask* but also in six novels that Daly published between 1929 and 1935.

Daly, who never fully understood the importance of the formula he helped create, also wrote stories about Vee Brown, a quick little detective who wrote music under his real name, Vivian.

Among the most talented of the pulp writers in those early days was an ex-private eye named Dashiell Hammett who had worked for the famous Pinkerton Detective Agency for several years. Hammett, a romantic realist, developed strong character studies in a melodramatic, objective and hard-boiled style that soon became everyone's favorite. Like Daly's work, Hammett's stories were told in the first person and featured a middle-aged, heavy set, nameless detective known as the Continental Op since he worked for the Continental Detective Agency of San Francisco. The Continental Op became one of *Black Mask*'s most popular characters and his appearance in any issue guaranteed it would be sold out as soon as it hit the newsstands. In 1929 Hammett published *The Maltese Falcon* as a serial in *Black Mask*, and in its pages he created one of the greatest of all the private eyes—Sam Spade. Curiously, despite the fact that Spade is one of Hammett's best known characters, Spade appears only in the *Falcon* and in three short stories written for slick paper magazines in the early thirties.

Daly's and Hammett's efforts to develop a convincing, tough, private operator quickly led others to imitate and even improve upon the work of the pioneers, and they had an eager outlet in the pages of *Black Mask, Detective Fiction Weekly, Dime Detective, Thrilling Detective* and *Street & Smith's Detective Stories*. Norbert Davis created Max Latin, a tough, suave, alcoholic PI who was always in trouble with the law. In the early 1940s the Max Latin stories ran as a regular series in *Dime Detective*. Also appearing in *Dime Detective* was John K. Butler's Steve Midnight, a Hollywood PI who told his adventures in the first person.

In 1933, Joseph T. Shaw, the most influential editor of *Black Mask*, bought and published a story called *Blackmailers Don't Shoot* by a 45-year-old English-educated Californian named Raymond Chandler. Chandler, a slow and careful worker, created two PIs for his short stories—John Dalmas and another dick named Mallory. Later, when Chandler tried his hand at longer works these two PIs merged and became the famous Philip Marlowe. Even though Marlowe's character was based upon the Hammett foundation, Marlowe was not only more philosophical and introspective than Spade but was also better educated and more articulate. He was, perhaps, the first thinking man's PI. As Ron Goulart has noted: "Marlowe had a gift for metaphor and simile that made his first person adventures vivid and poetic. It is difficult to be hard-boiled and poetic at the same time. Raymond Chandler managed to bring it off." With the birth of Philip Marlowe the PI novel was off and running, and Chandler's work soon became world renowned. All of the Marlowe novels became bestsellers and soon thereafter motion pictures. With the success of the Daly-Hammett-Chandler formula, a host of imitators was soon to follow and the PI novel became more popular than ever. Two of the most successful of the writers of detective fiction and two writers who have also created unusually memorable and successful private investigators—William Campbell Gault and John D. MacDonald—also began writing in the pages of *Black Mask* in the 1940s. MacDonald's Travis McGee and Gault's Brock Callahan and Joe Puma are as popular today as they were at the time of their creation in the 1950s and 1960s.

Beginning as a revolt against the gentility and pretentiousness that had come to characterize the detective story by the 1920s, the hard-boiled school was an American creation. Joseph Shaw wanted to create a new type of detective story that would break the mold that had encased the classic detective story into little more than a crossword puzzle embellished with cardboard characters, drawing-room dialogue and increasingly preposterous methods of murder. According to Shaw, there were several characteristics that these new stories should possess:

1) "We wanted simplicity for the sake of clarity, plausibility and belief. We wanted action ... (involving) recognizable human character in three-dimensional form."
2) The new pattern needed to "emphasize character and the problems inherent in human behavior over crime solution ... character conflict is the main theme."
3) Such distinctive treatment comprises a hard, brittle style ... a full employment of the functions of dialogue, and authenticity in characterization and plot.
4) To this may be added a very fast tempo, attained in part by typical economy of expression ....
5) We wanted writers who "observed the cardinal principle in creating the illusion of reality; they did not make their characters act and talk tough; they allowed them to ... they did not describe their characters as giants, dead-shots or infallible men ...."

The best of the pulp writers responded to Shaw's ideal. In his definitive essay, *The Simple Art of Murder*, Chandler expressed his impatience with the formalized mystery that had lost contact with the violence and physical reality of murder:

I think what was really gnawing at Miss Sayers' mind was the slow realization that her kind of detective story was an arid formula which could not even satisfy its own implications. It was second-grade literature because it was not about the things that could make first-grade literature. If it started out to be about real people (and she could write about them—her minor characters show that), they must very soon do unreal things in order to form the artificial pattern required by the plot. When they did unreal things, they ceased to be real themselves. They became puppets and cardboard lovers and papier-mache villains and detectives of exquisite and impossible gentility.

Hard-boiled writers created heroes with several qualities that set them apart from earlier detectives. First of all, they were tough, hard men who substituted action and the use of force for deduction and the analysis of clues. Street wise, these detectives trusted their instincts and their physical abilities more than their intellects. They pounded the pavement. As we have already heard from Race Williams, hard-boilers often shot first and asked questions later. Their method-of-operation depended on provocation, not ratiocination. Race concludes, "You can't make hamburger without grinding up a little meat." Chandler's recommended solution to plotting problems was, "when in doubt, have a man come through the door with a gun."

Hammett's Continental Op prefers above all methods "to stir things up." In *The Godwulf Manuscript*, Spenser, Robert Parker's modern-day tough guy, relies on this tried and true strategy: "I take hold of one end of the thread and I keep pulling it till it's all unraveled."

A second quality of these PIs is the complexity of their personality, a mixture of roughness and sentimentality. Their terse, laconic exterior belied a much more complicated soul that was troubled with the unfairness and inequality that plagued life's victims. Sad-eyed, world-weary, fed up, these sleuths worked at their trade not because they thought they could make the world better but because maybe they could postpone its becoming worse. The simultaneity of the Depression and the popularity of the hard-boiled hero was not accidental; maybe current economic woes and our interest in these characters isn't either.

Equal parts mercenary and philosopher, private eyes meted out the poetic justice that Nadya Aisenberg argues is the necessary contribution of mythic heroes. Protecting the underdog, fighting for a loser; these were routine activities that often drew the PIs into cases which their instincts told them would be nothing but trouble. The fact that the PI's clients were frequently fabulous looking women cannot be dismissed as an important motivator to take on the tough case. Timothy Harris' most recent Thomas Kyd novel, *Good Night and Good-Bye*, begins:

The first time I saw Laura Cassidy, it was four in the morning and she was trying to drive a fire-engine red Volkswagen out of the underground garage of a Harper Avenue apartment building. She nearly sideswiped the stone entrance, knocked over a garbage can at the end of the driveway, and turned right up the hill toward Sunset Boulevard. What held me rooted to the pavement wasn't her driving; it was the man spread-eagled on the hood of her car. A Volkswagen bug has a sloping hood and the man was having a hell of a time hanging on. His back was arched, his legs struggling to straddle the hood, his hands desperately clawing at the windshield wipers to prevent his sliding off. He was middle-aged, over-weight, and his face had the horrified, windswept look of someone who has just been pushed off a tall building .... And he was stark naked.

After rescuing Laura from this situation and returning her home, Kyd leaves.

All the way home I was aware of the scent of her perfume in the car and I kept recalling how her body had felt lying slack in my arms, and those arresting silver-blue eyes and the way they seemed to do something to the center of my chest. And another part of me kept recalling her medicine cabinet and the syringes and the slackness in her face. I'd been around long enough to know there was no percentage in falling for a junkie. I had my own self-destructive tendencies to deal with, there was no way I needed hers. I told myself to forget about Laura Cassidy and I decided I wouldn't try and see her again.

Compassionate and kind toward the innocent and the weak, hard-boiled dicks were cynical and suspicious toward politicians, wealth and institutional power. Nowhere is this attitude more pronounced than in the often hostile relationships between the PIs and the police.

A man in the blue-gray, jail uniform came along between the cells reading numbers. He stopped in front of mine and unlocked the door and gave me the hard stare they think they have to wear on their pans forever and forever and forever. I'm a cop, brother, I'm tough,...let's not forget we're tough guys, we're cops, and we do what we like with punks like you.
Behind me a rather remote and muffled voice seemed to be chanting the policeman's litany: "open it up or we'll kick it in." I sneered back at the voice. They wouldn't kick it in because kicking in a door is hard on the feet. Policemen are kind to their feet. Their feet are about all they are kind to.

(Raymond Chandler, *The Lady in the Lake*)

This animosity may have stemmed from the fact that many private eyes originally had been with the police or DA's office but then had resigned or been fired from the force. Inevitably, however, the PI had one cop on the force who was still his friend or did him an occasional insider's favor on the *quid pro quo*. The "honest cop" often shares the PI's sentiments about the force and abusive authority, but stays with the job despite his reservations. Captain Webber, Bay City chief of detectives, admits:

"Police business," he said almost gently, "is a hell of a problem. It's a good deal like politics. It asks for the highest type of men, and there's nothing in it to attract the highest type of men. So we have to work with what we get—and we get things like this."   *(Lady in the Lake)*

In the best of the current hard-boiled series, the police are treated with a much more even hand. Evidence is seldom withheld from them, cooperation between the PI and the cops is viewed as a necessity, the decent cop as the exception-that-proves-the-rule character is encountered less frequently. The police are seen as victims of the job society requires of them, much like the PI himself.

Bill Pronzini's Nameless Detective, Michael Lewin's Albert Samson and Arthur Lyon's Jacob Asch are the best exemplars of these new attitudes. Although the genre's commitment to realism demands that police corruption and excesses be examined, it also requires recognition that police will fight these evils themselves.

Similar to the American cowboy and Natty Bumppo, frontier hero before him, the PI often worked alone and lived a solitary, lonely life in and around the grimy back alleys and seedy speakeasies of the disorderly big American city. Isolated and unappreciated by the society he served, the private eye was often portrayed as the sole protector of society from the forces of evil and meanness. In a word, he was chivalrous.

In medieval Europe chivalry was the code of conduct to which all knights subscribed. Medieval knights pledged to protect the weak and oppressed—the poor, the widow and the orphan. In those days the chivalric code was based on courage, prowess, loyalty and generosity. These same traits mark our modern PIs. Knights of old, contrary to what you might have been told, could be terribly cruel to all who were not included in the code of chivalric obligation. Similarly with our modern knights who deal out swift punishment to those on the wrong side of justice and righteousness. Knights of old not only learned to use a sword, throw a spear, manage a shield and march—they were expected to entertain—just as our knights of today. Lastly, knights of old had to learn to wear armor, become accustomed to hardships and to choose a lady love just like our knights with guns. Like their chivalrous predecessors, our modern knights are loved by us because at times it seems they are the only defenders of truth, justice and morality in a world of deceit, senseless cruelty and immorality where life is never fair and nice guys finish last.

The attempt to be principled and loyal to a just but difficult moral code may be the quality which more than any other accounts for the appeal of the hard-boiled heroes. We admire their ability to master difficult situations without compromising their sometimes peculiar sense of honor. Their arrogance, rudeness and rowdiness can be excused because they are able to express to a world increasingly complex, endlessly bureaucratic and seemingly out of control, the power of one competent, determined individual.

In their introduction to the anthology *The Great American Detective* (New American Library, 1978), William Kittredge and Steven Krauzer suggest:

Society requires outlaws. It is bound by its own restrictions; in the name of democracy, it has handcuffed itself from taking the most direct, efficient route toward the maintenance of order and the abolition of disruptive forces .... Or as Mike Hammer complains, "The cops can't break a guy's arm to make him talk, and they can't shove his teeth in with the muzzle of a .45 to remind him that you aren't fooling." Social institutions such as democracy and due process are of course necessary; if they are not the most effective way of punishing the guilty, they constitute the most foolproof system for protecting the innocent. But if we can be morally certain outside the system that a person is culpable, we can sympathize with Mike Hammer's plaint. We will even accept the role of the outlaw as justice's guardian when we are convinced beyond a doubt that a criminal needs and deserves arm-breaking and teeth-shoving.

The private eye took his profession, his obligations and his skills seriously. As Spade says, "I'm a detective and expecting me to run criminals down and let them go free is like asking a dog to catch a rabbit and let it go." In a similar sense, Chandler's famous vision of his hero who walks the mean streets is both realistic and romantic:

> He is the hero; he is everything. He must be a complete man and a common man and yet an unusual man. He must be, to use a rather weathered phrase, a man of honor—by instinct, by inevitability, without thought of it, and certainly without saying it. He must be the best man in his world and a good enough man for any world. I do not care much about his private life; he is neither a eunuch nor a satyr; I think he might seduce a duchess and I am quite sure he would not spoil a virgin; if he is a man of honor in one thing, he is that in all things.
>
> He is a relatively poor man, or he would not be a detective at all. He is a common man or he could not go among common people. He has a sense of character, or he would not know his job. He will take no man's money dishonestly and no man's insolence without a due and dispassionate revenge. He is a lonely man and his pride is that you will treat him as a proud man or be very sorry you ever saw him. He talks as the man of his age talks—that is, with rude wit, a lively sense of the grotesque, a disgust for sham, and a contempt for pettiness. (*The Simple Art of Murder*)

Hard-boiled authors cultivated a style of writing that was distinctive of their new school. The narration was sparse and detached. Then and now, the best hard-boiled writers used language that created a taut, dangerous atmosphere full of moral decay, the threat of violence and characters who grab you by the throat. Howard Haycraft, a premier chronicler of mystery fiction, praised Hammett's prose as "economical, astringent, and muscular." Descriptions of violence were understated in a way that heightened their realism and physical impact. The writing had a bare-knuckled intensity.

> It was fists at first. He started it by throwing his right at my head. I went in under and gave him all I had in a right and left to the belly. He swallowed his chew of tobacco. But he didn't bend. Few big men are as strong as they look. Billie was.
>
> He didn't know anything at all. His idea of a fight was to stand up and throw fists at your heads—right, left, right, left. His fists were as large as wastebaskets. They wheezed through the air. But always at the head—the easiest part to get out of the way.
>
> There was room enough for me to go in and out. I did that. I hammered his belly. I thumped his heart. I mauled his belly again. Every time I hit him he grew an inch, gained a pound and picked up another horsepower. I don't fool when I hit, but nothing I did to this human mountain—not even making him swallow his hunk of

tobacco—had any visible effect on him. (Dashiell Hammett, *The Whosis Kid*)

However, at its extreme, hard-boiled violence could become sadistic, nasty and gory. Race Williams and his descendants, Mickey Spillane's Mike Hammer, and John B. West's Rocky Steele are probably the best known exemplars of the blood-and-guts overkill.

The goddamn bastards played right into my hands. They thought they had me nice and cold and just as they were set to carve me into a raw mess of skin, I dragged out the .45 and let them look down the hole so they could see where sudden death came from.

It was the only kind of talk they knew. The little guy stared too long. He should have been watching his face. I snapped the side of the rod across his jaw and laid the flesh open to the bone. He dropped the sap and staggered into the big boy with a scream starting to come up out of his throat only to get it cut off in the middle as I pounded his teeth back into his mouth with the end of the barrel.... For laughs I gave him a taste of his own sap on the back of his hand and felt the bones go into splinters. He wasn't going to be using any tools for a long time. (Mickey Spillane, *The Big Kill*)

In comparison to other mystery writing, the hard-boiled style emphasized human action at a fast pace. The dust-jacket cliches say it all: "break-neck," "breathless," "hair-raising," "gripping," "relentless," "hard-hitting," "knockout" and "staggering." Readers are lucky to survive. More good guys and bad guys are beat up, kicked around and punched out in hard-boiled fiction than in any other types of mystery.

A final element of hard-boiled style is its distinctive dialogue. Full of slang, earthy, street-wise, nasal and sneering, the tough private eye used words as weapons. He talked in an abrupt, aggressive, intimidating manner. He was wise-cracking and sarcastic. Occasionally witty but always tough, the dialogue captured the rhythm of the streets.

Pete leaned over. He looked both ways cautiously. He put his sleek head to one side and listened elaborately. He'd seen a gangster picture the night before and knew how it was done. Mark Hull waited with a pained but patient expression.

"I got a hot tip," said Pete mysteriously.

"Look out it don't burn your fingers."

"Do I get a cut?" asked Pete.

"You get a smack on the snozzle in about a minute."

(Norbert Davis, *Kansas City Flash*)

At its best with writers like Hammett and Chandler, this dialogue always served a purpose. Hammett was a master at revealing characters through dialogue while Chandler used the wise-crack as one of Marlowe's main defenses against his own vulnerabilities and emotions. At its worst, the wise-crack dialogue has often been imitated by writers who had no real purpose for it other than to copy a quality from the *Black Mask* tradition. Employed at this level, the slangy, wise-crack dialogue becomes a distraction, not unlike the quirky eccentricities of the British gentleman-detective who soon wears out his welcome.

Readers who are interested in studying additional characteristics of the hard-boiled genre—its political conservatism, its treatment of women and sexuality, its ambiguity about material wealth—should consult John Cawelti's definitive *Adventure, Mystery and Romance* (University of Chicago Press, 1976; especially chapters 6 and 7) which contains the following summary of the hard-boiled formula:

> The urban world of the hard-boiled detective story is, then, a surface of specious and ambiguous glamor hiding depths of corruption. It is ruled by a secret alliance between the rich and respectable and the criminal underworld .... The city is also a place of strong sexual temptation and excitement, but this very sexuality, embodied in stunningly attractive and seemingly approachable women, is a source of betrayal and of fundamental attacks on masculinity. The hero who confronts this nightmare world is a figure whose basic characteristics identify him with the lower middle class, those condemned by their lack of economic mobility to inhabit the decaying center of this urban society. He is a marginal professional with a smattering of culture, but on the whole his tastes and attitudes are ordinary. He is surrounded by continual threats to his safety and even his status. His sexual identity and masculine certitude is constantly being put on the line and threatened with betrayal and destruction. Yet the hard-boiled hero is potent and courageous. Though he must continually face the fears of loneliness and isolaltion, of status uncertainty and of sexual betrayal, he is the kind of man who can fight his way to the source of the pervasive evil and, meeting violence with violence, destroys it. In the process of his quest, he also lays bare the widespread corruption of the social order, thereby proving and maintaining his own moral integrity.

As the PI novel became more popular many literary critics began to tire of the genre and made a somewhat futile effort to steer the public away from this form of mystery fiction. In his 1969 book *Who Done It: A Guide to Mystery and Suspense Fiction*, Ordean Hagen defined the private eye as:

> A private detective working alone; not directly connected with any law enforcement agency, but generally cooperating with them. Don't look for them in the newer books, *as they are quite an anachronism.* (emphasis ours)

In another section of this same book Hagen is even *more* specific about the trend he sees in mystery fiction, stating:

> Today the trend is toward the novel of suspense. The detective is no longer the central character; the private eye has become obsolete, a parody if he appears at all. New police methods and cooperation between different bureaus of a modern police

department have made the lone wolf operator an oddity.

As an oracle or prophet Hagen leaves much to be desired. The year 1969 itself saw the publication, in both hard and paperback, of well over one hundred American mystery novels featuring a lone wolf private eye as the central character. Moreover in the decade that followed another six hundred odd novels, featuring private eyes of every conceivable shape, form and variety were released to eager readers by American publishers. Not only is the report of the PI's demise somewhat premature, he has grown in size, stature and popularity. Prophecy, Hagen should have known, is an extremely hazardous business.

The private eye novel is neither obsolete nor an anachronism. Instead, it has become one of the most popular forms of the always popular mystery novel, and it has even invaded other literary forms. Today there are a number of science-fiction private eyes, occult private eyes and religious private eyes and there is every good reason to suppose the invasions have firmly established beachheads. In the pages that follow we will explore in some detail these hybrid forms of the mystery novel and we will study at length the reasons for the perennial popularity of the heroic private investigator. By way of preview it can be noted here that our knights without armor come in every shape, form and fashion and in every human variety. There are young PIs (Chip Harrison) and old PIs (Jake Spanner), brilliant (The Hook) and stupid (C. Card), guilt-ridden (Mitch Tobin) and tough-minded (Sam Hunter and Mike Hammer), one who shoots first and asks questions later (Race Williams) and another who is fearful of guns (Neal Cotton). Many are alcoholics (Milo) and one drinks only milk (Humphrey Campbell). One of the most brilliant and effective is an active homosexual (David Brandstetter) and another is potentially suicidal and plays Russian roulette (Bernardo Thomas). One has the ability to see the soul mist rise from the bodies of his slain enemies (Joe Reddman). Another is a hypochrondriac and, because he smokes excessively, worries about lung cancer (Pronzini's "Nameless"). They also come from every walk of life. One is a member of the upper crust and a Harvard graduate (The Hook) and another is a self-confessed Bowery bum (Curt Cannon), while yet another (Murray Kirk) lives in a fancy hotel, owns a Cadillac, and has a glamorous mistress. Several of the detectives are well-to-do, middle-class, married and with children (Brock Callahan), while others find it impossible to make ends meet (Toby Peters) or have to do PI work in order to pay their taxes (John T. McLaren). As for physical infirmities, one is blind (Duncan MacLain), another is a dwarf (Mongo), one has only one arm (Michael Collins' Dan Fortune) and another is deaf (Joe Binney). They also come in all colors: black (John Shaft and Touissant Moore), white (Spenser and Goodey), brown (Jo Gar) and yellow (Tommy Lee). Both sexes are represented. Most of these private eyes are likeable, and gallant righters of wrongs and dispensers of justice in an oftentimes cruel and unjust world. They are, truly, our modern knights.

At one time it seemed that all the private eyes limited their activities to the larger cities—New York, Los Angeles, San Francisco, Chicago. *Black Mask* referred to Los Angeles and Hollywood as the New Wild West, and the Hollywood private eye novel became a sub-genre in itself. For a time there was even a pulp magazine called *Hollywood Detective*. While the West Coast area still has its appeal —the fictional private eyes have spread across the entire nation.

On the contemporary scene we find them in Cincinnati (Harry Stoner), Cleveland (David Stuart), Indianapolis (Albert Sampson), Oklahoma City (Cranmer and Maneri), Boston (Spenser and Jason O'Neil), Seattle (John Denson and Jonas Duncan), Atlanta (Jim Hardman), Denver (Joe Reddman), Detroit (Amos Walker), Philadelphia (Mike Dime), Miami (Mike Shayne), Ft. Lauderdale (Travis McGee), San Diego (Max Thursday) and Tampa (Ed Rivers). Admittedly, the metropolis still attracts the largest number with New York, Los Angeles, San Francisco, and Chicago predominating.

This book is first an attempt to rescue the strongest of the private eyes of the thirties, forties, fifties and sixties from oblivion and, second, an attempt to call your attention to a large number of fine, current-day mystery novelists who have created unusually memorable private eyes. Their creations often have been ignored by busy reviewers and Madison Avenue advertising hypes that push lesser, sensational works of sex and gore to the top of the heap. Although many of the PIs and the authors we review also include sex and gore, they distinguish themselves by giving us in-depth studies of character, by providing us insight into the workings of ordinary and not-so-ordinary human beings with whom we can identify and empathize.

The most accomplished of our authors give us much more than mere entertainment—even though there is no dearth of action. The best of their work is plotted with care and craft, and their villains as well as their heroes come alive. True, not every novel nor every private eye is a masterpiece. Some are weak and many are flawed but the best provide action, excitement and entertainment as well as a number of psychological truths about the human condition and that oldest of all conflicts—the conflict of good and evil. A number of literary analysts have made the point that the popularity of the mystery novel seems strongly correlated with the breakdown of our social institutions and increases in social disorder such as economic depression, political unrest, white collar crime and official malfeasance. Such may be the case on our contemporary scene and we may well yearn for people we can trust, for heroes we can believe in, and for situations in which evil is punished, the guilty are brought to justice, and the noble, the innocent, and the brave are rewarded. But such, we believe, is the case in all times and all climes and we can appreciate an honest rendering of the realistic triumphs of the knight errant at any time of man, in any place and in any setting. We agree with Philip Guedalla that "The detective story is the normal recreation of noble minds." And for those supersophisticates who would belittle and bedamn those of us who are addicted to the exploits of hard-boiled private eyes we agree with Rex Stout's theory that "people who don't like mystery stories are anarchists." If you agree, we welcome you to the world of the fictional private eye who, like Faulkner's modern man, not only survives but always prevails.

In 1983 we surveyed the membership of the Private Eye Writers of America (PWA), an organization of active authors of private-eye fiction, about their evaluation of past and present private eye novels. The survey was organized into two parts covering 1920-1970 (115 entries) and 1970-present (160 entries). The ratings of the PWA membership guided our selection of authors for this book. However, we retained the rightful prerogative of any author to base our final selections on additional grounds, not the least of which was personal preference. A brief summary of the survey's results are included below.

Part I (1920-1970)

Of the 80 questionnaires that were distributed, 27 were completed and returned. A response rate of 34% to a mailed questionnaire is lower than one would like to see, but still allows conclusions to be drawn with appropriate cautions. Interpretations of mailed surveys, particularly with a low return rate require the following caveats: 1) The results may not be generalizable from the respondents to the nonrespondents; this is particularly the case where there are reasons to believe that respondents and nonrespondents differ in some important ways. 2) The results may not be generalizable from the sample whose opinions were solicited (private eye writers) to some other sample (e.g., mystery fans in general). 3) The conditions under which respondents complete the questionnaire are likely to differ from person to person introducing many possible, but unknown, influences. 4) Ratings under conditions of anonymity may not be equivalent to other indicators of the same person's opinion (e.g., purchases of books, attributed reviews).

In order to broaden our base of opinion, we sent questionnaires to a number of very well-known critics and reviewers of mystery fiction as well as nationally known scholars in the area of popular culture. Therefore, the final sample of 27 is composed of 23 private eye writers and four reviewer-critics.

The "average" respondent rated 38 entries from a possible 115 listed in our questionnaire. Five respondents added a total of only eight different private eyes in the spaces provided indicating that the original printed list was very representative of the private eye domain. (In most cases, these additional private eyes did not appear in novels, a requirement we placed on our entries.) With respondents rating an average of 38 entries per questionnaire, one can fairly conclude that the sample was reasonably well-read and opinionated about this literature. The greatest number of ratings was 93; the fewest was 7. Ratings were scored 4 (Excellent), 3 (Good), 2 (Average), 1 (Below Average) and O (Poor).

Results for the 1920-1970 period are summarized in Table 1. The forty private eyes who were best known to the respondents are ordered in terms of the percentage of respondents who indicated they were "very" or "somewhat familiar" with the novels.

Two ratings are given in each of the six categories of evaluation: literary value (LV), overall entertainment value (OEV), character development (CD), plot (P), writing style (WS) and Final Grade. The upper rating is a *mean value* which is the numeric average of all ratings. The lower rating is a *mode* which is the rating that was most frequently given by respondents (on occasion, two ratings may be tied for the most frequent score, i.e., the distribution is *bimodal*). A mode is a useful statistic because it is less influenced than a mean by extreme scores. For example, an examination of the literary value score for Hammer-Spillane shows a mean of 2.8, a mode of 4. Although more respondents gave Hammer-Spillane a grade of 4 ("excellent") than any other grade, a few raters gave grades of 1 ("poor") thereby pulling the mean score down. In situations like this, interpretations of ratings are made most accurately by considering both the mean and mode values. An example in the opposite direction is illustrasted by the ratings of character development for Noon-Avallone.

The column labeled "Ratings Rank" lists the private eyes by the order of their Final Grade from highest to lowest. In instances when Final Grades were identical, we computed the means of the five component grades (LV, OEV, CD, P & WS) as a "tiebreaker."

The final column entitled "Not a PI" shows the number of respondents who disqualified the character as a legitimate PI in the hardboiled tradition which we defined as "a sophisticated, worldly-wise, full time private investigator drawing most—if not all—of his income from his PI activities and he is one who carries out his investigations in the tough but sympathetic tradition made famous by Hammett and Chandler." Of greatest interest here is the sentiment regarding *The Thin Man* characters and the two George Harmon Coxe series.

We computed a correlation coefficient between the Percentage Familiar score and the Final Grade for these 40 private eyes. A correlation coefficient is a statistic which shows the amount of relationship between two or more variables. It can range from -1.0 to 1.0; a positive correlation means that as scores on one variable increase so too do the scores on the other variable. The larger the correlation coefficient, the stronger the relationship. Percentage Familiar Score correlated .46 with Final Grade. This means that although there is a substantial positive relation between familiarity and opinions of quality, the two variables are by no means synonymous among this group of raters.

Part II (1970-82)

Twenty-eight respondents (35% response rate) completed the second survey covering 1970 to the present. Twenty-four of these respondents also answered Part I. Twenty-two private-eye writers and six reviewer critics comprised the sample for Part II.

The "average" respondent rated 37 entries from a possible 160 listed on the second questionnaire. Three respondents added a total of four different private eyes in the spaces provided indicating that, as with Part I of the survey, the original list was comprehensive. The greatest number of ratings for any respondent was 129; the fewest 6.

With an identical format to Table 1, Table 2 represents the data for the 40 private eyes best known by this group of raters. Scoring and determination of ranks were conducted in an identical fashion to Part I of the survey. We listed Pete Hamill's Sam Briscoe and Max Collins' Nolan out of sequence because of the relatively high frequency with which respondents viewed them as not meeting our working definition of a private eye. Three authors (Randisi, Lynds-Collins-Shaw, & Ellin) placed two of their detective-heroes in the top forty. In Part I, five authors (Hammett, Dewey, Gruber, Gault & Coxe) earned this honor.

The correlation in Part II between Percentage Familiar scores and Final Grade was .29, indicating that familiarity and opinions of quality were less related to each other than in Part I. A likely explanation for this finding is that with more recent books there has not been sufficient time for the discovery of quality to translate itself into wide readership. This explanation also fits the discovery that several recent authors who earned relatively high ratings of quality just missed the 35.7% familiarity criterion for the top 40 (Richard Hoyt, Sue Grafton & Jack Lynch are prime examples.)

To the inevitable question of how much confidence we have in the meaning of these results, we would reply "a good deal" for at least three important reasons. First, although the response rate was approximately 20% less than what we had originally predicted, a sample of 27 (or 28) experts is not an insubstantial one. Ask yourself this: on how many matters of taste or opinion do you have the comparative judgments of 27 people who are well-informed about the issue at hand? Second, the level of agreement between raters was extremely high. In the majority of cases, raters did not differ by more than one point in evaluating the various dimensions of quality. Agreement between raters becomes an increasingly important consideration as the number of raters decreases. Third, and to put it most directly, the ratings for the most part make good sense. For example, character development earns by far the lowest grades for Carroll John Daly, plot the lowest for Robert Parker, and overall entertainment value the highest for Stuart Kaminsky. Were these ratings different one would be concerned about the survey's credibility, but the pattern of scores for the individual authors is very predictable from a thorough knowledge of this literature.

As the final check on the reliability of the ratings, we deliberately included a number of authors on both parts of the survey. This enabled us to compare the ratings of a given entry made by the same respondent at two different times. We obtained separate-form ratings on very well-known private eyes (e.g., Travis McGee) and those of less notoriety (e.g., Bart Challis and Benjamin Smoke). In one case we obtained ratings of the same character (Paul Pine) under the author's real (Howard Browne) and pen (John Evans) names. In all instances, we discovered that the mean ratings in every category were identical from Part I to Part II. Modal ratings were also identical. This level of agreement indicates that raters were consistent across time in assigning their grades and were doing so in an attentive and conscientious manner.

We end where we began—with a caution about what these results mean. We believe they are a valid measure of the opinions of professional writers and critics within the PI field. How they might compare with evaluations by mystery fans in general or private eye fans in particular is not known but could be answered by additional survey work.

Table 1
Private Eye Survey (1920-1970)

Private Eye	Author	% Familiar	LV	OEV	CD	P	WS	Final Grade	Rating Rank	Not PI
Marlowe, Philip	Chandler, Raymond		3.9	3.9	3.9	3.8	3.9	3.9		
		100	4	4	4	4	4	4	1	
Spade, Sam	Hammett, Dashiell		3.9	3.9	3.8	3.8	3.8	3.9		
		100	4	4	4	4	4	4	2	
Archer, Lew	Macdonald, Ross		3.8	3.8	3.8	3.7	3.8	3.8		
		100	4	4	4	4	4	4	3	
Continental Op	Hammett, Dashiell		3.7	3.7	3.5	3.7	3.8	3.8		
		96.3	4	4	4	4	4	4	4	
Wolfe, Nero	Stout, Rex		3.5	3.3	3.2	3.1	3.5	3.4		
		96.3	4	4	4	3	4	4	7	**
Hammer, Mike	Spillane, Mickey		2.8	2.8	2.2	2.4	2.4	2.5		
		96.3	4	3	2	2	2	2	25	
McGee, Travis	MacDonald, John		3.3	3.5	3.4	3.2	3.3	3.4		
		92.6	4	4	4	3	3	4	6	**
Charles, Nick & Nora	Hammett, Dashiell		3.5	3.3	3.3	3.3	3.4	3.3		
		92.6	4	4	3	3	4	4	8	****
Shayne, Mike	Halliday, Brett		2.5	2.7	2.5	2.8	2.5	2.6		
		92.6	2	3	2	2	2	2	21	
Scott, Shell	Prather, Richard		2.3	2.5	2.1	2.3	2.5	2.5		
		85.2	2	2	2	2	2	2	27	

Private Eye	Author	% Familiar	LV	OEV	CD	P	WS	Final Grade	Rating Rank	Not a PI
Williams, Race	Daly, Carroll John		2.7	2.5	1.6	2.0	2.1	2.3		
		77.8	3	3	2	2	2	3	31	
Noon, Ed	Avallone, Michael		1.7	2.4	1.7	2.0	1.7	2.0		
		74.1	2	2	1	2	2	2	38	
Robinson, Mac	Dewey, Thomas		3.1	3.3	3.2	3.2	3.2	3.3		
		70.4	3	3,4	3	3	3	3	10	
Cool, Bertha, Lam, Donald	Fair, A.A.		2.7	2.9	2.5	3.1	2.5	2.7		
		70.4	3	3	3	3	2	2.5	19	**
Hunter, Ed & Am	Brown, Fredric		3.2	3.4	3.5	3.4	3.5	3.4		
		63.0	3	4	4	4	4	4	5	
Callahan, Brock	Gault, William		3.1	3.2	3.1	3.1	3.1	3.1		
		59.3	3	3	3	3	3	3	11	
Lash, Simon	Gruber, Frank		2.3	2.4	2.0	2.2	2.0	2.1		
		59.3	2	2	2	2	2	2	36	
Fletcher, Johnny	Gruber, Frank		2.1	2.1	1.9	2.1	1.9	2.1		
		55.6	2	2	2	2	2	2	37	
Puma, Joe	Gault, William		2.9	3.1	3.1	3.1	3.1	2.9		
		55.6	3	3	3	3	3	3	14	
Rome, Tony	Albert Marvin		2.1	2.7	2.6	2.8	2.6	2.6		
		51.9	2	2.3	2	3	3	2.3	22	
Liddell, Johnny	Kane, Frank		2.1	2.3	2.1	2,3	2.1	2.1		
		51.9	2	2	2	2.3	2	2	35	
Chambers, Pete	Kane, Henry		2.5	2.6	2.5	2.4	2.4	2.5		
		51.9	3	3	3	3	3	2.5,3	26	
Thursday, Max	Miller, Wade		2.6	2.8	2.6	2.6	2.7	2.6		
		51.9	3	3	3	3	3	3	20	
Crane, Bill	Latimer, Jonathan		2.8	3.0	2.5	2.7	2.9	2.8		
		48.1	3	3	3	3	3	3	17	
West, Honey	Fickling, G. G.		1.7	2.3	2.0	1.9	2.3	2.2		
		48.1	2	2	2	2	2	2	3,4	
Schofield, Pete	Dewey, Thomas		2.7	3.0	2.9	2.9	3.1	3.0		
		44.4	2	3	3	3	3	3	13	
Rivers, Ed	Powell, Talmage		2.6	2.9	2.8	2.9	2.8	2.8		
		40.7	2.3	3	3	3	3	3	16	
Havoc, Johnny	Jakes, John		1.8	2.4	2.2	2.1	2.1	1.9		
		40.7	2	2	2	2	2	2	39	
Pine, Paul	Evans, John		3.1	3.5	3.2	3.3	3.5	3.3		
		40.7	3	3	3	3	3	3	9	
Drum, Chester	Marlowe, Stephen		2.4	2.7	2.5	2.5	2.5	2.6		
		40.7	2	3	2	3	2	3	23	
Casey, Flashgun	Coxe, George		2.4	2.5	2.2	2.5	2.4	2.4		
		40.7	2	2	2	2	2	2	29	*****
Lennox, Bill	Ballard, W. T.		2.3	2.6	2.3	2.4	2.4	2.2		
		37.0	2	3	2	2	2	2	32	
Breed, Barr	Ballanger, Bill		2.3	2.5	2.6	2.6	2.6	2.4		
		37.0	2	3	3	3	3	2	28	
McGrath, Pete	Brett, Michael		1.6	1.9	1.9	1.8	2.1	1.7		
		37.0	2	2	2	2	2	2	40	
Cannon, Curt	Cannon, Curt		2.6	2.8	2.7	2.4	3.1	2.5		
		37.0	3	3	3,4	2,3	3	3	24	
Challis, Bart	Nolan, William		2.2	2.4	2.3	2.4	2.6	2.3		
		37.0	3	3	2,3	1,4	3	2,3	30	
March, Milo	Chaber, M.E.		2.6	2.4	2.2	2.1	2.3	2.2		
		37.0	2	2	2	2	2	2	33	
Moore, Toussaint	Lacy, Ed		2.8	2.8	2.9	2.8	2.9	2.9		
		37.0	2,3	3	2	3	3	2,3	15	
Ryan, Jack	Leonard, Elmore		3.1	3.3	3.3	3.2	3.4	3.1		
		37.0	3	3	3	3	4	3,3.5	12	
Murdock, Kent	Coxe, George		2.7	2.7	2.4	3.0	2.5	2.8		
		37.0	2	3	2	3	2.3	3	18	******

Table 2
Private Eye Survey (1970-1982)

Private Eye	Author	% Familiar	LV	OEV	CD	P	WS	Final Grade	Rating Rank	Not a PI
Spenser	Parker, Robert		2.8	3.0	3.1	2.1	3.0	2.8		
		96.4	3	3	4	2	4	3	22	
"Nameless"	Pronzini, Bill		2.9	3.3	3.2	3.0	3.1	3.2		
		92.9	3	4	3,4	3	3	3	8	
Scudder, Matt	Block, Lawrence		3.0	3.2	3.4	3.1	3.2	3.2		
		78.6	3	4	4	3	3	4	6	
Wine, Moses	Simon, Roger		2.9	3.0	2.9	2.7	3.0	2.9		
		75.0	3	2,4	2,3	2	2,4	3	20	
Kearney, Dan	Gores, Joe		2.9	3.3	3.0	3.2	3.1	3.2		
		71.4	3	3,4	3	3	3	3	9	
Peters, Toby	Kaminsky, Stuart		2.8	3.1	2.6	2.8	2.7	2.9		
		71.4	3	3	2	2	3	3	21	
Fortune, Dan	Collins, Michael		2.5	2.8	2.8	2.8	3.0	2.7		
		67.9	3	3	3	3	3	3	24	
Brandstetter, Dave	Hansen, Joseph		3.2	3.1	3.4	3.0	3.3	3.1		
		67.9	3,4	3	3	3	3	3	12	
Tanner, John Marshall	Greenleaf, Stephen		3.0	3.2	3.1	3.0	3.1	3.1		
		64.3	3	4	3	3,4	4	3,4	14	
Stoner, Harry	Valin, Jonathan		2.9	3.0	3.0	2.9	3.2	3.2		
		64.3	3	3,4	3,4	3	3	3	10	
Walker, Amos	Estleman, Loren		2.7	3.1	2.8	3.1	2.9	2.9		
		60.7	3	3	3	3	3	3	19	
Tobin, Mitch	Coe, Tucker		3.3	3.4	3.5	3.2	3.6	3.5		
		60.7	3	3,4	4	3	4	4	4	
Asch, Jacob	Lyons, Art		3.3	3.7	3.5	3.5	3.7	3.5		
		57.1	3	4	4	4	4	4	3	
Samson, Albert	Lewin, Michael		2.8	3.3	3.1	3.1	3.2	3.2		
		53.6	3	4	3,4	4	3	3.5	7	
Sughrue, C. W.	Crumley, James		3.6	3.7	3.8	3.6	3.6	3.7		
		50.0	4	4	4	4	4	4	1	
Shaft	Tidyman, Ernest		2,3	2.6	2.5	2.3	2.4	2.3		
		50.0	2	3	2	2	2	2	30	
Carpenter, Ace	Caine, Hamilton		1.6	1.8	2.2	2.2	2.2	2.0		
		50.0	1	2	2	2	2	2	38	
Levine, Jack	Bergman, Andrew		2.9	3.1	3.0	2.9	3.0	3.0		
		50.0	3	3	3	3	3	2	17	
Goodey, Joe	Alverson, Charles		2.3	2.8	2.9	2.7	2.8	2.8		
		46.4	3	3	3	3	2	3	23	
"Mongo"	Chesbro, George		2.3	2.3	2.7	2.3	2.5	2.5		**
		46.4	2	2,3	2,3	2	2,3	2	28	
Purdue, Chance	Spencer, Ross		2.0	2.3	1.4	1.3	2.1	1.9		*
		46.4	3	1,3,4	1	2	3	1	39	
Jacoby, Miles	Randisi, Robert		1.8	2.2	1.8	1.9	1.9	2.1		
		46.4	2	3	2	3	2,3	2	36	
Smoke, Benjamin	McBain, Ed		2.6	2.9	2.8	2.9	3.2	3.0		**
		42.9	3	2,3	3	3	3	2	18	
McCone, Sharon	Muller, Marcia		2.3	2.4	2.6	2.5	2.6	2.6		*
		42.9	2	2	2	2	2	2	25	
Kyd, Thomas	Harris, Timothy		2.8	3.4	3.4	3.2	3.3	3.3		
		42.9	3	4	4	4	4	3,4	5	
Easy, Johnny	Goulart, Ron		2.2	2.6	2.3	2.5	2.7	2.6		
		42.9	2	2,3	2	2	3	2	26	
Marlow, Sam	Fenady, Andrew		2.0	2.3	1.8	2.1	2.3	2.0		
		42.9	2	1,2	1	1	2	1	37	

Private Eye	Author	% Familiar	LV	OEV	CD	P	WS	Final Grade	Rating Rank	Not a PI
Po, Henry	Randisi, Robert		1.9	2.3	2.0	2.1	2.4	2.3		
		42.9	2	2	2	2	2	2	33	
Angel, Harry	Hjortsberg, Wm.		2.3	2.3	2.3	2.5	2.8	2.3		
		39.3	1	3	3	3	4	3	29	
Spanner, Jake	Morse, L. A.		2.3	2.5	2.4	2.1	2.2	2.3		
		39.3	1	1	1	1	1	1	32	
Haller, Mike	Byrd Max		2.1	2.5	2.4	2.4	2.4	2.2		
		35.7	2	3,4	3	2,3	4	2,3,4	34	
Roper, Max	Platt, Kin		1.9	2.1	2.1	2.2	2.2	2.1		
		35.7	2	2	2	3	2	2.5	35	
Cody	Reasoner, Jim		3.0	3.2	3.1	3.1	3.0	3.1		
		35.7	2,4	3	2,4	4	2,4	2.5,4	15	
Kirk, Murray	Ellin, Stanley		3.5	3.5	3.6	3.4	3.7	3.5		
		35.7	4	4	4	4	4	4	2	
Dekker, Jake	Ellin, Stanley		3.0	3.2	3.2	2.8	3.5	3.1		
		35.7	3	4	4	3	4	4	13	*
Shaw, Paul	Sadler, Mark		2.7	3.0	2.9	3.1	3.1	3.2		
		35.7	3	3	3	3	3	3	11	
Chandler, Ray	Denbow, William		1.5	1.1	1.0	0.9	1.1	1.0		
		35.7	0	0	0	0	0	0	40	**
Warshawski, V. I.	Paretsky, Sara		3.0	3.1	3.1	3.1	2.9	3.0		
		35.7	3	3	4	3	3	3	16	
Briscoe, Sam	Hamil, Pete		2.5	2.7	2.7	2.4	2.6	2.5		
		64.3	3	2	2	2	3	2	27	****
Nolan	Collins, Max		2.3	2.5	2.1	2.5	2.3	2.3		
		57.1	2	2.3	2	2	2	2	31	******

Chapter II
The King and the Royal Heir—
Dashiell Hammett & Raymond Chandler

NO ONE WOULD DARE TOUCH the subject of American detective fiction without paying homage to its twin deities, Dashiell Hammett and Raymond Chandler. So much has already been written about them that little we could add in the way of facts and literary commentary would be novel or enlightening. Nevertheless, since Hammett is the founder of the PI dynasty and Chandler is its master builder, homage in the form of a review of their accomplishments is demanded.

Most of what Hammett and Chandler attempted was a reaction to the type of detective story created by writers like S.S. Van Dine and Agatha Christie. Van Dine was, as Jon Tuska noted, the last of the great traditionalists. He was a gentleman who moved in a world of wealth, status and tradition, and he was totally lost in the world which Hammett in the twenties and Chandler in the forties depicted so vividly—a world of the common man, a world in which truth and justice were determined more by money and power than some abstract principle or some immaculate ideal. The new detective created by Hammett and Chandler, rather than seeking some collaborative social order in a chaotic world, became a law unto himself and administered his own brand of justice as he saw fit. In breaking new ground Hammett created not only a unique type of detective hero, but also a different type of literary morality. Not only did he bring contemporary America to the detective story, but he was the first to demonstrate the intimate connections between politics and organized crime on all levels.

In a capitalistic society money is power and how either the power or the money is acquired seems of little consequence. The position of the lonely truth seeker caught in the web of greed in a society strained by social injustice and economic inequities is clearly recognized by the average reader of escape fiction, the common man, the young, the idealistic and the romantic. It was to all of these readers that Hammett's hard-boiled seekers of truth appealed. The pulps were the escape hatches of the common folk. During the hard times, in the heart of the great depression, Hammett was their hero. It was many years later that Hammett, Chandler and the *Black Mask* writers were accepted by the privileged, and the literary elite. As Jon

20

Tuska observes:

Hammett was part of the heightened consciousness of his time in championing distrust over belief, skepticism over faith, cynicism over hope. It is the truly capable man who can sustain these mental postures and go on as confidently as the man who relies on all manner of comforting fantasies to get him through.

In this connection it is interesting that Andre Gide claimed his admiration for Hammett was based on the fact that his novels never drew moral conclusions. Hammett was a realist who depicted men as they are— too busy accumulating wealth, prestige, power and security to see life as it really is. This was an essential part of his genius and one of the prime sources of his impact on his readers.

The year 1983 saw a rebirth of interest in Hammett. As father of the hard-boiled style his influence on detective fiction, on television and on films has never waned, and biographers have found him to be as colorful a tough-guy hero as any that can be brought to life on the printed page. Although Hammett's literary output was relatively small—five novels and approximately thirty short stories—biographical material on him is growing rapidly. As his fame and reputation spreads, thesis and dissertation writers will escalate the interest. We make, here, no attempt to be definitive. Instead, we merely want to chart the peaks of the life of the true king of the PI genre.

Hammett

Samuel Dashiell Hammett was born on the 27th of May, 1894, in Saint Mary's County, Maryland. His father was Richard Thomas Hammett and his mother was Annie Bond. Baptized a Roman Catholic, he spent his youth in Baltimore and Philadelphia. He attended public schools there and in September, 1908, Hammett entered the Baltimore Polytechnic Institute. After one semester his formal schooling was finished. He left and went to work taking over his father's small business. The business folded a year later. From 1909 through 1915 he held a number of odd jobs including a stint with the B&O Railroad as an office boy. In 1914, at the age of 20, he began his lifelong attachment to alcohol. In 1915 he answered an advertisement and was hired as a Pinkerton operative. This job influenced him more than any other thing in his life. The Pinkerton logo was a single unblinking eye with the motto: "We never sleep," and the eye symbolized the Pinkerton Operative who saw everything and prevented crimes by recognizing criminal behavior. Although the agency had an excellent reputation, it became, at the turn of the century, more involved with the protection of business property and strike breaking than any other kind of activity.

As a Pinkerton operative Hammett was on call 24 hours a day, and in

1915 he started at the salary of $21 a week. Surveillance was his primary activity and even though he was tall—6 feet 1 1/2 inches—and weighed about 160 pounds, he could still shadow a suspect all day without being observed. Hammett was taught the rudiments of his job by a short, tough-talking operative named James Wright, and it was Wright who, years later, became famous as the model for Hammett's Continental Op.

Hammett embraced the Pinkerton code of anonymity, morality and objectivity wholeheartedly: the less known about a detective the less his chance of having personal information used against him; as for morality, the detective's job is to protect good people from exploitation by bad people, and if he takes a client's money he owes him loyalty, but even this must never supersede his own personal sense of right and wrong; and, finally, the detective must develop objectivity and emotional distance from the people with whom he deals. This code not only left its indelible mark on Hammett but it also colored his prose and gave his stories and novels an aura of authenticity and credibility found in no other mystery writer of his time.

Hammett worked in a number of Pinkerton offices around the country until June, 1918, when he enlisted in the Army. After basic training at Camp Mead, Maryland, he was assigned to the Motor Ambulance Company only 15 miles from his home in Baltimore. He was in the Army less than a year. Unfortunately, he fell victim to the flu epidemic that killed half a million people in the U.S. alone during the winter of 1918-1919. From February through May, Hammett was in and out of the hospital suffering from bronchitis and other respiratory disorders. In May it was discovered that he was tubercular. He was declared 25% disabled and discharged from the service as a very sick 25-year-old-man.

Hammett's small pension of a few dollars a week was scarcely enough to support him and he was back in the hospital a few weeks later with a 50% disability and a 40-dollar-a-month pension. As his health improved he went back to Pinkerton on a part-time basis. Shortly thereafter he moved to Spokane, Washington, to another Pinkerton office. Again, his health deteriorated and he went into the VA Hospital in Tacoma, where after spending a total of 6 1/2 months he was considered 100% disabled. While in the hospital he met a pert 23-year-old nurse named Josephine Dolan. As Hammett's health improved they left the hospital for dinner dates and even overnight trips to Seattle. In a short time they fell in love. In 1921 Hammett was transferred to San Diego. At the time, neither Hammett nor Jose knew she was pregnant. When she did discover her condition, Jose quit her job and went home to Montana. She corresponded with Hammett and, by letter, they arranged their marriage. A few months later Hammett had recovered sufficiently to leave the hospital. He then moved to San Francisco, reapplied to Pinkerton and was hired. Jose came to San Francisco and they were married on July 7, 1921, at St. Mary's Cathedral on

Van Ness Avenue. Because Hammett professed no religion they were married in the rectory rather than at the altar. They moved into a furnished apartment near the San Francisco Public Library at 620 Eddy Street which they rented for $45 a month. The steam-heated apartment was very small— a living room in front, a small bedroom with a folding bed and a kitchen. The landlady was a bootlegger who had the local police as customers.

Hammett's job with Pinkerton paid $6 a day, and at this time detective work in San Francisco was both exciting and dangerous. Hammett, who was called Sam at this time in his life, was good at his job and was an expert in tailing and usually drew these sorts of jobs. He learned a great deal as an operative. His on-the-job training taught him: 1) that in bonding a man, drinking has nothing to do with reliability; 2) that fingerprints are almost useless; 3) that as a profession, burglary provides a poor living; and 4) the best defense in court is to deny everything. During his Pinkerton stint Hammett worked on some fascinating cases, including the notorious Fatty Arbuckle rape case (Hammett called it "the funniest case I ever worked on . . . . In trying to convict him everybody framed everybody else.")

Because of ill health Hammett quit Pinkerton in early 1922. His bronchial condition became so bad that he was too weak to walk to the library and required assistance to get from the bedroom to the bathroom.

The Hammetts' first child, Mary Jane, was born in October, 1921. Because of his TB Hammett had to limit his contact with her. Since money was scarce, Hammett entered business school, training himself to become a newspaper reporter. This experience convinced him that advertising was the career he wanted and that more than anything else he wanted to write. Hammett went to work as advertising manager for Albert Samuels, who owned a jewelry store on Market Street. Though he was good at the job and a reliable and loyal employee, he started drinking again. After working all day on copy for Samuels, Hammett would go home to his apartment and drink most of the night. Hammett also smoked incessantly, rolling his own cigarettes. His drinking was done mostly to control the irritation of excessive smoking and the pain of recurrent coughing.

Hammett loved to read and he read avidly trying to educate himself. Science, biography, classical literature, history, the occult were favored topics. He discovered pulp magazines and, after reading a few of the stories, was convinced he could write better than the authors he was reading. So he set out to try. Another motive was his feeling that he had only a little time left to live and the only thing he really wanted to do was to write. In the fall of 1922, at age 28, Hammett started writing for publication and he chose George Jean Nathan's and H.L. Mencken's *Smart Set* as his outlet. The *Smart Set* paid little more than a penny a word and Hammett's first effort was a 600-word anecdote, published in October, 1922, about a woman who disliked her husband for his stubbornness and then discovers her six-month-old son takes after the father. Hammett called it "The Parthian

Shot" because the woman's final thrust before leaving the family is to have the son christened "Don." The reader is left to realize that the boy's surname is "KEY."

He published a second piece in the November, 1922, issue of *Smart Set* and began to send short pieces to other magazines. This success led him to try his hand at short stories which he typed out on an Underwood typewriter at his kitchen table. His first short story, "The Barber and His Wife," appeared in the December, 1922, issue of *Brief Stories*, the same time as his first *Black Mask* story, "The Road Home." It was for *Black Mask* that Hammett began to write about his former profession, using the pen name Peter Collinson (Peter Collins is criminal detective slang for nobody) for both.

After publishing several short stories under the Collinson and other pseudonyms, he published the story "Crooked Souls" in the October 15, 1923 *Black Mask* and signed it Dashiell Hammett. From then on—with one interesting exception—he signed all of his stories and novels Dashiell Hammett. The interesting exception was a story he sold under financial pressure to *Detective Fiction Weekly*, which he signed as Samuel Dashiell because he felt it was not up to the quality of his previous work.

By the end of 1923 Hammett was writing and publishing almost exclusively in *Black Mask*. In only 20 months, between November, 1922, and June, 1924, Hammett published 25 stories in the pulp magazines and nearly half were longer than twenty-five hundred words.

As his literary career improved, Hammett's physical condition worsened. From the summer of 1923 his life was consumed by his fiction. He was too ill to work at anything else, and since he had little or no social life he stayed home and wrote. But at a penny a word it was still hard to make a decent living. When a second daughter was born, Hammett sent his wife and daughters off to Montana to live with relatives.

With his family gone Hammett rented a cheap room on Pine Street. Many times he would write all night and would, on occasion, still work for Samuels. This regimen told on him. Often he forgot to eat and when he did it was dietetically inadequate. He lived on soup, Scotch, coffee and cigarettes, and occasionally slept with a girl across the hall or another female friend living nearby on Grant Street.

In the latter part of 1925 Hammett consulted a physician who told him his lung problem was "cured." Hammett did feel better, coughed less and continued to write, setting most of his stories in San Francisco and featuring as characters people he knew or had known in the past. Hammett could never write about anything or any place with whom or with which he was not intimately familiar. He acquired an apartment and when his surroundings improved he became more productive.

Hammett's work was not always eagerly accepted by his editors. When Phil Cody took over the editorship of *Black Mask* from George Sutton he started off by rejecting two of Hammett's stories. Hammett apologized to Cody and explained their inferiority as being due to his writing them solely for the money. He reworked them and they were readily accepted. When Captain Joseph T. Shaw took over the *Black Mask* editorship he also started out by rejecting one of Hammett's stories. Hammett was infuriated and threatened never to write for *Black Mask* again. Shaw then read several back issues of the magazine and saw that Hammett was exactly what he needed. He wrote Hammett a very apologetic letter begging him to write a novel-length story. Shaw also asked Erle Stanley Gardner—one of Hammett's pulp-writer friends—to intercede with Hammett on his behalf. Gardner did, and Hammett liked Shaw's suggestion. The result was the short novel "Blood Money," one of Hammett's best.

Josephine did not sympathize with Hammett's desire to become an important writer. It was primarily for this reason that Hammett was separated from his family. Nevertheless, he loved them dearly—particularly Mary Jane—and he wanted them near him. He moved them to San Anselmo and then to San Francisco where he rented them an apartment on the cable car line. He lived nearby in an apartment on Turk Street.

Shortly before this, while living at 891 Post Street, he completed his first true novel, *Red Harvest*. It was written in 1927, and the first of four parts was published in the November 1927 issue of *Black Mask*. *Red Harvest* featured the Continental Op. As the plot develops the Op is called to Personville—known as Poisonville—by Donald Willsson—the son of Elihu Willsson, a man who for forty years "had owned Personville, heart, soul, skin and guts." More than two dozen murders are committed in *Red Harvest*. Most of the people the Op meets are killed. Personville is gripped by corruption, and the Op arranges many of the killings in his effort to clean up the city. This novel was inspired by Hammett's own experiences in Butte, Montana, where he worked for Pinkerton as a strike-breaker. He used this book as an opportunity to reverse the anti-union activities that his former job had required of him.

In November, 1928, the first of four parts of *The Dain Curse*, Hammett's second novel, was also published in *Black Mask*. Like *Red Harvest*, this novel also grew out of an earlier short story called "The Scorched Face." Though it is generally considered to be his weakest book (in a 1932 interview Hammett himself called it "a silly story"), it is still a first-rate and entertaining novel. Laced with traces of mysticism, the novel centers around a beautiful woman, Gabrielle Leggett, who believes she has inherited a family curse from her mother. *The Dain Curse*, dedicated to Albert S. Samuels, was the second and last Op novel (and just about the last description of the Op, since he appeared in only three more short stories). Hammett's characterization of the Op is the novel's greatest strength. He is a model knight—noble and dedicated to the rescue of innocence.

By comparison to *Red Harvest, The Dain Curse* was not excessively violent. Yet in 1929, Hammett's novels were considered suitable for mature readers only. The book was both a popular and a critical success, but financially Hammett's profit was minimal.

In September, 1929, the first of five parts of *The Maltese Falcon*, Hammett's third novel and his masterpiece, was published in *Black Mask*. Five months later, in February, 1930, the entire novel was published by Knopf. According to Hammett himself, "If this book had been written with the help of an outline or notes or even a clearly defined plot idea in my head, I might now be able to say how it came to be written and why it took the shape it did, but all I can remember about its invention is that somewhere I had read of the peculiar rental agreement between Charles V and the Order of the Hospital of Saint John of Jerusalem, that in a short story called *The Whosis Kid* I had failed to make the most of a situation I liked, that in another called *The Gutting of Couffignal* I had been equally unfortunate with an equally promising denouement, and that I thought I might have better luck with these two failures if I combined them with the Maltese lease in a longer story."

It is in the *Falcon*, of course, that Hammett created his most famous private eye, the immortal Sam Spade. Hammett used the third person narrative to give Spade added strength. The novel, set in San Francisco, covers a five-day period—between Wednesday and Sunday, in December, 1928. Brigid O'Shaughnessy comes to Spade and his partner, Miles Archer, for help. She intends to use both to help her get rid of her criminal boyfriend, Floyd Thursby. Thursby served as protection for her while she was looking for the Maltese Falcon, a priceless statue. Brigid tells Spade and Archer that her sister had run away with Thursby and he won't tell her where her sister is hiding. She hires Spade and Archer under the pretense of shadowing Thursby in order to find her sister. This ruse will keep Thursby out of the way so she can collect the Falcon when it arrives by boat. If Brigid's plan works out, Thursby will kill his shadows as soon as he discovers he's being followed or be killed himself. If he doesn't behave like Brigid wants then she'll kill the shadow and blame it on Thursby. She gets Archer to do the shadowing, and on Thursday night Brigid kills both Archer and Thursby. In doing so she manages to have Thursby's murder tied to Spade, who must have murdered Thursby to revenge Archer's death. Suspicion is easily thrown on Spade because Spade not only disliked Archer but was having an affair with his wife. Spade, therefore, has to find the murderer and punish him to protect himself and his reputation.

Two other equally ruthless individuals are after the Falcon—Caspar Gutman, a criminal genius, and a homosexual named Joel Cairo. Spade manages to outwit Cairo, Gutman, the police and the DA and discovers that Brigid is the key. At the climax Spade is faced with the choice of turning Brigid in for the murders or going away with her.

The publication of *The Maltese Falcon* assured Hammett's reputation as a fine writer. Alexander Woolcott called it "the best detective story America has yet produced." The *Judge* critic, Tod Shane, said "The writing is better than Hemingway, since it conceals not softness but hardness." Frank P. Adams called it "the only detective tale that I have been able to read through since the days of Sherlock Holmes." Other critics were equally effusive, comparing Hammett to the greatest American writers of the day.

Hammett's next novel was *The Glass Key*. After finishing it Hammett was ruined as a novelist. His fame destroyed him as a writer. The fruits of this fame—the liquor, women, money and the notoriety—left him soft and weak. *The Glass Key* was serialized in *Black Mask* in four parts and, for some reason, was published first in England in January, 1931, and then in the U.S. in April of the same year. Most critics consider it and the *Falcon* as Hammett's strongest novels. *The Glass Key* is actually a hard-boiled love story, a story about human relationships and the corrupting effects of political power. It also features a non-detective gambler, Ned Beaumont, as the non-hero. Beaumont is a political organizer—a ward heeler—working for Paul Madrig, who controls an unnamed city near New York. The action occurs in the late 1920s or early 1930s.

The glass key is symbolic of the knowledge Ned and the others gain during the course of events—once the door is open and you know what's on the other side you have to live with this knowledge; it can't be unlearned. A "glass key" works only once—to unlock the door. This metaphor applies to all the major characters in the novel: Senator Henry, who learns the result of his lust for political power; Madrig, who cannot undo his attempts to cover up the Senator's crime; Janet Henry, who learns the extent of her father's corruption; and Ned, who, ironically, must break off with Madrig in order to save his friend's life.

In Hammett's opinion *The Glass Key* was his best book, and many critics agreed. According to Julian Symons:

> *The Glass Key* is the peak of Hammett's achievement which is to say the peak of the crime writer's art in the twentieth century. Constant rereading of it offers fresh revelations of the way in which a crime writer with sufficient skill and tact can use violent events to comment by indirection on life, art, society, and at the same time compose a novel admirable in the carpentry of its structure and delicately intelligent in its suggestions of truths about human relationships. As a novel *The Glass Key* is remarkable, as a crime novel unique .... *The Glass Key* can stand comparison with any American novel of its decade.

Dorothy Parker idolized Hammett and said so in the pages of *The New Yorker*. Will Cuppy in The New York *Herald Tribune* called *The Glass Key* "about twice as good as his *The Maltese Falcon*," and another critic, Walter Brooks, said that Hammett "has now written the three best detective stories ever published." He was referring to *Red Harvest, The Maltese Falcon* and *The Glass Key*. History has agreed. These three books are generally acknowledged as Hammett's masterworks.

In the summer of 1930 Hammett moved to Hollywood after signing a contract with Paramount to write original screen stories. Although he was never among the inner circle of Hollywood moviemakers, he did meet many other creative artists and made some lifelong and influential friendships. He began to carouse and drink heavily and in a short while he had spent everything he had made. He began to develop headaches and breathing difficulties and after one of his original screenplays was rejected he moved to New York in disgust and took on Ben Wasson as his literary agent. Wasson also handled William Faulkner. Hammett and Faulkner hit if off immediately and became fast friends. Wasson wanted something to sell while the good reviews of *The Glass Key* were fresh in the editors' minds. So Hammett obliged with the first sixty-five pages of *The Thin Man*. This fragment was completely different from the novel that was finally published which proved to be his last and his weakest. This was a novel that, in Hammett's own words, "always bored me." In it Hammett introduces Nick and Nora Charles, who are relaxed, carefree and urbane. They are the epitome of charm. Nick is an ex-private eye who retired when he met and married Nora. He would rather play, drink and party than solve crimes. Yet in *The Thin Man* he is required by circumstances, not of his own choosing, to solve three murders.

The novel is witty, bright, breezy and full of fascinating minor characters. One of the most interesting is the cross-word puzzle addict's darling, the Charles' dog, Asta. Of historical interest is the fact that the novel was considered risque at the time it was published. The mere fact that Nora went out with other men and Nick was attracted to other women was considered immoral as was the scene where after Nick scuffles with Mimi Jorgensen in her apartment, Nora asks, "Tell me something, Nick. Tell me the truth: when you were wrestling with Mimi, didn't you have an erection?" "Oh, a little." She laughed and got up from the floor. "If you aren't a disgusting old lecher," she said.

In the *Redbook* serialized version this passage was censored, but Knopf, the publisher, capitalized on it with an ad in the New York *Times* referring to the question. Nevertheless, because of this passage the novel was banned in Canada. Of further interest is the fact that the novel's dust jacket carried Hammett's photograph. Since Hammett himself was very thin and was posing as Nick Charles, little wonder that the public regarded Charles—and even Hammett himself—as the "thin man" the title referred to.

While Hammett was in Hollywood in late 1930 or early 1931 he met Lillian Hellman, who at the time was working at MGM as a script writer. This was the beginning of a thirty-year relationship which had a profound effect on both their lives. Hellman was 24 and Hammett 36 when they met. By March of 1931 he was calling her "darling" and in 1932 Hellman divorced her husband, Arthur Kober, and began living with Hammett on a periodic basis. The only details of their relationship come to us from Hellman's highly selective and subjective accounts. In Richard Layman's most apt and descriptive account:

What is known with some certainty is that Hammett loved Hellman, that he helped her realize her literary ambitions, and that the history of their life together includes his decline as a writer and his increased involvement in political causes that Hellman often espoused more vociferously than he did.

Although Hellman wrote about Hammett in four separate memoirs after his death, she also has been so protective of him she has inhibited biographical research. She approved Diane Johnson as the official Hammett biographer and the "truth about her and Hammett" was supposed to emerge in the pages of Johnson's long awaited opus, *Dashiell Hammett: A Life* (Random House, 1983). Whether it contains any more "truth" or merely some additional unreliable and highly subjective fantasy has been hotly debated by the critics.

By the end of 1931 Hammett was broke and had to start writing again. In the next two years he wrote seven stories and three short articles. Three of these stories were about Sam Spade, capitalizing on the popularity of *The Maltese Falcon*. These have been subsequently collected and reprinted in the volume called *A Man Named Spade*. Because they were written under the pressure of a need for money they were not up to the quality of the earlier Op stories. Nevertheless, Hammett was gaining popularity and with it increasing financial success, even though in the fall of 1932 he had to leave Hotel Pierre in New York City at the end of September with his bill unpaid.

Following publication of *The Thin Man* in 1934, Hollywood grabbed the movie rights and a movie based on the novel was released in June of the same year. This was the first of six movies based on the Thin Man characters released between 1934 and 1947. As a result of the first movie's popularity, Hammett became one of the most sought-after literary lights in the nation.

For this reason William Randolph Hearst's King Features syndicate persuaded Hammett to provide the continuity of a daily comic strip, "Secret Agent X-9," drawn by a young artist named Alex Raymond. Hammett received $500 a week for his efforts and was glad to get it. The strip was well received and equally well publicized, called by some "the greatest detective strip ever published." Hammett's name was associated with it, however, for only a little over a year.

Because of Hammett's popularity RKO, Warner Brothers, Paramount and Universal began to bargain for his services and movie rights to his work. In fact, between 1934 and 1936 six movies were made from his original stories or adapted from his work. In October 1934, Hammett became a screen writer for MGM and moved into the Beverly Wilshire Hotel in Hollywood. In June 1935 Paramount released the movie version of *The Glass Key* and Hammett's MGM contract was renewed.

In 1936, however, Hammett moved back to New York and was hospitalized briefly again because of excessive drinking and partying. When he was released he found himself in a tight financial spot because of his high living. As fast as the money poured in, Hammett mismanaged it. In December *After the Thin Man*, a movie based on Hammett's original story was released and in the following February Hammett sold MGM all rights to *The Thin Man* title and the characters for $40,000. Again Hammett moved back to the Beverly Hilton in Hollywood and resumed an extravagant, flamboyant lifestyle.

Hammett's work on scripts and revisions was not wholly satisfactory and his drinking increased along with his string of broken promises and failures to meet deadlines. Sadly, Hammett claimed he was working on a new novel to be titled "There Was A Young Man." Alfred Knopf, his publisher, disappointed time and again by Hammett's failure to deliver, washed his hands of Hammett. Hammett then went to Random House who gave him an advance on scheduled publication for the fall of 1939. But there was no book to publish and Hammett finally returned the advance, telling the publisher, Bennett Cerf, "I'm afraid I'll never write it. I'm petering out."

The words were prophetic. From this point on, Hammett's career went downhill. Largely because of Hellman's influence, Hammett became more and more interested in political causes, lending his support first to the Loyalist cause during the Spanish Civil War and then to the Screen Writers' Guild. In November 1938 Hammett spoke at a number of Communist-sponsored anti-Nazi rallies in New York. Although it was never established that Hammett became a member of the Communist party it seems likely, from the responsibilities he was given for party activities, that he did join the party sometime in 1937 or 1938. Hammett favored voter registration drives for blacks and immigration of foreign victims of persecution. He was anti-Nazi and anti-Fascist, promoted labor unions and believed that no government worker should be fired because of his political belief.

In May 1939, Hammett headed a project called *Equality: A Monthly Journal to Defend Democratic Rights and Combat Anti-Semitism and Racism*. The journal ran through 1940 and supported all anti-fascist and Jewish causes. In 1940 Hammett became National Chairman of the Committee on Election Rights and worked vigorously to get the Communist party slate on as many state ballots as possible. These activities plus his other supportive actions for leftist causes between April 1938 and December 1941 brought him to the attention of the House unAmerican Activities Committee and the FBI.

After Pearl Harbor, Hammett felt he should support the fight against facism, so he tried several times to enlist in the Army. Because of his tuberculosis, his age (he was 47 in 1941) and his rotten teeth he was always rejected. Finally, in the fall of 1942, when Army enlistment standards had softened, he had some of his teeth pulled and he was inducted and assigned to Signal Corps training at Fort Monmouth, New Jersey. A few weeks later Hammett was sent to Fort Lewis, Washington, and was then assigned to Adak, Alaska.

The commander of the Aleutians admired Hammett's work and gave him the priority assignment of starting a camp newspaper, *The Adakian*. Hammett successfully edited this 4-page newspaper for approximately fifteen months and was supremely happy with it. For the rest of the war Hammett received a number of writing assignments compiling campaign histories, and one history in particular, *The Battle of the Aleutians*, which is a collector's item today.

In August 1945 he returned to the US and was honorably discharged at Fort Dix, New Jersey, on 6 September 1945. Now, at the age of 51, Hammett moved to an apartment in New York City where his primary activities consisted of drinking and reading. By this time, however, Hammett was a confirmed alcoholic, and had given up all hope of resuming his writing career. He told one acquaintance that most days he saw no reason to get out of bed in the morning. He was careless and indifferent about money and tipped everyone extravagantly.

Because of his sympathies for the downtrodden, Hammett continued his political activities and in June 1946 he was elected president of the Civil Rights Congress of New York—a Communist affiliated group. In October he resumed his attempt to get Communist candidates on the ballot and he continued to lend his name and support to a wide range of liberal and leftist causes.

In late 1948 and early 1949 Hammett's health deteriorated and he was admitted to the Lennox Hill Hospital where the doctor told him if he continued drinking he would die. He did quit and with Hellman's help began to work again, assisting Hellman with her theatrical activities. Hammett even returned to Hollywood for a writing assignment and renewed his relationship with his daughter Josephine. He was not happy, however, and after six months returned to New York and Hellman.

By 1950 the FBI had compiled a 20-page report on Hammett and his alleged "subversive" activities. Finally, in July 1951, Hammett, as one of the trustees of the bail fund of the Civil Rights Congress, was called to court to testify about this fund as well as the whereabouts of four Communist leaders who jumped bail after being convicted of criminal conspiracy to teach and advocate the overthrow of the U.S. Government. When questioned on the stand, Hammett stubbornly refused any cooperation with the court. As a result the judge found him guilty of contempt and he was sentenced to prison for a six-month term. Hammett served the full six months, part of it in the Federal Detention Center on West Street in New York and the rest in the Federal Correctional Institute at Ashland, Kentucky. He was released in December 1951 after having served 22 weeks of his 26 week sentence, getting time off for good behavior. He was 57 years old when he left prison and found himself in dire financial straits as a result of suits for back income taxes which, again on principle ("I'd rather give it away than have it taken by the government") he had neglected to pay. During 1952 he became sick again and was unable to work. He was so ill when the House unAmerican Activities Committee came after him that Hellman testified in his place and refused to tell the Committee about anything except her own activities.

Hellman on several occasions stressed that Hammett was highly critical of many Marxist doctrines and was often contemptuous of the Soviet Union. William Nolan, in his biography, sums up Hammett's political beliefs as those of a humanist and a crusader:

An idealist and a visionary, an activist in the cause of human rights and social justice, Hammett chose what seemed to him the best (and only) means at hand with which to pursue this vision. He never wavered from his humanistic philosophy which in large part differed radically from the 'party line' to which he was connected.

Although the McCarthy hearings did nothing to Hammett, the Internal Revenue Service found him guilty of tax evasion and seized all royalties from his books, radio and motion picture residuals for the rest of his life. His books were removed from the State Department libraries for a short time until President Eisenhower ordered them replaced.

From 1952 Hammett lived rent free in a cottage on the estate of Dr. Samuel Rosen and he visited Hellman off and on in her house on Martha's Vineyard. In August 1955 Hammett had a heart attack which along with his lung and liver ailments totally disabled him from that date onward. During Hammett's remaining years Hellman took care of him, renting a cabin for them in the process. She refused to allow him to enter a veteran's hospital when he was no longer able to care for himself. When she learned that in addition to emphysema he also had an inoperable lung cancer she refused to tell him. As Hellman noted in her introduction to *The Big Knockover*:

His death was caused by cancer of the lungs, discovered only two months before he died. It was not operable—I doubt that he would have agreed to an operation even if it had been—and so I decided not to tell him about the cancer. The doctor said that when the pain came it would come in the right chest and arm, but that the pain might never come. The doctor was wrong. Only a few hours after he told me the pain did come.

Toward the end of his life Hammett rationed himself to one martini a day. Recognizing he had only a little while left, Hellman one day offered him a second martini. Hammett refused. Hellman said she never thought she would live to see the day that he would turn one down.

On January 10, 1961 Hammett died at the Lenox Hill Hospital in New York City. His funeral was held at Campbell's Funeral Home on Madison Avenue and paid for by the VA. He was buried at Arlington National Cemetery on January 13. Hellman delivered his eulogy and called him "a man of simple honor and great bravery. He didn't always think well of the society we live in and yet when it punished him he made no complaint against it and had no anger about the punishment."

The Continental Op—An Ordinary Knight

The Continental Op was Hammett's first private eye and there was nothing glamorous or heroic about him. He was short, thick-set, weighing about 180 pounds, balding and approximately 35 years of age. He had no name, no home and no personal existence apart from his job. He lived by a code which includes the rather strict rules laid down by the Continental Agency. He lived for his work. In the Op's words, "detecting is a hard business and you use whatever tools come to hand." The Op was a tough individual. If we follow his career closely we see him become tougher and more callous as he ages. The Op becomes a dispassionate and cynical professional—a man with a job to do, a rugged individualist out to right social wrongs. The Op is a knight out to expose corruption wherever he may find it, a hero who speaks for the majority of men everywhere who question the social values they see around them.

One of the reasons we are attracted to the Op is that he makes choices and sticks by his principles. He feels a sense of duty and loyalty to his clients and he fights to protect the lives of the innocent and the worthy. The Op's characteristics are those we have always admired in all men of action and our chivalrous PIs: courage, mental and physical strength, indestructibility, indifference to danger, honesty, knightly attitudes, pity for the weak and helpless, a deep sense of loyalty to worthy causes, and a passionate belief in honor and justice.

David Bazelon, curiously, does not see the Op as an opponent of evil. He, instead, sees him as a moral neutral. In Bazelon's words:

The Op is primarily a job-holder: All the stories in which he appears begin with an assignment and end when he has completed it. To an extent, *competence* replaces moral stature as the criterion of an individual's worth. The only persons who gain any respect from the Op are those who behave competently—and all such, criminal or otherwise—are accorded some respect. This attitude is applied to women as well as men. In *The Dain Curse*, the Op is attracted deeply only to the woman who has capacity and realism—and he fears her for the same reason . . . .

What is wrong with the character of the Op—the American—is that he almost never wrestles with personal motives of his own. The private eye has no private life. He simply wants to do his job well.

It is interesting, in view of the importance of job-doing to the detective, to remark the reasons for this lack of personal motivation. What the Op has as a substitute for motive is a more or less total projection of himself into the violent environment of crime and death. . . . The question of doing or not doing a job competently seems to have replaced the whole larger question of good and evil. The Op catches criminals because it is his job to do so, not because they are criminals.

Sam Spade—The Blond Satan

Like the Op, Spade also followed the agency's code. In fact Spade is the romantic embodiment of the private detective's creed. He takes his job personally and seriously and he would never allow his emotions to overrule his loyalty to the code—to give his client his best. Spade is the ultimate private eye, the epitome of the genre—smart, tough, insightful, worldly wise, painstaking and imbued with a personal sense of right and justice which overshadows all else. As Sam himself says, "There ought to be a law making criminals give themselves up . . . ." But since there isn't, no one is better qualified than he is to take the law's place. His job is to find out and he does. He detects, gets the facts and then figures the angles.

Samuel Spade was born in 1895 and, worked in Seattle for a time. He is six feet tall and weighs approximately 185 pounds. He has a V-for-Victory face with blonde hair and yellow-eyes, a big hooked nose, thick brows, flat temples, a widow's peak and jutting jaw. He looks like a blonde Satan. Spade is muscular, heavy-boned, with shoulders that have a slight droop, and his hands are big and strong with thick fingers. He prefers gray suits, dark brown shoes and a gray felt hat. He also likes green striped shirts with a green tie. In winter he wears a loose tweed overcoat. Spade is a heavy smoker and a heavy drinker. Rather than buying cigarettes, Spade rolls his own from Bull Durham loose tobacco and brown cigarette papers. He lights them with a pigskin-wrapped nickel-plated cigarette lighter. At home he drinks straight Bacardi from a wineglass and at the office he drinks premixed Manhattans from a paper cup.

As described by Ellery Queen in the introduction to a collection titled *A Man Called Spade*, Spade is a

rough-and-tumble operative who is most dangerous when his smile flickers with a dreamy quality; who hates to be hit without hitting back; who won't play the sap for anyone, man or woman, dead or alive; who can call a $2,000,000 rare avis a dingus and who, when asked in the latest movie version what the heavy lead falcon was made of, answered 'the stuff of dreams.' Meet the wild man from Frisco who always calls a spade a spade.

Spade—like Hammett—doesn't own a car or have a driver's license. He works out of a three-room, sparsely furnished office on Sutter Street near Kearney in San Francisco. There is an outer room, a reception-secretarial area, and two inner offices: one for Spade and one for his partner, Miles Archer. Spade's office is equipped with a beat-up desk with a desk blotter and an ashtray and an old armchair. His office help is a cake-loving, attractive secretary in her early twenties named Effie Perine. Sam will work for anyone with the wherewithal but he will not kill or commit burglary. He doesn't carry a gun and has no standard fee schedule. Fees are set on the basis of the client's ability to pay. Spade's greatest weakness is women although he distrusts them. He has been known to carry on more than one affair at a time.

In fact Peter Wolfe casts Spade in the role of a lover. According to Wolfe, what most readers and critics alike have overlooked is Spade's heart. In Wolfe's words:

[Spade's] toughness is leavened by both tenderness and subtlety; he has a feminine sensitivity to atmospheres and textures. Though basically a man of action, he doesn't exhaust his personality in man-talk or high-speed movement.

Wolfe points out that although Spade sneers at male authority figures and cracks wise with lawyers and other detectives,

He can extend both charity and charm to women without evoking something in return. He will rarely address Brigid or Effie Perine, his secretary, without using terms of endearment, like 'angel,' 'precious,' or 'darling.'

Philip Durham has summarized what we find so enjoyable and so worthy in Hammett and his heroes: although Hammett's heroes are violent, the violence is not mere sensationalism.

It was, rather, a kind of meaningful violence, sometimes an explicit description and implicit criticism of a corrupt society. Many Americans lost faith in the society of the 1920s, and Hammett's heroes tried both to expose the corruptness and to speak for men who, questioning the values of society, needed to be assured that somewhere—if only on the pages of a pulp magazine—there were heroes who cared.

This observation is equally true today. In a world of social inequities, of lavish wealth and grinding poverty, life is in John F. Kennedy's words, "basically unfair." Too often wrongs are not righted, justice is not served, truth is suborned and the guilty go unpunished. Hammett was acutely aware of such cruelties. He was a sensitive man who had to raise his protesting voice in support of concepts he believed would serve the causes of universal justice in an unjust world. When he created his fictional voices they were knights in the service of all that is right—speaking in a language universally understood by all who have suffered outrageous fortune and have yearned for revenge. Hammett's heroes are never dated. They are as vital and exciting today as they were at the time of their creation. And there is every reason to believe that they will remain so for readers in the years to come.

A Hammett Bibliography

Within the last few years a number of Hammett biographies have appeared and a Hammett revival has occurred; Hammett-study is a growth industry. Late in 1982 Stephen Talbot produced an excellent hour-long documentary, *The Case of Dashiell Hammett*, shown nationally on PBS. In 1983 Diane Johnson's long-awaited biography finally appeared. Ms. Johnson had Lillian Hellman's stamp of approval; therefore the Johnson biography is supposed to be the last and final word on what *really* happened between Hellman and Hammett. Our favorite sources, however, are William F. Nolan's *Hammett: A Life at the Edge* (Congdon & Weed, New York, 1983), Richard Layman's *Shadow Man: The Life of Dashiell Hammett* (Harcourt, Brace, Jovanovich, 1981), as well as his *Dashiell Hammett: A Descriptive Bibliography* (Univ. of Pittsburgh Press, 1979), and *Dashiell Hammett: A Casebook*, by William F. Nolan (McNally and Loftin,1969). Another important source, particularly valuable for its information about Hammett's Hollywood years is Chapters 5 and 6 of Jon Tuska's *The Detective in Hollywood* (Doubleday & Co., 1978). Peter Wolfe's *Beams Falling: The Art of Dashiell Hammett* (Bowling Green University Popular Press, 1979) is also particularly valuable for insights into Hammett's artistic richness and literary skill. Stephen Marcus's introduction to the Vintage edition of *The Continental Op* (1975) and Hellman's introduction to the Dell paperback edition of *The Big Knockover* in 1967 are also informative and insightful. Perhaps the most definitive list of articles, stories, radio and TV material concerning and related to Hammett and his work are William F. Nolan's three checklists published in *The Armchair Detective* in 1973, 1976, and 1984 (Vol. 6, No. 2, Vol. 9, No. 4 and Vol. 17, No. 4). Finally, no Hammett fan could afford to miss Joe Gores' superb novel—an imitation of the Hammett style set in the Hammett milieu—named appropriately—*Hammett* (Putnam's, 1975, and Ballantine Books, 1976).

Chandler

A very wise man once noted that every life is a failure when looked at from the inside. This has never been truer than in the case of Raymond Chandler. In the eyes of the literary world, however, few authors have been *more* successful. Matthew J. Bruccoli noted that after Chandler's death:

Raymond Chandler occupies a canonized position among twentieth-century detective novelists. Along with Dashiell Hammett and James M. Cain, he was one of the big three of hard-boiled fiction; but Chandler has always enjoyed considerable serious attention. His style has been justly admired. Indeed he has been regarded as almost a major writer in some quarters—especially in Europe. Such a judgement is not an absolute distortion for Chandler clearly merits respect. He, as much as anyone else, took a subliterary American genre and made it into literature. Hammett did it first, but Chandler did it better.

Chandler is generally regarded today as the most important writer of detective fiction in the history of the genre. Yet at the time his novels were first published they were poorly received and rather widely panned. Only seventeen people attended his funeral in March 1959 and at least a third of this number were strangers. Since this time Chandler's stature has risen considerably and we are fortunate today in having a number of critical biographical studies that more than compensate for the early neglect. While the definitive biography is Frank MacShane's *The Life of Raymond Chandler* (Dutton, 1976; Pelican, 1978) two other sources of great value are Jerry Speir's *Raymond Chandler* (Frederick Ungar, 1981) and Philip Durham's *Down These Mean Streets A Man Must Go: Raymond Chandler's Knight* (Univ. of North Carolina Press, 1963). Additional insights into Chandler's life and psyche are provided by Jon Tuska's superb work, *The Detective in Hollywood* (Doubleday, 1978)—must reading for anyone having any interest in detective fiction and detective films—and Matthew J. Bruccoli's *Raymond Chandler: A Checklist* (Kent State Univ. Press, 1968).

Raymond Thornton Chandler, in his own words, "was conceived in Laramie, Wyoming and if they had asked me I should have preferred to be born there. I always like high altitudes." He was, nevertheless, born in Chicago on 23 July 1888 where his American-English father, Maurice Chandler, and his Irish mother, Florence Thornton, had set up housekeeping a year after marriage in Laramie. Raymond grew up in Chicago and Plattsworth, Nebraska, where he and his mother spent their summers. Chandler's mother and father divorced when Raymond was eight. After the divorce Florence and Raymond moved to England where he was educated in the English public schools and where he acquired his sharpened eye for social distinctions.

Although Chandler attended Dulwich Public School and acquired a love for the classics, there were no funds to send him to Oxford or Cambridge where he had hoped to study law. Instead, he was sent to Paris to prepare for the Civil Service exam. Completing the preparatory courses in Paris—a city he loved—he moved to Munich, Nuremburg and Vienna to finish his studies. In June 1907 Chandler took the exam for the Admiralty Class I and Class II civil service clerkship. He placed third among the 600 candidates and began work as a clerk shortly thereafter.

Chandler's literary career began a year earlier while in Paris in the form of a try at poetry. "My first poem," Chandler stated, "was composed at the age of nineteen on a Sunday, in the bathroom, and was published in *Chamber Journal*. I am fortunate in not possessing a copy." Although he published 27 poems between 1908 and 1913, most are mawkishly sentimental and lacking literary merit. Even later, after he became a well-established writer, his verse was little improved.

Chandler soon found he detested civil service work and wanted more than anything else to be a writer. Leaving the Admiralty he worked for a while as a reporter for the *London Daily Express* and the *Westminster Gazette*. Chandler also published a dozen articles and reviews in a British literary journal named *The Academy*. Saddened by the suicide of a literary friend and an unrequited love affair with a girl with "cornflower blue eyes," Chandler, in 1912, at 23 years of age borrowed five hundred pounds from his uncle and came home to the U.S.

After spending a few weeks in Nebraska, Chandler moved to Los Angeles, working at a number of different jobs from picking apricots to stringing tennis rackets. He got a job as an accountant and a bookkeeper at a Los Angeles creamery and took up residence in the older residential section of LA northwest of Pershing Square. In 1916 Chandler's mother joined him and lived with him there the rest of her days.

In August 1917, at the beginning of World War I, Chandler went to Victoria, British Columbia and enlisted in the Canadian Army. In March 1918 he was sent to France. In June he suffered a concussion during an artillery barrage and was sent back to England. While there Chandler transferred to the Royal Air Force and was still in training when the war ended. He was discharged in Vancouver, returned to Los Angeles in 1919 and went into the oil business starting with the Dabney Oil Syndicate. As a returning war veteran in his early thirties, Chandler was considered a very eligible bachelor. Despite the efforts of friends to marry him off Chandler fell in love with Pearl Cecily Hurlburt, known as Cissy. Chandler knew her while she was still married and, in gentlemanly fashion, discussed their romance and his desire to marry her with her husband long before the divorce. Because Cissy was 18 years his senior, Chandler's mother opposed the marriage, so Chandler delayed it until Mrs. Chandler's death in 1924.

Although many said that Chandler "married his mother," Cissy was not only young in appearance but young in manner and heart. She, for example, often did her housework in the nude. During the early years of their marriage she proved to be a marvelous wife, having brains, beauty, maturity and a deep and sincere affection for her husband. The age difference was of no consequence. Gradually, however, as she approached sixty with her husband not yet forty the discrepancy began to show. Cissy tried to hide her age by dyeing her hair blonde and wearing unsuitable younger women's clothes. She also often feigned illness to win Chandler's attention and affection.

While MacShane in his biography takes pains to emphasize the stabilizing influence Cissy exerted on Chandler's life, she was also a source of great embarrassment in their later years together. However, she was the most influential woman in Chandler's life, and it is unlikely he would have become a successful writer without her strong support and constant encouragement.

Chandler became more and more successful as a businessman. Had it not been for the depression, he probably would be unknown today. The collapse of the oil business turned Chandler to the writing of fiction.

If the depression of the 30s was the primary motivator, Chandler's inability to resolve his own inner conflicts and to come to terms with the disparate elements of his personality was an important secondary driving force. The English Public School system had left its sexually devastating mark, and the presence of young women—secretaries and clerks around his office—both disturbed and excited him. Chandler courted his own secretary, and he took to weekending with other girls from his office and using his powers as office manager for private ends. Moreover Chandler began to drink heavily.

Chandler began writing by imitating others and his first imitations were of Hemingway. Then he discovered the pulps and in his own words, "It suddenly struck me that I might be able to write this stuff and get paid while I was learning." He found the stories in *Black Mask* and the other pulps "forceful and honest, even though it had its crude aspect."

Chandler became a student of modern American literature and began to study seriously his contemporaries and predecessors—particularly Dashiell Hammett. He later cited Hammett as the main influence on his work. Chandler wrote about Hammett: "He had style, but his audience didn't know it because it was a language not supposed to be capable of such refinements .... He was spare, frugal, hard-boiled, but he did over and over again what only the best writers can ever do at all. He wrote scenes that seemed never to have been written before." But in Chandler's words, "I thought perhaps I could go a bit further, be a bit more humane, get a bit more interested in people than in violent death." Chandler wanted to write detective stories where the people one encounters are more important than the plot. One of the advantages of the detective formula is its flexibility which enabled him to include characters from every walk of life and every social stratum.

Chandler was not prolific. He wrote very slowly. He spent five months on his first story, "Blackmailers Don't Shoot," which he sent to *Black Mask*. The editor, Joseph Shaw, sent it to W.T. Ballard with a note saying the writer was either a genius or crazy. Chandler's second story, "Smart-Aleck Kill," appeared in *Black Mask* in July 1934. The third story, "Finger Man," published in October 1934, was the first that Chandler said he felt at home with and the first that was not imitative.

Chandler experimented with a number of detectives before he settled on Philip Marlowe. Some of Marlowe's prototypes appearing in these early stories were John Dalmas, Ted Carmady, Johnny De Ruse, Pete Anglish, Sam Delaguerra, and the early literary father of Marlowe: "... a tall man with wide-set grey eyes, a thin nose, a jaw of stone. He had a rather sensitive mouth. His hair was crisp and black, ever so faintly touched with gray, as by an almost diffident hand. His clothes fitted him as though they had a soul of their own, not just a doubtful past. His name happened to be Mallory."

From the beginning Chandler's short stories were unique. His short stories were miniature novels. The writing was provocative and powerful, filled with impressive visual images and a sardonic sense of humor. For example, the short story "Red Wind" opens in the following manner:

There was a desert wind blowing that night. It was one of those hot dry Santa Anas that come down through the mountain passes and curl your hair and make your nerves jump and your skin itch. On nights like this every booze party ends in a fight. Meek little wives feel the edge of the carving knife and study their husband's necks. Anything can happen. You can even get a full glass of beer at a cocktail lounge.

The short stories Chandler published between 1933 and 1938 were among the best of their type ever written and during these five years his work steadily improved. He published only three stories in 1935; five in 1936; two in 1937; three in 1938; five in 1939; and no more until 1941. His earnings for 1938 netted him $1,275. It was Cissy's money that enabled them to survive.

Chandler began his first novel, *The Big Sleep*, in 1938 and he read detective fiction voluminously in preparation. Unlike Hammett, Chandler knew very little about crime, criminals or police procedures and he had to rely on his reading since he had little interest in or respect for the police. In his words, "cops are pretty dumb people." He also relied on his memory. If he wanted to write about a seedy hotel he would go visit one and sit in the lobby for half a day and observe the details around him. Like most good writers he used whatever was at hand—especially the city of Los Angeles and the state of California. Despite his wide reading he fell back on his own work—his earlier stories—as the basis for the novel. *The Big Sleep*, written in only three months, was based on two earlier stories—"Killer in the Rain" and "The Curtain."

The Big Sleep centers around the Sternwoods—a family headed by an old paralyzed ex-soldier and his two beautiful daughters: one a gambler and the other a degenerate; plus a strangely absent son-in-law. With all its money, vices and hidden scandals the family inevitably attracted blackmailers, criminals and people with something to sell. Marlowe, the private eye, is called in to break up a blackmail case but he soon finds himself involved in some odd and mysterious homicides which he proceeds, in one vivid scene after another, to gradually understand and finally solve. Although the plot is competently done, we do not read Chandler for his plotting. We read him—for the writing and the characterizations.

Chandler's second novel, *Farewell My Lovely*, is a comedic drama also based on two other short stories—"Try the Girl," published in January 1937 and "Mandarin's Jade," published in November of the same year. Chandler finished it in April 1940 but was working on his fourth novel, *The Lady In The Lake*, at the same time and this caused something of a delay. The plot of *Farewell My Lovely* revolves around the search by a giant named Moose Malloy for his lost love, Velma. The action is fast and furious and the tension in scene after scene keeps the reader as taut as the strings of a violin.

Involved in the search for Velma are a black with a broken neck, a gin-drinking floozie with a fine new radio, a lovely blonde of easy virtue with a rich and sadly helpless husband, and a charlatan consultant who calls himself a psychic. The character of Marlowe dominates and prevails. *Farewell My Lovely* is the only detective story that literary critic Edmund Wilson admitted to have read all of and enjoyed.

The third novel, *The High Window*, concerns the theft of a Brasher Doubloon—a rare coin—followed by two murders. This novel also contains a variety of richly assorted characters—some nice, some neurotic, and some nasty. Essentially, it is the story of Merle Davis (nice) who has been brainwashed into believing that she pushed Mrs. Murdock's (nasty) first husband out of a window because he made a pass at her. Marlowe (nice) finally discovers a blackmailer, Vannier, (nasty) who owns a photograph showing that Mrs. Murdock did the pushing. Merle is so very nice she, at first, refuses to believe that Mrs. Murdock did it.

The fourth Marlowe novel, *The Lady In The Lake*, was also based on his short story of the same name. It is both a morality play and a portrait of a troubled society. Everyone in the novel has a serious problem or is in some sort of deep personal trouble. The plot opens with Marlowe being hired by Derace Kingsley, a rich cosmetics company head, to find his missing wife. Kingsley admits that he hates her but he, nevertheless, wants her found. While Marlowe discovers what the missing wife was really like, a number of crimes also come to light. In the process of finding Mrs. Kingsley, Marlowe is threatened by the police, beaten up, arrested, blackjacked and forced to drink whiskey so he will appear drunk. He is jailed, knocked out, drenched with gin and framed for murder—all under the orders of a policeman named Lt. Degarmo.

Following the publication of *The Lady In The Lake*, Chandler sold himself and his skill to Hollywood. It was an arrangement that proved highly unsatisfactory for both Chandler and the movie industry. Chandler went to work as a screen-writer in 1944 for $1,750 a week. For the next seven years Chandler worked on at least seven separate screenplays. Although he was most closely associated with Paramount, he also worked with MGM, Warner Brothers and Universal.

Though he was well paid and treated fairly his relationships with the studios were highly strained. In 1947, for example, he was paid $100,000 to prepare a screenplay version of one of his novels—but it was never produced. The fault, however, was not entirely his. In translating his novels for the screen the studios made unforgiveable blunders. The earliest movie versions of his work attempted to superimpose characters created by other writers on Chandler's plots, and the results were monstrous. Chandler's first screenwriting assignment teamed him with Billy Wilder on James M. Cain's *Double Indemnity*. Though he received an Academy Award nomination for his efforts, Chandler was not happy. He disliked both Wilder and the finished product.

Chandler received a second Academy Award nomination for his original screenplay, *The Blue Dahlia*, which he had originally intended as a novel. Although he was not proud of *The Blue Dahlia* it was a financial success grossing over $2,750,000. Chandler never returned to his novel after the screenplay and no one knows whether it was originally conceived as a Marlowe vehicle.

In 1946 Chandler had his first chance to work on one of his own novels when MGM filmed *The Lady In The Lake*. He disliked everything about it. After two other aborted screen writings in 1946 and 1947 Chandler teamed with Alfred Hitchcock in 1950 to convert Patricia Highsmith's *Strangers On A Train* into a film. The collaboration was a failure and was his last Hollywood screenwriting attempt. Although two more movies were made from his novels after his death in 1959—*Marlowe* (based on *The Little Sister*) in 1969 and *The Long Goodbye* in 1973 it is unlikely he would have approved of either.

There was a hiatus of six years between *The Lady In The Lake* (1943) and *The Little Sister* (1949) the most completely plotted of all the Marlowe novels. This was *the* Hollywood novel. The plot revolves around Orphamay Quest's hiring Marlowe to find her brother Orrin.

The next novel, *The Long Goodbye*, followed four years later in 1953. This novel, in Tuska's words, "has to be considered as literature rather than in any way a thriller." The plot concerns Terry Lennox, a friend of Marlowe's, and his rich wife Sylvia. Sylvia turns up murdered and Terry asks for Marlowe's help to escape to Mexico. Terry insists that he didn't kill her. Marlowe takes him to Mexico. On his return he is arrested, thrown into jail and held as an accessory to murder. Marlowe is freed after the police tell him that Lennox committed suicide after writing a full confession, a confession which Marlowe subsequently disproves.

In 1955 Chandler was awarded an Edgar by the Mystery Writers of

America for *The Long Goodbye* and his work became even more popular. Recovering somewhat from Cissy's death in December, 1954, he attempted to find another woman to replace her. Most of his income from his books and subsidiary rights—which came to approximately $25,000 a year—he spent on potential candidates for marriage. He even went to England to try to find a new life. But Cissy's memory still haunted him and in an attempt to cheer him up several of his English friends tried to find him suitable female companionship.

In the meanwhile the hard drinking continued and, while he was invited to many parties and dinners in his honor his consistent failure to appear resulted in fewer and fewer invitations. The heavy drinking began to take its toll. Though he did try to stop drinking he had little success.

In 1957 he went back to work on the novel *Playback* and hired Helga Greene as his literary agent. Once more because of anxiety, depression and sexual frustration he drank himself back into the sanitarium. After drying out, with Helga's help he was able to finish *Playback* three months ahead of schedule in 1958. *Playback* is generally agreed to be his weakest and least successful novel. Nevertheless it is filled with some of Chandler's best paragraphs. *Playback* is the story of Betty Mayfield whom Marlowe is hired to keep an eye on. An arrogant attorney, Clyde Umvey, hires Marlowe to follow one Eleanor King and report on her activities. In the process of tailing her Marlowe is knocked cold, thrown in jail and then meets a blackmailer named Larry Mitchell who has something on Eleanor King who proves to be actually Betty Mayfield. Marlowe also finds he has PI company in the form of a Kansas City Shamus named Goble who is also on Betty's tail.

Though *Playback* is Marlowe's weakest chronicle it is eminently readable and rather sad. It is filled with autobiographical touches. One of the most poignant moments comes at the end of Marlowe's conversation with an elderly man named Clarendon. At the close of the conversation Marlowe starts to shake his hand: "I never shake hands," he said. "My hands are ugly and painful. I wear gloves for that reason. Good evening. If I don't see you again, good luck." It is fascinating that nothing could be more personal and relevant in Chandler's own life at this time. In MacShane's biography there is a photograph of Chandler with Helga Greene made shortly before he died. It is very clear from the photo made at a night club that Chandler is wearing gloves. We are also informed that Chandler suffered painfully from an unsightly skin disorder that forced him to wear gloves in public. The scene, at the end of the novel, in which Linda Loring introduced in *The Long Goodbye* calls from Paris and says she wants to marry Marlowe is also a reflection of Chandler's own dreams.

When the novel appeared, *Newsweek* ran a special news story on the character change and Marlowe's plans to marry. Chandler acknowledged the story with this comment: "I thought it was time Marlowe was given something worth having, some love of his own. You see there's a lot of him in me, his loneliness." This decision led to Chandler's plans for the next Marlowe story in which, though married, Marlowe would hate Linda's style of living as well as the house in Palm, i.e., "Poodle Springs," the name Chandler felt was most appropriate for the popular California oasis.

Despite Chandler's alcoholism, he was strong enough to fly to New York and attend the MWA dinner and give his inaugural address as their newly elected President. The weather in New York was bad and in his frail condition he picked up a cold. His incessant drinking weakened him to the point that he had no physical resistance. His cold grew worse and in a few days after his return to California he contracted pneumonia. In his weakened condition he could not fight off its effects. On 23 March 1959 he was admitted to La Jolla Convalescent Hospital. He died there three days later in his 71st year.

Chandler recognized, as Marlowe himself once observed, "There is no solution to life's puzzles and problems." And Jerry Speir observed that nobody could have written a better obituary for himself than Chandler did when describing the fictional author Roger Wade in *The Long Goodbye*:

> He worried about his work and he hated himself because he was just a mercenary hack. He was a weak man, unreconciled, frustrated, but understandable.

To this Speir adds, "Obviously, the complexity of the man himself, the internal strife he suffered and the external conflict he witnessed, were responsible for forging the works we now admire, and which surely merit far more attention than those of any mere 'mercenary hack'."

What is the critical estimate of Chandler's work today? Erle Stanley Gardner called him "A star of the first magnitude in the constellation of modern mystery writers." The Kansas City *Star* stated, some time ago:

> When the literary historians some years hence jot down the names of the Americans who developed a distinctive style of mystery story writing, Mr. Chandler will rank high on the list .... Raymond Chandler is, first of all, a *writer*—one who uses words consciously as a literary medium—and as such a master of his craft. Second, that he is worth reading, not only as an author of murder mysteries but as a *novelist*—whether you ordinarily read mystery stories or not. Third that his novels may be considered a part of contemporary American *literature*, along with those of such writers as Hammett, Cain, O'Hara, Burnett.

Typical of the accolades heaped on Chandler's head in recent years was a review of *The Midnight Raymond Chandler* published in 1981 by E.R. Hagemann:

> Chandler can dazzle and bewilder with a salvo of figurative language that should drive many writers to throw their typewriters in the garbage disposal. The style,

probably derived from Dashiell Hammett and Ernest Hemingway, has been filed down and honed until it is Chandler; and like any master, he has imitators but no school.

Julian Symons says that in the inevitable comparison between Hammett and Chandler, Chandler comes off second best. Symons says there is a toughness in Hammett that Chandler lacked and did not appreciate. But in Chandler's eyes, Hammett's toughness and the crude code of ethics followed by Spade and the Continental Op were deficiencies he specifically set out to remedy. While it is true, as Symons claims, that PIs are rough people doing rough work and that Hammett's vision is more accurate, Chandler's vision is more artistic—richer, more evocative and more insightful. Chandler has a literary depth and range Hammett was never able to reach. While it is, perhaps, futile and unfair to draw such comparisons, Chandler was a more sensitive and even more intelligent writer than Hammett and an excellent critic as well. He, better than others, wrote his own epitaph in one of his letters:

> To accept a mediocre form and make something like literature out of it is in itself rather an accomplishment. ... Any decent writer who thinks of himself occasionally as an artist would far rather be forgotten so that someone better might be remembered.

Chandler's singular accomplishment was that he did exactly that: he took the crude, unpolished, hard-boiled murder mystery and cut, shaped and polished it until it became a glittering work of art. We read him for the sheer joy of his arrangement of the words and the beauty of his phrases. This, for example, is his opening of *The Little Sister*:

> It was one of those clear, bright summer mornings we get in the early Spring in California before the high fog sets in. The rains are over. The hills are still green and in the valley across the Hollywood hills you can see snow on the high mountains. The fur stores are advertising their annual sales. The call-houses that specialize in sixteen-year-old virgins are doing a land office business. And in Beverly Hills the jacaranda trees are beginning to bloom.

And here, from *The Long Goodbye* is his description of a girl entering a bar:

> The old bar waiter came drifting by and glanced softly at my weak Scotch and water. I shook my head and he bobbed his white thatch, and right then a dream walked in. It seemed to me for an instant that there was no sound in the bar, that the sharpies stopped sharping and the drunk on the stool stopped babbling away, and it was just like after the conductor taps on his music stand and raises his arms and holds them poised. She was slim and quite tall in a white linen tailor-made with a black and white polka-dotted scarf around her throat. Her hair was the pale gold of

a fairy princess. There was a small hat on it into which the pale gold hair nestled like a bird in its nest. Her eyes were cornflower blue, a rare color, and the lashes were long and almost too pale. She reached the table across the way and was pulling off a white gauntleted glove and the old waiter had the table pulled out in a way no waiter will ever pull out a table for me. She sat down and slipped the gloves under the strap of her bag and thanked him with a smile so gentle, so exquisitely pure, that he was damn near paralyzed by it. She said something to him in a very low voice. He hurried away, bending forward. There was a guy who really had a mission in life.

Philip Marlowe

Chandler experimented with a nameless first person narrator in a series of short stories before he fused them into, perhaps, the best-known private eye in the world of detective fiction. And Philip Marlowe is the modern knight *par excellence*.

One of the principal reasons we admire Marlowe is his relentless pursuit of the ideal of justice. Chandler once wrote that "the emotional basis of the standard detective story was and had always been that murder will out and justice will be done." But, as Chandler emphasizes, justice will not be done "unless some very determined individual makes it his business to see that justice is done."

E.R. Hagemann described Marlowe as follows:

Philip Marlowe, private eye in L.A. Marlowe, the perversely virtuous knight in Corruption City. His charger is an out-of-style Plymouth; his lance, a well-oiled Luger . . . .
Forty dollars a day and expenses. Marlowe's fee for knighthood. He'll take 25 and he's been known to take less. Over in Hollywood he's got an office where 'the smell of old dust' hangs in the air 'as flat and stale as a football interview.' He meets all kinds (and in his kingdom there are *all* kinds); a fat man in a two-tone jacket which 'would have been revolting on a zebra'; a mortician whose 'composed gray face was long enough to wrap twice around his neck'; a shady doctor whose smile was 'like powder smell in the air after a gun is fired'."

While Cary Grant was the actor who most resembled Marlowe in Chandler's mind, he was very impressed with Bogart's portrayal in *The Big Sleep*. Yet, it might come as a surprise to learn that Chandler fully realized that Marlowe was far from being a realistic portrayal of the typical private eye. In Chandler's thinking: "The real-life private eye is a sleazy little drudge from the Burns Agency, a strong-arm guy with no more personality than a blackjack. He has about as much moral stature as a stop-and-go-sign."

MacShane in his biography of Chandler takes the position that the reader cannot, and is not expected to, identify with Marlowe the character but rather with Marlowe the narrator. Marlowe is never painted with sufficient depth or clarity that we know him ultimately. We do know, however, his moral stance and his essential honesty, his sense of social justice, and his hatred of pretense, cruelty and corruption. Marlowe's concern for others shows up time and time again in his novels. In *Playback*, for example, the heroine asks Marlowe:

'How can such a hard man be so gentle?'
'If I wasn't hard, I wouldn't be alive. If I couldn't ever be gentle, I wouldn't deserve to be alive.'

At another point in *Playback* Marlowe is talking to a young desk clerk whose girl friend operates the switch board. The desk clerk complains to Marlowe:

'Yeah,' he sighed, 'You work twenty hours a day trying to put enough together to buy a home. And by the time you have, fifteen other guys have been smooching your girl.'
'Not this one,' I said. 'She's just teasing you. She glows every time she looks at you.' I went out and left them smiling at each other.

The most valuable data about Chandler's conception of Marlowe comes to us from Chandler's letters where he insists that Marlowe is not to be taken seriously. In a 1951 letter he stressed: "You must remember that Marlowe is not a real person. He is a creature of fantasy. He is in a false position because I put him there." To know this fictional man we have to read long and carefully, and even then the facts are relatively few.

We know that Marlowe was born in 1906, is slightly over 6 feet tall and weighs 190 pounds. His hair is dark and his eyes are brown. He is of a husky build and women find him attractive in a rugged, brutish sort of way. He usually wears a hat and a trench coat. When he dresses up he wears his one and only powder-blue suit with black shoes and black socks. He has never married and he is a heavy smoker with a preference for Camels. He lights his cigarettes with kitchen matches, usually, and snicks them with his thumbnail. Like his creator, he also smokes a pipe—most often when doing some heavy thinking. He is a heavy drinker and keeps a bottle in his desk drawer for himself and his clients. He routinely serves Scotch and soda, or bourbon (Four Roses) with ginger ale when he is at home. He dislikes sweet drinks and for cocktails he prefers a double Gibson—usually two before dinner. He likes chocolate sundaes for dessert. He has a tough and cynical manner, supported by a steady stream of wise and stinging metaphors and similes (e.g., "Put some rouge on your cheeks. You look like a snow-maiden after a hard night with the fishing fleet.")

The well-turned simile became the recognized trademark of Chandler's metaphorical style and the literary device most conveniently imitated by subsequent authors. In his excellent study of popular culture,

Adventure, Mystery and Romance John G. Cawelti offers this analysis of how Chandler used the similes to reflect Marlowe's character:

These similes are sometimes sharply pointed and effectively witty; occasionally they degenerate into a mannerism. In general they are an effective means of stylistic characterization, reflecting Marlowe's personal style of perception and response. By contrasting such exaggerated comparisons with the understatement and lack of explicit emotion that also characterize Marlowe's narration, Chandler gives us a continual sense of Marlowe's complexity of attitude and character: He is intensely sensitive, yet carries a shield of cynical apathy; he is disturbed to a point of near-hysteria by the moral decay he encounters, yet always affects a wise-guy coolness and wit; he is bitter, exasperated, and lonely, behind a veneer of taut self-control, sarcasm, and indifference.

Despite the callous and flippant exterior he is, basically, a kind and altruistic man. For relaxation he occasionally goes to the movies—as long as they aren't musicals—and he plays an occasional game of amateurish chess. He lives in a sparse, sixth floor, three-and-a-half room apartment: living room with French windows and a small balcony, bedroom, kitchen and dinette, which he rents for $60 a month. He works out of a sixth floor one-and-one-half room office in the Cahuenga Building on Hollywood Boulevard. The office has a small waiting room and a larger interior office equipped with a glass-topped desk, a hat rack, a squeaky swivel chair, a wall calendar, five green metal filing cabinets, some wooden chairs and a stained wooden cabinet that contains a wash bowl. He cannot afford either a secretary or an answering service. He drives a big car—either a Chevrolet or an Olds—when he can and he also likes convertibles. He wears a Smith and Wesson .38 special with a four-inch barrel in a shoulder holster. He totes a Luger in the car and on occasion he will use a Colt automatic. He carries on his person a photostat of his PI license, an honorary deputy sheriff's badge, a number of phony business cards, a fountain pen flashlight and a penknife. He eats sparingly and often misses meals with one exception: breakfast.

He is strictly a loner—no living relatives and few friends—but he goes to Dr. Carl Moss for medical help and cooperates grudgingly with Bernie Ohls of the DA's staff, Carl Randall of the Central Homicide Bureau and Captain Gregory of the Missing Persons Bureau. His fee is $25 a day, later inflated to $40 plus expenses. Expenses are mostly gasoline and booze. Professionally he started as an insurance investigator. Next he worked for the L.A. County District Attorney's Office as a snooper until he was fired for "insubordination." He took up the PI business because it is all he knew. He will take most any case that is legitimate but he doesn't "do windows" (divorce work). His education consisted of two years at a college in Oregon—either the University of Oregon or Oregon State—and what he has learned prowling the streets of Los Angeles.

His sex life is a series of frustrating and unsatisfactory one-night stands and more than one psychologically-minded critic has hinted at a possibility of latent homosexuality because of too many contemptuous references to "queers," "fags," "pansies" and "queens," plus his ambivalent attitude toward the women in his life. Critic Gershon Legman, went so far as to state, "The true explanation of Marlowe's temperamental disinterest in women is not 'honor' but his interest in men . . . . Chandler's Marlowe is clearly homosexual—a butterfly, as the Chinese say, dreaming that he is a man."

Marlowe's attitude toward women was both romantic and chivalrous. His tendency to idealize them is unmistakeable. Like many English school graduates, Chandler had difficulty relating to the opposite sex and these difficulties come through in the character of Marlowe and in his relationships with nearly all the female characters. In *Farewell My Lovely*, for example, Marlowe had an opportunity to bed Anne Riordan but turns down her offer of an overnight accommodation and later tells Lt. Randall: "She's a nice girl. Not my type . . . . I like smooth, shiny girls, hardboiled and loaded with sin." While this could be interpreted as macho camaraderie with the lieutenant, much more plausible is Speir's interpretation that it shows: "a desire to keep his relationship with Riordan on a distant, impersonal level unsullied by a contemptible reality—to keep her on a pedestal 'in an enchanted valley.' So far as we know, Marlowe never has anything to do with 'shiny, hardboiled girls'."

Speir points to a second and even more important reason for Marlowe's avoidance of sexual entanglements, i.e., such romantic sub-plots would detract, significantly, from the singlemindedness of the main story—a literary tradition for most mystery novelists at the time. Further, in *The Long Goodbye* when Lennox attacks women for being deceptive Marlowe responds: "Take it easy . . . . So they're human . . . . What did you expect—golden butterflies in a rosy mist?"

Although, in most instances, he does avoid entanglements he does become romantically involved with Betty Mayfield in *Playback*:

I grabbed hold of her. She tried to fight me off but no fingernails. I kissed the top of her head. Suddenly she clung to me and turned her face up.
'All right. Kiss me, if it's any satisfaction to you. I suppose you would rather have this happen where there was a bed.'
'I'm human.'
'Don't kid yourself. You're a dirty low-down detective. Kiss me.'
I kissed her. With my mouth close to hers I said: 'He hanged himself tonight.'

Then, a few pages later the sexual encounter is clear and unmistakeable:

'I'm tired. Do you mind if I lie down on your bed?'
'Not if you take your clothes off.'

'All right—I'll take my clothes off. That's what you've been working up to isn't it?'

And apparently it is because on the following page:

I held her tight against me. 'You can cry and cry and sob and sob, Betty. Go ahead, I'm patient. If I wasn't that—well, hell, if I wasn't that—'
That was as far as I got. She was pressed tight to me trembling. She lifted her face and dragged my head down until I was kissing her.
'Is there some other woman?' she asked softly between my teeth.
'There have been.'
'But someone very special?'
'There was once, for a brief moment. But that's a long time ago now.'
'Take me. I'm yours—all of me is yours. Take me.'

This ends Chapter 23, and Marlowe obviously "took" her. At least it was Chandler's intent to persuade us this happened because at the beginning of Chapter 24:

A banging on the door woke me. I opened my eyes stupidly. She was clinging to me so tightly that I could hardly move. I moved my arms gently until I was free. She was still sound asleep.

It turns out that it is Sergeant Green at the door and the good Sarge inquires:

'You got a dame in there?'

Marlowe's reply is knightly and chivalrous:

'Sergeant, questions like that are out of line. I'll be there.'

Then, when Green goes away Marlow dresses and pens Betty a note which he leaves on her pillow. Later, when he sees Betty again:

'Will you take me back to the hotel? I want to speak to Clark.'
'You in love with him?'
'I thought I was in love with you.'
'It was a cry in the night,' I said. 'Let's not try to make it more than it was. There's more coffee out in the kitchen.'
'No thanks. Not until breakfast. Haven't you ever been in love? I mean enough to want to be with a woman every day, every month, every year?'
'Let's go.'

Marlowe must have seriously considered "wanting to be with a woman" because, in the final chapter, Marlowe receives a phone call from Linda Loring in Paris. In Linda's words:

'I've tried to forget you. I haven't been able to. We made beautiful love together.'
'That was a year and half ago. And for one night. What am I supposed to say?'

Marlowe confesses that he has not been faithful to her. Nevertheless, Linda proposes marriage and Marlowe accepts with the following statement:

I'll come, darling. I'll come. Hold me in your arms. I don't want to own you. Nobody ever will. I just want to love you.

These are hardly the words of a homosexual. Significantly, the last line of the novel states: "The air was full of music." In the unfinished Marlowe novel *The Poodle Springs Story,* Chandler did have Linda and Marlowe married but we are given to understand Chandler's intentions were to make sure that the course of their true love would not run smooth.

Marlowe's personal philosophy? This, also, is provided in *Playback*. Chandler works into the story a total irrelevancy in the form of an elderly gentlemen, Henry Clarendon IV, who sits in the hotel lobby and watches the passing parade. Clarendon is the vehicle used to express both Marlowe's and Chandler's philosophy of life:

'Very small things amuse a man of my age. A hummingbird, the extraordinary way a Strelitzia blooms open. Why at a certain point in its growth does the bud turn at right angles? Why does the bud split so gradually and why do the flowers emerge always in a certain exact order.... Do you believe in God, young man?'
It was a long way around, but it seemed I had to travel it.
'If you mean an omniscient and omnipotent God who intended everything exactly the way it is, no.'
'But you should, Mr. Marlowe. It is a great comfort. We all come to it in the end because we have to die and become dust. Perhaps for the individual that is all, perhaps not. There are grave difficulties about the afterlife. I don't think I should really enjoy a heaven in which I shared lodging with a Congo pygmy or a Chinese coolie or a Levantine rug peddler or even a Hollywood producer. I'm a snob, I suppose and the remark is in bad taste. Nor can I imagine a heaven presided over by a benevolent character in a long white beard locally known as God. These are foolish conceptions of very immature minds. But you may not question a man's religious beliefs however idiotic they may be. Of course I have no right to assume that I shall go to heaven. Sounds rather dull as a matter of fact.'

These are the ruminations of a very tired and disillusioned man who is growing old, who sees his time running out and who cannot help but wonder what all the sound and fury mean. A man who is trying to find some meaning in the patterns of his memories and dreams.

According to Jerry Speir, Marlowe is a "hero out of time." By this he means that Marlowe is not so much a fully developed character as he is an attitude or a tone of voice. Speir calls attention to the fact that Marlowe's idealistic sensibilities:

draw him spontaneously and sympathetically to the down-trodden, to characters like Merle Davis and Terry Lennox. He has open and ready contempt, on the other hand, for the societal powers responsible for their plight—the Elizabeth Murdocks, the Harlan Potters, the corrupt Bay City Police, etc. But even as Marlowe is quick to defend whomever he perceives as helpless, so is he—more often than not — disappointed in the results of his own well-intentioned heroics.

This disjunction between Marlowe's idealism and the imperfect world he is forced to live in comes through clearly in each of the novels. Marlowe is a *true* knight of old, an incurable romantic, an anachronism in the modern world. In the first short story he ever wrote Chandler called his detective hero Mallory in likely reference to Sir Thomas Mallory's Morte D'Arthur, a prototype of the idealistic and romantic knight. Marlowe is the modern extension of this chivalrous point of view.

Speir stresses the fact that Marlowe is never able to attain "an understanding of himself as operating within a fallen world and that is his major failing as a modern hero." If, on the other hand, it *is* a failing it is one that many of us share and it represents the kind of tough, but necessary, idealism that millions of people believe in and cherish.

Chapter III
Princes of the Realm
Ross Macdonald, John D. MacDonald, Mickey Spillane

Lew Archer—**The Psychological Knight**

ALONG WITH HAMMETT AND CHANDLER before him, Kenneth Millar aka Ross Macdonald was the last and many claim the "best" of the "big three." William Goldman has stated that the Lew Archer stories are "the best detective novels ever written by an American." Anthony Boucher in a *New York Times Book Review* declared Macdonald a better novelist than either Hammett or Chandler. Certainly Macdonald is the most cerebral and the most psychological of the three.

Macdonald added a new dimension to the PI novel that was sired by Hammett and shepherded by Chandler. Macdonald took the strong but callow youngster and gave it both education and polish. In Macdonald's hands the PI novel reached maturity and attained a level of respectability not known before. An anonymous reviewer praised Macdonald as follows: "His private eye, Lew Archer, helps him tie together a popular mythology that explores the ills of the modern world with a caustic compassion... [his novels about California] symbolize man's inability to cope with himself and the world."

When *The Underground Man* appeared in 1971, the book was given a rave review on page one of the *New York Times Book Review* by Eudora Welty, a giantess of American Literature. Her praise is well deserved because the novel is a modern classic. It is literature of the highest quality, a marvel of plotting, characterization, description of human emotions and sociological and psychological insights as well as brilliant and memorable writing. In the words of Jerry Speir, author of a Macdonald biography, *Ross Macdonald*, (Frederick Unger, 1978): "*The Underground Man* is Macdonald's greatest achievement because it constructs a world view that incorporates the author's well-loved themes of human pain and suffering within a vast sweep of sympathetic natural forces." Above all, Macdonald is concerned about people and the human condition. His alter ego, Lew Archer is, despite his world weary and often cynical attitude a compassionate and caring man doing his damnedest to bring a little humanity and justice into a too frequently evil and uncaring world. Archer is a moral man. He is concerned about simple values and human relationships. He believes in people and he knows the importance of human dignity. We can accept his view of the world and agree with his attitudes because they seem innately right.

Pity and understanding, the essential components of compassion, are dominant themes in all the Archer novels. Macdonald called Lew "a democratic kind of hero" and "a fairly good man... (who) embodies values and puts them into action." Macdonald's purpose, as Jerry Speir notes, was to confront evil, death, love, sexuality, all the deepest human conflicts and make clear the human condition. Archer is a medium through which the meaning of other people's lives emerge. In Speir's words:

Archer consistently functions not to achieve justice according to some preconceived abstraction but to assist the characters whose lives he touches in having their own revelations about their place in the world, their relationship to time and the avenues of action open to them. And, much as Archer serves as revealer of the truth to the characters of the novels, Macdonald plays the role of revealer to his reading public.

Lew Archer is the central character in eighteen novels and one collection of short stories. His name was taken from Hammett's *The Maltese Falcon*. Miles Archer was Sam Spade's murdered partner. Macdonald, however, says that Lew is patterned more after Chandler's Philip Marlowe. To know Lew it is necessary to extract bits of information scattered through each of the eighteen novels. In *The Moving Target*, which was Archer's debut in 1949, we learn he is "approximately" 35 years of age, he was born in Long Beach sometime late in 1914, went to grade school in Oakland, in 1920. He also attended Wilson Junior High but no city is mentioned. In *Find A Victim* he notes that he had a stormy adolescence and that he:

had lifted cars myself when I was a kid, shared joy-rides and brawls with the lost gangs in the endless stucco maze of Los Angeles.... Then a whiskey-smelling plain-clothes man caught me stealing a battery from the back room of a Sears Roebuck store in Long Beach. He stood me up against the wall and told me what it meant and where it led. He didn't turn me in. I hated him for years and never stole again.

In *The Doomsters* Archer remembers times when he was a gang-fighter, thief and poolroom lawyer. But in 1945 he reformed and joined the Long Beach police force, working his way up to Detective Sergeant. In *Find A Victim* we are told that he was in Army intelligence in World War II, and a gun battle makes Lew remember "the smells of cordite and flamethrowers and scorched flesh, the green and bloody springtime of Okinawa." After the war Archer returns to his work as a cop on the Long Beach force. After five more years Archer quits because:

There are too many cases where the official version clashed with the facts I knew... Most good policemen have a public conscience and a private conscience. I just have a private conscience, a poor thing, but my own.

After his police career he becomes a Private Investigator and opens an office at 8411-½ Sunset Boulevard. The office is a two-room affair on the second floor of a two-story building and is next door to Miss Ditmar's model agency. The office is sparsely furnished: in the waiting room is a sagging imitation leather green sofa and an armchair. The waiting room is bugged and there is a two-way glass in the door. Instead of a secretary Lew has an answering service. Sometime between his tour of duty as a policeman and his entry into the PI business, Archer marries and moves into a five-room bungalow in a middle-class residential neighborhood in West Hollywood. The marriage is short-lived, and his wife Sue divorces him on the grounds of mental cruelty. We are led to believe she divorced him because she did not like his line of work, his hours, or the company he kept. The intensity with which he works and devotes himself to a case provides little time for domestic felicities. Most of the novels occur within a two-to-four day period and he often goes for a day or two without rest or sleep. Following the divorce Lew sold the house and moved into a modest second-floor apartment in West Los Angeles.

Archer is six feet, two inches and weighs around 190. His hair is dark and his eyes are blue. When he was younger, i.e., in *The Moving Target*, *The Drowning Pool* and *The Way Some People Die* he resembled Paul Newman. In the latter novels, *The Underground Man, Sleeping Beauty* and *The Blue Hammer*, he resembles Brian Keith. Lew drives a battered, old, green Ford convertible. He rarely uses a gun but when he has to he prefers a .38 special and .32 and .38 automatics. Lew usually carries a photostat of his license, a number of phony business cards and an old, Special Deputy Sheriff's badge. For thirty years Lew was a heavy smoker— but never before breakfast. Sometime around 1968 (*The Instant Enemy*) he gave up the habit. Unlike most PIs Lew is a light drinker and usually only on social occasions. He never drinks while working or before lunch. When he does imbibe he prefers Scotch, bourbon, or gin and tonic. He also likes Bass or Black Horse Ale.

Lew is purposely vague about the details of his past. For example, in *The Drowning Pool* he states that he did divorce work in Los Angeles for ten years; on two other occasions he reports that he was fired from the Long Beach force in 1945 and then, again, in 1953. In 1958 in *The Doomsters* he states that his age was "forty." If he was 35 in 1949, then he is a little older than 40 in 1958. Nevertheless, in the latter novels we know he is close to sixty and, though rather sociable, somewhat lonely.

Like most PIs Archer started as a peeper "doing windows," i.e., doing divorce work and investigating blackmail and adultery. As he matured and his reputation grew he began to specialize in, as Richard Lingeman notes, "family murders with an Oedipal twist." In the early novels we encounter a rougher and tougher, more violent Lew Archer, but in the later novels his clientele are higher in social status and his own violence has mellowed.

In a 1973 *Time* magazine review of *Sleeping Beauty* John Skow chastised Macdonald for not giving Lew a raise. As Skow notes:

> When he began gumshoeing back in 1949 he made $50 a day and now he charges $100. It's just not enough. Even if he cracks one case a week, he has to solve 40 cases a year just to make $20,000.

Skow also maintains that Macdonald has "written the same detective story 19 times in a row..." This, of course, is an error. There are only 18 Archer novels and when Skow wrote his review in 1973 only 17 had been published. *The Blue Hammer,* the last Archer story, appeared in 1976. There is some truth in the charge that the plots are repetitive. It is also true that Archer gets more than his share of physical abuse. He is nearly drowned in *The Moving Target* and *The Drowning Pool.* He is burned seriously in *The Doomsters* and in *The Instant Enemy* he is run over by a truck. A severe beating in *Find A Victim* requires eight facial stitches. He is given a concussion and six stitches in *The Wycherly Woman* and in *The Galton Case* bullet wounds put him in the hospital near death.

Peter Wolfe in his book *Dreamers Who Live Their Dreams: The World of Ross Macdonald's Novels* has exhaustively analyzed the eighteen novels and has, as effectively as anyone, summarized the special qualities of Macdonald's work.

> Though most thrillers start quickly, his set their own pace, adding characters and information when both reader and plot are ready for them.
>
> Thus the novels give a great deal—action and credibility, sound plotting and something to think about: the meaning and mechanism of crime. The crime points to serious issues. Almost all his work shows how far society at large, the family and the individual have veered from what they should be. The idea is neither original nor profound. Ross Macdonald's strength lies not in idea but in his moral seriousness and power to convert idea into sharply observed and well-integrated details. He convinces us, through his artistry, of both the complexity and mystery of life. While persuading us that life is full of meaning, he does not define that meaning: rather, he invests detective fiction with a psychological dimension that fits well with its traditionally complex plot. More interested in private than in public crime, he uses psychology rather than applied science to probe motives and causes. This turning away both from the gadgetry of the novel of international

intrigue and the secular rationalism of the tec-yarn helps reveal his characters through speech and action.

And "psychological" is the keynote of both Archer and the novels. Archer is the most complex, the most intellectual, the best read and informed and the most thoughtful private eye in the genre. Archer probes the psychological depths of both the victims and the villains that he encounters. He tries to understand them as human beings with problems, passions and possibilities. In his own words: "Other people's lives are my business...and my passion. And my obsession too, I guess. I've never been able to see much in the world besides the people in it." Even Macdonald's villains elicit our compassion and understanding. Though thoroughly wrong they are still morally redeemable. The most sympathetic characters in *The Doomsters* and *The Zebra-Striped Hearse* are the murderers and the violent father, respectively.

The Archer Novels

Because of their subtlety and complexity it is difficult to summarize the plots of the Archer novels but it is possible to provide a general outline of their themes and settings.

The best summary of the "standard" Archer novel has been provided by William Goldman:

telling the plot of an Archer is impossible. The books are so ramified, Delphic and dark...[but] if there is no way of detailing a specific Archer plot, there is a kind of over-all structure that tends to fit the late novels: in general, perhaps a full generation before the present time of the novel, two people come together, neither of them lethal alone, but united, deadly. And they do something terrible. They murder or steal or assume different identities. Or all three. It is a wild compulsive drive that operates on them. Sometimes what they do they do for money or lust or power. But mostly they do it for love. And they get away with it. And everything is quiet. Until Archer comes. Usually he is hired for something standard: my wife has left me—find her; my husband has a mistress—tell me who; my Florentine box is gone—get it. So he begins and gradually, obliquely, the generation-old crime is scratched alive.

Over and over again, Archer confronts the failures of family, a concern that is often trivialized by critics' constant reference to the "Oedipal Theme" in Macdonald. Many of the novels involve a father quest, particularly those written after his own involvement in psychotherapy, but the motivation is not purely Oedipal.

In order of publication, the Archer novels were as follows:

1. *The Moving Target*, 1949
2. *The Drowning Pool*, 1950
3. *The Way Some People Die*, 1951
4. *The Ivory Grin*, 1952
5. *Find a Victim*, 1955
6. *The Barbarous Coast*, 1956
7. *The Doomsters*, 1958
8. *The Galton Case*, 1959
9. *The Wycherly Woman*, 1961

10. *The Zebra-Striped Hearse*, 1962
11. *The Chill*, 1964
12. *The Far Side of the Dollar*, 1965
13. *Black Money*, 1966
14. *The Instant Enemy*, 1968
15. *The Goodbye Look*, 1969
16. *The Underground Man*, 1971
17. *Sleeping Beauty*, 1973
18. *The Blue Hammer*, 1976

Not a bad book in the bunch and yet Macdonald was never awarded an Edgar for his Archer novels.

The only other appearance of Archer is in a few short stories Macdonald authored between 1946 and 1977. Seven of these were collected, first in a 1955 Bantam Paperback edition titled *The Name is Archer* and again in 1977 with the addition of two more stories by the Mysterious Press in a volume titled *Lew Archer: Private Investigator*. Macdonald wrote an introduction to the later volume and there, perhaps more clearly than anywhere else, enunciates his view of the detective story, the PI as a hero and why he chose this genre as a medium of expression:

At its very best, where it grazes tragedy and transcends its own conventions, detective fiction can remind us that we are all underground men making a brief transit from darkness to darkness.

The typical detective hero in contemporary American fiction speaks for our common humanity. He has an impatience with special privilege, a sense of interdependence among men and a certain modesty....

The private detective is one of the central figures of fiction in which the shift from aristocracy to democracy has visibly occurred decade by decade. This is true of the real-life detective as well as the fictional, for each imitates the other. The relationship of the imaginary and the actual is further complicated by the fact that fictional detectives tend to be idealized versions of their authors.... Everyone knows this, including the present writer ('I'm not Archer, exactly, but Archer is me').... One reason why detective fiction is important is that it serves as a model for life and action...

Possibly he became a detective originally in order to make his concern for, and knowledge of people possible and then useful. He felt a certain incompleteness in himself which needed to be fulfilled by wide and extraordinary experience. He discovered a certain darkness in himself which could only be explored in terms of badly lighted streets and unknown buildings, alien rooms and the strangers who live in them.

Ross Macdonald

Kenneth Millar was born on December 13, 1915 in Los Gatos, California, near San Francisco. His father was a sea captain and, apparently abandoned his wife and son when Kenneth was about five years old. In his childhood Ken lived with one relative after another and he estimates that he may have lived in as many as fifty different houses while he was growing up. He also spent two years in boarding school in Canada in his early teens and it was here that his writing career began in the form of poetry. The depression of 1929 forced him to leave the boarding school to live for a year with an aunt in Medicine Hat, Alberta. Then he moved back to live with other relatives on his mother's side in Kitchener, Ontario where he graduated from high school in 1932.

One of his high school classmates was a brilliant girl by the name of Margaret Sturm. They had both published stories in their high school magazine. Kenneth spent his summers working on the farm but during the rest of the year he attended college at the University of Western Ontario. In 1936-37, after the death of his mother, Millar spent time abroad touring England, France and Germany. In Germany he witnessed the Nazi's rise to power and while watching Hitler move by in a parade had his pipe knocked from his mouth by a storm trooper who informed him that smoking in the Fuhrer's presence was disrespectful. This incident and the general sense of foreboding in Europe sent Millar home. These experiences served as the background for his first novel, *The Dark Tunnel.*

Back in Ontario he and Margaret renewed their friendship which blossomed into marriage on June 2, 1939, the day after he graduated with honors from college. Millar immediately enrolled in summer school at the University of Michigan. In 1939 a daughter named Linda was born and Millar also sold some of his writings. During the next two years Millar taught English and history at his old high school and attended Michigan during the summers working on his Ph. D. In the meantime Margaret began writing mystery novels and her first (*The Invisible Worm*) was published in 1941. Because of Margaret's success Kenneth was able to quit teaching high school and become a full-time fellow at Michigan. Margaret got him interested in the mystery novel, and in the fall of 1943 he wrote *The Dark Tunnel.* With the war on Millar was inducted into the Navy and after OCS training at Princeton served as a communications officer on an escort carrier in the Pacific theatre. His second novel *Trouble Follows Me* was written while he was aboard ship.

After the war, in 1946, Millar joined Margaret and Linda in Santa Barbara where they had moved while he was in service. They have lived there ever since. Before the year was out Millar had written two more novels, *Blue City* and *The Three Roads.* In 1947 he started an autobiographical novel but suffered writer's block so severely he had to abandon the project. In his words, "I was in trouble and Lew Archer got me out of it... (Archer provided me with a shield) like protective lead, between me and the radioactive material." In 1949 the first Archer novel,

The Moving Target, was published. To avoid confusion and competition with Margaret, Kenneth first used as a pseudonym his father's name John Macdonald. However, that same year another famous Macdonald, John D. published a mystery novel and Kenneth's mother bought ten copies of it by mistake. Then he tried John Ross Macdonald, the Ross being a common Canadian name. To avoid further confusion with the other John he finally settled on Ross.

Despite his writing Millar maintained his academic interests and in 1951, after completing all requirements, he received the Ph.D. degree. His dissertation topic was *The Inward Eye: A Revaluation of Coleridge's Psychological Criticism*. This work led to his growing and abiding interest in psychology and, specifically, an interest in Freud and his disciples. Perhaps the most important influence on Millar's work, however, was the poet W.H. Auden who was on the Michigan faculty when Millar was there. Millar studied modern European literature under Auden, who was himself a lover of the detective story. Auden, in turn, encouraged both Kenneth and Margaret. Millar also pays homage to Dostoevsky, Proust who was his favorite author according to Matthew J. Buccoli's biography *Ross Macdonald* (1984) and, of course, to Hammett and Chandler. One of Millar's gravest disappointments was that Chandler did not like his work. He admits to patterning Archer on Marlowe and acknowledges his indebtedness to both Hammett and Chandler.

In 1956 Macdonald underwent psychotherapy and moved briefly to the San Francisco Bay area. Returning to Santa Barbara in the summer of 1957 he began work on *The Galton Case* and credited the psychotherapy with freeing him enough to be able to deal with the highly emotional experiences of his youth and to use this material in his work. This year, he also taught creative writing and began writing book reviews for *The San Francisco Chronicle*.

Beginning in the early sixties the Millars became very sincere and active environmentalists and were members of the Sierra Club, the National Audubon Society and the American Civil Liberties Union. Kenneth's 1964 article in *Sports Illustrated*, "A Death Road for the Condor," deplored the construction of a road through the Sisquoe Condor Sanctuary. California's forest fires and off-shore oil spills are featured prominently in *The Underground Man* and *Sleeping Beauty* respectively.

Millar summed up his philosophy of writing in a 1972 interview with Jon Carroll published in *Esquire*. After stating that his aim from the beginning was to write novels that can be read by all kinds of people he added:

"I don't think people become writers, for the most part, unless they have experienced a peculiar kind of distancing, which generally occurs in childhood or youth and makes the direct satisfactions of living unsatisfactory, so that one has to seek one's basic satisfaction indirectly through what we loosely call art. What makes the verbal artist is some kind of shock, or crippling or injury which puts the world at one remove from him, so that he writes about it to take possession of it.... We start out thinking we're writing about other people and end up realizing we're writing about ourselves. A private detective is just kind of an invented shadow of the novelist at work."

Although our attention has been focused on the works of Kenneth Millar, it is necessary to call attention to the fact that Margaret Millar is also an exceptionally able and accomplished writer. She has published eighteen novels that can be classified as crime and mystery fiction, three "straight," psychological novels, an excellent juvenile tale and a book about bird watching. She has created two memorable fictional private eyes: Joe Quinn in *How Like an Angel,* a truly superb novel and Steve Pinata, an orphan of Mexican parentage, in *Stranger in My Grave.* Her talents and accomplishments have not gone unrecognized. She won an Edgar in 1956 for her *Beast in View.* In 1957 she was elected President of the Mystery Writers of America and in 1965 the Los Angeles *Times* named her Woman of the Year.

The Millars' lives have seen considerable tragedy. In 1970, their daughter Linda died of a stroke at the age of thirty-one, leaving behind a husband and a son. In the late seventies Kenneth became seriously ill with Alzheimer's disease, a progressively crippling and fatal disablement. He died on Monday, July 11, 1983 at Pine Crest Hospital in Santa Barbara. He was 67 years of age. In November 1982, he received the prestigious Los Angeles *Times* Robert Hirsch Award for an "outstanding body of work by a Western writer." A number of outstanding American novelists, including Eudora Welty, came to Santa Barbara to honor him. In October of the same year, the Private Eye Writers of America awarded Millar its first Life Achievement Award. After accepting the award for Millar, his friend and colleague Dennis Lynds mourned that he "lost a friend, PWA lost a fellow writer and the world lost an American novelist."

Travis McGee—A Knight of Many Colors

One of the best known and most admired of our modern knight-errants is a powerfully built, six-feet-four, two hundred and five pound, deeply tanned, 45-year-old man sporting a boyish grin and going by the name of Travis McGee. Originally, he was called Dallas McGee but following the Kennedy assassination, his creator John Dann MacDonald changed his name to avoid the unpleasant connotation of the Texas city. A writer friend, MacKinlay Kantor, advised MacDonald, "Hell, name him after an Air Force base. They have good names. Like Travis in California." So Dallas McGee became Travis McGee who, when he is not out rescuing some maiden in distress can be found making love to them aboard *The Busted Flush* at Slip F-18, Bahia Mar, Fort Lauderdale, Florida.

To accommodate its oversized and sexy owner, the *Flush*, which McGee won in a poker game and named after the hand that started his run of luck, is equipped with an oversized bed and an extra large shower stall. McGee is a knight exemplar, an epic hero in the classical tradition, according to one critic, of guys "like Gilgamesh and Beowulf and Ajax and Sir Lancelot and all the rest."

McGee has appeared in 21 sagas each with a color in the title from *The Deep Blue Goodbye* (the first) to *The Lonely Silver Rain* (the latest). According to MacDonald he didn't want to number them because this would suggest they should be read in a certain order. For a time, he considered using months of the year, animals, geographical references, etc., to distinguish the books.

Each of the McGee novels opens with Travis taking it easy on his houseboat when his peaceful composure is disturbed by someone in trouble. More than likely the one in trouble is a fair young maiden. McGee, of course, must redress the wrong and see that justice is done. Although not strictly a private eye (more of a "private avenger" according to some critics) McGee works outside the law without a license and earns his living as a salvage expert. His standard fee in all his contracts is fifty percent of whatever he recovers. So far, McGee has managed to live comfortably, if not luxuriously. Though he drives a blue Rolls-Royce, it is of 1936 vintage and has been converted into a pickup truck. McGee calls the Rolls Royce, Miss Agnes, after his fourth grade teacher whose hair was the same shade of blue. We know very little about McGee's early history because as MacDonald says:

I had a full biography of Travis McGee in my mind when I started out and I had intended to drop little bits of his background in as I went along. But then in doing the books, I found I was very reluctant to do this. I didn't understand why until I read one of the papers which said that one attribute of the classical hero is that nobody knows much about his antecedents or his childhood—he's mysterious. I said, of course it's better to leave his background unknown and let people conjecture for themselves.

If the reader is careful he can construct the following outline of McGee's early years: 1) He is of Irish decent and his mother's name was Mary Catherine Devlin; 2) He grew up in Chicago; 3) He served a tour of duty in the Army during the Korean War; 4) He planned to go into business with his older brother after the war; 5) This brother was financially ruined and committed suicide; 6) McGee avenged his brother's death; and 7) He played professional football (as a tight end) for two years before an injury cut short his career. If you are interested in further factual detail about Travis you should get a copy of "The Special Confidential Report," a 34-page supplement to *The JDM Bibliophile* compiled by Jean and Walter Shine. This report is a comprehensive survey of the factual minutiae surrounding our hero. One finds, for example, every place he has visited since 1960, the name of every woman he has slept with, the name of every man he has killed, a catalog of every physical injury he has received, his personal habits and his special talents and skills.

Though such detail adds to the illusion of McGee's reality, we are more intrigued by his personality. He is neither beach bum nor playboy yet he does live a loose and unencumbered existence. Travis is a self-styled "reject from a structured society" and he avoids all things that "bind" or "tie one down"—things such as mortgages, time payments, credit cards, retirement benefits, payroll deductions, savings accounts and Green Stamps. He remains footloose and fancy free. In every respect a gentleman. He practices, "therapeutic sex"—sex that comforts and consoles, sex that is honest and sincere, and that occurs in the context of an emotional bond. Only fate, circumstance and MacDonald's clever and conniving narrative skill allow McGee to escape the eager jaws of wedlock. In *The Deep Blue Goodbye*, McGee admits to being "an incurable romantic who thinks the man-woman thing shouldn't be a contest on the rabbit level."

MacDonald has also further increased the credibility of McGee's image by allowing him to age naturally, grow in wisdom and become more cerebral and less physical as the years have gone by. MacDonald says "He grows older at about one-third the natural rate. Otherwise I could be senile before I'd finished with him." At one point McGee finds himself:

embedded in a life I had in some curious way outgrown. I was an artifact, genius boat bum, a pale-eyed shambling, gangling, knuckly man, without enough unscarred hide left to make a decent lampshade. Watchful appraiser of the sandy-rumped beach ladies. Creaking knight errant, yawning at the thought of the next dragon.

McGee seeks advice, wisdom and consultation from his friend Meyer, who lives seventy feet away in his cabin cruiser named appropriately, *The John Maynard Keynes* since Meyer has a Ph.D. in International Economics. A big hairy bear of a man, Meyer did not fully emerge in the series as an important character until the seventh novel *Darker than Amber*. Meyer is a splendid foil for McGee and a fascinating character in his own right. He understands McGee better than Travis knows himself. It is usually Meyer that provides us with most of what we know about Travis. At one point Meyer tells McGee that if he would only overcome his "ditherings about emotional responsibility," he would be a far happier man. But as David Geherin, MacDonald's best biographer, observes "he would also be a far less interesting one." Geherin also points out that McGee is "an ant with a grasshopper syndrome" and totally unsuited for a life of uninterrupted leisure. In Geherin's words, "The more one knows about McGee, the more obvious it becomes that retirement is the aberration, the temporary hiatus in his quixotic mission, not, as he would have us believe, the other way around."

A number of critics have stressed that Travis McGee is one of the most complex long-run characters in American fiction and McGee's own ruminations about himself support the claim: In *Pale Gray for Guilt* McGee reveals this complexity in telling us how he feels about being close to people:

Always we want some separation, some tiny measure of distance, regardless of how clumsily our culture mechanizes an inadvertent togetherness. The only exception is when sex is good in all dimensions, so that even in the deepest joining there is the awareness of that final barrier, an apartness measured by only the dimensions of a membrane and part of the surge of it is a struggle to overcome even that much apartness.

In *A Purple Place for Dying* he refers to himself as "beach-bum McGee, the big chaffed-up, loose-jointed, pale-eyed, wire-haired, walnut-hided rebel—unregimented, unprogrammed, unimpressed. I had even believed I had grown another little layer of hide over those places where I could be hurt."

In *The Quick Red Fox* McGee again tries to explain himself with these words:

Self-evaluation. It is the skin rash of the emotionally insecure. I felt as if I had spent a lot of years becoming too involved with some monstrously silly people. McGee, the con artist. I would fatten myself off their troubles and then take the money and coast for a time, taking my retirement in early installments. I was not a very earnest nor constructive fellow.

But, I thought, what are the other choices? I am not a nine to five animal.... I am not properly acquisitive. I like the *Busted Flush,* the records and paintings, the little accumulations of this and that which stir memories, but I could stand on the shore and watch the whole thing go glug and disappear and feel a mild sardonic regret. No Professional American Wife could stomach that kind of attitude.

But McGee recognizes his idealism even though he tempers his lofty dedication by using self-deprecating terms. His armor for example, is always "rusty." He himself is a "tin horn Gawain." His sword is "tinfoil" and his lance is "crooked." Embarrassed that he would like to be a hero, he admits, "whenever I hear that word the only hero I can think of is Nelson Eddy, yelling into Jeanette's face. And wearing his Yogi Bear hat."

As Geherin notes:

as long as he (McGee) is around, the spirit of Don Quixote lives on.... By evoking Quixote, McGee identifies himself with the tradition of the American private eye, at least as the figure has evolved ever since Philip Marlowe self-consciously likened himself to the knight in the stain-glassed window on the opening pages of *The Big Sleep*. . . . MacDonald has effectively combined the essential qualities of the classic private eye with several of these other heroic patterns to create a character of refreshingly unique dimensions.

MacDonald uses his PI as a spokesman for his own opinions. As MacDonald puts it, "McGee whips my dead bones" and McGee, as a rugged individualist living on the fringes of polite society, has a good-sized herd of horses to whip. He never passes up an opportunity to take pot shots at every flaw and foible of our contemporary culture. His eye is sharp, his aim is accurate and his wit is winning. After turning down an opportunity to bed one very luscious lady, McGee reflects on his behavior as follows:

Where is the committee, I thought. They certainly should have made their choice by now. They are going to come aboard and make their speeches and I'm going to blush and scuff and say shucks, fellas! The National Annual Award for Purity, Character and Incomprehensible Sexual Continence in the face of Ultimate Temptation. Heavens to Betsy any American boy living in the Age of Hefner would plunge at the chance to bounce that little pumpkin because she fitted the ultimate playmate formula, which is maximized pleasure with minimized responsibility.

And on racial relations and the problems of minorities he tells it like it is:

Regardless of all protestations, the whiter you are the better you live. Blondes have the most fun. One of the most thoroughly ignored aspects of the Cuban Revolution is how happily the black Cubans embraced the new order. Though the percentage is smaller in Cuba than elsewhere through the Caribbean, the pattern of discrimination was the same. Black Cuba was entirely ready for anything at all which promised equality in education, jobs and health care. (*A Tan and Sandy Silence*).

In reflecting on the deterioration of quality in the products we buy and use he muses:

There is something self-destructive about Western technology and distribution. Whenever any consumer object is so excellent that it attracts a devoted following, some of the slide rule and computer types come in on their twinkle toes and take over the store and in a thrice they figure out just how far they can cut quality and still increase the market penetration.

In *The Green Ripper* he refers to this senseless profit-at-all-costs attitude as the "perpetual farting of the great God Progress." And in *The Dreadful Lemon Sky* he jabs the Florida condominium craze:

On the tube the local advertising for condominiums always shows the nifty communal features such as swimming pool, putting green, sandy beach, being enjoyed by jolly hearty folk in their early thirties... But when the condominiums are finished and peopled and the speculator has taken his maximum slice of the tax-related profits and moved on to crud up somebody else's skyline, the inhabitants all seem to be on the frangible side of seventy, sitting in the sunlight, blinking like lizards, and wondering if these are indeed the golden years or if it is all a big sell, an inflation game that you have to play, wondering which you are going to run out of first, your money or your life.

McGee articulates his philosophy most clearly in a revealing passage in *A Tan and Sandy Silence:*

Wait a minute! What am I supposed to be doing? Making up the slogan I shall paint on my placard and tote in the big parade? Several things I could write on my placard and then carry it all by myself down empty streets.

Up with life. Stamp out all small and large indignities. Leave everyone alone to make it without pressure. Down with hurting. Lower the standard of living. Do without plastics. Smash the servomechanisms. Stop grabbing. Snuff the breeze and hug the kids. Love all love. Hate all hate.

The McGee Novels

There are 21 McGee novels so far, all published and available in Fawcett paperback editions. Since 1973, however, when Lippincott published *The Turquoise Lament*, the novels have been published in hardcover first. Also, most of the earlier paperbacks have been reprinted in hardcover form. The first McGee, *The Deep Blue Good-bye* published in 1964, has McGee helping Cathy Kerr, a friend of his friend, Chookie McCall. The problem turns out to be an ex-con named Junior Allen who served time with Cathy's father in Leavenworth. After his release Allen looks up Cathy and soon becomes her lover. Cathy quickly learns Allen is not interested in her but in jewels that her father has hidden. Allen finds the treasure, abandons Cathy and disappears. Cathy asks McGee to recover what Allen has stolen. Allen, a first class S.O.B., mistreats a number of women and almost destroys McGee before Travis sends Junior to a "deep blue goodbye."

Deep Blue begins what has come to be recognized as the well-formulized MacDonald story line. Reviewing MacDonald's work for Reilly's *Twentieth Century Crime and Mystery Writers,* James Gindin summarizes the standard McGee plot as follows:

Typically, he is drawn into a situation through some obligation from his past, learning that the wife or the daughter or the sister of some old close friend is being destroyed by one of the various corrupt forces. McGee pursues these legacies with fervor, with total involvement, relying on his strength, his intelligence and, sometimes, his contacts with people in positions of authority around the world who owe him favors. McGee's "salvage" is emotional as well as protective and financial, for he frequently restores his legacies by taking them, alone, for long cruises in his boat to little-known islands of the Florida Coast or in the Caribbean.

Most of the McGee novels combine the emotional salvage of a wounded woman with strong moral positions on a variety of social and individual evils that have gradually become more complexly conceived as McGee has matured. In order of their publication (not necessarily their conception), the McGee's are:

1. *The Deep Blue Goodbye* (1964)
2. *Nightmare in Pink* (1964)
3. *A Purple Place for Dying* (1964)
4. *The Quick Red Fox* (1964)
5. *A Deadly Shade of Gold* (1965)
6. *Bright Orange for the Shroud* (1965)
7. *Darker Than Amber* (1966)
8. *One Fearful Yellow Eye* (1966)
9. *Pale Gray for Guilt* (1968)
10. *The Girl in the Plain Brown Wrapper* (1968)
11. *Dress Her in Indigo* (1969)
12. *The Long Lavender Look* (1970)
13. *A Tan and Sandy Silence* (1972)
14. *The Scarlet Ruse* (1973)
15. *The Turquoise Lament* (1973)
16. *The Dreadful Lemon Sky* (1975)
17. *The Empty Copper Sea* (1978)
18. *The Green Ripper* (1979)
19. *Free Fall in Crimson* (1981)
20. *Cinnamon Skin* (1982)
21. *The Lonely Silver Rain* (1984)

John Dann MacDonald

McGee's creator John Dann MacDonald was born in July 1916 in Sharon, Pennsylvania into a solid middle-class family. When John was twelve his father, an executive with the Standard Tank Car Company, moved to a vice-presidency with the Savage Arms Company in Utica, New York. After graduating from the Utica Free Academy at age fifteen, John enrolled at the Wharton School of Finance of the University of Pennsylvania. He left, however, during his sophomore year and moved to New York City, working at a number of odd jobs. After a few months, John enrolled at Syracuse and received a B.S. in Business Administration in 1938. A year earlier, John met and married Dorothy Prentiss and after graduation the young couple moved to Harvard where John earned his M.B.A. in 1939 and Dorothy gave birth to their only child Maynard John MacDonald.

John worked for a collection agency, as an insurance salesman and for Burroughs Adding Machine Company before accepting a commission as lieutenant in Army Ordinance in 1940. Two years later he transferred to the Office of Strategic Services (OSS) and served in the China-Burma-India theater rising to the rank of Lieutenant Colonel by the end of the war. As a lark while in the OSS in India, John wrote a two-thousand word short story about life in New Delhi. He sent it to Dorothy in place of his usual long letter. Without informing John, Dorothy sent it to Whit Burnett's *Story Magazine*. Whit accepted it, paid Dorothy $25 and published it in the July-August 1946 issue. When John got back to Utica and heard the news he, for the first time, seriously considered a career as a professional writer rather than as a businessman. Since he had a little money saved from the Army, John decided to turn pro to see if he could make it. Five months later he had sold a story to *Detective Tales* for $40. This encouraged him further and by the end of 1946 he had published twenty-three stories in a number of the pulp magazines and had earned approximately $6000. His productivity continued unabated and he published at least thirty-five stories in 1947, fifty in 1948, seventy-three in 1949 and fifty-two in 1950! He also began writing novels and publishing in the "slicks"—*Playboy, Colliers, Esquire, Cosmopolitan, Liberty*—as well. Thus far he has published almost six hundred short stories, over sixty novels—most of these are paperback originals—as well as numerous collections of short stories, travel books, humor and science fiction.

Despite his staggering productivity his work is uniformly excellent and well received by both the general public and the critics. Although the McGee novels are the best known, MacDonald's non-mystery novels are also first-rate entertainment. *Condominium*, published in 1977, appeared on the *New York Times* best seller list for six months. *The Last One Left* (1964) was also a best seller and was nominated for an Edgar Award as the best mystery of the year. Anthony Boucher cited it as "one of the major suspense novels of the 1960s. In this novel MacDonald proves more conclusively than any living writer that "the distinction between the *thriller* and the *serious* novel is illusory."

Of the non-McGee novels several are of exceptional quality. MacDonald's novels about American businessmen: *A Man of Affairs, Area of Suspicion* and *A Key to the Suite* are as good as any that have been written on this theme. *A Flash of Green* (1962) about a war between a group of environmentalists and some unscrupulous local developers is an eloquent protest against the despoilation of natural beauty. The only non-McGee, PI novel MacDonald has written was his first published novel *The Brass Cupcake* (1950). Featured is one Cliff Bartells, a rough, tough ex-cop who is an insurance investigator for the Security Theft and Accident Company in Florence City, Florida. Because he refused to go along with the framing of an honest man Cliff is booted off the force. Cliff cynically refers to his gold badge as "The brass cupcake." Cliff is hired to investigate a jewel theft and a murder. During the course of the novel, which is definitely patterned after Hammett and Chandler, Cliff retrieves the jewels, solves the murder, exposes the corruption of his former colleagues and returns to the force as a Deputy Chief. In this manner MacDonald avoids having to continue Bartell's career as a PI.

MacDonald's work has received the following approval from David Geherin.

Far from being merely serviceable, MacDonald's prose is colorful, his language expressive, his rhythm graceful. One would not expect a writer who turned out three or four books a year to be as exacting as, say, Flaubert. Nevertheless, MacDonald is a consummate craftsman and his descriptions, observations and dialogue are the result of care, attention to telling detail, affection for the language and control over its power to generate emotional responses in the reader...

And Geherin is not alone. The best praise comes from fellow professionals. Chandler said MacDonald was one of a few writers he reread every year. Ian Fleming said he automatically bought every McGee novel as soon as it appeared. Richard Condon calls him "the Great American storyteller." Kurt Vonnegut, Jr., says that to archaeolgists a thousand years from now "the works of John D. MacDonald would be a treasure on the order of the tomb of Tutankhamen."

MacDonald was elected president of the MWA in 1962 and won the prestigious Grand Master Award in 1972. He is also the subject of an entire journal devoted exclusively to his work. From 1965 to 1978 Len and June Moffatt published the *JDM Bibliophile*. Since 1979 the Bibliophile has been edited by Ed Hirshberg and published by the University of South Florida. The University of Florida in Gainesville has 49 linear feet of shelf space devoted to his papers. In 1978 Hirshberg arranged a literary conference at the University of South Florida devoted to MacDonald's work. Hirshberg is currently writing MacDonald's biography for inclusion in the Twayne U.S. Authors series. MacDonald received the *French Grand Prix de Literature Policiere* in 1964 and the Benjamin Franklin Award for the best American short story in 1955.

Many of MacDonald's novels have been filmed: *Man Trap* in 1961 starring Edmond O'Brien, Jeffrey Hunter, David Janssen, and Stella Stevens was based on MacDonald's *Soft Touch; Cape Fear* in 1962 starring Gregory Peck and Robert Mitchum was based on *The Executioners*. In 1970 *Darker Than Amber* was filmed in Miami and the Caribbean with Rod Taylor as McGee and Theodore Bikel as Meyer. In 1980 both *The Girl, The Gold Watch, and Everything* and *Condominium* were filmed for TV and telecast. Sam Elliott as Travis and Katherine Ross as Gretel, starred in the 1983 ABC *Travis McGee* based on *The Empty Copper Sea*.

It is rumored that MacDonald has, inside a locked file cabinet in his home in Sarasota, Florida, an unfinished manuscript bearing the title *A Black Border for McGee*. As its name suggests the novel brings McGee's career to a close and has him dying a violent death. MacDonald says he keeps the manuscript ready "as leverage on my publisher." There have been times when MacDonald seriously considered bringing the McGee series to an end. After he finished *The Girl in the Plain Brown Wrapper*,

MacDonald swore it would be the last McGee, but he soon changed his mind. It is unlikely that we will be reading *A Black Border for McGee* anytime soon. After all MacDonald is still as inventive and energetic as ever, and there are hundreds of colors unused e.g., aquamarine, flame, auburn, avocado, brunette, beige, cherry, peach, pearl, puce, ocher, olive, honey, rose, violet, saffron, tangerine, umber, and white.

Mike Hammer—The Maligned and Bloody Knight

According to Pete Hamill, a novelist of no mean note himself:

> If Hammett was a Thirties Prizefighter, full of rough grace and a belief in the rules, and Chandler was a Joe DiMaggio, playing on ballfields of a summer afternoon, then Mike Hammer and Mickey Spillane were pro football: brutal, vicious, mean and literally pummeling their way into the American consciousness. Like pro football, Mike and Mickey reached their first large audience after World War II, telling them that winning wasn't everything, but—as Vince Lombardi would later say—it was the only thing.

As millions of readers are aware, Hammer's enormous appeal rests upon his toughness, his righteousness, his ruthlessness in the pursuit of justice, and the readiness with which he plays the role of judge, jury, and executioner. His willingness to dish out cruel and violent punishment, to revel in spilling the blood of the enemy, to deliver vengeance in rage and with extreme prejudice are literary traits that have fascinated readers who hunger for thrills and chills and for heroes of God-like proportions.

As an ex-comic book writer who helped create and insure the success of *Captain Marvel* and *Captain America*, Frank Morrison "Mickey" Spillane was clever enough to give the post-World War II public exactly what it was thirsting for. His first mystery novel, *I, The Jury* (1947), became the first mystery to sell over six million copies in the United States. Not only is Spillane the best-selling mystery novelist of all time but he is the best-selling *novelist*! At one time he was one of the most popular authors in the nation—having seven titles among the ten best-selling books of the century. Among the thirty top best-sellers from 1895 to 1965 seven were by Spillane. As of 1979 he has sold over one hundred million books at home and abroad. Most of these sales are due to the popularity of Mike Hammer. Spillane's popularity with the public is matched equally by his unpopularity with the established literary critics who hold Spillane personally responsible for, according to George Orella, "the perversions of the American detective novel," and who see in Mike Hammer "a hero who has descended to the bully, the sadist, the voyeur, no longer a hero at all, but merely a villain who claims the right always to be right." (Grella again.) And in John Cawelti's view, "By most traditional literary or artistic standards, the works of Mickey Spillane are simply atrocious. His characters and situations not only strain credulity to its limits, they frequently turn the stomach as well." The English critic and novelist Julian Symons is even more perturbed. He sees Hammer as a "monster masquerading as a hero" and after reviewing two of the Hammer novels concludes: "The most nauseating, and clinically disquieting, thing about these books is that Mike Hammer is the hero." Despite the critic's opinion, Hammer *is* a hero, and a hero, moreover, in a traditional sense.

Hammer is a single-minded fighting machine. Nearly all the plots of the Hammer novels revolve around Mike's redress of a terrible wrong done to his friends. The first Hammer novel, *I, The Jury* (1947), begins with the murder of his best friend, Jack Williams. During World War II Jack saved Hammer's life by taking a bayonet meant for Mike, in the arm. When Mike finds Jack dead with a .45 dumdum slug in his belly he swears revenge on the killer. Mike's friend Pat Chambers, Captain of Homicide, is also out to help. But as Mike points out,

> You're a cop, Pat. You're tied down by rules and regulations. There's someone over you. I'm alone. I can slap someone in the puss and they can't do a damn thing.... Some day, before long, I'm going to have my rod in my mitt and the killer in front of me. I'm going to watch the killer's face. I'm going to plunk one right in his gut, and when he's dying on the floor I may kick his teeth out."

As Mike begins his relentless pursuit of the killer the trail leads to a former gangster now in high society, a young man he is putting through college, a beautiful and seductive psychiatrist, a nymphomaniac and her normal twin sister, an ex-drug addict, and a retarded individual who raises bees. Mike slowly peels away the layers covering the truth, and the action leads relentlessly to a bloody and unforgettable climax.

In the second novel, *My Gun is Quick* (1950), Mike is out to avenge the murder of a red-headed streetwalker he calls "Red," who was killed by a hit-and-run driver. Mike suspects a combination chauffeur and bodyguard named Feeny Last, who works for a millionaire. Mike catches Feeny, beats him up, and dumps him in an open grave. After Mike absorbs several beatings himself, is shot at several times, and witnesses several killings, he meets a willing and winsome young lady named Lola, learns the identity of Red, and why she was killed. Mike is then able to wreak his terrible vengeance on the killers.

The third Hammer story, *Vengenace Is Mine* (1950), finds Mike drunk in a hotel room with a dead man. Mike is drunk because Lola, his love in *My Gun is Quick,* was killed. A friend of Mike's, Chester Wheeler, has been murdered with Mike's gun and the situation made to look like suicide. Hammer's friend, Pat Chambers of homicide, finds Mike and helps him even though Mike loses his license and his gun. Velda, his Secretary and right-hand woman, who also has a PI license and gun permit, takes over the business. Mike starts searching for the killer by contacting Wheeler's customers. In the process he meets Juno Reeves, a stunningly beautiful woman and the employer of one of the girls Wheeler was with the night he was murdered. He also meets Connie Wales who falls for Mike and takes him to a gambling den where he again meets Juno Reeves, who has located Marion Lester, the girl who was with Wheeler. With Velda's help Mike uncovers a blackmail operation and Chester's and other victims' killers. Then, as the title suggests, vengeance is Hammer's.

In *The Big Kill* (1951), the next Hammer novel, Mike is getting drunk in a bar one night when a derelict with a year-old kid comes in crying. He abandons the child and as he leaves the bar he is gunned down. Mike resents the fact the kid's father is killed and the kid has to pay. So he goes after the killers. In returning the killers' gunfire, Mike recognizes them as being in the hire of Lou Grindle. Next day Mike finds the kid's father was William Decker, an ex-con who was trying to go straight. Mike also learns the child's mother died of cancer a year before and that Decker was on the road back before he was killed. In tracking down the killers, Mike encounters a number of toothsome tootsies. Especially one Marsha Lee, an actress, who has her eye, and other parts of herself, set on Mike. Mike discovers that Decker got in deep with a loan shark and had to pull a robbery in order to pay off the debt. As in all of the Hammer novels, there are beatings and killings galore and the usual tense, Hairbreadth Harry ending.

The next novel, *One Lonely Night* (1951), has Velda captured by Communist spies. Mike pursues them relentlessly and manages to blow them away, but not before they manage to capture and torture Velda. In *Kiss Me Deadly* (1952), Mike picks up a big Viking-like blonde stranded in the middle of the highway. She is wanted by the police and has escaped from a sanitarium. Before Mike has a chance to know her, they are ambushed, she is tortured and killed, and she, Mike and Mike's car are shoved over a cliff. Mike manages to roll out at the last minute. The dead woman turns out to have been a witness for the FBI, and some Mafia baddies thought that Mike broke her out. When Mike swears to avenge the murder of the Viking he runs into trouble with the police, the FBI and the Mafia. As always, blood flows freely and shock is piled on shock at the novel's typically gory end.

Between *Kiss Me Deadly* (1952) and *The Girl Hunters* (1962) a decade elapsed. Spillane covered the lapse by having Hammer hit the bottle for seven straight years and wind up in the gutter. The reason for this behavior is simple: seven years earlier Mike sent Velda out on a job and she never came back. Mike assumed she was dead and overcome with despair began his slow suicide. First, Chambers rescues him, sobers him up, and tells him he needs Mike's help to solve a murder. A thug named Richie Cole has been shot and calls for Hammer. He tells Mike he was shot by someone called the Dragon and that Mike will never get "her" in time. "Get who?" Mike asks, and Cole's answer stuns him: "Velda." Seems Velda is still alive but the Dragon, a Communist conspiracy, will kill her unless Mike finds her first. Dragon masterminds an international network of spies and assassins. Mike, of course, completes his mission and gets Velda back but not before a number of assorted killings, seductions, near-seductions, beatings, bludgeonings and the usual final bloody act of vengeance.

In the next book, *The Snake* (1964), Mike is reunited with Velda after his seven-year intermission, Velda explains that it took her seven years "to learn a man's secret and escape Communist Europe with information that will keep us equal or better than they are." Velda has also taken in a 21-year-old blonde who is running away from a rich stepfather she fears and hates. When two gunmen try to shoot the runaway, Mike goes into action, and in the process uncovers an old crime that is haunting the present. Mike uncovers a million dollars in cash but before he can collect he is interrupted by the Snake, "the real Snake as deadly as they come," who gets the drop on him. Yet Mike prevails and lives to solve another case.

The Twisted Thing, published in 1966, is concerned with the kidnapping of a 14-year-old genius, Ruston York. The novel opens with Hammer witnessing the interrogation of Billy Parks, chauffeur to the father of the victim and an ex-con. A tough cop named Dilwick tortures Parks in front of Mike and when he threatens Mike, Dilwick is kneed and floored with typical Hammeristic dispatch. Mike goes to Rudolph York, the victim's father and a brilliant scientist, and starts tracking down the kidnappers. Along the way Mike encounters a he-man lady, an ex-stripper, and a nymphomaniac named Cousin Alice. Mike also learns that someone planned Rudolph's death and has succeeded in pulling it off. Mike has to get Ruston back and find the killer of Ruston's father.

In *The Body Lovers* (1967), Mike gets involved with an underground orgy cult made up of an international Who's Who of VIPs, Very Important Perverts, who throw sadistic soirees and hire sexy beauties to perform interesting sex acts. Unfortunately, on the morning after one of these orgiastic evenings two of the beauties wind up dead. Mike's job is to uncover the killers which, of course, he does. In *Survival Zero*, the last Hammer novel published in 1970, Lipton "Lippy" Sullivan, a friend that Mike grew up with, is knifed and left for dead in his bedroom. Mike gets to him before he dies, and Lippy tells him he was killed for "No reason, Mike, no reason." So Mike sets out again on a right-wing mission of vengeance. In the process he discovers a dastardly plot to destroy the nation. It seems that 22 Communist agents, working against their own government's best interests, have been planted in the country with a vaccine to protect a select few from a deadly bacteria that will destroy everyone except those innoculated with the vaccine. One key man has been assigned to release the deadly bacteria. Mike, of course, thwarts the plan, rounds up the agents and gets Lippy's killers.

Though he has been called vicious, brutal, bloodthirsty and worse, Mike is, nevertheless, a firm adherent to the chivalric code. Mike is a man of honor and a vigilante. He is a protector of the weak and helpless, and when he encounters the enemy and the oppressor he destroys them without a qualm. Furthermore, Mike's word is always good.

As for Hammer's personal life, we learn from the novels that he was born in New York in 1917 and went to school with Lippy Sullivan, and though he seldom mentions his early years, we do know he remembers fighting with the "Peterstown Bunch" and he also remembers growing up "watching Georgia Southern, Gypsy Rose Lee, Ann Corio, and the rest" on the stage of the old Apollo and Eltinge Theatres. Though he doesn't talk about his education, he went through the public schools, and it is likely he had some advanced training because he is well read and can recognize first editions and classical composers instantly.

Hammer opened his own PI office before World War II in either 1939 or 1940, and when the war came he enlisted, received desert warfare training and served in the Pacific theater where his friend Jack Williams saved Mike's life and lost an arm in the doing. After the war and back on the job in 1944, Mike reopened the "Hammer Investigative Agency" in a two-room suite, No. 808, in the Hackard Building in New York City. In 1944 Mike lured Velda to work for him as Secretary and Associate PI. Since she was with the Office of Strategic Intelligence during WWII, her experience qualified her for a PI's license which she obtained before joining Mike. Their office has an anteroom which holds Velda's desk and her typewriter, an antique bench, and two captain's chairs for waiting clients. Mike's office features a battered desk, a leather swivel chair, a file cabinet, a news clipping file, a trick lamp (for hiding important papers), a leather couch and a wash basin. Though the building is nondescript it is in a good location, has its own parking garage in the basement, good security with pickproof locks and watchmen as well as Nat Drutman, a good manager and one of Mike's friends.

Physically, Mike is difficult to describe since Spillane wants the reader to identify with Mike and see himself in Mike's shoes. In a 1979 interview with Michael Barson for *The Armchair Detective*, Spillane stated:

> I've never given a physical description of Mike Hammer at any time. I've described the girls or the adversary, but I've never described the hero . . . . This is one of the things you don't have to do . . . because a hero should be a figment of your imagination.

But on at least one occasion Mike has said "I'm no athlete," which is unnecesarily modest. Indirectly, we are led to believe that he is a fairly big man; at least six feet tall and weighing around 200 pounds, but at the end of his seven-year skid his weight drops to 168. His eyes are a mottled blue and brown, and facially he falls into the category of "rough ugly." Velda calls him ugly and he doesn't argue the point. On one occasion one of his many conquests tells him, "You're so ugly you're beautiful." He is a good dresser, wears custom tailored suits, ties and a pork-pie, battered felt hat eternally, both indoors and out. During inclement weather he wears a trench coat. His favorite weapon is a .45 automatic in a shoulder holster. When on a particularly demanding chase he may go several days without a shave or change of clothes. Mike's standard fee is $50 a day, including expenses, but he occasionally receives and cashes checks for $1,000, $5,000 and $10,000.

Without a doubt, Hammer is the most puritanical PI of all, refusing to sleep with Velda because, he says, "we're engaged." He has a hearty dislike of pornographers, homosexuals and personally eschews nudity, on one occasion refusing to go skinny dipping. Politically he is to the far right and has little affection for minorities, although he is friendly toward blacks "who know their place." He is imbued with a strong sense of patriotism and civic responsibility and wants to "clean up the world." Hammer's middle-America, right-wing leanings, more than anything else perhaps, have brought down the wrath of the critics, and to a certain extent the critics are right. Hammer is the antithesis of the sensitive intellectual. He is simple-minded, maudlin and sentimental. Spillane's plots are absurd. His style is a mess. The novels are an amalgam of soap opera and the comics. If anyone tries to take them more seriously or to read anything more into them, he is missing the target. The Hammer novels are comic strips without the pictures. They were written to entertain and to tell a good story. As a prime example of what a combination of soft porn, gore, rapid pace, retribution and horror, all put together in simple streamlined prose, can do to meet the entertainment needs of a bored, excitement-hungry population of paperback readers, the Hammer novels represent one of the most remarkable publishing triumphs of the twentieth century.

Spillane, a canny creator, has not only laughed all the way to the bank, but is still laughing. Within the last year or so his PI has begun to appear on TV and to acquire all the hallmarks of maturity and character that may, in time, make him a rival of Marlowe, Archer and Spade. The new, wiser and more sensitive Hammer, as recently portrayed by Stacy Keach, may even in the long run wind up winning the respect of the literary establishment. In 1984 The Mysterious Press published a collection of Spillane stories (*Tomorrow I Die*) under the editorship of Max Collins. One Hammer piece is included.

Frank Morrison "Mickey" Spillane was born in Brooklyn on 9 March 1918. He was educated in the public schools and later attended Kansas State

University in Manhattan, Kansas. He started his career writing for slick magazines and began selling stories in 1935. After some success he switched to the pulps and the comic magazines. He was instrumental in the development of Captain Marvel, Captain America and others.

During World War II he served in the Army Air Corps as a trainer of fighter pilots. Later in the war he flew a number of combat missions himself. In 1944 he married his first wife, Mary. They had four children but were divorced in 1962. In 1965 he married his present wife, Sherri. Sherri, a model, posed in the nude for the cover of his 1972 novel, *The Erection Set*. After the war he returned to the comics and then, doing what he always wanted, he got a job with Ringling Bros., Barnum and Bailey Circus as a trampoline artist. Following this brief period as a performer he joined the Federal Bureau of Investigation and helped break up a narcotics ring, receiving two bullet wounds and a knife stab during the investigation. He still carries the scars to support this claim. In 1952 he was converted to Jehovah's Witnesses and almost quit writing altogether. Following the success of the first five Hammer novels plus the one non-Hammer novel, *The Long Wait*, in 1951, he stopped writing until 1961. Although these first six books represent only a third of his output, they have accounted for two-thirds of his sales and have supplied the subject matter for two-thirds of the Spillane movies.

When Spillane stopped writing, a number of writers created new PIs to take Hammer's place and meet the public demand for this type of entertainment. Although the PIs who appeared and became popular during the middle and late fifties barely resembled Mike Hammer, a number of critics have erroneously accused Brett Halliday, Richard Prather, Evan Hunter (writing as Curt Cannon), John B. West, Michael Avallone and even John D. MacDonald, of modeling their heroes after Mike Hammer. Anyone familiar with the works of these writers—anyone who has read the novels rather than merely "reading about" them— obviously knows better. Most of them owe more to Hammett and Chandler than they do to Spillane and nearly all have added new dimensions and styles not found in Spillane's work. Spillane did begin to write again in the 1960s and between 1961 and 1967 published *The Deep* in 1961, *The Girl Hunters*, another Hammer novel, in 1962, and *Day of the Guns*, the first Tiger Mann novel, in 1964. Mann is involved in espionage work and is the American equivalent of James Bond. In their definitive Spillane biography, *One Lonely Knight: Mickey Spillane's Mike Hammer* (Popular Press, 1984) Max Collins and James Traylor describe Mann as "Mike Hammer, secret agent." *The Snake* (Hammer) also appeared in 1964. Then *Bloody Sunrise* and *The Death Dealers*, the second and third Tiger Mann novels, both appeared in 1965. *The By-Pass Control*, another Tiger Mann, and *The Twisted Thing* (Hammer) both appeared in 1966. In

1967, *The Body Lovers*, another Hammer, and *The Delta Factor* were published.

Following *The Delta Factor* Spillane shifted his literary gears and between 1970 and 1973 turned out three experimental novels: the last Hammer, *Survival Zero* (1970), *The Erection Set* (1972) a stated attempt on Spillane's part to write in the Jacqueline Susanne tradition "an even dirtier book than these women writers" and a novel called *The Last Cop Out* (1973), written entirely in the third person.

From the outset the Hammer novels were destined for the screen. United Artists signed a four-picture contract with Spillane in 1953 and filmed *I, The Jury* in 3-D with Biff Elliott as Hammer. Predictably, the plot was somewhat tamer for the screen. However, the film was not a huge success. *Kiss Me Deadly* appeared in 1955. Directed by Robert Aldrich, with Ralph Meeker as Hammer, the film grossed only $726,000. A disappointed United Artists went ahead with *My Gun Is Quick* in 1957 with Robert Bray as Hammer. The gross this time was a mere $308,000. Spillane was so upset with Hollywood's mangling of his work that he swore to never again allow his work out of his hands. He went so far as to establish his own film company with Robert Fellows, known as Spillane-Fellows Productions, located on East 37th Street in New York City.

Spillane is a *rara avis* in another respect: he is the only PI writer thus far to play himself *and* his private eye in the movies. In 1954 Spillane was cast as himself, a mystery writer, in the movie *Ring of Fear*. According to the plot, Clyde Beatty calls on his old friend Mickey Spillane to help track down and capture a psychopathic killer who is sabotaging Beatty's circus. Hammer was played by a real cop named Jack Stang. Although Stang looked the part he was definitely not an actor. Also in the early 1960s the Mutual Broadcasting System ran "That Hammer Guy" for a short while and in 1957-58 there was a television series featuring Darren McGavin as *Mickey Spillane's Mike Hammer*. The series was not renewed.

In the fourth and last film on the United Artists contract, *The Girl Hunters* (1963), Spillane was cast as Mike Hammer. The movie was filmed in England and despite an intensive promotional campaign and good solid performances by Spillane, Lloyd Nolan and Shirley Eaton, the picture still grossed less than a million dollars. People who were buying his books were not, it seems, going to the movies.

For the last decade Spillane has been content to devote himself to collecting his royalties, appearing on TV in Lite Beer commercials and enjoying the new Mike Hammer TV series starring Stacy Keach. It is very clear that we have not seen the last of either Mr. Spillane or Mr. Hammer.

Chapter IV
Knights of Old—The Hard-Boiled Standard Bearers
(1930-1970)

THERE WERE A NUMBER OF KNIGHTS who followed closely in the footsteps of the Princes of the Realm who were not of noble blood. Commoners though they are, their work has such skill that they deserve a place of honor at the table of champions only one position down from those of royal birth. The seventeen knights making up the body of this chapter have provided hours of entertainment and fully deserve the fame and glory a grateful kingdom can bestow. Since it is difficult to rank one knight higher than another, we will take them in alphabetical order by the author's last name. Since our first three knights work in or out of Chicago, we have dubbed them "The Chicago Knights."

The Chicago Knights: Ed and Am Hunter, Mac Robinson, Paul Pine
Ed and Am Hunter—Fredric Brown

Among the many pairs of PIs who are described in this volume, the tandem of Ed and Ambrose Hunter is the only uncle-nephew team to practice the detective business together. The Hunters were introduced in *The Fabulous Clipjoint*, Fredric Brown's splendid novel which won an Edgar for the best first novel of 1947. They are brought together when Am resigns his job with the carnival to come to Chicago to help Ed solve the murder of Ed's father (Am's brother). The title, one of the best in PI fiction, is drawn from a scene at the end of the novel when Ed and Am are looking out on Chicago from the top-floor cocktail bar of the Allerton Hotel:

We took a table by the window on the south side, looking out toward the Loop. It was beautiful in the bright sunshine. The tall narrow buildings were like fingers reaching toward the sky. It was like something out of a science-fiction story. You couldn't quite believe it, even looking at it.

"Ain't it something, Kid?"

"Beautiful as hell," I said. "But it's a clipjoint."

He grinned. The little laughing wrinkles were back in the corners of his eyes.

He said, "It's a fabulous clipjoint, kid. The craziest things can happen in it, and not all of them are bad."

Ed and Am were featured in six more novels. In *The Dead Ringer* (1948) they investigate the murder of a carnival midget (Brown had toured with a carnival in his younger days). *The Bloody Moonlight* (1949) and *Compliments of a Fiend* (1950) preceded *Death Has Many Doors* (1951) in which the Hunters open their own practice, the Hunter and Hunter Detective Agency, in Chicago. *The Late Lamented* (1959) and *Mrs. Murphy's Underpants* (1963) completed the series.

Ed and Am are a nicely balanced pair. Ed is a brash young man with lots of ambition. He has a weakness for beautiful murder suspects and is handsome enough to attract plenty of female attention. Ed is an innocent, but he learns quickly, especially under the seasoned tutelage of Uncle Am.

Am is middle-aged, chubby and wears a scruffy, black mustache. Though he has a twinkle in his eye, there is something else there—something deadly. Am is wily and streetwise, characteristics that stood him in good stead during his days as a carnival worker and private dick. He loves to play cards and often stays out all night at a good poker game.

Brown added Ed's idealism to Am's resourceful toughness to achieve a unique mixture that Ron Goulart praised as follows:

> He could work in the hard-boiled tradition . . . yet he comes across as a somewhat gentle tough guy, a man not quite as detached and cynical as some of his contemporaries. There is a sensibility underlying the book, an appreciation of the people who have to make their way on the mean streets and still manage to hold onto their honesty.

Throughout the Hunter (an apt name for PIs) series, Brown showcased his trademark skills: an imagination that soared beyond the genre's usual boundaries, clever wordplay (his friend, Robert Bloch reported that Brown once wondered aloud why people prefer a shampoo to a real poo) a tension between the romantic and the realistic, an ability to be tender and tough, narrative inventions, story twists, use of metaphor and a finely-tuned sense of irony that elevated some of his writing to the highest level.

Fredric Brown was born in Cincinnati in 1906. He attended the University of Cincinnati and Hanover College in Indiana and spent twelve years as an office worker in Cincinnati. Brown moved to Milwaukee where he joined the staff of the *Milwaukee Journal* as a proofreader and reporter. He sold his first short story in 1936 and over the years produced more than 300 stories—science fiction, mysteries, fantasy and detective stories were all in his repertoire.

Brown had a respiratory condition which forced him to move to the Southwest, living first in Taos, New Mexico and then in Tucson, Arizona. He worked in Los Angeles briefly writing scripts for TV shows such as the Alfred Hitchcock program, but his health problems required him to return to Tucson in the mid-sixties. He died in Tucson on March 11, 1972.

Brown was also well known for his science fiction writing. *What Mad Universe* (1949), expanded from a short story published a year earlier in *Startling Stories*, began his reputation as a sci-fi writer. *The Lights in the Sky are Stars* (1953) is regarded as one of his best novels. A collection of Brown's science-fiction stories edited by Robert Bloch appear in *The Best of Fredric Brown*. Brown also wrote one mainstream novel, *The Office* (1958), based on his own experience as an office worker in Cincinnati.

In addition to the Hunter series, Brown wrote more than 15 other mystery novels. Among the best are *The Screaming Mimi* (1949), *The Far Cry* (1951), *Knock Three-One-Two* (1959), *The Lenient Beast* (1956), and *The Deep End* (1952), an outstanding study of schizophrenia.

Several of Brown's works found their way to the big screen. Probably the most famous was Columbia's *The Screaming Mimi*, starring Anita Ekberg and Phil Carey. Brown's novels received considerable acclaim from critics and fellow authors. Anthony Boucher praised him, as did Ayn Rand. Mickey Spillane is reported to have called Brown his all-time favorite author. Robert Bloch singled out the following qualities of Brown's work:

The sardonic humor, the irony which at times brings to mind Ambrose Bierce. And yet there is a leavening element of playfulness which adds an extra dimension to his most savage satire or scaring cynicism. Add to this his gift for the realistic rendering of dialogue and accurate observation of character traits and the result is as impressive as it is entertaining.

Mac Robinson—Thomas B. Dewey

Another honorable Chicago knight is Thomas Blanchard Dewey's "Mac" Robinson. One of Mac's most likeable characteristics is his reluctance to use either a gun or his fists, although he will employ both with great skill for honorable and defensive purposes. Mac is one of the most humane PI's in modern fiction. He is also one of the wisest, most understanding and sympathetic. His heart is as big as a bushel basket and he is as compassionate as the Buddha himself. Mac is not only supersensitive to the frailties and foibles of humanity but also aware of the first noble truth: to live is to suffer.

Mac's motives, thinking and behavior are logical, reasonable, consistent and—above all—believable. More than most PIs, Mac is a true investigator rather than a brilliant logician, a hard-nosed avenger, or a don't-give-a-damn survivalist. When Mac gets to know his clients and the other people in his cases, he cares about them and tries to provide not only justice but counsel and guidance as well. If there is nothing else that Mac can do but sympathize, he does it intensely and we know there is nothing false about the emotions he reveals.

Another of Mac's winning traits is his modesty. In the first of the Mac novels, *Draw the Curtain Close* (1947), he says:

I'm just a guy. I go around and get in jams and then try to figure a way out of them. I work hard. I don't make very much money and most people insult me one way or another. I'm thirty-eight years old, a fairly good shot with small arms, slow-thinking but thorough and very dirty in a clinch.

Mac was a city cop when he was twenty-three. He started out in a uniform patrolling a beat on Chicago's west side. From the outset, however, he wanted to be a detective. Mac had a Sergeant named Donovan who trained him to be a detective in Mac's off hours. Donovan had him assigned to his own staff. When Mac did something of note Donovan saw that Mac got the credit. One night there was a nightclub hold-up and the robbers cleaned out the entire club. Pollard, the owner, was shot seventeen times. Donovan was on vacation and Mac cracked the case wide open. When Mac reported the facts and named the killers and their motives Mac started getting arguments all the way to the top. "When they fired me," Mac says, "for shooting off my mouth to one of the commissioners—Donovan helped me get this license. Being a cop was all I knew. I've done all right with it so far. Thanks to Donovan." Lt. Donovan figures in nearly every novel. Mac says, "I've known Donovan a long time .... He's more of a father to me than the real one I had once."

Mac is slow and methodical. On one occasion when one of his clients says, "be careful, please," his reply is, "Never fear ... I'm probably one of the most careful people in this town. I love life ...."

Mac's office and the place where he lives are one and the same. The office and the apartment are run together with the office in front and a bedroom, kitchen and bath in the rear. Mac also uses a call service in lieu of a secretary. He takes most of his food and drink at a bar-restaurant called "Tony's" directly across the street from his office. Mac likes beer and occasionally whiskey on the rocks. He also drinks a lot of coffee.

Although most of Mac's cases take place in Chicago, three of them occur in California where, in all three of the stories, he is assisted by another sympathetic cop, the fifty-year-old Lieutenant Lou Shapiro, a tough and reliable career man. For fifteen consecutive novels Dewey studiously avoids giving away Mac's family name. It is not until *The Love Death Thing* (1969) that finally, on page 41 when Mac is trying to reach Shapiro, the operator asks who is calling and he answers: "Mac Robinson, Ambassador Hotel, Room Seven Fourteen ...." Here, for the first time, we learn Mac's last name. This literary gimmick inspired Bill Pronzini years later when he created his now famous and totally "Nameless" PI.

The novels are consistently good, well-crafted, lucid and entertaining. One of the best is *Deadline* (1966) in which Mac in his quiet, easy-going way is hired to try to save a twenty-two year old from the electric chair. According to the condemned boy's lawyer, the accused is emotionally incompetent and is being railroaded. Mac has no clues, leads or help and only four days to come up with the right answers. He goes to a small country town where the crime occurred and despite the townfolk's opposition, manages to uncover the real murderer and stop the execution. Even though the reader knows the boy will be saved, Mac's beautifully orchestrated playing of the theme is a joy to follow.

One of the most compassionate and sympathetic of the cases is *A Sad Song Singing* (1963). Mac is hired by a teenaged singer to find her guitar-playing boy friend. Despite all of Mac's compassionate efforts, the search ends up in the discovery of a payroll robbery and an inevitable tragedy. The story and the characterizations are excellent and it is one of Mac's best. *Don't Cry for Long* (1965), *The Girl Who Wasn't There* (1960) involving twin sisters, *The King Killers* (1968) concerned with a neo-Fascist organization, *Death and Taxes* (1967) about gangland slayings and *The Mean Streets* (1955) concerned with juvenile delinquency are also well worth the reader's time.

Dewey clearly shows his sympathy and concern for the younger generation. For example, in *A Sad Song Singing*, when his seventeen-year-old client is crying for her lost boy friend, Mac says:

I had no words of comfort for her. There was too much time between us. What hurts like death at seventeen may be a muffled pang at my age, and there is no way to explain this across the years.

Dewey knew the Midwest well. Not only was he born in Elkhart, Indiana in 1915, but he traveled widely throughout Ohio, Michigan, Illinois, and Iowa as a child and young man. He received a Bachelor of Science in Education degree from Kansas State Teacher's College (now Emporia State) in 1936 and he did graduate work at Iowa in 1937 and 1938 before moving to California where he received his Ph. D. from UCLA in 1973. Dewey held a number of writing and editorial jobs during his career including a stint with the State Department, a magazine editorship, and several years with a Los Angeles advertising agency. He also taught English at Arizona State University for several years before turning to free-lance writing on a full-scale basis. So far Dewey has published a total of thirty-four mystery novels and over fifty short stories.

Dewey is also the creator of two other memorable detectives. A PI named Pete Schofield appears in nine novels: *And When She Stops* (1957); *Go to Sleep Jeannie* (1959); *Too Hot For Hawaii* (1960); *The Golden Hooligan* (1961); *Go Honeylou* (1962); *The Girl With The Sweet Plump Knees* (1963); *The Girl in The Punchbowl* (1964); *Only on Tuesdays* (1964); and *Nude In Nevada* (1965). One unusual fact about Pete is that he is a PI who is happily married. Dewey also created a non-PI detective named Singer Batts and featured him in four early novels: *Hue and Cry* (1944); *As Good as Dead* (1946); *Mourning After* (1950); and *Handle With*

Fear (1951). Batts owns a hotel in the fictional town of Preston, Ohio, is a bookworm, and a Shakespearean scholar who also thinks like a cop. Several of Dewey's stories have been adapted for television and he was elected a Director-At-Large of the MWA in 1960.

Readers interested in Mac are very fortunate. Pocket Books has recently reprinted a number of Dewey's earlier novels.

Paul Pine—John Evans (Howard Browne)

John Evans' Paul Pine is, in some ways, Mac's equal and in others, his superior. Though Paul lacks Mac's understanding and compassion he is, nevertheless, a considerate and sensitive individual who cares about others. At the end of *Halo in Blood* (1946), for example, when he is accused of being hard and bitter, Paul's answer is:

I don't think I'm hard or calloused or bitter. At least I don't mean to be. I get wet-eyed in the movies once in a while, and I think kids are wonderful. Maybe I give the impression you get, Leona, because my work makes me see people as they actually are. Oh I used to be a trusting soul. I thought people, even the shoddy ones, would give a straight deal if they got one themselves. And I used to go to bat for them, right down to the line. But after a few years of being lied to and cheated and doublecrossed—well I quit handing out halos. Too many of them were turning out to be tarnished instead of glowing; red instead of gold ... halos in blood.

While Pine is not as tough as Spade or Hammer he is tougher than Mac and equally as sophisticated in his dealing with cops. About his own occupation, he says, "You sat and listened or you stood and listened. And when the callouses got thick enough so you didn't fidget, then you could be a private detective."

In Pine's debut in *Halo in Blood* (1946) we learn that he worked as an investigator for two years in the State Attorney General's office before a change of administration encouraged him to get a PI license. Pine is thirty-one, five feet eleven, a hundred and seventy pounds. He sports a dent in his nose courtesy of high-school football, and he has an office—a reception room and an inner office—on the eighth floor of the twelve-story Clawson Building on the south side of East Jackson Boulevard, just west of Michigan Avenue in Chicago's loop. The reception room features a second-hand leather couch, two chairs and a reed table with old magazines. The inner office has an oak desk with a golden oak swivel-chair for Paul. There are also two brown metal filing cabinets, a padded leather customer's chair for clients and a Varga-girl calendar.

Paul likes dry martinis and bourbon. He lives in an apartment hotel—the Dinsmoor Arms—on Wayne Avenue. He prefers a .38 to a .45 but what he is really good at shooting is similes, metaphors and creative turns of phrase. Here are a few examples:

He was as clean as a commencement day neck...
His smile was as bleak as the Siberian Steppes...
...a hand the color and texture of Billy The Kid's saddle...
...as cold as a barefoot Eskimo...
...a rusted screen door that had long since stopped being a problem to flies.
He sat like that, not moving, carved out of stone, while the knives of memory cut him apart inside.
She said a few choice words that crackled like the weighted tip of a mule whip...
Her smile was as guarded as her eyes and her eyes were as guarded as the Philadelphia Mint.
She was sitting as stiff as a cement pretzel ...
...and her eyes were as dry as Carrie Nation's cellar.
...an alibi as shaky as the bed in a bridal suite.
The silence was as heavy as the bottom of a glacier.

Lest there be any doubt, John Evans—the pen name of Howard Browne—can write. He is a master of the nutshell characterization. Here is the description of a minor character in *Halo In Brass* (1949):

She was an inch or two over five feet but it took spike heels to put her there. She was too thin in the legs, you could knit a sweater with her arms and her waist looked like somebody's thumb. Her dark hair had a beauty-shop curl and she wore it piled high on top where it would look the worst. You see dozens like her around hotel lounges and cocktail bars any afternoon of any week—pretty in a standard way, shrill in the voice, feverish of eye and hard around the mouth.

In describing an older woman:

She was one of those small birdlike females who are active in church socials and the local chapters of the Eastern Star, and who work up quite a reputation for strawberry preserves. She would go into her eighties and die with patient resignation knowing in advance that the wings would fit and the harp would be in tune.

Even passing glances at people are marked with sharp and graphic insight:

Up to now his share of the conversation had been held down to breathing and knuckle popping. He was a tall gangling man who wore a necktie as though it were a hangman's noose and who would never really be at ease without a plan to lean on.

Ordinary landscape descriptions, in Evans' hands, are filled with life and wicked wit:

The sun was very bright and very hot, although this was nearly the end of September, and there was no breeze to speak of. I drove slowly on, sniffing at the strangely pleasant odor of what I finally decided was fresh air. They didn't have air like that in Chicago. They hardly had air there at all—just gas fumes with soft coal smoke to give it body....

Finally, his observations of human behavior are precise and as on target as a heat-seeking missile. Watching a number of well-to-do citizens gamble, he notes:

The motionless air carried the crisp rattle of chips, the dry even murmur of croupiers, the shrill voices of women. Put almost any woman in an evening gown and stick a glass in her hand and her voice automatically goes up three octaves. Change the glass for a stack of chips and the walls ring.

There are three Haloes—*Halo In Blood* (1946), *Halo For Satan* (1948) and *Halo In Brass* (1949). All three are well plotted and give us surprise endings. Only one manages to tip us off in advance.

Browne's narrative skill is no fluke. His ability is that of a professional who learned his trade writing for nearly all the media—newspapers, magazines, TV, radio and the movies. He was born in Omaha, Nebraska in 1908 and educated in Lincoln but he considers Chicago his home. After a stint as a department-store credit manager (1929-1941), Browne worked as an editor for the Ziff-Davis Publishing Company from 1941 to 1951 in both New York and Chicago. Moving to California in 1956 he made a good living as a free-lance writer turning out a number of movie and TV scripts for programs such as *Columbo, Destry, 7 Sunset Strip, Maverick, Mannix, Alias Smith and Jones, Cheyenne, The Fugitive, Mission Impossible, The Virginian, Kraft Mystery Theater* and *Playhouse 90.*

Between 1939 and 1955 Browne contributed over 300 short stories, articles and novelettes to the pulps as well as to a number of "slicks" including *Cosmopolitan, Redbook, Esquire* and *American Magazine.* Browne started writing as an escape from his 9 to 5 credit manager's job. Early in his writing career he came under the influence of James M. Cain and Raymond Chandler. In his words, "They were doing the kind of books I'd wanted to do before I'd read—or even heard of—either man." Unfortunately Browne published only six mystery novels: the three Halos and *Thin Air* (1954), *The Taste of Ashes* (1957) and *If You Have Tears* (1952). Pine is featured in all except the last one; this is an ironic story about a bank official who falls in love with his new secretary and plans to get rid of his wife.

When Browne retired in 1973 he had the enviable record of having been employed—at one time or another—by every major studio in Hollywood. Some of his movies include: *Portrait of A Mobster* with Vic Morrow portraying Dutch Schultz; *Capone* starring Ben Gazzara in the title role; and *The Saint Valentine's Day Massacre* with George Segal and Jason Robards. In a rare 1976 interview Browne said, "For the past 20 years I've written nothing except for the screen. Now that I'm semi-retired I'm going back to writing books." If he has turned out any additional Pines we have not been able to find them. Browne was an active member of the MWA for several years and he is also a member of The Writer's Guild.

The Mutt and Jeff Knights—Bertha Cool and Donald Lam—
A.A. Fair (Erle Stanley Gardner)

Under the pseudonym A.A. Fair, Erle Stanley Gardner, the famous California trial lawyer and world famous creator of Perry Mason, wrote a series of PI novels featuring as unlikely a pair of snoopers as the brain could concoct: Bertha Cool and Donald Lam. Bertha is "a sizeable hunk of woman with the majesty of a snow-capped mountain and the assurance of a steam roller." Bertha is somewhere in her sixties, with gray hair, sparkling gray eyes and a benign grandmotherly expression. She weighs in at over two hundred pounds. She is as penurious as Scrooge before his encounter with the ghosts, and when she puts a hammerlock on a penny it is permanently put. Bertha has a big neck, big shoulders, a big bosom, big arms and a big appetite. She is also head of *Cool Confidential Investigations,* a PI agency she inherited from her dead husband.

The first Cool and Lam novel, *The Bigger They Come* (1938), begins with Donald Lam, an unjustly disbarred attorney, applying for work with the Cool agency. Twenty-nine year old Donald is about five and a half feet tall and he weighs only one hundred and twenty-seven pounds. When he goes after the job his fortune is down to a dime and he hasn't eaten in over twenty-four hours. Because Lam is, in Bertha's estimation, such a good liar he gets the job despite Bertha's reservations about Donald's size and his ability to handle himself in a fight.

Bertha is a most remarkable character who, on her own admission, likes profanity, loose clothes and loose talk. In her words:

I want to be comfortable. Nature intended me to be fat. I put in ten years eating salads, drinking skimmed milk, and toying with dry toast. I wore girdles that pinched my waist, form-building brassieres, and spent half my time standing on bathroom scales.

And what in hell did I do it for? Just to get a husband.

It seems that Bertha got one and then one day after she caught him two-timing her, she gave up her diet and ate normally. Following Henry Cool's death Bertha assumed command—of his business, her life and everything else.

Of the two, Donald is the one with the smarts. In fact it was his cleverness and genius that got him disbarred. He bet one of his clients that it would be possible to commit a murder in such a way that there was nothing anyone could do about it. The client turned out to be a small-time gangster and when he was arrested he squealed about having the bet with Lam. Donald was right, there are legal loopholes; but the Bar Association felt what Donald had done was unethical and they disbarred him anyway. Later on in *The Bigger They Come*, Lam proves his point in brilliant fashion.

Another steady and likeable character in the series is Bertha's secretary Elsie Brand. Elsie and Donald have an off-and-on semiserious admiration society going, but nothing romantic ever seems to develop. Bertha is given to a numer of pet expressions from time to time. Whenever she is flabbergasted out comes, "Can me for a sardine," or "I'll be a dirty name," or "Why you little devil," or something equally archaic. Bertha also loves jewels and wears them on both hands. As far as the casework is concerned, Bertha's philosophy is simple. "A lot of agencies won't handle divorce cases and politics. I'll handle anything there is money in. I don't give a damn who it is or what it is, just so the dough's there." Bertha's mercenary behavior goes even further; she pays Donald a monthly guarantee which she keeps as low as possible and she in turn sells his services for as much as she can get—the exact amount is, of course, not communicated to Lam. She excuses her behavior on the grounds of having suffered so much during the depression of the early thirties. Donald is always after her to loosen up so he can get the job done. The by-play between Donald and Bertha in the struggle over money is reliably amusing.

Of the twenty-nine novels one of the best is *Spill The Jackpot* (1941) set in Vegas. It opens with Bertha in a sanitarium with both the flu and pneumonia. It is a well-plotted mystery combining a disappearance and a murder in an unusually effective manner. In *Double Or Quits* (1941), another of the better books, Lam is a suspect in one murder, is forced to confess to two more and then gets himself in real trouble by drinking from a bottle of poisoned Scotch. Donald also earns himself a full partnership and the agency changes its name to *Cool and Lam*. In *Owls Don't Blink* (1942) Bertha and Donald tangle with two women who switch clothes, names and identities to complicate the murder plot. *Bats Fly At Dusk* (1942) has Bertha wanted by the cops for burglary and suspected murder. In *Give 'Em The Axe* (1944) Donald has just gotten out of the Navy as the result of having contracted a tropical disease while fighting World War II in the South Pacific. Moreover Bertha's weight is now down to a hundred and sixty-five and Donald's is up to a hundred thirty-five. Elsie Brand—the loyal and likeable secretary—is still pounding away on the typewriter and the cases are still coming in—but not as fast as in pre-war times. Bertha has been accepting domestic cases and she hands Lam one in which all he has to do is get the goods on the new wife of a client's old flame. But, as in all domestic cases, there are two sides to the story. On one side Donald finds blackmail and on the other a murder. In *Crows Can't Count* (1946) Cool and Lam acquire a rich client who offers them $500 to find a piece of antique jewelry. Lam clears this up in no time but in finding the pendant he uncovers a murder and even more money than Bertha can shake a stick at—a trust fund, a gold mine, emeralds and a fat fee for the firm after Donald runs down the killers.

Of additional interest are the forewords that Gardner wrote for a number of the cases. The expressed purpose of these forewords beginning with *Beware The Curves* (1956) and dedicated to Arthur E. Bernard, Warden of the Nevada State Penitentiary at Carson City, is to alert the public to the need for prison reform. Others include *You Can't Die Laughing* (1957) dedicated to Percy Lainson, warden of the Iowa State Prison at Fort Madison; *Some Slips Don't Show* (1957) dedicated to Joseph E. Ragen, warden of the Illinois State Penitentiary at Joliet; *The Count of Nine* (1958) dedicated to Douglas C. Rigg, warden of the Minnesota State Prison at Stillwater; *Pass The Gravy* (1961) dedicated to Robert A. Heinz, warden of the California State Prison at Folsom; and *Kept Women Can't Quit* (1960) dedicated to Preston G. Smith, warden at the Terminal Island, California Federal Correctional Institution. An earlier dedication in *Some Women Won't Wait* (1953) for Thomas L. Sidlo, Chairman of the Public Relations Committee of the American Bar Association attempts to win greater support and respect for attorneys. The forewords all show Gardner's deep concern for our prisons and for prison officials. This same concern for miscarriages of justice underlay Gardner's work in founding *The Court of Last Resort,* a private organization devoted to helping men believed to have been unjustly convicted. Gardner's 1952 book of the same name was awarded an MWA Edgar for the best work in factual crime.

As for Gardner, Alva Johnston once called him "the Henry Ford of detective mysteries," and Frances M. Nevins referred to him as "one of the great natural storytellers." Certainly he is one of the best-selling writers of the twentieth century. Gardner sold his first mystery story to a pulp magazine in 1923 and between 1923 and 1932 he sold hundreds of stories—westerns, mysteries and even sex tales—to the pulp magazines of the time. Using a large number of pseudonyms—C.M. Green, Robert Parr, C.J. Kenny, Carlton Kendrake, Les Tellray, Kyle Corning, et. al.—he often had several magazines publishing more than one at the same time. In 1932 (when a dollar was worth something) he earned the astounding amount of $20,525 from magazine sales alone.

In 1933 he published the first Perry Mason novel, *The Case of the Velvet Claws.* Mason was an immediate success. The novels have been filmed, radioed and TVed in series after series from the 1930s to the seventies. At one time when Gardner was at the height of his creative output he employed six secretaries working full time transcribing his novels, nonfiction, articles and answering his voluminous correspondence.

Gardner, born in 1889, worked in a number of different occupations as a young man and traveled widely. From 1908 to 1911 he read and studied law and in 1911 was admitted to the California bar. He practiced law from 1911 to 1918 in Oxnard and became widely known as a champion of the underdog. In 1921 he joined a Ventura law firm and began to write fiction to increase his income. He wrote over 4,000 words a day for many, many years.

Gardner was a man of many interests including archeology, natural history, psychology and geology. He was an excellent photographer and a crack shot. He hunted for many years but as he grew older he gave it up on the grounds that it was not very sporting—the odds were weighted too heavily in favor of the hunters. Gardner had a great interest in and love for Mexico—particularly Baja and he wrote thirteen nonfiction accounts about Baja, the American desert, and the Sacramento Delta. When asked why he wrote mysteries he replied:

I write to make money and I write to give the reader sheer fun. People derive a moral satisfaction from reading a story in which the innocent victim of fate triumphs over evil. They enjoy the stimulation of an exciting detective story. Most readers are beset with a lot of problems they can't solve. When they try to relax their minds keep gnawing over these problems and there is no solution. They pick up a mystery story, become completely absorbed in the problem, see the problem worked out to a final and just conclusion, turn out the light and go to sleep. If I have given millions that sort of relaxation, it is reward enough.

Though there are a number of biographies of Gardner, two of the best are Alva Johnston's authorized *The Case of Erle Stanley Gardner* published in 1947 while Gardner was still alive, and Dorothy B. Hughes' *Erle Stanley Gardner; The Case of The Real Perry Mason* published by his own publisher, William Morrow & Co., Inc., in 1978, eight years after his death.

Gardner wrote eighty-two full length Mason novels which, in all editions, have sold more than 300,000,000 copies. In addition to the twenty-nine Cool and Lam novels, Gardner also wrote nine mysteries featuring the D.A. Doug Selby, seven non-series mysteries and four collections of novelettes and short stories, two non-fiction books concerning crime and countless short stories for the pulps and slicks. Among the giants of American mystery fiction, Gardner was one of the tallest giants of them all.

The Rock-Like Knight: Brock Callahan
William Campbell Gault

Of all the private eyes in this collection none is more knightly than William Campbell Gault's Brock "The Rock" Callahan. Moreover, of all the PIs Brock comes the closest to being a normal, middle-class, neighborly nice guy. He's as regular as rain, as ordinary as sin and as American as pie a-la-mode. In fact, he was an All-American in football at Stanford. He was one of the greatest linemen the Indians (now Cardinals) ever had. Following his collegiate career—which included playing in two Rose Bowl games—he moved to the Los Angeles Rams where he became the best guard in LA history: All-Pro three years in a row and, in the eyes of LA fans as good as, if not better than, Merlin Olsen. Among football experts Brock is ranked among the best linemen in the history of the game. After he became too old to play Brock got his PI license and settled down to becoming a full-time professional knight and problem solver.

Brock weighs two hundred and twenty pounds and would probably be in better shape and weigh a few pounds less were he not so fond of Einlicher beer—the finest beer in the world—which he consumes in prodigious quantities. This is the only thing he drinks except on rare occasions when he drinks Wild Turkey and water. Brock works out of a small pine-paneled office in Beverly Hills where the door letters spell out: *Brock Callahan—Discreet Investigations At Moderate Rates.* And in Brock's words, "My rates were still moderate, but my investigations covered some areas now to which the words 'discreet investigations' might not apply. Substitute 'muscle'." Brock has mixed emotions about his profession. He resents being tagged a "peeper." According to Brock, "In a country that extols private enterprise, private eyes should get more respect than they do." Brock does not do divorce work and he prides himself on his integrity. Brock also gets along well with the cops who, with few exceptions, admire and respect him. One of the primary reasons for this is Brock's own respect for others. As Anthony Boucher noted:

Observe his relationships with this clients, with the criminals he tracks down, with the police, and above all with women; and behold a subtle and admirable picture of an honest man trying not merely to maintain his own integrity but to concede to others their right to their own wholeness.

In many ways we are left with the feeling that Brock is, basically, too decent a man to be caught up in such a profession. In his own words in *Vein Of Violence* (1961):

In most murder cases, the obvious is the true, but the standard cases do not usually come to the direct attention of the private investigator. Men in my despised profession usually deal only with the devious and the deviates, and there are rarely any obvious conclusions to be drawn from the shenanigans of these kinds of people.

Brock's knightly qualities show up most prominently in his relationships with women. One woman primarily—Jan Bonnet, an interior decorator, who makes enough money for both of them to live on most comfortably were it not for Brock's manly pride that insists the man should be the breadwinner—or at least make more bread. Therefore, throughout eight of the nine Callahan novels, Brock lives alone in his small Westwood apartment. Brock, however, is no saint. Although he remains true to Jan, he has several lapses. He considers love-making to women, other than Jan, therapeutic. And though his services are not for sale, he likes being asked. As he puts it, "Don't get me wrong; no woman can buy me with her body. But only a prude would discourage them from trying." On another occasion he muses, "I am monogamous by instinct, but Jan is emotionally erratic, with long barren stretches for which I must maintain outside sources. Women . . . the poor bedeviled devils . . . . I fell asleep feeling sorry for the producer."

One of the most intriguing aspects of the Callahan novels is the continuity maintained from one novel to the next. Brock shows up first in *Ring Around Rosa* (1955) in which he has just gotten his license. In the next story, *Day Of The Ram* (1956) Brock investigates the blackmailing of one of his ex-teammates on the LA Rams. In the third, *The Convertible Hearse* (1957), Brock investigates the hot-car racket. In the fourth, *Come Die With Me* (1959), Brock looks into murder and larceny. In the next, *Vein of Violence* (1961), Brock investigates the murder of an aging ex-movie queen and befriends a Texas millionaire who, a few novels later, in *The Bad Samaritan* (1982) leaves Brock enough money for him to live comfortably on for the rest of his life and enough for him finally to marry Jan. As Brock says, "Hard work, honest dealing, persistence, intelligence—and being Aunt Sheila's nephew had finally earned me the financial security that is every American's birthright." In *County Kill* (1962) Brock helps an 11-year old boy clear his father of a murder charge. In *Dead Hero* (1963) Brock looks into the murder of a public hero. In his latest novel, *The Cana Diversion* (1982) Brock is bored with his new-found wealth and when a fellow PI, Joe Puma, is found with a bullet through his head Brock goes back to being a PI again and allies himself with CANA— Citizens Against Nuclear Armageddon—to bring the killer to justice. *The Cana Diversion* was good enough to win the 1983 MWA Best Paperback Novel award. In this novel, Joe Puma, the hero of six prior PI novels, turns out to be something of a villain. It seems that Joe was going to finger an FBI informant for a fee of thirty thousand dollars. This breach of ethics backfired. Brock blames Puma's death on their profession, "Dirty jobs are bound to soil the men who work at them . . . . Puma was in the same business I used to be in. It's a dirty business. He had a wife to support and a kid he hoped to get into law school. If he turned dirtier than the rest of us . . ." Brock ends the sentence with a shrug.

One of Brock's most interesting aspects is his relatively peaceful nature. Unlike most fictional PIs he seldom uses a gun, is only rarely knocked in the head, and his resorts to violence are most infrequent. He is, however, well up to the challenge when violence is required.

In *The Bad Samaritan* Brock takes on some porno film makers who are using underaged kids:

The lamp I hit Al with was smaller than the one Amos had thrown through the window, but it was cut glass and it had cut up his forehead pretty good. The blood running down over his eyes could have been the reason his looping overhand hand missed me by a foot.

I put my own right into his nose to hamper his breathing, as Angelo circled to get a side shot at me.

Together they could have taken me—maybe. But from the doorway Jack called, "Hey, Angelo, baby. This way. You're mine, Angie!"

Al had no partner now. It was man to man and I honored the tradition. I didn't try to disfigure him, only to make sure he would spend the rest of his life in pain. As I have mentioned before, I like kids.

Though Brock is a native Californian and has spent his entire career in the LA vicinity, he is no admirer of the City of Angels. Brock refers to it constantly as "smogtown" and in one acid comment says, "Los Angeles is not California, not in any way. Los Angeles is a fungus that will some day destroy California."

Brock's knightly qualities are abundant. In *The Bad Samaritan* one of Brock's friends tells him, "I always pictured you on a horse," she said, "A big white horse, strong enough to carry your armor. Go with God, amigo." To support her vision Brock picks up two teenage hitchhikers on their way to LA. With subtlety and wisdom, Brock convinces them there's no place like home. This vignette ends with Brock driving the two to the bus station—at their insistence—to catch the bus back home.

At the bus station in the San Fernando Valley, I bought them two tickets for San Francisco and gave Don a double sawbuck.

"Take a cab from San Francisco," I said, "Go home in style."

"If you'll give me your address," he said, "I'll——"

"Forget it. Go home and learn your trade, whatever that is. You sound like an engineer to me."

"I'm a pretty good mechanic," he said. "I've rebuilt a couple of old Jags and sold them."

"Could I kiss you?" Dianne asked.

"If you don't think it would excite you too much."

She kissed me, he shook my hand, and then they had to hurry for the bus, already loading.

I stood there. People sat on benches and read, or ate their lunches out of paper bags. Some bought tickets, some boarded buses, some got off. Not one of them had the grace to walk up and pin a Good Samaritan medal on me.

Gault's second PI, Joe Puma, is big and arrogant and not as well educated nor as middle class as Brock. His clientele are lower down in the social scale. In *End Of A Call Girl* (1958) Joe's client is a madam. In *The Hundred Dollar Girl* (1961) the client is the wife of a prizefighter. Joe is a licensed PI who carries a .38 and uses it when necessary. He is as hard-boiled as a two-hour egg and as honest as necessary. As he sees it, " 'Sergeant,' I said pompously, 'complete honesty is suicide in any business, any marriage, any art or any relationship. I'm as honest as any in my profession and much more honest than the majority of them." At another time Joe says, "I'm not exactly Galahad, but I do have to stay in business and that means I must be careful."

Puma, of Italian stock, shows up first in *End Of A Call Girl* in 1958 and appears in six other novels: *Night Lady* (1958), *Sweet Wild Wench* (1959), *The Wayward Widow* (1959), *Million Dollar Tramp* (1960), *The Hundred Dollar Girl* (1961) and the last, *The Cana Diversion* (1982) in which Puma is murdered. The Puma novels are terse, tough, well-plotted and worth any PI lover's attention. The biggest problem is finding them in second-hand bookstores and large libraries.

William Campbell Gault is one of the very best writers in the mystery and suspense genre and is deserving of all the praise that can be heaped upon his aging head. Art Scott has summed it up beautifully in commenting on Gault's work:

His work has been undeservedly neglected and long out of print, lost in the mass of mostly mediocre private-eye fiction that flooded the mystery field in the 1950s. His two series private eyes, Brock Callahan and Joe Puma, are memorable, believable characters, notable for their directness, integrity and—atypically for most 1950s private eyes—healthy, non-satyr-like relationships with women.

It is incredible that any writer with such abilty and skill and one who has never written a weak book could be so neglected by the quality-entertainment hungry public. In an interview not long ago Gault stated, "My Edgar winner—*Don't Cry For Me*—came out in 1952 and was out of print two months later. In 1952 I also wrote a juvenile novel, *Thunder Road*, which is still in print. So, one has to eat . . . . My only mystery fame lately has been in someone else's novel—Ross Macdonald dedicated *The Blue Hammer* to me."

Gault was born in 1910 in Milwaukee and attended the University of Wisconsin, graduating in 1929. On his way to becoming a great writer he worked as a waiter, busboy, shoe sole cutter and mailman. From 1932 to 1939 Gault was the manager and part owner of the Blatz Hotel in Milwaukee. During World War II he served with the 166th Infantry from 1943 to 1945. Writing professionally since 1941 Gault has contributed almost three hundred short stories to the pulp and slick magazines. He has written approximately twenty-five mystery novels and nearly forty juvenile novels. He is a superb writer of sports stories and he is one of the most widely read juvenile writers in the nation. In 1957 the Boys Club of America gave him a special award for his novel *Speedway Challenge* and in 1968 he received an award from the Southern California Council On Literature For Children and Young People. Thus far he has received two awards from the MWA—an Edgar in 1952 for *Don't Cry For Me* and thirty-one years later an Edgar for *The Cana Diversion*. Anthony Boucher was a great admirer of Gault and at a recent Bouchercon held in Milwaukee

Gault was given a shoe sole as a special award. This was done because in 1936 Gault operated a shoe-sole cutting machine at the Weyenberg Shoe Factory in Milwaukee. At this time he was 26 years old and had just sold his first short story. The late Fredric Brown was also a great admirer of Gault's work, and in a review of Gault's first novel he said, *"Don't Cry For Me* is not only a beautiful chunk of story but, refreshingly, it's about people instead of characters, people so real and vivid that you'll think you know them personally. Even more important, this boy Gault can *write*, never badly and sometimes like an angel." This was said about his very first novel and Gault has improved over the years. In a recent interview for the *Ellery Queen Mystery Magazine,* when Gault was asked whether or not Brock Callahan resembled him, he replied, "Brock is probably what I'd like to be—tall, fairly handsome, and muscular. I'm none of these things, though muscular enough for a little guy—5'7", 160 pounds." Little though Gault may be in physical stature he is a giant among mystery writers of the twentieth century. To parody James Reston, "Should we sing 'Hail to Brock Callahan and William C. Gault?' " "Hail yes!"

The Prolific Knight:
Michael Shayne—Brett Halliday (Davis Dresser)

Private eye creators come in all shapes, sizes and shades of narrative skill as well as productivity. Some have only one or two novels to their credit while others can turn out a book of acceptable or even exceptional quality in a week or so. Davis Dresser, aka Brett Halliday, is one of the most prolific of all our PI parents. Moreover, he is the proud pappy of one of the most personable and photogenic PIs in history—a red-headed, tough, two-fisted Martell-drinking Mick named Mike Shayne. Few American PIs are better known or more widely read, heard or watched. Written over a forty year period (1939-1974), over 30 million copies of Halliday's Mike Shayne stories have been sold thus far. To date, Mike is the hero in sixty-odd novels, hundreds of short stories. fourteen movies, a radio series, a TV series and along with Shell Scott is the only PI thus far with a magazine named in his honor. Although the first Mike Shayne novel, *Dividend On Death,* was published in 1939 most of the Shayne novels are still in print. Written in 1935, it took Halliday four years to get the first book published since publisher after publisher turned it down.

Dresser's own personal history is as fascinating as any novel. He was born in Chicago in 1904 and spent his childhood in Texas until he ran away at fourteen and joined the U.S. Army. After basic training he was assigned to Fort Bliss in El Paso on the Mexican border. Davis managed to escape detection for two years before the Army discovered his age and discharged him. He went home and finished high school and then, as he phrased it, he set out "in quest of adventure." The only work he could find was as a roughneck in the oil fields and he worked every oil field from

Burkburnett, Texas to Signal Hill, California for nearly four years. Tiring of the work, he signed on as a deckhand on an oil tanker. One night when the tanker put into port at Tampico, Mexico, Halliday went ashore and wound up in a tough waterfront bar filled with Mexicans who disliked American sailors intensely. When some sailors entered the bar the only other American there was an outsized redhead sitting alone in the rear drinking tequila. Inevitably, a fight broke out and Davis was slugged and knocked to the floor. Badly outnumbered and unarmed against the Mexicans who were armed with knives, the sailors faced a grim situation. Seeing the odds, the big redhead waded into the Mexicans and lined an escape path to the door with unconscious native bodies. The grateful sailors departed and Dresser never forgot the favor. Realizing the dead end of a sailor's life, Dresser left the sea and enrolled in Tri-State College in Indiana and earned a certificate in civil engineering. Still restless, he resumed his travels working as an engineer and a surveyor.

In 1927 he tried his hand at creative writing and despite his lack of success he persisted in sending stories to the pulps. As it did for Hammett, the depression aided his career. Since it was difficult to find engineering jobs Dresser kept writing. Using a number of pseudonyms—Anthony Scott, Asa Baker, Matthew Blood, Sylvia Carson, Peter Shelly, Kathryn Culver and others—he wrote dozens of adventure, mystery, western, love and sex sagas for the pulps.

One night in the early thirties, Dresser found himself in New Orleans' French Quarter in a Rampart Street bar looking for story material. Incredibly, he spied his savior—the big redhead sitting alone with a bottle of cognac in front of him. Dresser went over, introduced himself and the Irishman confided that he was a private eye in New Orleans on a case. Suddenly, the redhead stiffened and told Dresser to get up and get out of the saloon immediately and to forget he had ever seen him. Two toughs came into the bar as Davis was leaving. Watching from outside, Dresser saw the redhead leave with the two men—one on each side, hands in bulging pockets. Later that night Dresser decided to write a novel—a private eye novel—featuring the big, tough, cognac-drinking redhead whom he christened Mike Shayne.

It was not until 1938, however, that he had his first novel accepted by a publisher. This first one was called *Mums The Word For Murder* (1938) and he used the pseudonym Asa Baker. It took an additional year; before he was able to publish the first novel about his PI, Michael Shayne. This one was *Dividend on Death* (1939) and he used the pseudonym Brett Halliday. It was an immediate success and left both the public and his publisher clamoring for more.

Following his marriage to the mystery writer Helen McCloy, Dresser published a number of other books using the pseudonyms of Asa Baker,

Don David, Anderson Wayne and Hal Debrett—a joint pseudonym with his second wife Kathleen Rollins. None of these, however, brought him anywhere near the acclaim and success of his PI Shayne.

Halliday openly acknowledged his indebtedness to Hammett for much of the background and setting for his Michael Shayne novels. Also he gave credit to his wives, especially his last wife Mary Savage, who all were accomplished writers in their own right.

Mike Shayne, Miami's most famous shamus, is different from the typical PI in a number of ways. Though Mike uses his fists in nearly all of his sixty-some cases he seldom uses his gun, a .38 revolver. Brains, he argues, are always more effective than bullets over the long haul. Mike's affairs of the heart are also atypical. In the first novel *Dividend On Death*, for example, Shayne, meets Phyllis Brighton , a young beauty accused of murdering her mother. She falls in love with Shayne and tries to seduce him as the book ends. Shayne, much older, repulses her advances telling her to try again when she grows up. In the second book, *The Private Practice of Michael Shayne* (1940), Phyllis and Mike are engaged as the novel ends. Because of Hollywood's unwillingness to use married detectives in its movies, Dresser decided to kill off Phyllis and leave Shayne free. Therefore, between the next two novels, *Murder Wears A Mummer's Mask* (1943) and *Blood On The Black Market* (1943) Dresser has Phyllis die in childbirth.

After 20th Century Fox dropped the Shayne series, Dresser took Mike to New Orleans where he opens up an office much like Sam Spade's. Here Mike meets Lucille Hamilton. Mike is so smitten he brings her back to Miami as his secretary and she has occupied this position ever since. Dresser admitted that he, himself, didn't know what the situation was with Lucey and Mike. Though they are close and work together on most of the cases, there's neither mention nor suggestion of marriage. Mike often takes Lucey to dinner and drops by her apartment for talk and cognac (she keeps his special brand always on hand) but things stop there.

Because of his unwillingness to use a gun, Mike has taken some bad beatings over the years. Usually his fists manage to get him out of any scrape he gets into. Another reason for his escapes mentioned in several novels is "his ability to think like a criminal when necessary."

As for Mike's background, there is little to go on. According to Dresser he came into being in Tampico in 1938 and, in his words, "I don't know where or when he was born, what sort of childhood and upbringing he had. It is my impression that he is not a college man, although he is well educated, has a good vocabulary and is articulate on a variety of subjects." Mike's forte is his ability to use perseverance, ordinary common sense and guts. Moreover, there is more actual detection in the Mike Shayne cases perhaps than in any other PI series. Mike is one detective who detects. He doesn't need any gadgets or gimmicks. He approaches each case logically and systematically, follows the leads as they appear and when they evaporate, tries another one. Anthony Boucher has, on several occasions, praised Dresser for his ability to "play fair" with the reader in providing clues. Moreover, Barzun and Taylor note that even though the plots are often complex, they are reasonably and even adroitly worked through.

Mike has a number of acquaintances, but few good friends. One of the best is Timothy Rourke who manages to save Mike's skin on a number of occasions. Rourke, a crime reporter on a Miami paper, is tall, lean, disheveled and Mike's drinking buddy. He follows Shayne around for a scoop when the case is over. As for Mike's relations with the cops, he counts Will Gentry, the Miami Chief Of Police, as a friend and supporter. Peter Painter, Miami Beach's Chief of Detectives, is Mike's rival and his enemy. Painter comes out on the short end of every encounter. Sex, though always present, is neither excessive nor intrusive. At times, Shayne, like a true knight, appears almost virginal. In Boucher's anthology *Four and Twenty Boodhounds,* Dresser described Shayne as follows:

I think the most important characteristic in his spectacular success as a private detective is his ability to drive straight forward to the heart of the matter without deviating one iota for obstacles or confusing side issues. He has an absolutely logical mind which refuses to be sidetracked. He acts, on impulse sometimes, or on hunches; but always the impelling force is definite logic. It is this driving urgency and lack of personal concern more than any other thing, I think, that serves to wind up most of Mike's most difficult cases so swiftly.

Few of Shayne's cases last longer than one or two days. As Dresser says, on all of Mike's cases he gives the reader exactly the same facts and information that Shayne has at any one time.

Among the cases themselves, the most interesting due to locale and incidental characters are *Murder Wears A Mummer's Mask* (1943) set in the old ghost town of Central City, Colorado. After the death of Phyllis, Mike moved to New Orleans which figures prominently in *Michael Shayne's Long Chance* (1944). *Count Backwards To Zero* (1971) takes place partly aboard the ocean liner Queen Elizabeth II and partly in Bermuda. *Caught Dead* (1972) takes place in Venezuela, *Fourth Down To Death* (1970) is set in the world of big-time pro-football and *Million Dollar Handle* (1976) in the world of dog-track racing. In *She Woke To Darkness* (1954), Halliday himself is a character in the novel and the events take place in New York where Brett is attending the MWA Edgar Awards convention. *The Violent World of Michael Shayne* (1965) is set in Washington, D.C. and involves bribery and political corruption. *A Taste For Violence* (1949) is set in the fictional Kentucky mining town of Centerville.

Dresser was a prolific writer. In addition to the Shayne novels, he wrote a number of straight tales as well as a series of romantic love stories under the pseudonym of Kathryn Culver. He also wrote westerns under the names of Asa Baker and Hal Debrett. Halliday published an unusually good, frequently anthologized, series of crime stories involving construction crews at work on the Texas-Mexican border that Ellery Queen called Dresser's "engineering stories." These are now collectors' items. Dresser also was owner of a publishing firm—Torquil & Company and for a time he edited *Mike Shayne's Mystery Magazine*. Dresser was one of the founders of Mystery Writers Of America as well as a charter member of the Western Writers of America and the National Writer's Club. He made his home in Montecito, California. Unfortunately, there will be no more Mike Shayne cases written by his original creator. Davis Dresser died in Montecito on the 4th of February in 1977. Other admiring authors have kept Mike alive and use the magazine named in his honor to publish additional stories about his exploits. No greater tribute can a good knight have.

The X-Rated Knight: Pete Chambers—Henry Kane

According to the dust jacket of Henry Kane's first Richard Peter Chambers novel, Pete is a bombshell "who lives like a sybarite but is tough as an agent's smile; who can drink like a camel, but hold his liquor like a revenue snooper; who is equally at ease in the dignified inner sanctum of stately Curtis Wilde, Inc. on Fifth Avenue and Matty Pineapple's holy house of horrors down in Greenwich Village."

When Pete first got into the PI business he had a senior partner, Philip Scoffol. Pete and Phil worked out of an office entitled Scoffol and Chambers at 50 Rockefeller Plaza in Manhattan. Pete lives in a three-room penthouse with terrace at Central Park South on 59th Street near Sixth Avenue. Pete likes women—any and all kinds—and he likes Scotch and water almost as well. Pete also has a very competent secretary, Miss Miranda Foxworth, who is "built like an old-fashioned icebox but colder." She wears glasses, is bulgy and has marble-blue eyes but she is marvellously competent. Pete often frequents Trennen's Dark Morning Tavern directly across the street from his office. Pete is six feet two inches tall, one hundred ninety-three pounds heavy and in his words, "I'm a shamus, a private richard, a caper—kid. A wise guy private eye. Talks hard with the tough guys, purrs with the ladies. All the girls fall for him. You know, like what you read about."

Despite Pete's love of the opposite sex he is, like all good knights, the protector of fair young virginal maidens. When a young lady he has been ardently wooing tells him she's only eighteen, Pete hastily backs off:

"You ought to start dressing. It's dark out."
"What's the matter with you?"
"Nothing."
"What's the matter?" she said, bending over me touching my hair.

"Most people love it."
"Sure."
"Cleopatra was Queen of Egypt at seventeen."
"Sure."
"What's wrong?"
"Nothing." I tapped my wrist watch. "People are coming."

Pete tells it all in the first person and he is very handy with a quip. In describing a dress one of the lovelies is wearing he observes:

Her dress was less dress than any dress I had ever seen. Pink. Pink and simple and starting nowhere and ending nowhere but blending with the pink of her flesh and showing all of her, and where it didn't show, any imagination limping on one mongoloid cylinder could imagine and without any imagination, that wouldn't matter either. In back it was no dress all the way to the base of the spine, a smooth back, soft velvet over bones and in front it was more dress but not much more and from there it clung like a drunk to his last drink come closing time.

Pete's primary difference from other PIs is his sense of humor. Pete plays with words, pulls double entendres and puts his verbal two cents in where it always does the most good. Pete is also a nighttime person who does most of his work alone. He does accept some help from Homicide in the form of red-headed, freckle-faced Detective Lieutenant Kevin Cohen who respects Pete's reputation and integrity. Together they are an indefatigable and unbeatable team. Cohen, incidentally, is also featured as the cop character in Kane's Inspector McGregor series.

Since the Pete Chambers novels span a period of twenty-five years (1947-1972), there have been a number of changes in Kane's narration, plotting and style. The later Chambers are less hard-boiled, less stylistically cute and clever and generally better written. *Who Dies There* (1969) and *The Unholy Trio* (1967), for example, are two of the best novels in the series. Though most of Pete's cases are definitely PG or R rated, in 1969, during the sexual revolution Pete went to an X rating with a series of seven novels that had pornographic passages "inserted" to lend sexual spice to the blood and gore. Most of these had the word "job" in the title, eg. *The Schack Job* (1969), *The Bomb Job* (1970), *The Glow Job* (1971), *The Tail Job* (1971), *Come Kill With Me* (1972), *The Escort Job* (1972) and *Kill For The Millions* (1972). All these novels contain the irreverent, wisecracking, first-person punning that launched Pete's career and made him one of the most entertaining PIs of all.

Henry "Hank" Kane, according to the dust jacket of his first novel, "was born in 1918 with a golden pen in his fist." Incredibly, the first novel he ever wrote (*A Halo For Nobody* in 1947) was accepted by the first publisher he sent it to. Moreover, his first short story was snapped up by Esquire who was so enthusiastic they immediately contracted for five more. Kane was born and educated in New York City and he practiced law for a number of years before turning to writing. Besides the Pete Chambers, Kane has written a number of straight thriller and suspense novels. He has also written for television (the Peter Gunn series) and he has turned out many short stories. In addition to the thirty-two Pete Chambers books—twenty-eight novels and four collections of novelettes—Kane created another private eye who was a former inspector in the NYC Police Department named McGregor, an older, wiser, and more staid Pete Chambers, who appears in three novels: *The Midnight Man* (1965), *Conceal and Disguise* (1966), and *Laughter In The Alehouse* (1968). Kane also tried his hand at creating a female PI, Marla Trent. To our knowledge, her only appearances were with Pete in *Kisses Of Death* (1962) and by herself in *The Private Eyeful* (1959). Both McGregor and Trent were well conceived and executed. Why Kane failed to extend their lives is another mystery as yet unsolved.

The First Dark Knight: Toussaint Moore
Ed Lacy (Leonard S. Zinberg)

Toussaint Marcus Moore is a very black, 234 pound ex-World War II vet living in a small semi-tenement around 147th Street in a part of Harlem known as Sugar Hill. Toussaint shares the old-fashioned raiload flat with a "fireman named Ollie and a photographer called Roy." "It's a good deal," Toussaint says, "Splitting expenses three ways it costs each of us about twenty-five dollars a month, which is only slightly more than you have to pay per week for a room with 'kitchen privileges' in most parts of Harlem." The front room he lives in doubles as his office and a sign in the window says *Private Investigator*.

After his discharge from the Army in 1948, Toussaint went to NYU on the GI Bill while working part time as a guard in a department store. In 1950 Touie was called back into the service and when he got out in 1953 the guard job was gone. Ted Bailey, head of a PI agency and one of Touie's friends, puts him to work helping on some of the agency's cases. When Touie decides to try it on his own, Sid Morris, one of Touie's Army drinking buddies, comes to his aid by referring clients and keeping Touie afloat.

In *Room To Swing* (1957) the first of Ed Lacy's two novels showing off Toussaint's skills, we find our dark knight working for one Kay Robbens, a TV executive who hires him to shadow a rape suspect until they can arrange his capture on a nationwide TV crime special: *You Detective*. In doing the job Moore is framed for the murder of the rape suspect. The rest of the novel follows Moore's step-by-step movements as he tracks down the killer. Although Toussaint has a fiancee named Sybil, after meeting another young lady named Frances Davis, Touie gives Sybil the heave-ho.

Touie's indulgences consist of a red Jaguar, a pipe and London Dock—a spicy, sweet-smelling tobacco. Touie uses his fists often and a gun when necessary. Like so many blacks in a racist society, his greatest frustrations come from having to keep his feelings hidden and his strength under control. In his own words:

Ted, I'm sick of phonies. I want to be a mailman and mind my own business. Let somebody else be waiting to collar a babe shoplifting because she hasn't money to buy the clothes she needs. I don't ever want to dun an old woman into paying up on some goddamned sink on which she was screwed from the word go. Most of all I'm sick of being around people busy stepping on each other's backs, turning in their own relatives for a job, murdering them to keep the job.... In short I'm sick to death of playing in other people's dirt.

Though well-crafted, suspenseful and good enough to win an MWA award, *Room To Swing* is not as good as the second and last Lacy novel about Moore, *Moment Of Untruth* (1964). When the novel opens, Toussaint and Frances are married and Toussaint, now happy as a postman, discovers that Frances is pregnant. Although Touie pretends that he is happy about the news, secretly he is devastated: "Damn, just what the world needed—one more kid...another colored kid!" The problem is that on his income Touie realizes they will have trouble just paying the rent when Fran stops working. Looking for a part time job, Touie calls the Ted Bailey PI agency and finds that Ted has a PI job for him in Mexico. A wealthy widow, one Grace Lupe-Varon wants a "competent private detective, but who must not look like a dick." There is also the possibility of landing a big, long-term security guard account for Mrs. Lupe-Varon if she is happy with the agency's work. Since Touie has a vacation coming and the job will pay $2,000, he takes it.

On his arrival in Mexical City he discovers that Mrs. Grace Lupe-Varon is much younger than he thought, that she is a herpetologist (i.e. a snake expert) and that she wants Touie to find her husband's murderer. According to Grace her husband was murdered by someone who put a bushmaster in his bed. Most startling of all, Grace claims that she knows the killer. The killer, unfortunately, turns out to be a national hero—the famous bullfighter El Indio A.K.A. Jose Cuzo. Grace's husband Juan was the only journalist who dared pan El Indio in print and hint that there was something fishy in Cuzo's technique of bull fighting.

Touie's job is to "prove" Cuzo was the killer. At the end of the story Touie finds himself sympathetic with the murderer. The plot has a number of surprising twists and turns that make the story exciting. Touie, himself, is a credible and sympathetic PI who, though not a Superman, is a tough and courageous human being willing to put his life on the line when it becomes necessary.

There are only two novels featuring Toussaint Moore, but his personality and character are so well developed that he is a most memorable creation. This is even more remarkable when we learn that Ed Lacy—a pseudonym for Leonard S. Zinberg—was white. Zinberg was married to a black woman for a number of years and had many black friends. He wrote several other novels with black heroes. Lee Hayes, an ex-prizefighter, is a black police detective who gets along well with whites and is the hero of the novels *Harlem Underground* (1965) and *In Black And Whitey* (1967).

In addition to Toussaint, Lacy created two more PIs who each show up in only one novel. The PI hero of *The Best That Ever Did It* (1955) is one Barney Harris, a big tough rascal who weighs in at 248 pounds. At the opposite extreme is the PI Hal Darling, a five-foot one-inch former flyweight boxer and judo expert who is as fast with his mind as he is with his fists and feet. Lacy is, perhaps, best known for his stories about the fight game, and his *Walk Hard, Talk Loud* (1940) a straight, non-mystery novel about boxing was not only well received by the critics but was adapted for the stage. It had a long and successful Broadway run. Most of Lacy's work appeared as paperback originals and was generally unappreciated. Lacy, a New York City native, won an Edgar for *Room To Swing*. He was a correspondent for *Yank* magazine during World War II. There is little doubt that he would be better known and more widely read had it not been for his untimely death at 47 in 1968.

The Drinking Knight: Bill Crane—
Jonathan Latimer

Jonathan Latimer's PI William "Bill" Crane drinks alcoholic beverages in prodigious quantities. Although all the tough PIs drink—many to excess—Crane swims in booze. Among the hard drinkers, he is the hardest and the drunkest PI in the history of the genre. He, in fact, often solves the crime while recoving from a hangover. Bill not only drinks *before* breakfast, he drinks *during* breakfast, and he drinks *after* breakfast. One thing that can be said about Crane is that he plays no favorites—if it's alcoholic he likes it—beer, bourbon, scotch, wine, vodka, martinis, barcardis, rye, alcohol and water—and, by accident, in *The Lady In The Morgue*, embalming fluid. Unlike most boozers, Bill thinks when he drinks and he uses reason and logic to solve the cases rather than brawn and bullets.

Crane works for a New York agency headed up by one Colonel Black who is a pretty slick sleuth himself, although he only appears in a very minor background role. Crane, the second in command in the agency, seldom works alone. Most of the time he is aided by a good-looking younger PI named Doc Williams or an older gray-eyed Irishman named

Thomas O'Malley. The combination is unbeatable with Crane furnishing the brains and Williams and O'Malley the muscle.

Crane was, at the time of his debut, a different sort of detective. Not only is he smart and tough but he is also a master of repartee and the ad lib. As a wise-cracking wizard and deft dropper of the double-entendre Bill quickly endeared himself to readers. As Art Scott says:

Jonathan Latimer's Bill Crane series represents the very best of the 'screwball comedy' school of 1930s mystery fiction. Dashiell Hammett's *The Thin Man* (also published in 1934) is considered the archetype of the school, but Latimer's Crane mysteries, particularly *The Lady In The Morgue*, may well be considered the apothesis.

Crane shows up first in Latimer's 1934 novel *Murder In The Madhouse* in which he is committed to a mental institution. After three murders have been committed, the reader learns that Crane is a private detective who has been planted to find out what is going on.

The second Crane novel, *Headed For A Hearse* (1935), not only has Crane up to his usual antics drinking and wisecracking but it also is a first-rate "locked-room" classic. Robert Westland, a very wealthy man, is convicted of murdering his estranged wife (in a seemingly air-tight case) and is awaiting his execution on death row. Westland is resigned to his fate although he knows he is innocent. Six days before his execution he changes his mind and decides he wants to live. After Westland bribes the warden to let him talk to his lawyer, the lawyer brings in Crane and Williams to help out.

We are never given much information about either Crane's or Williams' appearance. In *Hearse* we are told:

He (*Crane*) was a tanned youthful man and he wore a brown tweed suit like Bolston's but his was lighter and looked as though he had slept in it. Williams was a dapper man with bright black eyes and a black moustache. . . . There was a dead white streak in his hair, over his right temple.

Later in the book Williams is described "with pouches under his eyes" and as looking "distinguished". Crane's libido, however, is healthy, and he never misses an opportunity to exercise it. Most of the time he has little opportunity and is left at the post wistfully wishing. Here for example:

Finklestein was watching Woodbury and Miss Brentino. Arm in arm, heads close in conversation, they were descending the steps. "Seem pretty intimate, don't they?" the attorney said.

Crane watched the sweeping curve of the woman's half presented profile, her narrow hips, her slender legs below the Persian lamb coat.

"I wouldn't mind being intimate with her myself," he said.

Crane never misses an opportunity to show off his wit. When one of the characters tells Crane:

"Don't think I'm doing this for you, because I'm not. I don't like you."
Crane said, "Kraft-Ebbing will never have to write a case history of my passion for you either."

And, a little later when one of the minor female characters remarks:

"I'm always thinking of the money first," Miss Hogan confessed.
"Like a mercenary soldier," Finklestein observed.
Crane said, "She belongs to an older profession than that."

One particularly interesting feature of *Hearse* is that the original edition contained a number of incisive comments on crime, the economy, the state of the nation, etc. When the book was reissued in paper in 1957 as one of the Dell Great Mystery Library offerings, all the social comments were deleted. Christopher Morley called the book better than *The Thin Man*. We agree.

The third Crane story *The Lady In The Morgue* (1936) is Latimer's masterpiece. It is as funny and bizarre as a Marx Brothers comedy and it is a cleverly contrived mystery at the same time. Crane is at his sparkling best. Trapped by the cops in a room where a young woman has just killed herself, Crane is forced to beat a hasty retreat through the only window, cling to a ledge and break into the adjoining room where a drunk and his naked wife are asleep. Crane dumps the drunk in the bath tub, ties up the wife and then jumps in bed with her to fool the cops.

Ten minutes later the police had gone and he had finished the whiskey. He felt a great deal better and not so sleepy and he climbed out of bed and put on his athletic top and his shirt. The woman's eyes, watching, brooded sudden death. He went to the bathroom, lifted the hairy man out of the tub and carried him back to the bed. He said to the woman, "I bet you could sell him to the zoo." He straightened his hair with his fingers, looked regretfully at the bottle on the stand, bowed gallantly to the woman. "I hope to see less of you sometime, madam."

The plot revolves around the identity of a young blonde found dead from having supposedly hanged herself in a cheap Chicago hotel room. To complicate things there is also a young heiress who is missing. After the body of the dead blonde is transferred to the police morgue, someone kills the morgue attendent and steals the body. Following some wild sequences involving professional hoods, a few shootings, a riot in a taxi-dance hall, a midnight grave-robbing expedition and a struggle with the killer in a room full of corpses—Crane comes up with the solution to all the problems.

In *The Dead Don't Care* (1938) Crane and O'Malley wind up in Miami and Key Largo assigned to protect a wealthy young man, Penn Essex. Essex has been receiving a number of mysterious messages signed "The Eye" that threaten his life unless he antes up $50,000 in unmarked bills. This is a little difficult since Penn hasn't yet received his inheritance and he's kept on an allowance of two thousand a month. Besides, he has run up gambling debts to the tune of $25,000 with a local gambler. Crane, who is described as belonging to the "pleasure school of crime detection" says that he never found that a little pleasure ever hindered him in his work. His best ideas come, he says, when he is relaxed. It is hard, however, to make the client see this. Clients are often stupid, that's why they have to hire detectives. Crane soon finds himself with a kidnapping on his hands—the snatching of Camelia Essex, Penn's sister—as well as the murder of one of the Essex's house guests. Again, Crane uses his wits to unravel the murder and recover the kidnap victim. In the process he is his usual witty self:

"It looks like snake country up there."
"My god! It does and I haven't any whiskey."
"Hell," O'Malley grinned at Crane, "Whiskey doesn't help you with snakes."
"It does before they bite you," said Crane.

And:

The thought of the Bugatti's swerve made Crane's stomach turn over. "How fast were we going?" he asked.
"A hundred and five," said O'Malley
"That fast?" Crane found he couldn't swallow. "I need a drink."
"There's some port in the dashboard compartment," said Essex.
"I'm afraid it's California port, though."
"Any port in a storm," said Crane.

The last Crane novel, *Red Gardenias* (1939) has Crane hooked up with Ann Fortune, Colonel Black's daughter. To solve the case of a death threat made against the family of an industrial magnate, Crane and Ann pose as husband and wife. By the novel's end Crane and Ann are, in reality, engaged.

The film versions of *Hearse* (*The Westland Case,* Universal, 1937), *Lady In The Morgue* (same title, Universal, 1938) and *The Dead Don't Care* (*The Last Warning,* Universal, 1938) were cinematic successes and starred Preston Foster as Crane. The transitions were fairly direct although the studio did change the setting of the last novel from Florida to California.

Born in Chicago in 1906, Latimer was educated in Arizona and at Knox College in Galesburg, Illinois. He served in the US Navy during World War II and learned the writing trade as a journalist on the Chicago

Herald-Examiner and later on the *Tribune.* In the late thirties he moved to California and became a screenwriter, writing the screenplay for Hammett's *The Glass Key* (1942), Kenneth Fearing's *The Big Clock* (1948) and Cornell Woolrich's *The Night Has A Thousand Eyes* (1948) as well as twenty others between 1939 and 1958. Latimer was also the writer for the Perry Mason TV series from 1960 to 1965 when the series concluded. Besides the Crane novels, Latimer also published *The Search For My Great Uncle's Head* (1937) under the pseudonym Peter Coffin. Perhaps Latimer's best novel, *Solomon's Vineyard,* was first published in 1941 in England. An abridged version was published here in paperback as *The Fifth Grave* (1950). The original text with the original title was finally published in 1982 in a signed, limited edition. Latimer's last novel, *Black Is The Fashion For Dying,* appeared in 1959. Latimer died on June 23, 1983 in his home at La Jolla at age 76 of lung cancer.

The Compassionate Knight: Jim Bennett— Robert Lee Martin

James Tobias Bennett likes double martinis, extra-dry and Miss Sandra Hollis, "a tall, rangy girl with close-cropped bronze hair and freckles," his secretary and bride-to-be. Jim also likes beer and bourbon and, on special occasions, a Gibtini—both an olive and an onion. Jim is in charge of the Cleveland, Ohio branch of the American-International, Inc., a private investigative agency. Like most other good PIs, Jim has a friend on the police force, Lieutenant Dennis Rockingham who refers to Jim as "the best in the business." Jim is a little better educated than most PIs. He has a Bachelor's and a law degree from Ohio State. Jim also has two very good assistants—Alec Hammond and Red Drake. For transportation they drive two late model Fords and a Mercury; all three are agency property.

Jim is one of the most "middle class" PIs in this book. He plays poker, swims, golfs, hunts and fishes and, like all good knights errants, saves old ladies, young maidens and friends from evil, bad men, killers and harm. All 11 Bennett novels are head and shoulders above the average, run-of-the-mill who-did-it. Martin can write and he knows how to hook the reader's interest. The characters, both major and minor, are interesting human beings with understandable drives and values. Bennett is world-weary, sophisticated and tough enough to do whatever is necessary to halt the heavy or crack the case but he is not so hard or insensitive that he fails to sympathize with the fallible creatures he hands over to the cops. The reader identifies with Jim Bennett and suffers with him as he endures his head-bashings and hangovers. Jim carries a Smith and Wesson .38 special which he uses only on rare occasions. Although one is reminded of Chandler and Marlowe, Bennett is physically bigger and tougher than Marlowe and also much higher up on both the social and the income scales. There is, nevertheless, the same brooding sense of melancholy and pity for the foibles of human beings.

Nearly all of Bennett's cases begin with Jim coming to the aid of a friend, usually on a social basis at first and then as the plot complicates, professionally. In *Sleep My Love* (1953) one of Jim's high school friends comes home to find his second wife with a knife buried in her chest. When the friend is accused Jim defends him and finds the true murderer. Shortly thereafter Jim is asked to help another friend beat another murder rap. In *To Have And To Kill* (1960) Jim and Sandy are invited to spend several days with the soda-pop king, Max Daney. Daney is one of Jim's Ohio State buddies. Max is getting married and wants Jim to be his best man. On the night before the wedding, however, the bride-to-be winds up dead on the beach clad only in a terry-cloth robe. Jim hangs on until the case is solved. In *Bargain For Death* (1964) Jim comes to the aid of another old OSU friend, Walter Larkin, head of personnel at a large manufacturing plant in southern Ohio. Larkin wants Jim to help him stop the theft of expensive tools and to uncover the sources of some insurance fraud. Jim clears these assignments up in short order but then finds himself involved in some bitter labor negotiations as part of the management team facing a brutal, power-hungry union boss. Bennett is up to the challenge and when this tyrant tries to bully the management team, Jim puts him in his place in the following scene:

"Stand up."

"Make me." He was grinning. He loved this.

I pushed back my chair, walked around the table to Fallon and slapped his face with an open palm.

He came out of his chair, fists swinging. Suddenly everyone was shouting, but I paid no attention. Several blows jolted me. I tasted blood on my lips, saw Fallon's grinning, happy face. I staggered back against the wall, came back at him, hating him, slammed his chin with a fist. He went down, but scrambled up, rushed at me. He knew how to fight, but the rage was on my side. He was wide open and I hit him again, easily. He hit the opposite wall, rolled there, his head down, blood dripping from his nose down over his mouth. Hands plucked at me, holding me back. Voices shouted at me as I jerked loose and hit Fallon again. He sank to the floor, head against the baseboard, arms and legs spread limply. He was still. I heard Walter Larkin say, "Jim, for God's sake...."

Frank Liggett and the committee members swarmed around me, pulled me away from Fallon, my enemy. My mortal enemy. Rage had always been my problem. Fred Simon's calm voice brought me back to sanity.

After Jim is shot at and becomes romantically involved with a beautiful blonde secretary, he helps bring a threatened strike to an end and he also uncovers a management spy who has been selling out the company.

Another of the Bennetts has an industrial setting. In *Killer Among Us*

(1958), Bennett is asked to investigate some industrial sabotage at the Buckeye Abrasives Company. Several of their grinding wheels, sold to the Portage Foundry, have shattered in use causing one employee's death and serious injury to a number of other workers. Sabotage is the only possible explanation. Jim takes the job and after a number of harrowing escapes from death, uncovers the motive for the actions and the saboteur.

In *She, Me, and Murder* (1962) Jim and Sandy befriend a young actress, Tracy Kent, in a nightclub. Then they discover that Tracy is the mistress of an aging movie tycoon, Harold McPherson. McPherson suspects Tracy of two-timing him and he asks Jim to do a routine check on her. Bennett quickly confirms Harold's suspicions. Tracy has been having an affair with a popular actor, Peter Ordway. A few days later Ordway is killed and McPherson is the prime suspect. It is up to Jim to clear Harold and come up with the real killer.

In *A Coffin For Two* (1962), one of the best, Bennett and an old journalist friend, Jake Camp, decide on a Sunday outing in Beech Forks, a Cleveland suburb. Camp needs to check on some burial markers in an old cemetery. Camp is something of an historian and has discovered a hidden burial vault holding the remains of some of Ohio's earliest settlers. While taking pictures Jim and Jake are interrupted by a lovely young crippled girl who is a descendant of the people buried in the vault. The girl is in pain and Jim rushes to her aid. After befriending her, Jim learns there are a number of unpleasant people who resent his and Jake's interest in the old burial ground. When an attractive woman hires Bennett to look for her missing banker husband, the various threads come together. The missing husband turns out to be missing from a board meeting of the Beech Forks Cemetery Association. Later Jim finds the missing husband, drunk, in the Beech Forks Hotel and he takes him home to his wife. The next morning the husband is missing again. When Bennett finds him the second time, it's at the scene of a head-on car collision. The husband is dead. From the evidence available it may not have been an accident after all.

One of the toughest and most melodramatic of all the Bennetts is *A Key To The Morgue* (1959), in which the corpses multiply as rapidly as in *Red Harvest*. This tale is quite different from the usual conservative Bennett case and Anthony Boucher, a great admirer of Bennett, was moved to say, "The events and actions would look better on Mike Hammer than on Bennett." Even the reviewer James Sandoe of the New York *Herald Tribune*, who routinely panned Martin's work, was lavish in his praise of this one.

The Widow and The Web (1954) is another Bennett set in a large industrial plant. In this story Jim comes perilously close to becoming entrapped in a torrid love affair with someone other than Sandy. Boucher says this story "places him very close to Bart Spicer among the humanizers of the hard-boiled private eye story." In another review Boucher opined, "I know few writers who can infuse into fictional murder so deep a sense of human sadness and pity as Robert Martin...." Boucher was only one of many critics who commented on Bennett's interest in people, his humanity and his decency.

Like Bennett, Robert Lee Martin was a quiet and conservative person with a warm sense of compassion for others. Martin was born in Chula, Virginia in 1908. When he was still a child, the family moved to Tiffin, Ohio, a small town about fifty miles southwest of Sandusky. After graduating from Tiffin's Columbian High School in 1927 he worked as a bank teller from 1928 to 1934. From 1934 to 1936 he worked as a stock clerk for the Sterling Grinding Wheel Company. This experience furnished the background for several of the Bennetts—*A Killer Among Us* in particular. From 1936 to 1941 he managed the stock department and moved into personnel work in 1941. He was promoted to assistant personnel manager in 1945 and personnel manager in 1950. The personnel background and experience is also obvious in the last Bennett, *Bargain For Death* in 1964. Martin, who spent most of his career with the Sterling Company, was one of Tiffin's leading citizens; he was active in the Community Chest, the Red Cross and Tiffin's Chamber of Commerce. Besides being a member of MWA, Martin served as an officer in the Seneca County Personnel Managers Association from 1950 to 1958. Martin wrote seven novels under the pseudonym of Lee Roberts and several other non-Bennet novels under his real name: *Just A Corpse At Twilight* (1955) and *Judas Journey* (1956) were two of the best.

Throughout his career Martin considered his writing only an avocation. Nevertheless his novels have been reprinted in nine countries, distributed to newspapers by four syndicates and serialized in magazines. Two of the novels were Detective Book Club selections and a number were adapted for television. Martin died at age 68 in 1976.

The Peripatetic Knight: Chester Drum—
Stephen Marlowe (Milton Lesser)

Chester Drum is the head of the Drum Agency located on the seventh floor of the Farrell Building on F Street in downtown Washington, D.C.. Drum works out of his Washington office—way out. In fact, of the twenty novels featuring Chester, he is kept stateside in only a few. And even in these few Drum is moving back and forth between the USA, Canada, Mexico, Rio and all points elsewhere. Drum is the most peripatetic dick in all of PI-dom. Nearly every Marlowe novel is a travelogue as well as a mystery story. Most of the nations Drum visits are clearly identified but in some the country is, for some reason, thinly disguised. In *Murder Is My Dish* (1957), for example, the Latin country is called the Parana Republic. *Trouble Is My Name* (1957) is set in East and West Germany. *Violence Is*

My Business (1958), set mostly in the Washington and Virginia area, sends Drum into Canada and the Laurentians for the climax. *Homicide Is My Game* (1959) takes our hero to Rio and Brazil. *Danger Is My Line* (1960) has a nordic heroine and sends Chester to Iceland and Sweden. *Death Is My Comrade* (1960) starts in D.C. but winds up in Russia and Finland. *Peril Is My Pay* (1960) takes Chester to Rome and the Olympics, and *Jeopardy Is My Job* (1962) has Drum investigating kidnapping and murder among the expatriates on Spain's Costa del Sol.

Of course in the Drum Beat series two of the titles alone betray the setting: *Drum Beat—Berlin* (1964) and *Drum Beat—Madrid* (1966). In *Drum Beat—Dominique* (1965) Drum prowls the back alleys of Paris and in *Drum Beat—Marianne* (1968) he is wandering the back roads of Yugoslavia.

Chester Drum is a 190-pound, crew-cut ex-FBI operative with extensive government connections. Drum will take most any sort of case except divorce work. He hangs out in Hamling's Bar and Grill—a small place on 16th Street a few blocks north of the White House and Lafayette Park. Hamling's is close to his office on F Street. Though tough, Chet also has his tender side. As his friend Jack Morley once testified: "Drum's the only private eye I've ever known who I'd let babysit with my kid." Although Chet does have an apartment, mostly he lives out of a B-Four bag. Like other PIs he keeps a bottle of Jack Daniels in his desk drawer and for defense and offense he carries a Magnum .357 in a shoulder rig. Every chamber is loaded except the one under the hammer. His friend, Morley, works in the State Department and comes in handy quite often—especially when Chet has trouble with foreign nationals.

Like all troubleshooters Chet is in for at least one or two headbashings and other assorted wounds in every novel. Though not quite as bloody as Hammer or Race Williams, he spills enough to stock a few blood banks. Marlowe also mixes intrigue and mystery with a dash or two of sex into a very readable product. The plots and the exotic settings give nearly every novel a James Bond-like taste. Though some critics have placed Drum in the Hammer tradition, Marlowe has given Chet more sophistication and intellect. The Drum novels—especially the Drum Beats—flesh out the characters with skill and finesse.

One of the nice things in the series is the collaboration that took place between Marlowe and Richard Prather in the late fifties when the two writers decided to collaborate and bring Chester Drum and Shell Scott together on a case. The result was called *Double In Trouble* (1959). Drum's opening comments in the story are:

I'm a private eye, operating out of Washington and points east, and I will pack a suitcase at the drop of a hat or a client's retainer or a blonde's smile. I've chased international gangsters across the sunny piazzas of Rome through the Iron Curtain to Berlin, tangled with Moslem fanatics—and belly dancers—in Arabia and professional assassins in India, battled revolutionists south of the border and gunmen on skis in Canada's mountains.

But I never knew what trouble was really like until I crossed the path of that West Coast shamus who calls himself Shell Scott.

Scott and Drum oppose each other at first but then collaborate while investigating the National Brotherhood of Truckers as the action alternates from Washington to Los Angeles. When the two wind up slugging it out with each other the chapter heading is: *Two Private Eyes Out Of Focus.* The fight is, as you would surmise, a stand-off.

Drum's creator is Stephen Marlowe, a pseudonym used by Milton Lesser, a native New Yorker. Lesser, born in 1928, was educated at William and Mary graduating with a BA in 1949. He served in the US Army from 1952 to 1954 and since the end of World War II has worked as a free-lance writer and teacher. He has been a writer-in-residence at William and Mary for many years. Since 1950 he has written over fifty novels—a number under his own name and the others under the pseudonyms Andrew Frazer, Jason Ridgway and C.H. Thames. Before turning to the mystery field Lesser wrote science-fiction very successfully. Although the Drum series ended in 1968, Lesser has continued to turn out suspense and straight novels. Among his better non-Drum novels published under the Stephen Marlowe name are, *The Search For Bruno Heidler* (1966), *The Summit* (1970), and *Come Over, Red Rover* (1968).

The Rugged Knight: Max Thursday—
Wade Miller (Robert Wade and Bill Miller)

In writing about Wade Miller (Robert Wade and Bill Miller) in John M. Reilly's *Twentieth Century Crime And Mystery Writers* Edward D. Hoch comments:

In an era when the private-eye novels of Hammett, Chandler, and Macdonald are the subject of serious literary discussion it's odd that virtually no attention is given to the early works of Wade Miller. Certainly Miller's private eye, Max Thursday is not in the same class with Spade, Marlowe and Archer, but he is still someone worth knowing and his six cases written during a five-year period (1947-1951) are still a pleasure to read.

They are indeed. The six novels are: *Guilty Bystander* (1947), *Fatal Step* (1948), *Uneasy Street* (1949), *Calamity Fair* (1950), *Murder Charge* (1950) and *Shoot To Kill* (1951). Max is introduced in *Guilty Bystander,* the writing team's second novel. Their first was a non-Thursday story called *Pop Goes the Queen* (1947). Max is a World War II vet who tried to make a living as a PI in San Diego but fell into the booze trap. Max's drinking drove his wife Georgia to a divorce and Max wound up as the house dick at the Bridgeway Hotel, a few blocks north of downtown San Diego. After Max's son Tommy is kidnapped, Georgia, now remarried, seeks Max's help. With the aid of Lt. Austin Clapp of the homicide bureau, Max recovers Tommy but not before Georgia's new husband is murdered. Max gets his revenge on the killers in a violent and surprising ending.

In the second Thursday, *Fatal Step*, Max (no longer an alcoholic bum) kills a gunman in an amusement park. In the third novel, *Uneasy Street*, Max is called by an old lady who wants him to deliver a mysterious package to one Count von Raschke in exchange for some unspecified property. Before Max can get further details the old lady dies from a knife wound that she had been hiding. Max starts to deliver the box but several characters try to steal it, and they are knifed by parties unknown before they can get away with the theft. When Max opens the box he finds it contains $100,000 in cash. Max seeks its rightful owner but before he can return it he becomes involved with a voluptuous blonde and a gang of international smugglers.

In *Calamity Fair*, the fourth Thursday, Max undoes a ruthless blackmail ring that specializes in framing lonely and wealthy ladies. In *Murder Charge*, the fifth and perhaps the best of the six novels, Max goes to work for Clapp and the San Diego police force by posing as a New York syndicate finger-man and then worming his way into one of San Diego's organized crime mobs. In the last novel, *Shoot To Kill*, Max—who is now a highly respectable and successful PI with offices on the fourth floor of the downtown Moulton Building—is the employer of four subordinate PIs. Max now also has a steady girl friend, Merle Osborn. One day, without warning, Max discovers that Merle has been seeing one Bliss Weaver behind his back. When Weaver's estranged wife is murdered, Max frames Bliss for the murder—even though he knows Bliss is innocent. When his conscience starts working again Max goes after the real killer who, along the way, also strangles Merle.

Plotting and characterization are excellent in all the tales, and Max is a likeable hero who takes his share of the lumps and gets his share of the breaks. At the outset Max is in his middle thirties sporting a gaunt, rugged face with a hook nose that only a woman in love could call handsome. His eyes are "sharp blue, eyebrows heavy, nose prominent and arched; his mouth—half-smiling now—could turn cruel easily. Not a friendly face unless he deliberately made it so. . . ." Max also has a heavy beard requiring frequent shaves. He drives an old gray Oldsmobile sedan and he smokes Camels. Later in his career, he takes up cigars. His hair is dark with a few short, grey hairs. When he is broke he drinks Old Cathedral which he calls "Old Sherman-Williams". When flush he drinks better stuff—usually bourbon and soda. When he's on a case Max often forgets to eat. He wears tweed clothes and a snap-brim hat. Max lives in half of a white stucco duplex in the Middletown section of San Diego, partway up the hill between the harbor and Balboa Park.

Max is less hard-boiled than he appears. After having killed four men, Max is so contrite he sells his .45 automatic and turns in his permit to carry a gun. His kindness and gentleness also show up in his dealing with women, children and elderly people. Max is always on the side of the underdog, protective of the mentally and physically crippled, sympathetic with people down on their luck and when, in *Shoot To Kill*, he attempts to frame his rival, he is so guilt-ridden he has to confess at the first opportunity and then risk his life in atonement for his fall from grace.

Bob Wade and Bill Miller have been working together as a successful writing team since their high school days at Woodrow Wilson Junior High School in San Diego. Both served in the US Army Air Force during World War II—Miller in the Pacific and Wade in the European Theater. Both were Sergeants. After the war both married and sired children: Miller, one daughter and one son; and Wade, two daughters and two sons. Besides writing a number of successful mysteries, while at San Diego State College Bob and Bill also edited The East San Diego Press—the largest weekly in the area—for a time. Their collaboration is one of the most successful in the history of modern crime fiction. Together they have turned out thirty-three novels, two screen plays, 200 radio scripts and countless novelettes and short stories. They have also written under the pseudonyms of Dale Wilmer and Whit Masterson. Wade has used the latter name since 1961 in writing a number of novels alone. He has also written two novels, *The Stroke of Seven* and *Knave Of Eagles* under his own name.

The Beat-Up Knight: Bart Challis—
William F. Nolan

William F. Nolan's Bart Challis is a savvy, quick-fisted shamus operating out of Los Angeles and the star of two crackling good yarns titled *Death Is For Losers* (1968) and *The White Cad Cross-Up* (1969) and a third planned one, *The Marble Orchard*, that for some reason or other never saw print.

Bart drives a Chevy Covair Sprint and is not above doing divorce work—in fact, for Bart it is very profitable. Bart carries a .38 special in a spring-clip holster and drinks Black Label scotch—on the job and off. He refers to the downtown section of Greater Los Angeles below Spring where his office is as "the armpit." Bart listens at keyholes, rousts bums for unpaid bills and runs down lost brats. Doing these things depresses him. Occasionally, however, he does get an interesting assignment, a variation on his normal "window work." Like the request he received from a fancy jeweler named Gibney Eugene Raphael who asks Bart to track down his wife's missing white Cadillac sedan. It seems that his wife's lover "borrowed" it. But the wife claims that it was stolen and she wants the insurance money so that she and lover-boy can run off. This situation, the start of *The White Cad Cross-Up*, sets Bart off and running. Before he gets launched Las Vegas way where the Cad is stashed, Bart stops by his own lover's nest to nestle with his own lovely, Lyn Marshal. Lyn practices Yogic sex, owns a .45 automatic and a bulletproof vest and loves to keep Bart sexually satisfied.

As soon as Bart gets to Vegas he finds the Cad in the lover's unlocked garage. Lover-boy is a small nightclub owner named Arlinger. When a pro hit-man tries to shoot Bart while he is still at Arlinger's garage, Bart shoots first and straighter. He then realizes he has been set up by someone out to get him. Checking the Cad's registration, Bart discovers that the car is registered to Arlinger. A few hour's later in Bart's motel room, Arlinger confirms that Raphael lied and was trying to set both of them up. Bart now goes to work for Arlinger and soon runs into another of Arlinger's girl friends who is promptly murdered. Following a trip to Mexico, Bart falls into the clutches of an expert in pain, finds the body of the murderer of the girl he was supposed to meet and winds up in the hands of the cops. After his release Bart has it out with Raphael, goes flying with a World War I airplane collector and gets beat up by Raphael's hoods. In fact, in breaking the case Bart is:

"Shot at by a triggerman, cracked in the neck by a fag, tortured by a pain-crazy dame, slugged on the head by a suicide, and worked over by two hoods."

The writing is superb. Nolan's pace is fast, his touch is deft and the dialogue is sparkling. For example, when Bart encounters a faggish and pretentious art salesman the following exchange occurs:

"Note Mayerburg's use of the small off-center dot," the salesman purred. "One's subconscious is held in thrall by the dot, representing womb desire."
"What's that?" I asked.
"The impulse shared by us all to return to the womb which gave us birth," he told me, the smile still pasted on his face like a stamp on an envelope. "The dot impels and beckons, irresistibly drawing us into its warm dark confines! We of Lamont's feel this is Mayerburg's triumph, the totally-realized end-product of his heated passion."
"Could be," I said.
He raised a quizzical eyebrow. "I take it that you are a collector?"
"You can take it that I'm a detective, the totally-realized end-product of a wasted boyhood. But I *do* peep a hot keyhole."

Ray Russell says, "The Nolan style is bright, fast, compulsively readable, often laced with sharp poetic images...(he) is a popular writer in the best sense of the term, a precise craftsman who always manages to reveal depth beneath the smooth commercial surface of his work." The first novel *Death Is For Losers* also got rave reviews and it is regrettable that Nolan didn't keep the Challis series alive. Of the first Challis, Art Goodwin said,

"Sparse writing, quick scenes, clipped dialogue all contribute to a fast-paced novel of suspense...Nolan's detective is very much in the tradition of hardboiled fictional private investigators that stretches in a line extending from Dashiell Hammett through Raymond Chandler to Ross Macdonald." Alan Hubin in his NY *Times* book review said, "Don't try to solve the case beforehand...just enjoy Bart Challis clomping through a California landscape decorated with recently deceased strippers and gangsters on his way to a killer. I did."

Nolan, besides being a first-rate PI novelist is also an authority on Hammett and Chandler, an excellent editor, a literary critic, a biographer and a science-fictioner. His *Dashiell Hammett: A Casebook* won an Edgar in 1970 and his 1983 biography *Dashiell Hammett: A Life On The Edge* is one of the best treatments of Hammett available. He is also the author of *The Black Mask Boys* (1985). His work has been cited by the American Library Association and his short stories have appeared in innumerable "best" anthologies of both science and mystery fiction. He is the author of *Logan's Run* (1967) that was purchased by MGM for a six-figure amount and became a hit motion picture and a short-lived TV series. In 1976 the Academy of Science Fiction and Fantasy gave him its annual award. In commenting on *Logan's Run* and *Logan's World* (1977) the sequel, Nolan makes the point that though they

are basically science-fiction books they also may be considered 'future crime' novels, since their 'hero' Logan is a policeman whose job it is to hunt down runners who defy the laws of the future state. In my novels the police are known as 'Sandmen.' Thus both Logan books fall into the SF/Crime—Suspense genre.

Also clearly within the genre is Nolan's tour-de-force merger of science-fiction, the PI novel, comedy and admiration for Hammett in his *Space For Hire* (1971) with his classical hardboiled shamus: Sam Space. As you can guess, Nolan says it was great fun to write. It is even more fun to read and it is one of the wildest and funniest PI novels ever written.

Nolan is an admirer of Ray Bradbury and he has compiled and edited the first serious critical study of Bradbury's work. Bradbury also admires Nolan and, in a collection of Nolan's short stories, *Impact-20* (1963), Bradbury wrote:

When I think of Bill I think of a tall lean-to, thrown together rucksack of bones. He was originally bonier and more wildly constructed, but while better years and good eating have rounded him off, the main impression is still of a windmill that runs swiftly even when becalmed. I would like to think that from time to time throughout my life I could look up to the horizon and see that brave, fast, furious and engaging windmill flourishing there.

In sum, God invented a pep-pill and dubbed it Nolan.

Nolan was also an intimate friend of the late great actor, Steve McQueen.

Bill was his biographer and in 1984 published the excellent *McQueen*.

In recognition of Nolan's many achievements, American River College of Sacramento awarded him an honorary Doctorate of Literature.

The Tampa Knight: Ed Rivers—
Talmage Powell

Ed Rivers lives alone in a small apartment in a run-down neighborhood on the edges of Ybor City, as the Latin Quarter in Tampa, Florida is called. Ed, who is in his early forties, has brown eyes and brown straight hair thinning at the crown. He is six feet tall and weighs approximately one hundred and ninety pounds. His face is heavy, bearish, dark tanned and creased. "Women either get a charge from the face or want to run from it. Men fear it or trust it to the hilt." Ed's office in downtown Tampa has a sign on the door which reads: *Nationwide Detective Agency, Southeastern Office, Agent In Charge: Ed Rivers*. Ed carries a .38 plus a knife in a sheath at the nape of his neck and he knows how to use both. Like most competent PIs, Ed has a friend at Headquarters—Lieutenant Steve Ivey who helps whenever Ed needs a buddy in blue. Ed's office is in two parts—an outer office with a cracked leather couch and matching chairs and an inner office that has a desk, a filing cabinet and a beat-up Underwood typewriter. The building is old and gloomy and the stairs creak under Ed's weight. Ed makes his own air-conditioning for his apartment—he puts a 25 pound block of ice in a dishpan, the pan on the table and an electric fan behind the pan pointed at the bed. Once upon a time, seventeen years ago Ed was a cop in Jersey. Ed also had a girl but she took off with a hood that Ed was after. They raced a fast freight train to a crossing and lost. After drinking and drifting for several years, Ed wound up in Tampa working as a stevedore. Then Nationwide gave him a chance and he took it. He's been at the PI business ever since.

Ed's first case after going to work as a PI was *The Killer Is Mine* (1959) and his second was *The Girl's Number Doesn't Answer* (1960). His third, *With A Madman Behind Me* (1961) shows most clearly Ed's knightly qualities. Sitting in his room one evening, Ed looks out his window and sees a fair young maiden in trouble in her apartment across the way. Rushing to her rescue, Ed finds himself under a gun held by a madman. The killer strangles the girl, bangs Ed on the head and dumps them both in Tampa Bay. Ed swims out of it and tries to find out why the girl was killed. After helping several other characters and breaking up a porno ring, Ed brings the killer and wrong-doers to justice.

In the fourth of the series, *Start Screaming Murder* (1962), Ed is sapped in an alley near his apartment. When he staggers into his pad he finds tiny Tina La Flor—a midget singer—hiding in his room after coming in over the transom. She was being chased by the sapper—Bucks Jordan—a heavy who was after her body. Ed comes to her aid for seventy-five bucks a day plus expenses—Ed's going rate. Ed manages to catch Jordan at Tina's house, beat him up and warn him about letting Tina alone. Bucks agrees and shortly afterwards Lt. Ivey shows up to tell Ed that Bucks is dead— murdered by his own blackjack. Now Ed has to find the real murderer as well as Tina who has mysteriously disappeared. In unravelling the knots, Ed is locked in a car trunk, hit on the head umpteen times and "angrified" something awful! And when Ed is mad he really plays rough. Witness:

I began to tremble with the effort to control myself. I started for the door. He moved toward me.
"Did I say you could leave big man?"
Somebody should have told him better. He mistook the whiteness of my face. He was too sure of himself and it gave me all the advantage.
When he reached for me, a grin on his face, I snapped his arm up, spun him, grabbed a handful of that black hair and threw him flat on the floor.
He lay dazed, the wind knocked out of him.
"I ought to kick your teeth in," I said...

In the fifth and last Rivers, *Corpus Delectable* (1964), Ed again comes to the aid of a fair lady. During Tampa's annual Gasparilla Festival a young girl comes to Ed's office for help but is murdered on the stairs. Since Ed was with her when she died the hit man can't be sure she didn't tell Ed everything. Checking on her background, Ed discovers she was the least likely candidate for a hit in all of Florida. As Ed examines the case, he runs into a nest of intrigue as well as some unpleasant relatives of a wealthy old Venezulan lady who died a few days before the girl was murdered. When Ed talks to the murdered girl's best friend he begins to see a motive for the murder. Soon after, the murderer returns and gets the drop on Ed. But as Ed says:

At the base of my neck my fingers had inched down. They touched the flat handle of the razor-sharp blade sheathed at my nape.
I didn't want to do it. I was so scared my spit glands had dried up. I steeled myself with a clinching argument: Rivers what have you got to lose?
As the knife slid free, I threw myself down and to one side. A man of experience, he didn't let the move rattle him. He was prepared. He danced backward to give himself room, to ensure himself from any flailing arms or legs. He thought he was still in control and had plenty of time.
"Okay," he said quietly. He was swinging the gun with deliberate care intending to make his first shot the last one.
My arm was snapping forward the second my body hit the floor.
I didn't expect the throw to be perfect. I was depending on the instinctive reaction of my screwed-tight nerves and muscles.
I needed luck.
He didn't know the knif existed until it glinted at him in the gloom. His startled cry mingled with the raw sound of the blade driving hungrily into flesh,

blood, and bone high on his left shoulder.

Further probing by Ed turns up the fact that the girl was an heir to part of the old lady's fortune and that blackmail and a missing portfolio have also entered the picture. After the killer is identified it then becomes a game of who will get whom first. Following the murder of the girl's roommate, Ed begins to uncover the motive: twenty million dollars. At the climax what began as a murder mystery winds up as a love story.

The Rivers novels are uniformly well-plotted, well-written, psychologically sound and entertaining from start to finish. Ed is a good knight, one who is a real pleasure to know.

Ed's creator, Talmage Powell, was born in 1930 in Hendersonville, N.C. He was educated in the public schools of North Carolina, New York, Tennessee, and California. He is married and has a son. Powell has been a free-lance writer since 1942 and during his career he has published over five hundred short stories and novelettes in the popular magazines. He has also written extensively for TV and the movies including several screenplays for Alfred Hitchcock. Powell is the editor of and contributor to one of the best humor anthologies of all time: *The Fireside Treasury of Modern Humor* (1963). Powell also published a number of mystery and suspense novels under the pseudonym of Jack McCready. Although Powell is best known for the five Ed Rivers, he has also published several other excellent mystery novels including, *The Girl Who Killed Things* (1960), *The Smasher* (1959) and *A Homicide For Surfside* in 1964. Powell is now living in semi-retirement in Asheville, North Carolina.

The White-Haired Knight: Shell Scott— **Richard S. Prather**

Me? I'm—Shell Scott. I'm a private eye. Most of you know me. You know I work out of Los Angeles and my cases are usually in the LA-Hollywood menagerie, that I'm six-two and two hundred and five pounds, with inch-long white hair sprouting, cropped-wheat fashion over my head and upside-down white Vs I call eyebrows, that I like bourbon-and-water and rare prime ribs, that I'm happy-go-luckie and my favorite hangouts are women.

In case you are one of the rare mystery fans who has missed the Shell Scott series you should know that Scott is a PI with a light touch and a broad sense of humor. Shell refuses to take himself too seriously and this is the primary reason why he has not been taken seriously by the critics. Shell heads up the business known as *Sheldon Scott, Investigations* located on the second floor of the Hamilton Building on Broadway, between Third and Fourth streets in downtown Los Angeles. Scott deals in burglaries, robberies, blackmail, murder, missing persons, assault, battery and you-name-it. According to Scott he's "handled half the crimes listed in the California Penal Code including 578 P.C. (Issuing fictitious warehouse receipts) and 653 P.C. (Tattooing of a minor).

Scott is six feet two inches tall, has gray eyes and is an ex-Marine. He has a scar over his right eye, a nose fractured several times and a little piece gone from the tip of his left ear. He is always deeply tanned. He usually dresses well and his favorite outfit is made up of a bright-blue blazer with interesting silver-nugget buttons, a pale-pink silk shirt and pink socks to match, sky-blue trousers (to match his robin's-egg-blue Cadillac convertible) and dandy white Italian shoes topped off by a bright tie with red seahorses on them. He carries a .38 special in a clam-shell holster. He ordinarily carries an empty chamber under the hammer "since I would hate to accidentally shoot off a chunk of my lattissimus dorsi or something even more desirable." Scott also uses other weapons when necesary. In *Gat Heat* (1967) he even uses a crossbow and a rocket gun. Scott likes women and women like him—lots. Though all the novels are narrated in the first person, the gentlemanly Scott is not one to kiss and tell. No Pete Chambers, all Scott's couplings are implied—never detailed. When Scott is not warming up some broad he is usually cooling off some hood with his fists or calming down an irate client with his wit. For example, in *The Cheim Manuscript* (1969), when a wealthy old Hollywood tycooon makes some uncomplimentary remarks to Shell his reply is:

Mr. Cheim, I do not ordinarily hit weak old men lying on their deathbeds, but you will have a better chance of living to an even riper state of canterkerous senility if you will kindly quit swearing at me.

Scott's best friend in LA is Phil Sampson, a career Captain at LAPD's Central Homicide. Hazel, the switchboard operator, is another buddy with a bosom. One of the very amusing gimmicks that Prather inserts into the cases is the tendency for the illiterate hoods and minor characters to butcher the English language. For example:

cold-blooded *premedicated* murder
like a *Sore of Damocles* over his head
(he slept with his daughter and) committed *insects*
(on taking a walk) I was taking a *constipational*
I feel an innocent citizen should *corporate* with the *farces* of law and order.
a sense of yumer

Scott also has a favorite lounging robe made of red silk with a flaming dragon embroidered on its rear. As far as his sex life is concerned, Scott is selective. Nearly all women find him attractive but the feelings are not always mutual. In *Gat Heat*, for example, Scott remarks about one of his admirers:

Friends, in my years as a private investigator in Los Angeles, I have looked upon death and destruction, blood and urp split brainboxes and disemboweled oxen. But I have seldom looked upon anything less appetizing than Aggie fluttering her bald lids at me.

Moreover, blood doesn't just flow in Shell's veins: "... blood does not creep in my veins, but rather, I like to think, sings and sometimes yodels in splendidly harmonious arteries. More, in my yodeling blood are several pounds of iron filings, each ounce of which is magnetically attracted to what I think of, fondly, as toothsome tomatoes. I have, in fact, a fondness amounting virtually to dedication for lovely lasses with lissome curves and eyes like silk, with smiling lips and boastful cleavage, with fire in their glances—and all that."

Shell lives in the Spartan Apartment Hotel on North Rossmore in Hollywood in Apartment 212 consisting of three rooms and bath complete with two tropical fish tanks, guppies and catfish, and with an oil nude painting, Amelia, on the wall of the living room. The carpet is yellow gold with a low chocolate-brown divan, two leather hassocks and a "much scarred coffee and booze table." The bedroom carpet is black. While his regular drink is bourbon and water he also is partial to martinis—very dry—and he is a cigarette smoker. Whenever Shell is asked his age he replies, "I'm thirty. In fact, I've been thirty for a hell of a time now." Moreover he gets tougher and more bullet-proof as he ages. If you like gunplay and violent action you'll adore Scott. Shell manages to eliminate anywhere from four to forty hoods per novel and manages to pick up two to four pieces of lead in the process.

Among the more intriguing of the thirty-six Shell Scott cases are *Dead Man's Walk* (1965) set in the caribbean and involving voodoo; *Dead-Bang* (1971) involving a nutty scientist with a combination health serum and aphrodisiac, a radio evangelist and a group of beauty contestants planning to strip nude on a live TV newscast; *The Kubla Khan Caper* (1966) set in a posh hotel in the desert near Palm Springs; *The Trojan Hearse* (1964) concerning an Elvis Presley-like national hero, psychiatry and the mafia; *Strip for Murder* (1955) which is set in a nudist camp; *Joker In The Deck* (1964) dealing with a truly amazing and unforgettable poker game; *Gat Heat* (1967) centered around a few sex orgies staged by a group of wealthy Californians; *Dead Heat* (1963) which delves into the stock market and stock manipulations; and, finally, one of Scott's toughest and bloodiest cases, *Too Many Crooks* (1953). Of unusual interest is *Double In Trouble* (1959), mentioned earlier, in which Scott teams up with Chester Drum, Stephen Marlowe's Washington PI.

Scott's creator, Richard Scott Prather, was born in 1921 in Santa Ana, California and attended Riverside Junior College in 1940 and 1941. When war broke out he entered the U.S. Merchant Marine and worked as a fireman, oiler and engineer from 1941 to 1945. After the war Prather married Tina Hager, got a civil service job and worked as a clerk at March Air Force Base until 1949 when he quit and became a full-time writer. Since the first Shell Scott, *The Case of the Vanishing Beauty* published in 1950, Prather has written over forty novels that have sold over 40,000,000 copies in the USA and over four hundred foreign editions in 15 other coutries. Under the pseudonym of David Knight, Prather published *Pattern For Murder* (1952), *The Scrambled Yeggs* (1956), and also published under his real name, *Dragnet-Case No. 561* (1956). Under the pseudonym Douglas Ring he published *The Peddler* (1952), also published under his real name in a revised edition.

Prather created another PI—an ex-GI named Mark Logan who worked out of Los Angeles—and he shows up in only one novel: *Dagger Of The Flesh* (1956). This novel is interesting since the plot involves hypnosis, drugs and post-hypnotic suggestion. Prather is the editor of one of mysterydom's finest anthologies—a collection of humorous mystery shorts entitled *The Comfortable Coffin* (1960). One of the funniest entries is a Shell Scott short called "The Live Ones." Excerpt: "Both of them (blonde cuties) were running about stark staring naked—they were stark and I was staring." The plot deals with attempts on the part of a local hood to have Scott's license lifted on a morals charge. Scott, of course, turns the tables on the crook. This collection, as Prather argues in his introduction, is "intended to make you feel good, jolly, even healthy." Prather is a former member of the MWA Board of Directors, resides in Fallbrook, California where he plays golf, raises avocados and collects books and royalty checks from the still in-print and ever-popular Shell Scott cases.

The Taciturn Knight: Carney Wilde—Bart Spicer

It is difficult to tell very much about Carney Wilde, a licensed Pennsylvania PI, because he is one of the most tight-lipped PIs in history. We know him only indirectly—through his actions, rather than from what he says about himself. Bart Spicer's Carney shows up first in the novel *The Dark Light* (1949) which won Dodd Mead's $1,000 Red Badge prize for the best first mystery novel.

Though Carney is big and tough he is also sensitive and intelligent. All seven of the Wilde novels, written in the first person, appeared between 1949 and 1959 and as Art Scott has noted "are among the very best private eye novels of that or any other decade." Carney, operating out of Philadelphia, heads up the CARNEY WILDE, INC. agency consisting of "two men on hand for assignment and four good retainers." Largely because of Eli Jonas, owner of the Jonas Department Store—the largest department store in Philadelphia—Carney is in good financial shape. A large portion of the Agency's income comes from Carney's services as the store's Chief Security Officer. Eli is not only Carney's sponsor but also a good friend who shows up in nearly all the Wilde stories. In the later stories, Carney is more affluent and his agency occupies a three-room suite in the Maritime National Building in downtown Philly.

Carney is tall—over six feet; heavy—over 240 pounds; strong—he often lifts and holds aloft men of normal construction. When he drinks he prefers straight rye whiskey, with a rye and soda chaser. He drives a Plymouth and carries a .38 revolver in a clam-shell shoulder holster. His fee is fifty a day plus expenses. In the third novel, *The Golden Door* (1951), when asked what his father was like, Carney replies, "He was a drunk . . . . He was a boss carpenter who stepped out of his line and tried to buck the stock market. He got caught holding short and he shot himself." This is about all we're ever told about Carney's background and there's even less about his present way of life and his likes and dislikes. Like most of his fellow professionals, Carney lives in a small, sleazy, three-room apartment that he describes as follows:

The soiled old corduroy couch with lumps at one end, the two bruised leather club chairs, and between them the cut-down library table I used for magazines and ashtrays—that was most of the sitting room. The other end had a weary dining room set of flimsy table and six hard-seat chairs that were used only for infrequent poker games. My bookcases were the unpainted variety and I had never got to the point of doing anything about them. Most of my books were old and looked it, but they were the ones I wanted. All that adds up to nothing much maybe, but it was my place, and when the door swung shut behind me, I breathed a different air and thought different, quieter thoughts.

Carney gets along well with the police and has a good friend on the Philly force—Captain John Grodnik who goes to Carney for help, and in turn helps Carney when he needs it. Carney's young right hand man, Penn Maxwell, is handsome, tough and impulsive. He is trustworthy and reliable when muscle is needed. Penn is also the husband of Jane Grodnick, the Captain's daughter. Carney has had a number of girl friends but he has never married because, as he says, "Hell, nobody in my racket has any business with a wife anyway. Particularly not with a wife who deserves a decent life."

Among the seven Wilde novels three are excellent: *The Long Green* (1952), *The Taming of Carney Wilde* (1954) and the prize winning *The Dark Light* (1949). In *Blues For the Prince* (1950), another good one, Wilde is involved with a group of jazz musicians which gives Spicer an opportunity to display his knowledge of New Orleans jazz. Spicer has a large collection of early jazz records—particularly the work of Jimmy Noone and Sidney Bechet. In *The Long Green*, perhaps the best of all, Carney is called to Tucson, where Eli Jonas is vacationing with his granddaughter Bibi. Soon after Eli's arrival Bibi is kidnapped and held for the long green—a fifty thousand dollar reward. Jonas calls Carney to find

Bibi and catch the kidnappers. *The Taming Of Carney Wilde* has Carney on a hunt for a killer-thief aboard a Mississippi excursion steamer. Also aboard are a beautiful young lady and Carney's quarry in disguise. *The Golden Door* (1951) is concerned with perfume smuggling, the illegal entry of foreign nationals, a seven million dollar inheritance and a number of murders. *Black Sheep Run* (1951) involves a number of underworld characters and a series of betrayals. The last novel, *Exit Running* (1959), in which Carney marries, retires and takes up another occupation, is the weakest of the seven.

Carney's creator, Bart Spicer, is a native Virginian who was born in 1918. In World War II, he enlisted as a private and rose to the rank of Captain after two years in the South Pacific. After the war he worked as a journalist for the Scripps-Howard Syndicate. He worked as a radio news-writer and then did public relations work for Universal Military Training and the World Affairs Council before turning to novel writing on a full-time basis. In the 50s Spicer also collaborated with his wife, Betty Coe Spicer, to write four non-PI mystery novels under the pseudonym Jay Barbette. Two of Spicer's best non-PI novels are *The Day of the Dead* (1955), set in Mexico, and *The Burned Man* (1966). Two other dramatic novels, *Act Of Anger* published in 1962 and *The Adversary* published in 1974, are well worth the reader's time. As Art Scott has pointed out: "The Wilde books are beautifully crafted: Spicer's plotting is coherent, with credible twists and surprises; his style strikes a satisfying balance between the telegraphic and the over-ripe; he writes convincing dialogue and makes imaginative use of the 'hard-boiled' simile. Wilde himself is an admirable, believable hero, not the formulaized caricature that can be found in too many tough-guy series of the period."

The Fat Knight: Nero Wolfe and His Squire, Archie Goodwin—Rex Stout

Rex Todhunter Stout's adventures of Nero Wolfe and his assistant Archie Goodwin span a period of forty-one years: from *Fer-de-Lance* (1934) to *A Family Affair* (1975). During this time neither knight ever ages. Nor did any other character in the forty-two books chronicling their activities. It was Stout's intention that his creatures would not change and he was determined to build a plausible, yet detached and romantic world that would avoid what he perceived to be an error on the part of other mystery writers. Their error, Stout believed, was allowing too much of the real world to intrude upon their imaginary one. Stout's advantage lies in the fact that none of the Wolfe novels are dated. They remain as fresh today as the day they were written. The powers of Nero, Archie, Fritz and Cramer and the rest have not diminished.

Stout, more perhaps than any other writer in this book, did his best to amuse and entertain his readers. He wanted his books to provide entertainment and at least as much pleasure in the reading as he had had in the writing. He once said, "If I'm not having fun writing a book no one's going to have fun reading it." Consistent with this view is Stout's passionate concern with the personality and character of his two heroes, Nero and Archie. No two detectives in the annals of American fiction are better known and none, perhaps, are more admired. In the August 1966 issue of *PS* magazine Wolfe was called "one of the most convincing, and certainly the most loveable [of] fictional detectives since Sherlock Holmes." Jon Tuska in his *The Detective In Hollywood* reports quite frankly:

If what I have to say in the following pages seems to reveal an unconcealed preference for Rex Stout's Nero Wolfe mysteries, I might as well admit that I have enjoyed his books more than those of any other of detective stories. I have enjoyed Hammett and Chandler, but I have enjoyed Stout more. I admire Erle Stanley Gardner, as will become apparent when I write of him, as one of the best plot artists and the finest champion of justice the detective story has known. I am charmed uncommonly by the Miss Marple mysteries of Agatha Christie and the Dr. Thorndyke adventures by R. Austin Freeman. But I am addicted to Rex Stout.

This admiration is mirrored by Otto Penzler who in *The Private Lives of Private Eyes* says:

Sherlock Holmes was not the first detective, but he was the first character to become more real than the flesh-and-blood personages of his time. The only other detective in literature about whom this is true is Nero Wolfe. A few other detectives may be greater in that they have solved more complex cases, and a few may even be more famous in distant regions of the world, and a few may sell more books, but none has achieved an emotional rapport with readers to equal that of Rex Stout's fat man.

What is the source of such admiration? If there is any secret to Stout's success it lies in the fact that he never fails to entertain his readers. No other writer provides us with more humorous commmentary on civilized living. And no other private investigator is more complex, colorful and convincing. Wolfe is a "character" in every sense of the word. He is not only intellectually entrancing but he is physically impressive. He is, in a word, FAT! He prefers "portly." In Archie Goodwin's words, Wolfe weighs somewhere "between 250 and a ton" and he was once said to weigh "a sixth of a ton." In later volumes Archie has settled on "a seventh of a ton" which is somewhere between 286 and 320 pounds—depending on whether you are referring to a short ton (2000 pounds) or a long ton (2240 pounds). According to Wolfe his justification for staying fat is "to insulate my feelings" but a more obvious reason is his fondness for the finest foods and his unquenchable thirst for beer—a minimum of five quarts per day.

From the novels we learn that Wolfe is five feet eleven and—even though corpulent—is well proportioned. He has been called "handsome"—at least once. His hair is brown, with a dash of gray at the temples, neatly trimmed and carefully brushed. Wolfe is immaculately clean and neatly dressed. His suits are conservatively dark and he always wears a vest in which he carries a large platinum pocket watch. To always appear fresh, he wears two yellow shirts every day. He is never without a tie and when, on rare occasions, he leaves the brownstone house on West thirty-fifth street he wears a brown or gray overcoat with a big fur collar and a black, felt pirate's hat—size eight.

According to William S. Baring-Gould, Wolfe's unofficial biographer, Nero and his twin brother Marko were born in Trenton, New Jersey in late 1892 or early 1893—even though on one occasion Wolfe claims he was born in the Black Mountains between Albania and Montenegro. Actually, Wolfe's mother returned to Europe in the early 1900s taking Nero and Marko with her. Settling in Budapest she married a man named Vukcic and had a third child. Nero and Marko grew up in the mountains herding goats and hunting dragonflies. In 1913 Nero entered the Austro-Hungarian civil service, became an intelligence agent and travelled to Egypt, Algeria and Arabia. In the Balkans during 1914-1915 Wolfe switched his allegiance to Montenegro and joined the Montenegrian army. When war broke out Wolfe came near to starving when the Serbo-Montenegrian forces were wiped out. In 1918 after the Allied Expeditionary Forces landed in Europe Wolfe hiked over 600 miles to join the Americans and fight the Germans. Nero tells us that he is personally responsible for killing over six hundred German soldiers.

After receiving an honorable discharge in 1918, Wolfe goes back to Montenegro and adopts a three-year old orphan named Anna. Leaving her in good hands, Wolfe returned to the US in 1921. Between 1921 and 1927 we know little of Wolfe's whereabouts. We do know, however, that in 1927 Wolfe became a private eye and clashed with Inspector Cramer. Meanwhile, Marko—who was also in London—returns to New York City and establishes Rusterman's restaurant. In 1929 Wolfe went back to Zagreb to look for Anna but he was arrested and forced to leave the country. Back in the US in 1930 Wolfe purchased the old brownstone house on West Thirty-Fifth street, hired Archie Goodwin as his assistant and launched his distinguished career as a private investigator.

Following a number of shorter cases between 1930 and 1933, Wolfe's first recorded case, *Fer-de-Lance*, was published in book form in 1934. The second book-length case, *The Case of the Frightened Man* (1935) was followed in 1936 by *The Rubber Band, The Red Box* in 1937, *Too Many Cooks* in 1938, *Some Buried Caesar* and *Over My Dead Body* in 1939, and *Where There's a Will* in 1940. From 1940 the remaining thirty-three book-

length cases were published at a rate of little more than one per year until
the last Wolfe, *A Family Affair* appeared in 1975. Many of the facts
surrounding both Wolfe and Goodwin are never revealed. For example,
little is known about the first meeting between the two. Both parties refuse
to discuss it. Rumor also has it that Nero's father was Sherlock Holmes.
While proof is missing it is known that Wolfe keeps Holmes' portrait
hanging in his office under the wall clock, over Archie's desk, where he can
see it at all times. Temperamentally, Wolfe is exactly like Holmes, and
physically Wolfe is the spitting image of Holmes' brother, Mycroft. Stout
clearly intends for us to make the connection.

Wolfe's true genius lies in his ability as a private detective to bring the
wicked to justice. As he says in *Too Many Cooks*, "I am not a policeman. I
am a private detective. I entrap criminals, and find evidence to imprison or
kill them, for hire." Like all true knights, Wolfe is a man of honor and a
man whose word is his bond. As he says, "I rarely offer pledges, because I
would redeem one, tritely, with my life." And on another occasion, "No
man alive can say that I have ever dishonored my word." As a PI he is
passionately thorough, possessing the patience of Job, and he is as
persevering as time. He has the deepest respect for facts as well as for the
environmental setting in which they are found. No possibility is
overlooked and Wolfe is devoted to the truth which he believes will always
come out. In his words, "You can't conceal truth by building a glass house
around it." Wolfe, however, is quite fond of lying—but only when the lies
are used to get at the truth. Inspector Cramer says, "In the past dozen years
you have told me, I suppose, in round figures, ten million lies." Wolfe's
reply is, "I tell only useful lies, and only those not easily exposed." Wolfe's
motives as well as his ambitions and his achievements are to right wrongs
and to serve the interests of justice in an often cruel and unjust world.

What we love most about Wolfe, however, is his prickly, peculiar,
egoistic, eccentric, captivating and cantankerous personality. Wolfe does
not like to be touched and whenever possible avoids shaking hands. Wolfe
hates things that move—airplanes and automobiles especially. They are
regarded as demons. He is, nevertheless, partial to his private elevator
which lifts him between floors. Wolfe despises cliches, hypothetical
questions, imprecise language, and he hates with a passion: arguing on the
phone, coarse talk, flies, geraniums, cinnamon rolls, gin drinkers,
interruptions, music, paper cups, the colors purple and red, rain,
restaurants, smoking, more than six at a table, television and violence. On
the other hand, he is "foolishly fond" of: crossword puzzles—the harder the
better; good rugs; books—he often reads two or more at the same time; food
and drink; unusual and abtruse words such as—acarpus, chouse,
gibbosity, intrigante, plerophory, rodomontade, subdolous and usufructs;
proverbs; languages—besides English he speaks seven languages: (French,
Serbo-Croat, Spanish, Hungarian, Italian, Albanian and Latin); and

orchids—his rooftop greenhouse holds 10,000 plants, many of them very rare. Wolfe moves only when necessary, and according to Archie, "Wolfe could have got a job in a physics laboratory as an Immovable Object if the detective business ever played out." If and when Wolfe leaves the brownstone it's because Archie is in trouble. On rare occasions Wolfe does visit the scene of the crime.

Wolfe's life revolves around his daily routine and the ministrations of his personal staff—Fritz Brenner his cook and major domo of the house; Theodore Horstmann the orchid nurse; and Archie Goodwin, Wolfe's PI assistant. Wolfe's day begins with breakfast (between 8 and 8:15 AM) served on a tray in bed or at a table by the window. While eating Wolfe reads two newspapers. After donning a three-piece suit with yellow shirt and tie, he takes the elevator to the greenhouse where he spends the next two hours with Theodore and with his precious orchids. Precisely at 11:00 Wolfe takes the elevator downstairs to his first floor office-sitting room where he greets Archie in the same way every morning, "Good morning, Archie, did you sleep well?" After placing a spray of fresh orchids in the vase on his desk he settles down to his mail, whatever business Archie may have, etc. At exactly 1:15 PM lunch is served and it is ample and delicious. Unless it is urgent or critical, business is not discussed while eating. After lunch Wolfe returns to the office and works until 4:00. Following two more hours with his orchids the day's business is then concluded between 6:00 and 7:15. Then dinner is served. Dinner, too, is a serious affair. It is followed by coffee in the office. At this time Wolfe will wax lyrical on any topic interesting him at the moment. The time when Wolfe comes closest to being human is after dinner. This is the time when he and Archie move from the dining room to Wolfe's office and Nero begins his conversational monologue. Wolfe never goes to bed early—having a case makes no difference.

Wolfe has no superior as a private eye. No stone remains unturned and no fact unpondered. After he gathers and analyzes all the clues on a case he will assemble all those involved in his office and then brilliantly solve the case by exposing the guilty. Inspector L.T. Cramer, head of the homocide bureau, is usually present, along with Sergeant Stebbins, to make all needed arrests. When Cramer calls on Wolfe he is usually in a foul mood. Wolfe, he claims, has lied to him, double-crossed him, withheld evidence, interfered with his work, etc. Cramer is a good cop and he respects Wolfe. The respect and admiration is reciprocated. As Wolfe sighs, "Inspector Cramer's indefatigable routine does have its advantages."

Archie is almost as intelligent as Wolfe and certainly more mobile. Yet Archie always plays the supporting role for, as Wolfe says, "two brilliant men under the same roof would be intolerable." Archie is the man of action in all Wolfe's cases and the necessary brawn to complement Wolfe's brain. Archie is always on the go and, in his words, "Wolfe never puts off till tomorrow what I can do today." Archie has a phenomenal memory and serves as Wolfe's memory file. "The only difference between me and a tape recorder," Archie says, "is that you can ask me questions." Additionally, Archie serves Wolfe as chauffeur, bodyguard, office manager, accountant, secretary, muscle man and gunman.

Archie was born somewhere between 1910 and 1914 to Mr. and Mrs. James Arner Goodwin. Archie was an outstanding athlete in high school starring in football and baseball. After high school he tried college but dropped out after only two weeks. Moving to New York City he got a job as a guard on a pier. On the job he shot and killed two men and was subsequently fired. He was recommended to Wolfe, however, for a job Wolfe wanted done. He did it so well Wolfe offered him a full-time job. Archie is tall—just under six feet—charming and good-looking. He has broad shoulders, narrow hips, brown eyes and a pleasant baritone voice. He has been told he looks like Clark Gable though he insists that he is more like Gary Cooper. He is attractive to women and he uses this charm to help break cases. Archie is also a skilled impersonator and a first rate burglar. He is good with a gun and he never leaves the office without one. According to Kittredge and Krauzer, "Wolfe is a daring creation, but Stout's most creative stroke is Archie Goodwin, because it is only through Goodwin that Wolfe's cases can be anchored to any kind of social reality." These critics go on to point out that these novels appeared during the depression of the thirties and that:

Depression America could hardly be expected to stand in quiet awe of a fat gourmand with clean, uncalloused hands and a great deal of money and conceit. But Goodwin is a working man, subordinate but skilled, absolutely essential to the smooth working of the operation. He has a forthright streak of independence: he becomes resentful when his own astuteness is questioned, and particularly peevish when Wolfe holds back details of a case, considering this a slur on his intellect and his discretion. When sufficiently provoked, Goodwin will even tell the boss to go to hell. Each time he does, of course, loyalty brings him back into the fold, but he makes his point: at a certain degree brilliance becomes arrogance, and when it is reached, Archie will not be pushed around.

Since Wolfe does not move any more than is absolutely necessary, it is up to Archie to do the legwork and gather the data for Wolfe to chew on and digest. Over the forty-two books Archie has successfully impersonated a policeman, a florist, a photographer, a financial secretary, a personnel expert, and a crook. When he first started carrying a gun he used two Colt revolvers and a Wembley automatic which he kept in the drawer of his office desk. Later he added a snub-nosed Farger and a Marley .38.

Archie's favorite drink is milk which he consumes in large quantities. As for liquor he does have an occasional drink and plays no favorites. He has Scotch and water, bourbon, cognac, martinis, gin and tonic, and rye from time to time. But, as he notes, "I seldom take a drink before dark." Like Wolfe he eats well and always has a big breakfast. While Wolfe is a "taster" Archie is a "swallower." Archie also dresses exceptionally well, is an excellent ballroom dancer, and likes to walk, swim and play billiards. At poker, gin, and bridge he is a consistent winner. The love of his life is Lily Rowan, a blue-eyed blonde. The odds are good that if he ever were to marry, Lily would be his choice. Archie has a key to her apartment which on occasion he uses.

Of the forty-two novels, some of the more memorable are: *Fer-de-Lance* concerning a most unusual murder by a most unusual means on a golf course; *The League Of Frightened Men* dealing with revenge; *The Rubber Band* in which there is a shoot-out in Wolfe's office and Wolfe is wounded; *Over My Dead Body* in which Wolfe is reunited with his long-lost adopted daughter Anna; *Where There's A Will* involving a strange legacy and a murder; *Not Quite Dead Enough* in which Wolfe and Archie both serve as assistants to the military during World War II; *Too Many Women* which Archie says is the most enjoyable case he ever worked on; *The Second Confession* in which Wolfe encounters and bests Arnold Zeck the infamous Mr. X; *Murder By The Book* in which two supposedly independent killings are connected and solved; *Before Midnight* involving a verse-writing advertising contest and the murder of the only man knowing the answers; *Too Many Detectives* in which—for the first and only time in his career—Nero Wolfe is jailed; *Might As Well Be Dead* which Archie calls the screwiest case he ever worked on; and *The Doorbell Rang* which many Wolfe admirers consider the greatest of all the cases and Nero Wolfe's finest hour.

Besides Archie, Wolfe uses the talents of a number of others in solving the mysteries. Though he is well informed on legal matters, Wolfe calls on the services of Nathaniel "Henry George" Parker when legal acumen is needed. Wolfe also uses other private eyes on occasion. Included are Saul Panzer, a free-lance PI that Archie says is "the best operative South of the North Pole." Saul, who is slight of stature—five feet seven inches and 140 pounds—is, nevertheless, an expert at shadowing and so good at his PI work he demands and gets double the standard fee. Saul has never refused Wolfe's requests. Then there is Fred Durkin, a bear-like, bald and burly, PI who is as equally effective as Panzer. Wolfe's third professional consultant is Orrie Cather who, in line with his name, is cat-like in his movements and who has a knack for getting information out of people. Orrie is also big— six feet 180 pounds—semi-bald, and a former professional football player. He also whistles while he works. If Wolfe needs additional help he calls on Johnny Keems—who, unfortunately, got himself killed in 1956—or Theodolinda "Dol" Bonner, who has her own detective agency, and her assistant Sally Colt A.K.A. Sally Corbett. There is also a mysterious Mr. Jones who delivers information about the internal affairs of the American Communist Party. Of course, Wolfe can always depend on Inspector Cramer and Sergeant Stebbins.

Rex Todhunter Stout bore little physical resemblance to his prize creation. Stout was a slender, 150 pounds with a scraggly beard and he was physically active throughout his lifetime. One of nine children, Stout was born in 1886 in Noblesville, Indiana but the family moved to Topeka Kansas when Rex was still an infant. A child prodigy, Rex had read through the Bible twice before he was three and, before he was ten, he had read over 1200 books in his father's library. At thirteen he was the best speller in Kansas and at eighteen he joined the Navy and wound up as a crewman on President Theodore Roosevelt's yacht. Leaving the Navy in 1908 he moved to New York City and worked at a number of jobs. During the next four years he moved about the country—Cleveland, Colorado Springs, Chicago, Indianapolis, Milwaukee, and New York City again— holding a total of thirty different jobs in the process. From 1912 to 1916 Stout tried his hand at magazine writing and he wrote and sold both fiction and fact to *Munsey's, Smart Set,* and other periodicals. In 1916 Stout married Fay Kennedy. To make enough money to allow him to devote full time to his writing Stout invented a school banking system that was quickly adopted and installed in four hundred cities and towns across the country. This thrift system was so successful that he had enough money to travel abroad and, in 1927, to settle down and write professionally. His first novel titled *How Like A God* was a non-mystery published in 1929. The next four novels, also non-mysteries, were competent and well-received but they also convinced Stout he would never become a true or "great" American novelist.

Convinced, however, that he was a good storyteller, Stout published his first mystery novel, *Fer-de-Lance,* which appeared as a serial in *The Saturday Evening Post* and then as a book in 1934. It was such a hit that his course was irrevocably set. The second novel, *The League Of Frightened Men,* published in 1935, was equally successful and his reputation as a great mystery writer was assured. In 1940 Stout interrupted the Wolfe-Archie chronicles to write propaganda for the war effort. He also served as chairman of the Writer's War Board from 1941 to 1946. From 1943 to 1945 he was President of the Author's Guild, President of the Author's League of America from 1951 to 1955, Vice President from 1956 to 1961, and President again from 1967 until his death. He also served as chairman of the Writer's Board For World Government from 1949 until 1975. He was active in the Mystery Writers Of America and was elected its President in 1958, and in 1959 he received the MWA Grand Master Award.

According to Stout he would rather have written *Alice in Wonderland*

"than any other book in our language in the last century." A close second
was T.E. Lawrence's *The Seven Pillars Of Wisdom* which Stout says he
read at least three times. In his opinion, *The Maltese Falcon* was the best
detective story written in this century and he was also an ardent admirer of
Graham Green and John Le Carre. Though he admired Ian Fleming he
turned down Fleming's invitation to have James Bond, Nero, and Archie
show up in the same novel. The reason, according to Stout, was that Bond
would have "gotten all the girls." Stout was, of course, devoted to Conan
Doyle and he was a long time member of the Baker Street Irregulars. As for
his own work, he called his Tecumseh Fox novel *Double For Death* the best
detective story he had ever written. Tecumseh, the least known of Stout's PI
heros, is of medium size and height, in his early thirties, and there is
nothing remarkable about his appearance—unless you happen to notice
the penetrating power of his dark brown eyes. On one occasion he was
described as looking "more like a chess player" than a private detective.
Unfortunately, there are only three Tecumseh Fox adventures: *Double For
Death* (1939), *Bad For Business* (1940), and *The Broken Vase* (1941). Stout
also created a female PI—Theodolinda "Dol" Bonner of Bonner and
Raffray Inc. Detectives, Dol and Sylvia Raffray are two more very
accomplished PIs. Dol is very independent and she not only detects but also
shoots when necessary. Sylvia plays a very minor role in the one novel
featuring these two ladies *The Hand In The Glove* (1937). Dol does,
however, show up as a bit player along with one of her employees, a naive
PI named Amy Duncan, in *Bad For Business*, a Fox novel. Finally, another
of Stout's fascinating PI creations is the funny-eyed and slow-moving
Alphabet Hicks. Hicks, a graduate of Harvard Law School was disbarred
during his first year of practice. Working then as a night watchman, a
subway guard, and a cabby, he finally graduates to PI work. In this
capacity Hicks uses calling cards that read:

A. Hicks
M.S.O.T.P.B.O.M.

which stands for *Melancholy Spectator Of The Psychic Bellyache of
Mankind* or:

A. Hicks
C.F.M.O.B.

which stands for *Candidate For Mayor Of Babylon.* Or
"A. Hicks"
L.O.P.U.S.S.A.F.

which stands for *Lover Of Peace Unless Someone Starts A Fight.*

This is why he is called "Alphabet." Hicks is a most interesting character and one with great potential for a series but Stout had him appear in only one novel, *Alphabet Hicks* (1941). This novel also appeared in paperback under the title of *The Sound Of Murder* in 1969.

Otto Penzler closes his short study of Nero Wolfe in *The Private Lives of Private Eyes* with the comment that Archie made when he returned to the old Brownstone on Thirty-Fifth Street and found a note announcing Wolfe's retirement, "If I actually had seen the last of Nero Wolfe," Archie says, "It was a damn sad day for me." Penzler remarks, "It was not the end then, but there will be no new adventures. It is a damn sad day for us all." We can only echo the comment and emphasize the sentiment. Rex Stout died in 1975 at the age of eighty-eight. Just a month before his death he published the last Nero and Archie novel, *A Family Affair*. With Stout's passing we lost some of the most colorful and memorable members of our PI family. Because of their perennial popularity, all forty-two of the Wolfe novels are still in print in inexpensive paperback editions.

Chapter V
Knights of Eld—The Best of the Rest

THERE ARE MANY BRAVE knights without armor who, for one reason or another, have not received the plaudits given to other servants of the Grail. These noble warriors should not be ignored. They are deserving of honor for their courageous deeds and conquests of dastardly villains. The sixteen creators of the PIs taken up in this chapter also did most of their work before the 1970s. While many of their tales are still in print, many more are difficult to come by. The tales of these lesser knights and their deeds of derring-do need to be told, so let us begin. Again, we proceed alphabetically by author.

John J. Shannon and Rex McBride—Cleve F. Adams

No historical survey of the private eye novel would be complete without reference to the work of Cleve Franklin Adams and his novel *The Private Eye* (1942) featuring that hot-tempered Irish PI John J. Shannon. Some critics have argued that everything Adams wrote was either second-rate Chandler or warmed-over Hammett. Such arguments, in our opinion, are unfair. Both of Adams' PI creations are unique personalities who add new dimensions to the genre. Rex McBride, in particular, is the antithesis of Philip Marlowe and Spade. We can empathize with Marlowe or Spade, but it is difficult to do this with McBride. Rex is an anti-hero, a male chauvinist PI-pig. Rex, a Humphrey Bogart type, is tall, slender, dark complexioned and handsome in a satanic sort of way. Despite his good looks, Rex is crude, uneducated, cynical, hypocritical and sentimental. Although the words of popular songs can bring him to tears, the soft exterior covers up a cynical, fascist heart. Rex broods, hates with a passion, explodes in fits of laughter over trivia, and he has the attitude of a Klansman toward minorities. In one of the early novels, Rex mutters, "An American Gestapo is goddamn well what we need." Rex's opinion of women is that they are good for only three things, and two of the things are cooking and cleaning. Despite his success in outwitting the crooks, Rex is a little on the stupid side. The only reason he comes out on top is that he's a little tougher and a little luckier than the crooks. There are five McBride novels: *Sabotage* (1940); *Decoy* (1941); *Up Jumped The Devil* (1943); *The Crooking Finger* (1944); and *Shady Lady* (1955). Only the first two were published while Adams was still alive. Most of the plots were direct steals from Hammett, and Adams admitted as much in a 1942 essay published in *The Writer* called, "Motivation In Mystery Fiction." The plots are chaotic, and the writing is repetitive. Adams uses the same scenes, story elements, and dialogue again and again. But it is in his characterizations that he has added something new to the PI genre. This is also true of Shannon, his other PI character, who is featured in Adams' best novel, *The Private Eye* (1942).

Unlike McBride, John J. Shannon does have a number of positive qualities and is much more knightly. Shannon, an ex-cop, a detective lieutenant in fact, discovered he could make twice as much money as a private investigator running a detective agency. He is good-looking with a "thick shock of dark hair, and very dark eyes under straight black brows, and a big nose and a fair share of chin. It was only when you looked at his mouth that you decided maybe he wasn't as tough as these other things would leave you to believe. The mouth was as fine and sensitive as a woman's."

Shannon is no superhero. He has a number of human weaknesses including a terrible Irish temper and a penchant for four-letter words which he utters in torrents on every occasion in which he meets the slightest frustration. Shannon is helped by two interesting assistant PIs. One, Miss Frances McGowan, is a good-looking, smart young lady whose feminity is a cover for the skills of a Ninja master. The other is an honest but stupid ex-cop named Gus Vogel. Gus makes up for his lack of brains with doggedness and loyalty. Shannon's secretary, Mamie Costello, a pert redhead with freckles, keeps order in the agency office. Shannon loves rye whiskey but will drink anything else alcoholic if he can't have his favorite.

The plot of the novel concerns the death of the husband of one of Shannon's former flames. Hubby was caught in the middle of a war between two mining corporations fighting over the copper ore in the mountains of Las Cruces. Under the guise of looking for a missing heir, Shannon goes after the murderer even though he is told it was suicide. Soon after Shannon's arrival someone tries to take him out with a stick of dynamite tossed in the window of his hotel room. Both sides in the war want to hire his services. Even the crooked Police Chief wants Shannon on his side. Meanwhile there are a number of interesting characters on the sidelines. One is the Mayor of Las Cruces, a golden-haired Polish giant who crushes empty liquor bottles in his hands. Named Pilsudski, the giant also wants Shannon to work for him. Before the case is closed Shannon is forced to kidnap the mayor, bribe the police chief, and make love to his employer's daughter while staying as healthy as he can when everyone he meets is trying to kill him.

Though Shannon was successful enough to form the base for a continuing series, Adams never followed through. It is interesting to note that Adams, born in Chicago in 1895, worked as both a detective and a copper miner at one time. His career also included a stint as a life insurance executive and the operator of a chain of candy stores before he turned to writing full time. His personal experiences obviously came in handy in writing the Shannon story. In addition to the McBrides and the Shannon, Adams wrote six other mystery novels under his own name and three featuring a character named Bill Rye under the pseudonym of John Spain. Between 1936 and 1942 Adams published nearly fifty short mysteries in *Detective Fiction Weekly*, *Double Detective*, and *Black Mask*. Adams was a friend and correspondent of Chandler and a disciple of Hammett and one of the best of the tough detective short story writers of the middle and late thirties. He died in December 1949. Acording to Francis M. Nevins Jr., the expert on Adams work, "in his own style Adams captured the gray and gritty feel of the time as powerfully as Chandler and created as enduring an image of the private detective." Nevins believed that had Adams lived longer he might have grown into a writer rivaling Chandler.

Tony Rome—Marvin Albert

Marvin H. Albert's Tony Rome is a hard-living, hard-loving PI who works out of his 36-foot sport crusier, *The Straight Pass*, that he won in a crap game. The boat, moored at a pier on Dinner Key, a small boating community in southern suburban Miami, serves as Tony's home. Although Rome has a two-room office in downtown Miami on the fifth floor of the Miller Building near the junction of Miami Avenue and Flagler Street, most of the action revolves around the boat. Tony's weakness is his love of gambling and nubile young ladies. Invariably, both have him constantly immersed in hot water. Tony also loves to fish. He smokes Luckies, drives a gray Olds sedan, has a battle-scarred tomcat friend named Tangerine, and carries a .38 Police Special as well as a Luger, which he also won in a poker game. Tony has a bad left shoulder as the result of a bullet that shredded one of the bones.

As for the PI business Tony is philosophical:

You get used to unfinished drama in my line of work. You're always dropping briefly into the middle of people's lives getting a short, disturbing glimpse of how mixed up they are, and leaving them that way. It's a series of second acts, in which you seldom arrive in time for the opening scene or stick around long enough for the final curtain. I had a memory full of cliff-hangers about which I still wondered whether those still hanging had finally managed to climb back up on solid ground—or had fallen to the jagged rocks far below.

Tony is also an ex-cop. His father was a captain on the force at the time Tony was a lieutenant. When Tony's father started investigating racketeering connections, many influential people became frightened and proved that Tony's father, while he was still a detective sergeant, had taken a bribe. The reasons for this were simple: Tony had started college and his mother was dying in the hospital; Tony's father's salary wouldn't cover the expenses. His salary was so small that he couldn't get a loan, despite the fact that he had three times been cited for bravery. Following the bribe charge Tony's father killed himself and Tony handed in his resignation. Shortly thereafter he became a PI.

Tony is, above all else, tough. In addition to his .38, he carries a tiny, six-shot .22 caliber, repeater automatic just four inches long which he conceals in the sleeve of his jacket. In *Miami Mahyhem* (1960), the first Rome novel, when on one occasion Tony is in danger of being snuffed, here's what happens:

I snapped my arms down as I jumped sideways toward the sofa. The roar of Langley's gun filled the room. I felt the bullet tug the back of my jacket as the tiny automatic fell out of my sleeve into my waiting hand. He was bringing his gun around for another shot when I fired. The automatic in my hand made a thin snapping sound....Oscar kicked the door open and came charging through, his gun swinging in an arc as he searched for me. I twisted around and swung the long brass lampstand like a baseball bat.

The heavy metal base of the stand caught him square in the middle of the forehead and knocked him back against the wall. There was the sound of splintering bone as the metal base caved in his skull. He slid down the wall and settled on the floor in an unwieldy heap that had no more life to it than a big bag of gravel.

To our knowledge there are only three Rome novels: *Miami Mayhem* reprinted by Dell in paper in 1967 as *Tony Rome; The Lady In Cement* (1962); and *My Kind Of Game* a Dell paperback original published in 1962. Both *Miami Mayhem* and *Lady In Cement* were made into fairly successful movies. The former starred Frank Sinatra and Jill St. John with Richard Conte. Albert wrote the screenplays for both. Of the three stories, *Miami Mayhem* was the most successful.

Albert is a professional journalist. Born in Philadelphia, he has been a magazine editor, a researcher for *Look* magazine, and a very successful TV and movie scriptwriter. During World War II he was the Chief Radio Officer on several Liberty ships. After the war he became a full-time professional writer. Between 1955 and 1975 he published over 25 suspense, western, and mystery novels and over a dozen screenplays.

Ed Noon—Michael A. Avallone

When Ed Noon, "like in High," was just a struggling PI trying to make ends meet, he had a swivel chair, Marilyn Monroe calendar and roll top desk in an auditorium on West Fifty-Sixth street in NYC. But only a few novels later Ed has come up in the world and now has an office on West Forty-Fourth street with a plate-glass door and a black secretary named

Melissa. Ed doesn't carry a gun religiously but he does have a .45 in his desk. Ed lives in a four-room apartment just a stone's throw from Central Park. He lives well.

Ed is a distinctive PI in a number of ways. First, he is the only PI in history to work closely with and for the President of the United States. Next, he is the most James Bond-like of all our PIs and he is almost as peripatetic as Chester Drum. In a dozen or so cases, Ed is off and running on spy-like missions of one sort or another for the USA boss man. Some of these cases are *The Doomsday Bag* (1969) in which Ed has to find a satchel containing the thermonuclear codes for total world destruction; *The Hot Body* (1973) in which Ed has to protect an ex-First Lady; and *Shoot It Again, Sam* (1972) perhaps the wildest plot of any PI novel. The book is dedicated as follows:

This one is for a couple of people who can never die, like Gary Cooper, because a part of my brain will always be Cooper territory. And for Ken Millar whose Lew Archer will exist wherever there are pages and printed words. And it is also lovingly dedicated to all people everywhere who still believe that nice guys don't finish last.

As for the plot, Ed is sunning himself at the beach one weekend and on returning to his office finds a wire from the Commander-In-Chief telling him to accompany the casket and dead body of a Hollywood superstar, Dan Davis, from New York back to Hollywood for funeral services and burial. On the train trip west, as Ed is riding shotgun on the coffin, the corpse rises from the dead, and Ed is knocked cold. When Ed awakens he is in a hospital being interrogated by the spitting image of Peter Lorre. Turns out the train was hijacked by a group of Chinese agents who have kidnapped Ed and then proceed to brainwash him with a group of professional mind-scrubbers made up to look like famous Hollywood stars: Clark Gable, James Cagney and Lorre as well. Pretty soon the Chinese have Ed convinced he is Sam Spade, as portrayed by Bogart in *The Maltese Falcon*. They have, of course, an ulterior motive. In a replay of *The Manchurian Candidate* movie of 1962, Ed is supposed to go back to Washington and the next time Ed sees his boss he is supposed to kick him in the shins with his cleverly prepared poison-needle-tipped shoes. As you would surmise Ed foils the plot and kills every evil-doer in sight. This novel gives Ed an opportunity to show off another of his passions: the movies and movie stars. As one critic has said, the fun of reading Avallone lies in encountering the most film-intoxicated man alive.

In another Nooner, *Little Miss Murder* (1971) Ed gets involved with another of his passions—baseball—in the form of the New York Mets. Altogether there is a total of thirty-five novels and over ninety short stories featuring Ed Noon; he showed up first in *The Tall Dolores* (1953) and last appeared in *Kill Her, You'll Like It* (1973). For those members of the

Nooniverse—what Noon's fans call all of his cases—Stephen Mertz has compiled a bibliography of Avallone's output, available in the February 1976 issue of *The Armchair Detective*.

Michael Angelo Avallone Jr. is a native New Yorker, born in 1924, and educated in the Bronx. He is one of seventeen children. After high school he went into the army and served in Europe during World War II, earning a battle star and working his way up to sergeant. Returning to NYC after the war he was determined to be a writer and, in his own words, "wrote his arm off for five years without success." Then, in 1951, he sold a short story to a sports magazine and launched a highly prolific and successful career in the pulp fiction field. He is known as a paperback novel specialist. Using seven different pseudonuyms (Priscilla Dalton, Mark Dane, Steve Michaels, Dorathea Nile, Edwina Noone [Ha!], John Patrick and Sidney Stuart) Avallone has written over a hundred and fifty paperback novels producing, for a time, nine to twelve paperbacks a year. Besides the Ed Noon series he has written a number of Nick Carter tales, many Man From U.N.C.L.E. novels, several romance and gothic novels and hundreds of short stories. Amazingly, from 1955 to 1959 Avallone was editor of twenty-seven publications in the men's magazine field as well as editor of *The Third Degree*, house organ of the MWA, from 1962 to 1965. As for his love of writing, Avallone says:

Ever since I discovered pencils, I have set out to prove the theory that a writer can write anything—or should be able to. I have ghosted when I felt the work was worthy (for me) of my individual aims. Liner notes, music biographies, personality articles, poetry, cover copy, all of these I have done because of a long-standing love affair with the English language. I intend to write forever—for I know of no other form of self-expression which so isolates collaboration and is the closest to 90% fulfillment of anything and everything one particular man thinks, sees, and feels.

In the golden era of TV, Avallone was often a guest or contestant on such prime time shows as "I've Got A Secret" as well as daytime favorites like "Play Your Hunch," "Who Do You Trust" and "Joe Franklin's Memory Lane." Finally, Avallone contributed a number of scripts for two of the better TV suspense series, *Mannix* and the very popular *Hawaii Five-O*.

Mark Foran & Tony Costaine & Bert McCall—W.T. Ballard

Mark Foran's PI philosophy is straightforward and simple:

Nobody forced me to become a private investigator, Mrs. Fremont. It was probably a mistake but it's one I made a long time ago and it's a little late to change now.

Foran appears in his first and only case in W.T. Ballard's *Murder Las Vegas Style* published in 1970. Mark is a competent, low-key, sensitive and perceptive operator in his middle thirties. Operating out of his LA office, Mark is hired on the recommendation of his ex-boss, the District Attorney, to accompany one retired Army Colonel to Las Vegas as his personal bodyguard. The good Colonel is attempting to persuade his niece to annul her marriage to a notorious gambler. On arriving in Vegas, Foran and the Colonel discover the niece has been murdered. Shortly thereafter they learn the new husband has also been found dead, apparently a suicide. Foran is quick to deduce both bride and groom were murdered by a third party. Set against the backdrop of Las Vegas like many of Ballard's stories, the novel is well written and well plotted even though the outcome is not as surprising as you might hope.

Ballard is an old and experienced hand in the mystery and pulp fiction field. He is best known for his skilled craftmanship in the Western genre, having written over thirty Western novels. He won the Western Writers Of America Spur award in 1956. Many of these novels Ballard wrote under the pseudonym of John Hunter. Ballard was also one of the original and most popular contributors to *Black Mask* when Joseph Shaw was serving as editor. Most of his Black Mask stories featured Bill Lennox, a tough PI-like character who worked as a trouble-shooter for a big Hollywood studio, General Consolidated. There were four Lennox novels: *Say Yes to Murder* (1942), *Murder Can't Stop* (1946), *Dealing Out Death* (1948) and *Lights, Camera, Murder* (1960). In the last three, Lennox has worked his way up to the level of an executive producer and is living much higher-on-the-hog than he did in the *Black Mask* short stories. While the Lennox tales are very good, Ballard was even better with a pair of fascinating private eyes named Anthony Costaine and Norbert McCall which he wrote under the pseudonym of Neil MacNeil.

Tony and Bert are tough and smart. Of the two Bert is the tougher and Tony the smarter. Both are the greatest threats to feminine virtue since Don Juan. Costaine is handsome enough to be a movie idol. Six feet tall, jet black hair, gray eyes, a heavy tan with a hint of Latin in the face, thin lips and dazling white teeth backed by a warm husky voice, Tony also dresses in only the best. He was educated at Dartmouth and Columbia Law School, and then worked for a while with the FBI and during World War II with the OSS. McCall, who served with Tony in both the FBI and the OSS, is larger and more rugged. In fact, Bert is just about as enormous and craggy as one can get. He stands six feet five-and-three-quarters of an inch tall and weighs in at two hundred and sixty five pounds. He is good-looking in a masculine way with heavy eyebrows, big bony hands, an infectious smile and the physical strength of a bull elephant. Bert drinks Scotch and Bourbon whiskey by the case and also plays the bagpipes. Tony and Bert make up the *Costaine and McCall Investigative Agency* that specializes in business problems and expects to be well paid for its services. As business detectives specializing in the investigation of industrial complexes they are probably the highest paid PIs in the business. For a typical case their asking price is $20,000 plus expenses, and their bare minimum is five hundred a week with a five thousand retainer. If on some difficult cases they are successful they expect $20,000 more. And they are worth it!

There are seven novels in this well-written series. Tony and Bert are fun to follow. They are cool, witty, cocky cut-ups and womanizers who manage to retain their credibility. The first tale, *Death Takes An Option* (1958) has the two looking into the strange suicide of the auditor of a large mining machinery corporation and the murder of one of the branch executives. It is an unusual plot with a surprise ending. *Third On A Seesaw* (1959), *Two Guns For Hire* (1959) and *Hot Dam* (1960) have the pair again looking into murder, extortion and financial hijinks at the corporate level. In the fifth, *The Death Ride* (1960), Tony and Bert come to the aid of their former OSS Commander, General Frederick Moss, who is now the owner of a Pacific coast amusement park where several patrons have been killed. Costaine and McCall go into action and nab the killers. The sixth, *Mexican Slay Ride* (1962), sends McCall to Mexico to steal back some stolen goods. When Bert is caught and slapped in jail along with the fifty men he hired to help, Tony has to come to the rescue. In the last story, *The Spy Catchers* (1966), Tony and Bert are brought into a top-secret aerospace industry to catch a thief, a murderer and a traitor who may be the same person. The plant is developing a revolutionary weapon—a cosmic ray gun—and the other side wants it too. As usual, there is a number of nubile maidens loose on the premises with much more than business in mind. It is light and pleasant reading. If you like your PI's competent and happy-go-lucky, you'll go for McCall and Costaine.

Willis Todhunter Ballard was born in Cleveland in 1903 and graduated from Wilmington College in 1926. The University of Oregon library in Eugene holds the collection of his manuscripts—over fifty novels and over a hundred short stories. Besides Foran, Lennox, Costaine and McCall, Ballard created another likeable hero—the cop Lieutenant Max Hunter. Hunter appears in three original paperbacks written in the early sixties.

Barr Breed—Bill S. Ballinger

Another Chicago private eye who is a master at deduction and logical thinking is Barr Breed. Breed is the head of an agency in downtown Chicago. Rather than a typical office of one or two rooms, Barr's office takes up a third of a floor. There are private, paneled offices for Barr, his three PI employees and his secretary. Breed's secretary is Evelyn Jones and as Barr says, "She is homely as hell." Breed wants it this way because it keeps her and his male employees' minds on their work. As Barr says,

"She's so homely, I figure she is one woman in the world who'll be honest." She is. The beauty in the office is furnished by his female PI Sylvia. Sylvia is an expert "shopper." When one of Breed's clients thinks some of his clerks might not be putting all the change in the cash register, Sylvia shops around and catches a lot of them "cause she doesn't look like she's got a brain in her head." Breed also employs Al Seevey, who's very efficient at digging up information and tracking down anyone who is missing, and Joe Dockert who is a rough and tough muscle man. Though Breed is not a college graduate he did play football at Southwestern State Teachers College for two years.

Breed's forte is using his brains to unravel complicated "locked room" type murders. There are, however, only two of these. The first, *The Body in the Bed* (1948), concerns a wayward husband who steps into the shower in his mistress' apartment. After finishing the bath and getting into bed, he discovers that during his ten minutes in the shower someone has strangled his mistress. Barr is called in to help and, after two attempts on his life, Barr decides that he had better cooperate with his friend on the force, Sergeant Cheenan. After the wayward husband and the betrayed wife are also killed, Barr begins to suspect the case is rather complex. Clearing it up takes the combined efforts of Breed and his staff, plus the cops. According to the critic John Muste, "*The Body In The Bed* is somewhat over-complicated and hides too many clues from the reader, but its Chicago setting, its violence, and its emphasis on sex mark it as a typical example of the hard-boiled novel from the period just after World War II." Muste and other critics have also argued that the novel is similar to Hammett's *Maltese Falcon* in that an antique wooden statue and a femme fatale are key elements in Ballinger's novel also.

The last Breed, *The Body Beautiful* (1949), has Breed dating a chorus girl. The first evening he goes to the nightclub to watch her perform in a golden bird cage fifteen feet in the air someone knifes her in the back and she falls into the orchestra pit. Breed, working again with his team and Cheenan, has to start from scratch to figure out the motive, find out who she knew and where she came from. Finally, he is able to capture the killer.

In addition to Barr Breed, William Sanborn Ballinger was also the creator of Joquain Hawks, a James Bond-like CIA ace who is part Spanish and part American Indian. Hawks is featured in a fine suspense series mostly with the word "Spy" in the title, e.g.: *The Spy In Bangkok* (1965), *The Spy In The Jungle* (1965), *The Chinese Mask* (1965), *The Spy In The Java Sea* (1966) and *The Spy At Angkor WAT* (1966). Another PI-like hero Ballinger created is Bryce Patch, chief of security at a large electronic company. Patch appears in one good novel, *Heist Me Higher* (1969).

Ballinger's generally acknowledged masterpiece in the suspense field is a marvellously crafted novel titled *The Wife Of The Red-Haired Man*

(1956). The plot concerns an Enoch Arden-like situation in which the second husband is murdered by the first. The husband and wife flee to elude capture by a detective trying to run them down. Part of the novel is written in the first person and told from the detective's point of view. Other chapters are written from an omniscience stance. The novel is beautifully plotted and has a double whammy of an ending—one ironic conclusion and another complete surprise. Another of Ballinger's interesting tales in a similar vein is *The Tooth And The Nail* (1955) featuring as its hero a magician whose wife is murdered. The magician goes after his revenge and gets it.

Ballinger, who was born in Oskaloosa, Iowa, in 1912, considers himself primarily a story teller who enjoys plotting more than any other aspect of writing. He was educated at the University of Wisconsin, graduating in 1934. From 1977 to 1979 he served as an associate professor of writing at California State University in Northridge. Ballinger, who has been writing professionally for over fifty years, is a member of the Writers Guild of America. He was an Executive Vice-President of the MWA in 1957. He also won an Edgar in 1960 and was the guest of honor at the Bouchercon II conference in 1971. Besides his thirty some odd novels, Ballinger has written over 150 scripts for television and the movies. He now lives in North Hollywood, California, enjoying his retirement.

Fergus O'Breen—Anthony Boucher
(William Anthony Parker White)

O'Breen, believe it or not, is Irish! Although he is a legitimate private investigator, he is hardly hardboiled. He is one of the softest boiled eggs in the book and he is a character. Whenever Fergus detects he exercises some peculiar habits. Number one, he paces. There are two reasons for this, according to O'Breen. First, it helps him think; second, it gets people so nervous they say things they didn't mean to say and provide Fergus with clues. Also, according to O'Breen, he becomes sweetness and light whenever he interrogates a suspect because Fergus believes that sugar catches more flies than vinegar. For Fergus it does. Another peculiarity is his dress. Fergus likes loud, bright colors in strange combinations. One of his favorite outfits is a yellow polo shirt which clashes beautifully with his flaming crimson hair and his bright green eyes. Fergus also knows hundreds of scatalogical limericks which he often starts but rarely finishes. He admits that his fondest ambition was to be a poet:

There's a family tradition that there's bardic blood in the O'Breens. I don't know how true that is; but if there is it came out in me. I used to want to be a poet; I still turn out some God-awful tripe for my own pleasure .... I took a hell of a ribbing for a while and then I got the feeling of "Well, I'll show them." I was too light for football, but I was, to speak with characteristic modesty, *the* best basketball sensation that Loyola has ever known.

It is true that Fergus did make thirteen baskets one year in a USC-Loyola game.

Fergus also sees himself as an "introspective extrovert with manic-depressive tendencies" who has to keep himself high as heaven to avoid getting low as hell. As a private investigator Fergus is "unorthodox as hell." He rarely drinks on a case and never before lunch. When he does drink he prefers, of course, Rye-Irish whiskey. Operating out of the O'Breen Detective Agency in Los Angeles, Fergus gets many of his cases through his older sister, Maureen, who is head of publicity at Metropolis Pictures. Even though Fergus is in his late twenties many people in the novels refer to him as "that boy detective." O'Breen's hobbies are reading, cooking, football, classical music and amateur theatrics. He drives a bright yellow roadster to match his shirts. Like other successful PIs, Fergus has a friend on the force, Detective Lieutenant A. Jackson in Homicide.

We know very little about O'Breen's early history but we are told he was born around 1910 and he never knew his mother. His father was an alcoholic and Fergus was raised by Maureen. Fergus is very bright and uses his wit and brains to solve the four cases he confronts. The first, *The Case of the Crumpled Knave* (1939), has an elderly inventor and card connoisseur, Humphrey Garnett, sending a telegraph to an old military friend, Colonel Rand, asking him to come to LA but warning him he might be a witness at "the inquest on my body." Sure enough, when Rand arrives Garnett is dead, poisoned, and in his hand is a crumpled Jack of Diamonds. Fergus solves the case and discovers the inventor was involved in the production of an anti-gas weapon that would be of great value in wartime. The second, *The Case of the Baker Street Irregulars* (1940), concerns a movie studio's plan to film a Sherlock Holmes story. The third, *The Case of the Solid Key* (1941), deals with two murders: the first, that of the managing director of a little theater group in a locked room; and the second, that of a crook and blackmailer that Fergus was involved with. Fergus manages to corral the killer in an off-beat climax. The fourth and last, *The Case of the Seven Sneezes* (1942), reveals that O'Breen is allergic to cats and that when he sneezes, he sneezes exactly seven times. The story is set on an island off the coast of California and involves a silver wedding anniversary party. Twenty-five years earlier at the wedding there was a murder. A bridesmaid had her throat cut and during the week before the wedding the same girl's cats had their throats cut as well. Now at the anniversary party a similar crime seems in the offing. Fergus is called in to clear up the earlier twenty-five year old murder and to head off the second.

O'Breen was the creation of William Anthony Parker White, better known as Anthony Boucher (rhymes with voucher). When asked why he adopted the pseudonym he said, "The Library of Congress lists 75 books by authors named William White." It is common knowledge that Tony Boucher was a star of the first magnitude in the galaxy of mystery fiction. Because of his voluminous critical and editorial output he attracted less attention as a writer of excellent fiction himself. Boucher was *the* premier mystery critic, the dean of critics, the man for whom the annual get-togethers of mystery writers is named: the Bouchercons. It would require an entire chapter in this book to list Tony's accomplishments and contributions to the field of mystery writing.

White was born in 1911 in Oakland, California, the son of two physicians. He was educated at Pasadena Junior College, the University of Southern California (BA 1932) and at the University of California, Berkeley (MA 1934). A Phi Beta Kappa, a Roman Catholic and a Democrat, Boucher wanted to become an admiral, then a physicist, then a linguist (he spoke and wrote French, Spanish, Portuguese, German and Italian) and, at one time, he wanted a career teaching languages.

He became interested in writing, acting and directing in the little theater movement. Next he tried playwriting and then got a job as theater editor of a LA newspaper. In 1936 he wrote a novel and sold it a year later. For the next few years he wrote at least one mystery novel a year. Then, in the late thirties, he developed an interest in science-fiction and wrote a number of science fiction stories for the pulps. This interest led to a job as book reviewer, specializing in science fiction and mysteries for the San Francisco *Chronicle* from 1942 to 1947. In 1949 he became one of the founders of and the editor of *The Magazine of Fantasy and Science Fiction*—an editorship he shared with J. Francis McComas from 1949 to 1958. During this period Boucher also reviewed mysteries for Ellery Queen's *Mystery Magazine* (1957-1968) and edited a number of mystery and science-fiction story collections.

In 1951 Boucher was chosen to edit the "Criminals at Large" column for the New York *Times Book Review*, a service he performed until his death in 1968. Over the years he wrote a total of 852 columns for the *Times*. For a seven year period (1961-1968) he was also the opera reviewer for *Opera News*. He also wrote scripts for the "Sherlock Holmes" and the "Gregory Hood" radio programs. Boucher originated the "Golden Voice" radio program featuring historical records which was broadcast in Berkeley, New York and Los Angeles from 1949 to 1968. During his career he wrote several hundred radio shows, wrote the introductions to over thirty books, edited more than twenty collections of stories and was the collector and editor of Dutton's annual *Best Detective Stories of the Year* from 1963 to 1968.

Boucher was also very active socially and politically. He was a member of MWA and was elected President in 1951. He belonged to The Crime

Writers Association, The Baker Street Irregulars, The Elves, Gnomes and Little Men's Science Fiction Chowder and Marching Society, The San Francisco Opera Guild, The National Collegiate Players and the Scorers and Molly McGuires of San Francisco. Boucher was a member of the central committee of the California State Democratic party from 1948 to 1952. He was a three-time winner of the MWA Edgar, receiving the honor for the best mystery criticism of 1946, 1950 and 1953.

After his death, one of his admirers wrote:

In the special world of writers and readers of mystery and science fiction books and stories, Anthony Boucher occupied a pre-eminent place, for his encyclopedic knowledge of those genres and for his ability to express his learning with pithy wit.

This accolade might also be apt as a review of a classic, non-PI mystery novel titled *Rocket to the Morgue* (1942) that Boucher wrote under the pseudonym of H.H. Holmes. This novel, which is the 1942 entry in the Haycraft-Queen *Definitive Library of Detective-Crime-Mystery Fiction, Two Centuries of Cornerstones, 1748-1948*, combines Boucher's interests in mystery and SF. The story is concerned with science fiction writers and a murder at a rocket-launching party. The victim is pushed into the path of the rocket just as it is emerging from its launching pit. After several attempts on the life of the hated son and heir of a literary legacy, the murderer is finally successful. Or so it seems until the surprising conclusion. Tony Boucher was someone special and his many contributions will not be forgotten as long as there are mystery and SF readers and writers.

Pete McGrath—Michael Brett (Miles Barton Tripp)

Another neglected Manhattan PI is big, tough and handsome Peter McGrath. Pete is the President, Vice President, Secretary, Treasurer and Chief and sole investigator of the *Peter McGrath Private Detective Agency*. He is also six-feet-three with jet black hair and blue eyes. This lovely ensemble is attenuated somewhat by a sullen and angry face. Pete has an office on Thirty-Fourth Street in Manhattan and he drives a three-year-old Chevy painted a respectable shade of inconspicuous gray because as Pete says, "A man in my business doesn't want to attract attention to himself." Under the hood "there's a monster of an engine on special mounts, there's a fast transmission and a heavy-duty, rear-end axle. The frame is reinforced. The trunk holds some of the melodramatic tools of my trade: a grappling hook, lengths of nylon rope, a filled two-gallon gasoline can and some empty, harmless looking soda bottles."

Pete says that even though he doesn't have any rockets or launching devices or passenger ejection seats, he does have a secret compartment built into the front seat where he keeps a number of electronic listening devices. He says he and the Federal Government have the same motto: Bug thine Enemy! Pete doesn't have too high opinion of his profession:

My business attracts a lot of sleazy characters. Television's stereotyped version of the private eye wearing three hundred dollar custom-made suits and driving around in Bentleys is phony. Most private investigators make their buck by snooping and gathering both legitimate and rigged divorce evidence. They're a shady, shabby bunch, scrambling for the dollar like hungry dogs after a chunk of old beef. Fiction writers have referred to them as muckrakers, troublemakers and jackals living off human misery, who'd sell out their mothers for a hundred-dollar bill.

Pete is a little better off than most PIs. He has a five-room apartment that faces the East River and the Borough of Queens. But he is usually behind in the rent and the phone bills. Pete, who talks to himself, likes Scotch whiskey, cigars and a blonde Viking named Samantha Conners who works as guide at the UN Building. His proverbial friend on the force is Detective Lieutenant Daniel Fowler, Homicide. Fowler helps Pete out with his cases and vice versa. Pete also possesses a wry sense of humor and uses it frequently. For example:

I'd seen some of Willie's women in the past. Usually they were outdoor types, which meant that Willie found them sleeping in public parks on benches or beneath bushes or weeping willing trees.

In describing the best features of a young lady, Pete remarks,

Her legs were long, the ankles narrow, calves rounded. There was enough buttocks bounce and hip sway to keep a marine battalion interested.

And, in dealing with a pro-football player who made the mistake of attacking him, Pete muses,

He made his move. I almost felt sorry for him. But my pity, what there was of it, was already used up on a guy in Jersey. I caught his jaw with my knee. His head lifted violently and he came to rest on his back with his eyes blank and went to sleep with a fine trickle of blood running from his nose.

Pete carries a .38 and a fake Police Lieutenant's badge that he uses frequently to grease his path. He also carries a set of lock picks and a microphone imbedded in a quarter-inch piece of rubber with a suction cup on it. There's a wire that runs from this to an amplifier in his jacket pocket which relays sound through an earplug. He uses these tools, along with his brains and brawn, to solve a total of ten complex cases.

The first, *Kill Him Quickly, It's Raining* (1966), has Pete mixed up with some ex-cons, some rapes and a couple of murders. In the second, *An Ear For Murder* (1967), Pete takes on a divorce case and in his efforts to find the husband gets a PI friend killed by a meat cleaver. Pete gets his vengeance with a machete and help from some hoods and the Treasury Department. The third, *The Flight of the Stiff* (1967), has Pete protecting a beautiful redhead whose beau has been murdered. A total of $40,000 has also disappeared. Pete goes in search of the money and the killer. Much blood, some of it his, is shed. In *Lie a Little, Die a Little* (1968), Pete gets a $10,000 fee to help clear Jason Dominique, a wealthy old eccentric, from being implicated in a murder as well as to help him deal with a blackmailer. Pete also gets a luscious redheaded assistant to help, but she turns out to be more of a pain than an assistant. *We The Killers* (1967) has Pete looking for a missing coed and breaking up an abortion ring. In *Dead Upstairs in the Tub* (1967) Pete finds himself looking into the supposedly accidental death of a girl on an LSD trip. Pete's friend who brought him into the case is also murdered and Pete is out to avenge them both. *Slit My Throat, Gently* (1968) has Pete involved in some gangland slayings and then looking for a missing girl and a murderer who likes to cut his victim's throats. *Turn Blue, You Murderers* (1967) finds Pete working for an underworld czar who wants Pete to find his missing wife. In *Death of a Hippie* (1968) Pete is hired to find a beautiful young hippie with a heroin habit who has disappeared along with $60,000 worth of jewelry. Pete has to reach her before a mobster does. *Another Day, Another Stiff* (1968) has Pete trying to clear a hell-raiser of a murder charge. Only his wife believes in the raiser's innocence and she hires Pete to prove it. He does but he is forced to do it the hard way—by leaving Manhattan and roughing it in Kentucky.

Most of McGrath's cases are set in and around Manhattan, but Pete is no lover of the Big Apple. Throughout the ten novels Pete takes opportunity after opportunity to criticize:

Daytime travel in New York can be treacherous. You have to watch out for chunks of ice blown by the wind, loose building cornices, falling flower pots, unleashed dogs, death-dealing traffic,bag-assed secretaries, harassed businessmen, pickpockets, opium peddlers, and con men.
    At night the city loses its grimy, sooty look. It becomes a fabled Arabian Nights municipality, glittering and mysterious. The aroma of the city also changes with nightfall. The odors of toil, of sweat, of concentration are replaced by the aroma of aphrodisiac perfumes, aftershave lotion, burnt Cherries Jubilee, roasted chestnuts, uuky puke, unwashed ankles, the emergency admitting room at Bellevue Hospital, formaldehyde, fresh wood alcohol. A half-ass fiction writer could go nuts with all these stinks and smells . . . .

The author of these astute observations is Miles Barton Tripp, alias Michael Brett, who was born in 1923 in Ganwick Corner, near Barnet,

England. During World War II he served in the Royal Air Force Bomber Command. He also studied law and was admitted as a solicitor in 1950. He practiced law off and on in Stamford, Lincolnshire from 1950 to 1952. Since 1953 he has been a member of the legal staff of the Charity Commission in London but has managed to find the time to write over thirty-five novels, many short stories, several plays and an autobiography. Besides Pete McGrath, Tripp has created another interesting character, Hugo Baron, a gentleman professional killer, and a skilled international investigator. There are three novels in the Baron series: *Diecast* (1963), *A Plague of Demons* (1965) and *A Cargo of Spent Evil* (1966). In a recent interview Tripp stated, "As someone who would rather plant characters than clues, and would prefer that the story evolves through the characters rather than by their being shaped to fit the structure of a plot, I naturally prefer psychology to technology and Simenon to either Christie or the imitators of Deighton." What is remarkable is that Tripp has such a mastery of the hardboiled American PI novel. Some reviewers have put down the McGrath series as poor derivatives of Chandler and/or Spillane. Such comments are misleading. If Pete McGrath is imitative then we need more such imitators.

Curt Cannon and Benjamin Smoke—Ed McBain (Evan Hunter)

One of our most sympathy-demanding detectives is Curt Cannon—a drunk and a bum. Curt crawls out of the gutter whenever a friend is in trouble and becomes an effective and sober investigator. Once the crisis is over and the problem solved, Curt crawls back. Most of the time when he is in the gutter he's barely alive and is only a ghost of his normal self. At one time, when he was still licensed, he was the best private eye in New York. Then one day he discovered that his wife was a tramp and that his best friend was a punk. Curt tried to pistol-whip them both when he found them in bed together, but someone called the cops. Cannon was charged with assault with a deadly weapon and lost his PI license. So he started some serious drinking and drank his way from uptown to the Bowery and Skid Row. Yet even in Skid Row people have problems, and people who knew Curt seek him out for assistance.

There are only two Cannons—one novel, *I'm Cannon For Hire* (1958), an original Fawcett Gold Medal paperback, and *I Like 'Em Tough* (1958), also a Gold Medal original, made up of six short stories published originally in 1953 and 1954 in the pulp magazines. When we first meet Cannon he tells us, flat out that he is a drunk:

THE NAME IS CANNON.
I'm a drunk. I think we'd better get that straight from the beginning. I drink because I want to drink. Sometimes I'm falling-down ossified and sometimes I'm rosy-glow happy, and sometimes I'm cold sober—but not very often. I'm usually

drunk, and I live where being drunk isn't a sin, though it's sometimes a crime when the police go on a purity drive. I live on New York's Bowery.

In the novel Curt has been a bum for five years running, when a friend, named Johnny Bridges, from Cannon's old neighborhood, asks for Curt's help. Johnny has not gone to a regular agency because he lacks the cash. The problem is that Johnny runs a tailor shop and someone has been stealing money from the cash register. Johnny suspects his partner but he isn't sure. Cannon agrees to help and goes to the shop for a look. When they arrive they discover that Johnny's partner is dead, two bullets in his chest, with Johnny's initials, in blood, on the wall behind the body. Cannon must clear Johnny and find the killer.

We learn of Cannon's background when he returns to his old neighborhood looking for the killer. Curt was a slum kid, born on the upper East Side of Manhattan of Irish parents. He wanted to go to college but couldn't because his father died and he had to support the family. Though he wanted to be a cop he went to work for a haberdasher. After his mother died he became a private eye. Cannon worked for an agency at first but then opened his own. Things were fine until he met Toni McAlister. After a year's courtship, he married her. Curt had a three-man agency and was doing well until he hired a fourth man, Dave Parker. Curt liked him— but so did Toni, too well. After four months of marriage, Curt came home unexpectedly and found Dave and Toni in bed together. Curt kept hitting Dave with his pistol until he destroyed Dave's face. Curt was hurt even worse, inside, and with his marriage destroyed he went to pieces, winding up on the Bowery.

The first story in the collection, *I Like 'Em Tough*, has Cannon helping the addict son of a man who is murdered after he asks Curt for assistance. The second tale has Cannon returning to his old neighborhood to look into the death of a boyhood friend. Moreover, the entire neighborhood is being menaced by a shakedown artist. Curt, in knightly fashion, ends the threat. The third short has Cannon finding a boy who impregnated and abandoned a seventeen-year old. In another one Cannon is called upon to solve his own murder! Seems that someone who's his spitting image is found with six .45 slugs in his carcass.

Curt Cannon is only one of Evan Hunter's pseudonyms. Hunter is the familiar Ed McBain, author of the famed 87th Precinct series consisting, at the moment, of more than thirty-five novels. Hunter also wrote seven fine novels under the name of Richard Marsten as well as sixteen serious works of fiction under his own name. Among these were a number of critical successes: *The Blackboard Jungle* (1954), *A Matter of Conviction* (1959), *Come Winter* (1973), *Strangers When We Meet* (1958), *Mothers and Daughters* (1961), *Buddwing* (1964), *Sons* (1969) and *Walk Proud* (1979).

Hunter has also written a number of science-fiction novels under the pseudonym of Hunt Collins, e.g., *Tomorrow and Tomorrow* (1955) and westerns, e.g., *The Chisholms: A Novel of the Journey West* (1976) as well as numerous short stories. He has written a number of tales for TV and the movies. Among these were the screenplay for *Strangers When We Meet* in 1960, the screenplay for Hitchcock's excellent *The Birds* (1962) and the script for *Walk Proud* (1979). He has written three plays produced and staged in New York, London and Michigan as well as a dozen juvenile books. One of Hunter's current successes is the lawyer Matthew Hope series—also written as McBain—which includes thus far four novels: *Goldilocks (1977), Rumpelstiltskin* (1981), *Beauty and the Beast* (1983) and *Jack and the Beanstalk* (1984).

Hunter was born in New York City in 1926 and was educated at Cooper Union and Hunter College where he earned a Phi Beta Kappa key. He served in the US Navy from 1944 to 1946. He is divorced and the father of three children. Awarded an Edgar in 1957 Hunter is one of the most readable writers in modern fiction.

We must also mention an additional character who is difficult to classify as PI or non-PI. Under the McBain name, Hunter wrote one novel about a six-foot three-inch, scarred, gray-haired, retired cop, Benjamin Smoke, who does not have a PI license and never expects to apply for one for the following reasons:

Whatever anyone may tell you about licensed private eyes, they're hired mostly to find missing persons or to get the goods on adulterous husbands; my aspirations are higher. I have a Carry permit for a .38 Detective Special, I would rather part with my pistol and my shoes than the magic little shield. I live fairly comfortably on my pension and on the dividends from some stock I inherited when my father died. I suppose I might be considered a happy man.
    In fact, I have only one regret.
    I've never investigated a case I couldn't solve. I've never encountered the perfect crime.

Smoke keeps hoping for a case tough enough to challenge his extraordinary abilities. He keeps looking for the perfect crime. In *Where There's Smoke* (1975), the only Smoke novel, Ben has to track down a psychopathic weirdo who is kidnapping corpses from funeral homes. It is a humdinger of a story and leaves the reader wishing that Hunter had never given up Smoke-ing.

Milo March—M.E.Chaber (Kendell Foster Crossen)
According to this armorless knight,

The name is March. Milo March. I'm an insurance investigator. With my own office—March's Insurance Corporation—on Madison Avenue, that little section of

New York famous for strong martinis and neat women. I'm for hire.

But don't make a big thing out of it and confuse me with those private eyes that wander around on your television screen. I wear a trench coat when it's raining. I carry a gun when somebody is trying to shoot me.

Milo has a "couple of pieces of paper that say I'm a private detective, but I work as an insurance investigator." Sometimes, that is. At other times Milo is a syndicate buster, a one-man commando squad and international rescue team, and a James Bond-like CIA operative. The gun Milo carries is a snub-nosed .32 caliber which he wears in a shoulder holster. March, on occasion, also carries a spare gun, an ivory-handled, old-fashioned belly gun with four revolving barrels that has been modified to fire regular .32 shells. The gun saves his live in *Hangman's Harvest* (1952).

Milo is featured in twenty-two novels written by Kendall Foster Crossen under the pen name of M.E. Chaber. Despite what March says in the quotation above, he uses his guns frequently and effectively. He also uses his fists, his wits and a number of other fighting skills he acquired as an OSS officer during World War II in Europe where he spent eight months behind Nazi lines. A little later Milo went to work for the CIA. Whether he likes it or not, his old Colonel, now Major General Sam Roberts, frequently calls March back to duty to do a job for him. This job is usually behind the Iron Curtain, which is the case in *Wild Midnight Falls* (1968) and *The Splintered Man* (1955).

Milo is tall, dark and handsome. A hit with the ladies in the early novels, as he grows older he finally marries one of the women he rescued from East Germany and adopts a young Spanish boy, Ernesto Pujol. These things occur in the novel *As Old As Cain* (1954). March met Ernesto when he went to Spain to recover a valuable diamond in *No Grave For March* (1952). Early in the series Milo operated from his office in Denver but he was finally lured to New York as the investigative business improved. His base of operations is of little matter, however, since like Chet Drum and Ed Noon he gets around. *A Man in the Middle* (1968) is set in Hong Kong, San Francisco, LA and Vegas. *So Dead The Rose* (1959) occurs in Berlin and Moscow for the most part. *A Lonely Walk* (1957) puts Milo in Rome. *Six Who Ran* (1964) finds Milo in Rio, and *A Hearse Of Another Color* (1958) has him in New Orleans. *Jade For A Lady* (1962) is set in Hong Kong, and *Wanted: Dead Men* (1965) has Milo working in Paris. *Green Grow The Graves* (1970) moves from Cleveland to Cape Town. While March is more of a private investigator than a spy, the intrigue and the exotic locale give the novels an extra dimension. Even those set in places like New York or LA exceed the average PI novel in entertainment value. *Flaming Man* (1968) and *Softly In The Night* (1963) are two of the better domestics.

Despite the volume of stories we are told very little about Milo or his personal habits. He loves martinis, very dry, and often drinks as many as ten or twelve in one twenty-four hour period. He also likes bourbon, scotch and soda, and brandy. And as one reviewer put it, "Milo doesn't miss a drink, a girl, or a wisecrack."

Crossen, writing under the name of Chrisopher Monig, authored a four-novel series about the activities of an insurance claims adjuster, Brian Brett, in the Hollywood-LA vicinity. *The Burned Man* (1956), *Abra-Cadaver* (1958), *Once Upon A Crime* (1959) and *The Lonely Graves* (1960) are the titles.

Kendell F. Crossen, who was born in Albany, Ohio, in 1910, also wrote under the pen name of Bennett Barlay, Richard Foster and Clay Richards. He attended Rio Grande College and moved to California soon after graduation. Starting first as a director and producer of stage revues, he quit to become a full-time writer in 1940. Between 1940 and 1965 Crossen wrote more than 400 dramas for radio and television and contributed over 300 short stories and 250 non-fiction articles to national magazines. In addition he wrote 45 novels—mystery, romance and science fiction— several hundred newspaper reviews and, somehow or other, found time to edit several collections of SF stories and edit and publish two journals, *Spark* and *Play*. For a while, early in his career Crossen was the editor of the famed *Detective Fiction Weekly*.

Flash Casey, Kent Murdock and Jack Fenner—George Harmon Coxe

According to George Harmon Coxe neither Casey nor Murdock was a professional detective, and they would be surprised to find themselves categorized as private investigators. However, other than not having the license, they fit the description to a P. Casey, originally known as Flashgun but later shortened to Flash, was born in the pages of *Black Mask* during the period when Joseph Shaw was editor. Flash needs to be considered a PI because as a professional crime photograher he used his nosey camera, itself an instrument of detection, to poke and pry into all of the circumstances surrounding the crimes he investigated. Shaw, it is reported, told Coxe that Casey should not compete with the detectives because he was unique since he was the only one carrying a camera. Casey began his career with the Boston *Globe* but when one of his photos was suppressed, he objected so strenuously he was fired. Casey moved to the Boston *Express* and resumed his career which is featured in six novels and around twenty short stories all published in *Black Mask* in the early thirties.

Casey was born somewhere near Boston, graduated from high school and perhaps even went to college for a year or so. Casey is six feet two and his weight varied from 210 to 220. He is a big and rugged fellow with solid muscles but he is still quick, agile and is considered handsome with dark eyes. His forehead is creased and he sports a thick head of dark brown hair which is usually long and in need of a trim. Like most Irishmen, Casey has a love of the grape as well as a quick and unpredictable temper. He gets involved in the plot most often because someone is trying to steal a negative or to destroy his equipment. Casey gets lots of tips and inside information from friends and acquaintances, and no such favors go unrewarded. Casey always returns the favor—tickets to see the Red Sox, pictures edited so someone will not be embarrassed, a few extra bucks when needed, etc. Because of such help Casey usually gets to the crime scene ahead of his competitors and the cops. Casey never married. His bedmates are usually young widows and divorcees who often proposition Casey.

Casey plays hero in six novels: *Silent Are The Dead* (1942), *Murder For Two* (1943), *Flash Casey, Detective* (1946), *Error Of Judgment* (1961), *The Man Who Died Too Soon* (1962) and *Deadly Image* (1964). In *Deadly Image*, perhaps the best of the six, Casey drops into one of his favorite bars, The Melody Lounge. One of his acquaintances, Shirley Farrington, asks Casey to take her home from the party where her husband is rapidly getting drunk. Farrington, a wealthy and honorable stockbroker, then asks Casey's help with his blackmail problem. Seems there are some snapshots showing Farrington in bed with a nude blonde beside him. Before Casey can clear up the blackmail, he finds himself entangled in a double murder which he feels obligated to help solve. This he does with style and good humor.

Unlike many series characters, Casey gets older along with the rest of us. Not only does Casey's hair show some gray and the bathroom scales point to an additional ten pounds, but he also slows down, matures mentally and mellows in outlook. According to Coxe, Casey was 32 in 1933, and in *Deadly Image*, the last book, Coxe says he saw him as a man of 45 or thereabouts. Coxe adds "in a matter of thirty-one years Casey has aged no more than fourteen. Wouldn't it be interesting if we could all age in a proportionate fashion?"

As Coxe began to write novels he felt that a slightly different version of Casey would be appropriate. In his words, "For some reason, perhaps from inexperience, I thought such a character, not unlike Casey in many ways as a photographer, but better dressed and better mannered, would be more appropriate for a book." So Kent Murdock was created and first appeared in *Murder With Pictures* (1935), an engrossing story in which Murdock divorced his first wife, married his second (Joyce Archer) and solved two murders. Kent is more sophisticated, urbane and socially acceptable than Casey. He is a little over six-feet, dark, with a lean, flat-muscled body that is loose yet well knit. His brown eyes sometimes show a glint of copper and, on other occasions, turn black. Murdock prefers scotch and soda, and he has a mocking smile. He lives in an inexpensive, second-floor rear, two-room kitchenette-and-bath suite. He is intelligent and well-educated, good looking, with a knack for wearing clothes well. He has a masculine vitality that makes him appealing to women.

The later novels find Kent and Joyce working as a team to solve other murders. All told, there are twenty-two novels involving Murdock and his cameras. Some of the best are *Mrs. Murdock Takes a Case* (1941), *Four Frightened Women* (1939) which also involves Jack Fenner in a minor role; *The Hollow Needle* (1948) in which Kent photographs the body of an industrial tycoon who has committed suicide and later hears the dead man "talk" over the radio; *The Big Gamble* (1958) which has Kent snapping pictures of a highway pileup and thugs trying to kill him for the pictures which seem relatively harmless; and *Murder On Their Minds* (1957) concerning the murder of a very good and very honest private eye who was investigating a member of Boston's blue-blood set. The Murdock series attained the most popularity of Coxe's works.

Less well known but certainly deserving of attention is the short, three-book series Coxe devoted to the legitimate private eye Jack H. Fenner. Jack shares a third floor office suite "just around the corner from Boylston" in downtown Boston with Frank Quinn, a lawyer. Fenner's fee is twenty bucks an hour plus expenses. Fenner, a "lean wiry-looking man a bit under six feet," has thinning black hair which accentuates the angularity of his face. Fenner combs his hair flat from the part to make the widow's peak more prominent. His eyes are quick, observant and seldom still. Fenner does not look nor dress like a PI. He normally wears gray worsted-flannel slacks, a well-cut Shetland jacket and highly-polished, wing-tip black shoes. He never neglects his wardrobe or his appearance. Before he became a PI Fenner was a plainclothes detective on the Boston Police Force. Then he worked for a national agency before going into business for himself.

Since Fenner shows up as a secondary character in several of the Murdock novels—*Four Frightened Women* (1939) and *Murder With Pictures* (1935)—Murdock reciprocates and shows up as a secondary character in *Fenner* (1971). Like Murdock, Fenner has a sincere interest in photography and he also has a closet full of electronic aids and surveillance gear that he uses when necessary. Fenner's not a muscleman although he does have a very fast pair of hands. Murdock says he has never seen him hit a man more than twice without dumping him. But when it comes to breaking down a suspect, he uses reason, logic and common sense rather than violence. In *Fenner* (1971), the best of the three novels, Jack is hired by George Browning to find his wife, Carol, an heiress to three million dollars. Carol escaped from a State mental hospital and her husband wants her found before she destroys him and herself with her insane behavior. Before Fenner catches up with Carol, George Browning is murdered in his wife's apartment and Carol is assumed to be the murderess. Soon afterwards Frank Quinn is also slain. Fenner goes to work and with wit, wile and a minimum of violence—plus Murdock's help—uncovers the killer.

As J. Randolph Cox notes in a review of Coxe's novels, "To some readers Coxe may seem dull. There is little explicit violence, just tales of people caught up in webs of their own spinning, told in a deceptively simple, formal style. For others that's entertainment." Coxe does manage to entertain without resorting to blood and gore on every page. For example, when one of the heavies pats Jack Fenner down he says:

"A private detective? Where's your gun?"
"What gun?"
"I thought they all carried one."
"Only in television. In television they carry guns and shoot the bad guys with no questions asked.... The whole thing is a breeze. In real life if a PI shoots anyone he's in trouble up to here .... A private dick has no more right to use a gun than any citizen who happens to have a permit to carry one.

While there are murders in Coxe's works they are quietly executed. Most of them occur off center stage.

Coxe was one of our most effective professional story tellers. Born in Olean, New York, in 1901 and educated at Purdue and Cornell, he first worked as a reporter on papers in Santa Monica, Los Angeles, Utica and Elmira for a five-year period after graduating from college. For the next five years, from 1927 to 1932, he worked as an advertising salesman in Cambridge, Massachusetts. Taking up writing full-time in 1933 he proceeded over the next 43 years to turn out 64 novels, over 150 short stories—about sports, love, adventure and the sea—and numerous screen, radio and TV plays. He was a contract writer for MGM for two years from 1936 to 1938 and again in 1945. He also wrote for the Kraft Television Theater in 1957 and oversaw the adaptation of his Flash Casey stories for radio. He authored the CBS radio series *The Commandos*. Coxe himself was very interested in photography and has written about it in photo magazines. Coxe was a member of the Board of Directors of the MWA from 1946 to 1948 and in 1969 and 1979. He was elected MWA President in 1952 and in 1964 he received the coveted MWA Grand Master Award.

Frank Gruber's PIs—The Pros—Beagle & Peel, And Simon Lash— The Amateurs—Fletcher & Cragg

Two of the most shiftless and irresponsible fugitives from poverty in the mystery genre are Frank Gruber's Johnny Fletcher and Sam Cragg. Working in and out of New York City in the late thirties, these two amateur PI con-men, book salesmen and detectives are among the funniest fictional teams in history. Eternally broke and having to scrounge for a buck,

Johnny Fletcher—the brains of the pair—always comes through with one scheme or another to net them a hotel room and a meal. Money flows through Johnny's hands like flood waters through storm sewers. He goes from rags to riches and back to rags two or three times in every novel. There are fourteen Fletcher-Cragg works beginning with *The French Key* in 1939 and ending with *Swing Low Swing Dead* in 1964. Whether they are legitimate PIs is a moot point. They are certainly not *professional* investigators even though they are superb at the task. The only professional "anything" they are is book salesmen. When desperate for a bed or a meal Johnny and Sam hit the city streets with a pile of $2.95 books called *Every Man A Sampson*. Sam takes off his shirt, flexes his overdeveloped biceps, puts chains and a wide leather belt around his middle and pops them with his muscle power. Johnny furnishes the sales spiel and the customers fork over. The take is sufficient to keep them alive and in business. Sooner or later someone is murdered and Johnny has to use his brain and Sam his brawn to put the killer in a cell.

Every one of the novels is fast-paced and amusing. In *The French Key* a dead man turns up in Sam's and Johnny's room clutching a $15,000 gold coin in his fist. In *The Laughing Fox* (1940) Johnny and Sam wind up in Cedar City amid a group of wealthy fox breeders who are holding their annual fair and fur auction. Before they split they find a dead man on their bathroom floor, his throat torn out supposedly by the victim's prizewinning fox. As a side benefit the reader gets a doctoral dissertation on the art and science of crap-shooting. In *Swing Low Swing Dead* Johnny wins a song in a crap game and after two people are murdered—one a rock 'n' roll songwriter—Johnny tries to solve the murders and evade a bookie seeking revenge and an insane chemist who likes to whip up explosives. *The Limping Goose* (1954) has the pair taking on a skip-trace job for the collection of a debt and running into a bevy of beautiful blondes and a dead playboy in a showgirl's apartment. *The Silver Tombstone Mystery* (1945) sends the two Times Square cowboys out west into an old abandoned silver mine. Along the way they meet a guy who wants more money than his services are worth, a beautiful blonde in trouble, an Indian snake charmer with a Ph.D. and a couple of corpses. *The Scarlet Feather* (1948) has the pair in Chicago with Johnny diving into Lake Michigan in November to rescue a young lady in a mink coat who has just left her Cadillac coupe in a suicide attempt. Broke as usual, they drive the Cadillac home and find a scarlet feather in an envelope addressed to the girl. When they return the car they meet the girl's father and Johnny gets a new outfit. They next wander into the Midwest Poultry Breeder's Association convention to stage their act and sell their books. A corpse is discovered under one of the chicken coops and the girl they rescued has come to the convention to meet the murdered man and his birds. The pair discover that the murdered man was involved in the illegal cockfighting business. Before the smoke clears Johnny finds himself penned up with a blood-crazed, steel-spurred fighting cock. Gamblers, cops and a blackmail plot involving a number of wealthy bettors complicate the plot.

In *The Gift Horse* (1942) Johnny is named heir to a million dollar estate that includes a race horse. In claiming his inheritance Johnny (and Sam) discover the eccentric millionaire who willed Johnny the money has been murdered, supposedly by the gift horse. *The Honest Dealer* (1947) has Fletcher and Cragg crossing Death Valley and running across a dying man who gives them a deck of cards which provides the key to his fate in Las Vegas. In Vegas the pair win money at the gaming tables and run into attempts on their lives before they clear up the mystery of the honest dealer.

Otis Beagle and Joe Peel are legitimate private investigators. In the first Beagle-Peel novel, *The Silver Jackass* (1941), which Gruber wrote under the pseudonym of Charles K. Boston, Joe Peel is working for Otis in the Beagle Detective Agency in a third floor office on Hollywood Boulevard. Beagle is a big, handsome fellow at six feet three and 210 pounds who wears a big (but fake) diamond ring on the third finger of his left hand. Joe describes Otis as "Big, flashy—and phony." Peel is five eight and around 160 pounds but he is tough and smart and a first rate shadower. He has the ability to "mix" in a crowd of six men and be inconspicuous. Otis threatens to fire Peel every hour, and every hour Joe threatens to quit. They spend a good deal of time insulting each other, but they are a skilled and effective team. They depend on wit, deduction and persistence rather than violence to solve their cases. Neither of the pair approves of guns. Otis, however, does on occasion carry a sword cane.

The Silver Jackass involves a fight over the inheritance of a silver mine in Nevada. At one point Joe is abandoned in an old mine pit. He manages to survive, cracks the case and earns a partnership in the Beagle-Peel Agency. In the second novel, originally called *Beagle Scented Murder* (1946) but changed to *Market For Murder* in the paperback, Beagle and Peel in a scoundrelly and unethical fashion get themselves involved in a double-dealing blackmail scheme. Their shakedown backfires and a murder then leads to the discovery of a dime-novel racket. During the doings, Beagle betrays Peel but Peel saves Beagle's life and harmony reigns. *The Lonesome Badger* (1954), also known as *Mood For Murder* when reprinted in paper, was their last adventure.

Simon Lash, the last of Gruber's fictional detectives, is a veteran, licensed, private eye, an ex-lawyer and as hardboiled as they come. He is a shamus who can smell a rat a mile away. As one of the characters remarks to Simon, "I remember one thing he said about you, that you were the most even-tempered man he knew—always mad." And Lash does have the world's largest shoulder chip. His generally hostile and cynical attitude toward the world is tempered only by his love of books and his distrust of his fellow man—particularly women. In Lash's words, "I hate good-looking women clients .... They think they can pay off with smiles."

Simon is aided and abetted in his efforts by an equally able and tolerant assistant, Eddie Slocum. Eddie provides quiet but competent support to Simon's leading role. There are only three Lash novels: *Simon Lash, Private Detective* (1941), *The Buffalo Box* (1942) and *Murder '97* (1948). In *The Buffalo Box*, perhaps the most enjoyable of the three, an old prospector forces his way into Lash's office on Hollywood Boulevard (having ridden up on a small burro) and hands Simon a small, hand-carved redwood box. Calling himself Lansford Hastings, the old-timer hires Lash to find the owner of the box. Lash is a bit put out because if the old man is who he claims to be then he must be well over a hundred years old. Moreover the original Lansford Hastings died in 1870. Hastings also claims he is the author of a book, *The Emigrant's Trail to Oregon and California*, used by the Donner Party on their way west in 1846. The Donner Party perished in the Sierra Nevada Mountains at what is now the Donner Pass. Lansford Hastings recommended the shortcut through the mountains that brought disaster to the emigrants. In trying to find the owner of the box, which is covered with carved buffalo, Lash discovers the box has a secret compartment containing a diary which describes a fortune in gold buried in Donner Lake. In tracking down the heirs to this fortune Simon encounters murder, mayhem and mystery as well as a second, identical buffalo box. Lash and Slocum survive it all and keep the secret of the "Japanese Box Trick"—a modern counterpart of the old box with the carved buffalo. The trick box, used by professional magicians, is full one moment and empty the next. When asked how it works, Lash replies, "If I tell you ... one hundred and eighty-four magicians will bawl the hell out of Frank Gruber for exposing magician's tricks."

Gruber was one of the most prolific crime fiction authors of our time. For years he wrote a complete mystery novel every sixteen days. During the thirties he wrote regularly for the pulp magazines—250 stories in more than 40 different magazines—and during the forties and fifties he turned out mysteries and westerns at the rate of five to ten a year. In the years between 1939 and 1969 Gruber published twenty some westerns as well as thirty-four mystery novels and, at the same time, authored twenty-five film and TV scripts. Some of his most famous movie scripts were *The Mask of Dimitrios* (1944), *Johnny Angel* with Steve Fisher (1945), *Dressed to Kill* with Leonard Lee (1946) and *The Great Missouri Raid* (1951).

Born on a farm near Elmer, Minnesota, in 1904, Gruber ran away from home at sixteen and enlisted in the Army. After the war he worked as an editor and writer on various farm and business journals. In 1934 he began to write fiction on a full-time basis. Gruber was a recognized authority on the frontier history of Missouri and Kansas as well as on the outlaws and guerillas of the Civil War. In a critical study of pulp fiction, *The Pulp Jungle*, Gruber attributed his success as a mystery writer to his use of an eleven-point plot formula which is worth repeating. To succeed, Gruber argues, good mystery must have:

1) A colorful hero; 2) a theme that contains information the reader isn't likely to have; 3)a villain more powerful than the hero; 4) a colorful background for the action; 5) an unusual murder method or unusual circumstances surrounding the murder; 6) unusual variations on the motives of hate and greed; 7) a concealed clue; 8) the trick that extricates the hero from certain defeat; 9) moving and carefully paced action; 10) a smashing climax; and 11) a hero who is personally involved.

There must be merit in this approach because in his way, Gruber was one of the most popular writers in the nation. Frank Gruber died in 1969.

Humphrey Campbell—Geoffrey Holmes
(Daniel Mainwaring)

According to his driver's license, Humphrey Campbell is 28 years old, six feet one, 195 pounds with green eyes and brown hair. Humphrey is an assistant to 65-year-old Oscar Morgan, head of Morgan Missing Persons Bureau of Los Angeles. Campbell gets very little help from Morgan, however, since Oscar is not only fat and lazy but somewhat corrupt. Humphrey is a "medium-boiled" PI who uses his intelligence and reasoning rather than his gun and fists to crack his cases. Unlike normal PIs Humphrey never drinks anything stronger than milk, his favorite beverage. Campbell also wears white suits and plays the accordian. Though Humphrey looks fat, he isn't; it's all muscle. Those unwise enough to underestimate Humphrey pay dearly. He carries a .38 in a shoulder holster and knows how to use it when he has to. Humphrey also claims that he is part Piute Indian.

In the first Campbell novel, *Then There Were Three* (1938), Humphrey ties up with a newspaperman, Robin Bishop, and the two go to Los Pinos looking for a missing girl. They find her dead in a pet cemetery. The rest is pursuit and capture. The second, *No Hands On The Clock* (1939) is set in the Reno-Lake Tahoe area and involves the kidnapping of a wealthy man's son, the murder of a red-haired girl who has been scalped and a case of mistaken identity. In *Finders Keepers* (1940) Campbell and Morgan are hired by a possible heir, Michael Burke, for the purpose of finding out who he is. Burke has an old diary that seems to prove he is the grandson and heir to half of the Dunecht estate. But if this is true then why did Burke come to them and why is he carrying a gun? Some of the Dunechts (Stephen Dunecht in particular, and purportedly Michael's uncle) want Burke to prove his case in court. Before anything can be settled,

Stephen is murdered. Humphrey is then left to solve the murder and to determine whether Burke really is the heir. *Forty Whacks* (1941) and *Six Silver Handles* (1944) close out the Campbell quintet. The former is unusually well-plotted and on a par with *No Hands On the Clock* and *Finders Keepers*. The latter is a very good puzzle.

Campbell's creator is Geoffrey Homes, a pseudonym for Daniel Mainwaring. Mainwaring was born in 1901 in California, the son of a forest ranger. After graduating from Fresno State College, he taught school for a year before becoming a newspaper reporter. He started as a copy boy for the San Francisco *Chronicle* and spent the next ten years as a reporter for a number of different papers before switching to publicity work. Moving to Hollywood, he worked for Warner Brothers for several years before becoming a scenario writer for Paramount. At RKO he began to write novels—mostly mysteries—and several of these became successful motion pictures. Some of Mainwaring's early novels—*The Man Who Murdered Himself* (1936), *The Doctor Died At Dusk* (1936) and *The Man Who Didn't Exist* (1937) featured a tall, handsome newspaperman, Robin Bishop, and his wife Mary who team up to solve these well contrived puzzles. Mainwaring also had an interest in special effects and developed special sound effects which he rented to numerous studios.

As a screenwriter, Mainwaring is best known for his script *Invasion of the Body Snatchers* (1956) adapted from Jack Finney's 1955 science fiction novel, *The Body Snatchers*; for *Baby Face Nelson* (1957); and for *Out Of The Past* (1947) starring Robert Mitchum and Kirk Douglas in a crime film classic, based upon his own novel, *Build My Gallows High* (1946). Mainwaring gave up novels for full-time screenwriting in 1946. Mainwaring says that he knows more about California than the President of the Chamber of Commerce. The claim is substantiated by the varied California settings he has written into his books. He says he came by this from the long wagon trips he used to take, back and forth across the state, with his father. In the decade between 1936 and 1946 Mainwaring published twelve mystery novels set in the valleys of north-central California. Most of his film scripts were "B" pictures but he wrote high quality "A" novels. In Bill Pronzini's words, "Each is distinguished by clever plotting, semi-hard-boiled realism, fast-paced action, witty and remarkably good dialogue and some of the finest and most vivid descriptive passages in mystery fiction." Mainwaring died in 1968.

Johnny Havoc—John Jakes

Handsome Johnny Havoc is the second smallest PI in our kingdom. Mongo, a dwarf, whom you will meet later, is the smallest. Johnny is only five feet and one inch above his shoe soles, but he is big of heart and has more guts than a tennis racket factory. When he is not getting his head bashed in or his block knocked off, he wears a pork pie hat, drives a convertible and is unencumbered by the formality of a license. His investigations are often directed at some fair young maiden's cleavage, boudoir or possibilities. He exercises his one-eyed wonder worm at every opportunity and the opportunities abound. Most of the time he uses his brain to get himself out of trouble, but his friend on the police force, Detective First Grade Fitzhugh Goodpasture, comes and rescues Johnny every time he gets in over his ears. At times Johnny goes so far as to deny that he *is* a PI. In his words, "I'm no eye. Merely an exponent of free enterprise." By this he means that he works as a private investigator but he avoids the license required because it hampers his freedom to do as he damn well pleases.

There are only three Havoc novels, *Johnny Havoc (1961)*, *Johnny Havoc Meets Zelda* (1962) and *Johnny Havoc and the Doll Who Had "It"* (1963). All three are zany romps. The action is fast and furious. The plotting is on a par with The Three Stooges. The physical violence is almost continuous with Havoc moving rapidly from bruise to bruise and from bosom to bosom. Every babe in each of the three books takes one look at handsome John and goes soft, sensual and sentimental. In spite of his passions, Johnny's lust is bridled and there is nothing remotely resembling an offensive passage in any of the books. All three are rated PG. Romantic? Yes. Pornographic? No.

John Jakes, best known for his best-selling American Bicentennial series, was educated at De Pauw and Ohio State and got his start as a copywriter. He next moved into the advertising business and became Vice-President of an agency in Dayton, Ohio, his home town, before becoming a full-time freelance writer. Jakes has written well over a hundred science-fiction, western, sports and mystery novels, most of which were published in paperback. Jakes has also written a number of musicals and the scripts for several plays. Under the pseudonyms Alan Payne and Jay Scotland, Jakes has written several fantasies and historical romances. He is a member of the Author's Guild, the Dramatist's Guild and Science Fiction Writers of America.

Johnny Liddell—Frank Kane

Despite the fact that Johnny Liddell appears in twenty-nine separate PI novels written by Frank Kane between 1947 and 1967 we know very little about him personally. Johnny first was an investigator for the Acme Detective Agency. By the fifth novel, however, Johnny had opened his own agency on the fourteenth floor of a building on West Forty-Second Street in New York. Johnny has a redheaded secretary, Pinky, who keeps the books. She and Liddell have a platonic love affair going as well. Johnny patronizes Mike's Deadline Cafe, a bar on 44th Street. He says, it's "the only place in town where I can feel like a detective anymore. I keep my hand in trying to see how many times I can spot the bartender beating the cash register." Frequently, in order to get information, Johnny calls on The Dummy, a enormous fat man, who operates a school for beggars out of an old warehouse. The Dummy's beggars—none of whom is blind, deaf or dumb—pick up information about people all over greater New York City. Liddell also has the usual contacts on the police force—Inspector Herlehy and Sergeant Ryan. These two keep him out of prison and fish him out whenever he gets into waters too hot or too deep. Though most of the action in the series takes place in New York City, Johnny does operate elsewhere at times: part of *Fatal Undertaking* (1964) takes place in Vienna; *The Guilt-Edged Frame* (1964) is set in San Francisco; *Poisons Unknown* (1953) occurs in New Orleans; *Maid In Paris* (1966) not unexpectedly takes place in Paris; *Bare Trap* (1952) is set in Hollywood as are many of the stories in the collection *Stacked Deck* (1961); *A Short Bier* (1960) occurs part of the time in Las Vegas; and *Crime Of Their Life* (1962) takes place on a Caribbean cruise ship.

Every novel has between two and ten killings, three or more fist fights, brawls and/or knifings, two to eight head-bashings and at least one to three kidnappings. Just about every object in Sears Fall Catalog is used as a weapon to cause breaks and bruises on the human anatomy. Moreover, Johnny acts, thinks and behaves in a tough and nasty manner to everyone except Pinky and Ronnie "Muggsy" Kiely, screenwriter and ex-reporter. Muggsy is the love of Johnny's life and she is also the daughter of Jim Kiely, managing editor of The New York *Dispatch*. Jim Kiely is about the only other person, besides those already named, for whom Johnny has kind words.

Characterizations in the novels are brief and superficial. Action—fast and pell-mell—is the keynote of a Johnny Liddell mystery. It kept his thousands of readers coming back to buy the Johnny Liddell novels one after the other. In fact, the novels sold five million copies in the twenty years during which they were being published.

Kane, who was born in Brooklyn in 1912, received his BS degree from City College and was a night law student at St. John's. He worked as a columnist for the New York *Press* for two years, as Editor-in-Chief for the Trade Newspapers Corporation, and as associate editor for the New York *Journal of Commerce* before World War II. After the war he worked in public relations for a while and then turned to freelance writing and radio and TV productions. He formed and served as President of the Frank Kane Corporation and Frank Kane Associates, producing regular and promotional films for several years before his death in November 1968. Besides the Liddells, Kane wrote several novels under the pseudonym of Frank Boyd, e.g., *The Flesh Peddlers* (1959) and *Johnny Staccato* (1960).

Staccato was a jazz pianist before he turned to private eyeing. He still plays an occasional gig at Hugo's, a Greenwich Village jazz club that doubles as his office. John Cassavetis played Staccato in the short-lived NBC series during 1959-1960.

During the early sixties Kane was a contract writer for the *Mike Hammer, The Investigators* and *S.A.7* TV series. For radio he wrote many contract scripts for *The Shadow, The Fat Man, Gangbusters* and *The Lawless Twenties* Series. Kane was also a member of The Overseas Press Club (which could be seen from Liddell's office window); the Author's Guild and the Writer's Guild of America East. He was on the Board of Directors of the Mystery Writers of America.

There is a good deal of authenticity to the Liddell novels because Kane's brother was one of New York's finest for many years and he served as technical advisor to the series.

Duncan Maclain—Baynard H. Kendrick

One of the most unusual PIs in history is Captain Duncan Maclain. He is unusual because he is blind. Maclain, a US Army Intelligence officer in World War I, was blinded at Messines in 1917. Maclain is not the first blind detective in mystery fiction; Ernest Braham's Max Carrados has this honor. It was Carrados, in fact, that inspired Baynard Kendrick to create Captain Maclain. Kendrick found Carrados' supersensory abilities so hard to swallow he was determined to set the record straight about blind people and to create a detective who could use touch, hearing, taste and smell alone to solve complex problems. Kendrick spent fifteen years working with and studying blind people to increase Maclain's authenticity. He was quite proud of the fact that in all the thirteen Maclain novels he never had Maclain do anything that he had not either fully authenticated or had actually seen done by a blind man. Kendrick based Maclain on a blind soldier living at St. Dunstan's Home, Regent's Park, London. Maclain denies that he is blind: "I'm not really blind .... I just can't use my eyes."

Maclain who is tall, dark, handsome and an elegant dresser, worked tirelessly to develop his remaining senses to the point that he no longer felt handicapped. He is a match for the toughest and most conniving of felons but Duncan is also kindly to all seeking his assistance. After his military service, Duncan moved to New York City and opened a private investigation office in the penthouse of a 26 story apartment house located at 72nd Street and Riverside Drive.

Maclain has crisp, dark hair salted with gray, a clipped black moustache, perfect teeth, a vigorous body and a mobile face always alive with interest. His eyes are dark brown and lively which makes it difficult for strangers to believe he is blind. Duncan is aided by his best friend and partner, Spud Savage, and his secretary, Rena, who is Spud's wife. Two of his assistants are Schnucke, a gentle female German Shepherd, and Dreist, another Shepherd a little larger than Schnucke, but who is as dangerous as a loaded gun. Dreist, has been trained to kill, is responsible for protecting Spud and Duncan from assault. Duncan works jigsaw puzzles for a hobby and to keep his fingers in training. He also reads voraciously in Braille and has, built into a corner of his office concealed behind the paneling, a large metal file containing in more than a hundred flat drawers a sectional map of greater New York. Engraved on its wooden surface are the grooves of every street and alleyway in the entire metropolitan area with the names of the most important streets showing in the grooves in tiny, raised Braille letters.

The first Maclain, *The Last Express* (1937) begins with a hand grenade exploding in the car of the assistant DA, leaving a pair of puzzling survivors: two caged white mice. The assistant DA lived long enough to letter the words *Sea Beach Subway—the last express* as the only clue. Maclain solves this murder as well as other killings and winds up the case with a wild chase on the subway—the last express.

There were thirteen Maclain novels. Among the best were *Blind Man's Bluff* (1943) in which Maclain investigates the murder of another blind man; *Out of Control* (1945) in which Maclain pursues a psychotic murderess across the Tennessee mountains; *You Die Today* (1952) in which Maclain comes to the aid of another blind war veteran who is being framed for murder; and *Reservations For Death* (1957) which concerns a madman who plants two bombs on an airplane—the first one doesn't go off but the second one does. Kendrick wrote about another PI named Cliff Chandler who worked on an ocean liner in *Death at the Porthole* (1938).

Baynard Hardwick Kendrick, who also wrote under the pen name of Richard Hayward, was born in Philadelphia in 1894 and educated in Philadelphia and Maryland. He was the first American to enlist in the Canadian Army in World War I and he served in England, France and Salonica from 1914 to 1918. During World War II he served as an instructor for blind veterans. He was married and had two daughters and one son. Kendrick was also a successful businessman as well as a successful journalist, writer and historian. One of the founders of the Mystery Writers of America, he held the first membership card. He was also their first President. In 1951 he received the Robert Meltzer Award of the Screen Writers Guild and he received the MWA Grand Master Award in 1967. Kendrick died in March 1977.

All of the Maclains are as entertaining today as they were at the time they were published. Maclain is a fascinating personality. Kendrick's novels served as the basis for the popular TV series *Longstreet*, starring James Fanciscus. The series which began in February 1971 ran for only one

season. It might have had greater success and a much longer run had the
script writers stayed with Kendrick's original conception.

Rocky Steele—John B. West

John B. West's Aloysius Algernon "Rocky" Steele first appeared in
1959 in a paperback original novel titled *An Eye For An Eye*. Like many
other PIs, Rocky has a two-room office in downtown Manhattan, a sexy
secretary, a .45 automatic in a shoulder holster, six feet three inches of
height and 198 pounds of muscle, guts and bone. Rocky is an ex-prize
fighter who is very hard to put down. As far as his job is concerned, it's
tough, like Rocky. In his words, "Now don't get the idea that the life of a
private eye is all ivory and green silk sheets. Most of the jobs I've been called
on were stinkers. Some old bag whose husband was chasing a new skirt,
and my job was to catch him with his pants down so she could stick him for
more dough at the divorce. Or some dizzy dame who had lost a dog and
went into hysterics every time you tried to talk about it, so you couldn't get
a description of the hound."

Rock is a commando veteran of World War II and Guadalcanal who
uses his combat ethics to good advantage in operating his Steele Special
Services, Incorporated. Rocky's secretary and handy-gal is Vicky Boston, a
sweet lovely that Rocky honors and protects like a good knight should. As
Rocky puts it: "Now don't get the wrong idea—I'd never asked her the
question you might be thinking. Like I said in the beginning, I always
figured I couldn't make her and still expect to get her to do the job, and she
had to keep the office straight." Vicky is no pushover—she is a karate
expert.

Rocky has an an old wartime buddy, Lieutenant Bob Evans, on the
Force. Bob is especially helpful in ballistics and other technical areas
where brains are necessary. Captain Johnny Richards, Chief of New York's
homicide squad, is another of Rocky's pals. Rocky drinks cognac, smokes
"Luckies" by the deck and plays solitaire when he's bored. He drives a 250
horsepower Caddy coupe—two-tone gray with real leather upholstery in
white.

Rocky is as hardnosed as an NHL goalie. In the second Steele, *Cobra
Venom* (1960), for example, the story starts with Vicky and Rocky fishing
up a concrete-laden corpse. Rocky sits happily with the corpse when the
cops are unable to go near it. In this thriller Rocky also gets involved with
the CIA. *A Taste For Blood* (1960) has Rocky looking into the murder of an
almost-client. Later there is an encounter with the beautiful mistress of a
crusading politician and a collision with a heroin ring. *Bullets Are My
Business* (1960) has Rocky involved in a complex inheritance and a series of
related murders that he solves after several razor-close calls. *Never Kill A
Cop* (1961) is most unusual in that it is set in Monrovia, Liberia, aboard a

passenger train and in the Canary Islands. Rocky decides to visit Liberia for a vacation and he has hardly unpacked before he runs into five bodies mutilated supposedly by a leopard. Next he encounters a priceless diamond and then a dangerous female before everything comes together.

The writing on the whole is not only as tough as Spillane—whom West is often accused of imitating—but it often becomes unnecessarily gruesome. West does not hesitate to describe blood, guts and gore in clinical detail and he has no qualms about trying to shock his readers. Bill Pronzini, in his *Gun in Cheek*, calls West's prose "nothing spectacular, a serviceable mutation of the Daly/Spillane style." His plots involve various and sundry gangsters, treacherous "frails," sympathetic and umsympathetic policemen, wicked government agents, a butler who *does* do it, and a great deal of violent ation and death. His characters are moderately well drawn examples of the type found in dozens of other private-eye novels of the period, including Spillane's; they neither say nor do anything outside the norm and concern themselves not at all with philosophical or sociological matters."

One of the most fascinating facts about the series is that West was a black man writing about a white PI and white characters. There are no black characters in any of the Rocky Steele novels. West was an unusual individual in a number of ways. Not only was he a licensed MD but he was also a specialist in the prevention and treatment of tropical diseases. West held five academic degrees and was a very successful businessman in Liberia where he was President of the National Manufacturing Company and President of the Liberian Hotel and Restaurant Corporation. He owned and operated the Liberian Broadcasting Corporation. Since West died in 1960 the last three Steele novels were published posthumously by his wife, Lineke, who also typed and proofread all the novels. Most of them were written in Monrovia where the Wests made their home, but West traveled widely and extensively in the USA and had many friends in New York, Las Vegas and California.

Chapter VI
The Modern Knights—The Best New Crusaders

WE BEGIN OUR MODERN ERA at 1970. This starting point may be arbitrary, although it is not without some justification. For example, 1967 saw the publication of Michael Collins' first Dan Fortune novel, *Act of Fear*, which won an Edgar for that year's best first novel and which inspired the by-now monotonous chant by critics about each new hard-boiled author being "the best since Hammett," "the new Chandler" and "the heir to Ross Macdonald." Fortune enjoys a senior status among the modern private eyes, but within five years of his appearance, Donald Westlake under the pseudonym of Tucker Coe, Joseph Hansen, Joe Gores, Michael Lewin, and Bill Pronzini had all written the first novels in their PI series (Actually, Westlake's first Mitch Tobin, *Kinds of Love, Kinds of Death* appeared in 1966.)

So the beginning of the 1970s is a reasonable date to mark the initiation of the private eye Renaissance. In this section we honor the best examples of the new tradition—The Modern Knights.

The Guilty Knights—Mitch Tobin and Matt Scudder

Two of the most sympathetic and inspiring PIs in all of fiction are two New York City ex-cops: Mitch Tobin and Matt Scudder. Their parallel plights are the respective creations of two of the best writers working the mystery field today: Donald Westlake, writing under the penname of Tucker Coe, and Lawrence Block, writing under his real name. What Tobin and Scudder have in common is a King Kong-sized clinical case of guilt. (Plus the fact that both work diligently to help solve one puzzle after another although neither has a PI license.) Their burden of guilt is as gargantuan a glob of the "sorrys" as any two human beings could grab. They do, however, deal with their problems in different ways. Mitch devotes himself to his family and forces himself to do hard physical labor; he builds a wall around his property. Matt Scudder on the other hand divorces his wife and takes to drink. But what is the source of all this regret and unhappiness?

Matt Scudder—Lawrence Block

Matt Scudder is an ex-cop who deliberately took himself off the force after almost sixteen years of exemplary service. One night, in a bar in Washington Heights "where cops didn't have to pay for their drinks," two juveniles held up the place and on their way out they shot the bartender in the heart. Scudder chased them into the street and shot one dead and hit the other in the thigh, crippling him. In Scudder's words, "That wasn't the first time I ever killed anyone. I was glad the one died and sorry the other recovered." Unfortunately, one of Scudder's shots ricocheted and hit a seven year old girl, Estralita Rivera, in the eye.

The ricochet took most of the stream off the bullet. An inch higher and it probably would have glanced off her forehead. Would have left a nasty scar but nothing much worse than that. This way, though, nothing but soft tissue and it went right on into the brain. They tell me she died instantly .... There was no question of culpability. As a matter of fact, I got a departmental commendation. Then I resigned. I just didn't want to be a cop anymore .... Or a husband or a father, or a productive member of society.

Scudder quit the force because he "lost faith."

To assuage his guilt, Scudder visits church, tithes and drinks steadily. Though left unsaid, the drinking is the obvious reason for Scudder's estrangement from his wife and sons. Matt sends his ex-wife Anita and his two sons some money from every case he is asked to solve.

Scudder's friend on the force, Lieutenant Koehler, sends business Scudder's way. Since Matt is not licensed, he is technically not a private detective. In his own words:

Private detectives are licensed. They tap telephones and follow people. They fill out forms, they keep records, all of that. I don't do those things. Sometimes I do favors for people. They give me gifts.

To date there are five novels in the Scudder series: *The Sins of the Fathers* (1976); *In The Midst of Death* (1976); *Time to Murder and Create* (1977); *A Stab in the Dark* (1981); *Eight Million Ways to Die* (1982).

In the first novel, Matt does a favor for Cole Hammford, whose daughter Wendy has been murdered, allegedly by her young male roommate who was arrested and charged with the crime. Two days later the accused is found hanging in his cell. Hammford is not satisfied with the resolution so he enlists Scudder to look into his daughter's background. Scudder is reluctant to take the job. "I don't need much money. My room rent is cheap, my day-to-day expenses low enough." But he finally agrees to go ahead.

Scudder's working arrangements with his clients are unusual.

I'm probably more expensive than one of the big agencies. They'd work for you either per diem or on an hourly basis. Plus expenses. I take a certain amount of money and pay my own expenses out of it. I don't like keeping records. I also don't like writing reports or checking in periodically when there's nothing to say for the sake of keeping a client contented."

"How much money do you want?"

"I never know how to set prices. How do you put a value on your time when its only value is personal? And when your life has been deliberately restructured to minimize involvement in the lives of others, how much do you charge the man who forces you to involve yourself?"

Scudder's two thousand dollar fee is split several ways: $500 goes into his bank account, $200 into St. Paul's poor box, $25 to Eddie Koehler, $25 for a bribe to get information, and the rest to his wife and kids.

Scudder systematically tracks down everyone who knew Wendy and gradually the picture of why she was murdered and who murdered her unfolds. Scudder is a gentle and introspective man, but he can be tough and ruthless under attack. Here for example in *The Sins of the Father* is how he deals with a young mugger:

I moved toward my inside breast pocket, and in an easy, rolling motion I dropped one shoulder, pivoted on my right heel, and kicked his wrist with my left foot. The knife sailed out of his hand.

He went for it and that was a mistake because it landed behind him and he had to scramble for it.

He was off balance and scrambling, and I got a hand on his shoulder and spun him like a top. I threw a right, my hand open, and I caught him with the heel of my hand right under the nose. He yelped and put both hands to his face, and I hit him three or four times in the belly. When he folded up I cupped my hands on the back of his head and brought my knee up while I was bringing his head down.

The impact was good and solid. I let go of him, and he stood in a dazed crouch, his legs bent at right angles at the knees. His body didn't know whether to straighten up or fall down. I took his chin in my hand and shoved, and that made the decision for him. He went up and over and sprawled on his back and stayed that way.

I said, "Listen to me. These are hard, tough streets, and you are not hard enough or tough enough. You better get a straight job because you can't make it out here, you're too soft for it...."

I bent the fingers of his right hand back one at a time until they broke. Just the four fingers. I left his thumb alone. He didn't scream or anything. I suppose the terror blocked the pain.

I took his knife along with me and dropped it in the first sewer I came to. Then I walked the two blocks to Broadway and caught a cab home.

Scudder is "about 6 ft. tall" and lives on pea soup, hamburgers, coffee and bourbon and does his best thinking in churches that he attends because they are quiet places. His friends are Trina, a waitress in his favorite bar, Armstrong's, and Lieutenant Eddie Koehler, Chief of homicide.

In the second Scudder novel, *In the Midst of Death*, Scudder looks into the activity of one Jerry Broadfield, a cop supposedly on the take who is allegedly extorting money from a number of people including a call girl named Portia Carr. Scudder has been hired by Broadfield to help clear him of the extortion charges. Shortly after Scudder interviews Portia, someone murders her and dumps her body in Broadfield's apartment and tips the police. Broadfield is arrested and asks Matt to help clear him. Scudder really doesn't like Broadfield and doesn't want to work for him but according to his personal philosophy, "As a matter of fact, I generally prefer to work for men I neither like nor respect. It pains me less to give them poor value."

After another friend on the force, Doug Fuhrmany, who is also looking into the police corruption, is murdered, Scudder is able to put the pieces together and solve the murders. Koehler then tries to get Matt back on the force but he refuses. The novel ends with a shocking but satisfying denouement.

The third novel, *Time to Murder and Create*, concerns a character named Jacob Jablon, "The Spinner," an ex-informant Matt knew when he was on the force, who entrusts Matt with a letter in which he names three people who are trying to kill him. One is a tycoon, Henry Prager, on a guilt trip. Another is a powerful politician, Ted Huysendahl, and the third is an ex-porn queen, Beverly Ethridge, who is now a social lionness. After The Spinner is murdered, Scudder finds that he had been blackmailing all three suspects. Scudder starts unraveling the tangled lives of the three to find which is the killer. Again, the climax is a surprise but quite logical. The characterizations are excellent and the dialogue unusually good.

In the fourth novel, *A Stab in the Dark*, Matt is hired by the father of a stabbing victim to reopen a nine-year-old case the police had closed. An attempt was made to pin the stabbing on a self-confessed multiple murderer. But there were differences in the M.O. of Barbara Ettinger's death that caused Barbara's father to hire Scudder to look into it. In this novel it becomes clear that alcohol is becoming more and more of a problem with Scudder. In one interesting bit of dialogue, Matt is talking to a sculptress who accuses Scudder of being an alcoholic:

"Don't patronize me. Let's face it. We're both alcoholics."
"I'm a heavy drinker. There's a difference."
"What's the difference?"
"I could stop anytime I want to."
"Well, why don't you?"
"Why should I?"
Instead of answering the question she leaned forward to fill her glass.
"I stopped for a while," she said. "I quit cold for two months. More than two months."
"You just up and quit?"

"I went to AA."
"Oh."
"You ever been?"
I shook my head. "I don't think it would work for me."
"But you could stop anytime you want?"
"Yeah, if I wanted."

As the novel develops Matt is able to find the real murderer and to recognize finally that he is an alcoholic.

The fifth novel, *Eight Million Ways To Die* (cited by PWA as the best Hardcover Private Eye Novel of 1983) is by far the most carefully developed and interesting for its psychological insight into the nature of alcoholism, and for the study of the intricate relationships between a pimp and his prostitutes. In this story Matt has become a regular at AA meetings and is making a serious attempt to stop drinking. The novel opens when Kim Dakkinen, a high class call girl, comes to Scudder and tells him she wants to get out of the life but she is afraid that her pimp, Chance, will kill her, mark her or talk her out of it. She hires Matt to get her off the hook. A few days later Matt picks up a newspaper and reads that Kim has been murdered. Matt assumes that Chance is the killer and goes after him. When Scudder finally tracks Chance down, he finds a man completely different from what he expected and it is soon clear that Chance is not the killer. In fact Chance himself hires Matt to find Kim's killer. As Matt tries to track down the murderer, other murders are committed and Matt's struggle with his urge to drink becomes more difficult. Uncharacteristically, in this novel Scudder uses a gun; in fact, it is necessary if he is to stay alive. Matt finally recognizes the seriousness of his drinking problem and at the novel's end confesses at an AA meeting: " 'My name is Matt,' I said, " 'and I'm an alcoholic'."

Whether Matt will conquer his alcoholism remains to be resolved in Block's next Scudder novel.

Lawrence Block was born in Buffalo, New York in 1938. He was educated in the Buffalo City schools and attended Antioch College from 1955 to 1959. In 1957 he began working for the Scott Meredith literary agency, then quit in 1958 to become a full-time writer. He was immediately successful, publishing three novels in 1961 and averaging at least a book a year ever since. In 1960 he married Loretta Ann Kallett. They had two daughters. In addition to the Scudder series, Block has also created two other series characters: 1) Evan Tanner, an international traveler, secret agent, womanizer and comedian; and 2) Bernard "Bernie" Rhodenbarr, a burglar and bibliophile with very expensive tastes. Both the Tanner and Bernie series are written with a light touch. At times the comedy is excellent, particularly in the Bernie series which began in 1977 with *Burglars Can't Be Choosers*. According to critic John McAleer:

Bernie wins our hearts because Block's keen comedy touch envelops him . . . .
Bernie is refreshingly forthright. He doesn't pretend to be Robin Hood
redistributing the wealth for the common good. Bernie knows his activities are
illegal and admits he steals.

In Bernie's own words, ". . . there are days when it bothers me. But
there's no getting around it, I'm a thief and I have to steal, I just plain love
it." At the same time, Bernie does have his own standards of right and
wrong. As McAleer notes:

In an inversion of normalcy that Lewis Carroll could not fault, a man bent on
supporting himself by breaking the law finds himself time and again, compelled by
necessity and his own bedrock decency, to restore to society the stability it professes
to cherish but which by its transgressions, it puts into jeopardy.

Block has also written under the pseudonyms Chip Harrison and Paul
Kavanaugh. The best of the Kavanaugh novels which are serious studies of
psychopathic individuals running loose in organized society is *Such Men
Are Dangerous* (1969). The four Harrison novels are semi-pornographic
comedies featuring a full-time, 17-year-old assistant private eye and part-
time lover called Chip Harrison. Chip is an assistant to a tough old private
dick named Leo Haig. Chip's major obsession is with losing his virginity
which he manages to do several times as both he and the series mature.
Block's strong sense of humor shows in a number of ways. For example, the
first Chip Harrison novel, *No Score*, is dedicated:

For *Lawrence Block* who is my favorite writer and who is as together a person as he
is a writer. And you can't get much better than that.

Sometimes They Bite (1983) is a collection of Block's short stories that
originally appeared in *Cosmopolitan, Alfred Hitchcock's Mystery
Magazine* and *Ellery Queen's Mystery Magazine*. It includes stories about
Scudder, Rhodenbarr and Martin Ehrengraf, a crafty criminal lawyer
whose clients are always innocent.

Block is also an authority on old coins, especially Australian and
Swiss medals, having published guide books on the subject. Since 1964 he
has served as an associate editor of the *Whitman Numismatic Journal*. He
also professes an interest in old subway cars, has taught fiction writing at
Hofstra University, is a contributing editor of *Writer's Digest* and, at the
moment, is working on additional Matt and Bernie novels.

According to the dust jacket of the latest Scudder novel, "Block's
acquaintances range across New York's social and geographical lives,
including men and women on both sides of the law." At present he lives
with his wife in Greenwich Village.

Mitch Tobin—Tucker Coe (Donald Westlake)

Mitch Tobin is trying to live down the fact that while he was shacked up with the wife of a man he sent to prison, his partner, Jock Sheehan, was shot and killed by a numbers runner who'd unexpectedly turned to narcotics. The arrest should have been a simple one-man job, but in Tobin's absence it led to Jock's death and Mitch's dismissal after 18 years on the force. Despite Mitch's unfaithfulness, his wife Kate stuck beside him, working to support Mitch and their son, Bill, while Tobin struggled to find employment.

In the first Tobin novel, *Kinds of Love, Kinds of Death* (1966) Mitch has involved himself in emotionless silence and impassivity. His only passion is his Sisyphean labor on his wall. In Mitch's words, "A wall is an unfortunate thing, a substantial thing, a thing worth a man's time and consideration. I was finding it possible to concentrate on this wall as I hadn't been able to concentrate on anything since ... for six months ... for a long time." Mitch's wall is two feet wide, ten feet high, and is designed to completely enclose the backyard of his property with no gates or openings. And Tobin does it right. As he points out, "If you're going to build a good wall, a wall to stand, then first you have to dig, because a wall should start down inside the earth, below the frost line. I figured in this climate two feet was deep enough."

Three days after Mitch begins to work on his wall he is visited by a punk representative of a mobster named Ernie Rembek. Rembek wants to hire Tobin to track down the murderer of his mistress who has absconded with a lot of the mob's money. Rembek is convinced it's an inside job and he can ill-afford to open his organization to the prying eyes of the police. The job is tailor-made for Tobin's talents. As he says, " ... in a small corner of my mind I felt a certain excitement, almost eagerness about the job, it would be a return to the life I'd lost, a task within my competence, and I couldn't help feeling a degree of hunger for it." Shortly after Tobin takes the job, the mistress is found dead at a motel and the money is missing. Tobin methodically interviews all the members of the mob who could have killed the girl and taken the money. As the personality of the suspects emerge one by one, Tobin begins to form a picture of the interrelationships between the victim and the members of Rembek's organization. After he discovers what happened to the money and who killed Rembek's mistress, Tobin goes back to work on his wall.

The second novel, *Murder Among Children,* is in many ways the most satisfactory of the five. Published in 1967 it combines the mystery and suspense of the classical locked-room puzzle with the systematic search for a motive and the killer. Mitch's work on his wall is disturbed one day by the visit of his cousin, Robin Kennely, who asks for Mitch's help. A restaurant that Robin, her boyfriend and a group of young people have just opened in

Greenwich Village is being haunted by a police detective who may be on the take. Because Mitch is an ex-cop, Robin thinks he can find out whether the detective actually wants protection money. Reluctantly Mitch agrees to help and goes to the restaurant where he meets one of the co-owners. While they are talking the only door to the second floor opens revealing Robin in shock, covered with blood and clutching a bloody butcher knife. Upstairs, Robin's boyfriend and a young black girl have been hacked to death. Since there is no other way out, Robin's guilt seems an open and shut case. Although Mitch himself is convinced of her guilt, he agrees to look into the case as a favor to Robin's mother. As Tobin begins to explore the situation and look for a motive, the restaurant's co-owner is murdered, an attempt is made on Tobin's life and the cop Tobin was investigating is killed. Robin is accused of the policeman's murder and thrown into jail. By this time, however, Tobin has solved the case. Again, after receiving the apologies of Captain Driscoll, Chief of the Homicide Bureau, Tobin goes back to work on his wall.

The third novel, *Wax Apple* (1970), is unusual because of its setting: The Midway—a halfway house for mental patients. Mitch is hired by hospital founder Dr. Cameron to enter the home as a "wax apple" (a fake patient) and nail the culprit who has been setting "little traps" that have caused a number of accidents to the residents. Five minutes after entering the house, Mitch is tripped at the head of a flight of stairs, leaving him with a broken arm, a headache and one dinger of a case.

In the fourth novel, *A Jade in Aries* (1970), Mitch is hired by homosexual Ronald Cornell, a men's boutique owner, to investigate the murder of his partner, Jamie Dearborn, who is also Cornell's lover. Astrology plays a prominent role in the novel since another homosexual friend of Dearborn's, Cary Lane, believes he can solve the murder by consulting the astrological charts. Tobin has to be very careful on this case because working without a PI's license constitutes a felony in New York, and the officer officially assigned the case, Detective Manzoni, is totally incompetent and jealous of Tobin's skill. Tobin manages, through dogged determination, to locate the killer and keep Manzoni at bay. Of equal importance is the fact that in this novel Tobin, for the first time, is beginning to assuage his guilt and end his self-imposed isolation from the rest of the world. In Tobin's words:

. . .I had started my wall to deaden the capacity for pain through physical work, to distract my mind from memory by filling it with simple questions of digging and building.

But suddenly this afternoon something had clicked into a different gear inside my head, and all at once I had found it possible to permit myself reactions that were not colored by guilt. I had found it possible to think and act like a living man . . . .
As Jock's surrogate, was I prepared now to forgive me, to declare my sentence

completed?

I couldn't be sure yet, I only knew I felt the way a man feels after a long illness just after the crisis point, when he is going to get better and knows it. He isn't strong yet, he isn't well yet, but he knows he's on the right road at last.

In the fifth and final novel, *Don't Lie to Me* (1972), Mitch is beginning to resume a normal existence. He gets his PI license, leaves his self-imposed prison and takes a job as a night guard in a Manhattan museum. One night, his old mistress shows up and begs Mitch's help for her husband, Danny, a professional criminal fresh out of jail, who is being pressured by some hoodlums to pull off a few more jobs. Tobin agrees, but before he leaves the museum he comes across a dead man in the middle of the floor. The police have no answers to this murder but they do catch the mob's revenge meant for Tobin. Is the past going to repeat itself? Not quite. This time Tobin forms a partnership with the police and with the man he cuckolded to resist the savage attack unleashed against him.

Donald Westlake was born in Brooklyn in 1933, grew up in Albany, New York, and attended Champlain College and the State University of New York at Binghamton. After serving a tour of duty in the Air Force (1954-1956), he worked at odd jobs until 1958 when he became an associate editor at a literary agency. In 1959 he took up full-time writing and published *The Mercenaries* in 1960. His second novel, *Killing Time* (1961), featuring a private eye named Tim Smith, has been favorably compared to Hammett's *Red Harvest*. Under the penname of Richard Stark, he has published a long series of novels featuring the professional thief Parker. The Parker novels are first-rate thrillers. MGM has filmed two of them: *Point Blank* (1967), starring Lee Marvin, Angie Dickinson, Keenan Wynn and Carrol O'Connor; and *The Split* (1968), starring Jim Brown, Diane Carroll, Julie Harris, Ernest Borgnine and Gene Hackman.

Westlake comments about Parker:

Parker is a Depression character, Dillinger mythologized into a machine. During the affluent days of the sixties he was an interesting fantasy, but now that money's getting tight again, his relationship with banks is suddenly both to the point and old-fashioned. He hasn't yet figured out how to operate in a world where heisting is one of the more rational responses to the situation.

Equally successful has been a series of humorous novels about inept criminals written under Westlake's own name. Included in the group are *The Fugitive Pigeon*, 1965; *The Busy Body*, 1966; *The Spy in the Ointment*, 1966; *God Save the Mark*, 1967, which won an Edgar; *The Hot Rock*, 1970; *Bank Shot*, 1972; *Cops and Robbers*, 1972; and *Jimmy the Kid*, 1974. Four of these novels have been filmed: *The Busy Body* (Paramount, 1967), starring Sid Caesar, Robert Ryan, Ann Baxter, Dom Delouise and Bill Dana; *The Hot Rock* (Twentieth Century Fox, 1972), starring Robert

Redford, George Segal and Zero Mostel; *Cops and Robbers* (United Artists, 1973), starring Cliff Gorman, Joe Bologna and Shepard Strudwick; and *Bank Shot* (United Artists, 1974), starring George C. Scott, Joanna Cassidy and Sorrell Brooke.

In an interview for Dilys Winn's *Murder Ink*, Westlake (who also wrote one novel, *Ex Officio*, under the pseudonym of Timothy J. Culver) explained why he decided to end the Tucker Coe series:

> The problem for me was that Mitch Tobin wasn't a static character. For him to remain miserable and guilt-ridden forever would have changed him into a self-pitying whiner. My problem was once Mitch reaches that new stability and becomes functional in the world again, he's merely one more private eye with an unhappy past. Not to name names, but don't we have enough slogging private eyes with unhappy pasts?

Westlake's recent novels have been termed "crime satire." They include *A Travesty* (1975), *Brothers Keepers* (1975) and *Enough* (1977). His latest book is *Levine* (1984), a collection of six police procedural novellas.

Dan Fortune—Michael Collins (Dennis Lynds)

Michael Collins, the best known pseudonym of Dennis Lynds, is the creator of Dan Fortune, a one-armed New York City private detective. Born in the Chelsea section of New York City, Fortune is of Polish-Lithuanian heritage. The Fortune was once Fortunowski but Dan's dad changed it. And Dan's middlename used to be Tadeusz but Dan dropped even the T. Dan is a legitimate, licensed **PI** but he prefers not to investigate much that is big or dangerous. Subpoenas, industrial work, some divorces and armed-guard jobs make up the bulk of his work. He gets five bucks for a summons and two dollars an hour for guard work. Industrial snooping pays more.

Dan prefers not to take on anything too dangerous because of his handicap—his left arm is missing. Most of the people at Chelsea regard **Dan** as a cop and Dan has, as a result, only two friends: his woman, Martine "Marty" Adair, and Joe Harris, the bartender at Packy Wilson's Pub.

As a kid Dan was known as "Danny The Pirate." This cognomen came as a result of the time when the young seventeen-year-olds Dan and Joe were looting a ship. Dan fell into a hold and broke his left arm in so many places the city hospital had to amputate just below the shoulder. Since Dan's old man was a cop, the force forgot the robbery and saved Dan the luxury of having a record. After Dan matured he got a PI license and opened up a one-room office with one luxurious window on 28th Street. Though Dan was born in New York City, lives and works there, he has lived and worked for short periods in most of the big cities of the world: London, Paris, Amsterdam, San Francisco, Tokyo. He has been a merchant seaman, a waiter, tourist guide, farmhand, actor, newspaperman and overage student—almost any work a man can do with one arm, a useless education and no special training.

Marty and Dan keep steady company and Marty, who has an apartment in The Village, is the beneficiary of Dan's insurance policy. She's also the reason why Dan stays in Chelsea.

Dan is not big—only five feet ten and 160 pounds—but he is unusually fast. One of his tricks is catching flies in midair and he can run the hundred in ten flat. He survives by using his wits. Normally, he doesn't carry a gun—he considers it too dangerous. When he does he prefers a .38 Police Special. Dan's philosophy is that it's not so important to win a fight as it is to not let the other man win.

The first Dan Fortune, *Act of Fear* (1967) won the Edgar award as the best mystery novel of the year. It begins with the mugging of a cop and the disappearance of a possible witness. One of the witness' friends, a kid, hires Dan to find the missing boy. Two girls and an innocent old man are murdered and Dan's client winds up in the hospital. Then the killers go after Dan.

In the second, *The Brass Rainbow* (1969), an aristocrat, Jonathan Radford III, is murdered and suspects are plentiful. Sammy Neiss, one of Dan's old friends, is accused of the crime. It is assumed Sammy killed Radford because he was unable to collect the money owed him from a gambling debt. Sammy, however, wouldn't hurt a fly. Dan gets involved with a B-girl, Jonathan's nephew, and a high society beauty before he unravels the tangle and turns up the killer. The third, *Night of the Toads* (1970), revolves around a producer, Richard Vega, and one of his actress girl friends, Anne Terry. After Anne saves Dan's life, protecting him from one of Vega's thugs, Dan finds himself indebted when she turns up missing. After it is discovered that she has been murdered, Dan goes after Vega with a vengeance. In the fourth, *Walk A Black Wind* (1971), an attractive young cocktail waitress, Franscesca Crawford, is found stabbed to death in her Manhattan apartment. Three months before her death she left home but only two of the months are accounted for. Dan is hired by a middle-aged salesman, John Andera, to find the killer. Dan succeeds, but before the killer is caught Dan is beaten up and shot and winds up on an Indian reservation in southwest Arizona. This novel perhaps more than any other Fortune is reminiscent of Ross Macdonald and the Lew Archer series. The fifth, *Shadow Of A Tiger* (1972), involves the murder of a quiet French pawnbroker, supposedly in a holdup. Yet the thief, who ransacked the shop, left behind three hundred dollars in the cash drawer. Nor were there any signs of forced entry. In solving this case, Dan encounters an assortment of unusual characters including an alcoholic Chinaman, a young beauty from Thailand, a hero of the French Resistance and a gang of hoodlums. *The Silent Scream* (1973), the sixth, involves Dan with the

Mafia and has him tracking down a blonde career girl and her boyfriends. It is as violent and as complexly plotted a novel as any in the series. The seventh, *Blue Death* (1975), brings Dan to the aid of a beautiful Armenian belly dancer. The dancer's new husband owes a corporation some money but he can't find anyone who will take it. Dan agrees to track down an elusive executive of the giant corporation. While doing it, Dan shuttles between Manhattan, Hoboken and the California mountains. As you would expect, he runs into murder.

In *The Blood Red Dream* (1976) Fortune is asked by Kate Vytantis, a Lithuanian, to find her eighty year old grandfather, Josef Stanic, who has disappeared over the weekend. What she fails to tell Dan is that the old man doesn't want to be found. Soon after Dan starts the search he runs into a bloody gun battle in a Yorkville alley, a gang of urban militants and a group of throwback, Eastern European "freedom fighters" who are still fighting World War II. When Kate Vytantis herself disappears Dan realizes that he has one complex mess on his hands. *The Night Runners* (1978), the ninth novel, concerns wealthy Wallace Kern, President of Kern Laboratories, and his wife Marjorie. The Kerns hire Dan to find Wallace's brother, Bill, a compulsive gambler who has disappeared with $8,000 intended as a bribe to get Bradley, Wallace's son, out of a Mexican jail. When the man who was to deliver the bribe is murdered, Kern asks Dan to find out what happened to the go-between and help him get his son out of jail. Dan winds up in Mexico getting Brad out of the Mexican prison at Piedras Negras but not before he becomes involved in a harrowing rooftop cat-and-mouse game, a Bolivian political struggle, additional murders and a showdown in Las Vegas. The tenth novel, *The Slasher* (1980), brings back Marty who last appeared in *Night of the Toads*. In the latest novel, *Freak* (1983), Dan becomes involved in a case of kidnapping and murder with the only clue being the scribbled word "Freak." This case takes Dan into the wild back country of Arizona.

Many critics believe Fortune to be the culmination of a maturing process that has transformed the private eye from the naturalistic Spade through the romantic Marlowe and the psychological Archer to the sociological Fortune. After naming Lynds the Best Suspense writer of the 1970s, the Crime Literature Association of West Germany praised him as follows:

The break in private eye novels started with Michael Collins. At the end of the 1960s, he gave the private eye novel something new and a human touch needed for years. They are much more than entertainment. There is a philosophy behind the detective. In each book we take a look at a special section of American society.

Actually, Fortune is derived from an earlier creation of Lynds, a private eye by the name of Slot Machine Kelley. Kelley was a crooked, cheap detective with one arm: a real one-armed bandit. He also worked in New York City and was based on a real detective that Lynds knew who hired cripples to serve summonses, figuring that no one would assault them. Kelley appeared in only short stories.

The significance of Fortune's handicap has prompted much speculation. As an example, Richard Carpenter wrote for *Twentieth Century Crime and Mystery Writers* that:

> His being one-armed is more than a gimmick, a diversion like Columbo's raincoat designed to mislead the wicked into underestimating him, although it often has that effect; it is a symbol of his alienation and the prime reason for his physical passivity. He is the wounded man whose wound makes him fearful—the thought that something might happen to his remaining arm fills him with dread—yet conversely makes him expose himself to danger in order to prove he exists.

Paul Shaw—Mark Sadler (Dennis Lynds)

The prolific Lynds has created a second PI that some critics feel is as good as, if not better than, Dan Fortune. Using the penname Mark Sadler, Lynds has given us Paul Shaw, another New York PI. Paul is the middle third of Thayer, Shaw and Delaney—Security And Investigations, New York and Los Angeles. Dick Delaney handles the Los Angeles Office, Hollywood on Wilshire, and John Thayer and Shaw hold down the New York Office on Madison Avenue. Shaw and Thayer are not your average run-of-the-mill shamuses. As Thayer says, "Brass knuckles and bottles in the drawer are out. We're Madison Avenue, not Tenth Avenue. No Tenth Avenue or Broadway hustle. No more hooch, heaters and 'stash the boodle, doll.' Today we're businessmen, and we need a successful business image." So they have two private seventh floor offices in a bank building and a large, impressive reception room. Their furniture is Danish modern, with wall-to-wall carpeting. The two secretaries are Finnish blonde. Clients get no surprises " . . . they see an office the same as all the other offices where they have spent their lives."

Paul also differs from most other PIs in that he is married. His red-haired wife, Maureen, is a successful actress and she and Paul live in a penthouse on Central Avenue South with a view all the way uptown. Paul carries a light, six-shot Colt Agent with a two-inch barrel and he drives a Ferrari. His cop friend is Lt. Marsh Baxter, a detective.

In the first Shaw, *The Killing Man* (1970), Paul comes home one night from LA to the office and surprises a burglar. In the struggle Shaw knocks the burglar through the office window seven stories down. Paul is not the callous type at all. In his words:

A cool killer of many men? I'm not. Few men are cool killers. Maybe we all do have violence inside us, maybe it is a dark part of all of us, but we also have a deep resistance to killing: in the so-called civilized countries anyway. We hesitate, most of us, even in the face of attack, or in defense of our children . . . . I had killed, except in war, only once before, and that one time had sent me alone into the mountains for a month to think about my life.

Since Paul can't accept killing a man he didn't even know and who had no known connection with any of his cases, he is forced to try to find out something about the victim. The trail leads to Greenwich Village, a college town in upstate New York, a small industrial center, and a mountain commune for alienated young people. There are additional murders before Paul manages to solve all of them.

The second Shaw, *Here To Die* (1971), begins with Paul receiving a telephone call at 2:05 AM one morning from a Frank Carlos in Malibu. Frank is the husband of Judy Tower, Paul's first love. Judy has disappeared without a trace. Paul flies out to California to look for her. When he arrives at the Carlos home he finds Frank lying in a pool of blood, stabbed three times. In finding Carlos's assailant and determining what happened to Judy, Paul is assaulted, thrown in jail and shot at before he clears up the mystery and despairs over all the senseless violence in the world.

Mirror Image (1972), the third novel, requires that Shaw clear a girl's dead father of an embezzlement charge. But this simple case gets complicated very quickly when Paul finds the bloody body of a man lying in the parking lot outside his motel window. Before it's over, Shaw is fighting for his life. The fourth Shaw, *Circle of Fire* (1973), has Paul flying to LA and then driving up to Northern California to explore the cases Delaney was working on before he was shot and seriously wounded. Paul quickly narrows it down to the case of the politician Russell Dobson whose car exploded while he was driving away with a girl he'd picked up in a roadhouse. Paul finds Dobson had a lot of enemies, including two opposing political candidates, a jealous girl friend and his sister's suitor who couldn't get Dobson's permission to marry the girl. The deeper Paul digs the more it seems Dobson was not the intended victim.

The most recent Shaw novel, *Touch of Death* (1981), has Paul investigating the murder of one Matt Jurgens. A few days before the murder Jurgens' wife hires Paul to find out what is going on between Matt and a small boy between 10 and 14-years old who has paid him three mysterious visits. Before Paul has the chance, Matt is stabbed four times with a foot-long antique dagger. Solving the murder and trapping the killer takes Paul into the Bowery, a skid-row hotel and the heart of East Harlem before nearly being killed himself.

Although the Shaw output has been relatively small, all of the novels were treated well by the critics. A reviewer for the New York *Times* said:

Dennis Lynds

One author who works in the Macdonald style without cliche is Mark Sadler. His latest Paul Shaw novel is a fine, sensitive book that has action without recklessness; a social point of view that presents no easy answers; and a well-plotted mystery that at all times is credible . . . . Two things about Paul Shaw: he is no Superman and he has compassion . . . . Sadler in addition is a smooth prose stylist who is remarkably successful working within what is, after all, a fixed form.

Dennis Lynds was born in St. Louis in 1924. He received his B.A. from Hofstra University in 1949 and his M.A. from Syracuse in 1951. Prior to this he served with the 12th Armored Division in France where he was decorated with a Purple Heart and three battle stars. Lynd's first career was as a chemist with Charles Pfizer and Company (1942-1943). Later he edited several publications put out by the chemistry industry.

Lynds started writing when he was still in high school and continued to do so during his college and army years. His short stories began to appear as early as 1951 in *New World Writing, The Gent* and *Prairie Schooner.* In the 1960s he began to publish mystery and detective short stories for *Mike Shayne Mystery Magazine, Alfred Hitchcock's Mystery Magazine, Manhunt* and *Shell Scott Mystery Magazine.* Under his own name he also published two "serious" novels during this time—*Combat Soldier* (1962) and *Uptown Downtown* (1963)—and later a novelization of a TV script called *Charlie Chan Returns* (1974).

In addition to the Collins byline, Lynds has written under several other pennames. As John Crowe, he has written the Buena Vista County mystery series which now numbers six novels. This series is unique because it is connected not by the presence of a central character but by the creation of a fictional area in California. Best among these novels are *A Touch of Darkness* (1972) and *Bloodwater* (1974).

Under the pseudonym of William Arden, Lynds has written a five-novel series about Kane Jackson, a specialist in the investigation of industrial espionage cases. Although the series was not commercially successful, it provided some interesting commentary on the relationship of government to big business. *Die to a Distant Drum* (1972) may be the best of this bunch. Arden is also the byline for the twelve juveniles that Lynds has written, all published by Random House.

Lynds has written one suspense novel as Carl Dekker, three novels under the Nick Carter house name and several "Shadow" paperbacks as Maxwell Grant. Under the Collins name he has written two science fiction novels—*Lukan War* (1968) and *The Planets of Death* (1970)—and as Lynds he recently published a collection of straight short stories, *Why Girls Ride Sidesaddle* (December Press, 1980).

Lynds currently lives in Santa Barbara, California. He writes seven days a week, 9-5 every day and 8-11 four nights a week.

James Crumley and His Montana Knights

James Crumley has two rules for survival in the tweed-and-sherry environs of university English departments: Rule one is "be genial, laid-back and mostly sober." Rule two is "if you don't like it you can always walk off." Jim Crumley is our *Numero Uno* Redneck Bohemian, who's leading a life as unchartered, as fast and sometimes as hard as any of our private heroes. Conceived in a tent somewhere in south Texas and born on Columbus Day, 1939 in Three Rivers, Texas, Crumley is a product of America's mid-century, roadside West; a frontier of mom-and-pop cafes, nickel pinballs, dusty bars and 15-unit motels along two-lane blacktops. The West before it was franchised to the urban cowboys. It's the West that Crumley still writes about and it's the home of the people he loves to write for, his favorite audience: "the good people who are rednecks and work hard and have a good time. The good rednecks—truck drivers, waitresses and field workers. I want to save their dignity."

The son of Arthur Crumley, an oilfield drilling superintendent, and his wife Ruby, a bookkeeper for a grocery chain, Crumley recalls that he taught himself how to read before the first grade. "Nobody in my family read much and nobody told me what to read. I didn't discover great writing until after college." After beginning at Georgia Tech, Crumley went to Texas A & I (Kingsville) where he received his BA in 1964. His formal training as a writer was at the University of Iowa Writer's Workshop from which he earned a Master of Fine Arts in 1966. "At Iowa I read everything I could. I learned what to read and that's all I did for a year. Dickens, Tolstoy, Dostoevski, Hemingway, James Jones, Durrell, Faulkner, Fitzgerald and O'Hara. I still reread them." At Iowa he also met Nelson Algren whom he remembers best for the perpetual poker game in which they both played. Crumley recalls, "Nelson finally lost his $7,000-a-year salary in the game, but I never got any of it."

In a dust-jacket tease for one of his novels, Crumley's life is summarized as a series of jobs: "an enlisted man in the U.S. Army, a roughneck, a bartender, and a college professor." He has itinerated up and down the heartland at a succession of teaching positions.

I taught a while at the University of Montana and then ran away. Then I taught at the University of Arkansas and ran away. Then I was Director of the Writing Program at Colorado State. From there I went to Reed College in Portland, then to Carnegie-Mellon in Pittsburgh.

Currently, he is teaching creative writing at the University of Texas at El Paso, "a good place where they like me."

In between the stops at academia have been some "on the road" periods where Crumley "drifted and drank a lot but tried not to misbehave too much." Married four times, divorced three, Crumley now lives in El

Paso with his wife, Bronwyn Pughe, and their young son. Crumley also has three grown children, all adopted in his previous marriages. He loves kids, books, motorcycles and Missoula, Montana. And he loves having a good time.

James Crumley published his first book, *One to Count Cadence*, in 1969. Set in 1962 with America about to plunge into the abyss of Vietnam, the novel describes the exploits of the 721 Communications Security Detachment, originally stationed at Clark Air Base in the Philippines and then ordered to Vietnam. It concentrates on the personalities of Sgt. "Slag" Krummel and PFC Joe Morning and their love-hate relationship. The tension between these two men and their dramatically conflicting views of life are reminiscent of Prewitt and Warden in James Jones' *From Here to Eternity*, the only book that might surpass Crumley's description of the enlisted men's U.S. Army. *Cadence* displays two of Crumley's most obvious writing talents later showcased in his novels about private eyes. First, there are the exuberant, unrestrained celebrations of rip-roaring masculinity. Crumley has bars and brawls and barrack life down cold. These scenes are raw and full of excesses, at one time hilarious and at another pathetic. Second, there is very talented writing about human relationships, whether they be between male buddies where all seems to be intuited and need not be spoken or between men and women where all is murky and difficult but wonderful.

Crumley started to write his first detective novel, *The Wrong Case* (1975), while he was at Colorado State and had decided he just couldn't face another section of freshman composition. It begins with a Lew Archer epigraph, "Never go to bed with a woman who has more troubles than you do," a bit of advice never followed by private detective Milton Chester Milodragovitch, simply known as "Milo" to everyone in his hometown of Meriwether, Montana. Milo is asked by Helen Duffy, a striking redhead, to search for Raymond Duffy, her younger brother who had come to Montana to work on his master's thesis in history. Raymond hasn't been heard from in three weeks, and Helen Duffy is convinced something has happened to him.

Helen Duffy's request comes at a time when Milo has just about decided to close up his private eye business, which after ten years of operation has fallen on hard times because the Montana legislature has passed a no-fault divorce law. Twice-divorced himself, Milo specialized in repossession and divorce work since "I never had to see anybody whose life was any better off than mine." Fact is Milo is quitting because he's disgusted with "a life that had become all hangover and no drunk."

I've got nothing to show for those years but bad debts and grief, I've not done a single thing in all that time I could be proud of, so maybe here at the end I should do something nice for a change, something for free, and maybe this shitload I call myself will feel better instead of worse for a change. Maybe.

So Milo takes the wrong case because he wants to feel human again. Because he wants Helen Duffy, "who behind the fluster, the dread and the sorrow, the fog of tears and pink tresses ... blossomed forth like a nightflower and the new moon; a woman so strong that she could believe in hope and trust and families and love, a woman who had survived without luck."

Milo offers the following deal to Helen: "I'll look for your brother in exchange for your nights ... my days for your nights." Offended, Helen leaves but later she accepts Milo's proposition. Milo soon discovers that Raymond Duffy was not the upstanding younger brother that Helen had claimed. His body is discovered in the men's toilet of an Indian tavern north of town, a shoelace tied around his biceps, a hypodermic needle hanging from his arm. Unconvinced that Raymond died of an accidental overdose or that he committed suicide, Helen pleads with Milo to investigate his death further. He does so with the help of his derelict buddies who reveal a spirit and sense of humor that the booze can't wash away. The death toll mounts as Milo is deliberately led down some blind and very nasty alleys until a denouement of sorts is finally reached. Closure of the case is not forced, and anyone who requires his mysteries to be fully resolved is likely to feel at the end as if only the first seven notes of the scale have been played.

Despite some derivative plotting, *The Wrong Case* is a private eye novel only in the obvious sense that main character Milo is a private eye. Mystery, action and the private eye as hero—these themes are subordinated to the book's larger concern of examining the requirements of relationships between people who suffer from all manner of weakness, grief and hardship. This is clear from the outset when Milo makes his proposition to Helen Duffy; he's taking the case because he hopes it will give him a chance to love. Milo himself disclaims any allegiance to the private-eye ethic and the sense of order it suggests. (Earlier, when Milo had been a deputy sheriff, he was a corrupt one, "on the take like every other deputy in the county."):

I had neither training nor experience as a detective, no matter what it said on my license. For God's sake, I didn't even read mystery novels because they always seemed too complicated. As a minion of justice or vengeance, I just didn't make it.

Another example of the distance between Milo and the genre private eye is his lack of heroic pretense. Late in the case after he has been severely beaten, Milo decides simply that he's ready to quit even though he hasn't solved the case. The idea that one would give up when things get tough is not what we expect from our modern knights.

I was through. Helen Duffy would have to live with what I knew about her little brother, and although I was fairly certain I had killed the wrong man, that was going to have to pass for vengeance this year. If Simon couldn't rest easy with that, then that was his problem, because I was tired and old and not nearly as tough as I thought I was, and I was through. As I drove away through the bursts of pain that came in bright flashes, I could see his laughing face, but the voice was still.

Although the book is full of violence, we soon realize that Milo doesn't have the sort of meanness that would appear necessary to survive in his business. He admits, "I lacked that abstract edge that makes violence calm and controlled, a tool for justice or vengeance." He has to crank himself up with a load of speed before he can get vicious enough to go hunting for a killer. Milo is basically a kind, generous man, a soft touch for every bum that comes near him. He runs a bar tab for the whole town.

The key to Milo's character is that as a man he's still looking for the family that he never had as a child. Milo's father was a rich drunk, his mother was an insane one. Both parents committed suicide. He remembers that after his father shot himself, his mother continued to shout at the body, "its heels still rattling on the hardwood floor." Ten years later his mother hanged herself with a nylon hose.

Milo adopts Simon Rome, a sad, lovable drunk, and then looks after him with a tenderness and devotion that suggests a son doting on his father:

"Take care," I said, standing and patting his shoulder. Beneath the heavy tweed, his body felt as feeble as an old woman's. Stringy flesh on the verge of corruption, bones nearly dust. I ruffled his hair for luck, touched the parchment scalp, the fragile skull, making my amends, then I left him there in his repose.

One of the most poignant passages in the book is when Milo gazes down on the streets of Meriwether from his office window and notices that Simon is finally wearing his father's beloved overcoat, a coat that Milo had also worn, "wrapped in it, unafraid in the solid odor of wool and sweat and whiskey." Milo's mother had given all of his father's clothes, even the favorite coat, to the Salvation Army so that the drunks and bums would wear them, a constant, hateful reminder to Milo that his own father was one of "them" and always would be:

I grew up as my mother meant for me to, watching my father's clothing parade up and down the streets of Meriwether, warming the backs of whatever dispossessed came into them. A retired NP engineer had been buried in his favorite tweed suit. His Russell snakeboots wore to greasy decrepitude on the feet of a local garbage man. Once I saw his Malone hunting pants on a drunken Willomot squaw, dirty and worn, the fly broken and a scrap of pink panties bulging out like a coil of gut.

Over the years I bought up what I could, haggling my allowance away to the Salvation Army, the Goodwill store, the secondhand dealers of Meriwether. On the streets and in the bars and skid-row hotels, I sought his clothes, bought and burned them. Once the winos found me out, I bought more clothing than my father had owned in his life, and if I had had enough money, the winos of our fair city would have been rich but naked.

Just before I went to Korea, I thought I had found all the clothes except the overcoat....

And now the overcoat had passed from deathbed to secondhand store to Simon. The coat wasn't an omen of death but of life; Simon had been dying for years. I leaned out the window and waved at him in the rising wind as the first splatters of rain shattered against my face. He didn't hear me; he turned into Mahoney's as if it were home.

Milo is a first-class drunk himself, a noble calling that is part of his family's legacy. The entire book is overcast with a purple alcoholic haze. Someone once said that *The Wrong Case* was the only book that always gave him a contact hangover. Drink is both Milo's curse and his blessing. He revels in the solace it can bring but regrets the pain it can never quite take away. Meriwether's drunks are now Milo's family. They're his brothers in drink, men who as they kneel before a toilet are "learning something about humility and (their) natural human foolishness, about how to survive (themselves)." They are the people Milo trusts and yet he knows that like him "all drunks have theories, endlessly tedious arguments, both vocal and silent, with which to justify their drinking .... Some of the theories may well be true, but because drunks lie so much, it's difficult to divide the sharp perceptions from the sorry rationalizations. Once, my father talked to me about drinking and drunks, and in my memory it sounds not at all sorry. Just sad."

Milo's life as a drunk is an attempt to recapture the few lucky moments of his childhood, a quest for the belonging and forgiveness of families. And still a quest for the coat, that last remnant of his alcoholic father, a man whose drunkenness he could always forgive, whose memory he could always cherish:

My warmest childhood memories are forged in bars. Not in zoos or camps, not on family outings or church picnics, not with gracious gray-haired lady English teachers helping me love Shelley and Keats. All those things happened, but the bars counted more....

After his death, I missed the bars just as hard as any alcoholic drying out. Perhaps my long quest after his discarded clothing was just an excuse to hang around the bars.

Just as Milo loves his father without forgetting his lies and his weaknesses and just as he finds Raymond Duffy without ever finally understanding the cause of his death, so too does he come to love Helen without ever fully comprehending her soul. Ultimately, *The Wrong Case* is a book about forgiveness—forgiveness for families who did not love, forgiveness for lovers who had to lie. It is this quality which finally raises Milo above the formulized private eye. Plenty of heroes have been betrayed by their women. Plenty have become bitter and cynical, preferring to live aloof and alone, protected by their proud autonomy from the risks of love. Spade cast the mold and ever since the male private eye has continued to claim the hollow victory of not playing the sap for any deceitful woman. It's a victory Milo doesn't want. He may be a drunk and a bum, and a man corruptible, but when faced with the decision all private eye fans will recognize, Milo chooses the woman over the principle. It's that choice for which we remember him.

Milo's back in *Dancing Bear* (1983), Crumley's newest and much awaited novel, this time fueled by peppermint schnapps and a snort full of blow but otherwise trying to keep his nose clean until he turns 52 and inherits his father's millions. He's hung up his PI spurs and now aimlessly rides the night shift for Haliburton Security—"rattling doorknobs, guarding twenty-four hour convenience markets, and holding the hands of lost children in shopping malls." When he's asked by Sarah Weddington, an old rich woman who was one of his father's former lovers, to satisfy her curiosity about the man and woman whose weekly parkside meetings she's been observing from her balcony, Milo sees his large fee as an easy ticket to Mexico's sunshine, away from Montana's "sear, frozen heart of winter."

What starts out as a simple tail assignment soon turns into explosive viciousness with Milo and his flaky Vietnam-scarred sidekick, Bob Simmons scrambling over the carnage they help create. Before Milo finally strikes the deal that saves his life, he's forced into combat with the forces of a multinational corporation where criminal greed begins but does not end with gun running, drugs, chop shops and stolen cars.

Sadder, older, a little tougher, Milo still fights the bottle he loves—"how I wanted a martini, but one would be too many and ten thousand wouldn't be enough"—and falls for the women who fool and fail him—"I would be their stooge, dance to their lies, dream of love in their arms." Still the warm heart who hands out his money to widows, orphans and old bums; afraid of a world that's too mean for him sober, he waits for 52 to roll around. Until then, "I live close to the grain, avoid even the appearance of evil, forgive all things, live alone in the tiny swamper's cubicle beside the alley, keep my nose clean."

And then we have *The Last Good Kiss*, a marvelous book, maybe the finest private eye novel written in the 70s. Its title taken from Richard Hugo's *Degrees of Gray In Phillipsburg* ("You might come here Sunday for a whim. Say your life broke down. The last good kiss you had was years ago ...") it is the PI novel of the 70s after *The Chill* in the 60s and *The*

Long Goodbye in the 50s.

Lauded by Greg Marcus as a novel about "the long hangover the 70s have had to suffer for the failure to face up to the conflicts of the 60s," *The Last Good Kiss* has earned raves from sources as diverse as *Rolling Stone* and *The Wall Street Journal*. The source of its appeal is hard to define. There is a special feeling that comes from reading it, an attraction that is immediate, almost precognitive. Many have praised the way it captures the semirural, modern American West. It is written with a melancholy appreciation of people whose lives have been hard. At times it is reminiscent of Steinbeck. Others have been struck by the pure craftmanship of the writing. Crumley's luxuriously long sentences blow across the page as naturally as the wind. Their phrasing is seamless and graced with sadness. The descriptions of the land and the country people are poignant. They can crack your heart.

> I reached for my wallet and took out her high school picture and handed it to her.
> "I killed that girl a long time ago," she said quietly, "you've been looking for a ghost." She touched her face in the picture, smearing it with blood. She didn't sob, but tears coursed unbidden down her cheeks. "That cameo was my grandmother's, you know, the only thing she had left when they got to California—that cameo and seven kids and a husband with a cancer behind his eye," she said. "She raised them all, made them all finish high school. She ruined her feet and legs slinging hash in a truck stop in Fresno, and when she got too old to work she went to the county home. She wouldn't live with her kids, wouldn't trouble them that way. When I was a little-bitty girl, my mother would take me to visit her, you know, and I hated that dry stink of the old folks. They were so crazy with loneliness, they always came out of their rooms to touch me and fuss over me, and I hated it, just hated it.
> "While she talked to Granny, my momma would kneel down in front of her chair and rest her legs on her shoulders and rub the varicose veins in Granny's legs, rub them until her hands began to cramp. Then she'd ask me to rub Granny's legs for a minute while she rested, and I wouldn't do it, wouldn't touch those veins like big ugly worms under her stockings. I couldn't make myself touch them, those legs she had ruined so her children would finish high school."

His sentences can play jokes on themselves but still leave you hurting.

> Once I even humped the same sad young whore in a trailerhouse complex out on the Nevada desert. She was a frail, skinny little bit out of Cincinnati, and she had brought her gold mine out West, thinking perhaps it might assay better, but her shaft had collapsed, her veins petered out, and the tracks on her thin arms looked as if they had been dug with a rusty pick. After I had slaked too many nights of aimless barstool lust amid her bones, I asked her again about Trahearne. She didn't say anything at first, she just lay on her crushed bed-sheets, hitting on a joint and gazing beyond the aluminum ceiling into the cold desert night.

The story's plot is not particularly original, relying on the conventional strategy of the lonely, down-but-not-quite-out PI following trails that are camouflaged by the lies of the innocent and the guilty, particularly a woman who is both. The opening scene pays obvious homage to *The Last Goodbye* ("The first time I laid eyes on Terry Lennox he was drunk in a Rolls-Royce Silver Wraith outside the terrace of the Dancers."):

When I finally caught up with Abraham Trahearne, he was drinking beer with an alcoholic bulldog named Fireball Roberts in a ramshackle joint outside Sonoma, California, drinking the heart right out of a fine spring afternoon.

Private eye C.W. (Chauncey Wayne) Sughrue is hired by Catherine Trahearne to find her ex-husband, alcoholic writer Abraham Trahearne, who's on one of his cross-the-West binges. Sughrue trails Trahearne through Wyoming, Montana, Oregon, Utah and Idaho before running him to ground in the dusty old bar in Sonoma. Trahearne promptly gets his butt shot up in a barroom tiff between Sughrue and a couple of good old boys. While waiting for the big man's backside to heal enough to allow him to haul him back home to Montana, Sughrue is asked by barowner Rosie Flowers to look for her daughter Betty Sue who ran away ten years earlier. For an $87 fee, Sughrue sets off on "his fool's errand" to look for Betty Sue accompanied by Trahearne and Fireball, certainly next to Carstairs, the best hard-boiled canine in all eyedom. Eventually we discover that Trahearne also wants to know about Betty Sue's past ten years but for very different reasons than Rosie's. Betty Sue's trail is a faint one, strewn with corruption, false death certificates, pornographic trade and personal trauma. Sughrue becomes as obsessed with the search as Rosie and Trahearne, and as the reader gradually discovers his is the most essential but dimly recognized reason of all.

Crumley originally planned *Kiss* to be the second Milo novel. However, a clause in an option contract with United Artists would have reduced the profits of any Milo sequel written within several years so Crumley adapted a character from a Texas novel he'd been working on for years and created Sughrue. The shift in characters became a major difference.

Sughrue and Milo share some superficial similarities. Both live in Meriwether. In fact there are some passing comments about Sughrue formerly having an alcoholic partner that suggest that he and Milo once worked together. Both are veterans; Milo from Korea, Sughrue from Vietnam, where he was court-martialled for unintentionally killing three generations of a Vietnamese family. Both have bittersweet memories of fathers, either drunk or crazy. Fathers loved but never fully embraced.

Both are drunks although Sughrue is not as reflective as Milo about his boozing: "I try to stay two drinks ahead of reality and three behind a drunk." Eight years younger than Milo, Sughrue can still maintain a smug, well-cultured matter of factness about his beergut and face of a saddle tramp. He drinks his beer and pushes his El Camino down the road admitting that "that's my act. And has been for years." At the same time Sughrue is beginning to show signs of self-pity and discontent, weary of a life where "home is where you hang your hangover." He's becoming old enough to have some regrets:

Nobody lives forever, nobody stays young long enough. My past seemed like so much excess baggage, my future a series of long goodbyes, my present an empty flask, the last good drink already bitter on my tongue.

For all this, Sughrue is a far different man from Milo. Sughrue has a natural-born mean streak which at times veers to the almost casually sadistic. In *One to Count Cadence*, Sgt. Krummel says, "Sometimes the good part of a man gets out of the cage, sometimes the bad." Crumley acknowledges, "Milo is my good side, Sughrue's the bad."

Sughrue's meanness makes him a persuasive interrogator. When a Denver hood refuses to tell him the whereabouts of Betty Sue, Sughrue flashes his viciousness:

'Are you going to tell me where she is?" I asked him, and he made the mistake of shrugging. "Get me the telephone book," I said to Trahearne.

"The phone book?" Stacy went into the bedroom and brought it back.

I lifted Jackson's feet and set them on the thick book. His genitals had balled up in his crotch and they looked like some vital organ that had slipped from his body. I stood up and took the .22 out of my belt.

"You don't know where she is?" I asked. He shrugged again, and I said, "Okay." I let the automatic dangle from my hand as I waited for the sound of a jet making its final approach over the motel. "Last chance," I said before the noise got too loud for him to hear. He shrugged again. "You know I'm not going to kill you, don't you?" I said. He shook his head, but his eyes smiled. He might be a piece of shit but Jackson had some balls on him. Either that or he was more frightened of his business associates than he was of me. That was a real mistake on his part. When the landing jet swept over the motel, I leaned down and pumped two rounds into his right foot. Blood splashed over the telephone book and the bathtub, as red as Jackson's face was white.

It is in this context of Sughrue's toughness and his machismo exterior burnt to a hard edge by the unremittingly arid West, always that most masculine of America's regions, that the real triumph of this novel emerges. After all the buddies have bonded for the night's last backslap and spent some good times with "strange ladies draped in denim and satin, in silver and hammered gold," they must still learn whether they can accept and love a woman without judging her. Driven by fear, Trahearne learns that he can't. Sughrue, coming closer to Milo than we might have thought possible, learns that he can.

I drank and smoked and watched the ceiling. When the ashtray beside the bed filled, I took it to the bathroom to empty it, and out of habit I wiped it clean. It was a lump of glazed clay, as formless as any rock, with a smooth, shallow depression in the center. As I wiped away the caked ashes, a woman's profile came into view, a high, proud face molded into the clay, a tangle of long hair streaming away from the face, as if the woman stood in a cosmic wind. When I looked more closely, I saw what seemed to be a ring of watchers, lightly impressed eyes around the rim of the depression, staring at the woman's face with a lust akin to hatred.

I had made my own bed and went to it to sleep, then to rise and do what I knew I had to do, to pay what I owed the women.

Like Abraham Trahearne in his prime, James Crumley has written about

the things he saw on his binges, about the road, about small towns whose future had become hostage to freeways, about truck-stop waitresses whose best hope is moving to Omaha or Cheyenne, about pasts that hung around like unwelcomed ghosts, about bars where the old survivors of some misunderstood disaster gathered to stare at their drinks sepia in their glasses.

From those simple people living their thin lives in a hard land has come the lesson that too many of our private eye heroes have missed, a lesson not lost on Milo, not even on Sughrue. The real life of courage is lived not by autonomous men but by forgiving ones.

The Big City Knights of Stanley Ellin

Stanley Ellin was born in New York City in 1916. At the age of 19 he graduated from Brooklyn College. Before becoming a professional writer at his wife's urging, Ellin held a succession of interesting jobs: dairy farmer, "pusher" for a newspaper distributor, teacher and steelworker. He served with the Army during World War II and then began his career as a full-time writer.

Ellin is probably best known for his short stories of crime and horror, which are rated by many as some of the finest crime stories written by an American. His unforgettable first story, "The Specialty of the House," won the Best First Story Award in the *Ellery Queen's Mystery Magazine* contest of 1948. It is often mentioned as one of the finest modern crime stories ever written. "Specialty" and several of Ellin's other award-winning stories (including the Edgar-winning "The House Party," 1954) were published in the volume *Mystery Stories* in 1956 (Simon and Schuster). This collection was praised by Julian Symons as "the finest collection of stories in the crime form published in the past half century," and Anthony Boucher described the book as "a permanent classic among short story collections."

In 1956 Ellin won a second Edgar for his story "The Blessington

Method" which became the title for another collection of Ellin's stories including "The Orderly World of Mr. Appleby," a superb study of a wife-killer and "The Nine-to-Five Man," about a day in the life of a professional arsonist. Ellin's third anthology is *Kindly Dig Your Grave and Other Wicked Stories* published in 1975. Once again Ellin's imaginative story-telling is showcased with offerings like "The Last Bottle in the World," which Edward Hoch called "one of the half-dozen best short stories about wine."

Ellin has written several non-PI novels including *Dreadful Summit* (1948), *The Key to Nicholas Street* (1952), *House of Cards* (1967), *The Valentine Estate* (1968), *Mirror, Mirror on the Wall* (1972), *Stronghold* (1975) and *The Luxembourg Run* (1977).

Ellin is also the author of two nonmysteries—*The Winter After This Summer* (1961) and *The Panama Portrait* (1962). Many of his works have been made into films and television plays by some of the world's most distinguished directors. Joseph Losey directed "The Big Night" (1951), based on *Dreadful Summit*, starring John Barrymore, Jr. "Leda" (1961), a French film directed by Claude Chabrol, was based on *The Key to Nicholas Street*, and "House of Cards" under the direction of John Guillermin was drawn from the novel of the same name. Alfred Hitchcock was one of several directors who brought Ellin's work to television.

Ellin is a writer of international reputation, with his works now translated into more than 20 languages. In addition to his three Edgars and numerous *EQMM* prizes, he was awarded France's Le Grand Prix de Litterature Policiera in 1975. A past president of the Mystery Writers of America, he was given that organization's most prestigious honor, the Grand Master Award, for lifetime achievement in crime fiction.

Four of Ellin's novels involve PIs. *The Eighth Circle*, which won an Edgar for best novel of 1958, introduced Murray Kirk, a different breed of private eye, but tough nonetheless. Jake Dekker, a freelance insurance investigator is the hero of *The Bind* (1970). The only private eye to appear in more than one Ellin novel is Johnny Milano whose debut in *Star Light, Star Bright* (1979) was followed by *The Dark Fantastic* (1983).

Ellin's detectives are cut from different cloth than the typical private eye. Outside of the characteristic persistence and hard edges, they share in few of the hard-boiled traditions. They are not isolated, either socially or in their work; they do not have a particularly world-weary view of life; above all, they are not poor. Ellin's detectives are wealthy and powerful men. They are accustomed to a world of political and economic influence in which they do their business with a big-city flourish and swagger that might be summed up as "New Yorkish." Their life-styles and their approaches to investigations are high-pressured. They are a well-connected group who often display corporate airs, drop the right name and use friendships for personal motives. Kirk is the senior partner in Conmy and Kirk, a top-drawer agency. Milano, a specialist in recovering merchandise for insurance companies, is a member of Watrous Associates with 30th-floor offices at Madison and 60th. Dekker flies solo but he purchases high-priced assistants along the way, in effect creating an *ad hoc* firm of experts.

They are all men with expensive tastes, verging at times on the extravagant. Big cars, Central Park penthouses and six-figure salaries with unlimited expense accounts. An Ellin detective is a cross between a straight Dave Brandstetter and a Park Avenue Dan Kearney. Kirk, Dekker and Milano's motivations are not the traditionally heroic ones of the knight exemplar. They are not self-sacrificing, noble nor resistant to temptation. They carry no special allegiance to the weak or the innocent. In each of his four private eye novels, Ellin shows his protagonist driven by personal, even selfish motives, most often an obsession with a woman for whom the case becomes the way by which her love can be captured.

This theme is established most dramatically in Ellin's masterpiece, *The Eighth Circle*, which Otto Penzler described as a "seminal publication in the history of mystery fiction." Murray Kirk is a detective at the top, a man-about-Manhattan with "health, wealth and women" who drives a Cadillac and takes his ice cream at Rumplemayers. College and law school graduate, Kirk was a West Sider who remembers being so poor he couldn't afford to bury his own father.

"When I left the cemetery that day," Murray said, "I knew that I had had it. I went right from there to the Conmy office, where there was a job open, and a chance to make real money, and a chance to be a human being. I know it sounds funny to hear talk like this when things are so different nowadays, but it wasn't funny to me then. I never went back to that law office I was working in, and I never turned around. I went straight to where I wanted to go, and that's why I can say I'm not being defensive about it. I know why I'm here, and any time I forget why, I can always take down the dime notebook the old man used to write his poetry in and remind myself. There's no place in this world for well-meaning fools. It's tough enough when you've got brains and know how to use them."

Kirk approaches his cases with a businessman's sense of ruthlessness and priorities. When he's asked by a defense attorney to investigate the case against Arnold Lundeen, a New York City cop charged with taking bribes from bookmakers, Kirk takes the job because he's in love with Ruth Vincent, Lundeen's fiance. Driven by his desire for Ruth, Kirk's goal is to prove Lundeen guilty so that he can win Ruth Vincent for himself, a to-the-victor-goes-the-spoils motivation which is anathema to the descendants of Spade and Marlowe.

The one problem was how to wrap up Lundeen so tight and sink him so deep that nothing could be salvaged of him. He had to be finished off so thoroughly that there wouldn't be more than a bad memory left of him while he rotted away his two-and-a-half-to-five in jail. That was it. That was everything. After that there would be no problems left, at all.

When Kirk enters the eighth circle, the level where Dante placed "the liars, flatterers, and sellers of office, the fortune tellers, hypocrites, and thieves, the pimps and grafters, and all such scum," he does so with unexpected results for his client and for himself.

In *The Bind*, Jake Dekker goes to Miami Beach for a surreptitious investigation of a widow who's trying to collect $200,000 from Guaranty Life Insurance for the death of her husband in an automobile accident. If Jake can prove the death was not an accident he can save Guaranty the pay-off and earn himself a handsome contingency fee. Jakes moves in next door to the widow along with Elinor, a young beauty whom Jake is paying to masquerade as his wife in order to establish his cover as the newest member of Miami's power society. Like Murray Kirk, Dekker is ice-blooded and calculating, at one point telling Elinor, who is falling in love with him, "Baby, don't ever weigh yourself against anything that's got to do with my job. You're in for a terrible disillusionment if you do." But, also like Kirk, Dekker has his soft side, well protected by a hard shell, but finally touched by Elinor despite all his attempts to keep their relationship strictly professional. The plot again presents a conflict between the needs of the client and the desire of the detective, this time reaching a less romantic ending than in *The Eighth Circle*. In typical Ellin fashion, the story telling is underpaced, particularly for a thriller, but taut with pressure and emotional intensity.

Johnny Milano, Ellin's third PI, is introduced in *Star Light, Star Bright*, a witty and sharply plotted novel that gives us a hard-boiled version of an Agatha Christie house-party mystery. Milano, splendid in his J. Press duds, is interrupted from his high stakes recovery work in New York by a call from Sharon Bauer, a beautiful superstar with whom he was once in love, but who dropped him to marry a crippled old billionaire named Andrew Quist, on the advice of an unctious guru called Kalos Daskalos. Someone is now threatening to murder His Highness who just happens to be visiting the Quist estate along with a pack of Hollywood mush heads. In exchange for $20,000 Milano is off to Palm Beach to guard the yogi and to ferret out the culprit from the guest list. A lot of wicked romance involving Milano, Sharon and Quist's art-scholar secretary takes place before someone dispatches Daskalos to eternity. The "someone" is not easily anticipated, but it's no problem for Milano who shines bright in this entertaining little sparkler.

Milano makes a much more serious appearance in *The Dark*

Fantastic, which proves to be one of the most ambitious and disturbing novels in contemporary mystery fiction. Although Ellin once again has his detective pursue a case in order to win a woman, the real theme of this novel is race and the extreme passions it generates. The story centers on the interplay between Milano and Charles Witter Kirwan, an aging historian who is dying of cancer. Although Milano and Kirwan are strangers to each other for most of the book, they appear in alternating chapters, providing a narrative device which slowly translates a coincidental meeting into a nerve-wracking contest of wills.

Kirwan lives alone in a stately Victorian mansion in the East Flatbush section of Brooklyn. Next door is a 24-unit apartment which is a crumbling, filthy, run-down eye-sore. Kirwan has come to despise the tenants of that building, most of whom are black, with a hatred so vicious and consuming that it is all that is keeping him alive. Charles Kirwan has a plan for the "Bulanga." A simple plan meant to give purpose to all his hatred; a final suicidal act of defiance and purification:

> Yes. Let's put it this way.
> Therefore, I, Charles Witter Kirwan, being of sound and disposing mind, am going to blow up that structure—that apartment building at 409 Witter Street—three weeks from this day.
> Blow it, in the fine old phrase, to hell and gone....
> There is intended to be—there should be—a heavy loss of life. At least sixty people reside in the building; I am choosing a time for the explosion when most will be right there to share it with me.

Meanwhile, Milano is trying to bust a big-time art scam. In the process he falls in love with Christine Bailey, a beautiful, black militant with an unnerving mixture of moves—two parts "put-down" for every one part "come-on." When Milano does Christine a favor and checks up on her strangely behaving younger sister, he encounters Charles Kirwan. It just so happens that the Baileys live at 409 Witter Street.

The rest of the novel slowly forces Milano and Kirwan to their inevitable confrontation, set against Milano and Christine's tumultuous but pleasing love affair.

The Dark Fantastic presents Milano as the epitome of the High-Style-But-Tough detective. Blessed with form and substance, Milano struts his stuff through all the right places; workouts at the Athletic Club, dinner at the Russian Tea Room, transportation in a regal blue 450 SLC Mercedes. As Christine observes, Milano is "not much like those late night movies."

Ellin's conception of the private eye as a paragon not of virtue but of success and competence eliminates self-sacrifice and chivalry as necessary components of heroism. Instead he emphasizes a more purely professional view in which skills are purchased (often at a high price) and a business ethic prevails. But if Ellin's heroes are sharp pros, they are still warm-blooded ones. Their pecuniary side is opposed by a compassionate quality which, although well-disguised much of the time, makes them attractive and desirable men. They are modernized Marlowes who, freed from introspection and self-inflicted isolation, still retain the hardness as well as the kindness of the good knight.

The Motor City Knight, Loren Estleman—*Amos Walker*

He is a solid, weight-trained 200 pounds with a surly, heavy-featured face that looks like it's felt its share of fists. Wrapped in the classic British trench coat squared with epaulets, the fedora curled down to meet the hard, steady eyes, he looks like somebody's hired muscle. Somebody who invests his money well. He's out of Detroit, drives a 69 Merc, rust-blotched blue, rolls on four slicks. Recent photos indicate that he works out of an upstairs office outfitted with the standard equipment—bottle of booze, Saturday night hand banger, "wanted" posters to cover the walls. Visitors are greeted by a "Trespassers Will Be Shot" sign that guards the entrance. Visitors should believe it; his own family does.

His self-evaluation: "I'm a good boxer, a fair wrestler, and . . . I saw my share of schoolyard fights. I don't belong to any organization, union or associations. I'm sort of antisocial that way; a loner." Acquaintances recall that leery busboys avoid tending to his cafe table. Our next private eye? Almost. He's our next author. Loren D. Estleman.

Most of the above description is accurate. The recent photo is a dustjacket put-on that reveals how much fun Estleman is having with his private eye series, featuring rough-cut Amos Walker.

Loren D. Estleman was born in Ann Arbor, Michigan, in 1952. Leauvett, his father, is a retired short-haul truck driver of French-German ancestry. His mother, Louise, is a first generation Austrian who worked for many years as a postal clerk. Loren and his older brother, Charles, a mail carrier, still live with their parents in Whitmore Lake, Michigan. *The Midnight Man*, the third Walker novel, is dedicated to "the Family Estleman: Four Against the World."

Estleman received his BA in 1974 from Eastern Michigan University, majoring in English literature, minoring in journalism. He says, "I just decided early in my life that my goal was to write books. That's all I ever really wanted to do." During high school, Estleman worked as a political cartoonist for the *Michigan Fed*, an AFL-CIO publication for federal workers. Throughout high school and college, he wrote several unpublished plays that gave him his first experience in writing dialogue.

Following graduation from EMU, Estleman was Editor-in-chief during 1975-1976 for the *Community Foto News*, a weekly paper in tiny

Pinckney, Michigan. From 1976-1977 he worked as a reporter, covering the courts and police beat for the Ann Arbor *News*. His last newspaper job was as staff writer for the Dexter *Leader* where he was required to be a jack-of-all trades. From 1977-1980 Estlemen was a writer, salesman, photographer and janitor for the *Leader*. He credits his newspaper experience with teaching him "how to research, how to find and talk to the right people when I needed some particular information." Since 1980, when he quit his position with the *Leader*, Estleman has been writing fiction full time, his dream finally realized.

Estleman's first book was *The Oklahoma Punk* (Major Books, 1976), a pulpy gangster story written in his senior year at EMU. It is no longer in print, a fact that does not greatly dismay Estleman. "For me, *Punk* represented an acceptable canvas upon which to base my own personal style .... Anybody in a creative field needs a place to be lousy while learning his trade, and for me, Major Books was that place."

Following *Punk*, Estleman began to write Western adventures. *The Hider* (1978) is a first-person, folksy narrative of a hunt for the last buffalo in the Pacific Northwest of 1898. A nostalgic youth, a grizzled old buffalo hunter and an Indian on the run are its trio of heroes. *The Wolfer* (1981) is a well-researched tale about hunting wolves on the Great Plains in the late 19th century.

The High Rocks (1979), *Stamping Ground* (1980) and *Murdock's Law* (1982) are period-piece accounts of the exploits of Page Murdock, a deputy U.S. Marshall for Judge Harlan Blackthorne in Montana. All are written in a hard-boiled style, well-suited to the always surly, usually likeable Murdock, who shares some qualities with his private-detective descendants. Trailworn and dusty, Murdock is as quick with the quip as any street-smart PI.

"We will draw straws. The holder of the short straw will go."
    I shook my head. "I don't like it."
    "Why not?" Hudspeth demanded. "It seems fair enough."
    "That's why I don't like it." (*Stamping Ground*)

Murdock is an interesting contrast with Amos Walker, of whom much more will be said soon. Unchecked by the Marlowe code of honor which inspires our admiration for Walker, Murdock is a man who can be purposefully brutal. He will kill for the sake of expediency and have few regrets afterward. In *Stamping Ground*, Murdock reflects on the fact that the sleeping Indian he is about to kill "had never done any of us actual harm." "It had me all torn up for maybe a second and a half. Then I brought the rock crushing down squarely onto his exposed right temple." So much for reflection. About the only code evident here is Murdock's Code, which is revealed by his answer to the question, "Just whose side are you on, Murdock?" "That's easy. Mine." The Murdock series has earned considerable critical acclaim. *The High Rocks* was a 1980 nominee for the American Book Award.

The award-winning *Aces and Eights* (1981) is an account of the trial of Wild Bill Hickock's murderer. It initiates a planned trilogy of historical western novels with the second and third novels to be portrayals of Buffalo Bill and George Armstrong Custer, respectively.

Following an assignment to write a newspaper article on the Ann Arbor chapter of the Baker Street Irregulars, Estleman wrote *Sherlock Holmes vs.Dracula* (1978), the first of his two deadpan recreations of Conan Doyle's famous sleuth. Told in the usual Watson narrative, Holmes pursues Dracula following the arrival of a Russian ship in England with all its passengers dead and drained. Along the way, Mrs. Watson gets kidnapped and Holmes has some near misses with his own mortality. In *Dr. Jekyl and Mr. Holmes* (1979), Holmes and Watson are asked to investigate the bizarre connection between the snazzy Dr. Jekyl and the unsavory Hyde. As usual, Watson tells the story.

Motor City Blue (1980) introduces Amos Walker (no kin to Hiram), a 32-year-old Vietnam vet working as a private eye in Detroit. *Angel Eyes* (1981), *The Midnight Man* (1982), *The Glass Highway* (1983) and *Sugartown* (1984) are the worthy sequels. Walker's Detroit is a scary extension of Marlowe's LA: decadent, corrupt, evil. It is the American city gone bad, so bad that its treachery fails to shock much anymore. Its dark streets are full of predators, driven by paranoia, greed and hate.

Visitors may gawk at the gleaming Renaissance Center; Walker sees another Detroit, the one "you never saw on the posters put out by the Chamber of Commerce":

Warehouses and tenements wallowed in the mulch of decades, their windows boarded up as if in an effort to shut out the world around them. Yellow mortar oozed out of brick walls covered with obscenities sprayed in black and candy-apple green; slat-sided mutts with glistening sores and eyes bright with the madness of hunger rooted among the offal spilled out of overturned trash cans; heaps of stale laundry shaped vaguely like human beings snored in doorways with their heads leaning against the jambs and their open mouths scooping black, toothless holes out of their stubbled faces. (*The Midnight Man*)

Walker's Detroit seethes with racial violence and tension. Estleman says, "race is an important part of this city, right behind cars and prostitutes. Anyone writing about Detroit can't ignore the issue of race." He doesn't. Walker crosses paths with enough bigots to clean and jerk a battleship. His clients are often happy to find out that a guy named Amos is white.

Walker's own racial attitudes are more complex. He acknowledges a considerable level of prejudice in himself and works to overcome it. He's got only three friends, two black. Walker is a true egalitarian; he believes blacks can be just as treacherous as whites. Each of the novels has at least one black villain richly deserving of our disgust. Estleman refuses to romanticize ethnics. They must answer to the same justice for their crimes as anyone else. No more, but no less.

What we know of Walker's past comes in bit-piece revelations. He's as taciturn about his past as he is about his cases. A prospective client is impressed by this quality: "You're supposed to be a man who keeps his mouth shut even at the dentist's."

Walker was raised in a small town west of Detroit. His father, now deceased, was a garage operator on Detroit's west side in partnership with the father of John Alderdyce, a black homicide lieutenant, who is an important figure in all the Walker novels. Alderdyce manages to be a fashion plate on a cop's salary and is Walker's oldest friend. But it's not a smooth relationship, tangled by the usual public vs. private-dick animosities. Amos trods a very rocky road when he strays into police territory. Cops hate him. "We get on like soap and dirty," he admits. Even Alderdyce thinks he's a pain in the butt and finds it necessary to threaten him no less than once or twice per conversation. A typical exchange with Alderdyce:

"Who's your client?"
"We've had this conversation before, John. Play back my answer from the last time."
He sucked in a long draft of stale air.
"You've never been involved in a cop-killing. The rules aren't the same. Do a fan dance with the facts and you'll have so many badges up your ass you'll clank when you sit down." (*The Midnight Man*)

Walker earned a BA in sociology and then entered the police academy. He dropped out of the twelve-week training course after eleven weeks when a fellow trainee, the nephew of a U.S. congressman, propositioned him in the shower. Since he was too insistent, Walker broke his jaw. That's the convenient reason Walker gives for quitting the academy. The real motivations run deeper than that. Walker could never be a cop just like Marlowe could never have been: they're not authorities. Walker subscribes to the motto of his ex-partner who was murdered while tailing a philandering husband: "It was the duty of every honest man to throw sand in the works whenever the opportunity presented itself." Walker does not trust the police to be able to overcome their own inefficiency and corruption and achieve a suitable justice.

Walker spent six years in the military with tours of Cambodia and Vietnam where he received the DSC. His three year stateside MP assignment taught him some useful tricks. "Never stick-fight with an ex-MP," he advises a very subdued former assailant.

Walker's got an ex-wife in California. She's got his much resented alimony payments and that's almost all you'll hear about her. His pastimes? Old movies, jazz (no music-to-shoot-up-by progressive, please) early rock, Haig and Haig, and Winstons. Lots of Winstons. A good cook but he goes heavy on the spices. He tends a one-bedroom house in Hamtramck and commutes to the dreary third-floor office on Grand River in a Cutlass with a transplanted 455 Coup de Ville engine. She "can hit 65 while you're still closing the door on the passenger's side."

Walker packs a Lugar in the Cutlass and a Smith and Wesson .38 on his hip. His fee is $250 a day, first day in advance. "I promise a day's work for a day's pay, which means I don't belong to a union." He's a good detective, and he works hard for what he gets. Above average in intelligence, a quick study and very physical, but his outstanding quality is his tenacity. You don't shake Walker, nobody scares him off; he "stick[s] like nuclear fallout."

Because his ethics place the client first, Walker is willing to break the law when he finds it necessary. As he explains to Lieutenant Fitzroy, a Detroit cop who'd very much like to see Walker's license filed away for good:

Everytime I take on a job I mortgage a piece of myself to my clients and I can't get it back until it's paid off. I have to do that and yet try not to step on the toes of the people who keep me in business. Sometimes that's impossible. I can't help it; it's the way I operate. (*Angel Eyes*)

But there are many things Walker won't do. He's a detective with principles, well-recognized now as the code according to Marlowe. "A private eye with a code may be nothing more than a pebble on the beach, but at least he stands out from the grains of sand" (*Angel Eyes*). He won't stand by and see someone victimized, particularly a woman. Men may kill one another for reasons he can understand, but you can't explain away killing an innocent. "That one you'll have to go down for," he informs an antagonist who went too far. Instinctively chivalrous, Walker doesn't use obscenity, especially in front of women. Also, he would never let a woman pick up a tab. On the other hand, he can be Spade-tough if he has to. Throughout the novels Walker embodies the classic ambivalence toward women that is a trademark of the hardboiled school. Pleasure vs. threat, desire vs. danger, romance vs. betrayal. Women are soft but double-edged. Chivalry always gives way to self-defense even for the most knightly.

Walker also won't play the executioner for anyone. In *The Midnight Man*, the contrast between Walker and the eye-for-an-eye code of the West represented by a man-mountain bounty hunter is drawn most sharply.

Walker is no Page Murdock. He's no Caspar Milquetoast either. Walker is very, very tough. He's so tough he crushes out cigarettes in his palm, "a habit I picked up in the jungle where there wasn't an ashtray handy." Walker usually doesn't throw the first punch, but he'll almost always throw the last. He will not suffer being laid a hand on or threatened. He meets violence with violence. When he catches a hired gun waiting to ambush him at his office, Walker gets two-fisted mean:

I reached out and slammed his forehead into the wall. He groaned. I brought a knee up hard between his spread legs, and as he was doubling over I grasped his belt, planted my feet wide, and whirled him clear across the room into the opposite wall. He struck on his back and began to slide. I walked over and hoisted him up by his damp shirtfront. Supporting him with one hand, I started batting his large face with the other, left to right, left to right, in rhythm. Blood spurted from his nose onto the T-shirt. (*The Midnight Man*)

At 32 (Marlowe's age in *The Big Sleep*), Walker is a bit younger than most private eyes. As a result, his frequent smartass routine in *Angel Eyes* and *Motor City Blue* is a little more brash than we might expect. Chandler would have called it a "rude wit." Age has not yet tempered his supreme confidence and need to always have the last word. Walker can be almost smug in his confrontations, "jauntily sardonic," in the words of one critic. Walker's the kind of guy you can't win with. An alcoholic, whom Walker is plying with liquor, places an order,

"God awmighty, that's a good booze. Keep 'em coming, Mr.—I didn't catch the name."
"I didn't throw it." I poured.

Walker is cut from lone-wolf cloth. Isolated and usually self-sufficient, he bears proud testimony to the independence of the Spade-Marlowe-Archer prototypes. He could never be an organization man. To a pretty-faced operative from a big investigative firm, Walker stakes his territory:

I'm saying I don't like glossy detective agencies that hire their talent off a movie lot and drop a bundle on miles of electronic spaghetti and window dressing and base their reports on the hard work of real investigators not on their payroll and then stiff them. But most of all I'm saying I don't like you. (*Angel Eyes*)

The Midnight Man finds Walker growing more disillusioned, scared like all of us by private demons. He has nightmares, begins to notice the sags and creases in the faces of people his own age and worries that death doesn't even disturb his appetite anymore. "I was growing a shell. The time would come when I'd be able to crack jokes in the presence of death, like some cops, because I'd be dead inside, deader than the stiff." A friend warns him, "You joke too much. Every time I get near what makes you run you crack wise. Ask a question, get a joke. Make an observation, get a joke .... Who the hell are you, Walker?" Walker knows his tough skin is stretching tighter and tighter over the tender parts: "Sometimes a sense of humor is what's left after everything else is gone ... it's the only thing keeping you from spraying your brains all over the ceiling." By *The Midnight Man*'s end, some self-doubt has grown through Walker's wisecracks. We wonder whether vengeance has loosened his once-confident grip on the code. Perhaps the mean streets have finally left him a little tarnished. Maybe vengeance and justice are not so different, even to him.

Neck and neck with Stephen Greenleaf as the finest stylist of contemporary private eye fiction, Estleman writes stinging prose with a visual, cinema-ready style. The language is modulated and economical at the same time, a legacy of his days as a reporter which taught him "how to give a fact its proper weight." The writing has a shadowy, smoky quality that suggests greater importance underneath the surface. The titles themselves are unequaled in evoking an around-the-corner aura of alley-dark danger.

Walker seldom announces a direct opinion of a character. He reveals emotions through his reactions to what people do to him or through his physical desriptions of them. Here's the dying gangster, Ben Morningstar, in *Motor City Blue*:

His eyes were huge wet plums that shimmered behind thick corrective lenses as they watched us come in. Farther up, hair as black and gleaming as a new galosh grew straight back from his forehead with a single, startingly white gash of a part following the path of a bullet long forgotten by everyone outside this room. Not a gray hair in sight. It made the rest of him look that much more worn out, like a shabby old chair with a crisp new doily pinned to its crown.

In *Angel Eyes*, a cop knocks everything off Walker's desk as a demonstration that they aren't such good friends. Walker insists that he pay him a dollar to replace the light bulb that was broken in the process.

Painfully, like a professional virgin saying yes, the sergeant hauled a tattered leather billfold from his hip pocket, peeled it open, and thumbed through some bills inside. There were a couple of crisp singles that hadn't been in circulation long, but he went past them and settled on a fuzzy one that someone had used to mop out a grease pit. He flung it down on the desk, from where Washington's dirty face leered up at me like a syphilitic degenerate. I pushed the eraser end of a fresh pencil under the crease, lifted it, and draped it over the telephone.
"I'll spray it later."
He growled and started around the desk. I rose to meet him. I said, "Let's do it. Two

moves, maybe three, and you'll be a detour in the street."

Estleman writes like Torme sings and vintage Desmond played. You can feel what's coming but the notes always tumble together just a little better than you ever anticipated. Robin Winks comments on this quality, "one keeps reading for the sheer joy of seeing the phrases fall into place." The style is polished, but Walker's voice, unlike that of many other Chandler derivatives, seldom seems practiced. It is original and improvised from the action. Walker's reverse similes are a trademark. Estleman dubs them "inverted exaggerations."

His shoulders were broad and square and he had no waist to speak of. He wouldn't be any harder to stop than a runaway oil tanker.
He scratched his head. He didn't make near as much noise doing it as a Rotomill tearing up pavement.
The drunk's hands didn't shake anymore than a go-go girl in an icebox.

The pace of the Walker novels is somewhere between urgent and furious. *Angel Eyes* and *Motor City Blue* wrap up in 48 hours. *The Midnight Man*'s spree of black militant terrorism, five homicides, one kidnapping and an assassination attempt are spent in less than a week. Estleman writes what he terms a "Freeway Style" mystery. The story opens with the detective working on a routine case. In *Motor City Blue* Walker is taking pictures of a man whom an insurance man suspects of making a false claim for injuries he sustained in a fall. *The Midnight Man* begins with Walker tailing a truck driver who his employer believes is hijacking the firm's goods. Soon the main case comes barreling down the fast lane with the detective still on the access ramp. He enters the flow at an angle and trailing. The rest of the way he races frantically to catch up, with what neither he nor the reader is sure until the final few pages. The "freeway" is full of some very heavy traffic. How Walker gets around and through it is what makes for a good read.

Estleman's plots are not straight-aways. They twist and turn like a Grand Prix course, making the "Freeway Style" all the more harrowing. Invariably, the story line pits Walker against forces that are much stronger than they first appear. Rooted in the dark underside of Detroit, organized crime, the labor rackets and racial hatred fuel the desperate motives that drive the city.

The series is populated with superb characters. Maintaining Walker's sense of isolation, Estleman has created a cast of only three regulars: Alderdyce, the friend-*cum*-foe cop; Iris, a snazzy black prostitute ("A medium dark face, like antique gold under a bright light . . . . A long neck. Nefertiti in a flame-colored blouse.") with two bad habits—heroin and being there for Walker when he needs her; and Barry Stackpole, a one-legged, eight-fingered investigative journalist at the Detroit *News* who trades information for Scotch and an exclusive.

Each of the novels presents additional memorable characters, drawn with distinctive physical qualities. Estleman admits he has a lot of fun with these figures and the fact that readers are able to remember them so well. Three characters deserve special mention. There's the previously described Ben Morningstar, who in *Motor City Blue* hires Walker to look for his missing ward, Marla. In *Angel Eyes*, Walker teams with Maggie, silverhaired, sixtyish, sharp-as-a-tack and one-woman staff for the Huron *Herald*, to search for a missing nightclub dancer. Walker calls her on the phone and asks, "Is this the Huron *Herald*?" (She has already told him twice that it is.) "No, it's the local office of the CIA. We answer the phone this way so the Communists won't know we're here." Then, there's *The Midnight Man*'s Munnis "Bum" Basset, a Moose Malloy-sized bounty hunter from Oklahoma who competes with Walker to capture a fugitive cop-killer with a vicious hatred for whites. Bum goes about 300 pounds with not "enough fat on him to fry an onion." He wears a cowboy hat, drives a souped-up, four-wheel drive pickup and calls people 'hoss.'

The racial tension and neon-lit grittiness that permeate all the novels are leavened by Estleman's ability to write laser-sharp humor. It's Grade A material. Walker gets off reliable one-liners that make him sound like a cross between Don Rickles and Groucho Marx:

I drew out my folded hankerchief, peeled it open carefully, plucked out the ring, and placed it in his outstretched palm.
"It's a diamond," he said.
"That'll settle the argument. The guy in the delicatessen said it was a ham sandwich." I slid a cigarette between my lips. "Can you put a price tag on it?"
"Please don't smoke. My asthma."
"I wouldn't dream of smoking your asthma. What about it?"
"Is it hot?"
"Brother, it's glowing . . . ." (*Angel Eyes*)

In addition to Chandler, Estleman ranks Poe and London as his favorite writers. He admires "the lyrical, poetical approach to action and adventure" which each of these authors demonstrated and believes they illustrate how "the literature of violence is purely an American development." Among contemporary writers, Estleman prefers the work of Greenleaf, Pronzini, Gores, Donald Hamilton and Douglas C. Jones, an author of historical westerns. He believes fellow Detroiter Elmore "Dutch" Leonard is the best writer of dialogue in the business.

Estleman claims, "I've never experienced what some people call writer's block. I just don't believe it exists. The best advice I can give anyone is what I give myself—if you don't *feel* like writing, write!

Anything else is just an excuse." He also believes that "you should never apologize for what you write. If there's something wrong with your work and you are a good writer, you can fix it."

The Walker novels reveal Estleman's diligent research efforts. He says that Walker is a closely studied composite of several police acquaintances, a couple of friends who are private investigators, a little Marlowe and a little of himself. The superb opening scenes of *Motor City Blue* and *The Midnight Man* are drawn from actual incidents reported by Detroit private investigators (Michigan law prohibits calling oneself a "private detective"). The nightmarish street scenes are based on walking trips of Detroit's toughest neighborhoods that Estleman took "at the risk of my life." He studied the history of Detroit back 300 years to its settlement.

Although the Walker mysteries have been critically and financially successful, Estleman believes that "six and out" is a good rule with books focusing on one character. After that they become too predictable and wear out their welcome. Because Walker is his favorite character, Estleman may be reconsidering the "six and out" rule: "I'll re-evaluate the work after six and make a decision." Whatever its eventual number, the Walker series will be recognized as works of fine quality. Their place in the top drawer of private eye fiction is secure.*

Joe Gores—His Own Knight

Other than Dashiell Hammett, the one real-life private detective to have written first-rate private-eye fiction is Joseph N. Gores. A writer with impressive range, Gores is the only person to have won Edgars in three categories: best short story ("Goodbye Pops" in *Every Crime in the Book* edited by Robert L. Fish in 1975), best episode in a television drama series ("No Immunity for Murder" for *Kojak* in 1976) and best first mystery novel (*A Time for Predators*) published by Random House in 1969.

Joe Gores was born December 25, 1931 in Rochester, Minnesota, the younger of two sons to Joseph and Mildred (Duncanson) Gores. He graduated from Notre Dame with a BA in English literature in 1953 and moved to California where he held a succession of unusual jobs. He has worked as a logger, a truck driver and a carnival worker, ran a weight-lifting gymnasium and managed a "hot sheet" motel on Geneva Avenue in San Francisco. He also served in the U.S. Army for two years during which he wrote biographies of American generals. His thesis on stereotypes in the fiction of the South Pacific earned him an MA from Stanford University in 1961.

---

*Several of the quotations and observations are drawn from Don Kubit's excellent article on Estleman which appeared in the December, 1981 edition of *Monthly Detroit*. We would like to express our gratitude to Mr. Kubit for his generosity in allowing us to quote freely from his article.

Joe Gores

An inveterate traveler, Gores has taught high school in Kenya, lived in Tahiti and visited all 50 states in the U.S. In addition to mystery and crime writing, Gores' *Marine Salvage* (Doubleday, 1971) is an accepted authority in that field and his *Honolulu: Port of Call* (Comstock, 1974) is a well-regarded anthology of South Seas stories.

Gores currently lives in San Anselmo, California with his second wife, Dori, their two children and several exotic pets. He continues to write short stories with now more than a hundred to his credit, screenplays and television scripts including the pilot episode of CBS' Mike Hammer series and an episode for the *Magnum PI* series.

While he was attending Stanford, Gores became friends with Gene Matthews, a San Francisco PI whom he accompanied on several of his cases. Gores recalls originally being attracted to PI work because he was "looking for something fun to do while I learned to be a writer." From 1955 to 1967 he worked as a private investigator in the Bay Area, first with the L.A. Walker Company and then with David Kikkert and Associates, specializing in repossessions, skip tracing and embezzlement cases. Not only did his years with Kikkert provide him with the raw material for his PI novels, Gores believes that the requirements of writing good field investigation reports helped him learn how to write compelling fiction— "concentrate on who, what, when, where, and why and do it in clear, vivid language." That simple rule is the blueprint for his creation of Dan Kearny Associates (DKA), a large Bay Area detective firm specializing in repossessions, skip tracing, collections and the investigations of thefts and embezzlements.

DKA was introduced in a short story entitled "File No. 1: The Mayfield Case" and has appeared in a total of twelve short stories, the majority published in *Ellery Queen's Mystery Magazine*. Three of Gores' novels are about the DKA and its cast of shrewd, professional agents.

The first novel, *Dead Skip* (1972), is dedicated to David Kikkert, Gores' former boss and the real-life model on which Kearney is based. After one of Kearny's field agents is nearly killed in a murder attempt disguised as a car accident, the DKA men and women begin an exhaustive search for the killer concentrating on the injured agent's current cases where they suspect a motive for the attack must be hidden. All the qualities of the later DKA novels are well represented here: the clipped prose, the tense and tough jargon of manhunters, a fast-moving, linear plot and descriptions of detective practices so technically authentic that these novels could serve as training manuals for the beginning agent.

Written deliberately in a spare, hard Hammett style, the DKA novels honor the professionalism of detectives who are well-trained and relish their work. They are the finest private eye procedurals ever written.

Five DKA regulars are featured in all the novels. There's Dan Kearny himself who has been a PI since age 14 when he began repossessing cars. An ex-boxer with "a jaw to batter down doors and gray eyes hard enough to strike sparks," Kearny has the hunt in his guts and a mastery of street tricks that make him "the best hunter there was." Office manager Giselle Marc is a tall blonde whose beauty often makes men overlook her intelligence, her MA in history from San Francisco State and her licenses for private investigations, repossessions and collections.

The primary field agents are Larry Ballard, 26, good-looking, reads Richard Stark, and Bart Heslip, ex-middleweight fighter and fiction's best black private detective since Touie Moore. Ballard and Heslip are almost habitual detectives, like old-timer Patrick Michael O'Bannon, a heavy drinking Irishman but a first-rate operative when he needs to be. They dig at every clue, follow each lead, track down all witnesses. It's tedious work, but with an insistent sense of urgency that keeps the DKA novels in high gear around all the curves:

And you went after them—for money. You found them, most of them. Damned tough to stay out of the way of an agency like DKA if it really wanted you. You had to change your name, dye your hair, keep your kids out of school, quit your union or your profession, tear up your credit cards, abandon your wife, not show up at your mother's funeral, run your car into a deep river, quit paying taxes, get off welfare.
Because every habit pattern was a doorway into your life, a doorway that the skip-tracers and field agents with the right key could open. (*Dead Skip*)

In *Final Notice* (1973) DKA gets pulled into a web of mob violence including two murders and a blackmail attempt against a Mafia boss. Although DKA finally discovers the killer, who was trying to gain control of the syndicate for himself, it is unable to gather enough sure evidence to turn him for the police. Instead Kearny fingers him to the mob knowing that it will deliver its own justice to the renegade.

Gone, No Forwarding (1978) opens with the mob's assassination of the killer in *Final Notice* and a seemingly unrelated attempt by someone to get Kearny's license revoked for an improper collection. However, the complaint against Kearny proves to be a complicated mob conspiracy to provide an alibi for its hit man. The DKA regulars must locate the seven possible witnesses to the disputed collection in order to save Kearney's shield and expose the mob's clever scheme. The action features superb private eyeing, bleached of its glamor and sentimentality, but vivid in the details of a nationwide search of streets thick with hypes, thugs and evil.

In one way or another, Gores' three other novels all deal with the theme of what he calls "the prehistorical qualities of man." In each instance, a civilized man is confronted with situations with which modern culture has left him unequipped to deal. The necessary behavior is some throwback to a time when a man had to be a hunter to survive the dangers around him. Each of these novels is a study of dual identities, where a veneer of social constraints, intellectual inhibitions and emotional sublimation covers an atavistic core of aggressive and deadly instincts.

A Time of Predators, Gores' award-winning first novel, examines this issue most directly. Paula Halstead, wife of Professor Curtis Halstead, witnesses four young toughs assault and blind a man they thought was a homosexual. In order to discourage her from identifying them to the police, the gang breaks into her house and rapes her. Unable to live with her own revulsion at this act, Paula commits suicide that same night. Curt Halstead is driven to avenge his wife's death and he reverts to the brutality of his former days as a British Commando in order to do so. This is one you'll feel in your stomach.

The revenge theme and the split between man's civility and savagery are treated more artistically in *Interface* (1974), featuring a fast, back-alley private investigator by the name of Neil Fargo, ex-football star, special forces officer and a non-practicing attorney. The story is as vicious as any ever written about a PI, and Gores' ability to capture the repetitively obscene vernacular of the urban underground distracts the reader from anticipating the novel's jolting ending. In fact, Gores personally regards *Interface* as the novel in which he came the closest to accomplishing all the goals he had set for himself.

Most critics believe that *Hammett* (1975) is Gores' *tour de force*. Set in the San Francisco of 1928, *Hammett* is a scholarly novel that presents Dashiell Hammett as a struggling, hard-drinking *Black Mask* writer **returning one** more time to his earlier profession of private eye to investigate the slaying of an old PI pal. The story introduces many little-known facts about Hammett's youth and his life in San Francisco but its most remarkable accomplishment is the reconstruction of San Francisco's Roaring Twenties ambience—prostitutes, bootleggers, corrupt politicos, hard-eyed cops and wicked orientals, all gliding through the sinister-slick streets of one of the world's most exciting cities. Once again, Gores dramatizes the issue of how man must rely on his instincts rather than his socialization to deal with the evil that the world can present. Hammett, the writer vs. Hammet, the manhunter is such an interesting conflict because Hammett is one of the few men who was both and was good at each. In his author's notes in the novel, Gores explains:

I wanted to write a novel about Hammett the detective because this experience *was* so seminal to his art. But it is not Hammett the detective who fascinates readers; it is Hammett the detective-turned-writer. My novel, therefore, had to prove the central tension existing between his two worlds.

Writing—even writing hard-boiled stories of mayhem and murder—demands insights and compassions (and allows self-delusions) that are destructive to the manhunter. Begin seeing your antagonist as a fellow human sufferer, rather than the enemy, and you lose that hard edge that lets you survive emotionally—and in rare instances, physically—as an investigator.

Because 1928 seemed to offer excellent possibilities to probe this essential tension fictionally, I chose it as the year in which to set my novel.

In 1975, Francis Ford Coppola bought the movie rights to *Hammett* and after commissioning 32 different screenplays (five by Gores), released his movie "Hammett" in 1983, more than six years after it went into production. Starring Frederick Forrest in the title role, the movie was pulled from distribution only weeks after its release, the victim of generally unappreciative audiences and the financial woes of Zoetrope, Coppola's production company.

Our only complaint with the crime novels of Joe Gores is that there are not enough of them. The most recent novel was released in 1978, and Gores indicates that although he has several more planned and under contract (including some DKAs), the economics of bookselling has him in no hurry to turn away from the more profitable television and screen writing he has concentrated on in recent years.

John Marshall Tanner—Stephen Greenleaf

Stephen H. Greenleaf was born in Washington, D.C. in 1942. When he was three, his family moved to Portland, Oregon. They remained in Oregon until 1947 and then returned to Centerville, Iowa, which was the original home of Greenleaf's mother and father. Centerville is a town of fewer than 10,000 located in southern Iowa. It is quintessential middle America—peaceful, cohesive, clean.

Greenleaf lived his childhood and adolescence in Centerville.His family was successful, well-known, well-liked. His father and both of his grandfathers were Centerville attorneys. Greenleaf graduated from Carleton College, a private, liberal arts school in Northfield, Minnesota, with a BA in history. He prepared for a law career, obtaining his J.D. in 1967 from the Boalt Hall School of Law in Berkeley. He was married in 1968 to Ann Garrison, a fourth-generation Californian.

Following two years of Army service that included a year in Vietnam, Greenleaf practiced law on the West Coast for six years, most of that time as an antitrust and securities fraud litigator in San Francisco. He worked for a year in Portland as a Legal Services lawyer.

Greenleaf's first foray as a writer was in 1972 when he tried to write the predictably autobiographical first novel. It was abandoned after his discovery that "it was awful."

As a lawyer, Greenleaf struggled to find his niche. He was not motivated by the "business side" of law and did not believe he was well-suited psychologically to succeed in the combative world of the trial

Stephen Greenleaf

attorney. Upon deciding to pursue a "people-oriented" small-office practice, he returned to Iowa. *Grave Error*, his first novel, was begun in 1977, while he was studying for the Iowa Bar Exam.

Greenleaf was about to accept a position with the Legal Services Office in Des Moines when Dial Press called with an offer to publish *Grave Error*. He stayed in Iowa City for five years, including two years as a student at the University of Iowa Writers' Workshop and two years as Adjunct Professor of Law at the law school. Like Tanner, his series hero, Greenleaf had reached the point in his career common to many lawyers: he decided he wanted to do something else. The job in Des Moines is still waiting.

In 1981, the Greenleafs left Iowa City and moved to Ashland, Oregon, a small town just north of the California border and home of the Oregon Shakespeare Festival. They currently live in Ashland with their teenage son, Aaron.

The first three Greenleaf novels are all set in the San Francisco Area. In *Grave Error* (1979), the action side trips through the San Joaquin Valley to "Oxtail, California." Ironically, the closest real California town to mythical Oxtail is Centerville. *Death Bed* (1980) traipses through Sausalito, Berkeley and Carmel. "El Gordo," a tough Bay area town where "every second building was an abandoned bowling alley or a taco stand," is the setting for *State's Evidence* (1982) although the scenery is improved somewhat by quick trips to Lake Tahoe and Contra Costa County, "decorator remnant of the wild west."

The California locales are painted with a sure hand; vivid, evocative, full of atmosphere.

We passed a sign that said Oxtail was a great place to grow. It didn't say what. Then the table-flat fields gave way to squat, dingy buildings which floated like a wino's nightmare out of the shimmering waves of heat.
It was a typical valley town. The cars in the used car lots were painted like ten-dollar whores and the dirt in the schoolyards was baked harder than an airport runway. Neon beer signs in the tavern windows twinkled dimly.

(Grave Error)

Lake Tahoe had once been something special even in a state where alfalfa sprouts and pyramid shapes and hot tubs are accorded the same status. The lake and the wooded shore surrounding it were a flawless gem cradled in an antique setting, a talisman of curative and regenerative powers. In my younger days a week at the old lake had, more than once, sucked the lowland poisons out of my systems and transfused my urban blood with something less adulterated and more noble. But the sports faddists and the nature culturists and the casino gamblers discovered the region. Newly hewn freeways made the lake as accessible as a Burger King, and now the waters are befouled with algae and the shore is blistered with glass-and-redwood sores and the air shimmers from the fumes of high rollers and show biz groupies. The mystical magic has been squashed flat by four solid lanes of tourist traffic and condo dwellers. *(State's Evidence)*

Greenleaf's thoughtful, colorful descriptions of the California scene are all the more impressive by virtue of their having been written while he was living in Iowa. The fourth Tanner novel (*Fatal Obsession*, Dial Press, 1983) is set largely in the Midwest. True to a somewhat perverse form, Greenleaf wrote it in Oregon.

Greenleaf credits diverse literary influences for his development as a writer. "I was sent home from the fifth grade for bringing one of Perry Mason's adventures to class. I wanted to be him." He admired Gardner for his power as a story teller and, in the A.A. Fair stories, for his humor.

In high school, he "went through my Shell Scott period," followed by preferences for Nero Wolfe and then Mickey Spillane. As a college student, he admired the stories of John O'Hara "for their surprise endings and their good structure." He believes the pre-Travis McGee stories of John D. MacDonald possessed distinctive power and variety and revealed the best of MacDonald's craftsmanship.

Outside the mystery genre, Greenleaf was inspired by the writers of "30s realism": Dreiser, Farrell and Faulkner. Even though Chandler's *The Long Goodbye* is his favorite detective novel, Greenleaf believes Ross Macdonald surpasses both Hammett and Chandler as mystery writers and must be considered one of America's finest modern writers. The Greenleaf novels are testimony to his great admiration for Ross Macdonald. All the familiar Macdonald themes are reworked beautifully: The deadly but never dead secrets of families who have lost their innocence and their love, the Age of Narcissus where nothing is quite what it seems or worth quite what it costs, the moral and environmental decay of California and the unhappiness of lives lived without spirit. Greenleaf describes *Grave Error* as a book "about love and death and friendship and duty and the ineradicable past and the inescapable future."

Like many of the featured writers in this book, Greenleaf has been criticized for being too derivative of the Hammett-Chandler-Macdonald tradition, for writing only pastiche. Pastiche maybe, but it's the best pastiche there is. We believe Greenleaf writes the most intelligent, most engaging prose of any modern private eye writer.

Greenleaf's detective John Marshall Tanner ("Marsh") is the hybridized namesake of John Marshall, the fourth chief justice of the U.S. Supreme Court and John Tanner, the hero of George Bernard Shaw's *Man and Superman*. The "Tanner" also owes a part of its inspiration to Greenleaf's like-named junior high school basketball coach and to its euphonic qualities.

Tanner tends his two-room office in the Jackson Square area, San Francisco; down an alley, up three flights of stairs to the top floor of a reconstructed firehouse built just after the earthquake. Jackson Square means high rent, but Tanner gets a two-thirds discount from his very grateful landlord, antiquary Carson James. James, who is homosexual, had been beaten up once by a disgruntled ex-lover. Tanner, using methods that earned him no pride, had "persuaded" the jiltee to stay forever clear of Mr. James, who promptly knocked down Tanner's rent "as a hedge against future imbroglios."

Now in his late forties, Tanner came to the gumshoe game as a second career. Following a stint in Korea, he graduated law school and became an attorney, a solo practitioner specializing in plaintiff and criminal defense work. One of his clients was a retired seaman, Luther Fry, who lost his life savings in a commodities market scam. Tanner filed suit on Fry's behalf against the principals in the deal and the case was assigned to Judge Charles Gooley. Through a combination of stalling, character assassination, intimidation and good-old-boying between the judge and the broker's attorney, Fry became afraid and accepted a nuisance-value settlement of $3,000. He then hung himself after sending his great-nephew the money as a scholarship for medical school.

Tanner proceeded to sue Judge Gooley for the wrongful death of Luther Fry. The case was dismissed but not before Tanner called the Judge "unfit and senile and a disgrace to the law." He was cited for contempt, suspended from practice and sentenced to six months in jail. Although the suspension has been lifted, Tanner "swore I would never practice law as long as Judge Charles Gooley was on the bench. Since the old cretin is still over there drooling all over his robes, I'm not playing lawyer" (*Grave Error*). Technically, this isn't true because he still advises clients in criminal investigations to hire him as their lawyer as a means of bolstering the confidentiality of their transactions.

Tanner finds PI work "short on glamour and long on moral ambiguity." His fee is $200 per day, $40 and $50 per hour depending apparently on the deepness of the client's pocket. Like any self-respecting maverick, he's not getting rich. Now in his late forties, he drives a battered blue '71 Buick. He "could stuff all of his assets into some carry-on luggage if he owned any carry-on luggage." "No tax shelters, no Keogh Plans, no Krugerrands. Just a five-thousand-dollar CD earning half the inflation rate." The only possessions that mean much to him are the original Paul Klee that hangs in the office, the desk given to him by his lawyer-grandfather and a real leather and walnut chair, a gift from the only woman he ever wanted to marry.

His work methods rely on most of the standard ingredients: No divorce work, keep the cops out even on cases where they assumed cooperation, a breaking and entering here, some tampering with evidence there. Tanner also is a good impersonator. In *State's Evidence* he plays a psychologist in order to get inside a very exclusive rest home. In *Death Bed*, he's a census taker; *Grave Error* finds him masquerading for a time as a muckraking investigator of mental health clinics.

Three supporting characters appear in Tanner's cases offering him information on the sly, a little support and sometimes a little muscle. There's Charley Sleet, the obligatory good policeman who provides some of the information and all of the muscle. Charley is a cop "24 hours a day," "going where he's needed," "immune to departmental politics." He's also big as a bear. Rooms seem a lot bigger after he leaves. Information also comes via Laverne Blanc, professional bay-area gossip who publishes a rag that "makes *National Enquirer* look like the *National Geographic*." Blanc is a foul-mouthed alcoholic who knows all the dirt that's to be known. He likes Tanner because Tanner saved his skin in a bar brawl precipitated when Blanc told a guy to go home and give his wife a shower ("If my pits smelled like hers I'd have them sandblasted.") Tanner tells Blanc he's just too sensitive.

Finally, there's rose-pretty Peggy Nettleton. She's Tanner's secretary-receptionist and "as competent as a fire hydrant." She offers him support. Tanner wishes it was more than that. He thinks a lot about her in off-hours, and you get the idea that she does the same for him. Tanner has made one pass at her in five years. He's afraid one more would be his last. Probably not. Peggy and Marsh are sure to heat up some day.

Tanner is a straight-ahead practitioner of the Philip Marlowe work ethic. Not talking to people is one of the things he does best. He won't be bribed, he won't take money to fail. The client comes first, right after his own pride:

I'm not in business to achieve the Humanistic Calculus; I'm in business to serve my client. Lots of times the interests of the client and the masses don't coincide. Once in a while they're completely at odds. So be it. (*Death Bed*)

He doesn't share Marlowe's prohibitions against mixing sex with business. Although Greenleaf professes that he finds it difficult to write about sex, he does it very well. Particularly in *Grave Error*, less so in *State's Evidence*, his female characters speak some very high-voltage eroticism.

Tanner rarely carries a gun but uses it when he has to. He shoots to wound. Only once has he turned Mike Hammer-nasty. This is in *Grave Error* when he seeks almost paternally intense revenge against a swaggering thug who has preyed upon a crippled young girl. Most often he gets through the tight spots by looking and talking like a mean guy. He is a master of the tough bluff. When a deputy sheriff challenges him: "If it wasn't so frigging hot, I'd come around there and wipe that smile off your face, pal"; Tanner's ready: "I'll start to worry when someone comes along to help you get that belly out of the chair." (*Grave Error*)

Because he believes the easy wisecrack is one of the great seductions in private eyedom, Greenleaf keeps a light muzzle on Tanner's quipping.

Tanner will sometimes restrain himself by grousing that he's starting to sound like a bad Bogart impression. Nonetheless, some of the dialogue is worth remembering for that chance-in-a-lifetime setup to get even with a snip:

"My name's Tanner. I'm here to see Mr. Loggins and his friend Fluto. We're starting a new chapter of the Sons of Garibaldi."
She had been inoculated at birth against mirth.
"Have you an appointment?"
"I do."
She wrinkled her lips and inflated her thickly swathed chest. "I don't have you in my book."
"And I don't have you in mine."

As PIs go, Tanner is among the most liberal. He's against Proposition 13 and hasn't had anything to vote for "since Adlai Stevenson was on the ballot." Reagan is anathema to him, a "puppet president" guided by advisors "with neither political philosophical or emotional fealty to [the poor]."

On matters of crime, Tanner is a realist who leaves ideology behind as he considers the universal motives for lives of violence and meanness. Modern-day criminologists are neither as succinct nor as insightful as Greenleaf's authorities:

You can find Duckie wherever men make their living with their backs instead of their brains—the docks, the loading sheds, the construction sites. Duckie's still fighting because what he likes best is hurting people, or maybe getting hurt himself. His trademark is the unprovoked assault, the irrational act of violence that makes reasonable men sweat in the night and lay awake till morning basted in the juice of their own fear.

Benson "Pencil" Marks, Oxtail's Ph.D. Sheriff and the best secondary character in the first two novels, cuts to the bone of underclass crime as Tanner and he discuss Oxtail's soaring rate of homicide: "Most of them run to a pattern of course. We've got a short supply of women and money and self-esteem. Men kill to get them and kill to keep them. Most of our crimes are pretty easy to figure out." (*Grave Error*)

We know little of Tanner's personal life, but then there's little to know. He thinks a lot about old movies and old loves; his favorites of both have unhappy endings. His home is furnished with memories and a few diversions. "I live with a television set and some printed words . . . . And a lot of dust. That's about it." Like all great West Coast private eyes, his examination of lives as they are lived has left him at times cynical and sentimental.

He is lonely and regretful. If a bomb dropped in his neighborhood "it

wouldn't kill anybody I'd ever spoken to more than twice." His best friends
are Charley Sleet and Ruthie Spring, widow of fellow-detective Harry
Spring. He sees them rarely and feels guilty about it.

For all this, Tanner is not a despairing character. His self-pity is kept
in bounds by a healthy capacity to find joy in music and books. Like Lew
Archer, he is literate, a man of refined tastes. Mozart, Beethoven,
Balanchine are favorites. He reads Donne, Tolstoi, Montaigne, Dickens
and of course Chandler and Macdonald. A highball and the latest Le Carre
soothe him. "The blunt and linear progression of my own life soon became
diffused by English indirection." Once in a while he'll retreat to a cabin in
Carmel bequeathed him by a former lover.

At times, Tanner seems almost breezy about his capacity to live alone
and enjoy it. Simple routines become uplifting. He likes to look at Jane
Pauley at the beginning of each day, eat his hearty breakfast at Zorba's
which is run by a Rumanian with an Anthony Quinn alter ego, read *The
Great Gatsby* on a stakeout. He listens to the car radio: "The girl singing
... was called Blondie, but she didn't sound like anyone Dagwood ever
knew."

Two qualities distinguish the Greenleaf novels. First, the quality of
the writing is superb. Greenleaf is a wordsmith who creates stylish, lively
prose. He believes character and style and aura are as important as plotting
and tries to emphasize all four equally. He admits that he is least secure
with the aspect of plotting and that he doesn't want to offer the Tanner
novels as exemplary plots. However, with the exception of *Death Bed* with
its two-cases-colliding-to-become-one experiment, the plots are quite
strong. Typically convoluted, they are like archaeological digs where
layers of artifice and debris are peeled back until we get to the core. *Grave
Error* has a twisty ending that owes much to *The Maltese Falcon*. *State's
Evidence* presents an original, well-controlled plot.

The Tanner books are a pleasure to read, because they were a pleasure,
we think, for Greenleaf to write. The man likes words. Robin Winks has
said that Greenleaf "spreads the metaphors with abandon and joy." His
similes and metaphors are well-tailored enhancements of atmosphere;
style that promotes substance. They are high-fidelity echoes of Chandler's
most characteristic literary device:

The tiny gold turtle pinned over her left breast was as smug as Governor Brown.

Charm oozed from his voice like jelly from a doughnut

The droplet left a trail like a surgeon's scar on the window.

His body was stiff and tilted, a puppet with a tangled string.

And our favorite description of impeccable tailoring:

His suit fit him as well as disgrace fit Nixon.

The second impressive quality is Greenleaf's emerging skill at characterization. The slower pace of *State's Evidence* is accounted for largely by the greater time spent on the secondary characters than in the first two novels. As an example, Ray Tolson, the ambitious but concerned DA, rises above the too convenient stereotype of the ruthless politico on the make and becomes a man with depth, a real person possessing a mysterious heart.

Greenleaf strives to create characters without generalizations. He defeats stereotypes by writing about people on a spectrum. Charley Sleet and "Pencil" Marks contradict the prevailing bully cop image. Women can be classic femme fatales of *film noir* renown or decent, vulnerable adults who struggle to keep a grip on what they value. In *State's Evidence* they run the gamut from randy to reserved. Blacks are portrayed also without abstraction.

Like the best of writers, Greenleaf can be reread and enjoyed. His books are therapeutic. They work the kind of magic unique to all good storytellers. We try to arrange a special time and place to absorb them. Greenleaf plans to continue the Tanner series but believes that he can maintain the quality best by writing other kinds of fiction on an alternating basis. After *Fatal Obsession*, his next book will be a nonmystery written with a different voice and a different style.

In his interview with us, Greenleaf had one request. He wanted by his own example to encourage aspiring writers to persevere and to believe that while professional writing is a difficult business to break into, it's not impossible. *Grave Error* was submitted "over the transom"; Greenleaf didn't have an agent or even know the name of an editor to whom he should send the manuscript. It was rejected seven times before Dial picked it up. A triumph of quality over position for which the mystery field is the real winner.

Dave Brandstetter—Joseph Hansen

Joseph Hansen was born on July 19, 1923, in Aberdeen, South Dakota, where his father, Henry, owned a shoe store. Later, the family migrated to Southern California. Soon after his self-proclaimed "escape" from high school, Hansen married Jane Bancroft. The Hansens, who have made Los Angeles their home since 1943, are parents of one daughter, a commercial artist in northern California.

Prior to becoming a full-time writer, Hansen held jobs as a bookstore clerk, a radio announcer and a library staffer. A writer who also teaches,

Joseph Hansen

Hansen has conducted poetry workshops and taught fiction writing at the Beyond Baroque Foundation in Venice, California, the University of California at Irvine, and the extension division of UCLA. He lived and wrote in England in 1974-1975 on a grant from the National Endowment for the Arts.

In addition to his own name, Hansen has published novels under two pseudonyms. As Rose Brock (Rosebrock was his mother's maiden name), he has written two gothics—*Tarn House* (1971) set in late 19th century Wisconsin, and *Longleaf* (1974), with a New Orleans setting, also late 1800s. He has written a collection of short stories (*The Corrupter*, 1968) and eight novels, some of them mysteries, under the byline of James Colton: *Lost on Twilight Road* (1964), *Strange Marriage* (1965), *Known Homosexual* (1968), which was later released without the explicit sex scenes as *Stranger to Himself* under Hansen's own name (1977), *Cocksure* (1969), *Hang-Up* (1969), *Gard* (1969), *The Outward Side* (1971) and *Todd* (1971). As Joseph Hansen, he has written two mainstream novels, *A Smile in His Lifetime* (1981), which he regards as his most important work, and *Job's Year* (1983). *Backtrack* (1982) is a non-series mystery, narrated in the first person, a departure from the third-person voice Hansen prefers for his narratives.

Hansen is best known for his series about Dave Brandstetter, a death claims investigator originally in the employ of Medallion Life, but recently free-lancing to various insurance companies in LA. Brandstetter was introduced in *Fadeout* (1970) and has continued his nicely polished act in *Death Claims* (1973), *Troublemaker* (1975), *The Man Everybody Was Afraid Of* (1978), *Skinflick* (1979), *Gravedigger* (1982) and *Nightwork* (1984). Both hard and soft cover versions of these novels are beautifully packaged by Holt, Rinehart and Winston in eye-catching high-gloss covers. Brandstetter has appeared in one short story entitled "Surf" published in the British magazine *Playguy*, in January, 1976. A shortened version was carried in the December, 1976 *Mystery Monthly* with the maladroit title "Murder on the Surf."

There are many differences between Dave Brandstetter and the generic Southern California private eye. He is older, now approaching sixty. He is rich, cultured and well-mannered and enjoys the accoutrements of success including fancy cars and fashionable, rustic digs in Horseshoe Canyon. No seedy fourth-floor walk-up with pebbled glass on the front door for him. When he worked for Medallion, the company of which his flamboyant father had been founder and chairman of the board, Brandstetter tended to business in a modern, spacious office.

As a freelancer, Brandstetter attains superstar status—appearances on the "Tomorrow Show," feature articles in national magazines. He's sophisticated, modern, urbane. He's elegant, the antonym of all the gritty gumshoes who've trudged the lost Eden of Southern California.

Brandstetter is also a homosexual. What a wonderful invention Mr. Hansen has wrought. Not only does he occupy Brandstetter with a profession where a leering philosophy of lechery toward women appears to be almost essential, he puts him in the employ of the insurance industry, an establishment renowned in the homosexual community for its suspicion and hostility toward homosexuals. (Medallion Insurance Company fires Dave almost immediately after his father dies, a decision he knew was inevitable.)

> "What you're saying is," she said, "that they always wanted you out, but they couldn't do anything while Carl was alive."
> "He warned me," Dave said. "There's an annual prize given to the biggest fag-haters. The front-runners are always the same—police departments large and small; governments federal, state and local; the Florida orange-juice crowd; the army, navy and marines; homosexuals themselves; and insurance companies. Only the last two are not sucker bets. And the insurance companies always win. Everything."

There have been homosexuals in mystery fiction before. George Baxt camped it up with Pharaoh Love, a black homosexual cop in *A Queer Kind of Death* and *Swing Low, Sweet Harriet*, and Gore Vidal, writing as Edgar Box, minced it up a bit in *Death in the Fifth Position*. A reasonably sound treatment of homosexuals' problems with the police is presented in Tucker Coe's *A Jade in Aries*. However, in Brandstetter, Hansen has created the most accurate portrayal of a homosexual in the mystery field. Never romanticized, never stereotyped, Brandstetter copes with the world around him, sometimes successfully, sometimes not. Writing in *Murder Ink*, Solomon Hastings praised the series for its quality in dealing with the "mundane everyday problems" that face Brandstetter: "he develops romantic relationships, but he does not let his personal life interfere with his work. It merely adds richness to his character in much the same way any ongoing heterosexual relationship deepens anyone else's life."

A homosexual himself, Hansen intends his novels "to deal as honestly as I know how with homosexuals and homosexuality as an integral part of the fabric of contemporary life, rather than something bizarre and alien. I chose the mystery novel form as a way to keep readers turning pages while I gave as faithful a picture as I could of a side of life I believe I understand and that needs no apology." Hansen believes there is a lot of bad literature about homosexuality particularly in the mystery field and points to Chandler as an example of an otherwise fine writer who had a very primitive attitude toward homosexuality. For the most part, he feels homosexuals still receive a lousy deal in crime fiction: "We're the dirty joke that society wishes would go away."

More than most series, it is important to read the Brandstetter novels in their chronological order to appreciate, in Robin Wink's words, how they are "linked through symbol, incident, and character, to the point that one sees them as a single, multi-volume novel, by which one may learn a great deal about what it means to be homosexual and male in modern America."

In *Fadeout*, Rod Fleming, Dave's lover of 22 years has just died from stomach cancer. Depressed, full of regrets and pity, Dave reminisces about his life with Rod, and in his recollection refuses to sentimentalize or romanticize homosexuality, a characteristic which may account for the discomfort some homosexuals have with Hansen's novels.

A conversation with lesbian and best friend Madge Dunstan reveals the sense of maturity with which Hansen graces discussions of aging, love and companionship, sex and friendship:

They ate in silence for a few minutes. Then, when he'd filled her glass again, she picked it up and studied him over its rim. Very grave.

"I'm through chasing beauty. Cuff was the last."

Dave told her, "There was a guy in the army. Name of George Starkovich. One of the ugliest men I ever saw. Squat, Hairy. But inside he was beautiful. He was one of the nicest things that ever happened to me in my life."

She shut her eyes a second and nodded. "I remember. You've told me. Any number of times. The point is lost on me, Davey. Sorry. If it can't be beautiful I don't want it. And if it is beautiful, it's not worth having." She drank from the glass, set it down businesslike, and her tone was brisk. "Granted, it took me a long time to figure it out. Figure it out I have done. And things are going to be different from now on."

The lasagne was as good as ever. Maybe better. He had a mouthful of it and could only raise his eyebrows to ask her to go on.

"Sex and companionship are mutually exclusive. Too bad. But a fact. Anyway a fact for me. However ... one gets more important as the other gets less. Right?"

He held out his hand and shrugged.

"I'm getting old, Davey. O-L-D, old."

He swallowed. "You, Madge? Never."

"Me most of all," she said. "When the thought of merry girlish chatter is enough to send you pawing through the medicine chest for that old set of ear plugs, you've had it. You're old. You begin wanting some nice, quiet, grown-up company. Somebody restful. Sex? You dimly remember something about it. A game for kids. Strenuous. You want to stretch limp in your easy chair and listen to Mozart quartets."

After Dave clears Doug Sawyer of the murder of an entertainment celebrity in *Fadeout*, they begin a relationship which lasts across the next four novels although plagued by memories of previous lovers never to be recovered or replaced. Through the death of his father, the mental deterioration of Doug's mother, the infidelities and disappointments, Dave lives a life always fully examined. In *Gravedigger* he begins to live with Cecil Harris, a young black television reporter, first met in *The Man Everybody Was Afraid Of.*

The novels are tinted with toughness but, with the exception of the more recent ones, contain very little explicit violence. Brandstetter never carries a gun and seldom throws a punch. In fact, he's winded after running across the street. But he is an accomplished, shrewd detective. Controlled and cool, he shows a touch of well-modulated irony. An excellent eye for the incongruous and a superb memory are his best tools. A colleague marvels, "There's something you don't know about people, there has to be." A woman compares his interrogative style to "a good priest's, a father confessor's . . . [but] something very different."

Brandstetter is good and proud of it:

My part was to play straight in a vicious game . . . . I liked it. I still do. That's why I am not quitting. I'm one of the lucky people getting paid to do what I love to do. Almost no one manages that in this life. Oh, I'd rather have written a good string quartet. I couldn't write even a bad string quartet. (*Skinflick*)

We know little of Brandstetter's physical appearance. Judging from both men and women's reactions to him, he is attractive, although probably not in the movie star mold cast by his father. He wears reading glasses. Thin, square-shouldered, blond and blue-eyed,he prefers habits of refinement. Glenlivit on the rocks, a quiet dinner at Romano's, chamber music, Mozart and Brahms.

Although Brandstetter is not a particularly funny or playful sort, there is subtle humor in the books, often in the form of inside jokes for the homosexual community and what one reviewer called "swish-hitting against [the straight] world." To begin, what should one make of the fact that Brandstetter is Scandinavian for "Brand's daughter"? And what of all those taken-for-granted "truths" about homosexual behavior? Like how "they" are fickle and impersonal, but Brandstetter lived with the same man for 22 years while his "Viking handsome" father had nine wives. And how "they" are all pedophiles, except all the seductions in the books are the work of a younger boy bedding down an older man. The names of the gay bars participating in the Mr. Marvelous contest featured in *Troublemaker* are all wry *double entendres*—The Bunkhouse, The Queen and Court, The Rawhide and The Hang Ten. But our favorite send-up occurs while Brandstetter is sipping a Scotch at LA's largest gay bar, The Big Barn, complete with US and THEM restrooms.

A voice at his ear said:
"I haven't seen you in here before."
David didn't look around. "Just passing through," he said. "As quickly as possible."

The owner of the voice turned away. "You're right—she's vice."

"Vice?" someone else said. "Impossible. She's wearing matching shoes."

Hansen's prose is widely admired. The style is terse, more in the tradition of Hammett than Chandler, but more sophisticated in the tone it evokes than either. The physical descriptions of the Southern California terrain are spare but remarkably pleasant. For example, a beach house

lay in the dunes like elegant wreckage. Nearing, he saw that the crazily angled upthrusts of varnished boards were walls and roofs. When he topped the last dune, clumped grasses snagging his pants legs, what had looked to be broken and strewn by accident shaped into a structure. Under wooden wedges of overhang, triangles of a smoke-dark glass drank light. The same kind of glass in very tall panes, sill to roof beam, mirrored surf, sky, horizon. A deck of gapped and biased planking reached high over jagged rocks. Blankness watched from towers bleak as prairie storefronts.

(Troublemaker)

Dialogue carries the pace. Hansen "jump cuts" from one scene to another entering them in the middle and leaving them before they end. Chapter transitions are minimal. In an April, 1980 article for *The Writer*, Hansen advises, "Let your characters live and move and have their being. Never explain. Let what happens next do the explaining. Always keep the reader a little puzzled. Just be sure he's never puzzled for too long about any one thing."

As mysteries, the novels are excellent. Clues are masterfully placed throughout the stories. The plots are tight but tend to follow particularly in the first four books what might be called the Hansen formula:

Ideally, the reader will suspect A for a while, then switch his suspicions to B, then to C, then to D, and back again to A. If you're writing your book well, you'll keep the reader off balance this way most of the time.

. . .A, B, C, and D, all, or each in turn, must appear to have had the opportunity, and motive. And means.

For a time. That's the key phrase. For now, the logic of the structure you've set up takes over, and will complete your book for you. Only one suspect can be guilty. And with each suspect the detective rules out, he moves a step closer to the real murderer. First A, then B, then C, turn out to be wrong guesses. A, cornered, sweating, red-faced, blurts that he was with E at the time of the victim's death; he's kept silent about this because E has a husband, perhaps the victim himself. B, grossly fat, could not have gone out on the rotting pier at the lake where the victim's body was dumped—the framework would have broken under his weight. And C? Suddenly C is found murdered. Which leaves the detective, the writer, and the reader, with D. *(The Writer, April, 1980)*

Beginning more or less with *Troublemaker*'s look at the gay bar scene, the series has taken a turn toward examination of a number of social issues and movements—law and order extremists (*The Man Everybody Was*

Afraid Of), zealous religious fundamentalists (*Skinflick*, probably the best book of the series), and the mass murder phenomenon in Southern California (*Gravedigger*)—all done in the cosmopolitan and literary style which has become the Hansen trademark.

Reviewers of a Brandstetter tend to assure prospective readers that the homosexuality is not intrusive or essential to the plot. That type of opinion says more about the reviewer than the books and is probably motivated by a desire to guarantee that the homosexuality is not exploited or that it is presented "tastefully." Surely this is true, but the idea that homosexuality is not germane to the plots and action of each of these books is nonsense. Homosexuality is central to the reason these books were written. By choosing the mystery story with its conservative message that good triumphs over evil and order over chaos, Hansen is able to take much of the threat out of a topic which if presented less obliquely would be largely avoided. What we have here is a fine demonstration of how the mystery can be used to illuminate the vital, troubling, often shadowy issues of human relationships.

Thomas Kyd—Timothy Harris

Chandlerphiles will recognize *Goodnight and Goodbye* as one of Chandler's many unused book titles, so when Timothy Harris used the title for his second novel about Thomas Kyd, he was serving notice of his intention to honor his favorite mystery author. "It's an homage to Chandler," Harris told the Los Angeles *Times*, "and I don't want anyone to think it's an original. Any writer moving into the mystery field is doing something derivative." Harris is one of the best modern-day Chandler imitators who, along with Stephen Greenleaf and Loren Estleman, can sing the Marlowe melody without dropping a note. You can almost hear that soft trombone moaning behind a rainy night's last torch song— "Lover Man (Oh where can you be?)."

Harris' detective, Thomas Kyd, works in LA in an office whose age almost instantly establishes its hard-boiled authenticity:

It wasn't much of a neighborhood but it was mine that year, and I liked my office better than the modern cubicle I'd had with the Beverly Hills outfit. The building was fifty years old, which in the Los Angeles time warp gave it the dignity of a classical artifact. The ceiling was very high, with an elegantly carved wooden cornice that went well with the polished wooden floors. The previous tenant had been a psychiatrist, and I'd inherited his furniture and the out-of-date magazines on the waiting-room table. I'd taped a few photographs around the walls, put my criminology degree and my license from the Bureau of Collective and Investigative Services in prominent positions, and left everything else unchanged.

Anyone who names his detective Thomas Kyd is no stranger to literary traditions. Alfred Harbage, a noted Shakespearean scholar who held faculty appointments at Pennsylvania, Columbia and Harvard,used Thomas Kyd as his pseudonym for four mysteries he wrote in the 1940s. Before that, there was Thomas Kyd (1558-1594), the pre-Shakespearan Elizabethan poet and dramatist who was a close associate of Christopher Marlowe, a surname that seems to crop up frequently in this field.

Our current Kyd is in his mid-thirties, six foot two, 190 pounds and shaggy-haired. He smokes Gauloises, swills ample loads of gin and as one might expect of a young widower and Vietnam vet with a combat stress reaction, is not unacquainted with other pharmaceutical ups and downs. Like Marlowe, Kyd's tough surface protects a tender core that hasn't been all burned up by Hollywood's evil flames. He's a Berkeley graduate, but he's no longer a liberal. He's tarnished with "the guilt I was starting to trail around, the suspicion that I no longer had any moral certainty of what I was doing." He's callous, tough and sarcastic; he tells one typically badly dressed cop, "You want to solve a crime, Granville? Why don't you go arrest your tailor?" (*Kyd for Hire*)

Kyd mistrusts power and money, and he's learned that nothing in Los Angeles is quite the way it seems:

I'm thirty-three years old. My wife is dead and I have a private business that brings in enough to keep me in clean underwear. I live alone. I'm not tough but I'll kill a man if he tries to act like an animal to me, which is to say, if he tries to kill me. If I'm suspicious, I'm not suspicious enough, because people are always surprising me. I've seen little kids in Vietnam, seven- and eight-year-olds, attack and kill old people for their clothes, so they could sell them. I've worked on a case where a man who'd lived fifty-three years with the same woman blew her brains out because he was tired of the way she fried eggs. I live alone because I want to and I drink because I'm weak and because I like to feel good enough though I'm not very good. And one way I make up for that is by being careful about my work, by forcing myself to question things that seem fine, or respectable, or lovely, like you. But the main thing is that I don't make speeches. Ever.

If Marlowe taught the class on how to hate cops, Kyd was his best student:

Every time Rabbit socked me, his partner would get mad and protest, "Stop shoving, pal," and poke me from the other side.

They weren't imaginative but they were predictable. Like bowel movements.

"I don't know why he isn't talking," Rabbit piped up cheerfully. "Just looking at him, you know this punk would sell his mother to a coon for a quarter."

"You paid one to put it to yours," I said.

"A live one," the partner remarked genially and socked me in the throat.

"You look like you're going to cry, Kyd," Rabbit said. "You aren't going to cry on us, are you?"

"Eat shit," I said.

"What should I do with your bones?" Rabbit grunted.
"Build a cage for your mother."

In the first novel, *Kyd for Hire* (Dell, 1978), Joe Elevel, a furniture tycoon, hires Kyd to search for his daughter, Charlotte, who vanished the same night that her mother killed herself, leaving a suicide note behind—"Charlotte knows. Soon you'll all know. It's unspeakable." The story behind the secrets of the Elevel family goes back 25 years, and Kyd has plenty of tough company interested with him in their past. Harris knows well the formula for this type of plot, perfected and repeated by Ross Macdonald. Credit Sophocles, no stranger himself to family secrets, with a strong assist.

Good Night and Good-Bye (Delacorte, 1979) begins with Kyd's rescue of Laura Cassidy, a fabulous femme-fatale, from the assault of a naked man sprawled across the hood of his Volkswagen. It is one of the best opening scenes you'll ever read, and part of it is contained in our first chapter. Laura has a way of disappearing from Kyd and from her husband, a high-roller Hollywood screenwriter who tries to hire Kyd to find her. Kyd does, just after it appears that Laura has killed her husband in one of your run-of-the-mill, Tinseltown, drug-tooting orgies. The motive for the additional murders that follow turns out to be a ripped-off movie script, a welcome relief from the drugs and sex scandals that fuel 75% of today's PI novels. Throw in two cut-rate Mafiosos, a psychotic Vietnam vet and some unctious semi-celebrities and the result is Harris' strongest novel.

As good as Kyd is, the real star of these novels is Los Angeles itself, and like all great characters, Los Angeles even has its fatal fault—San Andreas. No one since Chandler has captured the excess that is LA as well as Harris. Kyd calls it "Mutant City." A hollow, deadly city; organized decay glossed with glitter; Kyd's LA is the reason we need the word "sleaze":

The pavements of Hollywood Boulevard thronged with every variety of nightlife. There were fat ladies in print dresses with nylon stockings bunched up around their knees; bowed, elderly people on street corners trying to summon the courage to brave the traffic; old, broken-down queens; young hustlers with ravaged, restless faces; scornful, tight-mouthed whores; aging strong men; dwarfs; livid-faced drunks; and sullen, princely black pimps in Greta Garbo hats and flowing foxes and minks. There were businessmen in town for conventions, and tourists and teen-agers who'd drive from all over Los Angeles to participate in the evening traffic jam.

Timothy Hyde Harris was born in Los Angeles on July 21, 1946 to Donald and Mary Harris. The family left LA when Harris was six months old, and he grew up in various cities across Europe and Africa. (He read his first Chandler on a train trip in Switzerland.) Educated at Cambridge, where he wrote his first novel, the satiric *Kronski/McSmash* (Doubleday, 1970) featuring McSmash the far-out detective for the Monterey Narcotics Squad, Harris publishes under the name of Hyde Harris in England.

In addition to the two Kyds and *Kronski/McSmash*, Harris has novelized three screenplays. *American Gigolo* (Dell, 1979) was based on a screenplay by Paul Schrader. It is no worse than the movie which starred Richard Gere and Lauren Hutton. *Steelyard Blues* (Bantam, 1972) was taken from David Ward's screenplay and *Heat Wave* (Dell, 1979), a great PI story without an official PI, is based on a screenplay by Herschel Weingrod. Weingrod and Harris have collaborated on several original screenplays. "Cheaper to Keep Her," a romantic comedy starring Mac Davis as a private detective, Bill Dekker, was released by American Cinema in 1980. Their best-known effort was the screenplay for the Eddie Murphy-Dan Ackroyd comedy "Trading Places" which had a wonderful minor role for a cheesey private detective played by Paul Gleason.

Harris married Mary Bess Walker in 1980. He now lives in Los Angeles and is concentrating on film writing.

John Denson, The Olympic Knight—Richard Hoyt

Richard Hoyt worked counterintelligence for the U.S. Army in the mid 60s and later was a newspaper reporter in Washington, D.C. and Honolulu. His father was a moonshiner, horse trader and railroad man. Few of our private eyes have had better preparation for a life of adventure. Hoyt has been around the block, and his novels show it. If he sustains the initial quality of his John Denson series, he just may end up the best private eye writer of the 1980s.

Hoyt was born in Hermiston, Oregon, in 1941, to Clyde and Nellie Allen Hoyt. He received his BS (1963) and MS (1967) in journalism from the University of Oregon. From 1963 to 1967, following Army training at Fort Holabird, Maryland, he was a counterintelligence agent assigned to do surveillance and background investigation on the Olympic Peninsula. Toward the end of that stint, he was interviewing conscientious objectors and he began to get interested in politics. It was then that he decided to become a newspaperman.

Following a year in D.C. as a Washington Journalism Fellow, Hoyt went to Honolulu and earned a Ph.D. from the University of Hawaii (1972) in American Studies. His dissertation under the direction of Reuel Denney was on the American Indian myths of the Pacific Northwest. In Hawaii Hoyt worked as a reporter for the Honolulu *Star Bulletin* and then the Honolulu *Advertiser*. After returning to the mainland, he taught journalism at the University of Maryland where he was an Assistant Professor and then moved to Portland, Oregon, where he was appointed an Associate Professor in the Department of Communications at Lewis and

Clark College. In 1983 Hoyt resigned his position at Lewis and Clark to pursue a full-time writing career. He currently lives in Portland.

Hoyt divides his writing time between the Denson novels—there are now four of them—and his thrillers. His first thriller, *The Manna Enzyme* (1981), features a cast of colorful characters headed by Fidel Castro traveling *in cognito* in the US searching for an enzyme that will end global starvation because it makes all plant life digestible by human beings. *Trotsky's Run* (1982), a paperback original for Tor, was chosen as one of the Notable Crime Books of 1982 by the New York *Times Book Review*. Hoyt believes it is the best book he has written; it is his best seller. The plot involves two CIA agents trying to help Kim Philby come back to the West while they also try to determine the accuracy of Philby's claim that a U.S. presidential candidate is really a KGB mole. His newest thriller is *Cool Runnings* (1984) for Viking Press.

John Denson's debut in *Decoys* (Evans, 1980) marked him as one of a new breed—a softboiled detective. Along with Albert Samson, Denson epitomizes the soft boiler. He doesn't carry a gun, he doesn't knock heads, he's no Lothario. His style is unpretentious and vaguely blue collar. In each of the novels, Denson's life is saved by a woman; hardly the stuff of which Lancelots are made and a welcome twist of the damsel-in-distress cliche.

Denson is a flake, a quality which he always turns to his advantage:

Everybody underestimates a flake. I count on it. It's part of my act, has been for years. It's how I survive . . . . Self-depreciation. That's the trick. Put yourself down . . . . Lead with the obvious. Lulls 'em. (*Decoys*)

His investigative style is a product of his past careers as an intelligence agent and a reporter (sound familiar?). More cerebral than most private eyes, Denson takes special pleasure in besting the federal agents and intelligence agents who often cross his path. Cruising Seattle in his old Fiat and often bedecked in one of his many caps, Denson himself resembles a rakish spy more than he does a world-weary gumshoe in sharkskin.

Denson is a man of unusual passions and pasttimes. He is an expert at darts which he plays frequently at his favorite Seattle pub, Pigs Alley. He is a smoked-fish and fresh-vegetable freak with a special fondness for cauliflower and broccoli; he loves to judge the vegetable displays at the Pike Street market. Screw-top wine is his favorite beverage, but he also drinks a lot of beer especially in working-class bars; fancy bars and Hyatt atriums make him nervous.

Denson's apartment clues us to much of his character—part romantic, part dreamer, fully an individual. He has a stuffed English pit bull terrier named Winston hooked up to the doorbell. When the doorbell rings, Winston goes native, growling savagely like he's ready to go for the visitor's throat. Inside, the apartment is a "clutter of posters and memorabilia."

Denson is one of the great outdoorsmen among private eyes. These books sound like the workingman's version of the American Sportsman. Fishing for steelheads in Oregon's North Umpqua River. Hunting geese in the fields around Cayuse. Spending a night in the pine-sweet Siskiyou Mountains. Wildlife and wilderness are often essential to the plots and the way Denson looks at the world, and they allow Hoyt a special voice with which to tell his stories. The style is a bit reminiscent of Dick Francis, whom Hoyt admires greatly and discovered appropriately enough on a fishing trip of his own.

You don't have to be a duck hunter to appreciate *Decoys* but it might help. Because this is a book about deception, the double blind, "laying the spread" as the hunters call it. The action begins when Pamela Yew, a female private detective from San Francisco who says she works for a prostitute's union, enlists Denson's help in locating a pimp who Yew claims brutally murdered some hookers and is now hiding out in Oregon near Denson's old home. It doesn't take Denson long to figure out that Pamela is not telling him the entire story behind her mission, and so he wagers his $50,000 Thomas Eakins against a nonplatonic weekend with her that he can get to the bottom of the case before she can. The ensuing plot is a complicated affair with debts to "The Purloined Letter" and *The Maltese Falcon,* and it makes a spectacular beginning for Denson who admits that "a fool and his Eakins are soon parted."

30 For a Harry (Evans, 1981) is a splendidly titled novel about Denson's search for an extortionist connected somehow with the Seattle *Star.* "30" is newspaperman jargon for "the end" and that is what *Star* publisher Harold Balkan wants Denson to write to his paper's "Harry," a term derived from a true story about one Harry Karafin who was a much admired Philadelphia *Inquirer* reporter who was discovered to have been using his information and power to blackmail people. Denson goes undercover as a reporter to find the "Harry" whose identity ends up not being a total surprise.

The Siskiyou Two-Step (Morrow, 1983) begins and ends in water, but in between is an off-beat dance that finds Denson playing footsie with a British intelligence agent, the FBI, a bevy of beautifully rumped go-go dancers and a charmingly eccentric academician all of whom are after a manuscript that supposedly will prove that William Shakespeare was really Edward de Vere, Earl of Oxford, an old chestnut in the world of Shakespeare scholarship. Farfetched and wonderful, *Siskiyou* combines the extravagancies of Hoyt's international thrillers with the restrained, wry wit of his Denson adventures.

The newest Denson, *Fish Story* (Viking, 1984) is about the life of urban Indians and salmon fishing rights in the Pacific Northwest. The murder of a judge draws Denson to the deserted underground city that exists below old Seattle for a hair-raising Halloween night finale.

Hoyt is a clever writer who takes full advantage of his own background in creating some memorable scenes that work very well. *Decoy*'s surveillance sequence through Seattle is autobiographical and is simply as good as they come. The beginnings of *Siskiyou* with Denson shooting the white water on the naked corpse of a girl with a bullet hole between her eyes is, along with the first scene in Donald Zochert's *Another Weeping Woman*, the best opening you'll ever read. You can learn a lot about the way a big-time newspaper works from *30 For a Harry*, and the American Studies trivia quiz in *Siskiyou* is a great touch.

The Denson novels are stylish, suggestive of a heavy re-writer who is able to make his work sound relaxed and easy. The writing is witty but never silly. One reviewer dubbed Hoyt "John Le Carre with the giggles." But the real success of the Denson series is that Hoyt has created a character that you care about because of the interesting way he looks at his place in the world. Denson is an example of just how good the nonderived private eye can be.

Toby Peters, The Knight of the Stars
—Stuart Kaminsky

Do you pine for some pure enjoyment, some uncomplicated fun and humor? Do you yearn for the good old days of yesteryear when the Yankees always won, when you could order the luncheon special at Henrici's for 74¢, make a phone call for a nickel and buy your best winter suit for $40? When you could hire a private detective for $20 a day plus expenses? If nostalgia is your yen Toby Peters is your man. Set in the Hollywood of the 1940s, the Golden Age of Tinseltown, Stuart Kaminsky's series about Toby Peters is one of the most entertaining and charming creations in the genre.

This series is tailor-made for movie buffs and private eye fans. All the books involve real and famous characters who are threatened by fictitious calamities, blackmail schemes and gangsters. In each case, Peters is able, despite considerable ineptitude, to foil the treachery and scandal about to descend on some of Hollywood's most memorable stars. Along the way he's helped by a veritable "who's who" of mystery fiction and American literature.

Errol Flynn is facing blackmail because someone has a picture of him and a very young girl doing what Flynn was famous for doing. Flynn might even be facing *A Bullet For A Star* (1977), but Peter Lorre and Humphrey Bogart lend helping hands to Toby who directs the denouement on the set of *The Maltese Falcon*. William Faulkner is seen at a window smoking a pipe.

After someone murders a Munchkin, Judy Garland is afraid she might be next and calls Toby to prevent her *Murder on the Yellow Brick Road* (1977). With Louis B. Mayer paying the tab, Peters meets Clark Gable and William Randolph Hearst but receives his biggest assistance from Raymond Chandler whom he meets in a flop house lobby. Seems that Chandler likes to hang out in lobbies in order to pick up some good dialogue for his novels, but Toby is suspicious:

> I couldn't tell if he was putting on an act or if he was what he said. His story sounded dumb.
> "What books have you written?" I said. I put my gun back in my holster, but I didn't lean back.
> "Well," he said, "I did one called *The Big Sleep* and a few months ago another one of mine, *Farewell, My Lovely*, came out."
> I'd never heard of him or them, and I said so.
> "The number of mystery novels that have had even minimal success in the past five years can be counted on one hand of a two-toed sloth," he sighed.
> It sounded liked writer talk.

In *You Bet Your Life* (1978), Toby tries to discover why a Chicago hoodlum is putting the squeeze on Chico Marx for a $120,000 gambling bet, one of the few gambling losses which Chico really did not incur. Toby goes to Chicago by way of Florida and a meeting with a syphlitic Al Capone (Toby observes discreetly: "Something wasn't right with Big Al.") In The Windy City Toby catches a bad cold but cures it with a special remedy recommended to him by the rakish British agent Ian Fleming (raw egg in orange juice with a wine chaser). After finding out that Toby's a Democrat, a young state senator by the name of Richard Daly gets the Chicago police off his back.

The Howard Hughes Affair (1979) is a nifty blend of hard-boiled heroics, espionage thriller and real-life Sherlock Holmes ratiocination in the person of Basil Rathbone who's worrying about being typecast. Toby seeks to determine who might be trying to steal some military plans from the enigmatic Howard Hughes who's portrayed here with his full compliment of eccentricities. Bertold Brecht provides the key clue, Jane Russell the cleavage.

In the fifth Peters' novel, *Never Cross a Vampire* (1980), Peters is hired to find out who's sending Bela Lugosi some threatening letters. William Faulkner appears for a second time in the series, this time as a prime suspect in the murder of a literary agent.

Next to *You Bet Your Life*, *High Midnight* (1981) is the best Peters caper. Somebody very badly wants Gary Cooper to make a B Western. Cameo appearances are made by Babe Ruth, fat bellied and spindly legged; Bill Dickey; Cornell Wilde; and Ernest Hemingway, here a most obnoxious and pugnacious bwana. Mystery scholars will cherish a cop named John Cawelti who has to fetch coffee when the troops are thirsty.

After a circus elephant is electrocuted, Peters is called to Mirador, California, by Emmett Kelly who fears Toby may have to *Catch a Falling Clown* (1981). More trouble and more death hit the big top, and Toby needs all the help he can get from his band of ragtag cronies. A man named Alfred Hitchcock, incomparably macabre and scared to death of the cops, is an essential participant.

When Mae West calls, who wouldn't listen? Toby answers the call in *He Done Her Wrong* (1983) and meets Cecil B. DeMille and D.W. Griffiths for his trouble. The ninth book, *The Fala Factor* (1984), involves a case with Eleanor Roosevelt as the client. *Down for the Count*, featuring Joe Louis, is the newest Peters entry.

Toby Peters is not the best private eye in Los Angeles, but he is one of its most durable. At 5′ 9″, 160 pounds, he's got a bad back, sore feet, a nose that's been broken at least three times, usually by his older brother, knife scars from head to toe, and "reconstituted scar tissue and bone, tentatively glued together by a kid doctor in LA named Parry." In every case he takes more lumps than he gives, but he's philosophical about it all and even considers his corrugated face a professional asset. "My face was benign when I was 12, but it gradually became semimalignant . . . it announced that I had known violence." Agile and ugly, that's Toby Peters.

Toby became a private eye after seven years as a Glendale cop and five more as a security guard with Warner Brothers, a job he lost when he broke the arm of a Western star who thought he was as tough in real life as he was on the screen. Toby appears to have a strong aversion to telling the truth especially to his older brother, Phil Pevsner (Toby's real name is Tobias Leo Pevsner) who is an LA police lieutenant in charge of homicide. Phil is as straight as an arrow and thinks that Toby is a jerk who's lying about his involvement in the murders that he always seems to be calling in to the police usually with a phony Italian accent that he hopes will fool Phil. It doesn't. At its best, Toby and Phil's relationship is controlled animosity. At its worst, Toby is lucky to esape Phil's rage without having to do hospital time. Toby plays bait-the-brother with a virtuosity that has taken years to polish, and he need only ask "how are Ruth and the kids?" at the wrong moment to turn Phil into a lunatic bent on redestroying Toby's poor excuse for a nose.

Toby lives on the cheap because that's the best he can afford. The fact that he drives a '34 Buick doesn't establish his poverty so much as the sobering discovery that he can fit all his belongings into its trunk. He seldom uses a gun, at least not a real one. He is fond of the toy pistol he bought at Woolworth's. On those rare occasions when he has fired his .38, he's made sure to bill the client for the bullets he's used. He lives in an over-the-hill boarding house on Heliotrope run by the aged Mrs. Plaut, a woman so severely deaf that she believes her boarder "Tony Peelers" is a private exterminator. Mrs. Plaut is a bit hard-boiled herself as revealed by her cynical conviction that "this is a doggie dog world." Toby maintains himself on a junkfood diet that would embarrass Ronald McDonald. Tacos and Pepsi are staples. For variety—tacos and Coke. He carboloads on all the great cereals—Wheaties, Shredded Wheat and Puffed Rice. Outside of a very occasional beer he does not drink.

Toby's love life is also very impoverished. He still carries a torch for his ex-wife, Ann, she of the firm ideas and equally firm thighs. Ann, who appears briefly in all the stories, left Toby because she grew tired of his playing detective and refusing to grow up. Despite Toby's repeated efforts to win back her sympathy if not her body, Ann gives him little reason for optimism.

Toby gets seduced now and then but almost always for the wrong reason and in the wrong place. One fair fraulein nurtured him in a dental chair, an experience which his bad back did not let him soon forget. The only two women he pursues are Ann and Carmen, a tough-cookie cashier at Levy's Grill with a passion for professional boxing. Both elude him. Writing in *Mystery* (July, 1982) about the Peters series and its women characters, Jeff Pierce has observed that "women use Peters over and over. They are ego-soothers, pegs to fill up the holes in his self-confidence. He doesn't really care to understand them." The most decent woman in the series is Merle Gordon who in *You Bet Your Life* shows genuine affection and concern for Toby (Merle Gordon just happens to be the maiden name of Kaminsky's wife).

Toby's relationships with women reveal the basic qualities of his character. He is not a stupid man, but he is naive. His values and his motives seem more childlike than anything else. He faces danger with the sort of wide-eyedness that suggests a man who's going to hold onto the joys of childhood and the fantasies of the matinee movies despite everybody's attempts to make him change.

Toby's a kid and wants to stay that way:

I never grew up. Have no plans to. Took me almost forty years to find that out. I lost my wife when we both finally agreed on that, and I've been playing private detective ever since.

In addition to Phil and Ann three other characters play important supporting roles in the series. To say they help Toby solve his cases might be stretching it a bit, but they all do involve themselves in his dare-devil escapades with varying degrees of skills, and on occasion have been the difference between Toby's life and death.

The best of the bunch is Dr. Sheldon Minck, D.D.S., S.D., with whom

Toby shares a fourth-floor office in the Farraday Building, the run-down home of a bunch of shady operators including alcoholic doctors, a baby photographer with astigmatism, bookies and one Artistic Books under the management of the gargantuan Alice Palice. Shelly is fiftyish, sloppy fat and badly myopic, a condition which is minimally corrected by the cloddy glasses that always seem to be oozing down his nose. His business is very bad, a state of affairs entirely justified by the level of his dentistry skills and ethical standards. The S.D. after his name doesn't stand for anything, but Shelly thought it might attract some walk-in traffic, a very unlikely phenomenon on the fourth floor of The Farraday Building. One of Minck's few clients is a Walter Brennan look-alike by the name of Mr. Karl Stange. Stange is down to his last tooth upon which Shelly performs a root canal (he needed the practice). When Shelly tries to anchor some bridgework to this last pillar of enamel, Stange grabs one of the dental instruments and robs Shelly of all his office money—six dollars.

Minck's office is about as tidy as the inside of a shoe repair shop. His idea of a sterile field is blowing on his tongs after he uses them and then wiping them with his apron. The x-rays are kept in a pile with the LA *Times*. He's been known to pack gums with used cotton balls. Shelly spends a lot of time reading supply catalogues in order to figure out how all the dental instruments are supposed to be used. The only talent Minck shows for dentistry is "an indifference to victims that would have put the Inquisition to shame." While he is usually content to answer Toby's phone and leave cryptic, passive-aggressive messages, the temptation to play detective proves too great when Gary Cooper calls to hire Peters in *High Midnight*. After Shelly answers the phone, he identifies himself as Peters to Cooper and then investigates the case on his own. This venture lasts only a short time after Shelly discovers the life of a private detective may not be well suited to his temperament. One suspect with whom Minck made contact recalled him as "short, fat, obnoxious, and stupid." Cooper's description was "maybe fifty, roly-poly sweaty fella, bald head, smokes cheap cigars .... I've got to admit I wasn't impressed."

Then there's Gunther Whetherman, Toby's next-door neighbor at Mrs. Plaut's. Gunther is a midget who became Toby's best friend after Toby proved him innocent of the munchkin's *Murder on the Yellow Brick Road*. A dapper dresser, the immaculate Gunther is Swiss although his heavy accent misleads people to think him German, a most unfortunate mistake during the 1940s. Gunther works as a translator of the written word, but on occasion will work as a very intelligent and effective operative for Toby.

Finally we have Jeremy Butler, owner of the Farraday. The 250-pound Jeremy is an ex-wrestler turned poet who has had poems published in such stellar outlets as *Iliad Now* and *Southern Thought Magazine*. He too assists Toby on a case now and then, and at one point gives truth to that oldest of mystery cliches—"the butler did it." Jeremy's philosophy of life is an interesting blend of the poetic and the pragmatic as integrated by the wrestler-writer:

"I'll have you laughing through a toothless mouth," hissed Nelson to Jeremy, as we prisoners sat on the small wooden bench while Alex turned on the lights.
" 'And if I laugh at any mortal sting, 'tis that I may not weep.' Lord Byron," said Jeremy.
"A bunch of smartasses," said Nelson between his teeth.
"Know your enemy and break his arm," said Jeremy, answering Nelson's look of hate.
"That is not poetry," said Gunther.
"In a sense," said Jeremy. "It was said to me before a tag-team match in 1937 by Strangler Lewis."

Shelly, Gunther and Jeremy contribute to the comedy of the series, but beyond that the treatment Kaminsky gives them helps establish the overall optimism and good naturedness present in each of the novels. Whether due to Gunther's physical freakishness, Jeremy's devalued professions or Shelly's shysterish dental practice, each character would usually be regarded as one of society's marginal men, a person to be accorded little respect, an object of derision. However, Kaminsky manages to cast each in a sympathetic almost sentimental light so that we inevitably feel strong affection for them.

The humor in the series is first rate and quite diverse in form. There is clever word play such as the company "Edifice Wrecks," the building-demolition firm whose name Gunther is trying to translate into Polish and still retain the joke he only vaguely perceives.

There is a Woody Allen sense-of-the-absurd illustrated by Marco the gangster (*High Midnight*) who's trying to improve his vocabulary by forcing himself to use words like "environment," "plethora" and "calamitous" in complete sentences. The dialogue turns bizarre as well when Toby small-talks a hotel desk clerk in *You Bet Your Life* with the memorable line, "Large weather we're having." In *Catch a Falling Clown*, Toby attempts to interrogate Henry Yew, the animal keeper for the circus, a man whose English or cognitive abilities are obviously not sufficient for every occasion.

"What do you know about this morning?" I asked quietly as a few more stragglers went out of the tent heading for the big top.
"Monkeys," he said. "I know monkeys. Big ones mostly. I'm intense with monkeys."
"Intense?"
"Mr. Ringling said I was once," he explained.

"No," I said, trying to readjust the hat on my head. It was small and cardboard, which didn't bother me, but the rubber band holding it was cutting into my chin. "Tanucci and his wife, the younger Tanuccis, are dead, murdered," I said. "Did you see anyone fooling with the harness and rigging this morning?"

"I am poor with cats, horses, and people," answered Henry, examining one strand of straw that caught his eye. "Not intense with them. Just ain't."

"Few of us are," I tried.

One of the zaniest scenes in the whole series comes in *You Bet Your Life*. Toby is dashing through Chicago's Drake Hotel trying to elude three thugs—one who looks like Lou Costello, one who favors Lon Chaney and one who resembles a juke box. As he is about to be captured, Toby stumbles into a regional convention of the American Psychiatric Association. He is promptly mistaken for the guest speaker, Dr. Charles Derry from South Africa. Faced with the choice of rendezvousing with Costello, Chaney and the juke box or faking the speech, Toby soon finds himself introduced to the assembled throng for the featured address. Toby's ensuing lecture on Derry's master work, *Super-Ego, and Ego vs. Self and Ego: A False Battle* is a parody of psychobabble that comes embarrassingly close to the real thing.

The appeal of the Toby Peters novels is the air of nostalgia they create. We are swept along to the period Kaminsky so carefully and lovingly has recreated. A time when we huddled together around the radio and yielded to its magic, when our movie heroes were larger than life. A time of confidence and patriotism, wartime heroism and romance, a time of Gillette Blue Blades, Babo and Bromo Quinine Tablets. This strong atmosphere is owed to Kaminsky's diligent research which he described in an interview with Bob Randisi:

What I do is get a basic idea and let it work subconsciously for three, four, five months, while I'm doing other things. At the end of three or four months I'll start writing an outline. After I've done the outline, I'll then go back and do some research to give me a feeling for the period I'm going to cover. I usually select one or two periods, then I go to the library, spend a lot of time reading the *L.A. Times*. I do things like listening to old radio shows. I like it, I enjoy doing it, looking at old movies, a little reading of biographies, which I enjoy doing. After I do that, once I start the process of writing, I work very intensely. I can't put it away. (*The Armchair Detective*, 1980, No. 4)

The nostalgia actually takes two forms in the series. There is the obvious longing for the forties, one of America's most colorful and tumultuous decades. But there is also the more personal nostalgia within Toby himself—a longing for his own childhood, for the age when thrills-and-chills was all that mattered, before the demands of responsibility had taken over. It's significant that the most important fixture in Toby's office is a picture of him at age ten along with his father, Phil, and his beagle, Kaiser Wilhelm.

Toby faces the constant danger and hard knocks with a bravery of sorts; actually it's more like with a twinkle in his eye. Toby thrives on the close call, the near scrape. He's the naughty little boy that you can't help but love, the Dennis the Menace of private eyedom.

While there are elements of burlesque and parody in the series they are accomplished without any feeling of condescension or belittlement toward the genre. This is parody with the lightest of touches. Mockery is missing. The superiority complex that one feels with Richard Brautigan's *Dreaming of Babylon* or Thomas Berger's *Who Is Teddy Villanova* is not to be found here. Neither is plotting neglected as in the Chance Purdue capers by Ross Spencer. Kaminsky takes private eye fiction seriously and the comedy in his series is more an attempt to write unpretentiously than to imply that the genre is of little value.

Frankly, one feels that criticism of a series which is so much fun to read may be a bit pompous. It's true that the gimmick may be hard to sustain at an equal level through a large number of books (a problem most apparent in *Vampire*). Others have objected to the fact that Kaminsky can't seem to make up his mind whether to pitch the books as purely humorous pastiches or play-fair, clue-filled mysteries, a charge which invites a simple rebuttal: why should he? At times Toby slips into a too melancholy voice ("Yesterday's memories are filled with regrets and tomorrow doesn't look too good."), but then we do too. So while we could find several nits to pick, it might be better to ride along with that sage old advice, "if it ain't broke don't fix it."

Stuart Kaminsky was born on September 29, 1934 on Chicago's West Side. His father, Leo, ran a grocery store and his mother, Dorothy, worked at Goldblatt's and Lerner's, two long-time Chicago retail establishments. He attended the University of Illinois where he earned a BS in Journalism (1957) and an MA in English literature (1960). Following a two-year stint in the Army, Kaminsky worked at various writing positions at the University of Illinois, the University of Michigan and the University of Chicago where he was Director of the Office of Public Information. Married to Merle Gordon in 1959, he has three children. His two sons are named Peter and Toby.

In 1977 Kaminsky received his Ph.D. in Speech from Northwestern University. He wrote his dissertation on the film director Don Siegel. That same year he joined the faculty at Northwestern where he is now Professor in the Department of Radio, Television and Film and head of the Film Division. In academic circles, Kaminsky is best known for his books on filmmaking and biographies of important filmmakers. Among his publications *John Huston: Maker of Magic* (1978) and *American Film*

Genres (1974) are probably the most influential. He has also written *Don Siegel: Director* (1973), *Clint Eastwood* (1974), *Ingmar Bergman* (1975) and *Basic Filmmaking* (with Dana Hodgdon, 1981). The first Toby Peters novel was begun in 1973 when Kaminsky was working on the official biography of Charlton Heston, a project that ultimately fell through.

Beginning in 1981 with the publication of *Death of a Dissident*, Kaminsky started a new mystery series set in modern Moscow and starring Inspector Porfiry Rostinov, a fan of the '87th Pct. Novels which he purchases on the black market. Kaminsky describes the tone of these police procedurals as "serio-comic, more bizarre and surreal" than the Toby Peters novels (a hammer and a sickle are murder weapons in *Death of a Dissident*). The latest Rostinov tale is *Murder In Red Square* (1983). *When the Dark Man Calls* (also published in 1983) is a suspense novel which Kaminsky wrote as a "response to the criticism that I hadn't written anything with a strong female protagonist."

Kaminsky plans to continue to write Toby Peters novels for some time. He told Randisi:

I'm writing them chronologically, but that may have to stop, depending on how many books I do. He may cease to age. I've also thought about what would happen when I reach the postwar period. I don't know at what age I'm going to stop him, if I do at all .... I can see him getting into the early fifties, but I have trouble seeing him getting into the sixties. There's a radical difference and we've already had an enormous nostalgia and response to the sixties, in film particularly.

The Midwestern Knight (Albert Samson)—Michael Lewin

In the 1970s private eyes began to migrate from their California homeland to various areas of the United States. New England has Spenser, Detroit has Amos Walker, Joe Reddman hangs from the cliffs in the Rocky Mountains and Milo and Sughrue light up the Big Sky Country. But it is two Midwesterners—Albert Samson in Indianapolis and Harry Stoner in Cincinnati—who best represent the regionalization of the private eye.

Have the Mean Streets really come to Middle America? Judging from Samson's Indy and Stoner's Queen City, they have and they're being walked by a tough crowd. These are two of the country's most heavily populated small towns, rural in spirit behind their urban facades. But Indianapolis and Cincinnati are growing bad; their twilight dreams are turning into all-night neon nightmares. They could use a couple of good ops, and in Albert Samson and Harry Stoner they get two of the best.

Michael Lewin, creator of Albert Samson, was born in Springfield, Massachusetts, in 1942. He moved to Indianapolis at age five with his mother (Iris), a social worker and father (Leonard), a writer on athletic, political and social topics. He graduated from North Central High School in Indianapolis and then attended Harvard where he received a B.A. in

Michael F. Lewin

chemistry and physics. After a year of graduate study at Cambridge University in England he taught high school in Connecticut and New York City for three years and then began writing full time. He married Marianne Ruth Crewe in 1965; they have two children. Since 1971, the Lewins have lived in England where Lewin praises the quality of Indiana basketball and coaches the Frome Basketball Club's women's team.

Lewin began writing at Harvard when he elected to take some creative writing classes taught by Alan Lebowitz. He was introduced to mysteries by his wife-to-be whom he met at a party in Cambridge. She gave him a novel by Chandler who remains a Lewin favorite along with George Higgins, and, outside the mystery field, Jane Austen and Isaac Babel.

Lewin's first book was *How To Beat College Tests: A Practical Guide to Ease the Burden of Useless Courses* (1970). Intended as much to motivate good teaching as to instruct students how to pass, the book contains one helpful chapter on "how to cheat."

Lewin claims that he first created Samson as an inexpensive form of home entertainment during a visit to his mother in Los Angeles:

> We stayed six weeks, and at the beginning of the fifth we'd exhausted the low-budget entertainments of the area. So I decided to entertain the assembled company by writing a twenty-page take-off of a detective story.
> When I started my story, I began it where they all begin: with a female client walking into the office. Along with the obligatory wise-cracks, I included a few family jokes. Setting it in Indianapolis, for one thing. (*Murder Ink*, 1977)

After the royalties from *How To Beat College Tests* began to thin out, Lewin returned to Samson, "no longer the larkish self-amusement he started as," and in 1971 he published the first Albert Samson novel, *Ask The Right Question*, in which Samson is hired by a precocious 16-year-old to discover the identity of her biological father. In this novel which was an Edgar nominee for best first novel of 1971 the Lewin trademark of meticulous plotting and attention to detail is nicely established. The careful reader who remains attentive to the intricacies of dates, times and figures with which Lewin lines the story will be gratified by Lewin's play-fair story telling.

In *The Way We Die Now* (1973), Samson investigates the case of a mentally disturbed Vietnam war veteran charged with the murder of another private eye who had been blackmailing several husbands and wives in exchange for his covering up their philandering. *The Enemies Within* (1974) is a rarity in private eye fiction—it contains no murder. It does contain, however, a very unusual love affair between a woman and her step-brother. In it Lewin spins an eerie tale of obsessive deception.

The Silent Salesman (1978) finds Albert being visited for the summer by his teenage daughter, Marianne (known to her friends as "Sam"). Albert and Sam collaborate to discover why a woman is not permitted to visit her brother, a pharmaceuticals salesman who has ostensibly been injured in a lab explosion several months earlier. The case is full of people who aren't what they claim to be including the injured salesman. The book is memorable for its introduction of what we believe is the first father-daughter team in private eye fiction.

Missing Woman (1981) is the best of the Samson series. Attractively set in and around beautiful Brown County and the campus of Indiana University, the book is full of interesting plot reversals and excellent characterizations. There are many ways in which a person can be missing, and here Lewin explores them all.

The newest Albert Samson mystery is *Out of Season* (1984) which begins with a woman requesting that Samson help her find out who she is!

Lewin has created a second series character—Lieutenant Leroy Powder, originally in charge of the night-duty division of the Indianapolis Police in *Night Cover* (1976) and then the head of Missing Persons Bureau in *Hard Line* (1982). Tougher than Samson on the outside, Powder is an intelligent, sensitive, conscientious cop (at one of their infrequent encounters, Samson refers to him as a "legend in his own nighttime") and a more complex hero than we usually encounter in police procedurals.

Lewin has written another novel, *Outside In* (1980) about a mystery writer who tries to solve a real murder. In addition to his novels, Lewin has created several radio plays for the BBC, has been a contributor to *Sport* and *Penthouse*, and has written several short stories. His "Wrong Number" won a prize as one of the best short stories at the 1981 International Crime Writers Congress in Stockholm.

Albert R. (for Robespiere) Samson is a native Hoosier. He attended college but quit after his father (Bud) died. His mother still lives in Indianapolis and owns her own diner, Bud's Dugout, which has four well-maintained pinball machines that Albert likes to play. After trying his hand at security work, Samson returned to college, flunked out and wrote a book about his college days that made him temporarily rich and famous. He married, had a daughter and then divorced. He opened his one-man agency in Indianapolis in 1963, and he's been unsuccessful ever since, earning him the title of Indianapolis' cheapest private eye.

Samson's business is so bad that he advertises 20%-off sales in the paper—"Gigantic August Detective Sale." To help make ends meet he also constructs crossword puzzles, does photography and carpentry and other "odd jobs for odd friends." Albert's life-style seldom rises from the bargain basement. In five books, he's been evicted twice from Indianapolis relics about to feel the wrecking ball; his third office is in an abandoned west-side glass warehouse. He always lives in a couple of rooms behind whatever office he's renting, and isn't above taking baths in a vacant next-door room. When Albert finally trades in his '58 "gizzard-green" Plymouth, it's for a '65 Chevy panel truck.

Albert Samson is a very likeable private detective. His personality is bedrock Midwestern normal understated with a modest, wistful voice that charms as it entertains. Samson is common like the city where he works. He's well-enough adjusted, enjoys simple hobbies like basketball (what else in Indiana) and even lives with his mother for a while after his first eviction.

Introspective, plagued by self-doubts and a sense of indeterminate fear, Samson lacks any heroic pretense. After wounding a man during his earlier stint as a security guard, Albert refuses to carry a gun. He tries to avoid whatever violent options might present themselves to him. "I am not in the intimidation side of this business. I'm just not good at it." Elsewhere, he admits, "I get caught when I try to do things. It's not fair."

As a detective, Samson's strongest asset is his willingness to get involved in a case to the exclusion of almost everything else. He's a compulsive detail man who practices fundamental investigative work— facts and questions. "Work out what you know. Then what you want to know. Think about who knows it. Then move." Driven by what he calls his "promiscuous curiosity," Samson analyzes his cases carefully, frequently studying the notebook in which he writes copious notes on all his activities. Samson does more paperwork than any other private eye and the solution of his cases usually depends on him breaking the problem down into soluble parts and then asking the right questions. His one liability—a too active imagination—sometimes causes him trouble because more often than not his suspicions are groundless. When he thinks he's being followed, he's usually not; when he suspects someone is hiding in his office, it's usually empty.

Samson's singlemindedness makes him a hard man to know well. Although he has a steady female friend (always referred to as "my woman"), the relationship appears to be suffering from a chronic lack of attention. His only good friend is Jerry Miller, a black police lieutenant who went to high school with Albert.

Lewin has an excellent talent for creating a realistic feeling of loneliness around Samson who seems more estranged and disillusioned than one might expect in middle-of-the-map Indianapolis. The books manage to be pessimistic without turning sour and solemn, a balance achieved by Samson's self-effacing humor. As he tells an acquaintance in *The Silent Salesman*:

" . . . you haven't got any sense of Yuma."
"Any what?"
"Just an Arizona quip."

Lewin is an intelligent writer, who has created in Albert Samson a different type of private eye—a guy-next-door who shares in some of the genre's tradition but who shuns many of its extremes. Average, but because of it, very special.

A Knight in Poodle Springs, Jacob Asch—Arthur Lyons

"Poodle Springs." That was Raymond Chandler's derisive name for Palm Springs in his last but unfinished novel that satirized the hypocritical and empty lives of the tired rich in Southern California. Palm Springs is also the home of Arthur Lyons, author of the detective series featuring Jacob Asch, private eye working out of Los Angeles, a city that Lyons believes sets many of America's trends, "even the style of murder." And not since Chandler has a mystery writer surpassed Lyon's ability to portray the decadent and dark underside of Southern California's sunny high life. Lyons shows us California's rich and its powerful, belly-side up, bloated on their own excesses and greed.

Among the first echelon of contemporary private eye writers, Lyons is noteworthy because he is the only one who does not have either a full-time writing or teaching career. He devotes most of his time to managing Lyon's English Grille, a popular Palm Springs restaurant (on the advice of locals, Asch eats there once in *Castles Burning*). Born in Los Angeles in 1946, Lyons grew up in the saloon industry. His father, Art Lyons, Sr. came to Hollywood in 1936 and with his brother ran the Radio Room (now the Merv Griffin theatre), a renowned nightspot. He bought and managed several other bars and nightclubs in LA before the family moved to Palm Springs in 1957.

Art Lyons, Jr. attended the University of California at Santa Barbara, obtaining a BA in political science in 1967. Following graduation he entered the graduate program in international relations at UCLA but quit before the completion of one semester to return to the family's restaurant business. It was at that time that he tried his hand at writing science fiction. In a 1981 interview with Jeff Pierce for the *Willamette Week*, Lyons recalls:

> I thought for a long time that I could write science fiction .... And I'll never forget one [story]. I don't even remember what the story was, but I wrote to a throwaway, mimeographed little magazine in Regina, Saskatchewan .... And the editor wrote me a letter saying 'Don't ever send him anything again'; it was the worst story he'd ever read in his life, and I had my nerve to send him this ....
>
> But I just kept writing short stories. None of them ever got published. I came close a couple of times, and started getting some complimentary notes back. Then I started to work on *The Second Coming*.

The Second Coming (Dodd, Mead, 1970) was Lyon's first and still most widely read book. It is a nonfictional study of the concepts of devil worship and witchcraft that investigates the origins of Satanic groups and sporadic reappearance at various times in history. Lyons concentrates on the modern-day resurgence of Satanic groups in the US and Europe, paying special attention to Anton La Vey's Church of Satan which at the time claimed more than 7000 members. Because of the acclaim he received for *The Second Comng,* Lyons has served as a special consultant to several California law enforcement agencies on murder cases with suspected occult involvements.

The first two Asch novels continue to explore cultic phenomena and the willingness of people to give themselves over to some group in order to become more powerful. In *The Dead are Discrete* (1974) Asch investigates the torture murders of a young woman and her lover. The police are convinced that the woman's jealous husband is the murderer. Asch, however, wades through a morass of witchcraft, a Satan worshipping cult, Tarot cards, Egyptology, porno movies and necrophiles and finally exposes a different villain. In *All God's Children* (1975), a teenage runaway bounces back and forth between the Satan's Warriors, a vicious motorcycle gang, and the World of God commune, a sect of nasty Jesus freaks. The apparent dichotomy of these two groups evaporates as the reader comes to discover their basic equivalency in evil. Lyons comments: "I was always interested in the dark side of man. The people who are the most dangerous to me are the people who refuse to acknowledge that that side of them exists. Kill-for-Christ evangelists always get to me, the hypocrisy of it. You have to face the darkness in yourself, realize what you're capable of in order to purge yourself of it or be able to control it."

A central topic in the Asch series and one which Lyons believes has been overlooked in his work is *power*: how it's acquired, used and coveted. And how it becomes perverted. Usually, it's power wielded by groups, an indication of Lyons' fascination with social psychology. The ability to capture the influence and atmosphere of a subculture has become a Lyons trademark. *The Killing Floor* (1976) examines the meat packing industry and nefarious syndicate infiltration. *Dead Ringer* (1977) is as evocative a depiction of professional boxing as you'll ever find, and *Castles Burning* (1980) is a deft protrayal of kinky sex, dope-peddling and empty-soul psychopathy among the narcissistic. *Hard Trade* (1981) delivers a hard knock against politics and politicians, California style. It also gives new meaning to the term "child rearing." *At the Hands of Another* (1983) concerns the liability-accident industry and the world of crooked doctors, shady lawyers and ambulance chasers.

Power as the prime motivator is established from the beginning of the series when Lewis T. Gorman, a man of fabulous wealth and some very bent sexual tastes, boasts, "There are people who are superior and there are people who are inferior. The former rule the latter. It has always been that way and it will always be that way, no matter what social theories you may wish to expound to sugar-coat the fact."

That Lyons is half Jewish and created Asch in that same image accounts for his sensitivity to the oppressive potential of groups or tyrannical individuals. At one point Asch admits a strong cultural bond to his father's Judaism, speculating that he is "plugged into some common pool of paranoia shared by all Jews ... if there was a God up there watching over us, he had to be dressed in black leather." He expresses "a feeling of personal responsibility for being human and witnessing the cruelty and callousness of humanity."

Asch possesses the ideal PI pedigree. One critic called him "the very composite of the species, *genus Californiensis.*" Now in his mid-thirties, he is physical enough to protect himself from rough handling, but he does not play the enforcer. A former newspaper reporter for the *Chronicle,* Asch was fired for refusing to name his source for an article which broke a criminal case wide open. He was then sentenced to six months in jail for contempt by a judge "who had a castration complex and didn't think the First Amendment had anything to do with freedom of the press." The six months in stir has left him claustrophobic. He's been a private detective since 1969.

A self-proclaimed cynic ("things that make other people go wow usually just make me shrug or get me down on my hands and knees to look under the table for wires"), Asch is prone to existential questions and crises of identity. Across the years his brashness has given way to introspection, his ego bruised by the realization of his life's limits. Near the end of *The Killing Floor* he confides to Sarah, a woman he'd been involved with recently:

You just go on living, doing whatever it is you do and it's not that bad. It only gets bad when you wonder about what it all means ... and face the fact that none of it means a fucking thing.

For Asch life is "all an underwater bicycle race." But still he survives. He's willing to take life as it comes. When asked what he really wants out of life, Asch replies in true existentialist spirit:

I guess I'm trying to absorb existence. Most people I know don't have the capacity to do even that, life never touches them. It's like they're standing in the middle of a river in a rubber suit and the water's rushing by them but they never get wet. I don't know, I guess I'm just trying to get wet.

Despite the pessimism and self-deprecation, Asch is resilient in a way that links him with Stephen Greenleaf's Marsh Tanner. He does not drag us to despair. A Laker game on the radio, a chance to read a little Algren, a bottle of Kentucky bourbon, some good sex. They help him make it through the night.

In his interview with Jeff Pierce, Lyons described Asch as "doing something he doesn't particularly like and being stuck at it because he's good at it." Asch behaves like an authentic private eye. Lyons calls him "a plodder, a paper man and a good listener." Asch hardly ever is the beneficiary of the hot tip or the anonymous disclosure. He's not a lucky detective. Asch follows the paper trail we all leave behind. Into the County Assessor's Office, the Department of Motor Vehicles, the County Clerk's office, Asch is relentless. He is also a good listener. He almost never wisecracks, especially to prospective clients or people from whom he needs information. He is polite, almost solicitious. He is an excellent interviewer who'll encourage a client to fix him coffee simply because some people talk more when their hands are busy. One senses that Asch takes pride in his own competence, and he is well-respected by the cops for the most part. Few fictional PIs earn or receive as much cooperation from the police as Asch does.

As a stylist Lyons delivers some knockouts. He has raised death scenes to the level of art form. They are brutally beautiful, written with an eye for that one detail that brands the image into our memory. One such scene dominates *The Killing Floor*:

> The floor was slippery; my feet went out from under me and I went down on my can. I got up with a second effort and when I looked at my hands, I realized what I had slipped on. Blood.
> I turned to run and bumped into something large and heavy and pale.
> Terri wouldn't be making it tomorrow. She was completely naked but there was no sex in her now. She was hanging upside down from the chain attached to the ceiling and her long black hair nearly touched the floor. Her eyes were glazed and half-shut as if she were fighting a losing battle with sleep. The back of her head had been blown away and her throat had been cut from ear-to-ear.

The bizarre, surreal murder descriptions, always redolent of death in Lyons' novels, belie the debt that they owe to his careful study of *corpora delicti* particularly as set forth in Dr. LeMoyne Snyder's authoritative *Homicide Investigation* (Snyder was one of the original members of Erle Stanley Gardner's *Court of Last Resort*). In fact one of the most distinctive qualities of Lyons' writing is his realist perspective on murder and its motivations. He states, "when somebody dies in my books, the bodies smell." The graphic descriptions of murder in *All God's Children* were based in part on a satanic killing in San Francisco. *Dead Ringer* owes much to Lyons' research on the 1976 murder of heavyweight contender Oscar Bonavena (called by Muhammad Ali "the toughest man I ever fought") at the Mustang Ranch Brothel in Reno, Nevada.

Lyons bases his dislike for the mysteries of Ross Macdonald on the fact that Macdonald's insistence on Oedipal motivations for murder is simply not realistic. He believes that Macdonald tried to make murder too complex when it is really quite straight forward. "People don't murder people for Oedipal reasons. They murder them for revenge, money, or because they're nuts, or [out of] jealousy. There are very simple reasons, usually, for murder .... It boils down to one violent act, and you either have to be cold-blooded or pissed-off to accomplish it. That's why I've always been against very complicated murder set-ups."

Lyons believes that along with Chandler, Hammett, Hemingway and Ross Thomas, the writer who has most influenced him is Nelson Algren, an author unequaled in his ability to evoke the grittiness of the urban subterrain (*A Walk on the Wild Side; The Man with the Golden Arm; Never Come Morning*). Carl Sandburg praised Algren for creating characters "so terribly human that their faces, voices, shames, follies, and deaths linger in your mind with a strong midnight dignity." Lyons' expertise runs along a similar track. He creates scenes that attack our senses. Read any of the Asch novels and you'll squirm at least once. His "mean streets" are nightmares so real that they turn us inward, if only briefly, to that scariest of places—our own souls.

Spenser, The Autonomous Knight—Robert Parker

Among the many fine private eye writers debuting in the 1970s, Robert B. Parker has attained the greatest celebrity status—pictured in *Time* and many newspaper features, reviewed in *Newsweek* and *Playboy* and praised by such notables as Yale University President Bartlett Giamatti. A "reformed and redeemed academician," Parker resigned his Professorship in English at Northeastern University in 1978 to devote full time to his writing. He lives in Lynnfield, Massachusetts with his wife, Joan, who is an education specialist for the Massachusetts Department of Education. They have two sons—David, a professional dancer in New York City, and Daniel, a theater major at Sarah Lawrence.

Robert Brown Parker was born on September 17, 1932 in Springfield, Massachusetts, to Carroll and Mary Pauline Parker. He received his BA from Colby College in 1954, served with the U.S. Army in Korea for two years and then married Joan Hall in 1956.

After obtaining his MA in English from Boston University in 1957 he worked as a technical writer for Raytheon and an advertising writer for Prudential, wrote industrial films and even founded his own advertising agency. He returned to Boston University to continue his graduate work in 1962 and earned his Ph.D. in English from that institution in 1971. His dissertation, under the direction of Sterling Lanier, was entitled "The Violent Hero, Wilderness Heritage and Urban Reality: A Study of the Private Eye in the Novels of Dashiell Hammett, Raymond Chandler, and

Ross Macdonald." It linked the well-known heroes of the twentieth century hard-boiled novels with James Fenimore Cooper's Leatherstocking, describing them all as men of "armed innocence" who opposed corruption and confronted the world without accepting it.

Parker regards Chandler as the finest writer of hard-boiled fiction, but credits Macdonald with making the genre and its vernacular more acceptable as serious literature. He sees his own work as being in the tradition of Hemingway and Faulkner as well as Fitzgerald and Mark Twain.

Parker has held appointments at Massachusetts State College in Bridgewater, the University of Lowell and Boston University. He joined the faculty of Northeastern University as an Assistant Professor in 1968 and was promoted to Full Professor in 1976. Among his academic writings are *The Personal Response to Literature* (1970; with others) and *Order and Diversity: The Craft of Prose* (1973; with Peter Sandberg). He also wrote *Training with Weights* (1973; with John Marsh).

Shortly after receiving his Ph.D. Parker began to work on his first novel, *The Godwulf Manuscript*, which was published in 1973. It introduced Spenser—no first name and with an *s* like the English poet—a middle-aged, heavyweight who turned private eye after having been fired from the Suffolk County DA's office for insubordination.

Spenser is the consummate tough-guy, transplanted from Southern California to Boston. He is one bad dude who metes out the punishment and the wisecracks in equal (over)doses. He pursues adversaries with a vengeance and a physical competence which is seldom exceeded. Sharp-tongued and large of muscle, Spenser can lay on the big hurt. Parker admits that "sometimes Spenser administers justice for the sheer pleasure of it." He is physically, interpersonally and intellectually aggressive—a Dick Cavett with biceps. A typical confrontation begins with Spenser taunting a foe with smart-aleck repartee and then kicking the guy's raised dander into the next zip code:

From his place Sonny said, "Let me have him, Mr. Broz."

"What are you going to do, Sonny," I said, "sweat all over me till I beg for mercy?"

Phil made his little sighing sounds again. Sonny put his trench coat carefully on the arm of the couch and started toward me. I saw Phil look at Broz and saw Broz nod.

"You been crying for this, you sonova bitch," Sonny said.

I stood up. Sonny was probably thirty pounds heavier than I was and a lot of it was muscle. But some of it was fat, and quickness didn't look to be Sonny's strong suit. He swung a big right hand at me. I rolled away from it and hit him in the middle of the face twice with left hooks, getting my shoulder nicely behind both of them, feeling the shock all the way up into my back. Sonny was tough. It rocked him but he didn't go down. He grabbed at my shirtfront with his left hand and clubbed at me with his right. The punch glanced off my shoulder and caught me under the left eye. I broke his grip by bringing my clenched fists up under his forearm, and then drove my right forearm against the side of his jaw. He stumbled back two steps and sat down.

Spenser is proud of his skill in combat, but will usually not gloat over defeating an opponent, viewing his prowess as just something he knows how to do better than most other guys. At one point he says, "I've always been able to do most of what I needed to do." He takes the fighting victories for granted as we would hope he will take his defeats should they ever come along—"Everybody gets scared when they are overmatched in the dark; it's not something to be ashamed of . . . ."

Beyond the fist-fights is the more troubling matter of Spenser's penchant for firearms. He carries a gun everywhere, favoring a .38 Smith & Wesson. And in approximately half the books he kills people with it. Although at one point he says that one should never kill except involuntarily, he later relaxes this belief to a more utilitarian level: "I've never shot anyone when it wouldn't have been a lot worse not to." Spenser believes violence can be an honorable alternative and his reading material includes Richard Slotkin's *Regeneration Through Violence*. There are times when he loses control and becomes downright vicious.

Like most great private eyes, Spenser is not a clue-finder. He is a man of action with an M.O. reminiscent of the leading pulp heroes. "I take hold of one end of the thread and I keep pulling it till it's all unraveled" (*The Godwulf Manuscript*). He follows his instinct, a true believer in the wisdom of his gut reactions. Impulse and follow-through. Serve and volley. Because the impulses of the hero are almost always good ones, the need for reflection or caution is minimized; "over the years I've found that stirring things up was better than not. When things got into motion I accomplished more. Or I seemed to."

The result of this style is the diminution of plot in Parker's writing. The Spenser novels are less mysteries than what Parker himself calls "romantic adventures." They are not "whodunits" but "howdunits" with the question directed at how will Spenser act in order to do what must be done. Parker admits that "plots are not my strong suit. Plots in the Spenser books are a way for him to manifest what he is. I'm interested in the character and the way he behaves and the way one ought to behave when one encounters the issue of one's time."

A frequent theme in the early novels (*The Godwulf Manuscript*, 1973; *God Save the Child*, 1974; and *Promised Land*, an Edgar winner in 1976) is the harm that falls to children of broken families where parents have lost or forgotten their love. Although Parker is often compared to Chandler and less accurately to Hammett, it is actually Ross Macdonald whom he most resembles in the early novels with their attention to the emotional wasteland of disturbed families and the obligations we have to care for our children. *Early Autumn* (1981), a personal favorite of Parker's, finds Spenser once again concerned with the role of family and the proper way to nurture children. Praised and panned for its homage to Hemingway's themes of male mystique, self-reliance and courage, the story involves Spenser's playing adoptive father to Paul Giacomin, a fifteen-year-old son who is the spoils of a bitter custody battle between parents who care only about defeating each other.

In *Ceremony* (1982), Spenser rescues another child. This time it's April Kyle, a high-school dropout and family reject who's trapped in a violent and degrading world of prostitution and child pornography, a world where "the blood-dimmed tide is loosened, and everywhere the ceremony of innocence is drowned ... (from William Butler Yeats' "The Second Coming"). The book is memorable for its vivid description of Boston's rough-side Combat Zone and for its continuation of the detective-as-surrogate-father motif, this time with a morally painful solution that recognizes that the world just doesn't work the way it should and that some problems have no good solutions. This is a troubling book that takes Spenser's belief in the value of making one's own choices to its most anguishing extremes.

Parker believes that the relationship between men and women is the most interesting topic he knows of, and many of his novels deal with the joys and complications when a man and woman love each other. *Mortal Stakes* (1975), its title drawn from a Robert Frost poem, investigates the jock ethic played out on the fields of major league baseball, but beyond that, it is about the responsibility and sacrifice of marriage. In *Looking for Rachel Wallace* (1980), Spenser is hired to body guard a lesbian author who is on a promotional tour for her latest book. As with *Promised Land*, Parker examines today's modern sex roles and male-female relationships and casts a critical but not unsympathetic look at feminism. Spenser's commitment to his girlfriend Susan Silverman is used to authenticate the possibility and value of a nondestructive, mutually satisfying, romantic relationship.

Rachell Wallace recommends Spenser's body-guarding abilities to Candy Sloan, a Los Angeles TV reporter who is investigating mob corruption in the movie industry. Spenser heads for California and in *A Savage Place* (1981; from Coleridge's "Kubla Khan") does a little more to Candy's body than just guard it. The book is not one of the best in the series because Spenser's role in the case is forced, and the story fails to make the reader think in ways the other novels do. *The Judas Goat* (1978), Spenser's only other prolonged departure from Boston, is also a bit of a disappointment. Hired by the father of a family who was wiped out by a terrorist's bomb thrown into a London restaurant, Spenser goes to Europe and Canada to track down the nine revolutionaries who were responsible. The book never mentions that Spenser is a private eye, and in fact his contract with Hugh Dixon makes him appear to be a modern-day bounty hunter.

The Widening Gyre (1983), the second Spenser title to be taken from Yeats' "The Second Coming," is an important book in the series. It marks a transition in Spenser's relationship with Susan Silverman who embarks on a new career in clinical psychology and begins the process of self-creation that formerly was reserved for Spenser. Although the plot is recycled from the blackmail scam in *Mortal Stakes*, Spenser's solution forces him to the new realization that Susan's pursuit of independence is a strong woman's answer to the need for "a center, a core full of self-certainty and conviction." In the end after questioning his "one pipe dream" Spenser reaffirms his own need to believe in romantic love.

Parker is also the author of *Wilderness* (1979), a non-Spenser tale of danger, pursuit and courage, similar in many ways to James Dickey's *Deliverance*. With his wife, Joan, he has written *Three Weeks in Spring* (1978) about her ordeal with cancer. His most recent novels are *Valediction* (1984), the most elaborate Spenser novel to date, and *Love and Glory* (1983), a three-decade boy-meets-girl, boy-loves-girl, boy-wins-girl love story.

Derived from the Spade—Marlowe—Archer line, Spenser is, like his ancestors, a PI with a code. Parker has established two characteristics as the cardinal markers of Spenser's code: Honor and Autonomy. Parker has described honorable behavior as having no definition, but the hero "knows that there are things a man does and things he doesn't do, and it is not usually very hard to decide which is which. It is often wearisome to choose. The fact that such men elect to be honorable in a dishonorable world makes them heroic. As in most fundamental things that humans care for, honor is indefinable but easily recognized" (*Murder Ink*, p. 125). For Spenser, machismo is honorable behavior, and honorable behavior is a necessity when a man must act for people who lack honor.

Spenser has almost a fetish for autonomy. He hates systems, movements (they "put the cause ahead of the person") and politics ("too abstract for me"). Even his chronic rudeness to clients suggests a defense against his independence being violated. Spenser won't let circumstances dictate his behavior, won't accept anything other than self-directed action.

A special feature of Spenser, however, is his attempt to accommodate his drive for autonomy with his desire to love. This dilemma is one with which the series has always struggled. Spenser wants to believe in the love of families and the love of a man and a woman as parts of his expanded definition of machismo. The result is a sentimental character of mythic dimensions. Spenser is first and foremost a hero, a man able to integrate vastly disparate qualities, to live by firm principles which by their seeming incompatibility cause him to grow.

Spenser is our most androgynous private eye. A weightlifter, carpenter, jock and dedicated apostle of machismo, he is also an accomplished chef, an unabashed romantic and a literate man with considerable sexual and social sensitivity. He swigs Amstel beer one day, tips Pouilly-Fuisse the next. *Playboy* dubbed him the "Alan Alda of detectivedom." A coin with both sides shiny, Spenser is a romantic ideal—capable of a vigilante's violence at one extreme, a father's devotion at the other.

Spenser's heroism is enhanced by the series' two supporting characters—his steady girlfriend Susan Silverman and his black sidekick Hawk. Introduced in *God Save the Child*, Susan is a very attractive woman. Spenser's stomach does flip-flops whenever he sees her. Susan worked for many years as a high-school guidance counselor, but in *The Widening Gyre* she has returned to Harvard for her Ph.D. in psychology. Patterned after Parker's wife to whom most of his books are dedicated, Susan is a sexy, insightful, intelligent woman who happens to be very much in love with Spenser. They have an egalitarian relationship and engage in witty "Nick and Nora" conversations. Fidelity is their expectation; however, when Spenser proposed marriage "Suze" declined.

Hawk is definitely a horse of a different color. Appearing first in *Promised Land* as a man hired to kill Spenser, Hawk is an old adversary from Spenser's prizefighting days. After refusing to kill Spenser—"there ain't all that many of us left, guys like Spenser and me. He was gone there'd be one less"—Hawk returns in several of the novels as Spenser's hired muscle, a very efficient enforcer for the toughest cases. Hawk is an attention-getter.

Hawk was standing outside the Copley Plaza Hotel wearing a glistening black leather jacket and skintight designer jeans tucked into black cowboy boots that glistened like the jacket. He was a little over 6 feet 2 inches, maybe an inch taller than I was, and weighed about two hundred. Like me. He blended with the august Bostonian exterior of the Copley Plaza like a hooded cobra. People glanced covertly at him, circling slightly as they passed him, unconsciously keeping their distance. He wore no hat and his smooth black head was as shiny as his jacket and boots.

Hawk cares little about the traditional values. He is an amoral, practical hit man who kills and intimidates for a living. He doesn't particularly like to kill; neither does he particularly mind it. He does it as a job. The contrast between Hawk and Spenser is drawn most dramatically in *Early Autumn* where Spenser is faced with the decision of whether to kill the bigtime hood who tried to hire Hawk to murder him.

I said, "Never come near anybody I know. Never send anybody else. You understand me?"
Hawk said, "Ain't good enough. You gotta kill him."
"That right, Harry? Do I? Do I have to kill you?"
Harry shook his head. He made a croaking sound.
"You gotta kill him," Hawk said.
I stepped away from Harry. "Remember what I told you," I said.
Hawk said, "Spenser, you a goddamned fool."
"I can't kill a man lying there on the floor," I said.
Hawk shook his head, spit through the open door into the repair bay, and shot Harry in the middle of the forehead.
"I can," he said.

Parker has been criticized for Hawk, who some see as a subtly racist creation, made to do the dirty work which Spenser avoids. Parker maintains that Hawk represents an archetypal pattern in American myths—the dark companion of the white hero. Jim and Huck Finn, Tonto and the Lone Ranger, Cosby and Culp, Murphy and Nolte. However, the ultimate reason for Hawk's creation is that he illuminates and elevates Spenser. Hawk is in every way the opposite of Susan except for one quality—they both like Spenser. Hawk and Susan represent the extremes of Spenser's personality and because their admiration for him derives from their two opposing viewpoints, they help establish Spenser as the larger-than-life hero Parker intends him to be.

Reader opinion of Parker is highly polarized. You either like him a lot or you don't like him at all. For example, *Booklist* proclaimed *Early Autumn* to contain "some of the most sententious, nonsensical pronouncements on life ever to lope through literature," while Robin Winks lauded the same book for "[telling] it like it is, or might be, in lines that ring mostly true."

Two types of criticisms are raised by Parker's detractors. They either object to Spenser himself, viewing him as a character of unrealistic or unnecessary excesses or they protest what is often described as a pretentious, too literal treatment of social issues, particularly ones involving masculinity and femininity.

If you require your fictional private eyes to behave like real private eyes, if you regard most violence as gratuitous and if you want realism over an idealized fantasy of how men ought to behave, then Parker may not be for you. If, however, you possess a romantic streak which you like to indulge or sentimental impulses to which you can yield, Spenser will please you as a stylish and compassionate avatar of machismo and strong beliefs.

Whatever you may think of Parker as a social critic, he is a talented writer, able to convey heartfelt attitudes about life without sacrificing his novels' entertainment value. This series is fun to read especially when

Spenser lets loose one of his marvelous put-downs that hits your "Gee, I wish-I-had-said-that" bone. Parker has mixed some good medicine—a nifty dose of adventure, romance and heroics. Add Spenser's sass and his good taste and you have one of private eyedom's best anti-depressants and one of its most reliable good reads.

The Nameless Knight—Bill Pronzini

If you wanted to hire Bill Pronzini's private detective, you would have a very hard time for one very big reason. Pronzini does not tell you his name. It's not that he doesn't have a name, we just are never informed of it.

There are 15 novels either published or in press in the "Nameless" series. *The Snatch* (1971) is set in San Francisco but was written while Pronzini was living in Majorca. *The Vanished* (1973) sends the San Francisco detective searching for a missing person in Oregon, California redwood country and Kitzingen, West Germany. *Undercurrent* (1973), *Blowback* (1977), *Twospot* (1978)—co-authored with Collin Wilcox—and *Labyrinth* (1980) all take place in San Francisco-Northern California locales. *Hoodwink* (1981) is noteworthy for its unique setting—a West Coast Pulp Convention. *Scattershot* (1982) uses three unrelated cases that eventually merge to cause "Nameless" a serious personal crisis. *Dragonfire* (1982), regarded by Pronzini as his best novel in the series, tumbles through the squalid side of San Francisco's Chinatown as Nameless searches for the gunman who has put his closest friend, Lieutenant Eberhardt, in a coma. It is a book rich in moral dilemmas, the costs of friendship and the price of honesty. The tenth novel, *Bindlestiff* and *Casefile*, a collection of Nameless short stories, were published in 1983. In *Quicksilver* (1984), Nameless solves his last solo case before taking his first partner into his agency. The newest "Nameless" is *Nightshades*, published by St. Martin's in 1984.

The Nameless novels have a strong sense of continuity. Pronzini achieves a serial effect by aging Nameless accurately across the years and by ending several of the books with a major event still in limbo; will Nameless die of cancer, will he lose his PI license, will he get married? For the answers you must buy the next one.

The Nameless novels are admirably versatile. Some combine the best elements of the Hammett-Chandler tradition with the puzzle plots of the classic detective story; hard-boiled but with a locked room problem (e.g., *Hoodwink, Scattershot*). Others bear faint resemblance to classic detective story plotting (e.g., *Dragonfire*).

More often than we might care to admit, an author's important discoveries may be the benefits of good luck. In our field, for example (psychology), the subtle shadings that appear on the cards of the Rorschach Inkblot Test were the result of a printer's error, a mistake which

Herman Rorschach decided not to correct. Today shading responses are one of the most frequently interpreted associations on the Rorschach.

Pronzini's creation of a detective *sans nom* was likewise serendipitous. He and his editor "could not decide on a name they liked for an overweight, middle-aged Italian PI—Tony Rome was already taken." Regardless of the impetus, Pronzini's final decision to leave the detective nameless was a very wise choice.

The anonymity of the hero is no mere gimmick. It produces several effects and serves some important purposes. Initially, the reader anticipates that either Pronzini will slip and let the cat out of the bag during a routine introduction or phone call or that he will scatter a few tidbits which when carefully assembled will reveal the name to the most attentive readers. Forget it. In no time flat, you won't even be missing what obviously is missing in passages like the following:

The guy on the desk wore a western shirt, complete with green sleeve garters, and an air of professional hospitality. I asked him for the number of Charles Kayabalian's room, and he said he would see if Mr. Kayabalian was in and whom should he say was inquiring. When I said my name he smiled as if pleased by the sound of it and went to a small switchboard and plugged in. I heard him announce me; then he listened ... (*Blowback*).

A second effect of the anonymity is that the novels assume a pronounced autobiographical tone. Of course there's more than a little autobiography in almost all PI fiction, enhanced by the prevalent first person narrative. But Pronzini goes a step further. Without the character's name to act as a filter, we come to feel that we are really listening to Pronzini's voice, seeing his vulnerabilities, pursuing his commitments. Nameless seems more reflection than portrait. In a 1979 interview, Pronzini acknowledged, "what I was really doing was making myself. All the things he does are reflections of me ... what he and I are searching for is something more tangible than abstract ... searching for a way to make life fit."

At the same time leaving the detective unnamed allows Pronzini to use him as a prototype of what a good detective should be—"just a cop," "doing a job, helping people in trouble." He is the Everyman of PI fiction: honest, committed, compassionate and tough. Inspired by the nameless Continental Op but patterned after Thomas B. Dewey's "Mac," he is a hardworking professional.

Nameless grew up in the tough Noe Valley District of San Francisco. Following three undistinguished semesters of college and tours of Army duty in Texas, Hawaii and the South Pacific as a military intelligence noncom, he entered the Police Academy where his obsession with pulp magazines earned him the predictable nicknames of "Philip," "Sam," "Nick" and "Nero." It was at the academy that Nameless met Eberhardt, a fellow trainee, who subsequently becomes Lieutenant of Detectives and Nameless' best friend. "Eb" appears in all the novels; sometimes working on the case at hand, sometimes working through a personal problem like the failure of his marriage (*Hoodwink*), sometimes fighting for his life (*Dragonfire*).

Nameless was a cop for 15 years, the last four with the homicide division. He quit because of "the afternoon I had gone out on a homicidal sequel and found a guy who had hacked his wife and two kids to pieces with an axe." Six months later he passed his examinations and received a private investigator's license, ready to live out his pulp-inspired fantasies of being a lone wolf PI. His one-man agency has never been financially successful. He takes jobs for money but he doesn't turn them down because of a lack of it.

Originally, his office was located on Taylor Street, a couple of blocks off Market, in the Kores building "wedged between a dealer in old coins and a luncheonette." Worn and shabby, heated with steam, and equipped with a grimy hot plate and battered furniture, this office would have done any pulp hero proud. All it lacked was the obligatory office bottle in the right bottom desk drawer; Nameless drinks only beer.

In *Hoodwink*, after the office is vandalized in *Labyrinth*, Nameless moves his quarters to Drumm Street, near the Hyatt and the Embarcadero. Outfitted with chrome chairs, corduroy cushions, a pastel and beige color scheme, the new office is as bland as tapioca. Nameless yearns for his old digs, "dripping with character."

Off hours find him living in Pacific Heights in the same Queen Anne Victorian that he has occupied for more than 20 years, thanks to the graciousness of the long-term landlord who keeps the rent down. His apartment is the sort of mess that requires years of neglect and loneliness to create.

The only sign of decorative concern is the compulsively arranged collection of more than six thousand detective and adventure pulp magazines he has been collecting since his early twenties.

The Nameless series possesses a strong air of unromanticized realism. Pronzini has achieved this quality by concentrating on events which give continuity to the average life. Apart from his too infrequent cases, this detective's life is common, humorless, mundane. Nameless lacks notoriety, flair and sex appeal. Absent are the obvious conventions of the early hard-boiled writers which are so often copied by their modern-day imitators. Nameless never smarts off to clients because he knows they could put him out of operation (when he does break the law in *Labyrinth*, he gets in all sorts of deep water). He infrequently carries a gun and then it's a borrowed .38 that he finally throws into the ocean out of disgust for the violence it represents (*Dragonfire*). Self-conscious about his grayness and middle-age spread, he's too insecure to play the cocksman, and "secretaries are too expensive, especially beautiful ones." Instead, he worries about what the mainstream man worries about: work, health and being loved.

Nameless is the most hypochondriacal of all private eyes. Real or imagined ailments enfeeble him mercilessly. When he eats too much, he suffers heartburn and gas. When he exerts too strenuously, he frets over his sweat stains and body odor. Nausea swirls through his stomach, a vague weakness hits the back of his knees, his eyes look like "green agates floating in partially curdled milk," his phlegm changes color, and he has a lot of headaches and dizzy spells. Having lost an uncle to cancer, his greatest fear is that a relentless smoking habit will earn him his own carcinoma. For years, he tries to quit, unsuccessfully, despite the presence of all the warning signs. Finally in *Blowback*, a lesion on the left lung is discovered and Nameless takes on a case primarily as a diversion from waiting to hear whether the tumor is malignant (the answer waits in the next novel, *Twospot*). His work is "a tried and true antidote for self-pity and depression," it's "the only thing keeping (my) head together." In the course of solving this case Nameless is forced repeatedly to face his own mortality and he is able to purge himself of the fear of death through the realization that more than any illness, a person can victimize himself.

In *Twospot* Nameless emerges a slightly tougher, more hardened person as a result of the lessons learned in *Blowback*: "I was no longer inclined to care too much and too deeply about the lives of suffering of others ... human pain and human folly do not hurt me so much anymore." Maybe so, but Nameless is still brooding, still battling his emotional demons. Fears of rejection, lost youth, loneliness and too little love are constant companions. He is an adult version of the high school outcast—awkward, chubby, unpopular, sadly accepting the cruelty that life can hold for the unlucky. The fantasy world of the pulps and his own attempts to be the detective hero are only partly successful compensations. Although Nameless is a competent detective, he has never received the credit that he deserves. In fact, when he does his best detective work, the cops come down hard on him for making them look bad (*Scattershot*). His successes are due to a combination of Avis-we-try-harder diligence and well-developed investigative abilities. His work patterns are plodding, all nuts-and-bolts. He just gets the job done.

Nameless tries to fill his life with one great love, but here, unlike with his job, overachievement is no answer. In *The Snatch* he proposes for the third time to girlfriend Erika Coates, 37 and twice divorced. For the third time, she spurns him, and her rejection nags Nameless for years.

Unwilling to agree to Erika's ultimatum that he must give up his work to win her, Nameless longs for a woman who will return his love. Wearing his heart on his sleeve, he yearns to beome committed to a relationship. Despite some rare but promising opportunities, his love goes unrequited. Love-starved and sensing that time is running out, Nameless tries so hard to pull people close that he succeeds only in pushing them away. Critics have complained that he behaves like a love-sick, cloying teenager. But that criticism misses the point that Nameless is scared of a future where he still is alone. He acts like desperate people of any age act and it makes us uncomfortable to watch it.

Nameless is one of mystery fiction's sturdiest characters. Although he seems to care more about people than they do for him, he refuses to give in. He remains a gentle, sympathetic man who continues to trust the values he has held for a long time. Pronzini's great achievement is the creation of a private eye who confronts meanness and violence without the bravado, sarcasm and cynicism that has stereotyped the traditional hard-boiled dick. He is the most authentic private eye since Dewey's "Mac"—"working too hard, trying too hard, accomplishing a little but never quite enough."

Unlike his most human and lovable PI, Bill Pronzini does have a name. The youngest of two children, Bill was born in Petulama, California, to Joseph and Helen (Guder) Pronzini on April 13, 1943. He grew up there and went to the local schools. From the outset Bill was destined to be a professional writer. At Kenilworth Junior High, when he was twelve, he wrote his first mystery novel, *Devil's Island Mystery,* modeled after the Happy Hollisters. After High School he attended Santa Rosa Junior College for two years. Then, instead of accepting a Stanford journalism scholarship, he decided that writing was more fun and more educational than formal studying. While still in high school Bill became hooked on the pulp magazines. Like Nameless, he has an extensive private collection. Bill began his professional career as a reporter for the *Petaluma Argus Courier* and wrote news and sports stories from 1957 to 1960.

In 1965 when Bill was 22 years old he married Laura Patricia Adolphson and a year later sold his first story, "You Don't Know What Its Like," to the *Shell Scott Mystery Magazine* (November, 1966). Pronzini enjoyed a modicum of success as a pulp-fiction writer over the next three years. But to make ends meet, he was required to work as a newsstand clerk, a sports reporter, a warehouseman, a typist, a salesman and a civilian guard with the US Marshall's Office. The last named provided the training and experience that authenticated and improved his mystery fiction.

Bill and Laura were divorced in 1966, but his short stories and articles continued to sell. In 1968 Pronzini created the character of Nameless and became a full-time writer the following year. Also in 1969 Bill sold his first novel, *The Stalker,* which received an MWA scroll award for the best first

Bill Pronzini

novel of 1971. Shortly thereafter, Bill moved to the island of Majorca and there met a tour guide, Brunhilde Schier, whom he followed to Germany and married in July 1972. While in the Balerics, Bill expanded his short story character and wrote the first Nameless private eye novel, *The Snatch* (1971). In 1972, Bill managed to crank out several short stories as well as the novel *Panic* and another novel set on Majorca called *A Run in Diamonds* published under the pseudonym of Alex Saxon. In 1972 Bill also published *The Jade Figurine* under the pseudonym of Jack Foxx. In 1974 after returning to San Francisco with his new bride, Bill published *Snowbound* which sold over 12,000 copies in hardcover and over 100,000 in paperback. Following this came *Dead Run* as Foxx (1975), *Games* (1976), *The Running of Beasts* with Barry Malzberg (1976) and *Freebooty* also as Foxx (1976). Another collaboration with Malzberg resulted in *Acts of Mercy* (1977). *Hoodwink*, the seventh Nameless novel, was voted the Best Private Eye novel of 1981 by members of the Private Eye Writers of America. Pronzini was also elected the first President of this organization.

One unfathomable mystery is how one so prolific can write so consistently well. Bill Pronzini is prolific! Francis M. Nevins, Jr. called him the "last pulpster," like the pulp-writers of old who were paid only 1/2 to 1¢ per word and had to write steadily to stave off starvation. Bill learned early the rudiments of the pulpster's craft and has become, in Nevin's words, "tirelessly prolific behind the typewriter." Thus far Bill has published over 30 novels and around 275 short stories and articles. He has written in a variety of genres—mysteries, westerns, science fiction and sex-epics—not only by himself but with a number of collaborators. Edward Hoch has noted that probably no other writer has collaborated so successfully with so many different partners. As an editor he is equally skilled whether he edits and compiles alone as in the superb *Midnight Specials: An Anthology for Train Buffs and Suspense Aficionados* (1977) or the creepy *Werewolf: A Chrestomathy of Lycanthropy* (1979) or with Joe Gores *Tricks and Treats* (1976) or Barry Malzberg, *Dark Sins Dark Dreams: Crime in Science Fiction* (1978), *The End of Summer: Science Fiction of the Fifties* (1979) and *Shared Tomorrows: Science Fiction in Collaboration* (1979).

He has collaborated with Barry Malzberg in the production of 23 separate short stories and with Jeffrey Wallman in the writing of 30. Of these 30 stories half appeared under their combined first names—William Jeffrey—the others under the pennames Rick Renault, Robert Hart Davis and in the Westerns, as you might surmise, as by Romer Zane Grey. Bill has also collaborated successfully with Michael Kurland and in addition to the pen names Alex Saxon and Jack Foxx he has used the name Russell Dancer for at least one short story. Pronzini and Marcia Muller are co-authors of *Double* (1984), in which Nameless and Sharon McCone team up.

Like any writer Bill wants his work to be taken seriously. In his words,
"Basically, I'm an entertainer. My responsibility as a writer is to give the
reader honest prose and valid insights. He or she does with them what they
will. A book gives someone some pleasure for a couple of hours. But I go
back in search for worthiness. I haven't done much. That's the desire that
keeps me going ... to be respected and taken seriously". Pronzini admits
he would most like to be remembered for his Nameless novels. "In these
novels I have tried to create a character and a world in which people
matter—a character who cares about human life and human values. I
deplore man's inhumanity to man and I condemn the waste of the
potential we see all about us. In Nameless I see myself and all of us who,
being human, always seem to be in hot water. Nameless hates unnecessary
violence and seldom uses a gun—only when he has to."

Pronzini is not only an admirer of the great mystery traditionalists but
he is a dedicated student as well. This is admirably illustrated—along with
his puckish sense of humor—in his recent tribute to the trashier side of
mystery fiction called *Gun in Cheek* (1982). His own work, he feels, has
been most influenced by the pulp writers and literary notables like Conrad,
Hemingway and Steinbeck. He is particularly indebted to Evan Hunter,
Fredric Brown and Thomas Dewey, whose Mac Robinson, in Bill's
opinion, is the most underated Private Eye of all.

The Proletarian Knight (Moses Wine)—Roger L. Simon
The son of a physician, Roger L. Simon was born in New York City on
November 22, 1943. After graduating from Dartmouth College in 1964
with a BA in English, Simon obtained a Master of Fine Arts in playwriting
from Yale University in 1967. He then moved to Los Angeles and
concentrated on his screenwriting. Among his screenplays are the film
version of *The Big Fix* starring Richard Dreyfuss as Moses Wine and
Bustin' Loose featuring Richard Pryor. In 1965 Simon married Dyann
Asimow whom he met while they were both at Yale. They have two sons.

Prior to his Moses Wine series, Simon wrote two novels, *Heir* in 1968
and *The Mama Tass Manifesto* (1970). According to David Geherin's *Sons
of Sam Spade* (1980), which includes an in-depth study of Simon's work,
these first two novels display several of the themes that emerge in the Moses
Wine novels: the social and political inequities of American society, the
contradictions between socialist ideology and material success and the
temptations of wealth which interfere with the commitments of purists
whether they be radicals, artists or detectives. Although Simon spouts a
Marxist line, he conceded to Geherin, "I live a very bourgeois lifestyle. I
like money. In other words, I don't stand behind my beliefs, I only write
them."

The conflicts between radical beliefs, middle-class duties and richman luxuries are constantly challenging Moses Wine, whose debut in *The Big Fix* (1973) won Simon a Mystery Writers of American Special Award and Great Britain's John Creasey Award for Best First Crime Novel. The novel moved Ross Macdonald to proclaim Simon "the most brilliant new writer of private detective fiction who has emerged in some years." Wine is a graduate of Berkeley but his true alma mater is the peace movement of the 1960s where as a student protestor he belonged to the Fair Play for Cuba Committee and the Committee to Free Caryl Chessman. After dropping out of law school, afraid he'd turn out "like my New York relatives, riding through Harlem in their late-model Lincoln limousines," Moses began his PI career by helping a lawyer prove a cop beat up a peace demonstrator. Now he's a long-haired, in-debt, denim-draped "people's detective" who spends as much time stoking his hash pipe as he does investigating his cases.

The Big Fix opens when Lila Shea, a bed and soul mate from the SDS days, shows up at Moses' front door and recruits him to help out a liberal senator whose presidential primary campaign is about to be derailed by the unsolicited endorsement of Howard Eppis, an over-the-hill radical cut from Abbie Hoffman cloth.

Wine's activist ideals and bohemian affectations are always bumping into some very conventional concerns—like his jealousy of ex-wife Suzanne, who when she's not sexercising with her guru Madas is traipsing off to Europe to find herself, or his babysitting with sons Jacob and Simon always with the empty stomach and full diapers. Moses' wavering political commitments are kept on the straight-and-narrow by Sonya Lieberman, his 76-year-old aunt whose steadfast Marxism survived internment in a Stalinist labor camp.

The Big Fix sets up a gallery of political bo-bos and hypocrites for Simon to knock down, but the plot suffers from too many cliches and the hopeless improbability that a U.S. presidential aspirant would hire a shaggy proletariat like Moses Wine to drive around LA in a 1947 Buick in order to thwart the bombing of a freeway.

Improbabilities aside, Moses returns in *Wild Turkey* (1975), now a counter-culture hero of sorts. A feature article in *Rolling Stone* is planned, and the Buick has been traded for a '65 XKE. When a New York City anchorwoman is found murdered, Wine is hired to clear Jock Hecht, an aging sexologist with "Faustian lusts," who is the prime suspect. Hecht's alibi is that he was groping with a nude lovely at the Kama Sutra Sexual Phrontistery, but she can't be located until it's too late for her and Hecht who's found with a bullet in his head and a suicide note in his typewriter. The action also features a band of Cuban kidnappers and Cynthia Hardwick, a sex therapist whose name suggests she has a firm grip on her treatment goals. Sex is the target of Simon's satire in *Wild Turkey*, the way politics was in the first novel. For all the excesses of the sexual freedom movement, its proponents can remain just as empty and unfulfilled as the sexually repressed. Simon shows us a society so totally preoccupied with sexual gratifications that its people sacrifice their individuality and dignity. Wine is so frustrated by it all that he crawls under the covers and starts to masturbate. Although Simon has his plot under better control here, the characterization is reduced to transparent imitations of real-life celebrities.

In *Peking Duck* (1979) Moses joins up with a group of 13 archetypal Californians who under the spiritual leadership of Aunt Sonya are making a friendship tour to China, itself still reeling from the Cultural Revolution and the downing of *The Gang of Four*. Moses makes the trip in order to rediscover his liberal ideals, now further threatened by his recent purchase of a Porsche 911 that Aunt Sonya scorns as "the Gestapomobile."

Simon, who visited China in 1977, combines travelogue with a lot of wisdom according to Chairman Mao, but in the process he neglects the mystery. The book is half over before the central crime, involving the theft of a priceless Han Dynasty duck from a Peking museum is committed, but by then it's too late to rescue the reader's interest. Wise man say, "Maoist dogma not make good thriller."

Tastes in wine are hard to predict. This one is strictly sixties vintage, albeit well-aged. If those were your favorite years and you tend to think grass is something you hide in the refrigerator, then this Wine's for you. On the other hand, if you don't like ex-hippies in your neighborhood, chances are you won't like them in your mysteries either and will soon tire of Wine's funkiness. Simon's attempt to modernize the hard-boiled private eye by giving him a sixties mentality was an interesting innovation but one with little staying power. Wine is now more dated than the Continental Op, created almost a half century earlier.

Another Midwestern Knight Harry Stoner—Jonathan Valin

Southeast on Interstate 74, one hundred miles from Indianapolis lies Cincinnati, one of the Midwest's most interesting and least appreciated cities. With its strong German and Catholic backgrounds, Cincinnati is proud of its sedate neighborhoods, its gourmet restaurants and its all-American image. It is middle-class and old-fashioned and doesn't try too hard to hide its conventional morality. More ambivalent about the "strict moralist who hides inside me" is Cincinnati's tough-guy for hire, Harry Stoner, who peers into the shadows and dark corners that Cincinnati pretends it doesn't have.

Harry Stoner is a 6'3" hulk who weighs about 215 pounds, has the face of a busted statue and is a self-described "sucker for romance." A veteran of Vietnam where he was an Army MP, Stoner became a private dick following stints with Pinkertons and the DA's office. He drinks Scotch, hangs out at the Busy Bee, constantly listens to a Zenith Globemaster in his 2 1/2 room apartment in the Delores Building in Clifton and drives a Pinto.

Stoner is a child of the sixties who has retained that often infuriating blend of idealism and intolerance that was so common among the student protestors of that decade. Now in his mid-thirties, Harry still struggles with his desire to be unconventional and independent on the one hand and his almost reflexive morality on the other. Although Harry often belittles Cincinnati for its uptight Puritanism, he has to confront this same tendency in himself. When that control is lost, he begins to equate justice with revenge and sets out for one of the *mano a mano* finales that typify the novels. In an August 15, 1982 feature in the *Cincinnati Enquirer* written by Michael Paolercis, Valin described Stoner as follows:

> He's as moral as the city wants to be. He's not happy with it. He's a typical product .... He's a Cincinnatian. There's no question about it.

Valin's fire-fight endings have become a too easy resolution for an author who denies that his violence is ever gratuitous and claims that "the protagonist in a detective story is by convention the kind of man who reserves judgment" (*The Writer*, August, 1981). With the exception of Robert Parker's Spenser there is probably not a modern detective who is less hesitant to pass judgment and to kill for justice's sake than Stoner. In *Natural Causes*, the one novel that doesn't culminate in Stoner killing the villain, it's only because he gets there too late to realize his ambition—"I want to kill somebody, anyway." Illustrative of Valin's penchant for a concluding conflagration is the kill-or-be-killed scene between Stoner and Rafe, the sadistic black thug in *The Lime Pit*.

It is Valin's reliance on violence as an ultimate solution that cheats Stoner of the chance to be a hero rather than a near vigilante. The result is a character who somehow seems slightly dislocated, shaped by someone who doesn't trust in heroes to appeal to an audience who does.

Valin portrays Cincinnati's neighborhoods superbly throughout the series—trendy Mt. Adams, middle-class Clifton, rough-side Newport, Kentucky and Hyde Park, one of the city's most lovely areas. Behind Cincinnati's carefully tended facade of decency and civic achievement is the city Stoner sees—full of sexual predators, psychos and greedy hypocrites. Stoner's social conscience finds an easy target in Cincinnati, which he regards as "small-minded and drab and about as hopelessly parochial as any large group of people can be." We're introduced to this world in *The Lime Pit* (1980), Valin's first novel, when Stoner is hired by an old, dying man to find a missing 16-year-old girl who'd been living with him for the past year. The plot involves the well-worn sexploitation theme perhaps a little more sordid here than usual but told in a natural, unmannered style that is a Valin trademark. His narrative voice is among the very best of any current mystery novelist. The technique is nearly invisible so Stoner sounds fresh and realistic. He's seldom pretentious, a frequent character flaw in hard-boiled types.

Harry's second case, *Final Notice* (1980) involves his search for a maniac who's been mutilating the pictures of women in the art books at the Cincinnati library. Assisted by Kate Davis, a young female detective, Harry soon suspects a link between the library vandalism and an unsolved sex slaying in the area two years earlier. Stoner becomes convinced of the killer's identity based in part on the advice of a forensic psychiatrist who educates Harry about the etiology and correlates of violent psychopathology. Dr. Benson Howell's profile of the Ripper personality is clinically perceptive and factually accurate, the equivalent of the content you'll find in only the best abnormal psychology textbooks.

In *Dead Letter* (1981) Harry is hired by Dr. Daryl Lovingwell, a physics professor at the University of Cincinnati who suspects that his politically radical daughter, Sarah, has stolen some top secret government papers from his safe. Harry's client soon turns up dead, the victim of an apparent suicide that proves predictably enough to be a murder. Lovingwell was not without his enemies nor were they without their motives for killing him. Adultery, blackmail and espionage are all encountered as Stoner plows through a morass of sordid family secrets and dirty tricks in academia.

Day of Wrath (1982), Valin's fourth novel, is the most violent in the series. Valin says he intended the book to be a modern-day story of Orpheus and Eurydice and therefore deliberately made the climactic scene as hellish as he could. The plot is recycled from *The Lime Pit*, and while every author of PI fiction can be forgiven his one story about the libidinous teenage runaway, two such efforts are not so easily excused. The novel aims some of Valin's sharpest arrows at the conforming, shallow lives of the middle class for which Cincinnati becomes an emblem.

Harry goes to Hollywood in *Natural Causes* (1983) to investigate the death of Quentin Dover, the head writer for a daytime soap opera. It might have been an accident or a suicide or a murder, but the Cincinnati-based company United American, sponsor of the show, wants Harry to find out and help it maintain its squeaky clean image as much as possible. The premise gives Valin the chance to write about the inside workings of the daytime television industry, a setting he observed for a year while serving as a script consultant for an afternoon soap. The Hollywood of every Cincinnatian's fantasies is on florid display here—too much money and drugs and sex being chased by a group of jealous, callous narcissists with all the impulse control of leeches loose in a blood bank. Television's emptiness is mimicked by real life, or is it the other way around?

Natural Causes continues one unfortunate trend in the series—the declining quality of the women in Stoner's life. Jo Riley, the Busy Bee hostess in *The Lime Pit*, and Kate Davis, the sexy detective in *Final Notice*, are Harry's emotional equals, mature women with whom a sustained relationship might be possible. But in *Dead Letter* Harry goes for Sarah Lovingwell, his client's mixed-up daughter and possible killer, and then in *Day of Wrath* tumbles with Grace, a young, flakey, skin-and-bones jazz groupie who for reasons not immediately clear make him "feel a little adolescent fire in my own veins." Harry slips further in *Natural Causes* when he finds himself unable to resist Quentin Dover's voluptuous, air head wife, a woman whose nymphomaniacal behavior leads her mother-in-law to claim "she probably qualifies under state law as a public utility." Stoner's women used to be people too, just like Harry. Valin should let them return.

Jonathan Valin was born in Cincinnati, Ohio, in 1948. Shortly thereafter his family moved to Pittstown, Pennsylvania, and then Hawaii where his father, Sigmund, was a psychologist at the Oahu Territorial Hospital. After his father's death, Valin moved back to Cincinnati with his sister, Julie, and his mother, Marcella, who is an elementary school teacher in Cincinnati. Valin graduated from Walnut Hills High School and went to the University of Cincinnati where he met and married Katherine in 1971.

He earned an MA in English literature from the University of Chicago in 1974, returned to Cincinnati for a brief time to try his hand at professional writing and then took a position as a teaching fellow at Washington University in St. Louis, where he studied for a doctoral degree. It was during his two-and-a-half years at Chicago that he discovered Raymond Chandler and became excited about detective fiction.

In St. Louis, Valin began to write a novel based on the life of a woman married to a pro football star. After it was learned that the woman's story was not totally truthful, Valin discontinued the project, but his agent, Dominick Abel, asked to see anything else he was working on. Valin sent him the first 50 pages of *The Lime Pit*, Abel liked it and asked him to finish it as quickly as possible. Two weeks later Valin completed the manuscript, and Dodd, Mead took it within a month. At the time *The Lime Pit* was published, Valin had two other Stoners already written under the titles *Full Fathom Five* and *The Celestial Railroad*. By moving the setting from Chicago back to Cincinnati, Valin reworked *Full Fathom Five* into *Dead Letter*. Parts of *The Celestial Railroad* were inserted into several of the novels, most notably *Day of Wrath*.

The Stoner series is very popular abroad and has now been translated into ten languages. In addition, Valin has been nominated for Great Britain's coveted Silver Dagger award and received a Norma Lowery Memorial Fund Prize in 1978 for "Replay," one of his short stories.

Valin is the best mystery writer to come from Cincinnati since Fredric Brown. He casts memorable characters and draws vivid scenes, and it all hangs together because of that well-tuned voice that harmonizes Harry's insights with his Midwestern rhythms. Although Valin's conception of the hero has led him to some excesses, his mysteries are entertaining shockers that also convey a point of view on the quality of modern urban life. Valin's talent as a story-teller is that he produces real visceral thrills but never punctures them with too prickly social commentary.

Chapter VII
The Modern Knights—Best of the Rest

THIS CHAPTER FEATURES ADDITIONAL authors in the post-1970 period. In general, these private eyes have not sustained a lengthy series, either because the author moved on to other pursuits (e.g., Bergman) or because the character is still too new (e.g., Byrd, Schorr). In other cases the authors have not attained the literary quality or compelling characterization that distinguishes the writers in the previous chapter. However, they have given us some first-rate private eye yarns, often with very clever twists of the standard PI formula.

Here are the rest of the best Modern Knights.

Joe Goodey—Charles Alverson

In *Goodey's Last Stand* (1975) Joe Goodey's transformation from policeman to private detective required only one day, easily the fastest career change in private eye annals. Goodey lost his badge because he mistakenly shot an innocent old night watchman who just happened to be the mayor's cousin. But the very next day he gets his private eye's license in order to help the police conduct a discreet investigation of the murder of Tina D'Oro, a burlesque dancer who is also the mayor's mistress and who has a diary with his honor's name prominently featured throughout to prove it. The premise of the PI assisting the police investigate a sensitive crime is handled as effectively here as it is in Elliot Lewis' Fred Bennett series. Although the mayor initially is the most likely suspect, Goodey's attention is soon drawn to a list of suspects which includes an elderly gangster who fathered Tina's baby, a plastic surgeon who specializes in building bodies for girls like Tina and some dirt-bag flesh peddlers in the North Beach district.

In his second case (*Not Sleeping, Just Dead*; Playboy Press, 1979), Goodey enters a Big Sur commune run by a charismatic play-god named Hugo Fischer to investigate the death of a young girl with a drug problem. His client is the girl's rich grandfather whose deep pocketbook has been wide open to Fischer's Institute. It's fairly standard PI fare, but the development of Rachel Schute, Goodey's girlfriend who appeared in the first novel, provides some interesting characterization.

Goodey is an amusing character; a free spirit and a wisecracker but not annoyingly so. He's sort of a Spenser who's not hung up on himself and

270

who's not into machismo. Divorced, but reluctantly so; poor, but resigned to it; Goodey is a decent guy who makes an appealing hero. From his old Morris convertible to his apartment above a Chinese grocery store, his existence borders on the scruffy but never becomes despairing. He's a college dropout who hasn't done anything since the Army but be a cop. He has qualms about making money off other people's misfortunes, but he's not especially obsessed with heroics:

> Don't mistake me for a moralist, Rachel. You know better. I'm just an ex-cop scuffling after enough money to stay alive and operating. If some justice gets done in the process, that's fine. It makes the client feel better about paying.

There are stylistic echoes of Chandler throughout the two Goodey novels but they stop short of sounding pretentious. One scene is a particularly clever homage to Chandler. Goodey is summoned to the Mark Hopkins Hotel to see an ageing detective who's recreated his office in one of the hotel's suites, complete with hatrack, gooseneck telephone and a chess game in progress. If the chess set isn't a giveaway, the name of the detective is—Marley Phillips.

Phillips gives Goodey some background:

> "I expect you know something about me, Goodey," he said, "but let me fill you in a bit. For nearly thirty years I was a private eye in Los Angeles. I never got rich, but I did all right. I never took a dirty dollar or chased too hard after a clean one. There are some old cops, retired now or maybe dead, who'd have told you I was a sneaky, crooked son of a bitch, but they'd have been wrong. I lied to a few cops in my day, held out on them. But I never sold a client out or betrayed a confidence. I've seen the inside of a cell on that account."

And then he challenges Goodey to uphold the chivalric traditions he had perfected: " 'What I really want to know, Goodey . . . is are you going to turn out to be a shitheel like most of the dicks in San Francisco, or are you trying to be a real private investigator?' "

Alverson's first book, *Fighting Back,* published in 1973 by Bobbs-Merrill is a story about a man struggling to defend his fledgling business against the intrusion of a two-bit hood who tries to strong-arm his way into a partnership. Although it is not a PI novel, the book involves a brutal private detective named Alec Hoerner whose vigilante tactics place him outside the genre's usual boundaries.

Charles Elgin Alverson was born in Los Angeles in 1935 to William and Mabel Alverson. He received his BA in English from San Francisco State in 1960 and an MS in Journalism from Columbia University in 1964. He worked as a reporter for five years with *The Wall Street Journal* and was a staff writer for one year with the San Francisco *Chronicle.* Since 1969

Alverson has lived in Britain where he has worked as a freelance journalist and author. He has been a contributor to *The Sunday Telegraph Magazine, The International Herald-Tribune, Rolling Stone Magazine, Penthouse, Encyclopedia Britannica,* and has served as editor for *Vole Magazine* and *Insight Magazine.* Among his writing credits is a novelization of *Time Bandits* (1981). Alverson says that he "made Joe me with more balls, Philip Marlowe with a receding hairline and no illusions." He also claims that there will be no more Goodey books because Joe "can't stand the pace." That's the end unless Alverson makes good on his other idea of bringing Joe back to life as the first PI ghost.

Jack LeVine—Andrew Bergman

Andrew L. Bergman was born in New York City in 1945 to Rudy and Ruth Bergman. He earned a BA in history from Harpur College and then attended the University of Wisconsin where he was awarded a Ph.D. in American Intellectual History in 1970. His dissertation was entitled *Depression America and Its Movies,* and it examined the relationship of American films during the 1930s to such traditional American ideals as class equality and mobility. It was published by New York University Press in 1971 under the title *We're In The Money.*

After leaving Wisconsin, Bergman worked for a time with the publicity department of United Artists. He has written a biography of James Cagney (Pyramid, 1975). However, he is probably best known for his screenwriting where he has concentrated his efforts since 1975. His two most famous films are *Blazing Saddles,* co-written with Mel Brooks and Richard Pryor, and *The In-Laws,* starring Peter Falk and Alan Arkin. He also wrote and directed *So Fine* (1981) starring Ryan O'Neal, and recently finished the screenplay for a Warner Brothers film featuring George Burns.

Bergman has written two private eye novels: *The Big Kiss-off of 1944* (1974) and *Hollywood and LeVine* (1975). Both feature Jacob ("Jack") LeVine, a fat, balding, Jewish private eye who lives in Queens and works out of an office at Broadway and 51st Street. LeVine is an altogether unexceptional fellow who gets diarrhea on a stakeout and deprecates himself as a "schmendrick," "a basic model 1944 prole" and "a stocky Queens Jew sitting around in his underwear." He smokes Lucky Strikes, sweats a lot and has two preferred pastimes: baseball and poker. He drinks a Blatz everyday.

Levine is a man without glamor, doing a job without tribute. At one point he says, "People hire a dick to do dirty work, like they pay a colored girl to clean up the john . . . . And they do it for the same reason: neither of us counts. We do a job and disappear."

Both LeVine novels are an entertaining mixture of comedy, well-controlled parody, history and ably plotted mystery. Although *The Big Kiss-Off* is often described as parody, this label is misleading, because while Bergman has a lot of fun with Chandleresque dialogue and similes, he does not turn LeVine into a comic figure nor does he fail to develop a meaningful plot. The story involves a political blackmail scheme complicated by a serious outbreak of "every man for himself" among the lower ranks of the blackmailers. The target of this dirty plan is Eli Savage, a wealthy and generous contributor to Thomas Dewey's presidential campaign. Savage's daughter, who under a false identity approaches LeVine at the book's beginning, appeared in a couple of pornographic movies several years earlier. Now, a group of Democrats and military zealouts dedicated to Roosevelt's re-election are threatening to release the films if Savage continues to bankroll Dewey. Levine jumps into the fray with a spirit that allows the madcap finale to transcend all its improbabilities.

The tone of the book is nostalgic, similar to Stuart Kaminsky's Toby Peters mysteries. Real characters make cameo appearances, and there are a bountiful number of period details that capture wartime America at its best and its worst. The prose is witty and chock-full of good one-liners and send-ups.

Hollywood and LeVine, slightly more serious in tone than the first book, once again finds LeVine caught up in a case of national importance and political chicanery. Walter Adrian, a Hollywood screenwriter and old friend of LeVine's, asks him to come to LA to investigate why Warner Brothers is suddenly giving him the cold shoulder. Shortly after LeVine arrives, he discovers Adrian's body on a movie backlot. The police believe Adrian hanged himself, but LeVine eventually discovers that he was the innocent victim of the initial stages of the blacklisting campaign directed against suspected Communist sympathizers in the movie industry. LeVine has a private meeting with none other than Richard Nixon, the earnest Commie hunter ("attired in a suit of such a peculiar cut that it looked to have the wooden hangers and paper stuffing still inside"). LeVine rubs shoulders with many of Hollywood's biggest celebrities, but his most memorable encounter is with Humphrey Bogart, cinema's archetypal private eye, who, at the novel's critical point, gives LeVine a free ride and the proverbial shirt off his back.

In his *Sons of Sam Spade*, David Geherin quotes Bergman as claiming, "I never really saw myself as a mystery writer . . . . My novels are really historical novels." Both LeVine books examine the corruption, extremism and dirty tricks that have plagued American politics for years. Bergman's achievement was to place "a small-time shamus" right in the middle of some of this nation's most dramatic political events and then use those opportunities to poke a very sharp finger at our most pompous and powerful institutions—the FBI, the military, Republicans and Democrats. There's enough well-intentioned ridicule to go around for everyone. Bergman may gift-wrap his message in funny papers; nonetheless, the historian's famous warning is unmistakeable: learn from the mistakes of the past or be condemned to repeat them.

Sam Kelly—Jackson F. Burke

Sam Kelly, one of our black eyes, is a bald, amiable-looking stockily built man of forty-three who has a wealthy girl friend and client named Madam Bobbie. Her name also designates her profession. Sam, the PI hero of Jackson F. Burke's *Location Shots* (1974), has a round cherubic-looking face with fine features and the general look of "a friendly bulldog." Sam is about five ten and walks with a slight, almost unnoticeable limp. His speech is clear, clipped and precise: "It was his habit to speak softly, but the thunder was there." Though Sam is a licensed PI he is also the live-in house dick at the Hotel Castlereagh located in New York City at Verdi Square where Broadway, Amsterdam Avenue and 72nd Street come together. Sam's hotel suite also serves as his office.

When one of the Castlereagh's residents is murdered, Sam becomes very much concerned and, working with his friend Lt. Mike Moynihan of Manhattan North, Homicide, goes after the murderer. The murder victim was a friend of one of Sam's good buddies—one David Christopher. When Sam looks up David to find out more about the lady victim, he finds David also has been murdered. From this point on Sam is out for blood, puzzled why anyone would want to murder the easy-going Christopher, a writer of children's books. After some very clever sleuthing Sam manages to round up, and when the killer tries to shoot it out, execute the villain.

Although he is not as violent as Shaft, Sam is, in his own quiet way, equally as deadly. For example, when a midtown pimp cheats some of the girls, Sam puts the whoremaster and his buddies under the gun and turns the girls loose on them. After the girls are through, Sam takes the whoremaster outside at gunpoint:

put him in a gypsy cab and rode him down to Roosevelt Hospital. By the time they got to the hospital this creep was ready for the doctors. He had a broken jaw, a gouged eye, a cracked spine, and various internal injuries. How much of this was Sam's work and how much the girls' is a moot point .... The creep's buddies were found later and buried. There was a brief police investigation but nothing came of it.

From time to time, newcomers to the neighborhood—hoodlums and hooligans from the Bronx, Brooklyn or Harlem—would try to take on Sam but they never tried twice. Sam " ... carried his Astra .25 Colt 'Cub' automatic rather than a heavier weapon like the Colt .45 or an S&W .38

because he was not likely to kill with it unless he chose to. He could place one of those little .25 copper-jacketed bullets wherever he wanted it without fear of tearing too big a hole. He could put it in a man's kneecap and cripple him, or in his shoulder without utterly destroying the man. Of course, he could also place the shot in the man's head if he chose."

Sam, an interesting and complex character, is credible and well-drawn. He likes to sip Jack Daniels, smoke good cigars, listen to Chopin and read about classical music. He did occupational duty in Germany after World War II and married a German girl in Berlin at age 19. After the war Sam and his bride moved to the Big Apple and Sam joined New York's finest. He was a good cop until an incompetent superior got him shot and caused the death of a friend. When the incompetent was promoted, Sam resigned and started his PI career. After his wife's death, Sam moved into the Castlereagh and took on tougher and ever more dangerous assignments.

Location Shots, published first by Harper & Row in 1974, was reissued in paper by Charter in 1980. *Location Shots* is headed for the films, starring Billy Dee Williams as Sam. Kelly also shows up in *Death Trick*, published by Harper in 1975, and in a third novel, *Kelly Among the Nightingales*, published by Dutton in 1979.

Burke was born in Alameda, California, the son of an actor in 1915. He received his BA degree from the University of California at Berkeley in 1944 but abandoned his plans for a scientific career and pursued poetry. Burke reports that during the thirties he wrote a lot of formal verse but soon thereafter turned to prose. In 1945 he finished his first novel, *Noah*, and sold it to Alan Swallow. Swallow also bought his second novel in 1947. Before the Sam Kelly series, Burke contributed more than a hundred stories and poems to popular magazines. A few years ago he published another novel, *Juana*, based on the life of a real knight—Sor Juana Ines de la Cruz—a seventeenth-century Mexican poet and the first defender of women's rights in the New World.

Mike Haller—Max Byrd

Max Byrd was born in Atlanta, Georgia, in 1942. His father was a fiscal officer with the Veterans Administration, and the family moved several times during Byrd's youth. Following graduation from Dublin (Georgia) High School, Byrd attended Harvard where he earned a BA in American History and Literature in 1964. He studied at Kings College, Cambridge, on a Knox Fellowship before returning to Harvard for his MA and Ph.D. in English Literature. Byrd was appointed to the faculty at Yale University as an Assistant Professor of English in 1970 and was promoted to Associate Professor in 1975. He came to the University of California at Davis in 1976 where he is currently Professor of English in a department which also lists

Diane Johnson, the "official" biographer of Dashiell Hammett, among its faculty. A specialist in eighteenth century English literature, Byrd is a recognized scholar on Laurence Sterne's *Tristram Shandy*. He lives in Davis, California, with his wife, Brooks, who is a painter, and their two children.

Byrd has written three novels, all paperback originals for Bantam and all featuring Mike Haller, a San Francisco private eye who is a descendant of Marlowe if ever there was one. *California Thriller*, Byrd's first novel, was chosen best paperback of 1981 by the Private Eye Writers of America. It involves a missing person case as do the other two Haller novels. An investigative reporter disappears, and although his friends think he's just off with his latest chippie pursuing a week-end cure for a mid-life crisis, Haller finds a trail to a farm in the Sacramento Valley that's owned by Frank Brazil, one of the Bay Area's better-known thugs. Brazil just happens to be chummy with an internationally famous biochemist who specializes in chemical neurotransmitters and their effects on aggressive behavior. The plot may stretch too elaborately and the violence gets a bit excessive, but this is still the best private-eye novel ever written about the functioning and chemistry of the brain. Some right-wing politics as a motive and an inside look at a major newspaper make this an auspicious debut.

Fly Away, Jill (1981) takes Haller to London town searching for the runaway daughter-in-law of an old, wealthy Italiano who owns a fleet of oil tankers. The search is complicated by the fact that Papa is really stalking a different prey, a set-up which Haller discovers only after he's deep in an old-world network of family betrayals, heroin trades and unfinished vendettas from the Resistance movement. Byrd handles the change of scenery to Europe better than do most authors who bite their PIs with the travel bug. His London sprawls from tweedy to greedy traveling a very sinister subway, and the cave country of France's Dordogne Valley makes a chilling graveyard.

Finders Weepers (1983) has Haller looking for an heir to an $800,000 inheritance. The beneficiary is Muriel Contreras, a Mexican hooker whose life has been eroded by a hard rain of pimps, johns and dope. But somebody doesn't want Muriel Contreras found, and they're ready to snuff anyone who comes too close, including a feeble old private eye and Haller's girlfriend, Dinah. This one's as gritty as they get.

Mike Haller is a transplanted New Englander, having moved to California from Boston. After stints in college, the Army, Interpol in France, the wire services in London and the newspaper game with the LA *Times*, he put on his gumshoes in San Francisco. He says he's a "born drifter and slider, an uncommitted soul . . . which is what makes me such a good Californian." But "underneath the California mask was a Puritan's face" which reflects Haller's rather conventional morality.

Haller rumbles around San Francisco in a 1958 Mercedes 190SL, which he once described as his "faithful iron dog." His San Francisco isn't the one on the cable car postcards. It's a brutal city, coated with evil; a "Babylon by the Bay," a gorgeous demented old city ... cocktail glass in each hand, makeup cracked and hardening, lipstick smeared in a blood-red clot." The flatlands of Berkeley are "higher education's dirty hemline."

All rough and tumble with a very fast lip, Haller has a code of sorts— "some inscrutable combination of New England Puritan and bleeding heart." Haller's girlfriend, Dinah, who is a psychoanalyst at a San Francisco hospital and like Haller an opera buff, is an excellent supporting character in each of the books. Dinah is a cool-headed and warm-blooded woman whose ideal man "made passionate love to her every night until one-thirty in the morning. And then at two o'clock turned into a pizza." Haller also has a partner by the name of Fred, a retired cop. Sturdy as a rock and Irish to the core, Fred is never without his porkpie hat and he's never too far from the streets. Put him on the city map, he's part of the geography.

Byrd's novels cut with a sharp edge. Full of sly humor and inside jokes ("A p.i. in Boston named Parker is so good he's writing a cookbook." "What's it called?" "*The Thin Man*."), they are also packed with violence that blankets San Francisco and London like their famous fogs. The prose is interesting, and Byrd is a wry observer of the modern California scene. The style may derive from Chandler and Macdonald but there are topical plots and enough fresh flourishes to make Haller one of the most exciting California knights of recent years.

Mongo—George Chesbro

George C. Chesbro is a special education high-school teacher in Rockland County, New York, where he lives with his wife, Oranus, and their two children. He was born in Washington, D.C., in 1940 to George W. and Maxine (Sharpe) Chesbro. In 1962 he earned his BS from Syracuse University which is where he began his writing. He has published several short stories in various mystery magazines. One of his stories was included in *Best Detective Stories of the Year* (Dutton, 1973). His hobbies include chess, the occult and travel to Europe and Iran.

The hero of Chesbro's mysteries is Dr. Robert Frederikson, known as "Mongo" to his friends. "Mongo" is easily the strangest concoction in modern private eye fiction. He holds a Ph.D. in criminology which he earned while he was a headline performer in the Statler Brothers Circus. He was in the circus because he just happens to be a dwarf who is an expert gymnast. After he received his degree, he accepted a faculty position at a university in NYC where he teaches criminology. He also holds a black belt in karate, and is a licensed private detective: "Finding out things other people didn't want known was my way of trying to stay even with a society filled with people bigger than I was." His brother, Garth, "all disgustingly normal six feet of him," is a New York City cop.

Mongo was introduced in "The Drop," a short story that was published in the October, 1971, *Mike Shane Mystery Magazine*. Eight more short stories, many combining the occult with PI knowhow, preceded *Shadow of a Broken Man* (1977), the first Mongo novel. The plot is outlandish, involving a famous architect named Rafferty who despite being shot and falling into a smelting furnace five years earlier appears to be still alive. For reasons that become obvious, Rafferty is wanted by the Americans, the British, the French and the Russians who employ a gigantic freak to find him. Mongo is initially hired by the husband of Rafferty's "widow" to search for the architect, but he soon joins forces with the leadership of the United Nations in a bombing raid of the Russian consulate. If that seems improbable, wait till you get a load of the amazing psychic powers that make Rafferty such a hot item: "Somewhere out in that gathering light was a man many considered the most powerful and dangerous man who had ever lived, a man from whom no one could keep a secret, a man who could move objects with his mind. A man who could kill with a thought." Suspend belief all ye who enter here.

The second Mongo book is *City of Whispering Stone* (1978), another thriller built along international proportions, this time pitting Frederickson against SAVAK, the secret police of the Shah of Iran, in a complicated plot. Brother Garth, in love with a beautiful Iranian woman named Neptune, plays a major role, and the Iranian settings from Tehran to Persepolis are well-drawn.

In *An Affair of Sorcerers* (1979), Mongo is asked by Dr. Barnum, the Chancellor of the University, to investigate Dr. Vincent Smathers, a Nobel Prize winning psychologist on the faculty. Barnum is worried about the background of one of Smather's assistants who may have operated a brainwashing program in Korea and the fact that Smathers, who's an expert on sensory deprivation, seems to have a secret source of funds with which to run his department. Close to the heels of this case comes a request by a U.S. Senator for Mongo to look into the case of Estaban Morales, a psychic healer charged with murder, who is "treating" the senator's daughter, a victim of cystic fibrosis. Finally, a neighbor's daughter pays Mongo 57¢ and asks him to get "my daddy's book of shadows back . . . or something terrible will happen." These ingredients are mixed together to make an evil brew of witchcraft, occult ceremonies, ritualistic tortures and murder, seasoned with a bite of a rabid dog. Chesbro stirs the stew too long, and even a lightning bolt summoned at the climax fails to give the spark that could warm up this dish.

If you're a PI purist, the Mongo series may be a disappointment because its frequent forages into the occult and political intrigue seem to be an overindulgence of Mr. Chesbro's numerous hobbies. Still, Mongo is a captivating character who, even when overshadowed by all the paranormal and global shenanigans, possesses a pleasing blend of toughness, eccentricities and charm. You might say he grows on you.

Nate Heller—Max Allan Collins

Anyone who has read much Max Collins knows there has been a bona fide private eye novel perking inside him for many years. Widely respected by his fellow writers, Collins is a versatile writer with three successful suspense-mystery series to his credit, all of which by their voice and structure resemble the standard private eye yarn but lack an "official" PI hero.

Collins' first published novel, *Bait Money* (a 1973 paperback original for Curtis Books) introduced Nolan, a tiring ex-thief in the tradition of Donald Westlake's Parker. The series has continued with *Blood Money* (1973), *Fly Paper* (1981), *Hush Money* (1981), *Hard Cash* (1982) and *Scratch Fever* (1982), all published by Pinnacle Books.

A second series features Quarry, a hired killer. The titles, published by Berkeley, are *The Broker* (1976), *The Broker's Wife* (1976), *The Dealer* (1976) and *The Slasher* (1977).

Mallory is the hero of the third series. A Vietnam veteran, ex-cop, college student and aspiring mystery writer, Mallory is a tough amateur sleuth who solves cases in Iowa, the location for much of the Nolan and Quarry action. The first Mallory, *The Baby Blue Rip-Off* (1983) was Collins' first hardback novel. The second Mallory, *No Cure for Death* (1983) is also set in Port City, Iowa, a thinly disguised version of Collins' hometown. *Kill Your Darlings* (1984) is the newest Mallory, which takes place at a Bouchercon in Chicago.

Max Allan Collins was born in 1948 to Max and Pat Collins in Muscatine, Iowa, a town that claims to be the "Pearl Button Capital of the World." (Admit it. That's one you didn't know.) He began writing in high school and wrote five or six unpublished novels before hitting paydirt with *Bait Money*. During this period, he worked for the local newspaper and performed as a professional musician. Collins received a BA in English from the University of Iowa in 1970 and a Masters of Fine Arts in 1972 from Iowa's Writers Workshop.

Beginning in 1977, Collins took over for Chester Gould as the writer of the Dick Tracy comic strip which is syndicated in more than 500 newspapers. He is also the co-creator (with cartoonist, Terry Beatty) of Ms. Tree, a female PI who is the heroine of her own comic book. Collins says Ms. Tree is the answer to the question of "what if Mike Hammer had married his secretary, Velda and was then murdered on their wedding night? Wouldn't Velda step into her husband's shoes, take over the business and solve his murder?" Collins and Beatty also created Mike Mist, a private eye whose adventures are usually restricted to minute mysteries in comic format.

Collins names Dashiell Hammett, James Cain, Jonathan Latimer, Jim Thompson, Raymond Chandler, Horace McCoy and Mike Roscoe ("a style so clipped it makes James M. Cain look like a word horse") as some of his favorite writers. The two writers who have influenced him the most are Donald Westlake ("the best writer in mystery fiction today") and Mickey Spillane, of whom Collins says, "I love the guy...nobody can make readers turn pages like Spillane...I'm mainly talking about the early stuff, the first six or seven books Spillane wrote as a young man. There's nothing quite like them in literature." Collins' reputation as a leading expert on Spillane has been solidified by *One Lonely Knight: Mickey Spillane's Mike Hammer,* his book-length study of "The Mick," written with James Traylor and published by the Popular Press.

Collins lives in Muscatine with his wife Barbara and their son Nathan. He collects original comic art and claims to have put together one of the major private collections in existence.

Which brings us to *True Detective* (St. Martin's, 1983) and Collins' first genuine, A-1 private-eye, Nate Heller. This is a great book, probably the best historical detective novel ever written. It's more than a period piece in the entertaining Kaminsky or Bergman mold. It is the portrayal of an era—the tough-guy 1930s—with a broad sweep from the brawny shoulders of Chicago where most of the action takes place to the plastic paradise of Miami where Heller tries to prevent the murder of Chicago's mayor, Anton Cermak. The book is thoroughly researched and the many historical personages and events that are included are not mere grace notes of nostalgia; they are integral to the plot and they establish the novel's back-room, dark-alley atmosphere.

After Heller resigns from the Chicago police because of his **unintentional** involvement in a corrupt set-up, he goes private with the **help** of Eliot Ness, lightweight champion Barney Ross, and General Charles Dawes. Heller is employed by several clients on cases that ultimately converge, but his most improbable employer is Al Capone, a reluctant resident of Atlanta's Big House, who wants Heller to foil a contract that Frank Nitti has put on the head of Cermak. Those of you who know something about the history of American politics already know how successful that intervention turns out to be. But you couldn't have known about Nate Heller and the assistance he gets from the likes of George Raft, Walter Winchell and a young radio announcer named Ronald Reagan.

True Detective is a great read, a masterful hybrid of history and mystery with memorable tough-guy dialogue ("I haven't killed anybody all day. Help me keep it that way.") drawn against a vivid backdrop of depression-era America. A Heller sequel, *True Crime,* is coming from St. Martin's.

Carver Bascombe—Kenn Davis

Kenn Davis's Carver Bascombe is one of San Francisco's most exciting PIs. Like his predecessor on the East Coast, Toussaint Moore, Bascombe is black. As a young Vietnam veteran with a Military Police background and no other significant work experience, it was only natural that Carver would think of applying his skills to San Francisco's crime problems. In fact, his MP background triggered the San Francisco Permit Bureau's decision to grant him a PI license. Flamboyant Carver drives a twelve cylinder, baby blue, Jaguar XKE with tan leather bucket seats. Though Carver is studying law at night, his heart isn't in it. He's only a part-time student anyway and after a hard day's work there's little energy left for legal subtleties.

Carver's office on Fillmore Street is also his living quarters. The office is a single room with a cheap desk, filing cabinets and chairs plus some expensive Roberts recording equipment and a large color TV in the corner. A door in the side wall leads to his apartment. Carver's girlfriend, 34-year-old Gwen Norris, a Senator's daughter and a millionairess keeps Carver in Cesar trench coats, caviar and Colt .357 Pythons. Rather than saying that Carver has a white mistress, it is more accurate to say that Gwen Norris keeps a black stud. A product of the Detroit slums, Carver is regarded by other blacks in the Bay Area as a combination Superfly, Shaft and Virgil Tibbs.

Showing up first in *The Dark Side* (1976), Carver is hired by Gladys and Oscar Hart, art photographers, to look into the murder of their fourteen-year-old son, Ralphie. Ralphie, who also took snapshots as a hobby, was brutally beaten, sodomized and then given a fatal injection of heroin. Carver and Gwen manage to find Ralphie's body and get a lead on the motive for the slaying. Both the San Francisco art world and heroin smuggling are involved. Carver, who is intelligent, sensitive and well-read, is also steel hard. Before the case is brought to a close this hardness is well tested. There are several brutal killings, narrow brushes with extinction, and a fiery showdown in an art gallery.

The first Bascombe was a collaboration between Kenn Davis and John Stanley. The second, *The Forza Trap* (1979) is by Davis alone. It suffers from some serious flaws in both plotting and writing but it still gives us art-loving Carver, who is a most credible and likeable character. In *The Forza Trap* the world of opera furnishes the ground and the major figure is the black, world-renowned, opera star mezzo-soprano Marian Rooks. The novel, set in San Francisco again, opens with an attempt on Marian's life during a rehearsal. A member of the cast saves her by sacrificing himself. In his escape attempt, the sex-crazed assassin is accidently killed. Since someone wants Marian dead, Carver is hired to keep her alive. This proves to be a virtually impossible task. In the process of protecting Marian, Carver and Marian fall in love. Bascombe finds himself up against a black terrorist organization, homosexual thugs, and assorted murders. Following some slick sleuthing, Carver learns the attempts on Marian's life are coming from inside the opera company, and that an enormous quantity of the explosive cyclonite or RDX is being manufactured and that it has something to do with Verdi's opera, *La Forza del Destino*. Hence the title *The Forza Trap*.

The third Bascombe, *Words Can Kill* (1984), has Carver going to work for Jackson Fayette, one of his Army buddies. Fayette, author of a best-selling novel based on his experiences in Vietnam, wants Carver to investigate the murder of a third veteran, Ed Colfax, another novelist down on his luck in Sausalito. Because Carver's law school tuition has to be paid, he reluctantly takes on the case. On the dead man's body Carver finds a notebook containing the names of five other writers and it appears they are the best suspects. Carver also learns other things that make him wonder if Fayette actually wrote the novel he is famous for and why he was hired in the first place. Carver is particularly curious about another puzzle: how this murder case ties in with the twenty-year old theft of a rare thirteenth-century manuscript.

Kenn Davis, Carver's creator, is a talented West Coast artist and writer born in Salinas, California in 1932 and educated in Marin County and San Francisco. Davis took up oil painting in his late teens, studied both art and painting in College, and then went to art school. Davis, however, is unimpressed with the art marketplace. "I have had many one-man shows over the years," Davis says, "but have not shown my very odd, strange, and apparently disturbing art work for ten years. My paintings have been shown in galleries such as Gumps in San Francisco, the Sherman in Chicago, and others in Boston, Los Angeles, Denver, and New York City. I've had paintings on exhibit at the Dallas Museum of Fine Art, and the California Palace of the Legion Of Honor. And no . . . my paintings did not sell very well. I detest the marketplace in art."

Davis is currently employed by the *San Francisco Chronicle* as a staff artist. In addition to his writing and painting, he does low budget commercial films and industrial movies. He was recently Director of Photography on a low budget vampire movie, *Nightmare In Blood,* directed by John Stanley, a friend and collaborator who also writes for the *Chronicle*. Together, in 1979, Davis and Stanley published *Bogart '48* a novel with Humphrey Bogart as the hero. In the novel some terrorists are plotting to blow up the Academy Award banquet. All of Hollywood's film heroes and heroines play minor roles in the action and Bogart in his Spade-like role saves the day. Alone, Davis has published another chilling and first rate tale, *Dead To Rights* (1981), about three Vietnam veterans trying to pull off a $6,000,000 heist.

With Bascombe, Davis says the idea is "to have his stories take place in the world of the arts: painting, opera, writers and sculptors." So far Davis has covered the world of art, opera, and literature and he is currently working on a fourth Bascombe novel set in the world of sculpture. He is also at work on a novel set in Paris in 1927, another about a serial killer, a spy/love story, and a screenplay with Stanley. Davis also has plans for future Bascombe novels set in the worlds of music, poetry and ballet.

Joe Reddman—Warwick Downing

One of the more colorful of our American PIs operates in one of the more scenic parts of the nation—the environs of Denver, Colorado. We're referring to Warwick Downing's Joe Reddman, a private investigator with the conscience and skills of a Cheyenne Indian. Comparing Reddman to Hillerman's Tony Leaphorn, Newgate Callendar, critic for the New York Times Book Review, waxes eloquent about Reddman's "sheer atavism" and innate Indian characteristics: "They know nature; they can track and run endlessly; they are terrible machines when aroused." The only trouble with Callendar's praise is that Joe Reddman is *not* an Indian. Though white (according to Downing the name Reddman was probably a mistake because it is so misleading) Joe was raised by a Cheyenne foster-mother Blue Tree Woman "with the most beautiful skin in the world" whom his father lured to take care of him after his real mother died. She taught him to ride bareback and passed on to him thousands of years of Indian lore and wisdom. She promised him a Cheyenne name when he came of age. In Joe's words: "I finally did. Either that or she got tired of waiting. This was during World War II and I was an Officer Candidate at Colorado University, where I also played football. I had just been named an All American half-back, but getting my true Cheyenne name was a greater honor. It is *Nutaq, nha ewo-tsim-tsis*. It means, "Man Who Plays Games." According to Joe's cop friend Charles Riggs, Joe is

"Sometimes called the last wild Indian; sometimes called the player because of his fondness for games, known to the police as Mr. Cool and to me personally as a pain in the ass."

Joe not only uses his intelligence to solve the puzzles he confronts as a PI, he uses visions and has the Indian qualities of patience and stoicism.

Waiting is easy when you know how. It's a lot like sleeping, but there's a difference, usually when you sleep, you sweat more, and generally when you wait, you have better control over your dreams."

As for his stoicism and his ability to withstand pain, this excerpt from *The Player* is typical:

I laughed at him. "Go ahead, Charley. Start cutting."
With a sudden savage thrust he shoved the knife into my leg. I kept on glaring at him with contempt. My spiritual mother might have wept at the sight of the knife angled into my leg, but she would have smiled for my honor.... It was an ugly-looking cut. When Liston knocked the knife out, it levered out a hunk of muscle. She tore my trousers around it, her eyes and mouth soft and wet, and gently tried to push it all back.... I watched Liston as she worked, and grinned at her, and held my face and body still. I concentrated on the pain and let it wash through my body and purify it as though with fire.

Joe is close to nature and uses the native woodsman's skills and know-how to assist him in outwitting the villains. He not only loves all things natural but converses with them as well:

Spruce trees are like women who would prefer to be left alone and they will scratch and bite and slap you with their needles to keep you from violating them. I'd a lot rather get up in a ponderosa, because they just plain don't take offense.... When I got out of that old tree I kicked it, feeling good. You miserable witch, I thought. You scra¬hed my hands and wrists and face and neck and even tried to poke a stick in my eye. Then I told her I was going to get an axe and start chopping, but she knew better. I think she was just glad I'd gotten off"

Although it may be the dead of winter Joe goes after his enemies with as little outer wear as possible. For example, when he pursues the killers in *The Gambler, The Minstrel, And the Dance Hall Queen*, he philosophizes:

There are a lot of ways to dress for a fight. One is to cover yourself with armor, but that will slow you down. Another is to wear none at all, but then if you get hit, the war is over. Still, I like the second way best. I put my shoulder holster under a black wool shirt and put on dark cotton trousers and tennis shoes.

Joe also talks to animals and quiets them. When he encounters guard dogs he first identifies with them and then tries "to put my mind inside their hearts. They gentled down a little, like wolves that can't quite believe it, and I continued to talk to them in an easy voice."

Once Reddman goes after his enemies they have about as much chance of survival as an icicle in a blast furnace. Joe is not, however, a vengeful killer; he uses his weapons and brute force only when necessary. Because of his Indian training he, on occasion, can also see the spirits of the dying leave their bodies:

Sometimes when a person's ghost leaves you can see it, and I watched Mason's soul mist out of his body. He'd been trying with both hands to raise his pistol. "Have a nice trip, Mason," I said, and picked up his gun.

Reddman's creator, Warwick Downing, (born 1931) is a Colorado District Attorney residing in Cortez, Colorado, a small town in the southwest corner of the state near Mesa Verde National Park. Downing was born and raised in Denver, attended her public schools and then spent two years at the University of Wyoming before returning to Denver University and graduating with a major in English. After graduating from Denver University's Law School, Warwick moved to San Francisco and, after two attempts, passed the California Bar Exam. In San Francisco he worked as a prosecutor and criminal lawyer until 1968, when he moved back to Denver to a position in the U.S. Attorney's office. Downing got the urge to write after returning to Denver and observing the deterioration in the mountain environment brought about by increasing industrialization. Downing's first novel featuring Joe Reddman, *The Player,* was published in 1974. This was followed by *The Mountains West of Town* in 1975 in which Downing introduces his alter ego, Nathan Tree, a lawyer like himself who lives in a cabin in the moutains west of town. Reddman plays only a minor role in the second novel, but returns again as the hero and major character in Downing's third novel, *The Gambler, The Minstrel, And The Dance Hall Queen* published in 1976.

After two more unsold novels—one a blockbuster a la Clive Cussler and the other a juvenile about a 9-year-old boy growing up in Sheridan, Wyoming in the 1930s—Downing accepted a position as District Attorney in Cortez. Since moving to Cortez his legal duties have severely restricted his writing and he's done very little in the last two years. Fortunately for us, a new Joe Reddman novel *My Brother The Buffalo,* set on the Cheyenne Reservation in Wyoming, is underway. The plot hinges on Joe's visiting his foster mother Blue Tree Woman and her natural son Buffalo. The Cheyennes are divided over the issue of leasing coal mining rights and, while Joe is there, a murder is committed. Joe takes over and solves the crime.

As is often the case, Downing's novels have done much better abroad—especially in Europe where they are very popular. As for his skill as a story-teller, Downing received rave reviews for *The Player* including one from the *New York Times Book Review* which said "A smooth writing style, a fine storytelling ability, and a bang-up climax." The *Miami Herald* selected *The Mountains West Of Town* as one of the ten best mysteries of 1975. After reading *The Gambler, The Minstrel And The Dance Hall Queen* fellow mystery writer Tony Hillerman said "Joe Reddman makes you think of Travis McGee if he had been created by Raymond Chandler." Downing has also been frequently praised for his ability to capture the twangy dialogue of the current-day West and for the unusual places in which the *corpus delecti* is found, eg. inside a waterbed. To date, none of the three Reddman novels is available in paper—a gross oversight that badly needs correcting. Downing is a writer too good to miss and he deserves wider recognition. Downing's story telling skills are practiced, his powers of observation are strong and his sense of humor sharp. For example, in describing the moves of a drunk, "He wandered around like a three-legged dog after that, trying to figure out some way to relieve himself without falling over." And later, rationalizing his tolerance of drug pushers he says, "Waiting for a gang of drug peddlers rubbed my prejudice wrong. Although, what the hell I thought. I've hired out to banks that didn't sound as legitimate."

Fritz Brown—James Ellroy

With a symphony in his soul and a repo order in his hip pocket, Fritz Brown has prowled the mean streets just once—in James Ellroy's *Brown's Requiem* (Avon, 1981). But that solo is a virtuoso's performance, one of the best PI novels of the last decade, earning Brown a place in this chapter.

Brown is an ex-cop and an alcoholic who is known at age 33 as the repo king of Los Angeles owing to his working relationship with Cal Myers, one of LA's biggest car dealers. Fritz operates the Brown Detective Agency, a grimy little office on Pico in Rancho Park that gives him an $85 tax write-off and an air-conditioned room to read in. It's been years since he's handled anything other than repossession cases, back when he "had more illusions about myself as an urban manipulator." For now he runs his repo racket, tries to stay on the wagon and hangs out with his best friend and fellow alcoholic, the wildly wonderful Walter Cannon, a cultural guru obsessed with science fiction, music, TV and loads of T-Bird fueled fantasies ("the power of a Walter epigram can clarify the most puzzling day"). The love of Fritz's life is classical music with tastes that bespeak his German heritage—"Bach, Beethoven, Brahms, Bruckner and Brown—all German, all possessed of a mission, theirs musical, mine the destruction of evil."

The case starts out as a routine trail job initiated by a smarmy chunk-of-fat golf caddy named Fred "Fat Dog" Baker who wants Brown to follow his sister, Jane and the old benefactor with whom she lives named Sol Kupferman. It doesn't take Brown long to discover two important facts about his case: first, that he's in love with Jane Baker; and second, that Fat Dog is a raving, racist psychotic with a history of arson, exhibitionism, and unfathomable sadism. At that point the case becomes the dividing point in Brown's life, an opportunity for him to be involved in

something important, something vast and complex, and I was the sole arbiter of it.

Before this, September 2, 1967 had been the pivotal date of my life. I was twenty-one. On that date I had heard, really heard, music for the first time. It was Beethoven's Third Symphony. Walter had been trying to get me to listen to classical music for years, to no avail. The First Movement of the *Eroica* went through me like a transfusion of hope and fortitude. I was off with German romanticism, listening to Beethoven, Brahms, Wagner, and Bruckner six, eight, ten hours a day. I had found truth, or so I thought, and a strange metamorphosis took place: infused with the romance of giants, I gave up my vague academic dream and became a cop. An uneasy, malcontented one at first, until the booze came along and made the low-level administration of power exciting beyond my wildest fantasies.

Ellroy scores his plot with murder, extortion, police corruption, and the painful family past that Lew Archer loved to muck around in. The book is powerfully written, delivered with an intensity and boozy philosophy reminiscent of Crumley's best. The characterization is superb, particularly the more florid aspects of Walter and Fat Dog; and Brown's long fall off the wagon into a fifth of Scotch is a fine bleary eyed scene ("I had been away a long time, and mother booze was being generous, throwing me a mellifluous parade as a welcome home present").

The novel is marred by some overwriting. The moralizing comes a little heavy ("My mind was seized with a boundless hatred for America...with its optimism, boosterism and yahooism that opted for sentiment over truth every time"), and the soliloquies into Brown's love of music pad an already too long novel.

Fritz Brown is private eyedom's first German Romantic, one who can express his sentimentality with brass knuckles as well as concertos. He's a music lover with a vicious streak. *Brown's Requiem* was nominated for PWA's Shamus Award for best private eye paperback novel of 1981. We need an encore.

Ellroy's second novel, *Clandestine* (Avon, 1982), is about a policeman's attempt to solve a very brutal murder. Set in the 1950s and structured like a private eye story, *Clandestine* was nominated for an Edgar.

Ellroy's third novel, *Blood on the Moon*, published in 1983 by Mysterious Press has been described as a "neonoir urban horror novel." It is structured contrapuntally from the perspectives of a crazed mass murderer and the LA cop who pursues him. Ellroy has just finished his fourth novel, *Because of the Night*. In it he continues to examine his main concern as a writer: "I'm interested in people who tread outside the bounds of conventional morality; displaced romantics ill at ease in the 1980s; people who have rejected a goodly amount of life's amenities in order to dance to the music in their own heads" (Interview with Duane Tucker in *The Armchair Detective*, 1984, 17(2), p. 153.)

James Ellroy was born in Los Angeles in 1948. He was kicked out of high school, discharged as unsuitable from the Army after faking a nervous breakdown, and arrested about 50 times during a long booze and drugs hitch before going sober in 1977, "I opted for life," he explains.

Ellroy's mother was murdered when he was ten years old. The killer was never found. Ellroy admits that his tragedy has directed his writing; *Clandestine* was in part a fictionalized account of his mother's murder. Ellroy plans to continue writing LA police novels. He believes the cop will replace the private eye as the central hardboiled character in crime fiction.

B.F. Cage—Peter Israel

Peter Israel was born in New York City on August 1, 1933 to J. Leon and Ruth (Lustbader) Israel. Educated at Yale, Israel spent four years in Paris during the mid-1970s while he was the director of foreign services for the Albin Michel publishing house. In 1978 he became president of the Putnam Publishing Group in New York City. His former wife, Abigail (Pollack) Israel, by whom he had one son, is also an author (*A Boy and A Boa*, 1981), a translator of French literature, and a college teacher.

Israel's first novel was *The Hen's House* (1967), a nonmystery which won critical acclaim for its Kafkaesque version of interrogation and self-analysis in a mental-political institution of sorts.

It says "Public Relations" on B.F. (Benjamin Franklin) Cage's business card and that makes Cage a little different from the usual private eye because Cage isn't very interested in justice or the innocent of which there are very few in Cage's world. Cage is a specialist in the cover-up, "the gathering and suppression of information." His talent for putting in the fix is established in the appropriately titled *Hush Money* (1974) where he cuts himself into a fortune in stock certificates as compensation for keeping quiet about the deep, dark secrets of a very rich but very sordid California family. "Cagey" as he's known to some, hits such a jackpot with this blackmail scheme that he moves from Santa Monica to semi-retirement in Paris, the scene for the next two novels. The City of Light has its own forms of corruption and soon Cage is applying his special talents to a very nasty modern art scam—all crooked, hot and forged in *The French Kiss* (1976), and to European professional basketball (*le basket* where black American players display *le smash*) fast breaking into a mob-controlled hash network in *The Stiff Upper Lip* (1978). Cage brings each case to a close of sorts, but to say they are solved or that wrongs are righted would be stretching it. Of course, the Gallic mentality can be as appreciative of an amoral hero as the most sleazy California bigwig; Cage remembers one Frenchman's wisdom that "The only difference between us, Monsieur, is that you wash your hands after you urinate, and I before."

In most other respects, Cage runs the usual PI fast track. He's a first-class smart-aleck, cynical, with plenty of swagger and street smarts. He has a penchant for Air France stewardesses, a craving which Paris can satisfy in spades. Speaking of spades, there is an excess of racial slurs in the stories— at one point a black man's fear is attributed to the fact that "his storytelling was so good that he'd spooked himself."

Although the American-in-Paris novels give Israel a chance to write cleverly about the French and their gangster chic, neither comes close to the genuine tension of *Hush Money* which is as raw and as tough a mystery as you'll ever want. Israel has a stylish delivery, but his plots are cryptic and confusing. They can become almost as annoying as the fact that everywhere Cage goes he's being tailed; perhaps this is Israel's compensation for plotting that too often can't be followed.

Fred Bennett—Elliott Lewis

Elliott Lewis is a Los Angeles-based writer who has worked in the entertainment industry for many years as an actor, radio personality, producer, writer and director. Born in New York City in 1917 to Julius and Ann Lewis, he is married to Mary Jane Croft, an actress.

Lewis is the author of the Fred Bennett series which now numbers seven novels, all paperback originals published by Pinnacle. Five of the books are cursed by the stupid decision to put numbers in the titles, a characteristic which makes them seem to belong in the racks alongside the supermarket express lanes. *No. 1 Two Heads Are Better* (1980) is followed by *No. 2 Dirty Linen* (1980), *No. 3 People in Glass Houses* (1981), *No. 4 Double Trouble* (1981) and No. 5 *Here Today, Dead Tomorrow* (1982). We're spared the numbers on *Bennett's World* (1982) and *Death and the Single Girl* (1983).

Fredrick Bennett has all the characteristics of private eyeness. He is an ex-LA cop. He is an ex-husband. He drives a battered old Buick around the Southern California battlegrounds and lives a rather desolate life. One unique characteristic is his relationship with the police, especially Rufus Drang, his ex-partner on the force and now Captain of Detectives. Unlike most PIs who mix with the police about as well as Jesse Helms with the Communists, Bennett often works with Drang on cases that fall outside the department's official jurisdiction or which are too politically sensitive for the police to become involved. Bennett works without a license and without an office. He operates around the edges, showing an aptitude for the dirty work that Drang avoids: "I slice open the woodwork so all the hidden creatures have to crawl out," is his job description.

Written in third-person narration, each of the novels introduces Bennett in a case in which his involvement has a personal significance that drives the action. Often the immediate stimulus to Bennett's action is his proximity to a dead body. *Two Heads Are Better* begins with Bennett discovering the decapitated body of an old acquaintance in the trunk of his Buick, placed there by Drang who wants Bennett to help prevent a suspected kidnapping. The plotting suffers from some uncertainties, a problem that's remedied in the more recent novels.

In *Dirty Linen* Bennett investigates the death of Christine Walker, a Hollywood sex goddess and a woman whom he once loved. A corpse turns up in Bennett's apartment in *People In Glass Houses*, and one is dumped in the backyard of his rich stepfather's cottage in *Double Trouble*. Just your average maelstrom of mayhem, nothing out of the ordinary for a guy whose friends also include his sexy ex-wife Polly who happens to be very near the scene of a car-bombing homicide (*Death and the Single Girl*) and a skinny spacehead whom Bennett first spies at 1:30 in the morning walking a picket line outside a mortuary with a sign that reads "Sammy Lee Rogers on Strike Against Death" (*Here Today, Dead Tomorrow*).

The best book in the series is *Bennett's World*, in which Bennett, working as an undercover LA cop stalks a maniac who's slashing the throats of skid row derelicts. Although the book was not published until 1982, after four others in the series had already appeared, its action involves the breakup of Bennett's marriage, the suspicious financial dealings and insubordination that got Bennett fired and a nicely handled transition from cop to independent investigator. Either Lewis wrote this book first and its publication was delayed or he wrote it midway through the series in order to elaborate the personal crises that are alluded to in the other titles. Either way, do yourself the favor of reading *Bennett's World* before any of the others.

Bennett is an interesting character, prone to some unpredictable outbursts and amusing interrogative dialogue. He's a good impersonator, possesses a gutsy stubbornness and runs an excellent con. Although he knows his way around the streets, he seldom relies on fast-draw gunplay or physical intimidation.

Lewis is not a stylish writer, but his Bennett novels are always good reads. Uncomplicated, unpretentious and somehow rather tame in tone despite the usual California pathologies, they combine straight-away action with credible characters.

Peter Bragg—Jack Lynch

Another San Francisco investigator staking out a good reputation for himself is Peter Bragg, a Korean vet with a fifth-floor office on Market. Bragg used to be a reporter, first in Seattle, next in Kansas City, finally in San Francisco. After newspapering went sour and his marriage fell apart, he took to tending bar in Sausalito where he lives. He started doing some part-time work for an old lawyer friend and found out it wasn't much different from being a reporter. He liked it better than bar tending and so he went into the PI business for himself.

Bragg has appeared in three Fawcett paperback originals—*Bragg's Hunch* (1981), *The Missing and the Dead* (1982) and *Pieces of Death* (1982). Author John T. Lynch has three more on the way for Warner Books—*Sausalito, San Quentin* and *Monterey*. As the last titles suggest, Bragg's cases often take place outside of San Francisco proper, giving Lynch the chance to color the novels with some legitimate history of northern California.

This is a first-rate but we suspect underrated series owing in part to the prejudice against paperback originals. The narration is straight forward and unpretentious and the action sequences are excellent. The gangland gun battle that rages across Sun Valley in *Bragg's Hunch* is a superb scene that honors Hammett's famous short story, "The Gutting of Couffignal." Bragg is a restrained and believable hero, a good interrogator and physically competent enough with his fists and his guns to get done what needs to be done. He's cut more from the Hammett than the Chandler cloth. Durable, cooperative with the police and straight except for a joint now and then to relax, Bragg makes sense out of life by doing his work well—"bringing order out of chaos" as he tells a friend in *The Missing and the Dead*. His tastes are simple, like his requirements for a good woman—"You wash your face. You brush your hair. You smell nice."

The novels are well plotted. The death threats against the gangster in *Bragg's Hunch* favor Ross Macdonald's *Black Money*. *The Missing and the Dead*, nominated for a Shamus award in 1982, connects a missing-person case to the search for a mysterious murderer known as the Hobo who paints portraits of his victims as they look in the moment before death. *Pieces of Death*, an Edgar nominee in 1983, involves pursuit of a Mediterranean chess set, a six-million-dollar treasure that leaves a trail of death reminiscent of *The Maltese Falcon*.

Bragg is the very autobiographical creation of John T. Lynch who was born March 12, 1930 in Seattle. After graduating from the University of Washington with a BA in journalism in 1953 he worked for several weekly newspapers around Seattle and then joined the promotion department of a local radio/TV station. He also has worked for *TV Guide Magazine* and lived briefly in Davenport, Iowa, and Kansas City before returning to the West Coast where he clerked for a year in a San Francisco brokerage house.

Lynch began tending bar about 1960 at the No Name, a Sausalito tavern that is mentioned in several of the Bragg novels. He joined the San Francisco *Chronicle* in 1969, working first at the copy desk and then moving to the city side as a general assignment reporter and rewrite man. Lynch, a shirttail relative of General George Custer, currently lives in Corte Madera, California.

David Stuart—James MacDougall

Out of Cleveland comes David Stuart, another private eye derived from Lew Archer. Stuart is a philosophical, sensitive investigator whose techniques are as subdued as they are effective. He was trained to be an attorney but quit his position with his father's law firm early in his career because he "needed a value which the law, the courts, practice, the rules of evidence, and a dozen of other things did not prove . . . to know the truth was more important than any legal form of retribution." He's a widower; his wife was murdered shortly after she finished medical school. Stuart prefers moral certainties and his preoccupation with separating reality from assumption seems to be the primary motive behind his work.

The one problem with Stuart's introspectiveness is that it is too constant. He is virtually humorless. He doesn't have enough fun. His conversations are not easy; his observations are never simple. He has an irritating habit of answering a question with another question, and a glance at an antique vase prompts a monologue about how it resembles the human personality. The result seems to be that Stuart sometimes flaunts his moral superiority. He's too preachy, too insistent on his distinctions.

Stuart's first case was *Weasel Hunt* (Bobbs-Merrill, 1972) in which he's hired by a young man to find his long-missing father, a fellow that the rest of the too-wealthy family would prefer stay missing. He may be the headless skeleton found on the family's estate or he may be the person who put the skeleton there. The family conflicts are rather predictable as is the identity of the skeleton, but the book is intelligently written. MacDougall is a minimalist when it comes to action, but he has a real talent for revealing characters through everyday circumstances, slices of conversation and subtle interactions. He engages serious topics including the nature of friendship and the need for moral obligations.

In *Death and the Maiden* (Charter, 1980), Stuart travels to southern Ohio to investigate the kidnapping of the five-year-old daughter of a college professor. He's retained by his old college roommate, who is the attorney for the father. A more dramatic ending than in the initial novel makes this one a more satisfactory all-round effort.

James MacDougall was born in Cleveland, Ohio in 1940 to James and Augusta MacDougall. He graduated from Williams College in 1962 with a degree in American History and Literature and then went on to Case Western University where he received his MA (1965) and PhD. (1968) in English. His dissertation was on characterization in the novels of Charles Dickens. From 1966 to 1967 he was an Assistant Professor of English at Kent State. Since 1967 he has been at Ball State University in Muncie, Indiana where he is a Professor of English with a specialty in 19th century British novels and romantic poetry. He said that he began to read mysteries and think about writing one as a respite from grading exams. In addition to Macdonald, he likes the work of Dick Francis and Simenon.

Jake Spanner—Larry Morse

Larry Alan Morse was born in Fort Wayne, Indiana, on July 30, 1945 to Sidney and Ruth Morse. He earned a BA from Berkeley in 1967 and an MA from San Francisco State University in 1968. A resident of Toronto, Canada, Morse has worked as a production assistant for a Canadian educational television station and was the program coordinator of adult education for the University of Toronto 1970-1975. He has been a full-time writer since 1975, explaining that "upon returning from a long trip to Asia in 1975, I couldn't get a job. I still can't get a job, so I'm still a full-time writer."

Morse's first novel was *The Flesh Eaters* (Warner, 1979). It is based on a true story about a 15th century cave-dwelling family in Scotland who cannibalizes the travelers that pass by on the road. In 1980 he wrote his first crime book with co-author Carlos Yorio. Entitled *Who Did It* (Prentice-Hall) it was described by *Contemporary Authors* (Vol. 107) as "a text book of eight stories exploring all styles of the field, designed for students whose second language is English."

Morse's initial private eye novel was *The Old Dick* (Avon), a 1981 Edgar winner for best original paperback. The book's hero is Jake Spanner, a 78-year-old-private detective, long retired from LA's mean streets playing out his days on park benches and living in a dingy, two-bedroom tract house. Arthritic, plagued by insomnia and a craving for spicy foods, alone after his wife left him, Jake wheezes his proud way through one last bizarre case, assisted by the troupe of old cronies he recruits from LA's retirement homes.

The case begins when Sal Piccola, an old mobster whom Spanner put away decades earlier, asks Jake to help him recover his kidnapped grandson. Jake soon finds himself and his band of golden-age geezers chasing after $750,000 in ransom money, messing up LA's cocaine network, and suffering threats, ransackings and beatings before bringing the affair to a satisfying conclusion. Jake's brittle bones are comforted along the way by an unlikely coupling with a prostitute's young daughter aptly named Miranda Bliss and by frequent tokes from his hash pipe, a habit he picked up in the 1920s.

The novel's approach to crime is purely hard-boiled ("I wanted to smash those scum, inflict pain . . . ."), and it is matched by an unflinching look at the limits and the strengths of the aged. Jon Breen praised it for a "view of old age [that] manages to be unsentimental and uncompromising yet optimistic and good-natured." At one point Jake says, "When you get old, you either went soft or you got dry. Fortunately, I had gotten dry." Not so dry that he can't make one final go at it, living the fantasy of what you'd do if you had a last chance to do it.

The Big Enchilada (Avon, 1982), Morse's second PI novel, is a much less sophisticated effort, which while probably intended as a parody does not really succeed at any level. Its attitude goes far beyond hard-boiled—charred is more like it. The detective is Sam Hunter, a man of such Neanderthal sentiments and ugly excesses that he makes Mike Hammer look cerebral. Hunter is a very horny creep who has sex against the wall with his secretary on p. 10, on the floor with a client on p. 30 and in the shower with a 16-year-old on p. 53. Apparently these masochistic women are swept off their feet and onto their backs by Hunter's suave manners like when he throws his too-well done steak on a restaurant floor or pulls a gun on a motorist who's playing his car radio too loud. When really mad he gouges out eyeballs.

Hunter's idea of an interview is to grab a guy by his balls and squeeze, promising to "rip your balls off, and ... smash both of your knees, and both your ankles, and both your elbows and both your hands." His attitude toward violence—"I wanted to feel their skins rip and their bones snap beneath my fingers"—would give Race Williams a queasy stomach.

The plot is an extended improbability which begins when a 6'8" 500-pound giant barges into Hunter's office, breaks his desk and orders him to "stay away from Domingo," a warning as gratuitous as the rest of the book since Hunter has never heard of any Domingo. But he does have three ongoing cases involving 1) a "Bel Air rich bitch" with a kinky husband, 2) an obnoxious teenage punk doper and 3) the ubiquitous fourteen-year-old runaway porn star. Surprise, surprise! As Hunter backtracks these cases, he discovers they all lead not only to Domingo but to every conceivable form of sleaze and depravity that LA has to offer.

We recommend this book as the modern nadir of private eye literature, a classic of bad writing so noteworthy that it deserved to be honored in Bill Pronzini's *Gun in Cheek*. One critic praised the novel as a "parody of the parodies" whatever that is. In that same spirit, we credit that reviewer for great satire. Hunter returns in a second novel, *Sleaze* (1985).

Max Roper—Kin Platt

Kin Platt was born December 8, 1911, in New York City to Daniel and Etta (Hochberg) Platt. He attended public schools in New York and Connecticut and received a Bronze Star for his Air Force service in the China-Burma-India theater. Platt currently lives in Los Angeles where he can fully indulge his passion for golf.

Platt has been involved in several creative fields throughout his life. He has worked as a painter and a sculptor; however, his best known careers have been as a cartoonist and a writer. He was the illustrator and writer of the "Mr. and Mrs."comic strip (1947-1963) as well as "The Duke and the

Duchess" (1950-1954) both of which were carried by the New York *Herald Tribune* Syndicate. His theatrical caricatures have appeared in all the major New York papers, *Village Voice* and the Los Angeles *Times*, to name a few.

The author of more than twenty juvenile novels and mysteries, Platt won an Edgar for the best juvenile mystery of 1966 with *Sinbad and Me*. It initiated a popular series featuring youth-sleuth Steve Forester and his English bulldog Sinbad who solve subsequent cases in *The Mystery of the Witch Who Wouldn't* (1973) and *The Ghost of Hellfire Street* (1980). Platt has written several juveniles that deal with various forms of mental illness. The best-known of these is the Chloris series about a young girl who is emotionally disturbed (*Chloris and the Creeps*, 1973; *Chloris and the Freaks*, 1975; and *Chloris and the Weirdos*, 1978). Some of Platt's novels for young adults are quite lurid and pessimistic in tone. *The Doomsday Gang* (1977) and *Headman* (1979), both aimed at disillusioning kids about gang affiliations, are the best examples.

In addition to his private eye series, Roper has written one other adult mystery entitled *Dead as They Come* (1972) about Molly Mellinger, an amateur detective and editor of mystery novels.

Los Angeles private detective Max Roper was introduced in *The Pushbutton Butterfly* (1970) when he was hired to search for the wayward and strung-out daughter of a millionaire in the environs of San Francisco. Roper's second case (*The Kissing Gourami*, 1970), involves a girl who is killed by the piranha placed in her party dress, certainly one of the most pleasingly bizarre murder methods you're likely to encounter. In fact, the series presents a number of highly creative homicide techniques that occasionally fall outside reality's boundaries (another favorite is the muscleman who's poisoned by the spiked rubdown lotion he spreads on himself).

Roper specializes in cases involving sports stars and the distinctive atmosphere and lingo of various athletic locations are smoothly woven into the plots of the remaining novels. Horseracing (*The Princess Stakes Murder*, 1973), basketball (*The Giant Kill*, 1974), women's pro tennis (*Matchpoint for Murder*, 1975), bodybuilding and weightlifting (*The Body Beautiful Murder*, 1975) and baseball (*The Screwball King Murder*, 1978) give Platt, a self-described "half-ass jock," plenty of opportunities to reveal an insider's feel for the fine points of sport subcultures.

Roper is an operative of EPT (Emergency Procedure Terminus), a security, detection and espionage service run by O.J. Barr. EPT fronts a lot of government operations and helps "the average citizen if he was wealthy enough or if O.J. became interested in his particular problem." Many of its cases seem to involve illegal drug traffic. In his forties, Roper gets beat up a lot, but he always manages to deliver his licks and kicks. Roper's a karate expert and his assailants often meet with unpleasant exchanges such as *seiken jodan-uke* (left-forefist upper block), *hiji age-uchi* (rising-elbow strike) and last but not least *uraken hizo-uchi* (inverted-fist to the spleen).

The dialogue in a Roper novel has a snazzy, hipster tone but it often rings strangely old-fashioned. If it weren't for the *au currant* California movements and milieus, you'd swear that you were back a decade or two where somewhere somebody might say something like, "You keep smiling when you wanna deck some smart apple. You shake his mitt and wish him lotsa luck, all that crapola. Then, when you're ready, you make your move, you got the guy suckered out..." (*The Body Beautiful Murder*). Despite the fact that Roper's always leering after some "doll" who inevitably has "beautifully formed naked legs," his overt sexuality is largely repressed and slightly out of sync with the seventies.

The plots are uneven in quality. At their best they contain nicely placed clues and some competent detection by an easy-going uncomplicated hero. More often, they rely too much on quirks and coincidences with side excursions down alleys where the corpses keep piling up, albeit by some very imaginative finishing strokes.

Miles Jacoby—Robert J. Randisi

Robert J. Randisi is well-known among mystery writers as one of the leading champions of private eye fiction. A frequent contributor to and reviewer for *The Armchair Detective*, Randisi has probably forgotten more PI literature than most of us ever knew. He regards himself as the "world's foremost private eye nut."

Randisi was a founder of the Private Eye Writers of America in 1982, served as its first Vice-President and is the editor of its newsletter, *Reflections in a Private Eye*. He was one of the first authors to learn about the present volume, and his assistance was crucial to our being able to complete it.

A native of Brooklyn, Randisi was born on August 24, 1951. He has written more than 50 novels, the majority of them Westerns under various house names. He also has written fourteen short stories including the "Max Nolan Erotic P.I." series in *Beaver Magazine* with titles like "The Missing Bust" and "Hitch Humper." He is the editor of the first anthology of the Private Eye Writers of America published by the Mysterious Press in 1984 under the title *The Eyes Have It*.

Randisi has written four private eye novels under his own name. The first, *The Disappearance of Penny* (1980), was a paperback original for Charter featuring Henry Po, a licensed investigator for the New York State Racing Club, whose search for the missing daughter of one of the country's leading thoroughbred owners and trainers eventually runs into a large-scale race-fixing scandal. Dick Francis is the Triple Crown Winner of the

Murder-at-the-racetrack entries with his books about jockey-turned-PI Sid Halley, but Randisi knows this turf well enough to finish in the money with Po's first outing.

Randisi's second PI, Miles Jacoby (pronounced JACKabee, not JaCObee), known to his friends as "Kid" or "Jack" was introduced in *Eye in the Ring* (Avon, 1982), returned in *The Steinway Collection* (Avon, 1983), and his first hardback appearance in *Full Contact* (St. Martin's, 1984). Jacoby began his career as a part-time investigator for best friend Eddie Waters, a New York City detective who is murdered in *Eye in the Ring* with Jacoby's alcoholic brother, Benny, being the prime suspect. The conflict between loyalty to boss and loyalty to brother is complicated by an incestuous love affair and a professional hit man named Max Collins.

Jacoby is also a professional boxer, a "I-could-have-been-a-contender" middleweight with a 12-4 record whose retirement from the ring to take over Water's practice still leaves plenty of opportunity for Randisi to absorb some nice linament-and-resin ambiance into the Jacoby novels. Private eye fans will especially like *The Steinway Collection*, not only because it involves the theft of a priceless collection of pulp detective magazines, but because of the inside jokes and cameo appearances by PI celebrities. There's help from private eyes named Fortune, Po and a San Francisco op dubbed "lone Wolf," a pulps' expert named Kaminsky and cops called Abel and Seidman. Jacoby even takes up part-time residence in Bogie's, a favorite New York City hang-out for private eyers. The story-telling in the book is exciting and notable for its avoidance of hard-boiled posturing and cliches.

Cody—James Reasoner

American folklore suggests Texas as an ideal locale for PI exploits. Natural habitat for Hud, Teddy Blue, the Texas Rangers and J. Frank Dobie's *Cow People*, Texas has always loved its heroes. Even the "Lone Star" nickname inspires a spirit of dashing and defiant self-reliance. Although Texas has given us some of our most colorful real life private investigators (most notably, Jay J. Armes of El Paso), it has been a surprisingly infrequent setting for private eye novels. A welcome exception to this fact is James M. Reasoner's first novel, *Texas Wind* (1980), featuring a Fort Worth PI named Cody.

Texas Wind was the biggest surprise in our 1982 survey of private eye writers (see Chapter 1). Its high rating was achieved despite a distribution strategy by the publisher, Manor Books, designed apparently to keep the book a secret from as many people as possible. The book begins with a conventional Lew Archer problem. Mandy Traft, TCU student and daughter of a wealthy Fort Worth family, has disappeared. Her step-mother, Gloria Traft, hires Cody to find her before Mandy's father returns from a business trip. Cody's investigation leads him to conclude that Mandy has eloped with her roommate's boyfriend, Jeff Willington. This explanation proves adequate until Gloria Traft receives a ransom note demanding $125,000 for Mandy's return. Inside the box in which the note arrives is one of Mandy's fingers. Up to this point, the plot is pure Macdonald derivative, but Reasoner then supplies a few surprises as well as a satisfying alternative to the well-worn Archer motif that the young are always victimized by their overrich, underprincipled parents.

Reasoner has described Cody as "a sort of Lew Archer of the early books." In his early forties, Cody is a reasonably well-educated man with tastes in reading that run from Zane Grey to Herman Hesse. He is a connoisseur of modern western art and his office on Camp Bowie, just up the street from the Amon Carter Museum of Modern Art, is decorated with prints of Frederick Remington and Charlie Russell. Ably assisted by main-squeeze Janice Bryant, a "cool redhead who epitomized style and class. She would never see thirty again, but then she didn't need to," Cody is moderate with women and booze. He disdains Texas hype: "strictly ersatz cowboy, exploiting the Cowtown image for all it is worth. I . . . hadn't cared for it." Cody's only concessions to Texas myth are his boots and denim jacket.

Reasoner explains, "I didn't want to write a phony Texas story." As a result, Cody is drawn without any of the excesses that often stereotype Texas characters. In his effort to avoid misshapen machismo, however, Reasoner has left Cody a little flat. When he adds an extra dimension and lets Cody cut a fuller figure, Reasoner will have a detective that can hold his own with the best of the regional private eyes.

Born in Fort Worth on June 5, 1953, James Reasoner has spent most of his life in the small town of Azle, Texas. The youngest of three children born to Marion (an electronics technician) and Ora (an elementary school teacher) Reasoner, he attended public schools in Azle and then went to North Texas State University (Denton, Texas) where he received a BA in English in 1975.

In 1976, Reasoner married Livia Washburn, whom he credits as a major influence on his career: "Nearly everything I've written has been a collaboration with Livia to a certain extent . . . her input is an integral part of my work." Under her own name Livia has published "A Matter of Memories," a PI short story in the May, 1982 *Mike Shayne Mystery Magazine*. As by Brett Halliday, she wrote one Mike Shayne short story entitled "A Cry in the Night" (November, 1981, *Mike Shayne Mystery Magazine*). The Reasoners currently live in Azle where James manages "Reasoner's TV and The Book Place" with his father.

Reasoner began writing short stories for his own amusement at age eleven. His first short story, "Comingor," was published in the August,

1977 *Mike Shayne Mystery Magazine.* Since that time he has written more than 20 short stories under his own name and two pseudonyms, M.R. James and R. Mason. His "Man in the Morgue" and "Death and the Dancing Shadows" made the Honor Roll of Best Detective Stories of the Year in 1978 and 1980 respectively. The only Cody short story, entitled "Dead in Friday," was published in *Spiderweb* (Summer, 1982).

Beginning in 1978, Reasoner began to write Mike Shayne stories under the Brett Halliday byline. Between him and Livia they wrote 37 Shayne stories, all of which appeared between December, 1978 and October, 1982 in *Mike Shayne Mystery Magazine.* Jeff Banks, writing in *The Poisoned Pen,* called their "Mayhem in the Magic City" the equal of any of Dresser's stories of that length with the exception of "A Taste for Cognac." Reasoner admits, "I'm very fond of my Mike Shayne work; my primary goal was to remain true to Davis Dresser's original characters. Plots and settings change over the years, of course, but I like to think that my version of Shayne is the same character who first saw the light of day in 1939."

Reasoner feels a kinship with the original pulpsters like Norbert Davis, Lester Dent, Roger Torrey, W.T. Ballard and Carroll John Daly who tried their hand at all forms of fiction. In that tradition he and Livia are working on mysteries, Westerns and science fiction. They have published one historical romance, *Emerald Land* (Fawcett, 1983) under the penname Livia James and another, *Dawn at Sea* (Bantam, 1984), under their own names. Reasoner plans to write more novels about Cody, bringing him back to face once again "this damned Texas wind [that] blows all the time . . . . It blows all the good things away."

Red Diamond—Mark Schorr

Red Diamond Private Eye (1983) is a jewel. A novel of action, humor, parody and sensitivity to the plight of a romantic dreamer locked in the very unromantic routine of the anonymous working class, it could be placed in any category of mystery and shine as one of the brightest.

Simon Jaffe is a hefty, 42-year-old New York City cab driver trapped in a small and dismal world made up of a money-grabbing, castrating wife, two bewildering and stand-offish teenage children and a drab house slowly sinking into a Long Island marsh. He has two joys left in a life that "hadn't turned out the way he planned": he can drive his hack with the best of them ("The city was his. He knew every pothole, every one-way street, every slow traffic light") and he can lose himself in the finest collection of pulp detective novels this side of Bill Pronzini's Nameless.

Jaffe owns thousands of pulps, but his favorite is Red Diamond:

Diamond didn't waste his time talking. He was eloquent in several calibers. He always got his man, the girl, a couple of knocks in the head, and his fee. Red Diamond was the last person in the world you'd want to mess with. What a guy!

One day Jaffe picks up a fare by the name of Charlie Flitcraft who like his predecessor in *The Maltese Falcon* represents the opportunity to turn one's life around at random and create a new reality. Flitcraft asks Simon, "Do you ever want to chuck it all? Start again? Forget it all!" And upon returning to his flimsy, sinking house and discovering that wife Millie has sold his entire collection of pulps, except for the beloved *Diamond in the Rough*, for $2300, Simon does chuck it all and tumbles into his dream world as a new man, the man he's wanted to be for years; his Walter Mitty fantasies have come true at last:

He shut the door behind him and moved down the narrow corridor. There was a slight swagger in his walk, a bob in his shoulders.
Too long he'd been confined. Maybe he'd go down to the gym and shoot the breeze about old times. It was too early for that, he decided. It was never too early for a shot of bourbon.
He walked past the front desk. The clerk was nowhere in sight. He opened the heavy metal door and walked downstairs.
Red Diamond hit the streets.

From this point on, Diamond is hot on the trail of his girlfriend, the beautiful Fifi La Roche, whom he hopes to save from the clutches of his arch enemy, gangster Rocco Rico. Through Harlem bars, Times Square flophouses, Brooklyn shootouts and cross-country to Hollywood glitter, Diamond strong-arms his way through a pulp mystery that honors the Black Mask school as much as it parodies it. Red Diamond is as good as they come. Move over Spade and Marlowe.

Red is a hero five decades behind his time who mistakes every blonde for Fifi, looks for Rocco down every alley and gives us some of the best corner-of-the-mouth *double entendres* that ever spiced *Spicy Detective*.

Diamond had barely undressed in his room when he heard someone trying the knob. He stepped behind the door. As it was pushed open, he jumped out, grabbing the intruder from behind. His hands pressed on soft, feminine flesh.
Rosalie gave a frightened yelp, which he muffled with his hand over her mouth.
"You scared me," she said.
"You could get yourself killed coming in here like that. I've got dangerous reflexes."
She stepped back and watched the blood throb to his groin. "I see," she said with a lecherous smile. "You take a lot of showers. Got a dirty mind?"
"It's hot. And I don't like the smell of the people I spend my days with."
"What did you find out today?" she purred, coming in like a pirate about to board ship.

"A little of this, a little of that. I haven't put anything together yet. Why d'you ask?"

"Just curious," she said before pressing her lips against his. He didn't fight, but he didn't encourage her.

"My tub's going to overflow if you keep that up," he said, pulling away.

"I'd just love to hear what you do. It's so exciting."

"There's plenty I'd like to tell you. Even more I'd like to show you. But business before pleasure."

She grasped his most outstanding feature.

"You trying to pump me for information?" he asked.

"Maybe. You drive me wild."

"I've been through some tough interrogations. It takes a while to make me spill."

"Did you have a hard day?"

"Not as hard as the night's going to be." He took her hand away from him, spun her around, and gave her a pat on the rump. "Run along now."

"Are you coming back?"

He didn't answer. He walked into the bathroom, shut the door, and took a long, cold shower.

The closing scene with Jaffe, the "cabbie shamus," on trial for five counts of murder is a sentimental tour-de-force that will have the private-eye blood pumping through your veins as you call "More, Mr. Schorr, more."

Mark Schorr, the creator of Red Diamond, was born in Brooklyn in 1953 to Bernard and Vera Schorr. He attended the State University of New York at Binghamton for two years and then began working for a movie studio in New York City. He has worked as a freelance writer and investigative reporter for several years during which time he also has held a series of odd jobs—a bouncer at Studio 54, a clerk in a bookstore, a professional photographer and a licensed private detective. His articles have been published in *Argosy*, *New York* magazine, *The Village Voice*, *High Times* and several others.

In 1980 Schorr moved to California where for two years he covered the federal court beat and did investigative reporting for the LA *Herald Examiner*. He then joined the staff of KNXT, the CBS affiliate in Los Angeles, and was nominated for an Emmy for his investigative series on the LAPD SWAT Team. He worked for *USA Today*, an unsatisfying affiliation which lasted four months and ended appropriately on April Fools Day, 1983.

Red Diamond Private Eye is Shorr's first novel, but the good news is that it's not his last. The second Diamond novel, entitled *Ace of Diamonds*, was released by St. Martins in 1984, and a third is planned.

John Shaft—Ernest Tidyman

The roughest, toughest, meanest, hardest and most entertaining of the black eyes is Ernest Tidyman's John Shaft. Shaft appears in seven novels: *Shaft* (1970), *Shaft Among the Jews* (1972), *Shaft's Big Score* (1972), *Shaft Has A Ball* (1973), *Goodbye, Mr. Shaft* (1973), *Shaft's Carnival of Killers* (1974) and *The Last Shaft* (1975). The action in all seven is as violent as that of any of the Mike Hammers but it is more sophisticated and intelligent. Shaft is smart, sharp and sexy, a man that appeals to men as well as to women.

Above all, Shaft is tough. When two thugs go after him in the men's room of a bar Shaft's response is savage.

The door slammed open and Shaft was chuckling when he hit it with his shoulder just at the right time to catch the tall, rangy black with the edge of it. He caught him while he was still off-balance. Shaft reached out and grabbed the muscles of the man's solar plexis, as one grabs a basketball, and clenched steel fingers.

It is like having your gut torn out with a pitchfork. The man's jaw, bladder, and bowels all fell open in the excruciating pain and he rose in the air on the wings of agony and shock. Shaft yanked him forward with his handful of abdominal muscles and, like Homer in another odyssey, drove his fist into the small black head just below the left ear. There was a crunching, crushing feeling under his knuckles. This stray dog who chewed on the victims of a fat pimp was probably dead by the time he hit the urinal and bounced off to the floor.

Shaft was born in Harlem, brought up in Harlem, several times almost died in Harlem. His mother was on welfare and his father he never knew. After several juvenile busts he enlisted in the Marines and went through Boot Camp at Parris Island. He was a light heavyweight on the boxing team, made Honor man in the company and was rewarded with a fast trip to Nam. After being wounded and receiving a chest full of medals for "shooting up fourteen-year-old Cong kids because if you didn't they would blow your ass off," Shaft returned to the US where he still has bad dreams about those kids. NYU was next for the study of law. Since Shaft figured all lawyers were rich, like doctors, but they didn't have to cut people up, he wanted to be a lawyer. After a short while he gave it up and went into investigative work, first for a nationally known agency and then into his own business.

Shaft has no brothers, no sisters. His mother died when he was two. His father was a numbers runner and wound up with his throat cut. Shaft went into a succession of foster homes, in his words, "Some okay, some awful."

As for his PI business he says that "Ninety percent of the jobs, the bread-and-butter stuff that pays the rent, the answering service and the telephone bill is routine. Divorce crap, insurance claims—shit like that. Once in a while there's something bigger, and that's where the heavy bread is, and when there's heavy bread involved, they want you to put it on the line—your reputation, your license, your ass. So far I've been lucky with a few of those."

Shaft is thirty-two in the fourth novel but mentally he is older than Methusaleh. Though tough he has a tender streak and resents injustice with a passion. His buddy on the force, Lieutenant Victor Anderozi, admires him but considers him to be "an impertinent prick." Shaft is physically muscular, and has saddle-stitch scars across the back of his right hand and on his forehead—from a bicycle chain that almost cost him his sight. He wears a black leather coat and adds a black fur cap in winter. He frequents the *No Name Bar* across the street from his apartment on Hudson Street. His office has a desk, a chair, a filing cabinet and is located just south of Times Square on Forty-Sixth Street. His furniture depresses him—but so does the violence, squalor and wretchedness of all the hopeless victims in the city. That is why he is a one-man Angel of Vengeance when irked or irritated by the cruelty and meanness of the victimizers.

Shaft's creator, Ernest Tidyman, was born and educated in Cleveland and worked first as a newspaperman for the Cleveland *News*, the New York *Post* and the New York *Times*. Following this he became managing editor for *Signature* magazine. Tidyman also served in the Army during World War II. In 1966, after his 25 year newspaper career, he became a free-lance screenwriter and producer. His screenplays include *The French Connection* in 1971, for which he won an Academy Award; *Shaft* (1971); *Shaft's Big Score* (1972); *High Plains Drifter* (1973); *Report to the Commissioner* (1975); *Street People* (1976); and *A Force of One* (1979). His TV plays include *To Kill a Cop* (1978), *Dummy*—an adaptation of his novel by the same name—in 1979 and *Power: An American Saga*, also in 1979.

Though Tidyman is best known for his Shaft series he is an excellent novelist. Two outstanding examples are *Line of Duty* (1974), about a cop who is also a hit man for the Mafia, and the Western *High Plains Drifter* (1972), which he adapted for the screen. Other novels include *Flower Power* (1968), *Absolute Zero* (1971) and *Table Stakes* (1979). Another of Tidyman's successes is the case of Donald Lang—a deaf mute, illiterate, brain-damaged black—accused of two murders and a suspect in a number of others. Published under the title of *Dummy* in 1974, the novel shows clearly what cruelty and neglect can do to helpless children.

Because of the excellence of his work, Tidyman has received the Writers Guild of America Award, the MWA award and although he is white, the NAACP awarded him their Image Award in 1971 for *Shaft*. Tidyman was writing and producing films for his LA-based Ernest Tidyman Productions up to the time of his death in the summer of 1984.

Bernardo Thomas—Louis Williams

It is not easy to keep a novel as powerful as Louis Williams' *Tropical Murder* (1981) a secret, but somehow Tower Books managed. In our survey of PWA and mystery critics, not one respondent indicated a knowledge of this book. Other than a review in the *West Coast Review of Books* and one in *Best Sellers*, we were unable to uncover any attention from the critics. This book deserves a special award: The Best Unread PI Novel of the Past Decade.

The setting is Punto Fijo on the Venezuelan peninsula which is perpetually sweltering in a hazy miasma. The detective is Bernardo Thomas, son of a whore and a sailor who drowned at sea. Raised by relatives in the American South and trained to be a lawyer, Thomas comes back to Venezuela driven by the ghost of his lost father and by a Jungian shadow named Duarte who also affects a PI persona. Thomas is a "true solitary." He drinks too much. He is deeply depressed and plauged by existential crises. On occasion he plays Russian roulette, taking special joy in watching the pistol cylinder spin before his eyes. His life is smothered by the same dark glaze that clouds Punto Fijo:

I thought how most of life was not being able to find the toothpaste or was dropping your best pen into the toilet. It wasn't tragic. It wasn't dignified enough to be called absurd. It was simply trivial—a pig shitting on your doorstep.

The plot is secondary and a bit muddled. The death toll goes so high that the grave diggers and the priests don't even know the names of the people they're burying. The center of attention is Nelson Seed, an American oil worker whose disappearance causes his wife Wilda to hire Thomas, at first because she wants him found, later because she wants him dead. Wilda isn't the only person desperate to find Seed. Wilda's lover, local and not-so-local crime figures, and Thomas' own mother have their reasons for wanting to locate him. It's apparent from very early on that the drug rackets are at the center of all the grit.

Tropical Murder is not a quick read. It is a novel with a Crumley style to it, right down to some strong Texas roots. It's a long pull that leaves you feeling like Thomas feels at the end—"[like] you have given the party of your life and all the guests have gone home."

Despite extensive efforts, we have been unable to locate Louis Williams or learn anything about him. Tower Books is out of business. If anyone could provide the authors of this book with information about Williams, we would include it in a subsequent edition or some other suitable outlet with the proper acknowledgements.

Michael Brennan—Fred Zackel

Michael Brennan is another of the Lew Archer imitators. He's a medium-grade substitute; one injection of him might immunize you temporarily against the real thing. Down, divorced and destitute, Brennan is a San Francisco-based detective, recently fired from the Pacific Continental agency and now drawing unemployment checks while he waits for his investigator's license to expire. He can't recognize as much fauna as Archer can, but he does identify all types of fish during his stroll through a Butchertown smokehouse. Brennan is up to his eyeballs in cynicism ("Playing detective is like being a gravedigger. There's always dirt to be dug up, people willing to pay to have it dug up") and pity ("I wanted to be somone in my life . . . . Not just a peeping tom in lotus land") which fight for page space with the overwrought similes ("The twenty disappeared faster than Saturday night parking").

The end result is a nearly fatal case of the literary pretentions in Fred Zackel's *Cocaine and Blue Eyes* (Coward, McCann and Geoghegan, 1978), Brennan's first outing. The cocaine belongs to everyone in the sleazy downside of San Francisco, and the blue eyes belong to Dani Anatole, the missing girlfriend of Joey Crawford who sends Brennan an envelope with a thousand dollar bill in it and a note saying, "Find Dani for me." This amounts to a dead man's last wish because Crawford was killed the night before in a mysterious car wreck on the Golden Gate Bridge. Brennan begins to search for Dani simply to tell her that Crawford has been killed, but he soon learns that her disappearance is linked not only to the cocaine trafficking that pal Joey was pursuing but to several nasty and jealous relatives in her very wealthy family, owners of one of San Francisco's largest fish companies. The family, which is tied in with some unsavory Chinatown types, has enough past perversities it wants to keep hidden that Brennan's search for Dani touches off an epidemic of paranoia, revenge and meanness. The plot is undisciplined and the solution is ambiguous, but credit Zackel with some brass tacks dialogue and a couple of convincing action scenes that save the novel from its affectations.

Zackel has a better handle on the story line in *Cinderella After Midnight* (Coward, McCann and Geoghegan, 1980), the second Brennan. No surprise it's another missing person case, and as usual the missing person is a teenage girl. Her name is Julie Beaumont, and her mother is one of San Francisco's top-of-the-line call girls. As in *Cocaine*, all sorts of people want to hire Brennan in order to keep him away from their sercets which more often than not involve pornography, illegitimate kids, homosexuality, blackmail, and murder. Mix in the high-rollers like a female U.S. senator and a fabulously wealthy Calfiornia tycoon with some real scuzzy raunchers and put this one in the winner's column. Brennan still wallows too much, but he's not alone. His girlfriend, an investigator with PAC-CON, Brennan's old boss, keeps him a bit more cozy.

We haven't been able to find out anything about author Fred Zackel except that he formerly lived on a houseboat in the Bay Area.

Chapter VIII
Ladies of the Court—Female Private Eyes

THE PRIVATE EYE NOVEL has been dominated by men. Its authors are male. Its heroes are male. Its fantasies are male. For the most part, females have been relegated to the role of the passive victim or the conniving *femme fatale*. When Hammett, Gardner and Stout carved out larger roles for their female characters, the results were generally mediocre. In this context, the increased presence of females among the PI ranks is a noteworthy development.

The female private detective comes in two models—one created by a male author who more often than not emphasizes his heroine's long legs, big breasts and voracious sexual appetite, the other designed by a female author who stresses a woman's ability to achieve success in a world too long arranged for inflating the male ego. In this chapter we consider both perspectives, but we emphasize the female authors in an attempt to redress some of the male-favored imbalance.

A number of female authors also wrote about male detectives. One of the best writers of hard-boiled fiction was M(ary) V(iolet) Heberden who gave us some excellent tales about two private eyes—Desmond Shannon, a 1950s New York PI who appeared in a series of novels including the nicely handled *Murder Unlimited* (1953), and Rick Vanner in the Buenos Aires-based *Engaged to Murder* (1949). The noted science fiction writer Leigh Brackett whose *No Good From a Corpse* (1944) and *Stranger At Home* (1946) were her best pulp novels also had some memorable screen credits. She co-wrote the screenplay for *The Big Sleep* with William Faulkner and was the screenwriter for Robert Altman's version of *The Long Goodbye*. Hilda Lawrence's Mark East, a detective who often worked under cover, was showcased in three suspenseful tales—*Blood Upon the Snow* (1944), *A Time to Die* (1945), and *Death of a Doll* (1947). Lawrence wrote some very good non-East mysteries including *The Pavillion* and *Duet of Death* (1947).

Sara Scott—Karl Alexander
Karl Alexander's *A Private Investigation* (Dell, 1980) is an ambitious attempt at explaining what it's like to be victimized by crime and to put your life back together afterwards. The vehicle for this explanation is the life and career of Sara Scott who at the age of 28 witnessed the death of her

husband, Andy, an up-and-coming investigative reporter for *Rolling Stone*, killed by snipers in a passing car. The police are unable to find the killers, and Sara hires a crafty old detective by the name of Claude Casparian to take the case. She can't afford to pay him so she works as his secretary and then insists that he teach her the PI business in order that she can continue to search for her husband's murderers.

Four years and a BS in psychology later, Sara is working as a private investigator in Venice, California. It's been so long since the last client came through the door that her receipt book is covered with dust. Her life is going steadily downhill—she suffers constant nightmares about Andy's death, and her adolescent daughter Valerie is afraid her mother is going insane. Trapped by the past, Sara's emotional stability is deteriorating because of her obsessive need to understand and to avenge Andy's murder.

Just when Sara's landlord is about to evict her for being three months behind on the office rent, she finally gets a client, Helen Reardon, who hires Sara to follow her psychologist husband whom she suspects of having an affair. Sara discovers that Dr. Reardon has a secret, but it's not adultery. In fact, it looks like Reardon, who is also murdered in front of Sara, may have been a victim of the same people who killed Andy. Aided by Valerie, Casparian and her boyfriend Sam who does some nice undercover work in a suspicious halfway house for addicts, Sara unravels a scheme that includes high-ranking state officials and some real roughnecks from the Mexican mafia. There's quite a bit of tough stuff along the way with Sara practicing a few nifty moves copied from her favorite PI—Jim Rockford.

A Private Investigation tries the reader's patience. It is overly long and overwrought, qualities that also plagued its adaptation as a TV movie, entitled *Missing Pieces*, starring Elizabeth Montgomery as Sara. The repetition in the book is deadly as is Alexander's experiment with the stylistic technique of setting Sara's flashbacks and emotional broodings apart in italicized passages. The effect is to make Sara appear painfully vulnerable. Writing in *The Armchair Detective*, Richard Meyers quipped, "the girl would get hysterical at the drop of a discouraging word." This antagonism toward Sara is interesting because it illustrates the well-known psychological finding that we often tend to blame victims for their suffering. The fact that Sara makes us a bit irritable indicates that Alexander has captured the essential qualities of victimization—the overwhelming and seemingly endless sense of vulnerability, the loss of esteem and the anger—better than we may be able to tolerate.

Karl Alexander is probably best known for his novelization of Nicholas Meyer's science fiction-fantasy film *Time After Time*, which was published by Delacorte in 1979. The action involves a doctor (who is really Jack the Ripper) using a time machine (that has just been invented by H.G. Wells) to escape from 1893 London to 1974 San Francisco. Wells follows in hot pursuit. The Ripper and Wells suffer loads of culture shock in liberated lotus land. The sexual revolution leaves H.G. gasping for breath but ready for more. The result is whimsical and a lot of fun.

Honey West—G.G. Fickling

Honey West was one of the first super-sexy female investigators. She is a 5'5" blue-eyed, taffy blonde with a "baby-bottom complexion." Her 38-22-36 body is always being liberated from the swimming suits, negligee and miniskirts she wears. Sometimes she tucks her .22 automatic in her cleavage hoping that it won't fall into unfriendly hands. Men describe her as "delicious," "lucious," "miraculous" and "voluptuous." One guy claims Honey's got more dangerous curves than the Indianapolis speedway and makes him feel like an H-bomb about to be triggered. There's plenty of opportunity to make such observations because various parts of Honey are always spilling out into plain view. Count on her being naked on a beach at least once per novel. She's the original Big Tease of Private Eyedom.

Honey became a private eye after her father, Hank West, was murdered in an LA back alley. Following graduation from Long Beach City College, Honey became a detective in order to find her father's killer. At the beginning of her career she worked in Long Beach where she managed to resist the thousand or more propositions of marriage made to her by her good friend, Lieutenant Mark Strong of the Long Beach Sheriff's office. Honey is tough, knows judo and talks a liberated line.

But Honey is definitely not much of a feminist. These books, published by Pyramid, are unabashedly sexploitive. The titles tell it all: *This Girl for Hire* (1957), *A Gun For Honey* (1958), *Girl on the Loose* (1958), *Honey in the Flesh* (1959), *Girl on the Prowl* (1959), *Kiss for a Killer* (1960), *Dig a Dead Doll* (1961), *Blood and Honey* (1961), *Bombshell* (1964), *Stiff as a Broad* (1971) and *Honey on Her Tail* (1971). Late in her career, Honey moved from California to New York and began to work as an "international eye-spy" for the CIA. Age did not dull her beauty. One admirer marvels, "You have the look of a classical animal. Beautiful cast of creamy flesh . . . . Your blond hair is alive, like your body and the hungry curve of you would make a camera vibrate."

The plots of her CIA adventures are outlandish. Perhaps they were intended as parodies of James Bond. Formulas to make people invisible and micronized bombs in capsules small enough to swallow are key ingredients in *Honey on Her Tail*, for example.

The Honey West series was written by Gloria and Forrest Fickling, who used the pseudonym G.G. Fickling. They also wrote three books about Erik March, a totally forgettable character, and once appeared on Groucho Marx's *You Bet Your Life*. Their "Honey West" television series starring Anne Francis appeared on ABC between 1965 and 1966 making Honey one of the first female PIs on television. She had appeared earlier on the *Burke's Law* series. Honey was more scientific in her TV detecting than she was in print, a minor achievement for sure.

Kinsey Millhone—Sue Grafton

C. W. Grafton was born in China where his parents were missionaries. He practiced law in Louisville, Kentucky, and he wrote four novels during his life, three of which were mysteries. The first two are blessed with unforgettable titles, both drawn from the opening lines of a Mother Goose rhyme—*The Rat Began to Gnaw the Rope* (1943) and *The Rope Began to Hang the Butcher* (1944). *Beyond a Reasonable Doubt*, his last novel, is a crime story narrated by a likable murderer.

Grafton's youngest daughter, Sue, is now making her mark in the mystery field with her nicely conceived private eye, Kinsey Millhone.

I'm a private investigator, licensed by the state of California. I'm thirty-two years old, twice divorced, no kids .... I'm a nice person and I have a lot of friends. My apartment is small but I like living in a cramped space. I've lived in trailers most of my life, but lately they've been getting too elaborate for my taste, so now I live in one room, a "bachelorette." I don't have pets. I don't have houseplants. I spend a lot of time on the road and I don't like leaving things behind. Aside from the hazards of my profession, my life has always been ordinary, uneventful, and good (*"A" is for Alibi*).

Millhone first appears in *"A" is for Alibi* (Holt, Rinehart and Winston, 1982). Nikki Fife, a woman who has just finished an eight-year prison sentence for the murder of her playboy husband, asks Kinsey to find out who really killed him. Laurence Fife, the victim, suffered no shortage of enemies, and his wife also had plenty of reasons to want him dead. Not only was he a ruthless attorney and a skirtchaser but as Kinsey soon discovers, he had a handsome law partner with a lot of sex appeal— especially for Kinsey. Five corpses in this one, but most of the violence takes place off stage. Nominated by the Private Eye Writers of America as one of the best novels of 1983, this one deserves high marks for the crisp, shocker ending.

Millhone shares many characteristics with Sara Paretsky's detective, V.I. Warshawski. She has a tough edge that authenticates her competence. She is believable. It is interesting that Grafton began her book as a parody of Chandler and Cain, the same intention that Paretsky first pursued with Warshawski. Grafton says that her original introduction of her detective was

"My name is Kinsey Millhone. I'm what they call a 'dick,' though the term is somewhat of a misnomer in my case. I'm a woman . . . a female adult. Maybe you know the kind. I'm also a private investigator. I'm thirty-six, married twice, no kids. I'm not very tough, but I'm thorough . . . ." This piece of silliness set on my desk for a year. At intervals, I would try again, generally in the same hard-boiled mocking Mae West accent . . . . I knew that I could never sustain an entire book in this manner. Furthermore, I had no desire to do so. I wanted a "real" detective novel, not a *spoof* of one. It's clear to me now that because I felt ill-at-ease with the form, my own discomfort was getting in my way, rather like a telephone line being jammed by static (*The Writer*, January, 1983, p. 17).

As she became more comfortable with her creation, Grafton allowed Kinsey to become her alter ego, "the woman I might have been had I made different choices about my life." Kinsey is made of the right stuff. She is a risk taker who frequently pits herself against challenges, "imagining that a day might come when some amazing emergency would require such a test." Her only quirk is an affinity for cramped quarters; she drives a VW and lives in a converted, one-room garage. She also jogs a lot, carries an automatic and is not "good at taking shit, especially from men."

Grafton's plan is to take Kinsey Millhone through the alphabet. *"B" is for Burglar* is next and then there are only 24 more to go. This title plan is reminiscent of her father's use of the consecutive lines of Mother Goose verse. In the meantime, she continues to engage in a very diverse writing career. Prior to *Alibi*, she wrote two mainstream novels, *Keziah Dane* (Macmillan, 1967) and *The Lolly-Madonna War* (Peter Owen Ltd., 1969). More recently she has concentrated on writing for television. Among her several teleplays are "Sex and the Single Parent" (adapted from the Jane Addams book), "Walking through the Fire" (adapted from the book by Laurel Lee), "Nurse" (adapted from the book by Peggy Anderson), and two adaptations of Agatha Christie mysteries—"A Caribbean Mystery" and "Sparkling Cyanide," both written with her husband Steven Humphrey and aired in 1983 on CBS. With Humphrey she also wrote the pilot and two episodes for the CBS series "Seven Brides for Seven Brothers," and she wrote an episode for the popular CBS series "Rhoda." Her short stories have appeared in *Wind, Southern California Lit Scene* and *California Review*.

Charity Bay—Arthur Kaplan

Charity Bay is a private investigator in New York City. She got her start in San Francisco where she was a secretary to a private eye who was both sexist and stupid. Charity learned as much as she could from him, earned her own California PI license, and then went out and stole her first client "right out from under [his] nose."

Charity is very good looking. She must be because men are always looking at her breasts, her thighs, and then sometimes her face. Like Walter

Wager's A.B. Gordon, she has contacts around the world. At one point, she makes consecutive calls from the Hilton mezzanine to New York, London, Paris, Munich, Geneva, Rome, Montreal, Tampa and Chicago. Very impressive.

Charity has to be a good private eye. No one would hire her to enjoy her personality. She can be contentious and abrasive. She is misnamed. Charity acts like she's just graduated from an assertiveness training class with a specialty in how to act like a big cheese in restaurants. Don't smoke around her. Don't call her "darling." Don't give her a table by the radiator. Don't mix her salad. She and Spenser should square off and try to insult each other to death. She makes vague feminist rumblings from time to time which are incongruous with her introduction to the reader as a woman who uses sex as a tool of the trade.

In *A Killing for Charity* (Coward, McCann and Geoghegan, 1976), a lawyer for a group of New York diamond merchants asks Charity to investigate the robbery-murders that have been rocking the diamond trade. Almost a million dollars worth of diamonds are stolen in just a few days, all of it from men whose fetishistic secrecy would seem to make them unlikely robbery victims.

Charity gets beat up a lot, and she has to contend with a vain homicide lieutenant as she learns how a kidnapping and the diamond heists are connected. Her discoveries seem largely accidental; there's little good detecting in the book. What there is is a surfeit of information about the diamond business and a gripping, bitter ending that is skillfully done despite its repulsiveness.

As far as we know, this novel is Ms. Bay's only appearance. Readers may regard that as her one act of real charity. The story is a real downer, but a powerful one, and that might be just what was intended by the author, who once described himself as "an ironic and meditative pessimist."

Arthur Kaplan was born in 1925 in Brooklyn, New York. Educated at New York University and the Sorbonne, Kaplan served in the Coast Guard during World War II. He has worked as a newspaper reporter and a magazine editor. His first novel was *Hotel de la Liberté* (Dutton, 1964).

Angela Harpe—James D. Lawrence

Not only is Angela Harpe private eyedom's only black female, she is also one of its most extravagant characters. Known to friend and foe alike as "The Dark Angel" because of her penchant for sticking a black decal in the shape of a harp-playing figure with a halo and wings on the forehead of the criminals she runs to ground, Angie uses sex, violence and fancy gadgets in equally excessive portions to solve her cases, many of which involve recovery work for insurance companies. She makes James Bond look like a stick in the mud.

Angie is touted as the "highest-priced private eye" in Manhattan. With her background, it's no wonder. Born in Detroit to a junkie mother, Angie graduated Phi Beta Kappa from Radcliff, became a high-fashion model and a $1000 per night call-girl, worked for a year as a New York City cop, invested in the stock market and financed her training to become a private eye. Among her special talents are criminology, scuba diving, karate, flying, small-arms weaponry, electronics, gymnastics, zen, yoga and lock-picking. She reads Huxley and Patanjali, listens to classical music and collects original art.

Angie has many tools, broadly speaking that is. She has a gun strapped to one leg and a miniature burglar kit to the other. In her purse she carries a nylon-cable climbing rig, a nail file and lipstick that conceal picklock devices, and an inch-thick steel bar sewn into the bottom of the purse for the knockout punch. She drives a black Jaguar XKE. But her biggest weapon is her body which is barely covered by the peekaboo tops, microminis, lustrous dark nylons and bikini panties she invariably wears. Angie is an "incredibly sexy-looking black fox," who causes some men to look at her "popeyed with lust." Others are moved to whisper sweet nothings to her like "You're some dish, Mama" as they swoon over her "ripely swelling nudity."

Sex is what the Dark Angel is all about. The lid is off her id. All the way off. The Dark Angel novels feature Angie being forced to strip, perform fellatio, engage in group sex and pose for dirty pictures. She also gets tortured and anally raped. Later she does everything without being forced. Several times.

The books are pornography with a plot written in a style that sounds like a cross between a ghost writer of the letters to Penthouse with an ad writer for the Sunday supplement. ("The Dark Angel took from her bag the beautiful little ten-power electronically intensified night glasses specially crafted for her by Kensui of Tokyo.") The author prefers the metaphor of nuclear fission for the sex scenes. So we get such memorable passages as "they were ready to join in a pulsing, voluptuous crescendo of throbs and thrusts toward a final excruciating explosion of ecstasy," and "up, up, up to new peaks of ecstasy until again the universe exploded, blowing their minds." You could say the style and characterization are wooden, except that gives wood a bad name.

All the Dark Angel books were published by Pyramid in 1975 as part of a numbered series: 1) *The Dream Girl Caper*, 2) *The Emerald Oil Caper*, 3) *The Gilded Snatch Caper* and 4) *The Godmother Caper*. The plots usually involve Angie trying to find something for a client before the Mafia or some Harlem hoods find it. These contests always begin with a sadistic sex scene, repeated several times allowing Angie ample justification for the revenge she will wreak. The action is vicious, the writing racist and sexist.

The books were produced by Lyle Kenyon Engel who has also created such popular paperbacks series as "Nick Carter—Killmaster," "The Kent Family Chronicles" and "Wagon West." The author of the series is James D. Lawrence, described in *Contemporary Authors* as a writer of juvenile fiction books; Angela Harpe should not be included under that rubric.

Madge Hatchett—Lee McGraw

The most hard-boiled female private eye of all? That's Madge Hatchett (aka "Madge the Badge," "Black Widow" and "Bloody Madge"). As the name suggests, Madge is the female version of Mike Hammer. She is an ex-cop who works in Chicago where you have to be tough. But Madge is *really* tough. There's no hint she's a woman for the first 11 pages of *Hatchett* (Ballantine, 1976), her only appearance to date. Page 11 is where she caustically informs a client who has mistaken her for a secretary that "M.L. Hatchett, Investigations" is for *"Miz* Hatchett," and then she continues, "Let me guess. You're Bozo the Clown, right?" This novel was probably intended as a parody of Spillane's Hammer. Intended or not, it's pretty good pulp.

Madge pushes everyone around just like Hammer. Thugs, cops, winos—they all get rough treatment. First, Madge sweet-talks them with names like "fathead," "fatscum" and "stinking two-bit rats." Then she gets physical:

I reached out and grabbed a handful of shirt, yanking his face toward mine. He tried to jerk away. I helped him. I shoved a hand under his chin and sent him sprawling backwards. His legs got tangled up with the chair and there was a lot of racket as he went down. That really made him mad. He scrambled to his knees with a snarl, reached for the desk and stuck his hand into a partially opened drawer. I slammed it shut with my foot.

No doubt about it, Madge knows how to hurt a guy:

Taking a quick step, I lashed out with my foot and cracked a karate-kick right into fat boy's balls. I saw his face explode into a gargoyle of pain and then I didn't see anything at all.

All this action ultimately gets Madge into a lot of trouble with the cops. Of course she's unfazed. As she tells Captain Pete Connally, a character modeled after Spillane's Pat Chambers, "When you or the D.A. or anybody else can pin something on me, you're welcome to my license. Until then, screw off. All of you."

Madge is also very glamorous. She drives a Mercedes, lives in a stylish high-rise and packs a Baretta on her apparently voluptuous body. Judging from men's reactions to her, she is something to look at—tall, dark-haired and beautifully faced.

The plot has some interesting wrinkles, including an unlikely character who turns out to be Mr. Big, kingpin of Chicago's syndicate. Two murders, one of a friend and one of a neighbor, along with the disappearance of a *Playboy* centerfold give Madge plenty to worry about.

Hatchett is good enough to deserve a series but whether author Lee McGraw has plans for any future installments is something that he (or she) has kept a secret.

Sharon McCone—Marcia Muller

Among the handful of modern-day female private eyes whose creators are also women, Sharon McCone was the first to prove herself as a series heroine. Marcia Muller, author of the McCone series, had her first novel, *Edwin of the Iron Shoes* (McKay-Washburn) published in 1977. *Ask the Cards A Question* (1982), *The Cheshire Cat's Eye* (1983) and *Games to Keep the Dark Away* (1984) were all published by St. Martin's Press. All the novels are set in the richly diversified neighborhoods of San Francisco drawn by Muller with a fading, tattered quaintness. In addition to Sharon McCone, Muller has created another sleuth, Elena Oliverez, a museum curator in Santa Barbara, who makes her debut in a locked-room whodunit, *The Tree of Death* (Walker and Company, 1983).

Marcia Muller was born in Detroit in 1944 to Henry and Kathryn (Minke) Muller. She received her BA in English from the University of Michigan in 1966. She remained at Michigan for graduate work and earned an MA in journalism (1971). She has lived in Northern California for the past 12 years, after having spent one year in Asia.

Prior to devoting herself to a full-time writing career in 1981, Muller was a merchandising supervisor for *Sunset* magazine and then a field interviewer specializing in political and economic survey work for the University of Michigan Institute for Social Research. Throughout this period she also wrote free-lance magazine features. More recently she has operated a private consulting business specializing in the preparation of written proposals, corporate communications and in manuscript evaluation.

Within the mystery field, Muller holds the highest regard for Chandler and Ross Macdonald. Among contemporary PI novelists she prefers the work of Bill Pronzini, personal friend and collaborator with her on *The Web She Weaves* (a compilation of suspense stories written by women; William Morrow, 1983), and Sue Grafton, creator of Kinsey Millhone. Outside the mystery field, she admires the bittersweet novels of Larry McMurtry (*The Last Picture Show, Leaving Cheyenne, Cadillac Jack*).

As author of the McCone series, Marcia Muller is beginning to attract a widening circle of admirers. She states that her original aim for the series

Marcia Muller

was to "use the classical puzzle form of mystery to introduce a contemporary female sleuth, a figure with surprisingly few counterparts in the world of detective fiction." Because female private eyes were so rare, Muller believed that her character could not be too much of an eccentric or "superwoman," if modern readers were to identify with her. Nonetheless, she wanted McCone to assume the larger-than-life qualities that any crime-fighting hero must have—bravery, physical capability, diligence and independence. In an article for *The Writer* (October, 1978), Muller explained, "In order to reconcile these seeming opposites I chose to give Sharon a normal, perhaps pedestrian, family background and upbringing that produced a well-adjusted, uncomplicated adult. Sharon's problems are those we've all experienced at one time . . . ."

McCone became a private eye because of the most basic of motivations: she needed a job and wanted one that was interesting. She is not driven by revenge. She is not a zealot. McCone is so straight-ahead, so apparently well-adjusted that some critics have complained that she is "tepid." In her effort to avoid characterlogical quirks that might have interfered with plot, Muller may have initially made Sharon too normal for her and the reader's own good. She needs a bit more of a dark side, and Muller indicates that she now feels more confident in letting Sharon show us some of her private demons and become, in the process, a more interesting woman.

Sharon McCone is Scotch-Irish with her unusual but good looks dominated by her one-eighth Shoshone Indian inheritance. Her first job was with a San Diego department store where she started in management training but soon moved to store security. Bored with guarding skirts and blouses all the time, she resigned and went to Berkeley to earn a BA in sociology, a degree which proved of limited relevance to her subsequent return to security work with one of San Francisco's big detective agencies. Like many good fictional PIs she was ultimately fired from the agency because she had too much integrity.

In the first four novels, McCone works as the retained investigator for the All Souls Cooperative, a San Francisco legal service office run by attorney Hank Zahn and staffed by a group of young "eager-beaver" lawyers. The legal coop casts an atmosphere of sixtyish liberalism on the proceedings which is not very compatible with the personality of McCone who is neither political nor comfortable with the communal mentality that inevitably permeates such enterprises. In future novels, the cooperative will change. Muller says its members will "grow up" and become part of present-day society. But McCone will never be fully comfortable there because she is not one to blend into groups.

McCone is single, a status preferable for all private eyes but probably mandatory for female ones. Her initial romance is with Greg Marcus, an art-loving SF police lieutenant who was in charge of Sharon's first murder case. Their affair is tempestuous and complicated by occasional jealousies. McCone insists that Marcus respect her work and not threaten her autonomy, and Marcus has a most irritating habit of refering to her as "papoose." At its beginning the relationship is ambiguously asexual but it heats up in *The Chesire Cat's Eye* and then cools as McCone takes a new boyfriend in *Games to Keep the Dark Away*.

As far as her methods of investigation go, McCone most resembles the work style of Bill Pronzini's "Nameless" (astute readers will detect a cameo appearance by Greg Marcus in one of Pronzini's novels dedicated incidentally to Sharon McCone "the best of the lady private eyes"). Except in rare instances, McCone stays on the right side of the law and is cooperative with police. True, on occasion she flees the scene of the crime or carries a fake driver's license and might even break and enter, but such activities are aberrations from an otherwise do-it-by-the-book reliability. She is not a smark aleck. Neither is she very responsive to authority. In fact, if McCone has a sharp edge on her mostly smooth personality, it is because of the trouble she has with authority figures. This struggle is best embodied in the conflict of wills which plagued her and Marcus.

She does not rely on any unrealistic level of physical roughness to complete her work, but she is able to kill a man when she has to with the .38 she carries in her purse. She is never ridiculously courageous but neither is she easily deterred from doing her job. Muller comments on her strategy for creating what she regarded as the proper balance between her character's emotional and professional attributes: "How was Sharon to deal with the rough situations that came up in the course of her work without sacrificing her femininity? The qualities of empathy and intuition would be great assets to her, because as a woman she might realize or even be told things that ordinary investigative methods would not turn up. Still, she couldn't cry at every bump and bruise, or lose her gun in her purse at the crucial moment .... I constantly had to consider what I would do if I were a trained professional, how I would condition and curb my natural responses. I constantly made adjustments for this balance in every draft of the novel, and am still making adjustments now ...."

Is Sharon McCone a feminist? Readers' opinions are likely to depend on the requirements they impose on the label. McCone is a feminist in action and spirit but she is not feminist by virture of her rhetoric or a sexual-political view of the world. Her feminism is communicated by her success in a profession dominated by images and fantasized rewards that have always been masculine, if not misogynistic, in nature. More explicit indications of McCone's feminist beliefs appear in her exhortations to a recently divorced friend to make the life she wants for herself on her own terms, in her desire for a relationship in which a strong man and a strong woman are together "without diminishing each other or tearing each other apart," and in her commitment to be independent without being isolated from others.

These qualities have escaped the attention of some critics who have carped that McCone "trembles too much" when she discovers a corpse—presumably she could prove her mettle better by throwing up like male PIs do. In the same vein the mystery critic for *Library Journal* complained that McCone was "calculated to set the women's movement back by decades," a conclusion as absurd as the same reviewer's incorrect statement that McCone is a "woman lawyer."

The McCone series gives evidence of nicely controlled plotting, techniques which Muller describes in the previously mentioned article for *The Writer*. Although she has spared McCone a full compliment of peculiar traits (Sharon's ornithophobia is an exception), Muller introduces a nice assortment of charmingly eccentric supporting characters who serve to show that Californians, for all their unconventionality, are not that different from the rest of us. This same sense of easy, gradual identification with McCone, a character one initially expects to be less accessible, may be the secret behind her appeal as a detective-heroine: Women can admire her, men can trust her. She fulfills her own belief that strength in a woman doesn't require her to be ruthless or indifferent.

Delilah West—Maxine O'Callaghan

One tradition which Honey West helped establish was the motive of avenging the murder of a loved one as the basis for a woman becoming a private eye. In Honey's case she took over her father's agency after he was murdered. More commonly it is the death of a husband that drives his widow to a PI career.

An excellent example of this arrangement is Delilah West, who shares nothing with Honey but a surname. Actually Delilah became a private eye before anything happened to her husband. She resigned from the police force to join her husband, Jack, in the West and West Detective agency located in Orange County, California. He was murdered shortly thereafter while working on a missing person case. Delilah has been obsessed ever since with the search for his killer whose face she can see only in her nightmares; during conscious moments, she is vaguely amnesiac about the incident.

In *Death is Forever* (Raven House, 1981), Delilah is on a missing person case of her own, but what she finds one morning after being drugged in a skid-row hotel is a dead man with a knife in his back. He's not the person she's been hired to find. He's Jack's murderer—the same "pitted skin, a rim of black beard, staring black eyes." The police think Delilah killed the man out of revenge, so she's on the run from them during much of the novel as she tries to discover who first hired Jack's killer and then had him bumped off in the flop house.

For all her down-to-earth realism, Delilah is unusually felonious, even as private eyes go. She hides evidence, she breaks and enters, she assaults a police officer and she steals a car. Throughout the case, she has an assistant of sorts, in the form of Rita, a local woman who owns an answering service.

Maxine O'Callaghan has written two other Delilah West novels. *Run From the Nightmare*, a missing person case about a girl from Newport Beach, was published in 1982, shortly before the demise of Raven House. *Hit and Run*, in which Delilah develops a new romantic involvement, has not yet been sold to a publisher.

O'Callaghan was born in 1937 in Bells, Tennessee. She was raised on a cotton farm that her family sharecropped and was the first member of her family to graduate from high school. Following graduation from high school in Missouri, she worked as a waitress, a secretary and a long-distance telephone operator before meeting her future husband, in Chicago in 1957. O'Callaghan now lives in Mission Viejo, California, with her husband and two children. Her short stories have appeared in *Ellery Queen's Mystery Magazine*, *Alfred Hitchcock's Mystery Magazine* and numerous anthologies. Delilah's debut was in "A Change of Clients," a *Alfred Hitchcock's Mystery Magazine* short story which earned an "honor roll" citation in the 1975 volume of *Best Detective Stories of the Year*. She has also written one romance novel, *Dangerous Charade*, under the pseudonym of Marrissa Owens.

V.I. Warshawski—Sara Paretsky

V.I. Warshawski, Chicago's most appealing private eye, was the product of a New Year's resolution by author Sara Paretsky. "I resolved finally either to write a novel or accept my ambition as mere fantasy and nothing more on January 1, 1979," Paretsky recalls. Because she grew up with detective fiction and because she wanted a form that could accommodate her feminist beliefs, Paretsky decided to write a novel with a hard-boiled female protagonist. An attempted parody of *No Orchids for Miss Blandish* proved a false start but was followed by a more promising story over which she labored for nine months but which remained only one-third complete.

Following a friend's advice, Paretsky enrolled in an evening course on writing detective fiction offered by Stuart Kaminsky at Northwestern University. With Kaminsky's nurturance and advice, she was able to solve some vexing plot and character problems and finish the novel quickly. Her resolution had become *Indemnity Only* (Dial, 1982), the inauguration of V.I. Warshawski with Kaminsky as the worthy dedicatee.

Sara Paretsky

Sara Paretsky was born in Ames, Iowa, in 1947, the second of five children and the only daughter to David and Mary Edwards Paretsky. Her father had been born in Brooklyn, the son of Jewish immigrants. He is an internationally recognized microbiologist who received his Ph.D. from Iowa State University in Ames, Sara's birthplace. From 1951 his academic home has been the University of Kansas, where he has been a University Distinguished Professor since 1976. Sara describes her mother lovingly as "Mainline WASP." Mary now works as the children's librarian for the Lawrence, Kansas public library.

Paretsky attended country schools in Kansas and says that she played a lot of baseball through high school. Third base was her forte. She graduated from the University of Kansas in 1967 with a double major in political science and Russian. She then earned an MBA (1977) and a Ph.D. in American history (1977) from the University of Chicago. Her dissertation analyzed the erosion of influence by intellectual Calvinists (Moses Stuart, Bela Edwards and Edward Park) over the major academic centers of nineteenth century New England.

Following her doctorate, Paretsky settled in Hyde Park, Illinois, where she currently lives with her husband, Courtenay Wrighte, a University of Chicago physicist, her three step-sons and Capo, their golden retriever.

Among mystery writers, Rex Stout, Nicholas Blake, Sara Woods and Dorothy Sayers were Sara's early favorites. To that list, Sara adds Robert Parker and Sue Grafton as contemporaries she enjoys. Outside the mystery field, she admires the works of George Eliot, Alice Walker, Antonia White and Anne Tyler.

Other than the course on mystery writing with Kaminsky, Paretsky has had little formal training as a writer. She credits Dr. Neil Harris, a University of Chicago historian, with providing the single most intense, constructive critique of her writing in his capacity as the third reader of her dissertation. Paretsky admits, "The opportunity to receive such detailed analysis by such a fine stylist was one of the real lasting benefits of writing the dissertation."

Advertising, promotion and public relations have been Paretsky's primary career for several years. Currently she is manager of advertising and public relations for the malpractice division of CNA, one of the nation's largest insurance companies. She does not envision becoming a full-time writer at least in the near future: "Writing is fun. I'm afraid the financial pressure to produce would rob me of that fun and ultimately readers of some of the quality."

Paretsky's heroine, V.I. Warshawski, keeps office on the dark fourth floor of the "Pulteney Building" at the corner of Monroe and Wabash, a noisy, no-frills intersection in Chicago's Loop. This is a classic corner in the city that works, dominated by the el, a steel dinosaur that blocks the sun while trapping the grime and tension of the street.

Warshawski is a no-nonsense, fairly noncerebral, baseball-loving woman in her mid-thirties. Other than her jogging, she has not been captured by the health-and-hedonism life style of the modern, single urbanite. No tofu, no sprouts, no white wine; she goes for scotch and red meat. She's a bit like her Monroe and Wabash office: solid, down to earth, almost blue-collar although she specializes in white-collar cases, peppered with the brutality and insistent violence that Chicago has inherited as an unfortunate trademark. In *Indemnity Only* she unravels a missing-person case that turns into an insurance fraud put together by a bank vice president, an insurance executive and the head of the knifemaker's union (Paretsky's second stepson, Tim, is a professional knifemaker). Along the way she recruits help from Dr. Lotty Herschel, a physician who runs a medical clinic for the poor; Bobby Mallory, a cop who was a friend of her father, and Murray Ryerson, a seen-it-all reporter for the *Herald-Star*. All three characters make return appearances in *Deadlock* (Dial, 1984) when Warshwaski investigates the bombing of a thousand-foot freighter as it sits in the Sault Ste. Marie Locks. While her years of experience in the insurance industry proved adequate as background for *Indemnity Only*, Paretsky researched the second novel by taking a three-day trip from Thunder Bay to Niagara Falls on a freighter in the Canada Steamship Line.

Readers are apt to ask with a prospective client, "What does the V stand for?" Warshawski's crackback is "My first name." Later we discover it's for "Victoria," but friends call her "Vic." Vic's Polish father, Tony, was a cop in the Irish world of Chicago's police force. He taught her how to use a gun in between those afternoons when he'd take her to the Cub games. From her Italian mother she inherited her dark good looks, her middle name, Iphigenia, and her taste for opera.

Married several years earlier, Vic was divorced from her attorney husband after only fourteen months, explaining "Some men can only admire independent women at a distance." She is well-traveled in Chicago's law enforcement environs, having served as a Public Defender until she became disillusioned with the adversary system's tendency to confuse winning legal points for achieving social justice. After resigning her PD appointment she accepted a request to investigate a robbery charge against a friend's brother and cleared him by finding the real culprit. She's been a PI ever since.

Warshawski is a feminist. When a client worries whether a woman can handle his case, she answers, "I'm a woman ... and I can look out for myself. If I couldn't, I wouldn't be in this kind of business. If things get heavy, I'll figure out a way to handle them or go down trying. That's my problem, not yours." Warshawski's feminism is proven not so much by her rhetoric as by her competence. She works hard, fights through fatigue and pain and keeps her cool under intense provocation.

An interesting feature of Warshawski's feminism is that she carries it with none of the irritating arrogances so typical of some radical feminists. Her liberation is personal, not political. Confronted with a hostile group of staunch feminists who mistrust men, cops and capitalists probably in that order, Warshawski broods, "I kind of hoped Annette would try to throw me out: I felt like breaking someone's arm .... Maybe I'd break all their arms, just for fun." Like Robert Parker's Spenser, Warshawski allows masculine and feminine characteristics to coexist peacefully. She is a complex person who can admit to occasional maternalistic yearnings but lives a professional life that is obviously the result of a strong identification with her father. She is enthusiastically heterosexual in a warm, natural manner, willing to spend the night with a man because she'd "like the comfort of someone in bed with me." Still, readers who prefer their sex politicized will warm to Warshawski's one resort to women-on-the-street psychology: "You big he-men really impress the shit out of me .... Why do you think the boy carries a gun? He can't get it up, never could, so he has a big old penis he carries around in his hand."

Vic is a very physically capable private investigator. She is skilled with a variety of firearms and when necessary is an adept street fighter. Human enough to be scared by the violence that presses against her, Warshawski refuses to be intimidated. When two hired thugs mug her outside her apartment, she's ready: "Whirling reflexively, I snapped my knee and kicked in one motion, delivering directly into my assailant's exposed shinbone. He grunted and backed off but came back with a solid punch aimed at my face. I ducked and took it on the left shoulder. A lot of the zip was gone, but it shook me a little and I drew away." She eventually loses the struggle, but her opponents don't walk away unscarred.

Paretsky has succeeded at the very difficult task of creating a female detective who is both tough and credible. Despite an occasional wisecrack especially at the beginning of *Indemnity Only*, Warshawski is not a Spade or Marlowe derivative. This is a wise choice because, sexist as it may be, smartass female private eyes just don't ring true. They run the risk of sounding like a cross between Maude Finley and Joan Rivers.

Warshawski's toughness emerges largely from the fact that she is able to stand up to other people's anger and displeasure toward her. Paretsky says it is this quality of not being intimidated by anger that she most admires in her character. This is a revealing comment because it confirms the impression that the primary attribute of hard-boiled female detectives created by female authors is their emotional toughness. Male heroes fulfill their creator's fantasies of physical prowess and courage, but the best female operatives exemplify a psychological sturdiness in the face of others' resentment, anger and belittlement.

In Warshawski, Paretsky has created an excellent embodiment of this trait—she doesn't wilt or crumble, she wills herself straight ahead, never detoured by what someone else thinks she "should" be.

Kyra Keaton—Teona Tone

Among our authors Teona Tone is a one-of-a-kind for at least two reasons. She is the only female author to have worked as a private investigator herself; and her detective, Kyra Keaton, is the one investigator in this volume to operate in the nineteenth century.

Tone was born in Abilene, Texas in 1944 to Eugene and Pearl Tone. She received her BA in literature from the University of California at San Diego in 1970 and then worked as a full-time investigator for Nick Harris Detectives, a well-known Los Angeles agency. Later she worked part-time for California Attorney's Investigators. She gained special expertise in child-custody cases which she described in "They Have Ways to Make You Talk," a short nonfiction piece for *New West Magazine*. Tone returned for graduate work to UCLA where she earned her MA (1974) and Ph.D. (1977) in English and American literature. Her dissertation, "Picture and Text: A Theory of Illustrated Fiction in the Nineteenth Century," examines the way illustrations and text are integrated in the works of such authors as Mark Twain, William Dean Howells and Henry James. She has held teaching positions at UCLA and the University of California at Santa Barbara. She and her two children currently live in Santa Ynez, California, where she pursues her writing career and raises Holsteins and beef cattle.

Young, wealthy and beautiful with golden chestnut hair and "a tiger's eyes," Kyra Keaton operates a private eye agency out of her home in Philadelphia. Her father named her Kyra, which means *woman* in Greek because he believed she would embody the best qualities of the 20th century woman—"ready to handle anything." She learned Latin and Greek, studied psychology, physics, chemistry and engineering, and attended medical school. Her agency is well-known and employs a far-flung assortment of street urchins like the irrepressible Benny Mulchanney. She is also assisted by several of her upper-crust relatives including Aunt Lydia and cousin George Linton.

Kyra is an aristocrat and a feminist, a character inspired by George Sand, Henry Jamesian heroines and the real female private detectives who worked in America at the turn of the century. Headstrong and sexually liberated, she exerts her will with the confidence that comes from old money and many talents.

In Kyra's first case, *Lady on the Line* (Fawcett, 1983), she is hired by a U.S. Senate Committee to investigate the spreading battle between the Bell

Telephone Company and several fledgling independent companies over control of the nation's developing telephone system. Kyra craves the assignment because she believes it will finally enable her to solve the murder of her father, himself a business tycoon and communications innovator who died under circumstances that originally suggested his business partners may have been the killers. There are some nice twists on the plot which is itself a rarity in the PI genre—it's original!

Full Cry, Kyra's second outing, will be a classic weekend-in-the-country mystery set at a hunt club in Virginia. She's married now, the result of a romance torched in *Lady on the Line*.

Add Kyra Keaton to the list of successful PI originals. She's one of the more interesting hybrids you'll find —a private detective in a liberated historical romance. The rescue scenes are guaranteed to be favorites among feminists.

Alison B. Gordon—Walter Wager

Alison B. Gordon is a very beautiful, $400-a-day, Beverly Hills private eye, a ritzy female combination of James Bond and Stanley Ellin's John Milano. She can speak five languages, is a weapons expert and carries a .357 Magnum in her belly holster. She spent seven years in the CIA with tours in Africa, Vietnam and Thailand. A.B. is a classy dame. She drives a Porsche, vacations in Mexico and is well-known in Left Bank cafes. She is a widow in her thirties and when she meets a a man she likes, she makes love to him several times a day. That's not all she does to men—"I've used them, fooled them, exposed them, analyzed them, laid them ... and killed them." Her most annoying habit is a tendency to drop the names of famous and well-placed friends.

Blue Leader (Arbor House, 1979), the first of the "Blue" trilogy, is more an international thriller than a private eye novel. It tells the story of a fabulously wealthy eccentric who concocts an outrageous scheme to revenge the overdose death of his junkie grandson. Alison nails the pusher, the distributor and the importer of the heroin for a six-figure fee, but that's just the beginning. The bigwig recruits a World War II comrade, regarded as the greatest B-17 ace of all time, to head up a bombing raid of the Burmese jungles where the raw opium is being transported. A motley crew of Flying Fortress jockeys is assembled under the pretense of making a war movie, and the multi-continent action is on. Alison joins up as head of security for the outfit but she's soon brainy-head-over-sexy heels in love with the pilot hero. If you like Bond, you'll love this. It's so outlandish that it's great fun.

In *Blue Moon* (Arbor House, 1980), Gordon is asked to stop the May Fifth Gang who's planning to blow up all the casinos in Las Vegas unless they're paid $5 million in extortion money. The final novel, *Blue Murder*

(Arbor House, 1981), finds Alison foiling the plan of a secret, paramilitary organization named Lexington to accomplish nothing less than the takeover of the United States.

Wager's plots are marvelously grandiose, delivered in an arch third-party narration that makes each of the novels very good entertainment. The style resembles a gossip columnist with commando training.

Walter H. Wager is known as one of this country's best writers of international suspense novels. Two of his novels—*Telefon* (Macmillan, 1975) and *Viper Three* (Macmillan, 1971)—have been made into movies. He has also authored *Sledgehammer* (1970), *Swap* (1972) and *Time of Reckoning* (1979) as well as several other thrillers. Wager, who also uses the pseudonyms of John Tiger and Walter Herman, has written extensively for radio and TV. Born in New York City in 1924, Wager has degrees from Columbia (BA, 1943), Harvard (LL.B., 1946) and Northwestern (LL.M., 1949) and he was a Fulbright Fellow at the University of Paris during 1949. He has held numerous prestigious editorial positions including that of senior editor at the UN during 1954-1956, editor-in-chief of *Playbill* (1963-1966) and editor of *ASCAP Today* (1966-1972). In addition to his membership in several organizations of professional writers, he is a member of the governing board of the National Academy of Popular Music and has served as a public relations consultant for the National Music Publishers' Association.

Chapter IX
Court Jesters—Fools and Funnymen

WITHIN THE PI KINGDOM there are a number of jesters, clowns and comedians whose antics are not to be taken seriously. Their mission is to amuse, to entertain, to provide a sense of proportion and to insure that we do not take ourselves too seriously. Yet, as with all things human, some members of this "gun-in-cheek" crowd succeed admirably whereas others are dismal failures. We will briefly examine examples of both and we will begin with a failure which should have been a success, i.e., Thomas Berger's *Who Is Teddy Villanova* (1977) with its most strange PI, Russel Wren.

Russel Wren—Thomas Berger

Wren is supposed to be made in the classic mold but with a difference. He is a licensed PI with an unlicensed gun—a tiny, harmless Browning automatic in a .25 caliber. He has an office in New York City on East 23rd Street, with a plump maidenly secretary named Peggy Tumulty. Like the typical seedy PI, Russel owes Peggy two weeks back pay and is in arrears on the rent for his apartment as well. Wren is a bachelor, with a BA and MA in English but because teacher's wages are so low Wren got into the PI business. We would all have been better off if Wren had never left the classroom. Locked out of his apartment, Wren has set up housekeeping in his inner office. He uses the washbasin to wash in and mixes his coffee and cup-a-soup with hot water from the tap. The toilet is a communal one down the hall and is shared by both sexes and by a pornographic publishing firm.

In carrying out his PI assignments Wren is repeatedly hit on the head, held at gunpoint and interrogated by the cops. Moreover, the corpse of a large man keeps turning up at odd moments and no one knows why—not even the author. Wren's biggest problem, however, is proving that he is not Teddy Villanova—the international criminal that he has been hired to track down. This novel is supposed to be a parody and it is supposed to be funny. As a parody it is so murky and heavyhanded, so intellectually postured, so supercilious and showy, it winds up for any reader familiar with the PI genre as merely unreadable and silly. After the first chapter, the novel comes apart at the seams. The plot itself is a total mystery, at the beginning, in the middle and at the end. Every time the reader begins to believe that Wren's wretched behavior makes sense Berger brings in another idiotic twist. It soon becomes evident that as a parody of Hammett or Chandler or anyone else it is a failure. The best that can be said for it is that it is a pretentious putdown by an academic showoff. The majority of the critics at the time of its publication also felt that it left much to be desired. One said: "The style is strained and the plot tedious." Another, more forcefully opined: "The convoluted and brazenly preposterous plot is simply Berger's excuse to practice verbal gunplay with a license to kill." Only Leonard Michaels in a front page New York *Times Book Review* considered the novel "witty." Michaels also notes that Berger intends to be ridiculous. In this aim he succeeds. Why anyone with Berger's talent would publish such a mismash is the biggest mystery of the book, one that only his publisher and the most skilled operatives in this book would dare attack. The novel does, however, serve one useful purpose: it stands as a perfect example of what not to do for any writers setting out to write a funny, satiric or parodic example of the PI genre.

Thomas Berger is, of course, the famous American novelist best known for that classic anti-western novel *Little Big Man* (1964) and the Corporal Carlo Reinhart trilogy: *Crazy in Berlin* (1958), *Reinhart in Love* (1962) and *Vital Parts* (1970). Berger's only other venture into the mystery genre was *Killing Time* (1967) a non-mystery murder mystery. We call it a non-mystery because the killer is revealed early in the book and on the dust jacket. The question is not "Who done it?" but "Why?" More recently Berger has published *Regiment of Women* (1973), *Sneaky People* (1975) and *Neighbors* (1982). All of Berger's books with the exception of the Teddy Villanova lapse are elite works of fiction and worth the reader's attention—especially *Little Big Man* and the Reinhart trilogy. Berger is primarily a satirist and as every serious satirist knows you take a terrible risk every time out. When you succeed you are splendid and when you fail you fail miserably.

At the other end of the continuum is a very funny and intelligent effort by a lesser literary light who, without benefit of academic portfolio, shows how it should be done. We refer to Barry Fantoni's *Mike Dime*.

Mike Dime—Barry Fantoni

Fantoni has attempted the same thing as Berger with his novel *Mike Dime* (1981). But where Berger fails, Fantoni succeeds. Where Berger is merely silly, Fantoni is sharp and on target. He writes well. The very first page furnishes a typical example. Sitting in his office watching the rain outside, Mike watches his window leak and muses:

A small puddle was forming by the wainscoting under the window ledge. It was getting bigger. I could have used a Dutch kid with a big finger and a lot of dedication. I hauled myself out of my chair and shuffled through the groove in the carpet to the hat stand by the door. I put on my raincoat and hat and told the puddle in the corner I was going to drown somewhere else. Then something unusual happened. The phone rang.

The time is 1948, and the place is Philadelphia. Mike drives a 1939 Packard with bullet holes and a worn transmission. The plot, the style and the characters are vintage Chandler, with wit and humor. Mike is a World War II vet. He was a sergeant in Ike's First Army on the Normandy beaches in 1944. Mike uses a Luger and a .38 Detective Special when he needs a gun. He owns a soft-brimmed hat, a fawn gabardine raincoat, a full bottle of Jim Beam, an overdraft, a powerful imagination, a weakness for women between seventeen and forty-five and a private investigator's license issued by Philadelphia City Hall. Fantoni's parody is so good that the inattentive reader will fail to see it for what it is and will fail to appreciate Fantoni's artistry. Everything is here: nostalgia, seedy office, hard-boiled hero with the cynical attitude, brutal and bloody murders, gunplay, head bashings, colorful minor characters, hard drinking, fist fights, a complicated plot, false scents, several sexual encounters, a femme fatale or two, a tricky surprise ending and the final triumph of justice.

The writing is ever entertaining and the metaphors always amusing. In describing a cigar-smoking cop, for example, Fantoni says:

Uglo put the cheroot back in his mouth. Immediately the ash slipped off in a long thin roll. Some landed on his vest, some on his necktie. He lifted his hand and absently brushed at it once or twice without much success. But tobacco ash didn't worry a cop from Okie City. Compared to corn feed and horse shit it probably looked distinguished.

Then, in describing the movement of a wall fan, "Its head moved slowly from side to side slower than an octogenarian watching a tennis match." And in describing a woman,

She was in her late forties and her figure was spreading faster than spilled milk. A lot of her was almost into a peg-top velveteen skirt that was too long and a frothy organdy blouse that needed buttoning. She was the second woman in a week that I had met who didn't wear a brassiere. Her face was the color of uncooked bread, her lips were large and puffy and painted with less care than drunks count change. The shade of lipstick she was using was no brighter than a pink neon light. She had been doing something with her hair. It was piled high and dyed bright yellow. The style looked good on Ann Sheridan but on La Webster it looked like a heap of rope and was as attractive as scorched straw. It's commonly said that dogs grow to look like their owners. Masie Webster didn't have a dog. She had a room and it was every much the mess that she was. It hadn't made up its mind whether to be a bar, a den, an office or a boudoir. There were features and furniture from all. Mostly it looked like a storage room.

After a short dance, "The trance lasted to the end of the record. Then she stopped kicking and wriggling and came and sat down with a lot of gasping next to me on the studio couch. She landed like a Lancaster bomber." And then, "She added a wink that was meant to make me feel at home. It would have scared off a plague."

Finally, here is a sampling of other Fantoni metaphors:

She was colder than a nun's kiss.
Snoring as happy as a sow feeding piglets.
He looked like a hawk who had run out of shaving soap.
As neat and tidy as a parade of West Point cadets.
A smile that wasn't exactly warm enough to melt the ice, but a shade warmer than a layer of frost.
A silence powerful enough to bend steel girders.
The typewriter clattered on like an army of chipmunks with metal teeth.

If you are fond of this sort of writing then you're in for a love affair with Mike Dime.

Barry Fantoni, believe it or not, is an Englishman. Born in London's East End, he studied at the Commerwell School of Art and in 1963 he held his first one-man show at the Woodstock Gallery in Mayfair. So far he has had over 25 exhibitions of his paintings. Not only is Fantoni an artist, he is a professional actor with numerous TV and film appearances to his credit. When he is not acting and painting and writing he is serving as a regular broadcaster on BBC and on commercial TV and radio programs. He is also an amateur musician and has a collection of musical instruments at his home near Clapham Common in London. He and his wife are both animal lovers and at the moment support three cats and a dog. Barry's interest in detective fiction won him a position on the staff of *Private Eye*, Britain's complement to our *Armchair Detective*. Fantoni joined their staff in 1963 and now serves as a senior member of the editorial board. He has recently written a second novel featuring Mike Dime entitled *Stickman*.

C. Card—Richard Brautigan

Dreaming of Babylon (Delacorte/Seymour Lawrence, 1977) is Richard Brautigan's gift to the private eye field. If ever one would have appreciated an Indian giver, here was the time. Alas, Brautigan never took the book back, perhaps because he didn't want to be reminded that he wrote it.

A poet, short story writer and novelist, Brautigan was born on January 30, 1935 in Tacoma, Washington, to Bernard F. and Lula Mary Keho Brautigan. Although he never attended college himself he served as poet-in-residence at the California Institute of Technology during the 1960s. A recipient of numerous writing awards including a grant from the National

Endowment of the Arts, Brautigan was often viewed as one of the leading practitioners of the "New Fiction" with its odd or absent plots and unconventional forms and use of language. An author of international reputation, Brautigan's novels and poetry were first embraced by the youth and counterculture movements of the late 1960s whose dissatisfactions and disappointments Brautigan was able to evoke with a whimsical, imaginative style.

Often compared to Kurt Vonnegut, Jr., who helped promote his works on the national level, Brautigan lamented the promise and the loss of the American dream. He wrote with a gentle, humorous, often bizarre style which has on the one hand been praised as "gracefully complex," "inspired" and "divine idiocy" and panned on the other as vapid pop-writing of the worst kind. Brautigan approaches his theme of the lost American Eden with a shy, sometimes melancholy acceptance of things the way they are. Through the power of imagination, the literary equivalent to the flower child's drug experiences, Brautigan sends us on some cosmic trips, at times zany, at times sad, but seldom dark or pessimistic. Guy Davenport called him, "a kind of Thoreau who cannot keep a straight face," and proclaimed, "His imagination is magnificently nimble. His sense of the ridiculous is delirious, a gift from the Gods."

Among his collected poems *The Galilee Hitch-Hiker* (1958) and *The Pill Versus the Springhill Mine Disaster* (1970) are perhaps the best known. His most influential novel is *Trout Fishing in America* because it is here that the perverted American Eden theme is most artistically presented. Written in 1961 but not published until 1967, *Trout Fishing* has been called an "un-novel" because of its form—a medley of observations and vignettes. *A Confederate General From Big Sur* (1965), *The Abortion* (1966) and *In Watermelon Sugar* (1968) are other early novels of importance.

More recently Brautigan wrote parodies of science fiction (*Sombrero Fallout: A Japanese Novel*, 1976), gothics (*The Hawkline Monster: A Gothic Western*, 1975) and mysteries (*Willard and His Bowling Trophies: A Perverse Mystery*, 1975). In general these works have not been as well regarded as have his earlier writings, and their lack of substance caused more than one critic to wonder whether Brautigan did not know what he should write about. Richard Brautigan committed suicide in October, 1984 at the age of 49.

Dreaming of Babylon carries the subtitle *A Private Eye Novel 1942*. Brautigan has shown a strong affection for subtitling his parodies perhaps out of a fear that otherwise his readers won't get the joke. In the case of *Dreaming of Babylon* this fear is not entirely misplaced, for the book is as weak an effort from a major writer as one is likely to encounter. As parody, as humor, as any statement, the book fails. It is occasionally semi-amusing, aptly described by *Kirkus* as a "comic book without pictures." Brautigan must have had an off day when he wrote it. We certainly had one when we read it. We should have gone trout fishing instead.

Dreaming of Babylon features San Francisco private eye C. Card, the generic Sam Spade. Card is far-down and way-out, destitute and dead-beat to the point where he's two months behind on his apartment rent, has had to vacate his eight-dollars-a-month office, and now conducts his business out of a phone booth on Nob Hill.

Card's business is so bad he's taken to selling dirty pictures to the tourists and heisting change from a beggar. His last big "pay day" was when a car ran over him and broke his legs, earning him an insurance settlement.

On January 2, 1942, the day on which all the novel's "action" takes place, it looks like Card has finally been dealt a pat hand. Not only does his battleaxe of a landlady drop dead, thereby saving him from paying his past-due rent, but he's got a mysterious new client who wants to meet him at 6 PM in front of a radio station on Powell Street. The client informs Card that he'll need to bring a gun which is not a problem except that Card is so poor he can't afford the bullets. Approximately the first 20% of the novel is devoted to Card's attempts to scrounge up the bullets which he finally does from a friend who works at the city morgue.

The client turns out to be a shapely blonde who consumes massive amounts of beer without ever having to go to the toilet. She wants Card to steal the body of a prostitute from the morgue, for what reason neither Card nor the reader ever discovers. Although he accomplishes his mission against mounting odds, it's a pyrrhic victory, for in the end all Card has is the corpse of a whore in his refrigerator. Much of the novel takes place in the morgue or the cemetery, a suitable clue as to how lively this entire effort proves to be.

The title derives from Card's tendency to slip into fantasies of his living in Babylon where he assumes various heroic identities such as Ace Stag, private detective. In the Babylon of his dreams, Card is succored by a beautiful companion named Nana-dirat who makes good waffles and gives him rubdowns with erotic oils. The power, prestige and extravagance of Card's Babylon is a reprieve from the ridicule, humiliation and ineptness of his San Francisco reality. Onset of these fantastic fugues began the day Card tried out for a professional baseball team and got beaned during batting practice. He's been going back to Babylon ever since.

This is a sophomoric antic that attains a level of wit equivalent to a food fight in a cafeteria. We can find only two reasons to justify reading it: 1) to demonstrate how hard it is to write good parody and 2) to motivate your own escape into a more exotic dreamland—maybe "Dreaming of Cleveland."

Chip Harrison and Leo Haig—Lawrence Block

In our earlier discussion of Matt Scudder and Lawrence Block we made reference to Chip Harrison. Chip did not write the four Chip Harrison novels; Lawrence Block did. The first two Chip Harrisons—*No Score* (1970) and *Chip Harrison Scores Again* (1971)—are funny sex comedies recounting young, slight but handsome, seventeen-year-old Chip's erotic adventures. It is not until the third novel in the series, *Make Out With Murder* (1974) that Chip, i.e., Leigh Harvey Harrison meets Leo Haig and gets into the PI business. *Make Out With Murder* finds Chip, now in New York City, working as a trainee PI for Leo Haig. Chip answers an ad in the New York *Times* for a detective's assistant. Upon arriving for his interview Chip discovers that the four-story building on West 20th between 8th and 9th avenues is a whorehouse. The first two floors are occupied by Madame Juana and her charges. The upper two hold the office and living quarters of PI Haig.

Haig is five feet two and very round. He looks like a baseball. Leo has a head of wiry black hair and a pointed black goatee that he keeps well trimmed. Leo also collects and is an authority on tropical fish. His second hobby is his enormous library of mystery and detective fiction. Chip gets the job because he has had two books published (*No Score* and *Chip Harrison Scores Again*) and Leo wants to be immortalized in print as the world's greatest detective. Leo has one other peculiarity: he believes Nero Wolfe really exists and his greatest hope and ambition is that some day Wolfe will invite him over to the house on 35th Street for dinner. Haig hasn't been in the PI business long but Chip is to play the role of Archie Goodwin to Leo's Nero. Leo is also very choosy about the cases he takes: no divorce work, nothing that requires electronic gear, and nothing routine. What he does handle is baffling murder cases that he can solve using his incredible brain and Chip's legwork and typewriter. The last is for the recording of Leo's masterful triumph.

In Chip's first case—*Make Out With Murder*, one of his part-time girl friends, Melanie Trelawney, tells Chip that two of her sisters have died mysteriously and that she is afraid for her own life. A few days later when Chip goes to her apartment he finds Melanie dead, apparently from a self-administered overdose of heroin. Very quickly Chip discovers that she was murdered, since she had never used drugs and was terrified of needles. The Trelawney family lawyer hires Chip and Leo to look out for the family's interests—particularly the interests of the dead father and of the girls. On the heels of this, one of the sisters also hires the PIs to find Melanie's killer. Leo then meets what's left of the family and takes an interest in Melanie's sister, Kim. Chip, as one would expect, also gets to know the girls on the floor below the office. Very well, in fact, after someone throws a pipe bomb into the second floor of the building. The bomb, of course, was meant for

Leo and Chip. Next, the car of another of Melanie's sisters is blown to smithereens with her chauffeur still at the wheel. Other murders of family members follow. In between tracking down the killer Chip is between the limbs of a dozen or so assorted females. Finally in typical Nero Wolfe fashion, Leo assembles the remaining family members and unmasks the killer and his motive.

The second PI saga, *The Topless Tulip Caper* (1975), has Chip and Leo working for a beautiful topless dancer, Tulip Willing, aka Thelma Wolinski. They have been hired to find out who is murdering things: first, 123 tropical fish, and second, people in the strip-dancing business. In fact, one of the dancers, Cherry Bounce, aka Mabel Abramowicz, who is Tulip's roommate, is murdered right before Chip's eyes. After several other murders and the discovery that drug-smuggling is involved, Leo again gathers the principals and unmasks the killer. Although sexual escapades are scattered throughout this novel, it is the most serious of the series and places the most emphasis on plot and deduction. For information about Chip's creater, Lawrence Block, see Chapter VI.

Lou Peckinpaugh—Robert Grossbach

One of the funniest PI novels ever assembled is a literary oddity. It is a novel based upon a screenplay rather than vice versa. We are referring to Robert Grossbach's novel *The Cheap Detective* (1978) based upon Neil Simon's screenplay of the same title and the movie starring Peter Falk, Ann Margaret, Eileen Brennan, Sid Caesar, James Coco, Dom DeLuise, John Houseman, Madeline Kahn and Phil Silvers. Overall it owes a little to *The Maltese Falcon*, a little to *Casablanca* a little more to the Marx Brothers and a whole lot to burlesque and surrealism.

The PI in this instance is one Lou Peckinpaugh of Peckinpaugh and Merkle, Private Investigators. Lou is a short man with a tough, narrow-eyed, lined face and a gravel voice. He carries a Mauser, wears a soiled trenchcoat and pulls ready-made mixed drinks—Martinis, Creme d'Cacaos, Old Fashioneds, in the proper glassware—from his desk drawer, his coat pocket, his sleeve, et al.—at the drop of a hat (from there too). Lou also has a secretary, Bess Duffy, who has been his loyal aide for seventeen years. She has been in love with Lou as long as she can remember. But, as Lou tells her, "I'm saving you for a rainy day."

When the novel opens, Lou's partner, Fred Merkle, is shot and killed in a cheap hotel. Fred's wife, Georgia, with whom Lou has been having an affair for many years, asks Lou to investigate the murder. Next, she tries to frame Lou for the murder. Third, a crazy woman meets Lou at his office, pukes on his coat and asks him to find her niece. This is, apparently, the same job that Fred was on when he was murdered. Then a man with a stinking voice meets Lou in a chic waterfront dive and informs him that the "niece" is really a very valuable art object and he wants Lou to find it. At this same cafe Lou next meets a woman who once threw him over. Before he can sneeze, the woman's husband asks Lou to recover some stolen documents. In doing so, Lou discovers the stolen art object is a necklace made up of diamonds as big as hen's eggs. From here on the story becomes wilder and funnier. Puns, jokes, double entendre, witticisms and wisecracks follow one after the other from beginning to end. To wit:

"My niece is seventeen and attends boarding school at the Hail Mary Sister Theresa Convent and Kennels."
"Kennels? Isn't that for dogs?"
The woman nodded sadly, "I'm afraid none of the girls are very pretty."
"Two weeks ago, she climbed over the wall and disappeared. She hasn't been heard from since, and I've been worried sick. She could've been abducted and done God-knows-what-with. Raped, sodomized, tortured, forced to eat food with preservatives, given tuba lessons, anything is possible. Since then I've been frantic. I hired Mr. Merkle to find her. He called me tonight."

The book is as bristly with this kind of stuff as a petrified porcupine.

Silky Pincus—Leo **Rosten**

Sidney "Silky" Pincus is the creation of Leo Rosten and he is one of the most endearing characters you'll ever meet. Silky is a Vietnam veteran, an ex-cop and the partner of Michael X. Clancy in a PI enterprise called Watson and Holmes Incorporated. Silky is a member of the Israeli tribe, a comedian, owner of a weird dog named Mr. Goldberg, the uncle of a strange nephew named Hershell Tabachnik and the admirer of a walking dream named Kimberly Marsh. As one reviewer most aptly said, "picture Sam Spade as played by Groucho Marx." This is Silky Pincus, the chutzpah king of Manhattan.

The first Silky novel, *Silky* (1979), opens with Kimberly coming to Watson and Holmes (whose motto is: We never sleep) with a problem: someone is trying to kill her. Silky and Clancy take the case and Silky moves from one funny scene to another. The humor is beautifully supported and enhanced by the language and dialect. As the only fully Yiddish Manhattanite PI in the book, the street talk Silky uses often needs translation. Rosten obligingly provides a glossary. We are informed, for example, that a "shamus" is, actually, a sexton or caretaker of a synagogue—even though we use it to mean a PI or detective.

As for the plot of the novel, Silky and Mike run into their fair share of shootings and killings and, along the way, Kimberly and Silky fall in love. This development complicates things unduly and the conclusion is not only surprising but shocking in several ways.

The second Silky novel, *King Silky* (1980), has a beautiful brunette and a lawyer from Georgia offering Silky and Mike $2,000 a week to work for a mysterious reclusive billionaire, Howard Hughes Smith. Smith wants to build an expensive new casino in Atlantic City but a crime Don named Tony "The Snake" Quattrocino is standing in his way. Moreover, Mr. Smith's starlet girlfriend has disappeared and Silky is supposed to find her. In the doing Silky meets a beautiful older woman and falls in love. Things are fine until someone is murdered and Silky is the prime suspect. Then all hell breaks loose in a wild and funny mixture of corpses and comedy at a Western jamboree showdown. Again, the glossary is necessary and the translations are as entertaining as before.

In the two Silkys Rosten has managed to blend humor and homicide into a very harmonious whole. Both novels are like dry martinis: exciting, spirit-lifing and intoxicating.

Leo Rosen has been at the business of entertaining the American public for a long time. Author and/or editor of over thirty books, Rosen is best known for the *H*Y*M*A*N K*A*P*L*A*N* books, *Captain Newman MD*, *A Most Private Intrigue* and *The Joys of Yiddish*.

Julian "Digger" Burroughs—Warren Murphy

Digger Burroughs is a six-foot-three-inch 38-year-old, blonde, Irish-Jewish private investigator who works for Frank Stevens, President of the Brokers Surety Life Insurance Company, and drinks Finlandia vodka on the rocks. Digger is also one of the wittiest, most lady-lusting snoopers in Las Vegas and all points west. A master of repartee and the double-entendre, Digger lives on the fifteenth floor of a high-rise condominium on the Vegas strip and drives a white Mazda sports car. He likes alto sax solos by Freddy Gardner and a beautiful Japanese-Italian girl, Tamiko "Koko" Fanucci. At one time Digger was married and he occasionally sees his ex-wife, Cora. Digger is wired with a small tape recorder which he wears on his back and which comes in very handy on the job. When he is working everything makes him thirsty and he must quench his thirst frequently with strong drink. His areas of interest are very limited: fraud, suicide and beneficiary-as-murderer. Anything else belongs to the cops. Digger has an immediate superior—one Walter Brackler, a five foot bureaucratic martinet, that Digger calls "Kwash." The nickname is because Walter is, as Digger insists, "The only known victim in North America of kwashiorkor, an African disease that stunts the body and shrivels the mind." Digger also has a penchant for switching his name as the occasion demands. Though his aliases are not on a par with those of W.C. Fields they are close. For example, in the first Digger story (*Smoked Out*, 1982) he uses the name Orville Fudlupper, Tom Median—a highway expert (and at times Com Median)—Tim Kelp, Rico Bravo, Tom Lipton and Alrod Jettson—screenwriter. The plot has to do with the case of a doctor's wife who drove her Mercedes over a cliff. Was it accident or murder? The reason for suspicion is that a few weeks before the doctor took out extra insurance, with double indemnity for accidental death, and a pay-off of one million dollars. The doctor was the only beneficiary. Digger digs into this with cleverness and wit and, with Koko's help, sees that justice is done. The writing sparkles. For example, here Digger has told a redhead he has just shacked up with that he was a Hollywood screenwriter:

"What kind do you write?"
"Training films for the Army. You know, The Seven Warning Signs of Chancre. Starring Sperma Toesies and Spiro Keats and like that."
"Then what was all that dictation before into the machine, the scenes and stuff, the little Jap girl and all that, what was that all about?"
"That's my autobiography."
"You mean it's true?"
"It's the curse of most autobiographies. You should have seen the one I wrote for General Patton. It was a beaut. And all true."

The second Digger, *Fools Flight* (1982), has Digger looking into the crash of an airliner carrying forty newly saved souls, members of the Church of Unvarnished Truth in Ft. Lauderdale, who were enroute to a religious retreat in Puerto Rico. Strangly all were insured with Broker's Surety Life, Digger's employer. The beneficiary of this ten-million dollar bite is the leader of the C.U.T., one Reverend Damian Wardell. Digger and Koko go a-digging in another hilarious fun-to-read tale of homicide and highjinks. The third in the series, *Dead Letter* (1982), has a most unusual plot. Seems that someone has started a chain letter which requires that the recipient kill the person whose name appears at the top of the list. This letter is making the rounds at Waldo College in Boston. The second name on the list belongs to Allison Stevens, the daughter of BSLI's President Frank Stevens. When Digger goes looking for Allison he finds her shacked up with one of her boyfriends. Digger's job now is to keep Allison alive and find out who is killing whom. Things get both freaky and funny before Digger digs up the killer and pulls the chain on the psychos involved. The fourth novel is *Lucifer's Weekend* (1982). In this caper, following the accidental death of an electronics and planning specialist, Digger is asked to check on why the victim's widow refuses to accept BSLI's check for a million dollars. Although the verdict is *accidental death*, the widow is positive that it was murder. As soon as Digger begins his investigation someone takes a shot at him, a local cop kidnaps Koko, and the airtight murder plot springs a leak. Sharp and witty as ever, Digger leaves no pun unsaid and no killer unearthed before the fun is finished.

Warren Murphy, Digger's author, has written more than sixty novels and screenplays, including the satiric adventure series, *The Destroyer*, which now has more than twenty-five million copies of the twenty-some-odd novels in print. Murphy is a former newspaperman and political campaign consultant. He is also the creator of *Trace* (1983) aka Devlin Tracy who is another Las Vegas PI who works for the Garrison Fidelity Insurance Company. Trace's assignment in this instance is to look into the behavior of an idealistic doctor who may well be killing his patients rather than attempting to cure them. Trace is cut from the same cloth as Digger. He also appears in *Trace and 47 Miles of Rope* (1984) and *Trace: When Elephants Forget* (1984).

Murphy's hobbies are chess, mathematics and the martial arts. He currently resides in Tcaneck, New Jersey, where he continues to write full time.

Chance Purdue—Ross Spencer

Ross Harrison Spencer was born on August 21, 1921 in Hughart, West Virginia, to Ross and Virginia Spencer. He was married in 1952 and has three children. According to his entry in *Contemporary Authors* (Vol. 101) Spencer served in both World War II (Army artillery) and the Korean War (Air Force communications). He has worked as a truck driver, a steel mill worker, an aircraft worker and a railroad man. He owned and operated a landscaping and fencing business. A member of the Mystery Writers of America, Spencer has also written many poems which have appeared in *American Turf*. He lists his favorite writers as Ring Lardner, Damon Runyon, Stephen Leacock and Robert Service. Probably the best thing that Ross Spencer has written is *Echoes of Zero* (1981), a hilarious tale about a Clinch Mountain-drinking, good ole country boy, amateur detective named Rip Deston, who hails from Saddleback Knob, Ohio. A very entertaining book, full of surprises including a final classic punch line, this is Spencer's funniest novel so far.

Chicago-based Chance Purdue in Spencer's gift to private eyedom.

Purdue has appeared in several novels so far.

The Dada Caper (1978) *The Regis Arms Caper* (1979) *The Stranger City Caper* (1980) *The Abu Wahab Caper* (1980) and *The Radish River Caper* (1981) are their names.

There are several more to come.

Spencer writes all the novels without any punctuation other than periods and question marks.

All the paragraphs consist of only one sentence.

So the page looks like this.

This style doesn't make the stories any funnier but it does make them harder to read.

The Purdue capers are supposed to be hilariously funny.

Some people think they are.

Some don't.

Spencer does have a way with one-liners and nutty characters.

Sort of a cross between Rodney Dangerfield and Mel Brooks.

Earl Bargainnier called him "the Groucho Marx of detective fiction."

He writes some very amusing scenes too like the one about the all left-handed baseball team in *The Stranger City Caper* or the one about the decrepit Waupuwukee Downs racetrack in *The Abu Wahab Caper.*

The books are full of jokes, sports humor, satire, farce and outrageous action.

The characters have names like Miss Brandy Alexander...Dottie Piskay... Vito Cool Lips Chericola...and Oratory Rory McGrory.

Chance has his office in the third booth at Wallace's Tavern.

His wife Betsy is an ex-call girl who is the most beautiful blonde on Planet Earth.

Betsy is "sexier by accident than most women are on purpose."

His mistress is Brandy Alexander who is the most beautiful brunette on Planet Earth.

Purdue battles such diabolical organizations as DADA which stands for "Destroy America Destory America."

Purdue is very macho and patriotic.

He sings tenor on all the great national songs like "America the Beautiful."

Purdue drinks a lot of Old Washensachs and always plays *Alte Kameraden* on the juke box.

Each chapter begins with an aphorism by Monroe D. Underwood.

Underwood says things like oncet there was a female satyr but women's lib squelched the story.

Underwood says other things like once I knowed a feller who got arrested for unusual driving...they caught him without a CB radio.

It is a challenge to catch the relationship betwen the aphorisms and the contents of the chapters which are seldom more than three pages long.

This challenge is never compounded by having to worry about the plots.

There aren't any.

It only takes an hour or so to read one of the Purdue capers.

It takes a lot less to forget one.

But if you read one, you're going to laugh.

Before closing we should mention two other unsuccessful efforts at comedic satire using a private eye as the central character: Jules Feiffer's *Ackroyd* (1977) and Gary Wolf's *Who Censored Roger Rabbit* (1981).

Ackroyd, the better of the two, is presented in the form of a diary written by a young PI named Ackroyd. Ackroyd is neurotic and obsessive and he gets himself involved in the life of one of his clients, Oscar Plante.

Plante is a columnist who suspects his friends of stealing his idea for a novel. After solving this problem, Ackroyd is then hired to find out why Plante's old friends refuse to come to his parties. After a number of years go by, Ackroyd forms a detective agency, does CIA work for the Army in Vietnam and is then accused of betraying his country. Plante now dominates and haunts Ackroyd's every move. Finally Ackroyd takes over Plante's wife, son and mistress and maybe even becomes Plante himself. Unfortunately, the whole thing bogs down and becomes incoherent and tedious. The funny lines in the novel—and there are a few—are not sufficient to save it. One perceptive critic said the whole thing is presented like a great soggy bowl of raisin bran—but there aren't enough raisins to make it worth while. As you might suspect, the novel is a take-off on Agatha Christie's *The Murder of Roger Ackroyd* in which the crime is perpetrated by the author himself. As another critic observed, the novel lacks credibility but is "a fascinating bundle of neuroses that often uncannily mirrors our own." This is about the best that can be said about *Ackroyd.*

Jules Feiffer is the well-known cartoonist, humorist and playwright who has been in the entertainment business for over two and a half decades. One of his best black-humor bits was the novel, and then movie, *Little Murders* (1971) starring Alan Arkin, Elliott Gould, Marcia Rodd and Donald Sutherland. This story is about life in New York City and an aggressive urbanite who traps a passive photographer into marriage. Arkin is hilarious as a mind-blown detective. The funniest moments are, unfortunately, marred by the frightening and callous murders of innocent passerbys and by a very depressive atmosphere.

Gary Wolf's attempt at a humorous PI novel asks the reader to assume that cartoon characters in the newspaper and on the silver screen are alive and at times go about their everyday business like ordinary folk. At other times they dry up and blow away like they were made out of paper or are illusions. This strange and surreal novel is neither satire nor parody. Exactly what it *really* is is a good question. If you can accept this nonsensical casting and go along with your critical senses numbed and in suspended animation, maybe you can overcome your disorientation long enough to finish it. For Wolf's sake we hope some readers find it funny. Apparently some did because recent word has it that Disney productions has purchased the rights and intends to film it. Such courage is admirable. We have also been informed that Wolf has written a second and similar travesty entitled *Who Ordered Delancy Duck?* The only answer to such a query is: "It wasn't us!" Wolf has written a straight-forward PI novel called *What's Left of Alice Withers.* It features a reasonably sane PI named Ernie Hunter.

Chapter X
Seers and Prophets—Tomorrow's Private Eyes

A LOGICAL EXTENSION of the private eye format into the science fiction field was inevitable. In fact it is remarkable that this particular combination of mystery story and science fiction tale was so long in coming. Historically, the blending of the straight detective and science fiction genres is far from new. Anthony Boucher foresaw the amalgam and made a hesitant move in this direction as far back as 1942 with his *Rocket To The Morgue*. In an author's afterward Boucher said, "I hope that some of the regular readers of whodunits may find this picture of the field [SF] provocative enough to make them investigate further." Whether the readers did is conjectural, but the science fiction writers themselves have taken his words to heart and a number have made efforts to combine the two themes.

"Detective stories," according to Brian Stableford and Peter Nichols, "depend very heavily on ingenuity and generally require very fine distinctions between what is possible and what is not. It is difficult to combine SF and the detective story because in SF the boundary between the possible and the impossible is so flexible" (1979). Stableford and Nichols argue that only Isaac Asimov has achieved any real success in writing futuristic detective stories. This is incorrect, although Asimov certainly has been highly successful with his detective pair, Lije Baley (Human) and R. Daneel Olivaw (Robot) who investigate murders in the future in *The Caves of Steel* (1953) and *The Naked Sun* (1956). We had some other early precursors in which straight science and straight mystery were combined. One of the SF pioneers, Hugo Gernsback, published a pulp magazine, *The Scientific Detective Monthly*, in 1933. It lasted less than a year. Another original and more recent SF detective was Randall Garrett's Lord D'Arcy. D'Arcy works on an alternate world historically similar to our own where magic works and good progress has been made in ESP. D'Arcy, whose investigative procedures are clever and rigorous, showed up in a series written for *Astounding Science Fiction* in 1964 and 1965, and a novel, *Too Many Magicians*, featuring D'Arcy was published in 1967.

In general there have been more futuristic policemen than PIs. In Hal Clements's *Needle* (1950) an alien policeman pursues a criminal to Earth. *Logan's Run* (1967) deals with a policeman who refuses to die at his appointed time. H. Beam Piper's "Paratime Police" series (1948-1965) also featured some interesting and unusual cops. An excellent novel, made up of a number of short stories, about State Highway patrolmen enforcing traffic laws in the future, is Rick Raphael's *Code Three* (1966). Two rather unconventional female law enforcement officers also appear in *Sibyl Sue Blue* (1966) by Rosel G. Brown and Ian Wallace's *Deathstar Voyage* (1969). Larry Niven's 1980 investigator Gil "The Arm" Hamilton in spite of the fact that he is a member of the United Nations' police force, the Amalgamated Regional Militia, is closer in style, manner and behavior to the contemporary PI. Gil, the hero of *The Patchwork Girl* (1980), is tough, hard-boiled and he gets himself into scrape after scrape in the classic manner of our unarmored knights.

There is also a number of anthologies concerned with SF and crime. One of the earliest was *Space Police* (1956), edited by Andre Norton. Another was Miriam Allen DeFord's *Space, Time, and Crime* (1964) and more recently and best of all is Isaac Asimov's superb *Thirteen Crimes of Science Fiction* (1979), co-edited with Martin Greenberg and Charles Waugh. This last anthology does have one short, but splendid PI novelette, "The Detweiler Boy," by Tom Reamy. It is highly likely that Reamy would have produced more hard-boiled SF detective stories in the Chandler mold were it not for his untimely death at an early age. Finally, there is *Asimov's Mysteries* (1968), a collection of SF mystery stories. In the introduction to this collection Asimov argues that blending SF and mystery should be "pie easy" since science itself is so nearly a mystery and the research scientist so nearly a Sherlock Holmes. Asimov also provides some ground rules for such an amalgam that every would-be merger should heed. According to Asimov,

You don't spring new devices on the reader and solve the mystery with them. You don't take advantage of future history to introduce ad hoc phenomena. In fact, you carefully explain all the facts of the future background well in advance so the reader may have a decent chance to see the solution. The fictional detective can make use only of facts known to the reader in the present or of "facts" of the fictional future which will be carefully explained beforehand. Even some of the real facts of our present ought to be mentioned if they are to be used—just to make sure the reader is aware of the world now about him.

Once all this is accepted, not only does it become obvious that the science fiction mystery is a thoroughly accepted literary form, but it also becomes obvious that it is a lot more fun to write and read, since it often has a background that is fascinating in itself quite apart from the mystery.

There are, of course, a few select SF writers who have managed to move the private eye novel with its classical structure complete and intact into the years ahead. A good example is Philip K. Dick's *Do Androids Dream of Electric Sheep?* (1968). A part of this novel formed the base for the very successful movie *Blade Runner* (1982). Set in Los Angeles in 2019, the story is concerned with an overpopulated and polluted Earth. People are crammed into huge cities with skyscrapers as high as 400 stories. Traffic jams clog the streets and the city is drenched with continual rainfall. The police keep control with the Spinner—a flying car that hovers over traffic—and the Esper—a supercomputer that allows them to search a room without being present. Genetic engineering is one of Earth's biggest industries and genetically engineered human beings called replicants are sent to the space colonies and the military for use in deep space. The top replicant manufacturer, Tyrell Corporation, has created a new model, the Nexus 6, which has superhuman strength. Though replicants are outlawed on Earth some manage to return and pass as human. This is when the police call in the Blade Runners, special private detectives who use an elaborate type of detector called the Voight-Kampff to tell the difference between human beings and replicants. It is the Blade Runner's job to track down the replicants and eliminate them. After the police receive an emergency report that four Nexus 6 replicants have returned to Earth after taking over a space shuttle and killing the crew, they send for the one man most capable of finding them: Rick Deckard, played in the movie by Harrison Ford. Deckard is an ex-cop and an expert Blade Runner. The movie is the story of how Rick tracks down and eliminates the four replicants one by one. It is superb, both as science fiction and as a private eye tale of pursuit and capture.

Another novel in this category is Gardner Dozois and George Effinger's *Nightmare Blue* (1975), in which a PI named Karl Jaeger is the last private eye on Earth and the Earth is under attack from a race of aliens called the Aensas. The Aensas also control some vicious dog-like monsters, the Dktar, which they use to hunt down and kill human beings.

Karl Jaeger is "a huge man, cat-muscled, deeply tanned, dark blond, with a grim weather-beaten face; his expression was dominated by a strong almost unpleasantly massive jaw line and large, canny gray eyes, which were recessed beneath bushy eyebrows." Karl attended several universities on government scholarships, did post-graduate work in criminology and then went into the Intelligence Section of the Army. A hand grenade put a load of shrapnel into his leg and got him an honorable discharge. After earning a Master's degree he worked for the Southern European Police Group (SEPG) but then formed Jaeger Incorporated, selling only one thing: himself. Jaeger operates out of an expensive office suite in Nurnberg, likes Jack Daniels and Scotch, and is as tough as they come. After Karl is hired to find out exactly what the Aensas are up to, Jaeger and Corcail Sendijen team up against the Aensas and uncover the real purpose of their mission on Earth. In doing so they discover the Aenas have developed a horrible addictive drug called Nightmare Blue. With this drug the Aensas intend to conquer the Earth and the rest of the universe. Karl and Sendijen combine forces to defeat the monsters in this rip-roarer of a novel.

Another well-crafted series starring a future PI is Lloyd Biggle Jr.'s four-novel sequence recounting the adventures of one Jan Darzek. The biggest problem with this series is that they are hard-core SF and bear little resemblance to the PI novel. There is an element of mystery in the problems posed by evil alien forces, but on the whole SF characters, tools and techniques dominate the pages. Handsome, blond and blue-eyed Darzek is a late-20th century PI hired by the Council of the Supreme, rulers of our home galaxy, to solve the problems posed by the inimical Udef—a dark force that is destroying civilization after civilization in the Smaller Magellanic Cloud—a nearby galaxy. Darzek is aided in his missions by one of the most charming characters in either the mystery or the SF category: Miss Effie Schulpe. Schluppy, as she is affectionately called, is a little gray-haired lady slightly under sixty who wears old-fashioned rimless spectacles, types 130 words a minute from an office rocking chair, picks pockets with uncanny grace and drinks most any man alive under the table. "Three purse snatchers who thought her a likely victim had regained consciousness in hospitals with broken bones. Darzek loved her as he would have loved his own mother if she'd been a jujitsu expert and owned an unsurpassed recipe for rhubarb beer." Although Darzek is independently wealthy, he loves his detective work too much to retire and still takes on challenging cases—especially those commissioned by the Council of the Supreme. The four novels chronicling Jan's adventures are *All The Colors of Darkness* (1963); *Watchers of the Dark* (1969)—one of the best and one replete with comic interludes; *This Darkening Universe* (1975) and *Silence Is Deadly* (1977).

Lloyd Biggle is a professional musician who has a Ph.D. in musicology. He has had stories published in all the major SF magazines and in 1974 was elected Secretary-Treasurer of the Science Fiction Writers of America. Biggle is a veteran of World War II and he served in the infantry in the European Theater. He is married and lives with his wife and two children in Ypsilanti, Michigan. He has written a dozen novels, several collections of short stories and he also edited *Nebula Award Stories Seven* in 1972.

Two other novels blending SF and a PI are William Dorsey Blake's *My Time Or Yours* (1980) and David Bear's *Keeping Time* (1979). Both use the theme of time travel. In the former a PI named Reggie Moon takes a Concorde ride from Paris to attend a New Year's party in New York. After a truly **wild party** Reggie wakes up the following morning back in the year 1846. The beautiful girl he had been with at the party is also with him and very real. Equally real is a very dead sheriff and a murderer who is running loose. Reggie has to solve the murder and figure out how he can get back to the twentieth century. In *Keeping Time*, the better of the two novels, the time is 1991 and the setting is Manhattan. Jack Hughes, the world's finest PI and possibly the only one left, is hired by Ivory Wightman, owner of the world's only time-deposit bank to recover some missing tapes. The bank is a place where the rich and famous can store their most precious moments, literally, and at a later time relive them. Storage is on audio-visual, 3-D, holographic tapes. Not only are some tapes missing but two depositors are murdered. Hughes also has another problem: he has to work under the pressure of a four-day deadline. As he crawls through the dying remains of New York City he encounters mass suicides, Park Avenue slum dwellers, roaches that are indestructible and a host of apathetic people who have lost all will to live. The rough, tough, hard-nosed but knightly Hughes has to protect the other depositors on the thief's hit list, protect the remaining tapes and recover those already pilfered. Bear pulls it off in a very satisfactory fashion. The roaches, however, remain indestructible.

Mention should also be made of Katherine MacLean's detective George Sanford, hero of *Missing Man* (1975). Sanford is a telepathic PI who works with New York's famed Rescue Squad—an elite corps of Espers—who locate people in trouble by zeroing in on their mental distress signals. But even experienced tracers of lost persons like Sanford have trouble finding people in the New York of 1999. Rapid population growth has forced society into strict regimentation. Communal life has developed to the point where all human physical and psychological needs are met. There are various theme communes where you can live like a Medieval knight, or an Aztec, or even like people who lived in a country village back in 1949. There are over two billion people in the metropolitan area alone. George is challenged to find a missing computer expert who is being held captive by a band of crazed revolutionaries called Larry's Raiders whose aim is to destroy the city. After an exhaustive mental search George finds the Raiders and the computer man but in doing so he is captured. Larry, the Raider's leader, turns George's powers against the city and George now becomes the hunted "missing man."

Though it isn't exactly SF, James Gunn's fascinating story about Black Magic and a nice-guy PI in the middle of a magician's convention is very readable. Titled *The Magicians* (1976), it features a PI named Casey, who is hired by a sweet old lady to find the real name of a man known only as Solomon. Solomon, however, is a Magi and the head of a powerful organization of black magicians, witches and warlocks. Casey then meets a beautiful girl named Ariel and finds himself in a full-fledged war between the forces of good and the armies of evil. The reader should be warned, however, that the novel is more of a heart-warming love story than anything else.

Five other future PIs worthy of mention are 1) Anthony Villiers and his alien companion Trove the Trog featured in Alexei Panshin's *Star Well* (1968), *The Thurb Revolution* (1968) and *Masque World* (1969); 2) Miro Hetzel, the hero of Jack Vance's novel titled *Galactic Effectuator* (1981); 3) Victor Slaughter, hero of *Gomorrah* (1974), by Marvin Karlins and L.M. Andrews; 4) A. Bertram Chandler's John Petersen, a PI spaceman caught in a time loop in *Bring Back Yesterday* (1982); and 5) Asher Bockhorn in the employ of MexAmerica and Pacific Security in two novels by Barney Cohen, *The Taking of Satcon Station* (1983) and *Blood on the Moon* (1984).

Tomorrow's Champions—Bearers of the Grail

Four of the writers who have most successfully advanced the PI novel into the future are J. Reaves and his marvelous PI, Kamus of Kadizar, Mike McQuay's Matthew Swain, William Nolan's parodic Sam Space and Ron Goulart's Jake and Hildy Pace. All are vastly entertaining and should be read by every lover of the PI novel. Let us begin with Kamus of Kadizar and the novel *Darkworld Detective* (1982).

Kamus of Kadizar—J. Michael Reaves

Kamus (possibly Shamus?) is a young private eye, in fact the only PI on the planet Ja-Lur also known as the Darkworld. The time is far in the future when there are hundreds of populated worlds in the Unity of Planets System. Earth is only one of the older populated planets. Kamus is a half-breed. His mother was an earthling and his father a darkling. Kamus was the product of a situation in which his mother was raped by a darkling during a time called Shadownight when the two moons of Ja-Lur eclipse and form the Bloodmoon. "They don't roll around too often, the last time one occurred was when I was conceived." The Darklanders have the ability to cast spells merely by repeating magical phrases. These spells are powerful and can be used as deadly weapons.

Like all classical PIs', Kamus' office is located in a rundown neighborhood at the edge of the slums, the thieves' maze, in the city of Mariyad in the State of Adean. Mariyad is made up of a cosmopolitan group of visitors from other planets—Outworlders and the Darklander population. Mariyad is also the home of the planet's Spaceport. Ja-Lur is called the Darkworld because noon on Ja-Lur is just a little brighter than twilight on Earth. Communication on Ja-Lur is achieved by way of small pets, black furry creatures similar to a cat, called phonecubs. Kamus has a cub named Dash. You tell them whom you want to talk to and they call the other person's phonecub and the two cubs communicate via ESP mimicking the voices of sender and receiver. Instead of a gun Kamus wears a sword. Kamus doesn't smoke; he chews imported gum instead. As he explains, "Some private eyes smoke, but that habit isn't popular on the

Darkworld—polluting someone else's air is a good way to get hurt." With his spells—some of which are rather unreliable because he is only half a Darkling—and his sword, Kamus is capable of handling almost any problem that comes his way. Kamus' fee is seven hundred welhels a fortnight plus expenses. Kamus is licensed on both Ja-Lur and on Earth. When he is not working he patronizes the Blue Lotus Tavern, his second home, where he drinks ale and picks up bits of information.

The police on Ja-Lur are of two kinds: the locals, called the Guard and Guardsmen; and the Unity Service, similar to our FBI, who guard the Spaceport and have authority everywhere in the System. Kamus has a friend among the Guard—Sanris of Taleiday—who helps him out when he is in a bind.

Some years earlier Kamus was in love with an Earthwoman, Thea Morn. Five years previously Kamus applied for a cultural exchange program between Ja-Lur and Earth and he won the opportunity to study at the finest universities on Earth. Even though Kamus had to have genetic adjustments to shrink his pupils and protect his skin from sunlight he went to Earth. While there he met and fell in love with Thea, the beautiful blonde daughter of a rich man. Thea also loved Kamus and they were together for several years until Thea was accidentally killed by a teleportation malfunction. The tragedy has affected Kamus' relations with other women to the point that he, in knightly fashion, does all in his power to aid and abet the course of true love wherever he may find it. In his own words, "I think true love is a wonderful thing. It happens about as often as a snake wears sandals, but when it does, it's always worth waiting for." Kamus relies heavily on his suspicions and feelings, i.e., "those intuitions that form the bulwark of detective work." Kamus is tough, strong and a skilled swordsman. He is smart and he is superb at spotting a tail. He has a very suspicious nature and as he puts it, "Paranoia is an occupational hazard in my business."

Thus far Kamus has appeared in only one novel, *Darkworld Detective* (1982), which is made up of four separate but related cases. Each is named after a mystery classic. The first is entitled "The Big Spell"; the second, "The Maltese Vulcan"; the third, "Murder on the Galactic Express"; the last, "The Man With The Golden Raygun." The similarity of the plots to their classical predecessors is, however, remote.

Despite the somewhat comic-book aspects of the plot, the novel has wit, intelligence and credibility. It is both enjoyable and suspenseful, a well-concocted synthesis of the two fictional genres. J. Michael Reaves is a young TV scriptwriter under contract with Warner Brothers. He is a resident of Los Angeles. No stranger to science fiction, he has written a number of short stories, one of which was nominated for the 1979 British Fantasy Award. Another SF novel, *I-Alien*, was published a few years back and he is co-author with Bryon Preiss, of the well-received novel *Dragonworld* (1979). Reaves is also a regular contributor and reviewer for Delap's *Fantasy and Science-Fiction Review*. With his strong narrative skills and fertile imagination Reaves is a writer that lovers of mystery and SF should encourage to keep Kamus of Kadizar alive and kicking.

Mathew Swain—Mike McQuay

Our second major SF private eye, Mathew Swain, is thirty-three and operates out of an unnamed urban complex vaguely identified as somewhere in south-central Texas in the year 2083. Matt also operates at the edge of the slums. His office which is located in the low rent district is simple, "which suits my tastes and financial disposition." Matt's desk is old but made of real wood. He has two windows that let in the afternoon sun, a coat-and-tunic rack in the corner, a small, flowered, cloth-covered settee, a swivelchair and several folding chairs for conferences which never seem to occur. The Vis, i.e., the TV screen, takes up most of the wall opposite the sofa. Although he doesn't like guns, he uses a frump gun which fires pellets which explode on contact "leaving nothing but a pile of warm goo on the ground." He keeps a bottle of Black Jack—an unnamed booze of some sort, most likely bourbon—in his bullet (automobile) and in the big bottom drawer of his desk. Most of his regular work consists of follow-ups on death claims for the Continental Insurance Company. Matt refuses to do divorce work. He also has a girl friend, Virginia "Ginny" Teal, one of the "flowers of Texas" Matt has known for some time. Mathew lives about a kilometer from his office in the converted basement of a fifteen-story, also-ran building. The place is barely liveable, with paneled walls and a cheap but wearable carpet over a cement floor. Red brick pillars run, in double rows, through the length of the flat. Since they can't be ignored, Matt hangs dart boards, pictures and mirrors on all their sides. The place is naturally cool in summer and since the windows open to the sidewalk level he gets "a pretty good leg show" whenever he wants to watch.

Matt also keeps a sleek black cat named Matilda that attacks all enemies who invade the premises. Mathew's best suit consists of a black, form-fitting polyester one-piece that opens in the front down to the sternum. Over this he wears a tan waistcoat that remains open with the suit collar overlapping the lapels of the coat. Zippered boots the same color as the coat come up to mid-calf.

In knightly fashion Mathew says, "I'm a very elementary kind of guy, and the electronic limbo of the rich boys went right past me. Life was people to me—a shiv in the throat I could understand; good whiskey I could understand. The city, even crumbling and financially crippled, was real to me. Everything else was just confusing." His standard fee is three hundred a day plus expenses. In Matt's society garbage usually fills the streets most of the time. The government has given up the war against drugs and provides free, monthly welfare drug and food rations to the needy victims of Old Town. For pleasure, the average citizen wears alpha rings around his forehead. These rings stimulate the pleasure centers of the brain. To dance you merely stand on the dance floor and the floor jerks you around in time to the music. Death on the streets is so common that roving trucks, called Meat Wagons, scoop up and instantly atomize the corpses as a hygienic measure. Smog covers the city most of the time and there is a part of the city called Old Town and Ground Zero. Ground Zero used to be the city until sometime in the late 1980s when there was a meltdown of the fission reactors that provided power. As a result of exposure to the concentrated doses of radiation a number of mutants were created and they spread their contagion until a Quarantine Bill was passed forcing them to stay in Old Town where they lived off government handouts and got crazier and crazier. Enforcing the law is so expensive that the police have to charge for their services and bonuses are expected if quick service is wanted. Murders and killings—especially of ordinary citizens—are so common that only a rare few are ever investigated. Only the wealthy get anything in the way of priority from the police. Therefore everyone who can afford it hires personal and private bodyguards and security agents—known as Fancy Dans—for protecton. Most of the work and factory labor is done by androids called "andies."

This is the social milieu in which Swain operates and the backdrop for the four novels. Matt doesn't like it but his attitude is philosophical:

Maybe I *am* thick-headed. I'm just a poor slob trying to earn a living. But it seems to me that something has got to matter .... I do what I do because I like people, because deep down inside I feel like I'm helping somehow. That makes me feel good, Harry, helps me sleep at night. Now if that's a simplistic view of life to you, I offer my sincerest apologies—I guess I'm just a simple guy.

Hot Time in the Old Town (1981), the first Swain, has Mathew looking into the odd murder of one of his former clients—Phil Grover. Odd because Phil's corpse is only half there. The murder weapon is something completely new and unknown even in the year 2083. Phil's father, a wealthy old man, hires Swain to find his son's killer. Even though Swain has acquaintances on the police force he is still hauled in, beaten and given the third degree in the "truth chair" because he sticks his nose into the case. Once Matt's innocence is established, he and a blind friend, George Wesley, go after the weapon used in the murder. This trek leads to the Bermax Corporation, a government-sponsored advanced-weapons research project and to a sinister individual who owns and manages the laboratory—one Rick Charon. From the megalomaniacal Charon's questions and attitude Swain is convinced that Charon knows something about Grover's death. From this point on things get hot and heavy with Swain taking his life in his hands. Swain ventures into Old Town to see his friend and former lover, Maria Hidalgo, and to enlist her help with Charon. After Charon kills Wesley and threatens Ginny's life, Swain goes after Charon in a savage and shattering climax.

The second novel, *When Trouble Beckons* (1981), has Swain answering a call from Ginny who wants him to visit her on the moon. It is obvious, however, that something is very wrong. After Matt is almost assassinated by a zombie Fancy Dan he heads for the moon and Freefall City. Here he encounters another couple of murders and finds Ginny drugged and naked in a catatonic stupor with a dead man at her feet. Following a visit to the Psytronics Ward at the hospital, Swain learns from a friendly doctor that Ginny has been brainwashed with a strange new technique. According to the doctor, Ginny is dying of fright. Something has scared her so badly she is running away, consciously, subconsciously and physically. Swain's job is to find out what it is and how he can save Ginny. He finally manages this after an intriguing and exciting chase involving endorphins, hypnosis and alpha conditioning in a fantastic psychological plot.

The third novel, *The Deadliest Show in Town* (1982), has Swain, still reeling from Giny's narrow escape, taking a contract from a tycoon called The Fish Man. This character heads up a media conglomerate that plays with reality like a baby plays with fire. Swain's job is to locate the media's prize anchorwoman—a sleek redhead who gets her kicks in some of the city's sleaziest sex shops. While Matt is keeping ahead of a rival network that is trying to kill him, he uncovers a plot to assassinate the Governor. It takes all of Swain's luck, brawn and brains before the mess is straightened out. In the latest of the Swains, *The Odds Are Murder* (1983), we find Matt back in the DMZ, run down and flat broke. After obtaining psychiatric help Matt has his license revoked and he is out of business. To add insult to injury the entire city is suffering from a plague. While Swain is drinking at a nearby bar an old lawyer friend, Felix Bohlar, tells Matt that someone is trying to kill him and he needs Matt's help. Matt refuses but is persuaded when Felix shows him a list of victims and Swain sees, not only Felix's name but the names of several other friends on the list. Some of these friends are already dead. Before Matt can act Felix is murdered right before his eyes in the bar. Matt goes back to work with a vengeance and he quickly finds himself involved in a plot concerning millions of dollars as well as one of his former lovers whose husband was one of the hit-list victims. A lot of fist and leg work is necessary before Matt solves the case and avoids the plague.

All of the McQuay novels are interesting, and well-written in an exciting, witty and tough-guy style. McQuay is a very talented writer with a wry sense of humor. He has dedicated the entire series to the memory of Chandler. There are, on occasion, flashes of ironic, Chandler-like wit and insights. For example, in *Hot Time* Swain remarks, "I felt like I was sitting on a razor blade: no matter which way I slid, I was going to lose my ass." Again, a few pages later, "What they brought me was a cross between scrambled eggs and a piece of pebble board. They called it health food, and I figured that it was because a person had to be in peak physical condition to choke it down."

Mike McQuay is a Vietnam veteran who also served in Thailand, Japan and the Philippines. A Texan who graduated from the University of Dallas, McQuay currently teaches a science fiction writing course at Oklahoma State University. For fun he watches B movies on late night television.

Jake and Hildy Pace—Ron Goulart

The only conceivable word for the antics of a twenty-first century pair of private eyes dreamed up by Ron Goulart is "zany"—absolutely zany! Jake and Hildy Pace, a husband and wife team who operate Odd Jobs, Incorporated, one of the top private inquiry agencies in the galaxy, are as crazy and as funny as the Marx Brothers at their zenith. Odd Jobs, Inc. is no ordinary agency. It specializes in only the most difficult and most unusual cases with settings, characters and plots that would bring delight to Salvador Dali. Four of the Pace novels are already published and the fifth, *Brains, Incorporated,* is due out in 1985. Those still available are *Odd Job 101* (1975), *Calling Dr. Patchwork* (1978), *Hail Hibbler* (1980) and *Big Bang* (1982). One of the best novels is *Big Bang.* Set in 2003, thirty-four year old Jake Pace wakes up on a strange bed incarcerated in a murderer's cell accused of a brutal sex crime. It seems that a while ago Jake was found in bed with a dead call girl in underground Chicago, CHI-2. The girl had been killed by a lazgun still clutched in Jake's hand. Also it turns out that this girl had some information about one of Odd Job's former cases known as "The Big Bang Murders." When Jake went to see her he was knocked out and framed for her murder by persons unknown. To solve the Big Bang thing, the Paces are offered $250,000—in lottery tickets, not dollars. The Secretary of Security in Washington considers this a bargain price. The Secretary also gets Jake out of jail and he and Hildy are then off and sailing in pursuit of the killers. The Big Bang murders are exactly that: leaders of a new South American nation, the head of a Black African republic and five big business tycoons have all, quite literally, exploded. So far there have been no clues. Over fifteen agents assigned to the case have been killed— but none so far have exploded.

It quickly becomes obvious that the novel, written in typical Goulart fashion, is not to be taken seriously as either SF or mystery. In Goulart's world of 2003, Fergus O'Breen is Prime Minister of Free Ireland. A pair of Siamese twins—joined at the elbow—are the President and occupy the White House. Everything else in the nation is equally absurd. People drink "Chateau Discount Muscatel with Dr. Pepper added" or "Sparkling Burgundy with Hawaiian Punch and the MDR of Vitamins, A, B, et al." All characters in the novel have unusual names like "Ross Turd III, a fine old New England name" since "Boston has been full of Turds for generations." There is also an "Overweight Liberation Army," and a "House Committee on Fairplay for Gross and Disgusting People," and the "Plain Klothes Klan, an improvement on the Ku Klux Klan. A popular magazine is *Time-Life and Mammon*, and the two most popular weeklies are *The National Intruder* and *Muck*. After many adventures the Paces finally pin down the Big Bang gang and wind up the case.

Goulart is also the creator of the legitimate PI John Easy, who is the star of a four-novel series published between 1971 and 1974. The titles, all published by Ace are *If Dying Was All* (1971), *Too Sweet to Die* (1972), *The Same Lie Twice* (1973) and *One Grave Too Many* (1974). The plots typically involve Easy prowling Southern California in his dusty old VW searching for a missing person who usually happens to be a good-looking woman. Easy's Southern California is itself a strange universe worthy of science-fiction dimensions, an insane place where Easy is one of the last sensible survivors:

A sick character actor and three sailors went by Easy. A dwarf was standing on the opposite corner and threatening to expose himself to a cluster of broad, sweating motorcycle riders, who were sitting and standing around the curb. The dwarf ran through Easy's legs and planted a kick on the front tire of a death's-head-decorated Harley. "Screw your motorcycle," the dwarf said.

Easy walked on .... A female impersonator came out of a drugstore, stopped to dab just bought talcum under his red wig. "Ninety-two in the shade," he smiled at Easy.

"Yes, ma'am," replied Easy.

Born in Berkeley, California, in 1933, Ron Goulart attended the University of California at Berkeley where he began writing for *Pelican*, that university's humor magazine. Following graduation from Berkeley, he worked in advertising, writing copy for Skippy peanut butter and Ralston cereals. When he began his freelance writing career, he moved East and currently makes his home in Connecticut. He has written over a hundred books.

You might read Goulart anywhere. He has written under numerous pseudonyms and house names. His work includes private eye novels, science fiction, fantasies, romances and several anthologies including the excellent *Hardboiled Dicks* (Sherbourne, 1965). His trademark is the comic and the bizarre, both of which find their way into his mysteries and science fiction in plentiful quantities. Critics have favorably compared him to Kurt Vonnegut and note that Goulart is something of a cult favorite in Europe and the United States. The Chicago *Tribune*'s Jay Maeder praised him as "Science fiction's leading humorist."

Two other Goulart PIs are Jim Haley featured in *After Things Fall Apart*, an Edgar certificate winner in 1970, and Max Kearny in *Ghost Breaker*, published in 1971. Goulart has even created the first "private nose," a detective by the name of Les Moyles whose acute sense of smell helps him solve cases in several *Alfred Hitchcock's Mystery Magazine* short stories. A number of Goulart short stories have also parodied some of the genre's most famous names including Chandler, Ross Macdonald, John MacDonald and Ed McBain.

Sam Space—William Nolan

Finally, no survey of science fictional PIs would be complete without referring to William F. Nolan's Sam Space. Although he was referred to earlier in Chapter IV a little more needs to be added. Sam is, of course, a parodic tribute to Hammett's Sam Spade. As Nolan sees him, Space is the best private eye on this or any other Earth. Space is trained in seventeen forms of solar combat and he can snap the trunk of a small pine tree with a double-reverse dropkick provided his shoes are on. Seems he tried it once barefoot and broke a toe. Space is, according to Nolan, a hard-headed detective deliberately cast in the Warner Brothers mold of the 1930s, "out of Bogart by Chandler, a Hammettized op thrown gun-first into the future."

In *Space for Hire* (1971) set in 2053, Nolan runs Sam around the entire Solar System and pops him in and out of alternate universes. Sam also manages to change his shape, sex, age and mind while struggling with monsters, mad scientists and quirky time-machines. In a veritable orgy of outlandish situations Space, in true knightly fashion, beds a robot, fights a fire-breathing dragon, rescues a three-headed damsel in distress, gets cursed by a witch in a candy forest and goes to work for a client who keeps losing his body. In the process, Space gets hypnotized, seduced, slugged, double-crossed, tortured, brainwashed, drowned and fatally shot. Space drinks imported Scotch and as an Earth-Op working Mars and as an ex-rocket jockey out of Chicago, he reminds all of his clients that the detective business is in his blood. His great grandfather was a PI named Bart Challis in a place called Los Angeles, California, back in the 1970s. Space is licensed to pack a .38 notrocharge, fingergrip Colt-Wesson under his coat and he's had to use it more than a few times in his somewhat checkered career. Sam's lusts are twofold: hard drink and soft women. While a sucker for a sob story, he's nobody's patsy. With this background Space takes off in a wild and funny space opera with totally fantastic, improbable and surrealistic situations. It's great fun that no lover of either science fiction or mystery should miss.

Nolan is also the author of the famous *Logan's Run* (1967) and *Logan's World* (1977). Logan, as mentioned earlier, is a policeman who refuses to die at his appointed time in an overpopulated world of the future. The novel was made into a successful movie and then a popular, but short lived, TV series.

With the current popularity of both science fiction and the private eye it is likely we will see many more such blends in the years ahead. Maybe also in the movies and on the watching box. How about *Hans Solo: Private Eye* or *Mike Hammer In The 23rd Century* or *Thomas Magnum: Star Rover* or *Star Cases?* Only time will tell.

Appendix
Jousters and Contenders

WE'VE COVERED OUR 101 KNIGHTS and we find we are only half-way home. So our last section is devoted to at least 101 more private eyes sorted into a collection of categories that we hope you'll find useful in pursuing those topics or locales that interest you and avoiding those that do not. Our categories are arbitrary; some characters could fit under many headings,others do not fit very well anywhere.

Finally we must admit that we've missed a few. Sorry, but that will leave some fun for all of you reader-detectives out there in tracking down your own list of world-weary warriors. We doubt that you'll find another 101, but if you do, write us and we'll think of some appropriate award—maybe a patch for your tired eyes. We'll call it the Eye Saver.

Bad Eyes

Chandler (1977) by **William Denbow** earned the dubious distinction of being rated the worst novel among the post-1970 private eye fiction in our national survey of writers and critics. The novel casts Raymond Chandler in the role of a private detective coming to the aid of Dashiell Hammett and in the process thoroughly distorts Chandler's character. Perpetual reading of this book would make a viable alternative to the death penalty.

Phyllis Swan has scored a point for women's liberation although it surely is an unintentional one. Her series about Anastasia Jugedinski (just call her "Anna J.") proves that a woman can write just as poorly as any man. Anna J. is the bastard daughter of the police chief of some place called St. Mary. She lives with her studious brother who seems to have some incestuous interest in her. Not that Anna J. would notice; she's been frigid ever since she was raped at age 13. If you find all that a little improbable, wait till you try on the plots.

In *Trigger Lady* (1979), a notorious racketeer hires Anna to be his companion and bodyguard for an upper-crust charity ball he wants to attend. He needs a bodyguard because he expects a rival is going to try to snuff him at this swanky affair. If the idea of a big-time hood hiring the illegitimate daughter of a policeman to be his muscle strikes you as a bit odd, how about his logic for the arrangment: "as my companion, you would be constantly beside me without causing undue suspicion."

You've Had it Girl (1979), *Find Sherri* (1979) and *Death Inheritance*

(1980) are the other novels in the Anna J. series in which we learn that Anna graduated from the Police Academy and worked for a time as a cop. The books have a down-and-dirty tone to them, established by frequent ethnic taunts and the seemingly endless torment that Anna suffers from her rapist, Angelo. Angelo must own the record for most pages devoted to a juvenile delinquent in a mystery series.

Best-Named Eyes

Angel Graham is a man. And he is anything but an angel. Smart, tough and deadly with a gun, Angel stars in three fast-paced paperbacks written by **Richard Russell** and published by Tower in 1979. The titles are *Paperbag* (the best of the three), *Reunion* and *Point of Reference.*

Another great PI name is Pete Brass, hero of **Robert Donald Locke's** 1957 novel *A Taste of Brass.* The story, set in LA, is classic hard-boiled stuff that has the tough and cynical Pete working for a dwarf who hires him to find a beauty named Cherry D'Armand. This is not an easy task, and it gets Pete into all the trouble he can handle. When he finds Cherry, she tries to kill him, but Brass is as durable and serviceable as his name.

Another PI with an unusual name is **William Kaye's** Chickie French who was introduced in a 1981 release from Leisure Books entitled *Wrong Target.* The novel follows Chickie's attempt to find the people who killed his sister by mistake in an assassination scheme apparently aimed at her husband. Kaye spins a clever tale with an unusual, double ending.

Larry Hornblower is a good name for an ex-cabbie who now works in New York City as an unlicensed PI. He's placed his ad in the yellow pages so it appears right under "X Yourself: Divorce." As a result he gets lots of calls from unhappy and suspicious wives. In *Death of a Punk* (1980), Hornblower, who tends to the chubby side, is searching the East Village for a missing teen-age boy. Lenny is an appealing character in a nicely written paperback original by **John Browner.** Another cab-driving PI working out of NYC was Jigger Moran who appeared in *Jigger Moran* (1944) and *There Are Dead Men In Manhattan* (1946). Moran was the creation of **John Roeburt** who was best known for his Edgar-winning novel of 1949, *Tough Cop.*

Coast-to-Coast Eyes

Next time you're in a strange city and need a private eye, chances are you can find one. Private eyes are everywhere, and they may be watching you. A quick tour of the country and some other fictional detectives to put on your map:

Arizona

Dallas Webster is a Bull Durham-smoking, reluctant PI from

Yavapai, Arizona. Reluctant because Webster is a kicked-back cowboy who has no hankering to be a detective. He has sworn off violence ever since World War II where he distinguished himself as a Mustang Fighter Pilot. Easy-going, laconic and funny most of the time, Dallas becomes a death-dealing dynamo of destruction whenever he's riled up. His riling takes place in two enjoyable cases written by **Donald K. Stanford** in the 1950s— *The Slaughtered Lovelies* (1950) and *Bargain in Blood* (1951).

In the topical and unusual category is **Edwin Gage's** *Phoenix No More*, which was published in hardback in 1978 and in paper in 1980. Gage's PI, Daniel Falconer, is hired by a pop singer, Jinx Boulding, to play bodyguard to her father, Cass Boulding, a rich and conniving construction millionaire. Seems that Cass's life is threatened and no one knows why. Falconer takes the job and shortly thereafter someone does murder his charge. In uncovering the killer we are taken into the depths of the nuclear power industry and the problems of corruption and politics in the Sun Belt, as well as into the dangers surrounding nuclear reactors and nuclear waste. In an afterword Gage notes, "Although this novel was conceived as entertainment, recent worldwide news regarding nuclear power is making it all too clear that the thrills of a novel are derived from the dangers of life." The novel's epilogue also contains excerpts from Cass Boulding's diary. Here it is clear that Boulding, realizing the money he had made from constructing nuclear power plants is tainted, wants to expose the entire nuclear industry and the threat it poses to future generations.

One entry from the diary is noteworthy:

Had nuclear power plants been spread over Europe when World War II was fought, Europe would be uninhabitable today. Conventional bombs would have blown open the containment vessels of the power plants, causing meltdowns and releases of immense amounts of radioactive gases. One of these plants contains a thousand times the radioactivity of the Hiroshima bomb. Nuclear waste dumps would have been blown apart and unimaginable quantities of radioactive material would have entered the water table, seeping slowly toward the oceans. Every man, woman and child would have died of radiation sickness. Every cow, bird, horse, eagle, seagull, fox, rabbit, bear, deer and fish would have died.

Although critics may feel that the PI novel is not the place for soapbox oratory, Gage's message is integral to the plot and reminds us of a peril only the foolish would choose to ignore.

Boston

Michael Spraggue is an ex-PI who, nevertheless, keeps investigating to help his friends. Spraggue, who works out of Boston, gets along well with some of the cops like Lt. Hurley but not Captain Hank Menlo who sent Mike a congratulatory note when he turned in his PI license. In his first case after he gives up the PI business, *Blood Will Have Blood* (1982), Spraggue helps out his friend, Director Arthus Darien, who is staging a production of *Dracula*. Someone is determined to close the play before it opens and is playing a series of vicious and sick practical jokes: a garlic nosegay for the leading lady, a blood bath for the bride of the vampires, a bit player's Bloody Mary spiked with real O Negative blood, etc., and there's a murder. Darien persuades Mike to accept a part in the play and to find the enemy. After Mike's brilliant detective work both motive and murderer are unmasked.

Linda J. Barnes followed her first Spraggue novel with *Bitter Finish* (1983) which is set in the wine-growing country of the Napa Valley. Spraggue has allowed his license to expire after finding more congenial work—acting in Hollywood films. When his old flame and current wine-business partner, Kate Holloway, is accused of murder, Spraggue returns to the field to sort out the deception, intrigue and lies he finds growing in the valley. The newest Spraggue is *Dead Heat* (1984).

John Kincaid is another Boston PI who in his first and only case, *Death Be Nimble* (1967) by **Richard Smith**, is sent an embossed invitation to a yacht club party with an enclosure of five $100 bills. His task is to find the killer of a prominent society woman who raced greyhounds for a hobby. Kincaid runs a fast and somewhat lucky track in this competently written novel.

If you need an art education you should read the two novels of **Oliver Banks** featuring Amos Hatcher, a Boston PI specializing in art crimes. Murder and theft form the plots of the excellent *The Rembrandt Panel* (1980) and *The Caravaggio Obsession* (1984). Education of a different sort is available in **Lawrence Kinsley's** *The Red-Light Victim* (1981) which finds Jason T. O'Neil privately investigating your usual pornography-goes-to-campus scandal; this time at Boston University

Buffalo

Barney Calhoun is a six-foot-two, 210 pound ex-cop who works in Buffalo around Lake Erie. He is the anti-hero of *Hit and Run* (1964) in which he tries to commit the perfect crime but fails. Calhoun's creator was **Richard Deming** who also wrote about a second PI named Manville Moon (*The Gallows in My Garden*, 1952; *Whistle Past the Graveyard*, 1954). Deming wrote for TV and also novelized several *Dragnet* and *Mod Squad* scripts.

Chicago

In 1955 a Chicago PI named Jim Rehm appeared on the scene in an unusually good novel, *King-Sized Murder*, written by **William Herber**. Rehm is a memorable and likeable character who inspires the antipathy of the police because he is so efficient. The novel, as hard-nosed as any in the genre, was well-received by the public and critics, and Herber brought Rehm back a year later in another toughie entitled *Live Bait for Murder* (1956). Rehm holds his own with the best of the Windy City detectives including Mac Robinson, Ed and Am Hunter and two detectives created by **Milton Ozaki,** a Chicago-based writer and tax accountant. Ozaki's detectives were Rusty Forbes (*Dressed to Kill*, 1954) and Carl Guard (*Maid For Murder*, 1955).

Ellery Queen (Frederic Dannay and Manfred B. Lee) also created two private detectives. The first was Barney Burgess, a Chicago PI who appeared in a single, well-written novel, *Kiss and Kill* (1969). Barney is your classic tough PI; he models himself after Humphrey Bogart. Queen's second PI was Micah "Mike" McCall who was featured in three mysteries: *The Campus Murders* (1969), *The Black Hearts Murder* (1970) and *The Blue Movie Murders* (1972).

Denver

Nick Caine, a Denver detective with a murky past and a long list of prejudices, debuted in *Another Weeping Woman* (1980) and appeared a second time in *The Man of Glass* (1981) by **Donald Zochert**. We found the affected style of both novels more than a little annoying but must admit that the opening scene of *Another Weeping Woman* in which a girl is attacked by a crazed grizzly bear in a national park is as well done as any beginning in modern private eye fiction. Zochert is perhaps best-known for his clever *Murder in the Hellfire Club* (1978), a highly praised locked-room mystery.

Kansas City

Johnny April was the PI in five razor-sharp, lean novels written by **Mike Roscoe** (a pseudonym for **John Roscoe and Michael Ruso**) in the middle 1950s. All of April's cases are fast-paced pleasures written in authentic *Black Mask* style. The titles are *Death is a Round Black Ball* (1952), *Riddle Me This* (1952), *Slice of Hell* (1954), *One Tear For My Grave* (1955) and *The Midnight Eye* (1958). Anthony Boucher once said that April was "the only genuine private eye I know."

Los Angeles

If you haven't been taken for a ride on a cliche lately, hop on board **Allan Nixon's** *Get Garrity* (1966) which features Tony Garrity, a half-Aztec, half-Irish, unlicensed private eye out of LA. Garrity is a disbarred attorney with a bad drinking problem and way too much guilt and self-pity. His reputation as a tough guy accounts for people's interest in hiring him to get them out of blackmail schemes like the one faced by the movie mogul in this story. Written with about as little taste or virtue as you'll ever find.

Ace Carpenter, formerly a professional guitar player, is another Los Angeles private detective. He drives a VW, smokes a pipe and drinks lots of Stolichnaya. In *Carpenter, Detective* (1980), a paperback original from Charter, Ace makes like a warmed-over-Lew Archer searching out the ugly secrets of the rich and rotten St. John Family. *Hollywood Heroes* is the second book written by **Hamilton Caine**, a pseudonym for **Steve Smoke**. Smoke was also the editor of *Mystery Magazine*.

Nicholas (*The Seven-Per-Cent Solution*) **Meyer's** *Target Practice* (1975) is about LA private eye Mark Brill's investigation of an apparent suicide by Harold Rollins, an American prisoner of war who had just been accused of collaborating with the North Vietnamese. Brill criss-crosses the country to question the few prison camp survivors about what happened to Rollins in "The Swamp." A memorable interview with a quadruple amputee who believes he's dead haunts this novel which packs a triple whammy of sordidness: murder, massacre and incest.

Nathan Brightlight is an experienced Hollywood PI who shows up in **Trevor Bernard's** *Brightlight* (1977). Hired to find the gorgeous wife of a fading movie star, Brightlight meets intrigue and murder in a very low-key story that is both sad and ironic.

A generally overlooked PI of the 1960s was **Raymond Bank's** Sam King, a PI formerly from Denver but now operating an agency in LA that specializes in the recovery of stolen goods. King travels from one western state to another in plots that are a bit too pat to be convincing. One of the more cleverly conceived ideas is contained in *Meet Me in Darkness* (1960).

Another old timer beating his gumshoes on the LA pavement is Steve Mallory, seasoned pro in the "snitch racket." Assisted by partner Harry Jellison, Mallory was one of the early Marlowe derivatives right down to the sad cynicism: "There was nowhere to go but home. And home was nowhere to go." Mallory appeared in one novel we know of—*The Kiss-Off* (1951) by **Douglas Heyes.**

Warren Hearst and **Harry Herbold** are two LA private investigators hired to investigate the drowning death of a woman shortly after her husband took out a double indemnity insurance policy on her in **Robert Carson's** *The Quality of Mercy* (1954). Thomas Chastain praised this novel, which reads more like a procedural mystery than a hard-boiled tale, as "one of the most—if not *the* most—fascinating private eye novels ever written."

Stan Bass is a tough, but honest, professional gambler and a free-lance private eye working out of California and Las Vegas. He likes detective work because "it gave me some W-2 forms to file, a must for a professional gambler, and partly because it was work that suited my temperament. It was solitary work and I didn't mind the loneliness." Bass deals his deck in two excellent novels by **David Anthony**—*The Organization* (1970) and *Stud Game* (1977).

Howie Rook is another Hollywood PI, an ex-newspaperman, who in his first case, *Unhappy Hooligan* (1956) by **Stuart Palmer**, helps the police solve a murder that was made to look like a suicide. To do so he has to risk his life by joining the circus and posing as a clown. Rook showed up in a second novel called *Rook Takes Knight* (1968). Stuart Palmer also created a famous female detective, the irrepressible Hildegarde Withers, star of 15 amusing mystery novels. Palmer, who died in 1968, was an interesting character who played polo, raised poodles and exotic fish, was a guest clown with Barnum and Bailey and worked as a private eye for Jack Hardy, Al Matthews and other LA defense attorneys. Palmer was once President of the MWA and was a founder of the Screen Writers Guild.

Several other entries in what William L. DeAndrea has called the "Southern California Gloomy Private Eye Novel" are Harry Lake in **Peter Fine's** very stylish but somewhat hackneyed *Troubled Waters* (1981), John Steele in four novels by **Jerome Odlum** (e.g., *The Mirabilis Diamond*, 1945), Alan Macklin in E.V. Cunningham's *Sylvia* (1960), Terry Traven in **Geoffrey Miller's** *The Black Glove* (1981), Nichole Sweet in **Fran Huston's** so-so *The Rich Get It All* (1973) and John T. McLaren, a rancher in a state that might as well be California who does some part-time PI work in order to pay his taxes, but who apparently does it only once in **Will Cooper's** *Death Has A Thousand Doors* (1976).

Minneapolis

Nathan Phillips is a superb Minneapolis PI whose first and only case thus far has been *April Snow* (1982) by **Nick O'Donohoe**, a college English professor who has written a splendid novel of pace, dialogue, plot and characterization. Phillips is an investigator with the soul of a poet and the eyes of a hawk. Outwardly tough but inwardly tender, Nathan is wise beyond his years. He's a "clean big man" in a "nastly little profession" trying in this case to find the no-good, drug-dealing son of an old, rich, and bitter client. Trivia buffs will please note that *The Armchair Detective's* article on "The Rise and Fall of Raven House" (Vol. 17, No. 1) incorrectly places this novel in Cincinnati.

New Orleans

Jerry "Renegade" Roe is the half-Cherokee Indian, PI partner of Stuart Worth in the New Orleans firm of Worth and Roe Detective Agency. He's hard to miss, what with his blue eyes, shoulder-length black hair, headbands and moccasins. And, of course, he drives a Mustang. Worth and Roe are the stars of **L.V. Roper's** "caper" series—*The Red Horse Caper*

(1975) and *The Emerald Chicks Caper*(1976), etc. Roper wrote about another detective named Mike Saxon who worked in Kansas City in *Hookers Don't Go To Heaven* (1976).

New Orleans' best PI is a six-foot Cajun by the name of Johnny Bordelon. Once with the New Orleans Police Department, Bordelon now works out of a studio apartment on Rampart Street in the French Quarter. Besides private eyeing, Bordelon makes some additional income from his paintings—landscapes are his specialty. Tulane dropout and LSU graduate, he frequently cooks enticing Cajun specialties and holds a black belt in karate. He prefers the company of Danielle Focault, a legal secretary for a prominent Crescent City attorney. He is sometimes assisted by Leon Briggs, also an ex-cop and former house dick at the Monteleone. Bordelon appears in three novels written by **George Ogan** and published by Raven House Mysteries. The titles are *To Kill a Judge* (1981), *Murder in the Wind* (1981) and *Murder by Proxy* (1983). Some nice New Orleans color, so-so plots.

A third PI working in New Orleans is Neal Rafferty who is both tough and sensitive as he searches for a missing set of the works of William Blake in **Chris Wiltz**'s *The Killing Circle* (1981).

New York City

Next time you need help in the Big Apple (and who doesn't), check out one of the following ops:

Roger Levin and ex-marijuana middleman, ex-owner of a Chinese restaurant named Long Hai, and now a sometimes unlicensed private investigator gets himself into some very exciting escapades in a series of novels by **Richard Furst**. Best of the bunch is *The Caribbean Account* (1983), an original, if occasionally overwritten, thriller with a marvelous villain.

Peter Braid is a Manhattan PI in the classic mold. A noteworthy fact about Pete is that he is a colleague and drinking buddy of Mike Hammer. An ex-marine WW II veteran, holder of the Navy Cross and a judo expert, Pete's first, and as far as we know only, case was *Dragon Hunt* (1967), in which both Mike Hammer and Pat Chambers lend their help. The author, **Dave J. Garrity**, is a personal friend of Mickey Spillane, and it is obvious that "The Mick" had considerable influence on the plot and style of this novel.

William T. Ard was born in Brooklyn and worked as a detective for a short time after World War II. Ard wrote thirty books, most of them in the hard-boiled tradition. Anthony Boucher praised him as "just about unmatched for driving story-movement and acute economy." Ard wrote under several pseudonyms including **Ben Kerr, Mike Moran, Thomas Wills** and **Jonas Ward**. Ard's best character was Timothy Dane, a handsome New York City private eye with an excellent reputation for decency and honesty. Dane appeared in nine novels, the best of which were *Hell Is A City* (1955) and *.38* (1952). He was one of the so-called soft-boiled dicks, a forerunner of the later Archer and modern-day characters like John Denson and Albert Samson. He also was the model for a second private eye named Lou Largo, whom Ard introduced in *All I Can Get* (1959) and reprieved in *Like Ice She Was* (1960). Four Largo books were ghost written after Ard's death in 1960, one by **Lawrence Block** and the remainder by **John Jakes**.

The highly regarded mystery author **Thomas Chastain** has created two excellent New York City detectives. One is a cop by the name of Max Kauffman who goes after a crazy bomber in *911* (1976). The other is a private detective named J.T. Spanner, the only PI we know who has both of his ex-wives working for him in *Vital Statistics* (1977). Kauffman and Spanner collaborate in *Pandora's Box* (1974).

Sid Ames is the PI hero of four action-packed mysteries by **H.W. Roden**. He is often assisted by John Arden Knight, a New York City PR consultant. The four titles are *You Only Hang Once* (1944), *Too Busy To Die* (1944), *One Angel Less* (1945) and *Wake For A Lady* (1946).

Shepard Rifkin's one novel about Joe Dunne, a NYC private detective, is *The Murderer Vine* (1970). In it Dunne is hired to revenge the murder of a young man who was working for the voter registration of blacks in the South. You have to read this book to understand why Dunne never appeared in a sequel.

Hillary Waugh, one of MWA's past presidents, is best known as a pioneer of the police procedural (e.g., *Last Seen Wearing*), but he has created two private eyes, neither of whom quite matches the quality of his other fiction. Philip Macadam is a NYC private detective featured in *The Girl Who Cried Wolf* (1958) and Simon Kaye is a series character who sometimes gets a helping genuflection from his regular chess partner and boyhood chum, Father Jack McGuire. Simon specializes in protecting young women from harm; *The Doria Rafe Case* (1982) and *The Glenna Powers Case* (1981) are examples.

Nash Kanzler is a New York PI called out of retirement to track down one Stinger Brown who is offing black leaders and Mafia chieftains at a rapid rate. Both groups want revenge on Stinger and they want it quick. Nash's chase makes for a funny and harrowing tale entitled *Stinger* (1978), written by **Nathan Gottlieb.**

A Creative Kind of Killer (1984) is the pseudonymous beginning for Fortune Fanelli, a Soho resident who takes on a private case now and then. Fanelli is off to a strong start in this novel written under the name of **Jack Early**. He may be the only PI who is raising two teenagers and who has a mother who is a butcher.

Harry Fannin, a private eye from the Village, receives a late-night visit from Cathy, his nymphomaniac ex-wife, who shows up to die on his door step with a knife wound in her chest. Fannin tracks down her killer in **David Markson's** *Epitaph for a Tramp* (1959), a gritty and well-written paperback that takes you for a fast ride through the Village subterrain. Fannin appeared in a second novel: *Epitaph for a Dead Beat* (1961).

Edward D. Hoch's *The Shattered Raven* (1969) concerns a murder committed at the MWA's annual award banquet in NYC. Featured is Barney Hamet, a one-time private investigator and now a successful mystery writer who's just been selected as executive vice-president of MWA. He has to turn sleuth one more time to find the murderer of the famous recipient of the Reader of the Year Award. A lot of name-dropping, interesting MWA trivia, and a chance to rub elbows with some great writers. It's a good read.

Dale Shand is a handsome, romantic, Scotch-drinking PI working out of NYC. All the women—young, middle-aged and old—go for him. Schand is an ex-newspaperman who tangles with a blackmailer in *The Deadly Quiet* (1961) and a runaway blonde with $25,000 in her handbag in *The Shining Trap* (1965). The author is **Douglas Enefer** who has attracted a better following in England than in this country.

Steve Drake was one of the better Manhattan PIs working in the late forties and early fifties. Drake was an actor at one time, but admits, "I wasn't a very good actor. I didn't have the temperament for it, or maybe it was the profile." He is skilled at wisecraking, repartee and drinking brandy and charges a very reasonable $30 a day plus expenses. Drake appeared in five novels beginning with *Shoot the Works* (1948) and concluding with *Shakedown* (1955). The series was written by **Richard Ellington**, himself an actor and radio entertainer.

John Thomas Ross is a PI in the Mackelroy agency of NYC. In Ross' first case, *Closet Bones* (1977), written by the Washington, D.C. writer **Thomas Bunn,** he goes to a small town on Lake Champlain to investigate the disappearance of his client, Richard Buehl, heir to a chemical corporation fortune. A few hours after his marriage to a beautiful New York painter, Buehl disappears from his yacht. The bride has no explanation nor does she explain why the wedding took place in secrecy and was attended only by members of a hippie commune and a guru named the Boo-hoo. The deeper Ross probes into the family's affairs the more skeletons he finds in their closets—including connections with the drug world and a prostitution ring.

Berkeley Hoy Barnes is a hypochondriacal NYC detective who got his name from the fact that his mother was reading Bishop Berkeley's *A New Theory of Vision* during the last stages of her pregnancy and "became sort of convinced that the whole thing was an illusion." Barnes, who started out as a corporation lawyer, turned to criminal law and then to private eyeing, becomes very upset when he meets strangers causing him a nervous stomach. So his right-hand man, Larry Howe, keeps all sorts of medicine handy to take care of the problem. Barnes' brains and Howe's legwork are well-employed in three cases: *Murder Trap* (1971), *The Money Murders* (1972) and *The Bold House Murders* (1973). The pair's creator, **Eugene Franklin**, is actually **Eugene Franklin Bandy**, who also writes about Kevin Macinnes, "the world's most expert operator of the Psychological Stress Evaluator (PSE)." Macinnes is not a PI, but he acts like one in each of his novels thus far—*The Blackstock Affair* (1980) and *Deceit and Deadly Lies*, an Edgar winner in 1978.

Other New Yorkers who ply the PI trade are Shep Stone in two novels by **Jeff Jacks** (*Murder on the Wild Side, 1971; Find the Don's Daughter,* 1973); Steve Conacher in an eight-novel series written by **Adam Knight** (the best entries are *I'll Kill You Next*, 1954; *Murder for Madame*, 1952, *Kiss and Kill*, 1953 and *Knife at My Back*, 1952; Pete Shay in *Minnesota Strip* (1979) by **Peter McCurtin**; Bump Harwell in **Burt Hirschfield's** *The Verdugo Affair* (1984); Kirby Hart in **Dexter St. Clair's** *The Lady's Not for Living* (1963); Peter Cross in the pseudonymous **Jim Thomas's** *Cross Purposes* (1971); Ben Gates in five **Robert Kyle** novels beginning with *Blackmail, Inc.* (1958) and ending with *Some Like It Cool* (1967); and Kevin Fitzgerald, a broker and seedy investigator who appeared in only one novel, *Bloodstar* (1978) written by **Tom Topor. Will Squerent's** *Your Golden Jugular* (1970) is an excellent tale about Sampson Roach, a Madison Avenue investigator with money for a change, and **Niles Peebles'** two books about Ross McKellar (*See the Red Blood Run*, 1968; *Blood Brother, Blood Brother*, 1969) are effectively authentic stories about an aging PI.

Pacific Northwest

Jonas Duncan, a retired LA homicide investigator, is the PI hero of **Jackson Clark Gillis'** *The Killers of Starfish* (1977). The setting is the area around Puget Sound where Duncan has settled to get away from crime and violence. Before he can take root a petty ex-con is crushed by a ferry. Duncan's name is found on the body and he is drawn, unwillingly, into a search for the killer. The hunt takes him to Seattle, Seattle's Skid Row and to Starfish, a beautiful private island owned by a rich alcoholic. Gillis, a prolific and talented TV writer, worked on both the *Perry Mason* and the *Columbo* shows and, in 1974, won an Edgar for the latter.

Conan Flagg, a rich and handsome bookseller and part-time PI works in Oregon in a so-so series written pseudonymously by **M.K. Wren**. The two most recent titles are *Seasons of Death* (1981) and *Wake Up, Darlin' Corey* (1984). Seattle-based Thomas Black debuts in *The Rainy City* (1985) by **Earl W. Emerson.**

Peter Cory is one of several of **Stuart Brock's** PIs from the late 1940s. In *Just Around the Corner* (1948), Cory focuses on several murders in one of Seattle's swankiest hotels. Though hardboiled, Pete has soul and on one occasion he is brought to tears. A second Brock detective was Bert Norden, who also worked in Seattle. In *Killer's Choice* (1952), Norden is hired ostensibly to serve as a secretary to Jonathan Decker, a wealthy millionaire. His real job is to protect the old man from all his relatives who want to kill him for his money. Norden is a skilled PI with an eye for beauty, both environmental and feminine.

Pittsburgh

Casey Carmichael is a Pittsburgh PI and a good one. He is big, tough and cheap, charging a modest fee of only $75 per day (on selected cases he doubles this rate). When he needs to think, he plays solitaire. His most interesting case, written by **John Nicholas Datesh**, is *The Janus Murders* (1979). He is asked by the beautiful Diana Winter of the Winter National Bank (one of Pittsburgh's biggest) to exonerate her fiance, Tony Hiller, who has been accused of killing her father, Harold Winter, the president of the bank. Unfortunately for Tony, he was overheard telling a friend exactly how he was going to commit the murder and get away with it.

Dimitri Gat is the creator of Yuri Nevsky, a Russian-American private eye who lives in Pittsburgh. The first Nevsky book was *Nevsky's Return* (1982); however, it was the second title, *Nevsky's Demon* (1983) which earned the author considerable attention. Too bad for Gat that all the publicity was bad, because of the discovery by Bob Sherman, an investigative reporter for Jack Anderson, that it was a copy of John MacDonald's *The Dreadful Lemon Sky*, a Travis McGee novel published in 1974. Gat admitted that his book was "modeled" on the MacDonald book. Both books deal with drug smuggling—McGee investigates pot being brought into Florida, Nevsky is concerned with cocaine being smuggled across Lake Erie. After MacDonald's publisher alleged 32 instances of copyright infringement, Gat wrote a letter of apology to MacDonald and Avon recalled 60,000 copies of the book. If you have a copy, it's a bit of a collector's item; if you don't, you can still read the original—by MacDonald.

San Francisco

A playwright who tried his hand at the PI genre is **Robert Upton** who gave us a most loveable detective named Amos McGuffin in *Who'd Want To Kill Old George?* (1977). McGuffin has a good sense of humor and a plentiful thirst. His search for the killers of Old George takes him to the Institute of Dynamic Consciousness where he almost loses his own consciousness—permanently. McGuffin returns in *Fadeout* (1984). San

Francisco is also the home of Walter Brackett, a transplanted Englishman who has to solve two mysterious murders in **Derek Marlowe's** *Somebody's Sister* (1974), and Martin Windrow who uncovers about as much kinky sex as even San Francisco can stand in **Jim Nisbet's** *The Gourmet* (1981).

Tommy Lee, our only Chinese PI, works in San Francisco's Chinatown. Tommy is a one-man gang, the terror of the Tong. He has the physical skills of Bruce Lee and the wisdom of Charlie Chan. In his only case to our knowledge, *The Chinatown Connection* (1977) by **Owen Park**, Lee is called upon to break up an extortion scheme aimed at the Mafia by a group of Orientals. The entire community is threatened, and it is up to Lee to stop the danger. He does. Although the novel is of average quality, the glimpses into the Sino-American culture and West Coast gang behavior make the book worthwhile.

The South

Ace Chaney shows up first in **Christian Garrison's** *Snake Doctor* (1980) as a policeman in an old-fashioned city in the New South. Ace is a bit of a "good ole boy," but he's also a family man with a tremendous dedication to his job. Unfortunately for Ace, his investigation of a corrupt State Senator costs him his job, and so he goes to work for the Paragon Detective Corporation as a PI in *Paragon Man* (1981). When a fellow PI, Sam Clayton, is killed and the quarter-million dollars worth of diamonds Clayton was guarding is stolen, Ace is assigned to help the owner of the diamonds get them back. Ace gets a strong assist from Jake Spicer, a tough black detective on the police force who made a very strong showing in the first novel. This series has gotten off to a fine start.

Nathan Hawke runs a one-man PI agency in Sun City, Florida, but he gets plenty of help from Detective Lieutenant Toby Duane. Hawke was featured in a ten-novel series written by **Bob McKnight** and published by Ace in the late fifties and early sixties. Various Florida attractions are featured in the plots which have Hawke and Duane shooting, slugging and sleuthing away on their fast-paced cases. Some of the best chases are *Downward, Swamp Sanctuary, Running Scared* and *The Flying Eye*.
Anna Peters, a former chief of security for a corporation, goes the PI route in **Janice Law's** *The Shadow of the Palms* (1980), set in Sarasota, Florida.

Texas

Embodying many of the Texas myths is **Robert Ray's** Clayton Yankee Taggert whose only appearance to date has been in *Cage of Mirrors* (1980). Taggert, a Vietnam vet, is unwillingly dragged into investigating the murder of an old army buddy who once saved his life. The novel is an uneven amalgam of Ludlum, LeCarre, Ross Macdonald and Louis L'Amour—very good at times, very bad at others.
In *The Leo Wyoming Caper* (1978), a Texas cowboy-like PI named

Deuce Ramsey is hired to track down a 35-year old millionaire named Leo Wyoming who has disappeared. Wyoming is a practical jokester; one of his tricks is to reenact the Kennedy assassination in Dallas. **Jamie Mandlekau** has written one weird but entertaining tale.

Washington, D.C.

James (*Six Days of the Condor*) **Grady's** *Runner in the Streets* (Macmillan, 1984), introduces John Rankin, a former investigative reporter who has turned private eye. Short on mystery but long on the corruption that drives Washington, the book examines power and influence in the nation's capital as well as the unrequired love affair that ensnares Rankin. Pretentious at times but good enough to make us enthusiastic about a return visit.

Defective Detectives

The exploits of handicapped detectives have amazed readers for years, beginning with **Ernest Bramah's** blind 'tec, Max Carrados and continuing with the one-armed Dan Fortune. In their 1983 anthology **Ray Browne** and **Gary Hoppenstand** have collected some of the best in the wonderfully titled *The Defective Detective* (Popular Press). There have been numerous private eyes with various afflictions, none of which, of course, proves disabling.

The most recent example of a handicapped investigator is Joe Binney, the only totally deaf PI in the genre. **Jack Livingston** has written two Binneys—*A Piece of the Silence* (1982) and *Die Again, Macready* (1984), both published by St. Martins Press. Binney talks, reads lips and handles his problem so well he neither needs nor wants anyone's sympathy. Joe is so hard and efficient that you almost feel sorry for his opposition. The plots of both novels are straightforward but compelling and realistic enough to hold even a jaded reader's attention. Enough murders, sex and puzzling personalities to please everyone. Livingston is a pseudonym, but for whom we do not know.

Alo Nudger is an ex-cop who also played Mr. Happy, the clown cop who introduced safety cartoons on TV. Nudger's handicap is that he is afraid of everything. He is constantly taking antacid tablets for his nervous stomach; fear overwhelms him; he's scared of pain; fear is always leaving an aftertaste and sometimes he can smell his own fear. Nudger first showed up in **John Lutz's** *Buyer Beware* (1976). Now he's making a comeback in *Nightlines* but we can't figure out why he puts himself (and us) through the misery.

One of the fattest PIs in history is Jim Hanvey, a gargantuan slob of a man with quadruple chins, short fat legs and an omnivorous appetite. Jim is fat enough to be defective. He picks his teeth with a gold toothpick hanging on a chain across his chest. When he isn't chasing a crook, he can usually be found sitting down, resting with his shoes off. Jim showed up in two novels, *Jim Hanvey, Detective* (1923) and *Scrambled Yeggs* (1934) written by **Octavus Roy Cohen**, a native of Charleston, S.C. and a regular contributor to *Saturday Evening Post, Colliers* and other popular magazines in the thirties. Cohen wrote about another PI, David Carroll, who appeared in at least one novel, entitled *Gray Dusk*, which suffers by comparison with the Hanvey books.

Steve Silk, the only detective we know to have but one lung, appeared in a series of 15 novels written by **James Brendan O'Sullivan**. Silk is a well-dressed ex-prizefighter, a witty and sexy master of repartee, and a very good detective. Many of the plots involve clever gimmicks for catching the reader's attention. For example, *I Die Possessed* (1955) begins with a death letter from the author who also happens to be the corpse, making it one of the few mysteries told from the corpse's angle. Most of the novels suffer from a bad case of cliche-itis as well as terminal inauthenticity of dialogue. People are always referring to their guns as "roscoes" or saying "curtains to you." The plot twists are the major compensations.

Samuel Clemens Tucker was a pro golfer before a tour of Vietnam sent him home minus his left foot and his left ball. One-legged golfers are notoriously short off the tee so Tucker was forced to return to his other career—private investigations which he conducts in the Bay Area assisted by his psychiatrist-wife, Trudy, who went all the way beyond the call of duty in restoring Tucker's morale and good health. Author **Jerry Allen Potter** provides moderately interesting plots in *A Talent for Dying* (1980) and *If I Should Die Before I Wake* (1981).

Harold "Schill" Schillman, a complex ex-cop turned PI, was almost terminally defective. Schill got so depressed that he attempted suicide. The bullet bounced off his thick skull, and he decided to live. Since detective work is all he knows, he sticks with it when a notorious gambler asks him to locate his wife in **Eric Bercovici's** *So Little Cause For Caroline* (1980). Schill obliges and shortly after the not-too-hard-to-find-wife is found, she's murdered, but an attempt is made to have it look like suicide. This very Chandler-like novel was made into an excellent TV movie entitled "One Shoe Makes It Murder," starring Robert Mitchum and Angie Dickinson.

Eyes of the Prophets

A couple of writers who distinguished themselves in the science fiction arena also tried their hands at a PI novel.

Manly Wade Wellman who was well-known for his science fiction stories and screenplays tried his hand at the PI tale and produced one very good novel entitled *Find My Killer* (1949). Jackson Yates, the PI hero, is well-drawn, and Wellman took pains to authenticate every detail in the book by checking with the police, doctors, lawyers and even professional criminals. All this care results in a very good story about a supposed suicide that turns out to be murder. The difference in this case is that the victim's will provides $5,000 for anyone who can find his killer! Yates collects the reward but not before he runs into forgery, poison, blackmail, antique guns that work, a seductive widow, a lonely lady lawyer and a number of narrow escapes from extinction.

Keith Laumer, the well-known science fiction writer and creator of the Retief SF series, wrote a PI mystery entitled *Deadfall* (1971) starring Joe Shaw, a superb detective in the Chandler mold. In fact, the novel is dedicated to Chandler and Marlowe. Shaw is a cynical, wisecracking student of human behavior who is hired by an ex-mobster to find his daughter who was taken away from him 25 years earlier. A little too pat at the end and a little too lucky elsewhere, the novel is still a very well-written tale.

Funny Eyes

In addition to the detectives in Chapter 9, several other humorous investigators and parodies have dotted the PI landscape. The majority have made only one or two appearances and then beaten a fast retreat.

Andrew Fenady's *The Man With Bogart's Face* (1977) is about a guy who undergoes plastic surgery to make him the spitting image of Humphrey Bogart. He then opens an LA office under the name of Sam Marlowe. Some funny dialogue, some crazy scenes, it was made into a movie by 20th Century. Sam returned in *The Secret of Sam Marlowe* (1980).

A well-educated, image-conscious private eye who makes most of his money selling burglar alarms, Roger Dale is called upon to solve *The Talk Show Murders* (1982), a cleverly wrought novel by the multi-talented entertainer **Steve Allen**. The mayhem begins when an obnoxious rock star is poisoned on Toni Tennille's talk show. The fatalities soon become a media event as members of Phil's, Johnny's and Dick's guest panels are bumped off. Dale, who likes to wear Edwardian suits and comes across like a hip Philo Vance, concentrates on constructing psychological portraits of his suspects, a practice originally known as *portrait parle* in the days of Bertillon, but called "P.P." by Dale. That's just one of many double entendres, puns and wisecracks invented by Allen, who functions as a narrator through some of the novel. Good fun, good parody, good looks behind the scenes. You can almost hear that naughty Allen cackle in the background.

Pete McCoy is a contemporary LA private eye, but most of the action in *The Murder of an Old Time Movie Star* (1983) by **Terence Kingsley-Smith**, is recalled from events that took place in the Hollywood of the

1930s. An inferior attempt to be nostalgic and funny in the tradition of Kaminsky and Bergman. One of the main characters is even named Kasimir Kaminsky. All the name-dropping and irrelevancies become tedious and rather mean spirited. The best that can be said of this effort is that there are a few scenes that may not annoy you.

Jock Eyes

The hardcourt, the ring and the playing field have been the training grounds for a number of obviously well-coordinated private eyes. An example is Tony Boyle, a big Vietnam veteran who usually beats people senseless when they assault him. If they try to gun him down, he kills them. Tony was an undefeated boxer in the service. His hands are considered lethal weapons. Tony appeared in only one novel, *Wake Up the Dead* (1974), by **William Wall**, but he does just about everything a PI can do in any novel before the missing person case he's on is concluded.

Bill Lockwood, also known to his friends as The Hook because of the boxing prowess he demonstrated in World War I, is the chief detective for the Transatlantic Underwriters Insurance Company. Despite the connotations of his knickname, The Hook is a suave investigator. A graduate of Columbia Law School, he drives a gunmetal grey '37 Cord convertible, prefers accessories by Dunhill, and likes to spend his evenings dancing at the Rainbow Room. His boss envies the fact that Lockwood always looks like he just stepped out of an ad for Arrow Shirts. This series, by **Brad Latham**, is set in the late 1930s; the titles are *The Gilded Canary* (1981), *Sight Unseen* (1981), *Hate is Thicker Than Blood* (1981), *The Death of Lorenzo Jones* (1982) and *Corpses in the Cellar* (1982).

Just what is a "Tut Claw"? It's a private eye-lawyer-special-agent; real name, Theodore Claw. It's also an ex-boxer, wrestler and baseball pitcher who was once in the Green Berets and taught karate. The only thing Tut hasn't done is appear in a good mystery. He's had to settle for jobs like *The Cocaine Caper* (1978) and *The Castilian Caper* (1978), two uninspired books by **Vincent A. Paradis.**

An ex-minor league second baseman, Mark Renzler became a private eye after he was beaned with a fastball that blinded him in his left eye and ended his baseball career. Renzler works in NYC which he knows well from his two years as a New York cop. In *Dead In Center Field* (1983), by **Paul Engleman**, Renzler is working on two cases—the blackmail of a beautiful blonde and several threats against the life of Marvin Wallace, a slugger with the New York Gents who's closing in on Babe Ruth's home-run record. Not in the same league with Parker's *Mortal Stakes*, but still a solid performance that goes the distance.

Paul Benjamin's Max Klein, one of the 1984 crop of new PIs, is also one of the most appealing. Max is bright, tough, enterprising and down on his luck. A Columbia University graduate and a college baseball player, Max tried law but couldn't hack it and turned private eye. His office is on the third floor of an ancient West Broadway building, two blocks south of the Chambers Street subway station. It is decrepit, run down and cheap. The walls are covered with Brueghel color reproductions. Max's first appearance is in *Squeeze Play* (1984) and it is an auspicious beginning. The plot is about a major-league baseball hero who, at the height of his career, loses a leg in an accident. After recovery the hero wants to run for the Senate. When he receives a death threat he comes to Max for help. One of the newest sporty detectives is John Byron Hyde, karate instructor—PI, in **Benjamin Wolff's** *Hyde and Seek* (1984). Good California ambience in the solid hard-boiled tradition.

Pairs of Eyes

Two eyes are better than one especially when they are PIs. When the one eye is a man and the other is a woman, there is a whole new outlook on things. Beginning with Nick and Nora and Bertha Cool and Donald Lam, male-female teams have made occasional appearances on the scene, but they have never gained the popularity of the lone-wolf.

One of the better new couples is the LA team of Fritz Thieringer and Maggie McGuane whose only outing to date has been in **Brad Solomon's** *The Open Shadow* (1978). To make ends meet, Maggie writes movie reviews now and then, and Fritz does a little shoplifting. Good dialogue and a vivid look at grimy-crimey Los Angeles, qualities that distinguished Solomon's other private eye novel (*The Gone Man*, 1977) featuring Charlie Quinlan, an actor turned private detective.

Attractive newcomers to the mixed-double set are Bridget O'Toole and Harry Garnish who made a strong debut in **Frank McConnell's** *Murder Among Friends* (1983). Bridget is an ex-nun who runs a Chicago detective agency that she took over from her ill father. Harry is her smart-aleck chief detective. The ecology-based plot is a bit scrambled, but this pair has the potential for a good series.

Samson's Deal (1983) by **Shelley Singer**, introduces Jake Samson, a soft-boiled unlicensed PI who works out of Oakland. Hired by a radical professor to investigate the death of his wife, Jake is assisted by his unofficial partner, a lesbian carpenter named Rosie who wields a mean two-by-four. Jake is an ex-cop, a former hippie, Jewish and not very physical. Tame by typical PI standards, the novel gives some interesting Bay Area culture lessons.

In **Reed Stephen's** *The Man Who Killed His Brother* (1980), Mick "Brew" Axbrewder, an unlicensed PI, teams up with his partner, Ginny Fistoulari, a licensed detective who runs Fistoulari Investigations to look for his niece who is the latest of nine young girls to have disappeared in a city named Puerta del Sol. "Brew" is a drunk with a Scudder-Tobin case of guilt over the fact that he accidentally shot his brother, a policeman who was chasing a purse-snatcher at the time. "Brew" has been a drunk and Ginny's reclamation project ever since. He also appears in *The Man Who Risked His Partner* (1984).

Ben Shock and Charity Tucker are the partners of the New York firm "Shock and Tucker—Investigations." Ben is an ex-cop who spouts reactionary rhetoric, and Charity is beautiful but frigid, the result of being a rape victim (Ben was the cop who killed her assailant). Their cases sound like a visit to a cut-rate zoo—*A Sounder of Swine* (1974), *A Requiem of Sharks* (1973), *A Murder of Crows (1971)* and *A Parliament of Owls* (1972). The author is **Patrick Buchanan,** a pseudonym of **Edwin Corley.**

Johnny Marshall is a fast-talking, street-smart Los Angeles PI who gets a frequent and able assist from his wife, Suzy, a good-looking brunette Johnny constantly refers to as "the little woman." Now and then their great Dane, Kahn, puts the bite on somebody, but "only on orders, or when he sees a gun." An inferior derivative of the Nick and Nora Charles idea, this series, written by **James M. Fox** (penname of **James M.W. Knipscheer**) includes such titles as *The Iron Virgin* (1951), *The Gentle Hangman* (1950) and *A Shroud for Mr. Bundy* (1982).

Al Delaney is another of the lesser-known PIs of the 1950s, who works out of the Redman Detective Agency in a place called Chancellor City. When Giles Redman, who started the agency, is killed in the line of duty, Delaney and a lovely lady PI named Dolly Adams keep things going. One of the best of **Thomas Black's** novels about Delaney was *Four Dead Mice* (1954) retitled *Million Dollar Murder* in the paperback edition (1954). Delaney has a keen intelligence, a knightly attitude and even though he hates violence he inevitably finds himself in the middle of it.

William Schaefer lives in a New York City Westside apartment and works for the Worldwide Detective Agency. Standing six feet two and usually needing a haircut, he is in his middle thirties and tough enough for all purposes. In his first case, *The Moment of Fiction* (1979), written by **Daniel Estow**, an important financier asks him to track down a book written by the associate of a number of important literary figures. No one is sure whether the book exists, but Schaefer is willing to find out. Along the way he meets an attractive lady, Ann Lang, who helps his search. In the second novel, *The Moment of Silence* (1980) Schaefer and Ann are now operating their own PI agency and are hired to find a businessman's runaway daughter.

Marvin Kaye's five-novel series about Hilary Quayle is centered in the world of show business because Hilary is technically not a private eye. She runs a public relations firm. The real PI in the books is Hilary's right-hand man, known only as Gene. He functions as secretary-legman and boy-Friday for Hilary whose powers of deduction typically uncover a murderer who's used some rare poison as the means of mayhem. A mildly entertaining series (especially *The Grand Ole Opry Murders,* 1974 *and The Soap Opera Slaughters,* 1982), but with little to offer fans of the hard-boiled school.

Other Pairs

It's a rough game of two on two in **Steve Knickmeyer's** *Straight* (1976), nominated for an Edgar "Best First Novel" award. Two Oklahoma City PIs—the lame, Demoral-popping Steve Cranmer and womanizing, pool-shark Butch Maneri—pursue a pair of hit men named Straight and Coady. They've just executed a contract on a businessman who was blocking a building project in a small Oklahoma town, and Cranmer and Maneri are hired by the victim's mistress to find the killers. Cranmer and Maneri earn more gambling on football games than they do sleuthing. They're a couple of fast-lane good ole boys.

Our nomination for the funniest detective team goes to Doan and Carstairs, creations of **Norbert Davis**, one of the best pulp writers of the 1930s. Doan is a short, chubby detective working in California. Carstairs is a Great Dane that sometimes eats the evidence and stands at stud for some of society's most demanding lady Great Danes. They appeared in three novels published in the mid-40s—*The House in the Mountain, Sally's In the Alley,* and *Oh Murder Mine.* Davis' trademark was his ability to combine zany humor with tough-guy action. His Max Latin stories in *Dime Detective* were highly regarded.

The South's version of Spenser and Hawk—that's Jim Hardman, an unlicensed, pudgy Atlanta PI and his black sidekick, ex-football player, Hump Evans. They're a rough pair, and Atlanta makes a surprisingly good setting for this well-written, fast-action paperback series by **Ralph Dennis**. The titles are numbered; twelve in all, beginning with *Atlanta Deathwatch* (1974) and ending with *The Buy Back Blues* (1977).

Schyler Cole and Luke Speare run their own agency, The Cole Detective Agency, located on Lexington Avenue in downtown Manhattan. They charge $50 a day plus expenses, and they'll do anything legitimate. Schy is uncommonly honest; as he says, "I don't pad my expense accounts excessively, or stretch out my cases to fraudulent lengths. On the other hand there's such a thing as being too smart and efficient for your own good." Cole and Speare showed up in six novels written by **Frederick C. Davis** in the mid 1950s. Three of the best were *Another Morgue Heard From* (1954), *Drag the Dark* (1953) and *Nightdrop* (1955). Davis also wrote about an unusual detective named Cyrus Hatch, professor of criminology, and his ex-pugilist bodyguard, Danny Delvan. *He Wouldn't Stay Dead* (1939) and *The Graveyard Never Closes* (1940) were two of the strongest efforts.

Huntington Cage is a NYC private eye with a secret advantage—he has a twin brother, Hadley Cage, allowing him to be in two places at the same time. Hadley is a painter who lives in New Jersey, but once in a while he helps "Hunt" out on a case when he receives their secret signal consisting of two tones transmitted by Hunt's specially designed watch. Other than a planned rendezvous for a case, the brothers Cage make no contact. No one cares either because the series, initiated with *The Lady Killers* (1975) by **Alan Riefe** is pretty thin stuff. Riefe also created another private detective by the name of Tyger Decker, introduced in *Tyger at Bay* (1976). Tyger also works in NYC and has a twin brother who wants to be a PI but ends up a corpse instead.

Shean Connell is a piano-playing private detective who gets a lot of help from his young assistant, Lester Hoyt, a nineteen-year-old budding criminologist. Connell and Hoyt appeared in at least one novel that we know of—**Roger Torrey's** *42 Days For Murder* (1938) which is set in wide-open Nevada, complete with "gangsters, white slavers and dope runners."

Real Eyes

We would be remiss if we failed to mention some of the real life counterparts of our fictional heroes. Most private detectives spend their days repossessing automobiles, serving subpeonas, trailing wayward husbands and wives and engaging in similar sorts of mundane activities. There are, nevertheless, some PIs whose real life careers are considerably more exciting. A recent issue of *Life* magazine, for example, told of the exploits of two PIs in Fremont, California, Melody Ermachild and Barry Simon, who managed to clear a 13-year old of a murder she didn't commit and who also worked on the De Lorean case and the Jonestown mass suicides. A number of others have written autobiographies that read like fiction or have told their stories to journalists. Among the latter are **Gil Lewis, Irwin Blye** and **Jay J. Armes**. Gil Lewis is a missing persons expert working out of Boston. Gil's exploits are set forth in **John Sedgwick's** *Night Vision: Confessions of Gil Lewis, Private Eye* (Simon & Schuster, 1983). **Irwin Blye** is a New York PI who specializes in debt skippers but over a period of twenty years has seen and done just about everything that PIs do. His career is the focus of **Nicholas Pilleggi's** *Blye, Private Eye* (Playboy Press, 1976). By far one of the most colorful and brilliant investigators in the nation is the real-life six-million-dollar man, **Jay J. Armes** of El Paso, Texas. Armes, whose deeds are set forth in **Frederick Nolan's** *Jay J. Armes Investigator* (Macmillan, 1976), is a self-made man with no hands but with specially designed prosthetics that give him the skill and ingenuity of a James Bond. He has, for example, a .22 magnum pistol surgically implanted in his wrist. Armes has worked for some of the most famous names in the world: Marlon Brando, Howard Hughes, Elizabeth Taylor and Elvis Presley. Moreover, he's never lost a case. Finally, there are some real PIs who have written a novel. One of the best examples is **Jerry Kennealy's** *Nobody Wins*, published by Manor Books in 1977.

Reflective Detectives

Hank Bradford is another ex-cop who turns to teaching and PI work after his former partner is killed and the partner's wife holds him responsible: "You should have been there backing him up, protecting him like he always protected you." Bradford has appeared in three mysteries written by **Mike Warden**: *Death Beat* (1980) where he plays bodyguard to a rock star, *Dead Ringer* (1980) which is concerned with several murders in a laundry room and *The Topless Corpse* (1981) where the lead dancer in a musical review is murdered onstage in front of a thousand witnesses.

Dion Quince is one of the few PIs who operates totally undercover. On the surface, Dion is a well-known writer who has already won the National Book Award in the nonfiction category. Somewhat like George Plimpton, Dion writes about dangerous occupations from the point of view of those doing the work. Secretly, however, Dion is a PI in the employ of Univest, the world's largest private investigation firm. In **Timothy Welch's** *The Tennis Murders* (1976), Quince's boss, Edmund Groom, assigns him to revenge the murder of a female professional tennis player. The player's father has put up $30,000 for the killer's capture, dead or alive. The smooth and skillful Quince gets the job done in a taut and gut-gripping story of ruthless professionals on and off the court.

Ben Helm differs from most PIs in two ways: he is happily married and he writes and lectures on criminology. In the best of the five Ben Helm novels, *The Silent Dust* (1950), Ben is asked by a former sweetheart to supply a perfect murder technique for a novel she's writing. Ben obliges, but a few days later the lady writer is killed and to cover up a possible scandal, the murderer is forced to kill a second time. Ben, an expert on murder, has to use all his cunning to outwit the killer. Helm was one of the most popular PIs during the late forties and early fifties. His creator, **Bruno Fischer** (who also wrote under the pseudonym of **Russell Gray**) was a prolific author who wrote several novels about another detective named Rick Train.

The newest cerebral detective is the New York-based Alexander Magnus Gold who debuts in **Herbert Resnicow's** *The Gold Solution* (1983) and follows in *The Gold Decline. (1984)*

Scary Eyes

William Hjortsberg's *Falling Angel* (1978, also serialized in short form in *Playboy*) is one of the few novels that stretches the PI genre. A marvelously macabre mix of the occult, mystery, voodoo and the dark arts, the story centers on Harry Angel's search for a famous 1940s singer named Johnny Fortune who disappeared from an asylum shortly after his return from WW II. Everyone seems to think that Fortune is dead except one Louis Cyphre with whom Fortune once had a financial agreement. Cyphre now wants Angel to run Fortune to ground in order to redeem his debt. Angel's eventual discovery of Fortune is one he could have lived without, and his terrifying fall through a never-more-hellish New York City is propelled by some of the most gruesome murders the mind can conjure up and by a final Faustian shock that will spin your brain.

Hired originally to follow a wandering son, a private detective known only as "The Eye" watches his quarry marry a beautiful woman and go off on their honeymoon. Through the window of the newlyweds' honeymoon cottage, The Eye sees the young woman, who we later come to know as Joanna Eris, calmly murder the groom and make off in his Porsche with $18,000. The Eye becomes obsessed with Joanna and follows her across the country as she continues to rob and murder men she has just married, usually on their wedding night. The Eye morbidly looks on acting, at times, like a voyeuristic accomplice, at times, an active protector of this eerie death woman. The pattern goes on for years. Joanna kills nearly 30 people. The Eye only watches. **Marc Behm's** novel bears little resemblance to the classic PI tale. The Eye has no hero's code, his only quirks (besides following Joanna everywhere) are a fascination with crossword puzzles, and the creeping suspicion that Joanna could be his long-lost daughter. The edgy energy that drives *The Eye of the Beholder* (1980) at its beginning dissipates with the endless globe trotting leaving you sad and just plain tuckered out by the end.

The Longest Eye

In 1966, when **Roderick Thorp** published *The Detective*, the novel shot to the top of the best-seller list and stayed there for many weeks. The reason for its popularity was, in the words of one reviewer, that it "combined the techniques of both the police procedural and private eye novel with the domestic realism of a John O'Hara novel." The story of Joe Leland is probably the longest PI novel we have. Leland is a complexly developed character who becomes involved in a case which blows the top off a town's darkest secrets. To solve the case, Leland must come to grips with five different personalities: a nymphomaniac, a psychiatrist, a sexual deviant, a woman in love and himself. Leland next appeared in *Nothing Lasts Forever* (1979), a book in which Thorp executes one of the most harrowing plot situations you'll ever read. Leland is now a police consultant and an expert on SWAT tactics. He finds himself pitted against a band of international terrorists with his daughter's and his own life at stake. You're going to be emotionally drained when you're done reading this one.

Transplanted Eyes

A number of Americans have moved abroad to practice their detective work. An example is Tim Parnell, an ex-CIA agent and now a PI specializing in cases involving aircraft. His office is in Amsterdam's airport. In his first case, *The Man Who Played Thief* (1971), by **Don Smith**, he recovered some stolen diamonds and made enough money to retire. Instead he continues his investigative work, and in *The Padrone* (1971), he solves the bombing of a millionaire's jet. The next two cases were *The Payoff* (1973) and *Corsican Takeover* (1973). Smith also wrote about a secret agent named Phil Sherman who was featured in sixteen secret missions.

Burns Bannion was an American PI who worked in Japan. His adventures are chronicled in **Earl Norman's** "Kill Me" series beginning in 1958 with *Kill Me In Tokyo* and continuing with *Kill Me In Shimbashi* (1959), ... *Me in Yokahama* (1960) and ... *Me in Yoshiwara* (1961). There were at least three more. Bannion's greatest weapon is Karate which he studies very seriously in Tokyo. Most of the Orientals in the books say things like "Ah so" and "I'm big sick," and drop all the pronouns and verbs from their dialogue. For his part, Bannion is always meeting some luscious young woman with a dreamy superstructure. Norman belongs in Bill Pronzini's *Gun in Cheek* as one of the best of the worst.

Curt Stone was another private eye transplanted to Oriental shores during the 1950s. The titles in this series by **Jack Seward** are *Case of the Chinese Skeletons* (1964), *The Eurasian Virgins* (1969), *The Frogman Assassinations* (1968), *Assignment: Find Cherry* (1969) and *The Chinese Pleasure Girl* (1969). One reviewer called Stone "a combination of Mike Hammer and Travis McGee." Killing comes easy to him "because he's done so much of it." One interesting feature of the books is that Stone can translate from Japanese into English "without conscious effort."

Raou F. Whitfield was one of the original *Black Mask* writers under the editorship of Joseph Shaw. Whitfield lived in the Philippines for a time, and those islands are the setting for his best stories involving Jo Gar, the Island Detective. The 24 Gar stories were written under the name of **Ramon Decolta**. Gar carries a .45 Colt automatic, squints a lot, rides in a horse-drawn *carromatta* and specializes in solving murders that inevitably have been committed with a knife. Whitfield wrote three tough-guy novels: *Green Ice* (1930), *Death in a Bowl* (1931) and *The Virgin Kills* (1932). Ben Jardinn, the detective featured in *Death In A Bowl*, is a cynical distrusting hard-boiler in the Chandler tradition.

TV Eyes

Some of the most interesting PIs proved to be more successful on television than on the printed page. Three that come immediately to mind are **Roy Huggin's** Stuart Bailey, the star of Warner Brothers' series *77 Sunset Strip* from the novel by the same name; Miles Banyon, a 1930 character on NBC, starring Robert Foster from the novel *Banyon* by **William Johnston**; and perhaps the fattest PI on TV, **Richard Gallagher's** Frank Cannon played by William Conrad on CBS.

Bailey was featured in two novels and a very successful five-year series. *Banyon* ran for two seasons, and *Cannon* lasted from 1971 to 1976, with a brief return in 1980. To list all of the TV eyes would require a book in itself, and fortunately such a book is already available. It's **Richard Meyer's** *TV Detectives* (1981) which traces the history of television's detectives from NBC's 1949 *Martin Kane, Private Eye* with William Gargan as the first Kane to 1981's *Magnum PI* starring Tom Selleck.

Author Index

Private Eyes Index